M000159346

A Feminist Companion
to Reading the Bible

BS
521.4
.F46
1997

A Feminist Companion to

Reading the Bible

Approaches, Methods and Strategies

edited by
Athalya Brenner &
Carole Fontaine

Sheffield
Academic Press

Theology Library
SCHOOL OF THEOLOGY
AT CLAREMONT
California

Copyright © 1997 Sheffield Academic Press

Published by
Sheffield Academic Press Ltd
Mansion House
19 Kingfield Road
Sheffield S11 9AS
England

Typeset by Sheffield Academic Press
and
Printed on acid-free paper in Great Britain
by Cromwell Press
Melksham, Wiltshire

British Library Cataloguing in Publication Data

A catalogue record for this book is available
from the British Library

ISBN 1-85075-674-0

To the memory of

Fokkelien van Dijk-Hemmes

ת·נ·צ·ב·ה·

CONTENTS

PREFACE

This introductory volume to the *Feminist Companion* series is in many ways a testament to what this series has already achieved: the previous volumes leave the reader asking for more. This multi-volume set of feminist biblical interpretations has not only made available the work of feminist scholars from around the world, many of whom published in obscure but welcoming venues early in their careers, but it has also inspired and commissioned new works for upcoming projects in the series. While it may have originally been envisioned for a scholarly audience interested in feminist perspectives on the Bible, it has become a favorite of students at all levels of higher education hoping to supplement the standard historical-critical fare found in existing 'commentary' series.

So far, the series has approached its task on a more or less book-by-book basis, with articles presenting both larger topical discussions as well as ones that explore specific feminist readings of a given passage or set of interrelated passages. The present volume follows that same pattern, but is directed not at a single book or related corpus of books of the Bible. Rather, the goal of *Approaches, Methods and Strategies* is to raise the kind of structural and systemic issues of method that are largely glossed over or merely implied in most non-feminist works on the Bible. To that end, we include broadly theoretical essays on feminist methods and the various roles they may play in research and pedagogy, as well as non-feminist essays that have direct bearing on the methods or subject matter feminists use, and a variety of readings that illustrate a variety of methodological strategies adopted by feminist scholars.

The question of method is always an intriguing one, and increasingly, such questions are becoming critical for readers who want to understand both the liberating and reactionary potentials within the text. Under the persistent press of feminist interrogation, historical critical scholarship, perhaps the most dominant paradigm for research in this century and the one preceding it, has been required to offer proofs of its claims to be 'value-neutral', 'objective' and 'bias-free' in its methodology. Such proofs have not been particularly easy to demonstrate, so avoidance of feminist questions seems to have become the method of choice for dealing with this challenge to the authority of elite, male interpreters. In fact, historical-critical methodology has been shown by feminists to be neither particularly historical (given its simplistic understandings of history, and the writing of history), nor particularly critical of its own perspectives, situated as they are in the modern period. What was supposed to have been a universally valid starting point for inquiries of the text some communities hold as 'Scripture' has turned out instead to be a startling example of the particularity of race, class, and gender of the established group of 'authorized' readers, namely, men of educational and ecclesial status whose personal or group power interests have been marketed as 'universal' and 'human' of view.

Unfortunately, this blindness to the limitations of one's own method as an expression of one's 'social location' continues to be the rule for great segments of the discipline of biblical studies, as well as among those who write and interpret for the world of the church and synagogue. While we do not wish to rehearse at length here the entrenched animosity between religious groups and the academic guild,[1] what *may* be said confidently is that the fiction of unbiased interpretation is common coin in both realms. Neither group is particularly willing to undercut the authority of its interpretations by admitting to any inherent limitations in its source materials or the methods used to study them. Into this gap of credibility we insert this set of essays in order to examine the state of our methodologies as they pertain to bias, including gender bias, in interpretation, and the strategies used to unmask and overturn that bias.

In many ways, this project is a direct response to the excitement of student readers of the previous volumes of the series. Why, they have asked, do we never see these kinds of questions raised in *introductory* textbooks or courses on the Bible? Surely these are the sorts of considerations that ought to be discussed with students *before* they embark on their studies, not tacked on *after* the fact as 'optional' feminist perspectives. Editor Athalya Brenner's strategy of suggesting that feminist authors respond to their own reprinted work has been especially instructive to student readers at the introductory levels:

---

1.   In many cases, members of the guild are in direct conflict with the goals and methods of the believing communities by their very insistence on asking historical and 'truth' questions of a corpus of writing which, according to some religious bodies, is to be hallowed, believed, and appropriated more or less uncritically.

watching a scholar voluntarily deconstruct her or his previous work allows readers to gauge both the scholar's growth in a certain area of discourse, as well as allowing them to judge the role that professional allegiances and responsibilities (i.e., 'social location') may have played in structuring the writer's earlier handling of source and secondary materials.

To be sure, there may well be an introductory preface here or there that discusses the nature of artifactual (anepigraphic) and epigraphic sources used to reconstruct a socio-cultural or political history of 'ancient Israel' or the New Testament communities, but the role of the *interpreter's* method in the making of meaning is seldom addressed. Feminist and liberation theologians who *do* engage in such contextualizations of their own work often find, to their dismay, that such methodologically self-reflective enterprises do not seem to serve to foreground these questions for others. Rather, the scholar who regularly regards herself or himself as part of the hermeneutical circle of interpretation is usually labeled as 'subjective' and 'partisan', as compared to the mainstream or 'malestream' commentators who present themselves as 'objective' and engaged in their research for purely disinterested motives.

In fact, no one learns all the ancient languages and background subjects needed to become a professionally competent biblical scholar without some powerfully motivating force at work, whether the scholar is aware of it or not. The investment of time and money, and the uncertainty of a successful outcome, are simply too overwhelming to allow anyone engaged in biblical studies to view the pursuit as merely 'objective'. 'Experts' are not created by accident; there is always some intentionality on the part of one being so credentialed. Under such conditions, it is not an 'out of bounds' question for readers to wonder what motivates the authors they read, *especially* if and when those expert authors fail to divulge their contextualized starting points for discussion of something as important as biblical literature. This volume, then, hopes to be a self-critical reflection on the 'whys' and 'hows' of studying the Bible.

The task of interpreting biblical texts, as we understand it as feminists, involves not just the listening for ancient voices of various timbre, but also the discovery and recovery of one's *own* voice as a interpreter engaged in the circular of activity of reading and making meaning. It is appropriate then in such volumes as this to give explicit space to that modern voice: many of our authors will reflect here on the 'day-to-day'-ness of their work as feminist scholars who study the biblical record. Contexts of research, teaching, and even faith commitments have not been considered some 'lesser', incidental feature of the work we do, but have been deliberately foregrounded by those for whom such 'situatedness' is itself a powerful hermeneutical entry point into the text.

We make here no claim for 'universals', choosing instead to preserve a babble of critical voices, some at cross-purposes with others. Some authors doubt that genuine 'female experience' can be retrieved from a patriarchal text; others find that 'thick' contextualization of their source materials produces a dramatically different evaluation of the text's liberating potential than one might have supposed. Jewish and Christian voices have been allowed to speak from their own particularities without being flattened or reshaped into the presentation of some putative, so-called 'Judeo-Christian' heritage. Nor do all the voices speaking here necessarily concern themselves with communities of faith; many direct their critique to the malestream scholarly establishment as the central nexus of their concerns.

We offer these volumes, then, in the hope of challenging, exciting, annoying, angering and liberating readers of all stripes and kinds. What you do not find in one place, we have tried to provide in another. The New Testament suggests that all the books of 'Scripture', Hebrew and Greek, are 'Spirit-breathed' (2 Tim. 3.16a); we remind *you*, Gentle Reader, that it is for *you* to decide how and in what way that may be so.

This volume is dedicated to my students, without whose questions it would never have been envisioned, and without whose assistance, it could never have been completed. Professor Barbara Geller of Wellesley College willingly listened to early versions of my essay which appears in this volume, and encourage me with perceptive comments. Among my students, I especially wish to thank Reverend Cara Davis, Reverend Carol Ramsey-Lucas, Therry Neilson-Steinhardt, Margaret Tabor, Carole Yorke, Mary Jane Jenson and Jean Sangster for their help in the preparation of this manuscript. To Athalya Brenner, who was always gracious about matters both great and small, go my continuing thanks and respect.

Carole R. Fontaine
Newton Centre, Massachusetts

ABBREVIATIONS

AB	Anchor Bible
AfO	*Archiv für Orientforschung*
AION	*Annali dell'istituto orientale di Napoli*
AJP	*American Journal of Philology*
ANEP	J.B. Pritchard (ed.), *Ancient Near East in Pictures*
ANET	J.B. Pritchard (ed.), *Ancient Near Eastern Texts*
AOAT	Alter Orient und Altes Testament
BA	*Biblical Archaeologist*
BARev	*Biblical Archaeology Review*
BASOR	*Bulletin of the American Schools of Oriental Research*
BDB	F. Brown, S.R. Driver and C.A. Briggs, *Hebrew and English Lexicon of the Old Testament*
BHS	*Biblia hebraica stuttgartensia*
Bib	*Biblica*
BibB	Biblische Beiträge
BJS	Brown Judaic Studies
BO	*Bibliotheca orientalis*
BTB	*Biblical Theology Bulletin*
BZ	*Biblische Zeitschrift*
BZAW	Beihefte zur ZAW
BZNW	Beihefte zur ZNW
CAD	*The Assyrian Dictionary of the Oriental Institute of the University of Chicago*
CBQ	*Catholic Biblical Quarterly*
CTA	A. Herdner, *Corpus des tablettes en cunéiformes alphabétiques*
EncJud	*Encyclopaedia Judaica*
ExpTim	*Expository Times*
HAR	*Hebrew Annual Review*
HAT	Handbuch zum Alten Testament
HBT	*Horizons in Biblical Theology*
HR	*History of Religions*
HSM	Harvard Semitic Monographs
HTR	*Harvard Theological Review*
HUCA	*Hebrew Union College Annual*
ICC	International Critical Commentary
IEJ	*Israel Exploration Journal*
JA	*Journal asiatique*
JAAR	*Journal of the American Academy of Religion*
JANESCU	*Journal of the Ancient Near Eastern Society of Columbia University*
JAOS	*Journal of the American Oriental Society*
JBL	*Journal of Biblical Literature*

JBTh	*Jahrbuch für Biblische Theologie*
JEA	*Journal of Egyptian Archaeology*
JFSR	*Journal of Feminist Studies in Religion*
JJS	*Journal of Jewish Studies*
JNES	*Journal of Near Eastern Studies*
JPSV	*Jewish Publication Society Version*
JRE	*Journal of Religious Ethics*
JSOT	*Journal for the Study of the Old Testament*
KAI	H. Donner and W. Röllig, *Kanaanäische und aramäische Inschriften*
NRSV	New Revised Standard Version
OBO	Orbis biblicus et orientalis
OLP	Orientalia lovaniensia periodica
Or	*Orientalia*
OTG	Old Testament Guides
PEQ	*Palestine Exploration Quarterly*
PRU	*Le Palais royal d'Ugarit*
RB	*Revue biblique*
REg	*Revue d'égyptologie*
RHR	*Revue de l'histoire des religions*
RSO	*Rivista degli studi orientali*
SBL	Society of Biblical Literature
SBLDS	SBL Dissertation Series
SBLMS	SBL Monograph Series
SEÅ	*Svensk exegetisk årsbok*
SJT	*Scottish Journal of Theology*
TDOT	G.J. Botterweck and H. Ringgren (eds.), *Theological Dictionary of the Old Testament*
ThB	Theologische Bucherei, Kaiser Verlag
TTod	*Theology Today*
UF	*Ugarit-Forschungen*
USQR	*Union Seminary Quarterly Review*
UT	C.H. Gordon, *Ugaritic Textbook*
VT	*Vetus Testamentum*
WBC	Word Biblical Commentary
WMANT	Wissenschaftliche Monographien zum Alten und Neuen Testament
WUNT	Wissenschaftliche Untersuchungen zum Neuen Testament
ZAH	*Zeitschrift für Althebraistik*
ZAW	*Zeitschrift für die alttestamentliche Wissenschaft*
ZDPV	*Zeitschrift des deutschen Palästina-Vereins*

INTRODUCTION

Athalya Brenner

At the beginning of May 1995 I put the typescripts of the tenth volume of the *Feminist Companion to the Bible*, in the mail to Sheffield Academic Press. At that moment I experienced a sense of closure: I thought that the volume, *A Feminist Companion to the Hebrew Bible in the New Testament*, would be the last in the series. I came back to my office (in Amsterdam at the time) and had a look at my e-mail. There was a message from my good friend, Carole Fontaine, entitled 'What we need is...' What we needed, according to Fontaine and as set out in her Preface (above), was an introductory volume to the *Feminist Companion* series: a volume to do less with specific texts (like the first ten, explicitly text-oriented, volumes) and more with the methodologies, guidelines, strategies and approaches current in contemporary feminisms, as applied to the Bible and exemplified by current teaching and publications. We pondered the idea together for some time and, finally, decided to co-edit. The following collection of essays, then, is hopefully a step towards the goal Carole envisaged.

Each of the earlier volumes in the series contains reprints of previously published articles, although their number varies from one volume to another. In this collection, most of the essays are newly commissioned; only six are reprints. This is a matter of editorial decision. In the first ten text-oriented volumes, the focus is on a representative sample of recent and contemporary work, the 'state of the art', so to speak, as exemplified in discussions of particular biblical texts: hence the necessity for reprints and translations from other languages. Also, at the time, the body of feminist works on the Bible was much smaller than it is now. Many feminist works—single articles in particular—were at best scattered, and it was difficult to publish such works in reputable periodicals (see Milne in this volume). Relevant materials were therefore often non-accessible or unavailable. This situation has changed: in the last few years feminist Bible criticism has proliferated. In this collection, therefore, and in dialogue with recent research, the focus is on *present* research trends and on some guidelines for future developments: hence the attempt to include as many new works as possible, with a much smaller number of recently published but important essays.

I. *Metacritics*

What can be stated about the relationship between feminist Bible criticism and other main [male] streams of biblical studies? What can be stated about the relationship between feminist criticisms and feminist biblical studies? The first question, which is posed by Adele Reinhartz in 'Feminist Criticism and Biblical Studies on the Verge of the Twenty-First Century', is directed inwards: to the so-called 'guild' of biblical scholars and students, including the often still marginalized feminist (mostly women) practitioners. The second question, posed by Pamela Milne in 'Toward Feminist Companionship: The Future of Feminist Biblical Studies and Feminism', entails a critical examination of feminist Bible studies in the dual light of its own past performances *and* the general, external to the Bible, feminist value systems. Consideration of these two questions leads to another, namely, how and to what ends can or should the future of feminist biblical criticism be shaped in view of its recent and admittedly short history, and in view of its [often tenuous] links with non-biblical feminist criticism? Although the third question, which is closely related to the first two, is partly and generally answered by Reinhartz and Milne, a more detailed answer—together with a survey of major theories and trends in the last decades—is supplied by Heather McKay in her 'On the Future of Feminist Biblical Criticism'. All three articles are metacritical articles: after a few decades of developing feminist biblical criticism, the time for assessment has clearly come. But, although all three deal roughly with the same materials, each is different in perspective. Reinhartz discusses the Bible, its study and the interrelationship between its mainstream studies and feminist studies through the metaphors of story and plot. Milne, after surveying attitudes and convictions, calls for the development of non-confessional modes of criticism, a strategy which would bring feminist Bible criticism closer to other feminist practices and theories. McKay ends her classificatory survey of past and present feminist approaches by contemplating the possibility of more balanced approaches in the future, in order to help create a 'gender-neutral scholarly environment' in which both gynocentric and androcentric study could flourish side by side and together.

Concurrently with hoped-for movements toward non-confessional

and more balanced approaches, confessional and traditional contexts for the study of the Bible and its socio-political usage continue
to exist in many of the current worlds inhabited by feminists, as
Milne and McKay amply demonstrate. In her 'The Abusive Bible: On
the Use of Feminist Method in Pastoral Contexts', Carole Fontaine
applies feminist critique to such life and scholarly situations. The
Bible can be and is abusive in many places: for feminists who wish to
retain their socio-religious links with their own communities this is a
serious challenge. Previous feminist criticism too often absolves the
Bible while blaming its [mostly male] commentators for the abuse.
Fontaine's analysis and suggestions for the future—to reopen, reassess, resist and reappropriate biblical texts—take in previous models and, in so doing, draws a multiple blueprint of fresh possibilities
for applying scholarship to contemporary life predicaments.

The last two essays (one with a response) in this section exemplify
how contemporary feminist criticism of the Hebrew Bible has been
moving to include within its course not only narratives and other
materials pertaining directly to woman figurations or female concepts, but also towards considerations of larger critical issues; and
how new feminist works now rely on as well as criticize previous
ones. Both articles are anchored in the two trends that have been
emerging concurrently: feminist critical consciousnesses, and literary
theory (the now widely legitimized strategy and praxis of readerly
response). Carol Smith, in 'Challenged by the Text: Two stories of
Incest', is a test case of how narratives and notions of the Hebrew
Bible have been approached by scholars, and how a more secure
feminist approach can bear on the results of the interpretive process.
My 'Identifying the Speaker-in-the-Text and the Reader's Location in
Prophetic Texts: The Case of Isaiah 50' is another look at the textual
and ideational complexities of a so-called 'servant poem', and the
literary 'identity' of this 'servant' in the light of developments in
teaching the Prophets and feminist critique. In her 'Response' to my
essay, Carole Fontaine discusses the implications of my reading for a
number of scholarly issues, including issues referred to extensively in
the first four articles of this section.

II. *Differences and Otherness*

As Sharon Ringe writes in 'An Approach to a Critical, Feminist,
Theological Reading of the Bible', projects such as hers entail
'perspective, experience and commitment'. For her, using 'experience' as a critical category entails, among other things, that 'data of

one's existence—gender, race, class, ethnicity, physical condition, relationships' and so on—are considered as significant perspectives and commitment-creating. The four articles in this section illustrate, each in its own way, how feminist writers are moving from the general notion of woman's marginalization in the Bible and in Bible-conditioned cultures into a new centering/positioning of women—and other 'others'—in discourse and psycho-social situations.

The recognition and acceptance of diversity in biblical studies is amply accommodated in Elisabeth Schüssler Fiorenza's edited volumes, *Searching the Scriptures.* The four essays here follow the example of that volume in maximizing and championing *difference,* traditionally obliterated in biblical studies. Difference—of interpreters, of interpretation, of audience—is seen as a value rather than a reflection of circumstances only. Ringe offers Phil. 2.5-11 as a case study to support this, and notions of mutuality in matters of 'texts of life and life of texts'. Alicia Ostriker, in 'A Triple Hermeneutic: Scripture and Revisionist Women's Poetry', surveys the Bible for elements that may encourage challenges to its authority. Through a look into appropriations of themes by women poets, she suggests that biblical revisionist hermeneutic may be of three kinds: of suspicion, desire and intermediacy. In 'Overcoming the Teaching of Contempt', Katharina von Kellenbach analyzes how and why recent Christian feminist scholarship has marginalized Judaism as patriarchal in comparison to early Christianity and 'reinstate[d] traditional anti-Jewish arguments'. She concludes her analysis with a call for feminists to proceed in the two parallel projects: critique of the Bible and its worlds; and dialogue between Jewish and Christian feminist critics. In 'Overlapping Communities and Multicultural Hermeneutics', Kwok Pui-lan looks at the latest developments in New Testament studies, in the creation of 'alternative interpretive space[s]' by decentering the hegemony of what she terms 'Eurocentrism' and by condoning 'multiculturalism' in Bible interpretation. Kwok shows by her test case, the story of the Syro-Phoenician woman (Mk 7.25-30, Mt. 15.21-28), that different models of interpretation are derived from the interpreter's life location. She demonstrates how postcolonial interpretation enables re-visioning of individual texts, has implications for anti-Judaic readings, is relevant to women and raises the question of the validity of interpretive (academic, mainstream/malestream) discourse.

III. *Other Worlds*

Comparative studies of the Bible in light of ancient Near Eastern civilizations and cultures, especially of ancient Mesopotamia and ancient Egypt, have been current in biblical studies for the last hundred years at least. The assessment of any comparative approach's value for understanding biblical texts and worlds has been changed and modified many times. Meanwhile, studies of these ancient Near Eastern worlds—originally developed as auxiliary methods for Bible study—have become independent and separate disciplines which, nevertheless, are still relevant for Bible scholarship. Not surprisingly, feminist and gender approaches within those disciplines is encountering difficulties not dissimilar to those encountered by feminist Bible criticism. The two essays in this section were written by women scholars of such disciplines who are not Bible scholars. They demonstrate the validity of their ancient Near Eastern (ANE) materials for feminist Bible study *and* the problematics of comparative methodology and gender in both fields.

In 'Feminist Research and Ancient Mesopotamia: Problems and Prospects', Julia Asher-Greve states that it is premature to assess feminist scholarship in ANE studies, which is still 'in the initial phase of *engendering*'. She then proceeds to consider methodologies, concepts and terminologies from the perspectives of general considerations about history and civilization/culture; mainstream Mesopotamian studies; general feminist–gender studies and feminist–gender Mesopotamian studies. Her methodological observations are equally applicable to biblical as well as ancient Near East scholarship.

Lana Troy, in 'Engendering Creation in Ancient Egypt: Still and Flowing Waters', supplies Egyptian materials for the comparative study of the biblical creation stories. Egyptians sources about the creation of the world are diverse and vary from one location or time grid to another. Troy shows how, in individual Egyptian myths and in the corpus viewed as a whole, 'creation was patterned on female and male reproductive modes, on the mechanics of conception and birth'. The existence of differently sexed/gendered creation models is potentially meaningful not only for feminist Egyptologists but, by application, also for feminist biblicists.

IV. *Other Close Contexts*

In section III, especially in Asher-Greve's essay, the methodology of transdisciplinarity and contextualization is discussed. The materials are presented in an etic mode (from outside the field of biblical studies). This section contains three essays written in the emic mode, from within biblical studies. In each of these, diverse materials from outside the Bible are judiciously but differently utilized to display their comparative and complementary worth for contextualizing biblical literature and cultures; and this contextualization focuses on questions of gender and gendering. The three disciplines/contexts (and Asher-Greve's essay may be consulted here for this terminology) for this essay are, in order: archaeology, iconography and cross-cultural [sociological] analysis.

In 'Recovering Objects, Re-Visioning Subjects: Archaeology and Feminist Biblical Study', Carol Meyers focuses on how 'ethnoarchaeology can provide a new vision of gender in the biblical world and, thus, a new understanding of female images in the biblical word', something that has been almost totally absent from so-called biblical archaeology and its applications to the Bible until now. Methodologically, Meyers's position is close to Asher-Greve's. Conceptually, it represents a similar project to that of Ostriker's. In 'An Iconographic Approach to Genesis 38', Eleanor Ferris Beach reviews the Tamar and Judah story against its biblical and exegetical contexts, then moves to what she terms 'visual exegesis', the utilization of iconographic images from the ancient Near East to explain and re-vision textual, narrative and socio-religious items. Beach concludes by showing how her visualization, derived from archaeological artifacts, creates a re-vision of the power structure and its gendering in Genesis 38. Power structures in family and community are also the social locus for John Pilch in his 'Family Violence in Cross-Cultural Perspective: An Approach for Feminist Interpreters of the Bible'. Pilch reviews current cross-cultural approaches and available research. He then suggests a sociological, socio-cultural model for investigating violent abuse of females and other weak groups in ancient Mediterranean cultures, including the worlds of the Hebrew Bible. As the model shows, Pilch's findings are applicable to the interpretation of biblical abuse phenomena from the perspectives of individuality, family and society, socialization and cultural norms, gender divisions and more. In many respects, then, Pilch's essay is a companion piece to Fontaine's 'Abusive Bible', illuminated from another perspective.

V. *Otherness and Translation*

One of the fields feminists have not been active in is Bible translation; another one is text criticism. Although modern translations and their gender biases are often referred to in feminist writings, alongside instances of biased commentary, feminist study of Bible translation *per se* is scant.[1] And, although in certain academic interpretive communities—such as the Dutch ones—translation from biblical source languages is considered a prerequisite to any study, this praxis by and large does not lead to feminist interest in text criticism, ancient versions or modern theories of general and Bible translations. The trend is changing, however. The two essays in this section are addressed to issues of translation in ancient and modern languages and apply their methodologies to specific texts.

In 'Septuagint and Gender Studies: The Very Beginning of a Promising Liaison', Kristin De Troyer looks at the nature of translation as interpretation, which leads her discussion to modern text criticism and assessments of the nature of the Septuagint and other Greek versions. By asking gender-specific questions and by recognizing gender subjectivity (covert or overt) in the ancient translator, De Troyer claims, the reader may come to evaluate a translation and its relation to the source text differently. Her examples are taken from the book of Esther in the Hebrew and the two Greek versions. Tod Linafelt, in 'Surviving Lamentations', sees Lamentations in terms of its concern for the 'perishing children'. He relies on Walter Benjamin's theory of translation as survival, Derrida's commentary on Benjamin, and Detweiler's concept of 'overliving'. Linafelt gives a reading of the Hebrew text of Lamentations 1–2, in which Zion is posited as a frustrated mother appealing to Yhwh on behalf of her tormented children, but to no avail. The poet, according to Linafelt, focalizes (to borrow a term from Mieke Bal) on the mother and shares her despair and final silence. A subsequent reading of several verses from the expansionist Aramaic Targum to Lamentations 1–2 shows an imaging of survival there, while a hopeful 'afterlife' can be found in passages of the so-called Second Isaiah. In all the passages cited the governing metaphors are of mothers—and children. Thus, the application of modern translation theory enables Linafelt to reconsider Lamentations and its translations in terms of source and target, survival and ideology, gender and metaphor.

---

1.   But see now Sherry Simon, *Gender in Translation: Cultural Identity and the Politics of Transmission* (London: Routledge, 1996).

VI. *Goddesses and Wisdom*

The search for 'original' goddesses or goddess characteristics of the divine (male) figurehead was frequently undertaken by Euro-American, especially Christian, feminist Bible critics and feminist theologians in the 1970s through to the early 1990s. This search was often motivated by devotional urges to renew goddess veneration in some way and produced some amazing ideological results, namely accusations of goddess suppression in the Bible and in Judaism (see von Kellenbach's essay). Fortunately, the goddess discussion has moved beyond this initial phase to more responsible treatments of biblical texts and archaeological artifacts (see Asher-Greve, Meyers): the extraction of goddess figures from their admitted suppression in or by biblical literature seems to answer other agenda in current research.

Both essays in this section share some underlying notions: goddesses existed in some Hebrew Bible worlds and socio-literary contexts; they were transformed into concepts in others; the modification of goddess figure into concept can be traced and perhaps historicized; comparative data from the ANE, in particular from the southern Levant and Mesopotamia, and elsewhere are necessary for the mapping and delineation of this process.

Judith Hadley delineates this development in 'From Goddess to Literary Construct: The Transformation of Asherah into Ḥokmah'. Asherah is seen first as a female deity worshipped as Yhwh's consort during the Israelite and Judahite monarchies—a notion absent from biblical texts. She is then demoted to a wooden object (an asherah), much as the goddess Astarte is demoted to a fertility idiom. Finally, Hadley examines 'the personification of the figure of Lady Wisdom, perhaps as literary compensation for the eradication of the worship of goddesses such as Asherah and Astarte'. Bernhard Lang proceeds from the personified figuration of Wisdom and works his way backwards to the goddess idea in 'Lady Wisdom: A Polytheistic and Psychological Interpretation of a Biblical Goddess'. Lang moves from a socio-historical placement of Proverbs 1–9 to a Jungian analysis of the Wisdom figure. His next step is to examine Wisdom's status as goddess and daughter of the creator god in light of the (Aramaic) Ahikar text and in Ugaritic and Mesopotamian mythology. He then charts Wisdom's mythological 'career' from scribal goddess to patroness of nature wisdom in polytheistic times, to 'her' poetic ideation in later monotheistic times. In his analysis of Wisdom, Lang moves from history to myth to psychology, so as to connect the biblical text with 'the timeless world of human experience'.

VII. *Intertextuality*

The notion of 'intertextuality' has come to denote many things since it was developed out of Bakhtin's notion of dialogics. So much so that it may and is so loosely used nowadays in Bible criticism as to render it useless unless rethought and redefined. Clearly, the issue of 'intertextuality' requires methodological revaluation as well as re-assessment of its usefulness for feminist criticism. The two articles presented here include such theoretical reconsiderations as well as extended examples.

In her 'Intertextuality: Ruth in Dialogue with Tamar',[2] Ellen van Wolde traces the notion from its beginning through to its current usages. She distinguishes between intertextuality as text production and text reception, as diachronic and synchronic, as general and particular, external and internal; and proposes a step-by-step procedure for intertextual Bible research. Van Wolde's project in this essay is to redefine intertextuality in a narrower, inner-biblical sense. By way of an extended example, the Ruth narrative and the Tamar narrative (cf. Beach) are read as if in dialogue with each other. Van Wolde concludes by pointing out how a dialogic and analogic reading of the two stories that adheres to a firm program enriches the reader's appreciation of each and both.

Elaine Wainwright, on the other hand, has 'chosen intertextuality as a way of studying relationships between the testaments' because the method reveals aspects of both the Hebrew Bible and the early God Movement's worlds through a new 'lens'. Her understanding of the intertextuality notion in 'Rachel Weeping for her Children: Intertextuality and the Biblical Testaments—A Feminist Approach', is similar to van Wolde's, but relies more on Kristeva's notions. Wainwright uses intertextuality specifically for difference and for its enabling force of creating space for multiple modes of criticism, including feminist criticism. Wainwright therefore reads the Matthean narrative of Jesus' infancy in dialogue with relevant Hebrew Bible narratives (such as the creation/beginning passages in Genesis, Joseph's dreams in Gen. 37, Moses' infancy in Exod. 2) and prophecies, ending her reading of the New Testament infancy narrative with Rachel's weeping in Jeremiah 31. Thus, her reading has

---

2.   For an earlier study of this subject, cf. Ramona F. West, *Ruth: A Retelling of Genesis 38?* (PhD dissertation, Southern Baptist Theological Seminary; Ann Arbor, MI: University Microfilms, 1987).

implications for the issue of difference and multivocality far beyond the textual sections chosen for intertextual analysis (see section II).

VIII. *Forays into Rabbinics*

Viewed as a whole, the New Testament—and its exegetes—interpret the Hebrew Bible/Old Testament as a prooftext for its own practical and ideological ends. The same observation can be applied to the literatures of so-called rabbinic Judaism. In both instances, the claim for and of interpretation in actuality authorizes claims related to the interpreters' circumstances inasmuch as, if not more than, it explicates biblical texts. The essays in this section are commentaries on how rabbinic Bible reading may have operated in Jewish communities. As such, they also constitute a contribution to the issues of the establishment of women's socio-communal role by referral to the Hebrew Bible.

Judith Hauptman's 'Rabbinic Interpretation of Scripture' moves from an introduction of the rabbinic corpus to a review of the relatively new and limited feminist criticisms of it. Hauptman reads her texts not for the Bible-derived patriarchal oppression of women, which she understands as obvious, but for the 'challenge...to look beyond such a finding and determine where the system as a whole was heading'. She concludes her discussion of sex crimes against women in the Hebrew Bible, the Mishnah and Babylonian Talmud by observing that (at least some of) the rabbis' interpretations of Scripture was 'socially motivated and tendentious': the rabbis invented rules of exegesis that allowed them to deconstruct and reconstruct Scriptures in favour of, rather than against, abused women.

Miriam Peskowitz, in 'Rabbis, Feminists and Patriarchy's Ordinariness', poses a series of methodological questions concerning critical concerns of feminist readings for women, men and gender. She then analyzes a passage from the mishnaic tractate, $K^e t\hat{u}b\hat{o}t$ (marriage contracts), with referrals to the complex literary and socio-historical features underlying the rabbinic sources. The Hebrew Bible is almost totally silent on gender relations within the legal transaction of marriage. Peskowitz demonstrates that gender relations matter to the rabbis, some of whom attempt to transform the *sense* of husbandly authority over a wife's property—already much in evidence in the Hebrew Bible—into a *legal* concept. Throughout her essay, Peskowitz emphasizes that a plurality of readings for the same passages and ideas is, of course, viable and valuable.

Although, with notable exceptions, women have been by and large excluded from the formulation, study, exegesis and transmission of canonized texts in Judeo-Christian communities, this exclusion has included, first and foremost, Scriptures. In 'Torah Study and the Making of Jewish Gender', Daniel Boyarin outlines the decisive significance of such female exclusion from education and equal participation in sacred literatures for gendering females and males in the Jewish Ashkenazi traditional settings, then traces the changes introduced by several women in the modern era. Boyarin's study is about a specific community of orthodox Judaism in which the 'Torah study' was typically talmudic (rather than Hebrew Bible) study, and the women who tried to break away from the exclusionary gendering were orthodox women interested in staying within the community. However, the implications of his description and analysis are clearly relevant to feminist projects related to biblical studies, and are thought provoking.

IX. *The Personal/Autobiographical*

Perhaps paradoxically, a growing awareness of the 'death of the author' is augmented and supplemented, in biblical studies as well as in other fields of knowledge, by a growing awareness of the reader's life. Feminist insistence on 'experience' as a critical category may have contributed its share to this not particularly feminist trend. In recent years, autobiographical or 'personal' criticism, in which the critic emphasizes her or his life situation as an asset for, rather than hindrance to, his or her craft, has been legitimated by, and allotted a small space in, at least some academic circles. This section, which complements section II (in which the emphasis is on 'experience' and 'difference' as *abstracted* personal and group categories rather than on an *individual*, autobiographical, 'personal' category) has two such 'personal' essays. No claim is made by any of the contributors for universal validity or privileged status. On the contrary: the value of such contributions lies in their promotion, once again, of the diversity that creates space for feminists and all other readers.

David Gunn has written extensively on his biblical namesake, king David. In his 'Reflections on David' Gunn charts his personal journey as a Bible scholar from his earlier work on biblical texts in which the king plays a major role, twenty years ago, to his latest and current work. My essay, '"My" Song of Songs', maps relevant factors of my earlier life in Israel and the retrospective ramifications of this life for my critical comprehension of the Song of Songs.

X. *Back to the Traditional*

Feminist criticism of the Bible emphasizes certain issues while relatively or wholly neglecting other concerns: not all or even most possible perspectives current in critical Bible discourse are studied or developed by its practitioners. Yet, feminists clearly do and may benefit from elements of mainstream interpretation (in addition to being damaged by it). We thought that all of us needed to be reminded of this. To that end, we reprint here Claus Westermann's study of 'Beauty in the Hebrew Bible', translated into English for the first time.

Carole Fontaine's 'Preface' to the essay explains why it was chosen as a non-feminist source that may be of value for feminists in their own projects. In the essay itself, Westermann classifies the concept of 'beauty' as 'being' and 'event', then applies his classification to various texts and genres of the Hebrew Bible. His work is a reminder that, ultimately, feminist criticism of the Bible—whatever its allegiance—at the present stage cannot and perhaps should not break away from the communities of academic and religious discourse that are still far from accepting it fully.

I

METACRITICS

FEMINIST CRITICISM AND BIBLICAL STUDIES ON THE VERGE OF THE TWENTY-FIRST CENTURY*

Adele Reinhartz

The year 1995 marks a hundred years since the publication of *The Woman's Bible*, by Elizabeth Cady Stanton. Although one can by no means draw a direct line from Cady Stanton's efforts to the shape of feminist biblical criticism in the present,[1] this anniversary provides an appropriate occasion for an assessment of the current relationship between feminist criticism and biblical studies, as well as an attempt to foresee its future course. I approached this task with the intention of providing a reasoned analysis, cataloguing achievements and challenges, and outlining a vision of the shape of the field in the twenty-first century. These intentions came to naught, however, when I discovered, to my horror, that my capacity for reasoned analysis has been damaged by my lifestyle. I refer specifically to my near-total immersion in narrative. From Judges, Judith and campus intrigue during the day, A.A. Milne, E.B. White and complicated schoolyard anecdotes in the evening, to Toni Morrison, Tony Hillerman and/or the evening news at night, my days and my thoughts are bounded by stories. For this reason, every effort to approach my present task was thwarted by a still, or rather, shrill small voice, demanding, 'read me a story'. But what story, or stories could I read into, or read out of, the relationship between feminist criticism and biblical studies?

As every child, and the occasional narrative critic, knows, there are two essential ingredients to every story: character and plot. By resorting to gross overgeneralization, oversimplification and reductionism, I managed to construct two protagonists out of the abstract terms

---

*   This article is a slightly revised version of a panel presentation on the 'Impact of Women's Studies on Biblical Studies', at the Society of Biblical Literature Annual Meeting, Philadelphia, 19 November, 1995.

1.   For an assessment of Cady Stanton's work, see Elisabeth Schüssler Fiorenza, 'Transforming the Legacy of *The Woman's Bible*', in Elisabeth Schüssler Fiorenza (ed.), *Searching the Scriptures*. I. *A Feminist Introduction* (New York: Crossroad, 1993), pp. 1-24.

'feminist biblical criticism' and 'biblical studies'. To begin with the former. Most, though by no means all, participants in feminist criticism are women; all are concerned with issues related to women, and are engaged in diverse activities: writing women into biblical history, society and cult; examining the representation of women in canonical and non-canonical texts; searching for evidence of women's hands in material artifacts; addressing androcentrism and patriarchy in texts as well as in scholarship, and exploring the relationship between biblical texts and women's lives in all their complexity. Here there is, then, a female protagonist for our story. As for biblical studies, if not all biblical students are male, it is the case that many of us sat, or currently sit, at the feet of male teachers, where we are taught the norms and practices of what Elisabeth Schüssler Fiorenza has termed 'malestream' biblical scholarship. Unlike feminist criticism, this form of scholarship does not describe its agenda in terms of gendered interests and perspectives. Rather, its explicit goal is to reconstruct the original text, context and meaning of Scripture by applying objective, value-free, scientific methodology enshrined in historical and related criticisms. Yet it is clear, at least to feminist critics, that the interpretive activities directed towards this goal, far from being value-free, express the norms and world-view of the exegetes themselves. Even now, despite the adoption of gender-inclusive language, many major institutions, academic societies and their sponsored journals continue to embody the voices of the patriarchs of our field. Voilà: biblical studies as male protagonist.

Now for the plot. What kind of story do these protagonists act out? A heart-warming romance, perhaps, in which the woman's reluctance is overcome by the male protagonist, with the resulting passionate love and living happily ever after? Or romantic comedy, in which bumbling male anti-hero is found and re-educated by beautiful, talented, persistent, forgiving heroine, and again, they live happily ever after? Or, to reverse the roles, a story in which ageing professor transforms young, brilliant, but uneducated flower girl into his fair lady, and is in turn transformed by her, with the requisite happy ending?

More promising, and more appropriate, perhaps, are biblical love stories. Again, there is a range to choose from: the pastoral romance of Ruth and Boaz in which rich, older male relative rescues beautiful young widow and provides her, and her mother-in-law, with a proto-messianic offspring. Or, on another reading of Ruth, the love between Ruth and Naomi, which transcends or, perhaps, erases the boundaries of age, gender, religion and ethnicity. Or, for a more sinister plot, the perversion of the love story in biblical tales of terror—the incestuous rape of Tamar, daughter of David (2 Sam. 13), the gang rape and murder of the Levite's concubine (Judg. 19), or the death by fire of Samson's Timnite wife (Judg. 15.6).

How fitting are these stories as allegories of the relations between feminist criticism and biblical studies? There are, without question, scholars who, though trained in the traditions of the fathers, have taken serious account of feminist scholarship and allowed it to have a profound impact on their work. And certainly there are feminist critics whose encounters with a patriarchal establishment have left them rejected and violated. Yet I have misgivings about choosing the love story in any of its permutations as the appropriate basis for an allegory on the relationship between feminist criticism and biblical studies.

First, the biblical love story frequently results in either the literal or the figurative erasure of the female partner. Victims of tragedy such as the Levite's concubine and Samson's Timnite wife are blotted out through their murder, while Tamar, raped by her brother Amnon, 'dwelt, a desolate woman, in her brother Absalom's house' (2 Sam. 14.20). The only way in which Naomi can provide security and a future for her beloved Ruth is to marry her off to Boaz, in compliance with levirate law. Indeed, after the conception and birth of her son, Obed (Ruth 4.13), Ruth is mentioned no more.

Secondly, the very act of overgeneralization that permits the gendered personification of feminist criticism is misleading precisely because it lifts feminist criticism out of its intellectual context in contemporary critical theory. For the challenge that feminist criticism poses to biblical studies does not lie specifically in its interest in women's history, theology, rituals and representation, but in its radical rethinking and re-evaluation of the norms and canons of biblical criticism. In the formulation and deployment of its critique, feminist biblical criticism has benefited not only from women's studies and feminist theory but also from generous interaction with a range of other 'isms' and 'ologies', including literary and social-scientific criticism, post-colonialism, gay and lesbian studies and African, Asian and Latin American liberation theology. Feminist criticism comes well armed to do battle with mainstream biblical criticism on grounds that go beyond androcentrism and patriarchy to the foundational assumptions of our discipline. The feminist battle itself must be seen as only one front in an all out war within Western intellectual thought.

These military metaphors suggest that efforts to tell the story of feminist criticism and biblical studies might be better served by an apocalyptic paradigm, a cosmic struggle between the forces of Good and Evil, a feminist Star Wars, perhaps, or, better, a feminist Revelation, complete with an eschatological vision of a future world in which the ecclesia of women is the new Jerusalem. In this model, the battle lines are drawn between believers in the primacy of value-free scholarship and those, including feminist critics, who argue that complete objectivity is neither possible nor desirable.

In a generally favorable review of two recent collections of feminist biblical writing, Yair Zakovitch confesses, 'If I squirmed nervously in my armchair while reading, this was principally because of what I am: a man and a Biblical scholar who tries, as much as posssible, to silence his inner voice in order to listen to the voices of the Biblical verses. Turning the Bible into a mirror [as Zakovitch claims feminists try to do] prevents one from seeing the depth of literary creativity and sophistication in it and tends to distort its significance.' Such a reading, in his view, is not capable of revealing 'the secrets of the Bible', even though it opens a window for understanding the mind of the reader.[2] In contrast, Carolyn Osiek argues that 'biblical interpretation cannot function in isolation from the social and intellectual world of the interpreter' and that the notion that traditional scholarship is value-free is simply false.[3]

The language in which these scholars define and defend their opposing perspectives does indeed call to mind the conflict inherent in the apocalyptic paradigm, if not the extravagance and phantasmagorical nature of its imagery. But the apocalyptic model, like the romantic paradigm, is undermined by its own reductionism. The apocalyptic plot presumes a monolithic vision of each side which, I would venture, does not do justice to the complexity of the situation. Efforts to be 'right' on gender issues may inscribe other wrongs such as anti-Judaism, as in studies that attempt to vindicate Christianity by assigning its patriarchal elements to early Judaism. On the other hand, even as feminists draw from the well of women's studies and critical theory, so do we also utilize the specialized tools of biblical

2.   Yair Zakovitch, 'Bible, Bible on the Wall', *Jerusalem Report*, 26 January, 1995, p. 48. The review is of Judith A. Kates and Gail Twersky Reimer (eds.), *Reading Ruth: Contemporary Women Reclaim a Sacred Story* (New York: Ballantine, 1994), and Christina Büchman and Celina Spiegel (eds.), *Out of the Garden: Women Writers on the Bible* (New York: Ballantine, 1993).

3.   Carolyn Osiek, 'The Feminist and the Bible: Hermeneutical Alternatives', in Adela Yarbro Collins (ed.), *Feminist Perspectives on Biblical Scholarship* (Atlanta: Scholars Press, 1985), p. 96.

scholarship and seek entry into the institutions that it has created.

This becomes clear as we consider the fundamental question at stake in the discussion: does the text have a voice of its own, which can be heard only if one suppresses one's own; or, is the text itself mute, capable of being heard only through the diverse voices of those who read it? Though the two sides in the debate may have clear if divergent responses to this question, to my mind the answer is not an 'either/or'. Rather, it requires a more complex model of the relationship between interpreter and text. Readings from a variety of social locations not only reflect the minds of the readers, as Zakovitch suggests, but also bring to light or illumine different aspects of the text. Further, to read out of one's own identity and social location does not make one incapable of hearing and learning from the readings of others. To read an Asian-feminist interpretation of the book of Ruth opens one up not only to the authority structure of the traditional Japanese household in which the mother-in-law exerted considerable power, but also to potentially oppressive undertones in the relationship between Ruth and Naomi within the biblical story itself. Similarly, African-American readings of the story of Hagar can become a touchstone for discussions of racism, the Eurocentric bias of standard commentaries on Genesis and the dynamics of class, ethnicity and economics in Genesis 16 through 21.

My own experience in biblical interpretation, and my readings of the work of others, have convinced me that reading from an 'invested' perspective does not, in fact, render us incapable of hearing the voice of the text, of imagining the way in which that text might have been heard or read by its earliest audience, or of considering its impact on a contemporary reader who is unlike oneself. As a particular Jewish feminist reader of the fourth Gospel, I am particularly sensitive to a number of issues, such as its portrayal of Jews and its use of the term Ἰουδαῖος, the depiction of Jewish-Christian women, the use of the language of wisdom and paternity in Johannine Christology and theology. Yet other issues, such as the parable—or is it allegory?—of the shepherd and the sheep, the structure of the signs stories, the use of prophetic motifs in the characterization of Jesus, are also of interest. A daughter of holocaust survivors, I am concerned with the contribution of the fourth Gospel, and interpretations thereof, to Christian anti-Judaism. But, though not a Christian, I also care about its implications for the role of women in contemporary Christian life. These contemporary questions do not obscure an intrinsic curiosity about the historical, social and religious setting of the Gospel in the first century CE. In investigating these and other issues

I will not hesitate to draw on the range of historical-critical method while acknowledging that the basic facts of my identity, as well as many other factors that may or may not always be visible to me, will shape the exegetical process and its results, just as they have for all readers of this text.

Not only the polarized characters but also the plot structure of the apocalyptic paradigm compromise its use as a model for the relations between feminist and biblical studies. The conflict between right and wrong implied in apocalyptic stories is ultimately one between the self (defined as right) and the other (defined as wrong), and is resolved when right, that is, self, asserts power and domination over wrong, that is, the other. Yet the goal of feminist criticism is not to substitute female hierarchies and modes of scholarship for male ones, but to transform the system as a whole. A crucial element of transformation is the breaking down of hierarchies, and the emergence and positive evaluation of a broad range of voices. As the Bible and Culture Collective has noted, 'It is perhaps this refusal of mastery that is womanism's and feminism's most radical edge, offering not a new system of domination but a continuous critique of all such systems'.[4]

If the apocalyptic model, like the romantic model, is flawed both in terms of character and plot, perhaps we should search specifically for a third narrative paradigm, one that challenges hierarchy, and both values and gives voice to difference. Such stories do not abound in the biblical corpus, though stories concerning the structure of power and authority are not hard to find. In Numbers 12, for example, Miriam and Aaron challenge the authority of Moses, saying, 'Has *HaShem*[5] spoken only through Moses? Has *HaShem* not spoken through us also?' (12.2). The issue recurs in Numbers 16, when the Levite Korah and 250 community leaders assemble against Moses and Aaron, and say, 'You have gone too far! All the congregation are holy, every one of them, and *HaShem* is among them. So why then do you exalt yourselves above the assembly of *HaShem*?' (16.3). In both cases the text has *HaShem* weighing in on Moses' behalf and punishing those who would challenge the established human authority figures; Miriam (though not Aaron) gets leprosy, and Korah and his cohort are swallowed by the earth. The biblical accounts therefore

4. Bible and Culture Collective, *The Postmodern Bible* (New Haven: Yale University Press, 1995), p. 270.

5. Literally 'The Name' (in Hebrew), a Jewish circumlocution for avoiding the explicit mention of God's name.

uphold the principle of a single, divinely appointed human authority figure who brooks no challenge.

Nor are there many stories that uphold the value of diversity. The Tower of Babel story in Genesis 11 provides an etiology for the dispersion of peoples over the face of the earth and the diversity of human language. When the people of the whole earth attempt to 'build [themselves] a city and a tower with its top in the heavens' (11.4), *HaShem* frets: 'They are one people and they have all one language; and this is only the beginning of what they will do; nothing that they propose to do will now be impossible for them' (11.6). The dispersion and confusion of languages was *HaShem*'s way of creating obstacles for large-scale co-operative projects and circumventing a potential threat to divine hegemony, power and authority.

The difficulty in finding biblical support for challenging central authority and supporting multiple voices is not surprising, given the struggle for monotheism that pervades the Hebrew Scriptures. But the fact remains that while each of the three paradigms explored thus far goes some distance in describing the current relationship between biblical studies and feminist criticism, none provides a reasonable or appealing vision of the future of our field in the twenty-first century.

This unfortunate situation leaves me with two options. One is to acknowledge the limitations of my attempt to tell this story on the basis of biblical paradigms, an admission which could be followed up by the sort of academic analysis of my own motivations, underlying assumptions and social location that I was hoping to avoid. The second is to follow time-honoured tradition and simply rewrite these biblical stories to suit my own purposes. While the former option is likely the more honest, the second is undoubtedly more fun.

So in the spirit of narrative pleasure, allow me to don my rose-coloured glasses and revisit our three paradigms. I begin by recounting the long-suppressed, alternative ending to the Book of Ruth. In this version, Naomi and Ruth's efforts to support themselves lead them to hire a real estate lawyer, who searches the title to Elimelech's land and discovers that in fact it belongs to Naomi outright. The two women settle down on the land, plow, sow and harvest their own crops, and rejoice in the knowledge that they have secured their future without having to bow to the patriarchal strictures of levirate law. Their story becomes an inspiration to those feminist biblical scholars who, ambivalent towards existing institutional structures, work together in teaching, research, publication and social activism to create their own.

Turning to the apocalyptic paradigm, I will read a section from a newly discovered pseudonymous work, attributed to the prophet Danielle and set in post-exilic Israel. Based on internal evidence, however, scholars believe it was written approximately twenty-five centuries later by a Canadian, sometime after October 30, 1995. In ch. 7 Danielle, traumatized by the near-defeat of the 'no' side in the Quebec referendum, dreamed of a time when the forces of good would triumph unequivocally over the forces of evil. In her dream she saw the winds of heaven stirring up the great sea and many great beasts came up out of the sea, each different from the next. She watched as each beast was successively devoured by the one that came after it, culminating in the destruction of the final beast, who was put to death and its body destroyed and given over to be burned with fire. She recounts,

> I, Danielle, then saw one like a daughter of woman, coming with the clouds of heaven. To her was offered dominion and glory and sovereignty, that all peoples nations and languages should serve her. But the one like a daughter of woman refused, saying, 'Thanks, but no thanks'. As for me, Danielle, my spirit was troubled within me. Luckily, the angel Raphaella was available to reveal the truth concerning all this. She said, 'The beasts are the successive waves of biblical criticism, each of which claimed to supply the truth and supplant its predecessor. The last, and most persistent beast is the chimera of value-free scholarship, to which the others were also enslaved. The one like the daughter of woman is a collective image for feminist biblical scholars, who strive not for dominion but for the transformation of our intellectual frameworks 'so that they become truly inclusive of all human experience',[6] including, alongside many others, that of the conquered beasts themselves.

Finally, there is the little-known sequel to the Tower of Babel story. Despite their geographical dispersion and the confusion of their languages, the people of the earth experienced the irresistible urge to get together and learn each other's tongues or, as they came to be called, modes of discourse. And so the historical-critics spoke with the literary critics, the structuralists interfaced with the social-scientific critics, the post-colonialists and the womanists discovered a common vocabulary, the liberation theologians and speech-act theorists attempted polite, if strained, conversation, while the postmodernists did their best to deconstruct everyone else. Building a common city and tower were now out of the question due to divine fiat, the rising cost of real estate and frozen academic salaries. Instead, the people of the earth decided to meet together on an annual basis, in a different metropolis every year, in order to listen to each other speak,

---

6. Schüssler Fiorenza, *Bread Not Stone* (Boston: Beacon Press 1984), p. 2.

try out each other's modes of discourse, and buy each other's books at an attractive discount. Though the sacred writings were much in evidence on these occasions, God remained inconspicuous. I imagine, however, that she did not fear *this* babble but rather enjoyed it even if, like her creation, she did not quite understand it all. Her greatest joy, however, was to hear the women's voices with the men's, each with its own accent, timber and range. And indeed, it was very, very good.

TOWARD FEMINIST COMPANIONSHIP: THE FUTURE OF FEMINIST BIBLICAL STUDIES AND FEMINISM

Pamela J. Milne

Introduction

The *Feminist Companion to the Bible* is a celebration. It is a celebration of feminist biblical scholarship as a viable and vibrant area within the discipline of biblical studies. It is a celebration of the dynamic growth and diversity of feminist biblical scholarship over a century, but particularly over the last twenty years. It is a celebration of intellectual interest in women and women's issues related to the Hebrew biblical tradition, an interest that has finally found extensive expression after millennia of neglect and suppression. It is a celebration of women scholars and their scholarship in a field that had been so heavily dominated by men. And it is a celebration of the fact that some male biblical scholars are learning to include women and women's issues in their own scholarship on the bible.

Unique Contributions of the Feminist Companion

As a multi-volume series, The *Feminist Companion to the Bible* not only celebrates feminist scholarship but also makes a unique contribution to this rapidly emerging field. Unlike a commentary in which numerous feminist analysts attempt to provide general introductory information on each biblical book and to illuminate all relevant biblical passages from a similar interpretive perspective,[1] or an edited collection of articles which may include studies of a variety of texts by several interpreters,[2] the *Feminist Companion* seeks neither to

---

1.   For example, Carol Newsom and Sharon Ringe (eds.), *The Women's Bible Commentary* (Louisville, KY: Westminster/John Knox Press, 1992).

2.   For example, Peggy Day (ed.), *Gender and Difference in Ancient Israel* (Minneapolis: Fortress Press, 1989) or Alice Bach (ed.), *The Pleasure of Her Text: Feminist Readings of Biblical and Historical Texts* (Philadelphia: Trinity Press International, 1990).

include all biblical texts nor does it attempt to achieve uniformity of method or perspective.

It is, rather, a reflection of the diversity and creativity which now characterize feminist scholarship on the Hebrew bible. It gathers the work of a wide range of feminist commentators, some of it previously published and some newly written, some of it focused on specific texts and some on more general issues. Its historical scope takes in a century of feminist biblical criticism. Studies from the 1990s are placed in the context of work from the 1890s[3] and from the 1970s[4] with the result that the attentive user of this *Companion* can hear the voices of the foremothers who dared to challenge the interpretive orthodoxies of male religious establishments and can observe how those early voices have inspired and empowered subsequent generations.

Methodological diversity also characterizes the *Feminist Companion*. Literary approaches do predominate, but this simply reflects the current emphasis in biblical scholarship as a whole. However, literary criticism is itself multifaceted and this is well reflected in the articles which comprise this series. There is no prescribed or privileged critical methodology or analytical focus. Historical, sociological, anthropological, archaeological and psychological approaches are all evident alongside or in partnership with literary approaches. The community which produced the biblical text, readers of the text, the history of interpretation of the text are among the foci included along with the text itself.

Phases of Feminist Biblical Criticism

The *Feminist Companion* series also provides the best representation to date of what are often described as the phases or generations of feminist biblical criticism.[5] The first phase coincides with the rise of

---

3.   Elizabeth Cady Stanton (ed.), *The Woman's Bible* (New York: European Publishing Co., 1895) is probably the best know work among nineteenth-century efforts of women to interpret the Bible from a feminist perspective. Selections from Stanton's work are included in several volumes of the *Feminist Companion: Genesis, Song of Songs*, and *Ruth*.

4.   For example, Phyllis Trible's 'Love Lyrics Redeemed' in A. Brenner (ed.), *A Feminist Companion to the Song of Songs* (The Feminist Companion to the Bible, 1; Sheffield: JSOT Press, 1993) is reprinted from Trible's classic, *God and the Rhetoric of Sexuality* (Philadelphia: Fortress Press, 1978).

5.   For discussions of the perceived phases of feminist biblical criticism seen principally from a North American perspective see Pamela J. Milne, 'No Promised

the feminist movement in the United States. At its very roots in the late eighteenth century, the emerging feminist movement raised critical questions about the bible. This phase culminated in 1895 with the publication of *The Woman's Bible* by Elizabeth Cady Stanton and was followed by a period of relative feminist silence on this subject lasting until the 1960s.

The second phase began shortly after Valerie Saiving's article, 'The Human Situation: A Feminine View', asked fundamental questions about the inclusivity of contemporary Christian theological models.[6] In the 1970s, the work of Phyllis Trible, particularly her investigation of Genesis 2–3, stands out as the most influential and can be said to mark the beginning of the second phase of feminist studies focusing on the bible.[7] Working from a literary-critical perspective and with the rhetorical-critical method which had recently made its appearance in North American biblical scholarship,[8] Trible, along with women scholars like Phyllis Bird,[9] began the process of placing feminist questions within the framework of professional biblical scholarship.

During the first decade of the second phase, feminist biblical scholars struggled to have their work accepted. They struggled to win

Land: Rejecting the Authority of the Bible', in H. Shanks (ed.), *Feminist Approaches to the Bible: Symposium at the Smithsonian Institution* (Washington: Biblical Archaeological Society, 1995), pp. 47-73; Eileen Schuller, 'Feminism and Biblical Hermeneutics: Genesis 1–3 as a Test Case', in M. Joy and E.K. Neumaier-Dargyay (eds.), *Gender, Genre and Religion: Feminist Reflections* (Waterloo: Wilfid Laurier Press, 1995), pp. 31-46. Elisabeth Grössmann's 'History of Biblical Interpretation by European Women', pp. 27-40, in E. Schüssler Fiorenza (ed.), *Searching the Scriptures. I. A Feminist Introduction* (New York: Crossroads, 1993), reminds us that women have been interpreting the Bible in unique and interesting ways for centuries prior to the development of an explicitly feminist consciousness and political context.

6. Saiving's article was originally published in the *Journal of Religion* (April, 1960) and is reprinted in C. Christ and J. Plaskow (eds.), *Womanspirit Rising: A Feminist Reader in Religion* (New York: Harper & Row, 1979), pp. 25-42.

7. 'Eve and Adam: Genesis 2–3 Reread', *Andover Newton Quarterly* 13 (March 1973), pp. 251-58, reprinted in Christ and Plaskow (eds.), *Womanspirit Rising*, pp. 74-83. In the same year, Trible also published 'Depatriarchalizing in Biblical Interpretation', *Journal of the American Academy of Religion* 12 (1973), pp. 39-42.

8. James Muilenberg played a key role both in introducing this method of analysis to the United States and also in influencing Trible's development as a biblical scholar.

9. See, for example, Bird's important early survey article, 'Images of Women in the Old Testament', in R. Ruether (ed.), *Religion and Sexism: Images of Women in Jewish and Christian Traditions* (New York: Simon & Schuster, 1974), pp. 41-88.

space in conference programmes; they struggled for space in traditional scholarly journals; they struggled for teaching positions. One of the most telling examples of these struggles was the fate of feminist scholars and scholarship during the centennial celebrations for the [American] Society of Biblical Literature (SBL) in 1980. The special programme planned in celebration set aside just one session for the topic 'women and the Bible' within the general category of 'The History and Sociology of Biblical Scholarship'. A group of women scholars used this time for a panel focused on 'The Effects of Women's Studies on Biblical Studies'.

While a minimum amount of space was found for women in the conference programme, the same was not true for the centennial publications. Three volumes on the history of the discipline, planned by the SBL in connection with the centennial celebration, contained no articles on women.[10] Rather than continue allowing women's voices to be silenced by the malestream SBL, the women on the panel took their papers to the British *Journal for the Study of the Old Testament* published by Sheffield Academic Press. In what surely must have been an embarrassment to the SBL, their papers appeared in *JSOT* 22 in 1982.

It is my sense that only after this publication of the papers from the women's panel did significant change begin to occur in the SBL. Although anything faintly resembling a feminist article remains a rarity in the *Journal of Biblical Literature*, the journal of the SBL,[11] women scholars, scholarship about women and feminist scholarship are all highly visible at both the American and the international SBL annual meetings. Indeed, many of the best attended sessions in recent years have been those in women's sections such as the 'Women in the Biblical World'. A similar pattern can be observed in some of the other professional biblical society meetings around the world.

By the 1990s, the sheer volume and diversity of woman-centred critical analyses of the bible suggests that we have now entered a third and very complex phase. For one thing, the term 'feminist' is no longer adequate to describe or include the analytical and ideological interpretive concerns of all women. Having established the validity and necessity of including women in the interpretive process, we are

10. For a fuller account see P. Trible, 'The Effects of Women's Studies on Biblical Studies', *JSOT* 22 (1982), pp. 3-5.

11. *The Journal for the Study of the Old Testament* remains a much more 'feminist friendly' journal than *JBL* or most other professional biblical studies journals.

now engaged in exploring the multitude of characteristics and qualities which distinguish groups of women. Woman-centred analyses today may examine factors of social and economic class, race, nationality and sexual orientation in relation to the literary characters in a biblical text, the women of the ancient community, the later faith community that preserved and transmitted the text, as well as in relation to the contemporary analyst and women in contemporary society.

Continuing Barriers to Feminist Scholarship

It is probably safe to say that the advances observed in professional biblical societies and publishing forums have not been equalled in the classroom or curriculum. Women scholars, and particularly *feminist* women scholars, still encounter difficulties in the job market. At a time when few teaching positions are available, and when departments of religion and religious studies are being 'down-sized' or eliminated[12] in favour of more 'essential' disciplines, women—who have entered the discipline in record numbers over the last decade—find themselves shut out by economic factors that compound the problem of sexist bias that has traditionally been a systemic barrier to women in this field. Personally, I do not think the economic argument is unrelated to the problem of sexist bias. The devaluing of the field that we can now observe at many institutions may well be linked to the fact that what was once a virtually all-male discipline is now no longer so. Obviously the place of scripture studies in theological schools is not at risk, but the same cannot be said for biblical studies, or even the more general study of religion, in non-theological contexts.

While feminist scholarship in biblical studies may be quite vibrant now, its long-term viability may be endangered or at least impeded by the gradual disappearance of teaching positions, which are the essential vehicle for ensuring that feminist perspectives on the study of the bible and religion are integral parts of the post-secondary educational curriculum. Given the centrality of the biblical tradition to Western culture and society,[13] feminist literacy with respect to the

12. In Canada, for example, the departments of religion at the University of Alberta and the University of Ottawa have recently been merged with other departments. At the University of Windsor, the religious studies department has been disbanded.

13. In a recent article in *Time* magazine, the biblical book of Genesis was described as 'central to Western culture'. The focus of the article is a two-month

bible ought to be seen as a necessary and very useful tool in the struggle to deconstruct patriarchy. Making it so represents a significant challenge to feminist biblical scholars.

Issues for the Future

In what follows, I wish to identify some issues I believe have been somewhat neglected by feminist biblical scholarship as it has developed into its current form. In so doing, it is not my intention to suggest that the development that has taken place has not been significant, important or useful. Nor do I wish to suggest that the kind of feminist analysis that has been done since the 1970s should stop.

Rather, it is my contention that there is now a need to focus more attention on some other aspects of feminist biblical scholarship that have not yet been adequately explored or developed. There are encouraging signs in recent years that a significant change is beginning to occur in a direction I think needs to be supported and advanced.

Feminist and Feminist Biblical Scholarship

Specifically, I want to suggest that feminist biblical scholarship needs to pay more attention to its relationship to other areas of feminist scholarship and activity. Even though it continues to draw on the work of feminists in other disciplines, feminist biblical criticism remains relatively isolated from feminist scholarship as a whole and from the contemporary feminist movement. One of the reasons for this is that feminist biblical scholars have often undertaken their work without raising the question of what makes their analyses feminist or for what feminist purpose their analyses are undertaken. As a result, feminists in other fields may be uncertain about how, or to what extent, feminist analyses of the bible contribute to wider feminist goals. Finally, I want to look at feminist biblical scholarship in an academic, non-theological context and argue for the

television series on Public Broadcasting Service (PBS) entitled, *Genesis: A Living Conversation*. There is no mention in the article of any of the contributions of feminist scholarship to the interpretation of Genesis. Although a few women are mentioned, the main emphasis is on what men are thinking and writing about this text. It tells us that 39 people are featured in the series. Among them are Catholics, Protestants, Jews, Muslims, a Hindu, preachers, Bible experts, psychologists, novelists, artists and poets. There is no mention of feminists. *Time*, 145.20 (October 28, 1996), pp. 66-75.

importance of developing this side of the feminist project more fully.

The marginality of feminist biblical criticism is not difficult to observe. For the most part it is evident in the absence of feminist work on the bible from mainstream feminist discourse. A survey of feminist journals or multi-disciplinary collections of feminist essays shows that they rarely include works by feminist biblical scholars. More general articles on religion occasionally find their way into such places, but analyses of biblical texts or traditions are rarely presented as part of the larger feminist intellectual world.

There are, however, more overt indications of marginality. Feminist scholars have themselves occasionally reflected on the situation. Historian Gerda Lerner, though taking note of feminist biblical studies, is generally critical of them. She cites the work of Phyllis Trible, Phyllis Bird and John Otwell, but finds unconvincing their efforts to counterbalance what she regards as an overwhelming amount of evidence of patriarchal domination in the bible with a few examples of heroic or independent female characters. For Lerner, such examples are insufficient to sustain an argument that women in the biblical tradition or in ancient Israel had a high status or were equal in status to men.[14]

Christian feminist theologian Letty Russell is even more explicit in identifying the marginality of feminist biblical scholarship. For her, the principal reason for this situation lies in the belief held by feminists in other fields that no matter how great the patriarchal bias against women within the biblical tradition, feminists biblical scholars will 'continue to uphold the value of biblical materials...'[15]

Two points can be made about the assessments offered by Lerner and Russell. The first is that they were both made in the mid-1980s and largely reflect the status of feminist biblical scholarship in the second phase. The second point is that the suspicion they identify among feminists generally in regard to feminist biblical scholarship relates to the issue of the 'authority' of the bible. Feminists in other fields seem concerned that no matter how sexist the bible proves to be, feminist biblical scholars will defend its religious authority and spiritual value. In other words, there appears to be a suspicion that much feminist work on the bible subordinates feminist ideologies to theological ones, a suspicion that the usual goal is to find ways, no

14. Gerda Lerner, *The Creation of Patriarchy* (Oxford: Oxford University Press, 1986), pp. 176-77.

15. Letty Russell, 'Introduction', in L. Russell (ed.), *Feminist Interpretations of the Bible*, (Philadelphia: Westminster Press, 1985), p. 14.

matter how tenuous, of making the bible into a positive resource for women. The logically prior question of whether or not the Bible is of value and what kind of value, if any, it has for women is side-stepped in preference to developing strategies for finding or creating ways of encouraging women to claim the biblical tradition as a women-friendly religious authority.

Indeed, there was a great deal of truth to the critique in the mid-1980s. Since then, however, there has been a significant increase in the amount of feminist work on the bible that is not specifically aimed at 'recovering' or 'reclaiming' the bible as a woman-friendly sacred text. Such work is still in evidence, of course. Phyllis Trible has continued to produce studies in the context of a commitment to Christianity and with the goal of demonstrating that the intentionality of the biblical tradition and faith is not patriarchy and sexism. Though she concedes that the bible is a patriarchal document, she is firm in the conviction that it can be redeemed from the 'bondage of patriarchy'.[16] She has always been very clear about her commitment to the biblical tradition in a Christian context and she works to overcome, resolve or confront the problems presented by the bible and its interpreters for herself and others, like herself, who believe it is possible to be both feminist and Christian.

But many others now either do not work within a confessional framework at all or at least do not attempt to minimize, rationalize or find ways around the problems presented to women by the biblical tradition. Mieke Bal, for example, explores the biblical text as a feminist narratologist but neither as a believer nor as a biblical scholar. She is decidedly not interested in the question of the religious authority of the bible but she is very much interested in the ethical responsibility for, and the political consequences of, reading texts such as the bible.[17]

---

16. See, for example, her articles, 'Eve and Miriam: From the Margins to the Center', in Shanks (ed.), *Feminist Approaches to the Bible*, pp. 5-24; and 'If the Bible's So Patriarchal, How Come I Love It?', *Bible Review* 8.5 (1992), pp. 44-47, 55.

17. Mieke Bal, 'Introduction', in M. Bal (ed.), *Anti-Covenant: Counter-Reading Women's Lives in the Hebrew Bible* (Sheffield: Almond Press, 1989), pp. 11-24. Bal has worked extensively on the book of Judges and one of her studies, 'A Body of Writing: Judges 19', is included in A. Brenner (ed.), *A Feminist Companion to Judges* (The Feminist Companion to the Bible, 4; Sheffield: JSOT Press, 1993), pp. 218-30. *A Feminist Companion to Ruth* (The Feminist Companon to the Bible, 3; Sheffield: Sheffield Academic Press, 1993), pp. 42-69, reproduces a chapter (together with a later Afterword) entitled, 'Heroism and Proper Names, Or the Fruits of Analogy',

Esther Fuchs is a biblical scholar who has consistently raised feminist concerns about the subtle and insidious ways in which the biblical text communicates patriarchy. Her work has not attempted to reclaim or reform but only to reveal unapologetically the patriarchal strategies woven into the bible. For many years hers was a scholarly voice crying in the wilderness and it has fallen silent in recent times.[18]

The work of Cheryl Exum offers an example of how some feminist biblical scholarship has changed focus. This is particularly well documented in the *Feminist Companion* volume on Exodus to Deuteronomy, which contains two articles by Exum on Exodus 1.8-2.10. The first was originally published in 1983[19] and the second, a critique of the first, was written for the *Feminist Companion* volume published in 1994.[20] In the second article Exum tells her readers that the biblical text, Exodus 1.8-2.10, was not one she herself chose for analysis. Rather, it was one she was invited to reflect on for a joint symposium entitled the 'Feminist Hermeneutic Project', held by the American Academy of Religion in 1981. From her vantage point in the 1990s, Exum notes that in the early 1980s 'one of the goals of the emerging feminist biblical criticism was to uncover positive portrayals of women in the Bible...' At that time, few feminist biblical scholars stopped to assess the validity of such a goal. Today, however, Exum challenges the very idea of 'pluck[ing] positive images out of an admittedly androcentric text, separating literary characterizations from the androcentric interests they were created to serve'.[21] In many ways, she is recognizing the very issues Fuchs tried so hard to raise in the 1980s. The key problem Exum sees with her earlier approach,

from Bal's book, *Lethal Love: Feminist Literary Readings of Biblical Love Stories* (Bloomington: Indiana University Press, 1987), pp. 68-88. The articles illustrate Bal's focus on literary dimensions and show how she examines biblical texts in wider cultural contexts.

18. See, for example, Esther Fuchs, 'The Literary Characterization of Mothers and Sexual Politics in the Hebrew Bible', and 'Who is Hiding the Truth? Deceptive Women and Biblical Androcentrism', in Adela Yarbro Collins (ed.), *Feminist Perspectives on Biblical Scholarship* (Chico, CA: Scholars Press, 1985), pp. 117-44.

19. The first article was entitled ' "You Shall Let Every Daughter Live": A Study of Exodus 1:8–2:10', and appeared in *Semeia* 28 (1983), pp. 63-82.

20. 'Second Thoughts about Secondary Characters: Women in Exodus 1.8–2.10', pp. 75-87 in *A Feminist Companion to Exodus to Deuteronomy* (Sheffield: Sheffield Academic Press, 1994). In this article, Exum also critiques the article by Jopie Siebert-Hommes, ' "But If She Be a Daughter... She May Live!": "Daughters" and "Sons" in Exodus 1–2', in the same volume (pp. 62-74).

21. Exum, 'Second Thoughts', p. 76.

and that of many other feminist scholars who focus on the literary
dimensions of the biblical text, is that it ignored ideology. It noticed
that women characters were presented in a positive light but it failed
to inquire about whose interests were being served by such a portrayal. By recommending such texts as positive for women readers
today, this kind of approach functions to make women complicit in
the androcentric gender ideology of the bible.

Exum views her recognition that women's experience has been
'displaced and distorted' in biblical texts as in other patriarchal
texts,[22] (even ones which appear to present women in a positive light)
as a 'step in the right direction'[23] for feminist biblical criticism. I
could not agree more. But it is just one step that needs to be taken
more explicitly and by more feminist biblical critics if our work is to
be viewed less suspiciously by our feminist colleagues in other
disciplines, and if our work is to play a significant role in the feminist
movement's struggle for gender equity.

Implications of Gender Ideology in the Bible

A necessary next step, I would argue, is to consider the political and
social implications of biblical gender ideology, not only as it affects
women characters in the text but as it has affected women in society
through the millennia and in our own time.

When we examine the phases through which feminist analysis of
the bible has developed during the past two hundred years, we can
observe that there has been a process of professionalization that has
involved a de-politicization of feminist work on the bible. This process, I believe, is precisely what has led to the marginalization of our
work from the larger feminist enterprise.

One could argue that the first phase of feminist analysis of the bible
in the United States grew out of political necessity. Ironically, perhaps, in a country so dedicated to the separation of church and state,
the bible was a major authoritative weapon wielded by some white
Christian men in denying basic human rights to African Americans
and to women: the rights of self-determination, freedom, education,
along with the right to vote.

In 1790, when Judith Sargent Murray published her essay, 'On the
Equality of the Sexes',[24] she attached to it a piece she had written

22. Exum, 'Second Thoughts', pp. 86-87.
23. Exum, 'Second Thoughts', p. 87.
24. Reproduced in Alice Rossi (ed.), *The Feminist Papers: From Adams to de*

privately to a male friend ten years earlier that makes reference to the Adam and Eve story. An advocate of equal educational opportunities for women, Murray found that traditional interpretations of the bible were being used in defence of a *status quo* that saw women as inferior and subordinate to men and, thus, not worthy of an education equal to that of men. From the reply to her male friend, we can infer that he must have used Genesis 2–3 in support of an argument for male superiority. Such a use of this text was long and well-established.[25] Murray did not seem to be intimidated by such a tactic and responded with a taunting feminist reinterpretation of the text:

> Thus it should see, that all the arts of the grand deceiver…were requisite to mislead our general mother, while the father of mankind forfeited his own, and relinquished the happiness of posterity, merely in compliance with the blandishments of a female.[26]

By the mid-1800s, the efforts of American women to be active and public workers in the abolitionist movement further highlighted the need to challenge traditional male biblical interpretation. So long as women remained in the domestic sphere and within the society of women, their work drew little opposition. But when women such as Angelina Grimké began delivering her anti-slavery lectures to mixed audiences of men and women in New England, she was quickly and forcefully attacked by Christian clergymen who appealed to New Testament texts such as 1 Tim. 2.9-14, 1 Pet. 3.1-7 and other 'household code passages'[27] to insist that women should be silent and

Beauvoir (New York: Columbia University Press, 1973).

25. See B.P. Prusak, 'Woman: Seductive Siren and Source of Sin?', in R. Ruether (ed.), *Religion and Sexism: Images of Women in Jewish and Christian Traditions* (New York: Simon & Schuster, 1974), pp. 89-116; J.A. Phillips, *Eve: The History of an Idea* (San Francisco: Harper & Row, 1984); Elaine Pagels, *Adam, Eve and the Serpent* (New York: Random House, 1988); Pamela J. Milne, 'Eve and Adam: A Feminist Reading', in H. Minkoff (ed.), *Approaches to the Bible: The Best of Bible Review* (Washington: Biblical Archaeological Society, 1995), II, pp. 259-69.

26. As quoted in Rossi (ed.), *The Feminist Papers*, p. 24.

27. This term refers to a group of late New Testament texts that assume the notion of the patriarchal Greco-Roman household structure as the ideal model for the early Christian community. In this model, the *paterfamilias* held ultimate authority over all others, human and animal, in the household. Eventually, the state was imaged as the macrocosm of the ideal father-led household, hierarchical and imperialistic. Col. 3.18–4.1 is the earliest Christian text to employ this pattern exhorting subordinate members of the community—wives/women, slaves and children—to submit to their superiors—husbands/men, masters, parents. Extensive discussions of household code texts can be found in David L. Balch, *Let Wives be Submissive: The Domestic Code in 1 Peter* (Atlanta: Scholars Press, 1981); Elisabeth

submissive. The Council of Congregationalist Ministers of Massachusetts issued a pastoral letter in 1837 denouncing such public activity by women:

> The power of woman is her dependence, flowing from the weakness which God has given her for her protection... We cannot, therefore but regret the mistaken conduct of those who encourage females to bear an obtrusive and ostentatious part in measures of reform, and countenance any of that sex who forget themselves as to itinerate in the character of public lecturers and teachers.[28]

Women activists were virtually forced to address women's rights in the context of biblical interpretation at this time. The issue of the role of the bible and institutionalized religion in oppressing women was on the agenda of the first women's rights convention at Seneca Falls in 1848.[29] Women had to take up the task of interpreting the bible from a feminist perspective because many of the churches used the authority of biblical proof-texts to justify keeping women out of the public sphere and denying them the key political right to vote.

There appear to have been two main feminist approaches to the problem. In a social context which was overwhelmingly Christian, most feminists seem to have adopted the view that the locus of the problem was in the translation and interpretation of the bible by men rather than in the bible itself. They were convinced that the bible was being misused by those claiming that women were created inferior to men by the god of the bible. This misuse was analogous to its misuse in support of slavery. These feminists were convinced that once the bible was properly and accurately interpreted, no evidence would be found to sustain the argument that women were inferior and subordinate to men.

Few women at the time had any professional scholarly training in biblical or theological studies, so some, like Lucy Stone, undertook

Schüssler Fiorenza, 'Tracing the Struggles: Patriarchy and Ministry', in *In Memory of Her: A Feminist Theological Reconstruction of Christian Origins* (New York: Crossroads, 1983), pp. 243-342; Mary Rose D'Angelo, 'Colossians', in E. Schüssler Fiorenza (ed.), *Searching the Scriptures. II. A Feminist Commentary* (New York: Crossroad, 1994), pp. 313-22; Sarah J. Tanzer, 'Ephesians', in *Searching the Scriptures*, II, pp. 325-48; Kathleen E. Corley, '1 Peter', in *Searching the Scriptures*, II, pp. 349-60.

28. 'Pastoral Letter from The General Association of Massachusetts (Orthodox) to the Churches Under Their Care', in Rossi (ed.), *The Feminist Papers*, pp. 305-306.

29. Miriam Gurko, *The Ladies of Seneca Falls: The Birth of the Women's Rights Movement* (New York: Schocken Books, 1974), pp. 9-10, 257.

the study of Hebrew and Greek in order to gain direct access to the biblical text in its original languages. With the ability to interpret on the basis of their own direct reading of the bible, feminists offered two main counter strategies. The first was to reinterpret the key texts that had been used to bolster the belief in woman's secondary nature and status—texts such as Genesis 2–3—in more woman-positive ways. The second was to find alternative texts that presented women in what appeared to be more positive roles—texts such as Judges 4–5 or the stories of Ruth and Esther.

But the efforts of these feminists seem to have had little effect on the way the bible was being used by the opponents of women's suffrage. By the end of the nineteenth century, there was still substantial opposition to the idea of women's equality from the major Christian churches, and feminist efforts to reinterpret the bible had met with limited success. As a result, most feminists attempted to ignore the opposition from organized religion as best they could, as they struggled for political enfranchisement.

However, others such as Matilda Joslyn Gage[30] and Elizabeth Cady Stanton,[31] chose to confront the opposition more directly. Whereas earlier feminists had chosen to work from within the structures of institutional religion, Gage and Stanton critiqued more from the outside. Moreover, they both located the problem within the biblical text itself, identifying the bible as a patriarchal document containing degrading ideas about women. Unlike many of their feminist sisters whose goal was to change the way people understood the bible in relation to women, feminists like Gage and Stanton were more interested in exposing the bible for what they believed it actually was and thereby minimizing its appeal and authoritative influence.

Gage launched a broad attack on Christianity setting forth the thesis that the oppression of women was part of this religion's very fabric, not merely a cultural overlay that could be removed through reinterpretation. She argued that belief in the secondary and subordinate status of women was a cornerstone of Christianity, one that it inherited from Judaism.[32]

30. In her book, *Women, Church and State: The Exposé of Male Collaboration Against the Female Sex* (repr.; Watertown, MA: Persephone Press, 1980) published in 1893.

31. *The Woman's Bible* (repr.; Seattle: Coalition Task Force on Women and Religion, 1974).

32. *Women, Church and State*, pp. 237-38. Although Gage saw Judaism as the forerunner religion that promoted the subordinate and secondary status of women,

Stanton's focus was more specifically directed to the Christian bible. She and a group of other women, none of whom were professional biblical scholars, produced the most extensive feminist-critical analysis of the bible ever undertaken to that date. *The Woman's Bible*, published in 1895, attempted to examine all biblical texts pertaining to women. As a result of this exercise, Stanton reached the conclusion that the bible contains degrading teachings about women that have become the foundation of the Christian religion's view of women.[33] Having reached this conclusion, Stanton's feminist goal was to convince other women that the bible should be regarded simply as a collection of historical and mythological writings by men, not the authoritative word of god.[34] If people could be persuaded of this, then the moral force of efforts to use the bible to restrict women to the domestic sphere and to limit their political and social rights would be undermined.

Elizabeth Cady Stanton did not engage in feminist biblical criticism for the sheer intellectual excitement of reading from a woman's perspective or of giving voice to neglected female characters. She engaged in a feminist analysis of the bible because she was profoundly aware of the impact of the biblical tradition on the attitudes and values of Western society. She felt compelled to engage this tradition as part of her struggle to improve women's lives.

Although well-received in some circles, Stanton's work was predictably denounced by the clergy as the work of the devil. Surprisingly, however, it was disavowed in 1896 by the National American Suffrage Association, whose wealthy and conservative leadership was apparently concerned that *The Woman's Bible* would damage the credibility of the movement.[35] Not only did the publication of *The*

she did not appear to shift blame from Christianity to Judaism. She seems to have thought that the Christian religion took this belief to new heights. Her criticism focused on Christianity insofar as it was such a pervasive influence on the Western world. On this point Gage and Stanton seem to be in agreement. Judith Plaskow, in an article discussing the problem of anti-Judaism in feminist Christian scholarship, notes that when Stanton presented a series of resolutions to the Annual Convention of the National Women's Suffrage Association criticizing Christian theological teachings about women, the leaders of the convention shifted the blame from Christianity to Judaism. What Stanton had laid at the door of Christianity, these leaders prefered to 'hand over to the Jews…' See J. Plaskow, 'Anti-Judaism in Feminist Christian Interpretation', in Schüssler Fiorenza (ed.), *Searching the Scriptures*, I, pp. 117-30.

33. Stanton, *The Woman's Bible*, p. 214.
34. Gurko, *The Ladies*, p. 286.
35. Carolyn De Swarte Gifford, 'American Women and the Bible: The Nature

Woman's Bible mark the culmination of the first phase of feminist biblical criticism, it also seems to have marked the beginning of a separation, or distancing, of the emerging feminist movement with its related feminist disciplines from feminist study of the bible.

When the second phase of feminist biblical criticism appeared in the 1970s in the United States it was decidedly apolitical, except perhaps within the context of biblical scholarship itself. The feminists who inaugurated this second phase were very different from feminists like Murray, Gage or Stanton. They were professionals, trained by professional biblical scholars in seminaries and universities. Their challenge, it seems, was to gain recognition for their work within the setting of professional biblical scholarship. They needed to demonstrate that they understood and could work competently with the tools and methods of biblical scholarship: philology, linguistics, archaeology, historical-critical and literary-critical and other methods, and apply these to aspects of the biblical text and tradition that had been neglected by their non-feminist colleagues.

Using traditional methods of analysis to investigate non-traditional questions (i.e., questions of relevance and interest to women and about women) from feminist perspectives, the majority of scholarship in this phase was focused on changing the way individuals interpreted biblical texts about women. Trible's work is classic, insofar as it exemplifies the effort to teach us how to read the text in less woman-hostile ways. Much of the work in this phase was highly technical in nature, reflecting the technical sophistication of biblical studies as a whole. And much of it had as its larger goal the improvement of women's role and status within organized religions for whom the bible was the authoritative document of faith.

Little attention was paid, however, to examining the impact of the bible on women as a group or on groups of women. While there was considerable interest in examining the literary depiction of women as female biblical characters and several efforts to explore the lives of women in ancient Israel and early Christianity, there was almost no focus on exploring how the bible shaped or was used to shape the lives of women through the centuries to the present. Nor was there much reflection on how white women's experiences with the biblical

of Woman as Hermeneutical Issue', in Yarbro Collins (ed.), *Feminist Perspectives on Biblical Scholarship*, pp. 28-30; Margaret Hope Bacon, *Mothers of Feminism: The Story of Quaker Women in America* (San Francisco: Harper & Row, 1986), pp. 184-85; Elizabeth Clark and Herbert Richardson (eds.), *Women and Religion: A Feminist Sourcebook of Christian Thought* (New York: Harper & Row, 1977), pp. 213-17.

tradition in its multiple interpretations might be different from the experiences of native, African or Hispanic women. The questions of how racism and colonialism interact with sexism to impact on specific racial, ethnic or social groups of women in different ways were not being asked by many. So much attention was being devoted to the examination of specific biblical texts that the larger question of the relationship between the bible and general societal attitudes toward women and/or patriarchal societal structures was overlooked. Perhaps this is not surprising, given that so much feminist biblical scholarship has been done in the United States where, traditionally, the individual takes precedence over the group. In a society where the rights of the individual are almost always valued above the rights of groups of people,[36] it seems natural to focus on the individual

---

36. Affirmative action legislation is now under serious attack in the United States. Central to this challenge is the assertion that the rights of individual white men cannot be outweighed by the rights of members of a racial minority or women who have suffered discrimination based on membership in a group. In Canada employment equity legislation, though not particularly more effective in overcoming the effects of centuries of discrimination, has not been as easily overturned through the legal system because of a more developed legal concept of systemic discrimination and more integration of principles of substantive equality, as opposed to mere formal equality.

The notion of formal equality goes back to Aristotle. In the formalist model (which is the dominant model in the United States), individual citizens are regarded as political and legal equals. Rights and freedoms, entitlements and opportunities attach to individuals not to groups. Thus, these cannot be assigned on the basis of group characteristics such as sex, race, ethnicity, nationality, religion, etc. Although this model does not pretend that individuals actually are equal, it holds that they should be treated by the state as if they were. The notion of substantive equality (the recently established legal model in Canada), by contrast, begins with an awareness of the actual inequalities which exist between citizens. It does not assume the existence of an abstract formal equality to which all citizens have access. This model seeks to show how the powerful define values to rationalize existing distributions of power. Its goal is to construct mechanisms for eliminating actual inequalities by achieving equality of concrete outcomes, rather than merely providing the opportunity for abstract equality. The difference between the two models can be seen in the approaches to maternity leave in Canada and the USA. Maternity leave is a right of all women in full-time employment in Canada. The legislation upon which this is based recognizes that since only women get pregnant and give birth to children, providing leave recognizes and accommodates the sexual difference in reproductive functions between men and women in a way that equalizes women's ability to participate in the workforce. In the United States, by contrast, so long as men and women are equally denied maternity leave they are deemed to be treated equally. For a more extensive discussion of these notions of equality see Sheilagh McIntyre, 'Backlash Against Equality: The "Tyranny" of the

interpreter and the individual interpretation.

Trible, for example, is an individual who loves the bible, for whom the biblical tradition is central to faith, despite its patriarchal short-comings. Her work has undoubtedly provided many other individual women with a mechanism for seeing the biblical text differently. Stanton, on the other hand, was more concerned with how the bible was used in denying equal social and political rights to women as a group in society as a whole.

Both the technical nature of second phase feminist work and its generally inward focus may have played a role in rendering feminist biblical scholarship of relatively little interest to feminists in the wider feminist movement.

Politicized Scholarship and Ethical Responsibility

Certainly not all feminist biblical scholarship in the second phase followed this path. Esther Fuchs was one who had been attempting to draw our attention to the subtle and subconscious ways in which the biblical text communicates a gender ideology that is problematic for women as a group. Although it has taken some time, it does appear to me that we are now beginning to see more feminist biblical scholarship examining where our work fits into the bigger picture. For this reason, I think we can now speak of the emergence of a new phase of feminist biblical criticism within the last few years.

This phase may be marked by some of the work mentioned earlier. Cheryl Exum, in examining the ideology of the text and the consequences such ideology has, is now seeing the connection between biblical gender politics and the larger phallocentric symbolic order.[37] Mieke Bal, in examining the political consequences of reading a text like the bible, attempts to hold both text and reader ethically responsible.[38] Feminist scholarship on the bible functions on one level to allow us to analyze the 'positions of power which underlie the social circulations of readings'.[39] As politicized scholarship it leads us to examine what governs access to 'the privileged channels where readings can become public goods...'[40]

Likewise, David Clines has also raised the question of ethical

"Politically Correct"', *McGill Law Journal* 38.1 (1993), pp. 1- 63, especially pp. 26-35.

37. Exum, 'Second Thoughts', p. 86.
38. Mieke Bal, 'Introduction', in Bal (ed.), *Anti-Covenant*, pp. 11-24.
39. Bal, 'Introduction', p. 15.
40. Bal, 'Introduction', p. 15.

responsibility and the politics of social power. Clines has pointed out that biblical scholars have in the past rarely questioned the effect on readers of texts like the Bible.[41]

In this kind of work I see a shift away from a focus on the reader and his or her individual interaction with the biblical text toward a consideration of the broader social implications for women of reading or otherwise encountering a text like the Bible. Even in societies that are essentially secular in nature, the social impact of the biblical tradition on sexual standards, sex-role stereotyping and gender ideology can be significant.

Perhaps because, as already mentioned, so much of the second phase of feminist biblical scholarship emanated from the United States, where the historic legal emphasis has been on the rights of the individual rather than on the rights of the group, efforts to teach individual readers how to 'reread' biblical texts in a more woman-friendly way so that they might pluck the 'intentionality' of the word of god out of the patriarchal cultural baggage of the tradition, was to be expected. In this context, few have been raising the question of how the bible and biblically based traditions (such as legal, political, or family traditions) continue to impact on women as a group within society. This, of course, was Stanton's focus but it was not one which won wide acceptance in the United States.

Today, feminist analysis of the bible is very much an international activity. It is being carried out in contexts that have, historically, developed more balance between individual and group rights. This, in turn, may be a facilitating factor in the appearance of more scholarship that seeks to investigate the influence of the bible on our lives as women.

In addition, it is interesting to note that the questions about ethical responsibility are now often arising in non-confessional or non-theological contexts of biblical study. The emergence of the second phase of feminist biblical scholarship was associated largely (though not exclusively) with theological schools. Although this remains a significant source of feminist scholarship on the bible, the third phase is characterized, I think, by considerably more feminist analyses originating from secular, academic contexts.

For the most part, feminists have not made much of the distinction between these two valid, but very different, contexts for their analysis of the bible. Doing so, however, might provide an avenue for greater

41. David Clines, 'Why is there a Song of Songs? And What Does it Do to You if You Read It?', *Jian Dao* 1 (1994), pp. 14-26.

connection to, and interaction with, feminists in other disciplines. Although there may be an understanding among biblical scholars about how confessional and non-confessional approaches differ, such a distinction is not often appreciated by those outside the field.

Confessional versus Non-Confessional Scholarship

Philip Davies has recently reflected on this distinction and offered some clarification of terminology which would be useful in building greater understanding by feminists in other disciplines of what feminist biblical scholars do. Davies suggests the use of the term 'scripture' to designate confessional, theological approaches to the study of the bible and 'biblical studies' to designate non-confessional, humanistic studies. Each constitutes a separate discipline defined by methodology, aims, practices and presuppositions, though focusing on basically the same material.[42] Key presuppositions in a confessional approach include the belief that the word 'god' refers to a real entity and that the bible is, in some way, the inspired, authoritative and revealed word of god. The non-confessional approach presupposes only that the bible is the product of human literary creativity.

Davies calls for a more conscious effort to distinguish between these two different 'discourses' and for scholars to be clear about which discourse they are using, within which discipline they stand. His comments, though made generally about ways of studying the bible, are relevant for feminist biblical studies as well. As a third phase emerges, it seems to be growing more in a non-confessional direction than was typical of feminist analyses in the 1970s or early 1980s. But relatively little overt discussion of this shift in emphasis has yet taken place.

Feminist Biblical Studies and Feminist Scholarship

It is precisely here where I see the possibility for developing closer connections with feminists and their work in other areas. The major

---

42. P.R. Davies, 'Two Nations, One Womb', in *Whose Bible is it Anyway?* (Sheffield: Sheffield Academic Press, 1995), pp. 17-55. Davies is highly critical of work done by Brevard Childs and Francis Watson. The former, he claims, attempts to absorb the non-confessional approach within the confessional, while the latter tries to banish the non-confessional approach. The appearance of work such as theirs leads Davies to emphasize the separation of the two approaches or 'disciplines', as he calls them.

suspicions voiced by feminists outside the field pertain only to feminist analyses of scripture which belong to the confessional 'discipline' or 'discourse'. The suspicion is that feminists who study the bible subordinate their feminism to their faith commitments. But this cannot be said of feminist scholars who engage in non-confessional biblical studies.

Davies suggests that:

> A non-confessing discourse about bibles subjects them to evaluation from a range of perspectives, allowing the biblical literature to interact with different value systems and to have its own varied value system compared and judged by what is analogous to a 'free market'.[43]

A non-confessing feminist discourse, rather than subordinating the feminist perspective, subjects the biblical text and tradition to evaluation from feminist value systems. Feminist biblical scholars who are working in non-confessional contexts might well promote dialogue with other feminists by emphasizing this and by making a greater effort to articulate the feminist goal or purpose of their work.

A third phase of feminist biblical scholarship which is more self-consciously non-confessional and less American-centred than that of the second phase will be in a better position to raise questions about the relationship between the biblical tradition and women as women, and groups of women in a variety of social and historical contexts.

Even in the most secular of societies and even for the most secular of feminists there is much value in understanding the ongoing influence of the biblical tradition on societal attitudes toward women. Athalya Brenner, in a study of anti-woman bias in prophetic texts, has seen this quite clearly. She correctly and forcefully observes that '[r]eligious propaganda is not divorced from social norms but rather builds on them and perpetuates them'.[44] We need only reflect on the messages carried in the popular symbol for one of the largest computer companies in the world (an apple with a bite out of it), or the popularity of films with the 'dangerous woman' theme to realize that biblical images and values are woven into the fabric of many societies.

The effort to make the connections with the larger feminist movement and feminist scholarship in other disciplines will have to come from feminist biblical scholars. We need to do a better job of 'selling' the relevance and importance of our subject matter to a feminist

---

43. Davies, *Whose Bible*, pp. 48-49.

44. Athalya Brenner, 'Pornoprophetics Revisited: Some Additional Reflections', *JSOT* 70 (1996), p. 84.

movement that has regarded our work as marginal and irrelevant.

The location and integration of feminist biblical scholarship in non-confessional, academic departments of religion, religious studies or biblical studies facilitates this task. It is here particularly that the biblical text can be set beside other texts, including women-authored texts, in an unprivileged way and examined as a thoroughly human product. The tendency in my own country, and elsewhere, to reduce or eliminate such academic departments as funding for post-secondary education decreases is cause for concern. At the very moment when feminist critiques of religion are gaining a place in the curriculum and when feminist scholars of religion are available in significant numbers, the academic study of religion, including biblical studies, appears to be an easy cost-cutting target.[45] One of the urgent challenges facing feminist scholars in biblical studies, in my view, is to ensure that the emerging non-confessional, academic critique is not only not lost, but becomes an integral part of the growing field of feminist women's studies.[46]

As I look toward the twenty-first century, I look toward the potential of non-confessing feminist biblical scholarly discourse for reconnecting my discipline to those of my sister feminists; and for reconnecting the work of feminist biblical scholars to the task of the feminist movement in making the idea of women's equality (along with the equality of other marginalized peoples) a social, political, legal and economic reality. To realize this potential it will be incumbent upon those of us who practise this kind of discourse to develop

45. It may not be coincidental that the academic study of religion incorporating feminist-critical thought is a prime target for administrators seeking to make budgetary cuts. Feminist thought is still largely regarded as 'dangerous knowledge' in malestream post-secondary educational institutions insofar as it questions the very foundations of the masculinist epistomology upon which the academy has been built.

46. At the 1995 Annual Meeting of the SBL, the fifteenth anniversary of the 1980 panel on 'The Effects of Women's Studies on Biblical Studies', a session on 'Biblical Scholarship in the 21st Century' again had the theme of 'The Effects of Women's Studies on Biblical Studies'. I was surprised, even dismayed, to see the extent to which the 1995 panel interpreted the title in a way similar to the 1980 panel. The actual topic was the effect of feminist biblical studies on traditional male biblical studies. 'Women's Studies' was interpreted quite narrowly. Perhaps in another fifteen years we can ask what effect women's studies as a multi-disciplinary endeavour has had on biblical studies as a multi-perspective discipline, including feminist perspectives.

its political consciousness more fully, to set out more clearly the feminist objectives of our work, and to demonstrate more transparently the importance of our contributions to the goals of the feminist movement.

ON THE FUTURE OF FEMINIST BIBLICAL CRITICISM

Heather A. McKay

The Aim of this Study

It is perhaps stating the obvious to claim that the 'very speed of development of feminist criticism has scarcely given it time to reflect...',[1] but Sally Minogue's description of the intellectual maelstrom within which feminist criticism is struggling to furnish an identifiable voice draws attention to a clearly definable need. Feminists—and others—need answers to these questions: 'Why is it so difficult to "do" feminist biblical criticism today?' and 'What is the way forward for feminist biblical scholarship?'[2] In this study I aim to suggest answers to both those questions, by analysing factors that handicap practitioners of feminist biblical criticism and by exploring possible avenues through which feminists may professionally practise critical analysis of biblical texts.

Any answer to the first question demands a recognition of feminists' varied intellectual engagement with the competing claims of different disciplinary approaches and methods, and of the cognitive clamour—not to say, dissonance—aroused by this engagement. The differing arenas in which biblical studies are pursued and the different agendas that inform those studies multiply the difficulties. For, to some scholars the Bible is both cultural product and religious literature—that is, Scripture. To them, the text of the Bible offers more than interest, education or entertainment; it exercises a normative function within their lives, thoughts and scholarship. They seek to elucidate the theological relevance of the biblical writings within the framework of their own religious and cultural contexts. To others, the importance of the Bible is located in the influence its texts and their interpretation has on almost all modes of human discourse, personal, socio-political and ideological. They seek to lay bare for scrutiny

---

1. Sally Minogue (ed.), *Problems for Feminist Criticism* (London: Routledge, 1990), p. 5.
2. I do not exclude male scholars from this category.

the means by which the texts of the Bible can be used to manipulate human behaviour. Their wish is that the Bible will exert authority only where its meaning has been fully understood and accepted.

To address the first question, I will consider the warring strands of reaction and pro-action to be found in feminism. Feminism arose as a response to, and reaction against, the conceptualizations of the patriarchal symbolic universe where men were at ease and women at a disadvantage; it was originally reactive. Feminist criticism reacted against the misogyny of (some) male writers, against the frequent omission of women from texts supposedly describing events in the 'real' world and against the dangers of writing feminist discourse as a mirror image to the existing (male) discourse.[3]

But is a reactive response to androcentrism to be the sum of feminism's ambitions? Should there not be envisaged a time when the reactive animus will have cooled? Could there not come a time when that debate will no longer occupy the centre stage? And this would happen not because the issues have been suppressed or repressed, but rather because the symbolic universe will have been enlarged and contain regions of both types of single-sex populations and a large area of mixed-gender *Lebensraum* or, rather, *Redensraum*? In such a world, feminist scholarship will certainly be pro-active, possibly assertive, but the need for aggression and the attacking of embattled positions will be long gone.

I strongly believe it is time to resile from the recent (and current) practice of blaming and apostrophizing male-authored and androcentric texts. Admittedly this has been a necessary procedure to make plainly visible the false consciousnesses that they—in common with the texts of any dominant group—perpetuate,[4] but the procedure should now be modulated, if not abandoned. That negative and angry stance will no longer serve the purpose of forward-looking feminist scholars who wish to move beyond a rhetoric of blame and who wish to foster the creation of, and be able to work within, a

3.   Minogue, *Problems for Feminist Criticism*, p. 6; however, to be fair to Minogue, she also refers to feminist critics who realized the dangers of believing that all that needed to be said about women and their interests could be said by women

4.   Heather A. McKay, '"Only a Remnant of Them Shall Be Saved": Women from the Hebrew Bible in New Testament Narratives', in Athalya Brenner (ed.), *A Feminist Companion to the Hebrew Bible in the New Testament* (The Feminist Companion to the Bible, 10; Sheffield: Sheffield Academic Press, 1996), pp. 33-61 (33, 61).

gender-neutral, or, better, a both-gender-friendly, climate of discussion in biblical studies.[5]

An answer to the second question will require a combined focusing on both the present state of feminist scholarship and on the ideal style of academic debate that can be envisaged as a future possibility were the aims of critical feminism to be successfully realized. To address the first point my strategy will be to examine techniques applied to biblical texts by feminist scholars,[6] with the particular aim of identifying in their work aspects both of critique of the patriarchal world-view expressed in the primary and, secondary literature,[7] *and* of any adhering complicity with the very perspectives under critique.

My final section will consider what a both-gender-friendly climate of discussion would be like; and how committed scholars working in such a climate might proceed with their continuing work of biblical criticism.

As in my previous piece addressing this subject,[8] I invite readers of the Bible—and of this essay—to observe *for* themselves, and *in* themselves, any 'false consciousnesses'[9] inserted in their minds by the subtle skills of authors and narrators.[10]

Red Herrings to Be Put to One Side

The intellectual project of moving towards a situation of gender-equal writings and criticism is bedevilled by red herrings. Often the ideas expressed sound relevant to the discussion but they actually arise from flaws within the present discourse and, therefore, tend to trap the discussion there. The questions they raise remain difficult to discard, but should be held in suspicion as probable time-wasters.

5.   See discussion of this topic in Athalya Brenner, 'Women's Traditions Problematized: Some Reflections', in Bob Becking and Meindert Dijkstra (eds.), *On Reading Prophetic Texts: Gender-Specific and Related Studies in Memory of Fokkelien van Dijk-Hemmes* (Leiden: Brill, 1996), pp. 53-66.

6.   A survey of the aims and strategies of feminist readings of texts may be found in Catherine Belsey and Jane Moore, 'Introduction: The Story So Far', in Catherine Belsey and Jane Moore (eds.), *The Feminist Reader: Essays in Gender and the Politics of Literary Criticism* (Houndmills, Basingstoke: MacMillan Education, 1989), pp. 1-20.

7.   I do not exclude female scholars from this category.

8.   McKay, 'Only a Remnant', pp. 32, 61.

9.   I use the Marxist term 'false consciousness' to mean any of those diverse internalised mental straitjackets of self-restriction engendered in the 'oppressed' by, or to the advantage of, their more subtle 'oppressors'.

10.   Myself not excluded.

Being Fair to Both Genders All the Time
This red herring distracts from the main task because of the number of ways the word 'fair' can be understood. Some feminists say that since there has been androcentric control of the symbolic universe for many millennia then there should be gynocentric control for at least one; to be 'fair' there must be for a long time an equal and opposite dominance given to female discourse modes. Other scholars say that since any person can read texts from only one perspective at a time anyway, attempts to be 'fair' could only lead, at best, to an alternation of gender favouritism. Still others say that since the symbolic universe, as it exists today, is androcentric, then all gynocentric positions are no more than secondhand, derivative positions in that they have to be articulated in andocentric language and concepts—so actual equality and 'fairness' can never be achieved.

I believe a way to avoid this cluster of impasses is to begin from a declared stance of believing in the value of both genders in all forms of human discourse with acceptance that males and females owe their gender to their socialization, and, thereafter, to try to be as even-handed as one may. If this is a naïve stance, at least it is genuinely and purposefully naïve, though perhaps falling within the category of 'feminism's somewhat pragmatic and *ad hoc* approach to some of the most profound problems of explanation confronting social theory'.[11]

Uniform Resistance to the Use of Stereotypes
There is a current view that the use of stereotypes in discussion is *per se* bad. Stereotypes are thought to be unable to carry truth since they express generalizations from particular (biased) perspectives. All individuals, it is argued, have the right not to be bracketed within a stereotype, so, stereotypes should not be regarded as representing reality in any way whatsoever. This position should, however, be contested and forced to yield some of the moral high ground that it claims. After all, every mature human understanding is reached by the adoption and modification—or discarding—of a succession of stereotypical views or statements by means of which the subject can think, consider and reflect.[12] The stereotypes are *useful*, though not

11. Caroline Ramazanoğlu, Up against Foucault: Explorations of Some Tensions Between Foucault and Feminism (London: Routledge, 1993), p. 6.

12. Descriptions of stereotypes and provocative stereotypical statements are used extensively to promote reflection and understanding in Julia T. Wood, *Gendered Lives: Communication, Gender and Culture* (Belmont, CA: Wadsworth, 1994), especially pp. 260-88.

real, or *absolute*. They are aids to a developing understanding, no more, but certainly also, no less.

Gendered False Consciousnesses

The false consciousnesses that restrict or modify both men's and women's involvement in the academic discipline of biblical criticism include more than a tinge of gender focus or bias. It will be useful to consider these and notice the effects that they have produced and that we can recognize in scholarly debates within biblical studies.

Male-Generated and Female-Internalized False Consciousnesses

The more publicly stated false consciousnesses that operate to limit women's involvement in the academic domain arise from, or express, male consensus perspectives.

In General Discourse. The following examples, expressed or implied by male speakers and writers, have operated over a long period of time to hobble women intellectually[13]—as the long tight skirts given that name once did physically.[14] The first set of statements reduces the hypothetical women to child or servant status.

— Women do not belong in the coterie of educated cognoscenti.[15]
— Women have little to say of importance in the 'real' world.
— Women spend a lot of time talking about unimportant things like feelings, food, shelter and children.
— Women always overreact on issues of authority and power.
— Women always overreact in sympathy with silenced or suppressed opposition.[16]

13. See the extended discussion of these and similar misprisions in Carol Gilligan, *In a Different Voice: Psychological Theory and Women's Development* (Cambridge, MA: Harvard University Press, 1982), especially in Chapter 1.

14. The hobble skirt is a long narrow skirt that restricts the wearer's leg movements down to mid-calf at which point the skirt becomes a wide ruched valance to the ankles. The original meaning of hobbling is tying the front legs of a horse together to allow it to graze without being able to run off.

15. Kate Campbell, 'Introduction: Matters of Theory and Practice—or, We'll Be Coming Out the Harbour', in Kate Campbell (ed.), *Critical Feminism: Argument in the Disciplines* (Buckingham: Open University Press, 1992), pp. 1-24, especially pp. 3-13.

16. Elaine Showalter's attack on the 'textual harassment' of women could be

— Women's communication is always of a more emotional, less rational, and, therefore, less valid form than
men's.
— Women actually prefer to be told what to think and do.

Sadly, it is only gradually that these internalized beliefs are being
examined by women and modified or discarded. It is with similar
sluggishness that they are being dismissed from male discourse.

Other such statements ask 'sensible' women to shrink from being
bullies to 'get their own way' by painting an unappealing picture of
rampant, slightly out-of-control, female power.

— Now women want all the power for themselves—which
is just as bad as what they claim to be opposing.
— Fishwives always had a name for a good command of
English.
— There's nothing worse than a hectoring woman.[17]

The extreme images depicted above are definitely not such that many
women, 'sensible' or otherwise, would espouse them with equanim-
ity.

In Feminist Biblical Studies. The following beliefs, expressed or implied
by some female speakers and writers have operated recently to muzzle women intellectually—as the scold's collar once did physically.[18]
Only gradually are they being critiqued and modified.

— The Bible *must* have good things to say about women
too.[19]
— If we read the Bible very carefully and subtly we will
find parts that value women.[20]

read by some as an overreaction: see discussion in Minogue, *Problems for Feminist
Criticism*, p. 6.

17. Note the use of Hector's name in this statement.

18. A mediaeval instrument of punishment attached to the head of condemned
'nagging' wives. The metal headpiece incorporates a sharp spike that pointed up-
wards from under the wearer's chin. Any attempt at speech was thereby discour-
aged.

19. Rosemary Radford Ruether, 'Feminist Interpretation: A Method of Correlation', in Letty M. Russell (ed.), *Feminist Interpretation of the Bible* (Oxford: Basil
Blackwell, 1985), pp. 111-24 (115); Elisabeth Schüssler Fiorenza, 'The Will to
Choose or to Reject: Continuing Our Critical Work', in Russell (ed.), *Feminist Interpretation*, pp. 125-35 (130).

20. Carolyn Osiek, 'The Feminist and the Bible', in A. Yarboro Collins (ed.),

— If we study biblical symbolism we will find attractive and powerful female images.[21]
— If we focus on the present and the future we can forget past damage and hurts.[22]

Feminist biblical scholars who accept these views are constrained in what they write by what they believe *must be true* about the Bible.

On the other hand, the following provocative statements, expressed or implied by other feminist speakers and writers, have had the effect of freeing women intellectually—as incitements to avoid self-stifling by throwing off corsets once did. These represent the most vociferous opposition to the androcentric *status quo.*

— All men, both in the Bible and in commentaries and preaching, exclude all women from the category of valued humans.[23]
— Every textual depiction of women's physical attractiveness in the Bible and in male-authored secondary literature is little more than male voyeurism.[24]
— Every textual depiction of heterosexual congress where the woman is silent and her subjectivity is denied is an act of literary rape that is repeated over and over again through the reading process.[25]

These feminist biblical scholars resist the constraints generated by

---

Feminist Perspectives on Biblical Scholarship (Atlanta: Scholars Press, 1985), pp. 93-106, states (p. 94) that the 'biblical tradition contains enough of lasting and universal value that it is worth salvaging', and later (p. 100) praises the 'loyalist' approach because it has a 'carefully worked out biblical method' that allows many 'intelligent American women' roles as believers and interpreters *within* their faith tradition.

21. Brenner, 'Women's Traditions Problematized', pp. 55-66.

22. Schüssler Fiorenza, 'The Will to Choose or to Reject: Continuing Our Critical Work', pp. 133-34.

23. 'Not only is scripture interpreted by a long line of men and proclaimed in patriarchal churches, it is also authored by men, written in androcentric language, reflective of religious male experience, selected and transmitted by male religious leadership' (Fiorenza, 'The Will to Choose or to Reject: Continuing Our Critical Work', p. 130).

24. Susan Durber, 'The Female Reader of the Parables of the Lost', in George J. Brooke (ed.), *Women in the Biblical Tradition* (Lampeter: Edwin Mellen, 1992), pp. 187-207 *passim.*

25. J. Cheryl Exum, *Fragmented Women: Feminist (Sub)versions of Biblical Narratives* (JSOTSup, 163; Sheffield: JSOT Press, 1993), Chapter 6, 'Raped by the Pen', pp. 170-201.

what has been taught about the Bible and ask that other intellectual stances (for example, materialist or structuralist) are used like the second blade in a pair of scissors in conjunction with religious or androcentric perspectives to cut open the meaning of the texts. They have decided on their answer to the question posed by Letty Russell: whether to be blindly 'faithful' to scriptural teachings, or to apply their 'talents' and integrity to their work[26] and risk an unwelcome outcome.[27]

Female-Generated and Male-Internalized False Consciousnesses
Women, no less than men, have held some truths to be self-evident when it comes to describing the differing intellectual strengths of males and females. These are equally liable to be false consciousnesses.

In General Discourse. The following statements represent women's claims to intellectual supremacy in certain areas of life. Many men accept them as containing some truth and opt out of, or hesitate to opt in to, particular spheres of human discourse.

— No man can write with any sensitivity about women's feelings.
— Men are less skilled than women in interpreting human relationships.
— Men are less skilled than women in expressing and understanding their own, and others', feelings.
— Men cannot relate well in father–son relationships, from either side of the bond.
— Men see only half of every problem they are discussing.

Of course, the vast body of poetic literature written by men belies the universality of these generalizations, but many women who are keen to claim expertise in traditional male preserves of power and influence are reluctant to relinquish supremacy in these, traditionally female, areas.

In Feminist Biblical Studies. The following statements, expressed or implied by some female speakers and writers, have recently reconfigured, that is, revalued at a lower level, the 'objective' value of the

26. Letty M., Russell, 'Authority and the Challenge of Feminist Interpretation', in Russell (ed.), *Feminist Interpretation*, pp. 137-46 (137).
27. Their interpretations might be unwelcome to themselves, their community or to other scholars.

intellectual contributions of men to critical biblical studies.

— Men are more concerned with their status in the discipline than the subject they are ostensibly discussing.
— Men are too competitive to be genuinely involved in cooperative scholarship.

As with all the statements above, these may well hold some truth but should not be allowed to condition our perception of the scholarly community so that we discern two opposing (gendered) camps within it. That can serve no one's interests in the long run.

Current Exegetical Strategies

Feminist writers tend to be uneasy about accepting traditional androcentric interpretations and try to offer more woman-friendly exegeses, though that turns out to be more difficult than one might imagine. Feeling themselves intellectually disgendered and thereafter regendered or other-gendered by their male-dominated education they are discommoded, even partially disabled, as they think and write.[28] They recognize the dissonance with the concomitant loss of power, but remain at a loss as to how to reinvigorate their writing in ways that celebrate both feminist ideals *and* traditional forms of rational thought. They are torn two ways.

Often feminists try to interpret the biblical texts in ways that generate readings that are more acceptable to women, and there are several approaches possible. These have been usefully, though not exhaustively, characterized as *loyalist, rejectionist, revisionist, sublimationist* and *liberationist*,[29] because they represent different attempts to produce valuable discussions from engagement with the biblical texts. They result in: proclamation of the Bible as essentially good to women; rejection of the Bible; recovery of parts of the Bible that value women; retrieval of positive feminine images in the Bible or universalization (for women too!) of the Bible's message of salvation for men. In spite of the helpfulness of this outcome-based analysis, I believe that the driving forces, the religious and political agenda, behind different feminist approaches offer another important means of analysing and classifying them.

28. Gerda Lerner, *The Creation of Patriarchy* (Oxford: Oxford University Press, 1986), pp. 224-29.
29. Osiek, 'The Feminist and the Bible', p. 103; see also fuller discussion of the terms below.

Prioritizing the loving-both-genders aspect of God as he is portrayed in the Bible and writing in a *reactive* way are Osiek's loyalist, sublimationist, revisionist and liberationist scholars who seek to show either that the biblical text does not actually denigrate women, or that it contains powerful and admirable female images, or that once revisioned, rewritten and reinterpreted in inclusive language the biblical texts offer equal promises and roles to both genders. These groups of scholars claim that the Bible can be culturally updated to serve the needs of all members of, usually, the Jewish and Christian religious communities.

But those placing the highest priority on preserving the integrity of women take what I would describe as an independent and *pro-active* stance. They include Osiek's rejectionist scholars who will not agree to the value of texts that ignore, denigrate or violate women, and so prefer to discard them totally. Other forms of rejectionism aim to deconstruct the 'divine' authority of the Bible and demand that its propositions be valid without that *imprimatur.*

So, taking a similar, but not identical, stance is a further group of scholars, typified by Athalya Brenner and Fokkelien van Dijk-Hemmes, who focus their attention on the certainty of women being involved equally—at least somehow and somewhere—in the production of the cultural product that we know as the Bible. They do not adopt the quasi-apologetic stance of revisionists or liberationists, being firmly convinced that women have always been important in society. What they recognize and wrestle with is the fact that women's inscription in the texts has been muted.[30] It has been filtered through the perception and through the writing of male authors. So, while the loyalists and others wish to preserve the gender neutrality of God and affirm that the biblical message is equally available to both genders now (though not necessarily *portrayed* in that way in the past) *they* wish to prioritize and affirm the gender inclusiveness of human life and culture throughout time. For this reason I would designate their approach as *inclusivist.*

Other scholars, of whom Cheryl Exum is typical, similarly demand that the biblical texts be read (no more than) fairly. As they work with the biblical narratives, they do not accord the Bible any special treatment or employ special pleading to excuse the atrocities against women recounted in its texts. If the God they find portrayed in the

---

30. Athalya Brenner and Fokkelien van Dijk-Hemmes, *On Gendering Texts: Female and Male Voices in the Hebrew Bible* (Biblical Interpretation Series, 1; Leiden: Brill, 1993), Introduction, and *passim.*

Bible is especially cruel and heartless in his treatment of women, then they say so.[31]

Unfortunately, however, on closer inspection, each of the feminist approaches addressed above contains within itself the danger of affirming what it seeks to deny, or of becoming complicit in (at least part of) what it seeks to eradicate.

Reactive Positions

Loyalist Approaches. Osiek herself writes as a *loyalist*, believing that the Bible as 'Word of God' must be life-affirming for all creation. If an interpretation does not discover that, the reading method is faulty and must be remedied.[32] She admits that the approach has its weaknesses, namely manipulating the literal meaning of the text at times and giving the text 'the benefit of the doubt' whenever it is at odds with history or advocates practices discordant with modern societal norms.[33]

Typical of male loyalist writing are apologetic attempts to show that the Bible treats women with dignity and equality.[34] Throughout Thierry Maertens's book about how the dignity of women advances through the course of the Bible, the biblical assumptions that women are second-class citizens, and depend on men for their actions, names, titles and descriptions remain unchallenged.[35] His persistent and over-protesting loyalty to the text does not, in the end, serve his aims, but, rather, underscores for modern readers the unstated, and perhaps unrecognized, need for its 'repair'. Similarly, Ben Witherington in his book about the high status of women in Christianity states that through the generosity of Jesus women *became* equal with men,[36] and assumes that 'Jesus' positive attitudes towards children can

---

31. See also the work of Phyllis Bird, such as, 'The Harlot as Heroine: Narrative Art and Social Presupposition in Three Old Testament Texts', *Semeia* 46 (1989), pp. 119-39; also Phyllis Bird, 'Poor Man of Poor Woman: Gendering the Poor in Prophetic Texts', in Becking and Dijkstra (eds.), *On Reading Prophetic Texts*, pp. 37-51.

32. Osiek, 'The Feminist and the Bible', p. 99.

33. Osiek, 'The Feminist and the Bible', p. 100.

34. Thierry Maertens, *The Advancing Dignity of Woman in the Bible* (trans. Sandra Dibbs; De Père, WN: St Norbert Abbey Press, 1969).

35. McKay, 'Only a Remnant', pp. 34-35.

36. Ben Witherington, *Women and the Genesis of Christianity* (Cambridge: Cambridge University Press, 1990), pp. 118-19.

only reflect a positive estimation of women in their role of child-bearer'.[37] But if that is the most positive aspect of Jesus' views on women that even a 'loyalist' critic can find it is scarcely a matter for feminist rejoicing.

In similar vein, though from a more precarious starting point, female loyalists struggle to defend the Bible. They put forward such claims as that God appreciates, and sometimes rewards, the faith of oppressed and marginalized women,[38] or that women can some-times be 'more than' various epithets they have been given by men,[39] or else they attempt to vindicate the biblical depiction of women by providing readings that over-emphasize the role and status of women or that take politically 'innocent' stances towards ambiguous stories.[40]

I see a serious flaw in the loyalist approach, and one that makes it difficult for many women to follow. The exegete of this school has to behave like Virginia Woolf's 'angel in the house'[41] and solve the problems created by others in her or his faith community. The meth-od demands complicity in helping one's (textual) oppressors to avoid admitting guilt, shouldering blame and making restitution.[42] The text, its God and its message remain as they always were for these scholars—above reproach.

Sublimationist Approaches. Sublimationist writings begin from a female-centred position and prioritize all the virtues and abilities classically attributed to women. Women are seen as caring and supportive, making life possible and pleasant, whereas males show initiative and power merely to order that life in the way that suits their needs and desires.[43] Proponents of this feminist approach avoid confrontation with patriarchy and escape to their corner of the symbolic universe—a realm to which they ascribe greater impor-

37. Witherington, Women and the Genesis of Christianity, p. 48.

38. Ann Brown, *Apology to Women: Christian Images of the Female Sex* (Leicester: Inter-Varsity Press, 1991), pp. 119-36 (135).

39. Katheryn Pfisterer Darr, *Far More Precious than Jewels* (Louisville, KY: West-minster/John Knox, 1991), Contents and *passim*.

40. Sharon Pace Jeansonne, *The Women of Genesis: From Sarah to Potiphar's Wife* (Minneapolis: Fortress Press, 1990), pp. 14-30 (1, 6, 7).

41. Virginia Woolf, 'Professions for Women' in *The Crowded Dance of Modern Life* (ed. Rachel Bowlby, Harmondsworth: Penguin Books, 1993), *passim*.

42. In this case the 'oppressors' are anti-women statements or stances in the texts that are still perpetuated in preaching and comment.

43. Osiek, 'The Feminist and the Bible', p. 102.

tance. They can rejoice in the glorious images of virgin Israel, bride of God, Mary as virgin-mother, and so on, and avoid the harsh messages from biblical narratives about raped virgins, bereaved brides and lonely, neglected widows.

A weakness of this approach is that it majors on the superiority of femaleness over maleness and so rules out any genuine equality of the genders.[44] But I see a more serious difficulty and regard this approach as intellectual 'cheating', its objective being achieved by relocating the discourse in a psychological realm—that of symbolic womanhood or the divine feminine—where no pain or slights can be felt. The 'bride of Christ' and 'virgin Israel' did not have to make their way in the real, patriarchal society of the narrative world—nor in the real world today. By concentrating on the religious imagery of the Virgin Mary one may imagine a symbolic existence for women that is as joyful and untrammelled, and avoid confronting issues of power and freedom either in the narrative world of the texts or in the exigencies of one's own material culture.

What these images are useful for is to explain and illustrate joyful and uplifting emotions and prospects that must continually be held in tension with their opposing miserable and despondent counterparts: the virgin sitting in the dust wearing sackcloth, the sonless widow, the starving and the wretched. To focus on the positive images alone is to present an imbalanced picture of reality, and to claim that this approach functions as a critical stance is, to me, an inappropriate application of an essentially explicative strategy.

Revisionist Approaches. Revisionists regard patriarchy as historical, certainly, but not as absolute; the male-centredness of texts can be dislodged and the full roles of both men and women, which they played in real life, be seen again. Women's roles are researched and re-evaluated by this school in order to show the crucial parts that women play in narratives or events.[45] The outright anti-female (sometimes pornographic) material in biblical texts can then be set in its historical and/or literary context and may be disowned as being culturally conditioned and belonging firmly to the past.[46]

44. Osiek, 'The Feminist and the Bible', p. 102.

45. Phyllis Trible, *God and the Rhetoric of Sexuality* (Overtures to Biblical Theology; Philadelphia: Fortress Press, 1978), especially Chapter 4, 'A Love Story Gone Awry', pp. 72-143, where she re-attributes the gendered roles within the Creation story from Genesis 2–3, so that Adam becomes a *human* rather than a *male* creature.

46. See , for example, the discussions of the anti-woman imagery in Hosea by

One weakness of the revisionist approach is that it attacks the symptoms of patriarchy, that is, its inscription in the texts, and not the root causes of its confident continuation in the subsequent interpretation of texts, that is, its un-self-critical presumption of the right to know what's best for everyone. As a result, this approach uses selective application of the critical process to (only) the alteration of the language of the biblical narrative and thereafter focuses on the harmonious outcome achieved by the revision. However, those who employ this approach are, nonetheless, forced into the position of implicitly accepting that the picture of women presented in the texts must stand, as it is written, for all time, and may be 'changed' only in (their) secondary literature.[47]

The revisionist approach also causes cognitive dissonance in the scholars adopting it since, in its practice, it demands willing repetition of the 'offensive' material every time comments are being made on texts. But, of course, those who take a *loyalist* stance are not rendered uncomfortable by these passages because they have avoided making such negative judgements about the Bible in the first place.

Liberationist Approaches. Liberationist approaches take their starting point from texts that refer to the future freedom and glorious status of human existence, expressed in universal language. The kingdom of Heaven is assumed to be a place where all inequalities will be set aside and a radical new acceptance of shared rights and powers will be freely available to all.[48] The approach also demands that anything that does not give women full place must be, by definition, not divine, and, equally, any text that does is truly reflective of the divine.[49]

Rosemary Radford Ruether, for example, begins with the prophetic message of the Old Testament read without gender connotations and applied universally.[50] She accepts that the message is not designed for women but argues that it can be adapted for an ever-expanding understanding of being fully human.

Mary Joan Winn Leith, in 'Verse and Reverse: The Transformation of the Woman, Israel, in Hosea 1–3', in Peggy L. Day (ed.), *Gender and Difference in Ancient Israel* (Minneapolis: Augsburg–Fortress, 1989), pp. 95-108 (97-98).

   47. Osiek, 'The Feminist and the Bible', p. 101.

   48. Osiek, 'The Feminist and the Bible', p. 103.

   49. Radford Ruether, 'Feminist Interpretation: A Method of Correlation', p, 117.

   50. Radford Ruether, 'Feminist Interpretation: A Method of Correlation', pp. 117-24.

Elisabeth Schüssler Fiorenza likewise concentrates on a critical evaluation of biblical texts combined with proclamation, reconstruction and celebration.[51] She reads New Testament texts that look to a time of humanity restored and redeemed, believing that the 'word of God' contained therein cannot desire the detriment of women and demanding suspicion only of historical exegeses and modern interpretations.[52] After careful scrutiny and inclusive translation, chosen biblical texts that affirm the 'discipleship of equals' may be presented and proclaimed in liturgy.[53]

Osiek rightly identifies the main weakness of this stance as giving the highest authority to the religious revelations discerned in biblical texts and as developing a 'canon within the canon',[54] by employing a form of special pleading that prioritizes favourite texts—texts that can fulfil the criteria set by the approach, namely an application to a future heavenly realm and an ability to be interpreted in terms of guaranteed equality of powers and freedoms for all.

I, on the other hand, resist the required complicity with male views of salvation and the belief that the end of biblical interpretation is to annex these understandings for women as well as men (for whom they were written). This seems no more a critical endeavour than brushing cobwebs off obscured church carvings in order to polish up the few figures of women represented there. I state this because the central beliefs of this position seem to me to be quite independent of the texts, and arise from a determined independent belief in the equality of women with men—a view that is seldom expressed in the Bible.

Proactive Positions

Rejectionist Approaches. By definition, 'rejectionist' scholars do not write much biblical criticism, especially since in its most basic form this approach rejects the biblical texts completely as providing no useful guidance or role models for women's personal and family lives.[55] The first famous proponent of this position is Elizabeth Cady Stanton, who recognized that the Bible functioned in her society as a political book, because it was interpreted in ways that allowed it to be

51. Fiorenza, 'The Will to Choose or to Reject', pp. 125-35.
52. Fiorenza, 'The Will to Choose or to Reject', p. 130.
53. Fiorenza, 'The Will to Choose or to Reject', p. 130.
54. Osiek, 'The Feminist and the Bible', p. 104.
55. Osiek, 'The Feminist and the Bible', pp. 97-98.

used to confine women in restricted gender roles.[56]

The more extreme form of this approach rejects the entire biblical tradition and goes on to reject Christianity as a whole on the grounds that patriarchy cannot be eliminated from its essence.[57] The works of Mary Daly[58] and Daphne Hampson[59] best illustrate this position where thoughtful, self-aware women decide to leave men (behind) in sole possession of extant patriarchal religion and form a feminist post-Christian religion.

As Osiek notes, this stance would lead to a new dualism and the valorizing of new binary oppositions where female products are unquestionably good and superior to unquestionably evil male products.[60] She believes that a successful outcome for this stance is unrealistic in cultural terms because of both the sharp separatism and sudden upheaval that it demands.[61]

My main quarrel with this approach is that it demands acceptance of the premise that the norms of *one* gender should become the honoured norms. If this ideal was wrong under patriarchy, it should be equally wrong under feminist rules. This point is also made by Catherine Belsey and Jane Moore, who further point out that the 'danger here is that the emphasis on difference tends either to have the effect of leaving things exactly as they are, with women eternally confined to a separate sphere, or to lead to a politics of separatism, which despairs of changing patriarchy and settles instead for an alternative space on the edges of it'.[62] To my mind, any free choice by women of a *marginal* position in the critical arena would be a seriously retrograde step.

A less extreme rejectionist stance treats the biblical texts as sources of various voices from the past. The variety of the voices, and of the

56. Elizabeth Cady Stanton, *The Woman's Bible: The Original Feminist Attack on the Bible* (first edn; New York: European Publishing Company, 1895, 1898; abridged edition, with Introduction by Dale Spender; Edinburgh: Polygon Books, 1985), pp. 7-13.

57. Osiek, 'The Feminist and the Bible', p. 98; Cady Stanton's position is thoroughly discussed in Elisabeth Schüssler Fiorenza, *In Memory of Her: A Feminist Theological Reconstruction of Christian Origins* (London: SCM Press, 1983), pp. 7-14.

58. Mary Daly, *Beyond God the Father: Towards a Philosophy of Women's Liberation* (Boston: Beacon, 1973); and *Gyn/Ecology: The Metaethics of Radical Feminism* (Boston: Beacon, 1979).

59. Daphne Hampson, *Theology and Feminism* (Signposts in Theology; Oxford: Blackwell, 1990), pp. 1-6, and *passim*.

60. Osiek, 'The Feminist and the Bible', p. 98.

61. Osiek, 'The Feminist and the Bible', p. 94.

62. Belsey and Moore, 'Introduction', p. 10.

silences—often women's silences—can be discovered, and then the reader can choose to agree or disagree, to internalize the image or not. Any authority the biblical texts gains with readers has to be earned by relevance to their lives, not, *a priori*, as a matter of unthinking commitment. Typical of this position is the work of Cheryl Exum, who reads narrative texts to see what is said about women, what is not said about women and what these sayings and non-sayings mean.[63] She also observes what the woman says or does not say and what that implies about her role in the narrative, and notes who it is that observes and describes the woman and how she 'suffers' under that observation and description.[64]

This approach allows a valuing of women's roles and struggles to find a way to let biblical women speak in the public reading—or, rather, interpreting of the texts. The downside is that each step of each exegetical manoeuvre reminds the scholar and her readers of the severity of truncation and marginalization that has been exerted on women characters by the authors of the texts.

Inclusivist Approaches. Athalya Brenner and Fokkelien van Dijk-Hemmes read between the lines of the biblical narrative to find material that deals with women or their concerns in a positive, or informed, way, characterizing such texts as 'double-voiced'—implying by this term that women's voices may be heard though in a muted way in the writing of the male biblical authors.[65] This approach offers an inclusive analysis of all texts that refer to women or to women's concerns and so includes the full variety of styles and language used about women in the (Hebrew) Bible.

I am, however, still somewhat disappointed with the 'inclusivist' approach because it demands complicity in the inviolability of the text as it stands and settles for tinkering with the interpretational weight given to male and female concerns. To its credit, though, it does have the advantages of operating with the biblical texts *as they stand*, of treating all the texts as open to equal scrutiny, and of identifying a locus for women's involvement within the production

63. J. Cheryl Exum, '"Mother in Israel": A Familiar Story Reconsidered', in Russell (ed.), *Feminist Interpretation of the Bible*, pp. 73-85.

64. J. Cheryl Exum, 'Murder They Wrote: Ideology and the Manipulation of Female Presence in Biblical Narrative', in A. Bach (ed.), *The Pleasure of her Text: Feminist Readings of Biblical and Historical Texts* (Philadelphia: Trinity Press International, 1990), pp. 45-67; J. Cheryl Exum, *Fragmented Women: Feminist (Sub)-versions of Biblical Narratives* (JSOTSup 163; Sheffield: JSOT Press, 1993).

65. Brenner, 'Women's Traditions Problematized', pp. 61-66.

of the writings *as cultural products*—though not as having a direct input to the composing and writing. Even 'inclusivists' know that men kept a tight grasp on those powerful roles.

As we can see from the foregoing accounts of possible strategies of working with the texts, each method carries a bitter pill that the exegete must swallow.

Future Exegetical Strategies

My final section will consider what a both-gender-friendly climate of discussion would be like and how committed scholars working in such a climate might proceed with their continuing work of biblical criticism.

Recently, the search for other visions of this ideal future intellectual milieu has led to the formulation of a few 'programmes', some defined by negative criteria—what the future should *not* be like—and others more positively, though somewhat idiosyncratically, envisaged. And it is within the general ambience of the more proactive approaches to whole-human discourse that I believe the future of feminist criticism lies.

Working within the realm of the history of ideas, two French feminists attempt to predict the outcomes of present trends in Western feminism. First, Hélène Cixous, writing somewhat lyrically, looks forward to a situation where women will radically transform their role '"within" man's discourse', displacing the within-ness and exploding it. Not that women will appropriate anything from male discourse nor merely adapt aspects of it; rather they will ignore, transcend or, even, give it a shattering side-swipe.[66] She believes that 'displacement' is the key and that through 'ceaseless displacement' the enormous resources sealed up within women's imaginations will enrich and expand the complete human intellectual enterprise. The extravagance of the language she uses makes the prospect seem a little overwhelming, but if the eruption foreseen is no more violent than the brilliance of fireworks or the dancing of *jets d'eau* then human scholarship will indeed be enriched by this feminist input.

Julia Kristeva has similar hopes though she expresses them rather

66. Hélène Cixous, 'Sorties: Out and Out: Attacks/Ways Out/Forays', taken from Hélène Cixous and Catherine Clément, *The Newly Born Woman* (trans. Betsy Wing; Minneapolis: University of Minnesota Press, 1986), reprinted in Belsey and Moore, *The Feminist Reader*, pp. 101-16, and notes, pp. 229-30, especially pp. 114-16.

differently.[67] She sees feminism as having three phases. Its initial ambition was to take its place within the temporal structure of history. This was later replaced by a move towards explorations of meaning lying outside sequential time, and doing this by embracing atemporal ideals of femininity through aesthetic and religious re-appropriation of archaic myth. The final phase involves combining the two earlier moods and formulating a demand, not for equality with men, but for provision of rights and freedoms that celebrate the potential of (all) human difference and (all) human specificity. She hopes that this feminism will free itself from a one-to-one connection with 'Woman' and spread respect for difference and singularity throughout the whole of human discourse. As with those of Cixous, these objectives would also enlarge the range and language of critical studies—but they are expressed in something of 'the grand manner'. Her ideas sweep through one's conception of scholarship like the lavishly-clad entourage of an energetic empress undertaking a wave-making royal progress through the realm.

Contributing a combined British and American flavour to the discussion, Daphne Hampson writes as a post-Christian feminist—a title she might regard as well-nigh tautologous.[68] She envisages feminism as combining ethics, politics and spirituality,[69] with a strong focus on the interconnectedness of humanity and the others of earth's life forms.[70] She encapsulates her feminist vision in the one-word image of 'connectedness', quoting with approbation Eleanor Haley's view that feminism 'offers us individually and collectively the possibility of making connections with ourselves, one another, the earth, and all that is and can be'.[71] Interestingly, the concentration on both *individuality* and *collectivity* reminds us of the vision of Kristeva outlined above.

For myself, a rather cooler, and more congenial approach, would be to look forward to some interesting additions to the range of

67. Julia Kristeva, 'Women's Time', taken from 'Women's Time', *Signs* 7 (1981) (trans. Alice Jardine and Harry Blake), pp. 13-35, reprinted in Belsey and Moore, *The Feminist Reader*, pp. 1197-217, and notes, pp. 240-42, especially pp. 197-200, 213-17.

68. Hampson, *Theology and Feminism*, p. 1, claims that feminism has proved the 'death knell' for Christianity.

69. Hampson, *Theology and Feminism*, p 120.

70. Hampson, *Theology and Feminism*, p 132.

71. Hampson, *Theology and Feminism*, p 145, quoting from Eleanor Haley, 'What is Feminist Ethics? A Proposal for Continuing Discussion', *JRE* 8 (1980), p. 124.

scholarly discussions and debates in books, articles, conference papers, seminars, e-mail discussion groups, and even to the desultory chats that occur as two scholars browse in a library or at a bookstall. What will be additional will be a greater openness of attitudes, more awareness of the range of attitudes and perspectives held by other scholars worldwide, and an ability to see, describe and explain arguments from more than one perspective.

I also expect that some current practices and positions will lose ground, have less currency or become marginal. Absolutes such as 'right' and 'true' will be used more sparingly and will often be relativized, as in 'right at that time' and 'true for me'. There might even be less risk of incurring wrath by the mentioning of the name of a scholar from the 'wrong' school. And the phrase 'the new methods' will not be used as a term of abuse.

Balancing the Approaches

Is it possible to consider drawing up a balanced approach involving all these possible strategies for the future? Or, is it perhaps wiser and more productive to focus on naming—in order to avoid—the downside of each of the current approaches to biblical study?

The loyalist stance offers women (and men) with a faith perspective one way of trusting the biblical texts, but it demands their complicity in helping the sources of gendered oppression, *and their successors nowadays*, to avoid any guilt or to accept responsibility now and initiate reformation.

The sublimationist stance offers a more pleasant Bible reading strategy, but demands the complicity of blinkered vision in focusing exclusively on certain female roles, such as virgin Israel, bride of God, church as bride of Christ, and mother of the faithful, Mary as virgin-mother, Christ-Sophia, maternal images of Christ and of the Holy Spirit.[72] As well, it allows an opting out of the implications of unpleasant narratives by relocating the discussion in a psychological realm where no pain is felt.

The revisionist stance offers religious women a way of accepting the Bible with the proviso that the reader recreate a more gender-neutral past for it by rereading and rewriting it within its own history. The flaw I identify here is that the method demands acceptance of the authoritativeness of the text as it stands and operates only in the detail of interpretation.

72. Osiek, 'The Feminist and the Bible', p. 102.

The liberationist approach begins outside the Bible, in a world of historical actuality where men and women 'have' equal roles and rights. But, to offer this perspective to Christian and Jewish women (and men) it must in return demand their agreement that the definitions of salvation formulated by males are rich enough to merit translation into universal terms. The approach is an avowed advocacy committed to upholding religious beliefs based on interpretations of the Bible as Scripture, and it contains the limitations to be expected of such a stance.

The rejectionist stances offers feminists two choices. Complete rejection of the Bible gives independence and integrity in exchange for exclusion from the debates about interpretation of the Bible, and demands complicity in accepting the asymmetric conclusion that the norms of *one* gender, namely, female, should become the norms of all. The post-Christian position allows the appropriation of the best of biblical and Christian insights into a new feminist package that recreates a religion that values women's life roles more highly, though it is not clear if there is a place for men in that world-view. Less vigorous rejectionists ask that the Bible earn every crumb of its authority by validation of its precepts and role models against rigorous controls, but their work demands a revisitation of narratives of women's humiliation in order to overstrike and rewrite them.

The inclusivist position offers a prioritization of scholarship over faith interests but involves an agreement that women *were* somehow involved in the production of the Bible—other than as the mothers and nurturers of the authors, that is. To those who see the Bible as a purely masculine production this path is closed.

Conclusions

Feminist readings and feminist critiques can only help dissolve gendered false consciousnesses if they are applied in a wide-ranging and persistent way *and* accompanied by approaches from other standpoints as well, such as materialist and structuralist, or from other disciplines, such as sociology, psychology and cultural anthropology. Feminist strategies can succeed only if they are not assumed to contain all that is best in scholarship and if they prevent the critical pendulum from swinging too far towards a single-mindedly feminist stance.

It is important to remember the following points about scholars, and especially about female scholars. First, in order to succeed in the world of scholarship, whether spoken or written, they must be:

— trained in the methods and jargon of the discipline;
— able to compete effectively using the rules and logic of the guild;
— able to function as (pseudo-)males.[73]

But it is also vital to remember that by so being and doing they become complicit in:

— the maintenance of the androcentric symbolic universe, and complicit in acceptance of the top-down symbolic understanding of society that supports legitimation by power and authority rather than on one's contributions to community survival and productivity;[74]
— maintenance of the androcentric modes of expression and legitimation, and of communication and arrival at consensus, that is, complicity in Western, liberal, classical modes of education, argumentation and validation of statements and premises about the symbolic universe.

This in turn means they also become complicit in:

— acceptance that female modes of communication are inferior to, or less effective than, male;
— the use of gender-biased psychological language and norms in order to be intelligible and convincing to those who accept those norms as standard;
— continued suppression of female modes of expression and continued delay in their incorporation into whole-human modes of expression and legitimation;
— retardation of development of a complete, whole-human symbolic universe.

If there is to be a successful development of a gender-neutral scholarly environment where scholars of either gender *as a matter of course* give both androcentric and gynocentric readings of texts along with whatever other forms of criticism are helpful to their work, it will not

73. Deborah Thom, 'A Lop-Sided View: Feminist History or the History of Women?', in Campbell (ed.), *Critical Feminism*, pp. 25-52 (29, 46), reports that successful women were spoken of as if they were 'men in petticoats', quoting Mary Astell writing at the beginning of the eighteenth century, and notes that those who, in the twentieth century, were considered too extreme and deviant were thought of as 'women in trousers'. By either appellation the point is being made that they, though biologically female, are really 'men' if they can succeed in a male sphere.

74. Such as food production, health care and child-rearing.

come about without a fair degree of support from male scholars—whether they are feminists or not.

Reflection on the nature and functioning of false consciousnesses can help only those who consider them, and can, thereafter, help only them to acknowledge the influences that shape their scholarly work. So this route is open to a self-selected group—currently a minority, but perhaps possibly soon a majority. However, if some groups of male scholars continue to regard feminist criticism as a threat and as dismantling or reclaiming or removing something valuable and rightly theirs...then the best strategy for the non-entrenched groups—of whatever provenance—is to declare determinedly the marginal quality of such self-serving beliefs and to claim the centre of the field for more even-handed modes of discourse.

THE ABUSIVE BIBLE: ON THE USE OF FEMINIST METHOD IN PASTORAL CONTEXTS

Carole R. Fontaine

A trusting child is bound for sacrifice and placed by his father upon an altar waiting to receive his blood. It is God's will, we are told, and the father's willingness to kill his son is reckoned to the father as 'righteousness' (Gen. 22).

A lone wife is shoved out of the door of safety to satisfy the desires of a lustful crowd seeking to 'know' her husband and master. After a night of rape and abuse, she is found with her hands stretched across the threshold of the house that offered her no sanctuary. To announce the results of the deed, her husband dismembers her body and sends the pieces as tokens to the males of the surrounding tribes (Judg. 19).

A royal princess is raped by her half-brother, who goes unpunished by their father. The full brother who takes up her cause does so for his own political ends, which leads in turn to the tragic end of his quest for power. The innocent victim dwells 'desolate' in her brother's house. The father says nothing (2 Sam. 13).

A queen is commanded to appear before her husband's feasting nobles and satisfy their lust. When she refuses, she is 'disappeared' from the story and replaced with a more appropriately submissive beauty (Est. 1).

A neglected wife questions her husband's behavior. When she does, she is narratively 'disappeared' from his story. She is replaced with a more docile female, another man's wife (2 Sam. 6.20-23).[1]

An unknown woman raises her voice in blessing of the messiah who is passing by. 'Blessed is the womb that bore you' she says, 'and the breasts that you sucked'. She is silenced immediately and her

---

1. For a discussion of this text and the fate of Michal, daughter of Saul and sometime wife of David, see J. Cheryl Exum, *Fragmented Women: Feminist (Sub)versions of Biblical Narratives* (JSOTSup, 163; Sheffield: Sheffield Academic Press, 1993), pp. 42-60.

blessing nullified, as the messiah replies 'Blessed rather are those who hear the word of God and keep it!' (Lk. 11.27-28).[2]

When students in the Jewish and Christian traditions turn to their heritage in search of answers to the questions and problems that beset them today, it is natural and not at all surprising that the Bible should occupy a central position in their struggles. It is a formative complex of texts and traditions, treasured and revered for centuries. In many respects, the Bible has performed its function well: generation after generation, it has told the story, 'kept the faith' and enlightened the human journey by continuously indoctrinating each successive generation into the 'faith of the fathers'. Communities created the Bible and proclaimed it 'Sacred Scripture'; now that Scripture creates communities by serving as an ongoing resource of faith and practice.

Within the seminary, church or synagogue setting, the pastoral engagement of such issues as domestic and sexual violence in society most typically might take the form of 'Bible studies', sermons, or topics dealt with in prayer or study groups. These are not, however, the only contexts in which such topics might legitimately be studied, although such questions posed by a community of faith may well offer the most poignant settings for this type of inquiry. The discussion presented here seeks to ask how such subjects may be handled in teaching for pastoral contexts, especially Christian seminary settings where the Bible is taught as course subject matter. In fact, the Hebrew Bible may be taught in many different ways: in secular settings it may be seen as literature, as a (semi- or pseudo-) historical document, or as a source for sociological and anthropological reconstructions of early 'historical' religions (as opposed to archaic and primitive religions which, it is usually supposed, biblical religions supersede in a more or less orderly evolutionary development).[3] In seminaries, Jewish or Christian, in contrast to departments of 'Religious Studies' that contain 'Biblical Studies', the starting point for the consideration of the biblical text also (typically) includes some notion of its 'inspiration' and/or 'authority' as a foundational text for the communities which accord it the status of 'Sacred Scripture'.

2.   This text is beautifully interpreted in Kerry M. Craig and Margaret A. Kristjansson, 'Women Reading as Men/Women Reading as Women: A Structural Analysis for the Historical Project', *Semeia* 51 (1990), pp. 119-36.
3.   Robert Bellah, 'Religious Evolution', in William A. Lessa and Evon Z. Vogt (eds.), *Reader in Comparative Religion: An Anthropological Approach* (New York: Harper & Row, 3rd edn, 1965), pp. 36-50.

In these settings, how does existing methodology handle the evidence of 'abuse', first found in stories told by the text and then perpetuated by the commitments of the text itself, as interpreted by its believing communities?

One of the basic assumptions with which Christians and Jews seem to operate is that the Bible is a document that stands wholeheartedly and unreservedly on the side of human dignity. The faithful assume that the Bible has words of comfort for the victims, mostly women and children, of sexual and domestic violence; that the Bible is clearly against such violence; that it is a major resource on such questions for people of faith, a friend and not an enemy. Critical feminist biblical scholarship—which attends to the consideration of what the Bible is and how it does what it does—does not, however, automatically endorse these basic, positive assumptions.[4] The brief synopses of biblical stories with which this essay began should raise at least the suggestion that something may be terribly wrong with the uses made of the Bible by its communities of faith, if not also with the Bible itself.

The objection might be raised that the feminist biblical scholar's view of the role of the Bible in shaping the thoughts of society and believers on these issues is a rarefied academic perspective not applicable to the world-views of the contemporary sufferers themselves. Perhaps. But let us turn to some case studies of how abusees interpret the biblical God's role—and, by implication, the Bible's role—in their distress:

> A 55-year-old woman was raped by a stranger who broke into her home during the night. Her explanation for why this had happened to her was that God was punishing her for having divorced her husband ten years earlier.

> A 19-year-old woman had been sexually abused by her older brother since she was 10 years old. Her explanation was that the incestuous abuse was God's punishment for her being a bad person. In addition, at age 15 she had an abortion because she had been impregnated by her brother. The incestuous abuse continued and then she was convinced that God was punishing her for having had the abortion.

---

4.   See, for example, essays in A. Brenner (ed.), *A Feminist Companion to the Latter Prophets* (The Feminist Companion to the Bible, 8; Sheffield: Sheffield Academic Press, 1995); and Kwok Pui-Lan, 'Racism and Ethnocentrism in Feminist Biblical Interpretation', in Elisabeth Schüssler Fiorenza (ed.), *Searching the Scriptures*. I. *A Feminist Introduction* (New York: Crossroad, 1993), pp. 101-16.

A battering husband, in addition to physically beating his wife, also regularly raped her. She interpreted this pattern of abuse as God's way of correcting her tendency to rebel against the authority of her husband.

A gay man who had just begun to be more open about his sexual orientation was kidnapped and brutally raped by three men. He...concluded that God was punishing him for his positive feelings about his homosexuality.[5]

These case studies are taken from Christian pastor Marie Fortune's groundbreaking work, *Sexual Violence: The Unmentionable Sin*, which has become a standard text in the field of Christian pastoral response to sexual and domestic violence. Anyone who counsels parishioners or students, or listens closely to stories of friends and family, could add other stories: the 20-year old rape victim who was told by a clergyman that the event had been God's will because she was not a virgin; the devastated 24-year old victim of three separate attacks of rape who concluded that she did not even deserve to be alive, since such violence against her could only be a sign that God's love had been forever withdrawn from her; the 34-year old incest survivor who recalls being sexually active from the age of two, now an outcast to her family because she would not visit her abuser as he lay dying in a hospital.[6]

We all know these stories; if they are not our own, then they might belong to people we love. In some sense, even those of us who are lucky enough not to have been physically or sexually abused have shared, through love and empathy, in the emotional wreckage wrought on abusees as we have reached out to our broken friends, relatives, students and parishioners. No doubt those who love their god, cherish their religious traditions and are in some sense the propagators of those traditions, regularly cringe as they hear victims voice their understanding of how God was present or absent in the midst of that suffering. Clearly, those suffering from this sort of trauma may be prone to shaping their theologies of suffering in ways that echo the reality of their experience of abuse.[7] Most pastors and rabbis have tried hard to assist the survivors of violence and their families and friends in moving from what Joy M.K. Bussert has characterized as a 'theology of suffering' to an 'ethic of empowerment'.[8]

5. Marie Fortune, *Sexual Violence: The Unmentionable Sin* (New York: Pilgrim Press, 1983), p. 194.

6. These examples are drawn from pastoral counseling sessions with my white, middle-class seminary students.

7. Judith L. Herman, *Trauma and Recovery* (New York: Basic Books, 1992).

8. Joy M.K. Bussert, *Battered Women: From a Theology of Suffering to an Ethic of*

But there comes a point when one must wonder whether we are all reading the same Bible, since the interpretations made in these situations seem to be so divergent. Are the abusees all crazy, suffering from well-earned paranoid delusions and post-traumatic stress, when they express their belief that somehow God was 'out to get them' and that the betrayal and abuse they endured were a manifestation of that divine enmity?

While most feminists do not believe in a God who punishes in such a fashion, I do *not* think the abusees who speak in these terms do so without justification. They have read their Bibles and in doing so inhaled the toxic fumes of the patriarchal ethos of the biblical tradition, especially where it deals with the topic of bodies. The 'theological' problems raised by the fact of human embodiment are played out differently in each testament. The Hebrew Bible, while it maintains a more wholesome view of the entire body 'complex' (i.e., it does not divide persons into 'soul' and 'body', but sees them as a unity), is deeply fearful of women's bodies and the powers of procreation and blood that they hold.[9] The New Testament's apocalyptic world-view and affirmation of a savior embodied in *male* (*not* female) form caused its writers to place a low valuation on female embodiment, and its anthropology does see a 'soul–body' split. The position taken by the New Testament has traditionally worked to disadvantage women in theological discussions, since women are associated with 'body' (because they are the vehicle for the production of new ones), and body is clearly inferior to spirit in such theological thinking.[10] Paradoxically, however, it is through their bodily states that Christian women receive 'salvation', either as humble, consecrated virgins[11] or as devoted mothers (1 Tim. 2.14-15). Given the dysfunctions that survivors of sexual violence often face in the area of

Empowerment (New York: Lutheran Church in America, 1986), pp. 65-66.

9.   Alice Bach, 'Good to the Last Drop: Viewing the Sotah (Numbers 5:11-31) as the Glass Half Empty and Wondering How to View it Half Full', in J. Cheryl Exum and David J.A. Clines (eds.), *The New Literary Criticism and the Hebrew Bible* (JSOTSup, 143; Sheffield: Sheffield Academic Press, 1993), pp. 26-54; Mieke Bal, *Lethal Love: Feminist Literary Readings of Biblical Love Stories* (Bloomington: Indiana University Press, 1987), pp. 1-8, 65-67.

10. For further discussion see C.R. Fontaine, 'Disabilities and Illness in the Bible: A Feminist Perspective', in A. Brenner (ed.), *A Feminist Companion to the Hebrew Bible in the New Testament* (The Feminist Companion to the Bible, 10; Sheffield: Sheffield Academic Press, 1996), pp. 286-301.

11. Bernard of Clairvaux, *Magnificat: Homilies in Praise of the Blessed Virgin Mary* (trans. Marie-Bernard Said and Grace Perigo: Cistercian Fathers Series, 18; Kalamazoo, MI: Cistercian Publications, 1979), pp. 9-13.

their sexuality, it is worth hearing the reformer Martin Luther's words on this text in Timothy, as he envisions the spiritual wellbeing Christian salvation offers to Protestant women believers:

> *She will be saved.* That subjection of woman and domination of men have not been taken away, have they? No. The penalty remains. The blame passed over. The pain and tribulation of childbearing continue. Those penalties will continue until judgment. So also the dominion of men and the subjection of women continue. You must endure them. You will also be saved if you have also subjected yourselves and bear your children with pain. *Through bearing children.* It is a very great comfort that a woman can be saved by bearing children, etc. That is, she has an honorable and salutary status in life if she keeps busy having children. We ought to recommend this passage to them, etc. She is described as 'saved' not for freedom, for license, but for bearing and rearing children.[12]

It is no wonder, then, that survivors of sexual and domestic violence have devised the explanations that we saw above: they have read the stories of Genesis, Judges, Samuel and Job; they have heard the discourses on sexuality by Paul and those who spoke in his name; they have heard their clergy send them submissively home to abuse in order to protect the 'sanctity' of the family and 'traditional family values'. They are *not* crazy. On bad days, I tend to think that those of us who seek to use the Bible in a liberating, empowering way are the crazy ones. To turn again to Marie Fortune's work, she writes in *Keeping the Faith*, in the 'Appendix for Clergy and Laypeople',

> The Bible has often been misinterpreted and misused in response to the Christian battered woman by those who have wanted to help her. This has been sometimes due to ignorance, sometimes due to denial of the seriousness of wife abuse, sometimes due to a desire to control the battered woman and limit her options.[13]

While deeply appreciative of Fortune's desire to make the Bible part of the solution instead of part of the problem, I cannot second the analysis quoted here. I only wish that it were so simple as a case of misinterpretation that could be solved with better translations and more thorough historical-critical research. Unfortunately, the problem goes deeper than that, into the core of the Bible itself.

It is important, then, to take a closer look at what is going on in the ways communities of faith, as well as academic communities, view

12. Martin Luther, *Luther's Works* (ed. Jaroslav Pelican; 30 vols.; St Louis: Concordia, 1955–), XXVIII, p. 279.

13. Marie M. Fortune, *Keeping the Faith: Questions and Answers for the Abused Woman* (San Francisco: Harper & Row, 1987), p. 81.

the Bible, and the uses made of it. Most of my remarks will be illustrated from the Hebrew Bible since that is my area of major competence, but the critique offered here applies to the New Testament as well, and is in no way meant to imply that the Hebrew Bible is theologically or morally inferior to the New Testament, or 'incomplete' without it. Things do not become instantly better with the appearance of Jesus. This is due to the thoroughgoing underlying patriarchal assumptions of the New Testament writers and communities, as well as to the apocalyptic world-view that caused them to think rather differently about sexual and domestic issues than they might have otherwise, had they not been expecting the imminent end of the world (and hence, the end of sexuality altogether).[14] Even after the appearance of the Christian church, Judaism continued to be a viable and vital tradition to which its women adhered. In fact, differences between Jewish, Christian, and pagan women in the early centuries of Christianity may well have been exaggerated by Christian triumphalist readings.[15]

It is also important to emphasize here that there is no one 'Christian', 'Jewish', 'academic' or even 'feminist' way to understand the Bible; there is a broad range of variation in how differently Christian and Jewish communities deal with the issues of interpretation, and the disagreements among feminists are legion. Further, I am asking questions of the text and making interpretations that clearly reveal my philosophical and social location as a Caucasian woman born in the United States, raised in poverty in the American South and baptized as a Protestant Christian, now a feminist seminary professor on the edge of the twenty-first century. My allegiances are with the abused. The whole notion of 'individual

---

14. The role of the NT and Christianity in perpetuating such abuse as discussed here is amply reviewed in Joanne Carlson Brown and Carole R. Bohn (eds.), *Christianity, Patriarchy, and Abuse: A Feminist Critique* (Cleveland: Pilgrim Press, 1989). On the role of NT theology, see especially Joanne Carlson Brown and Rebecca Parker, 'For God So Loved the World?', pp. 1-30 in that volume. For a critique of the implicit anti-Judaism inherent in Christian feminist interpretations which make Jews responsible for patriarchy and the death of the Goddess, see Judith Plaskow, 'Anti-Judaism in Feminist Christian Interpretation', in Fiorenza (ed.), *Searching the Scriptures*, I, pp. 117-30. The tendency on the part of some Christian feminists to make the 'Jewish' heritage of Jesus and Paul responsible for any anti-female elements of the text, while ascribing any liberatory properties to the 'new' Gospel, is as unhelpful as it is unhistorical.

15. Barbara Geller Nathanson, 'Toward a Multicultural Ecumenical History of Women in the First Century/ies C.E.', in Fiorenza (ed.), *Searching the Scriptures*, I, pp. 272-89.

rights' is a fairly modern one and has little support in the texts of antiquity, nor does the idea that the destiny of women is or should be anything other than the role of mother and wife receive much attention there.[16] I honestly do not know if ancient women ever asked themselves the questions raised here; the classically trained biblical scholar in me believes that probably they did not, but the feminist is not so sure.[17] Bearing in mind these qualifications in the way texts will be handled here, let us turn to the primary materials. The Bible contributes to the past and present exploitation of women, children and gay, lesbian and bisexual persons in three areas: by its *nature*, by its *content* and by its *function*. I shall examine each of these in turn.

The 'Nature' of the Bible

What exactly is the Bible anyway? The direct, literal words of God? The words of humanity about God? God's word back to humanity's word? An imaginative record of humanity's musings about the nature of human life and the deity? A factual, historical account? The record of a people? A great and compelling work of literary artistry? A recipe book that can teach anyone, anywhere, anytime how to cook up a successful, rewarding life? There are communities that endorse each of these views, and do so in good faith according to their best understanding of these complex questions. While I suspect that many who attend Christian seminaries—as well as those who teach there—might opt for some version of the progressive 'middle' view that the Bible is a divinely inspired *human* product, we must not forget that the literal interpretation (i.e., the view that the Bible is the *actual* Word of God) holds sway for a large number of the faithful in the United States and around the world. And for those subscribing to that view, 'biblical' theology's stranglehold on the lives of women and children is felt most keenly and with its most deadly and deadening effects. For some, 'bibliolatry', that is, turning the Bible

16. The exceptions here are Mesopotamian creation epics, which suggest that certain classes of females (she-demons who prey on children, priestesses and *naditu*-women) were created by the gods for human population control. 'Story of the Flood' (Atrahasis Epic), in Benjamin R. Foster (trans.), *From Distant Days: Myths, Tales and Poetry of Ancient Mesopotamia* (Bethesda, MD: CDL Press, 1995), pp. 76-77.

17. The fact that wives and slaves run away (for which we have textual indicators) is a sure indication that they were not happy with their individual lots; whether or not they questioned the existence of structures that caused their conditions is difficult to assess from the extant records available.

into an idol whose authority is worshipped *instead* of God, is a reality. Further, by any progressive reading, the reality of literalism is one that can rob sufferers of abuse of the comfort of a faith in a real God: not the punishing patriarchal tyrant who sexually humiliates the female Israel (so with Hosea, the so-called 'prophet of love')—but the one who bends low to comfort the abused and humiliated (Jn 8.1-11); the one who could no more forget humanity than a mother could forget her nursing child (Isa. 49.15); the one who is *god* and *not* man, who does not come to destroy (Hos. 11.9).[18]

It is precisely because religious communities have held a privileged view of the Bible's 'nature' as some sort of divine product with divine content and purpose that it has been so difficult to analyze the ways in which the Bible might be contributing to the various oppressions visited upon different groups—women, children, foreigners of other faiths, homosexuals and the created universe. Those engaged in scholarly research on the Bible have also been blinded by inherited religious sensibilities about the nature of the Bible, refusing to ask some of the common-sense questions which they would put to any other ancient document as a matter of course. This may be seen particularly in the ways the *character of God* has been exempted from the rigorous critical study that is usually applied to human characters.[19] One could read the Hebrew Bible for years using the 'value-neutral' mainstream/malestream scholarly methodology developed in historical criticism, without ever asking the kinds of questions about character and action, human and divine, raised by feminist scholarship.[20] Given the problematic behavior displayed by the Father God of the Bible in both Hebrew and Christian Scriptures,[21] the careful reader is certainly entitled to some serious doubts when being asked to affirm the standard Christian theological metaphor,

18. For a discussion of the imagery in Hosea see T. Drorah Setel, 'Prophets and Pornography: Female Sexual Imagery in Hosea', in Letty M. Russell (ed.), *Feminist Interpretation of the Bible* (Philadelphia: Westminster, 1985), pp. 86-95; and C.R. Fontaine, 'A Response to "Hosea"', in Brenner (ed.), *A Feminist Companion to the Latter Prophets*, pp. 60-69, as well as other essays in that volume.

19. Danna Nolan Fewell and David Gunn, *Gender, Power and Promise: The Subject of the Bible's First Story* (Nashville: Abingdon Press, 1993), pp. 18-19.

20. Phyllis Trible, *Texts of Terror: Literary-Feminist Readings of Biblical Narratives* (Philadelphia: Fortress Press, 1984). While flawed methodologically in various ways, this work represents one of the firstfruits of feminist literary analysis of abusive texts.

21. Male deities from the ancient Near East share in the abusive tendencies seen in the Bible, especially Enki, Marduk, Chemosh/Molech, Ba'al and so on.

'God is Love', for the truth of that claim is by no means clear. If the patriarchal God is *really* an impartial and loving Redeemer, then let him redeem: we the readers should not be forced to make humanity 'guilty' in order to preserve the innocence of a god who does not act.[22] If the combined impact of historical-critical scholarship allied to the feminist method has worked to erode some of the Bible's traditional authority as the Word of God and branded it for what it is—the words of elite males projected onto deity to protect and legitimate the powers of patriarchy[23]—then we are truly living in a time of signs and wonders. Furthermore, even those who prefer a literal interpretation must make room somewhere for the human element in the production of the actual manuscripts of the Bible, and there we find a wedge for enlightenment. Perhaps God *did* whisper the words of the Torah in Moses' ear or sent Living Word into the world, but between the ear and the hand there is tremendous room for 'sin' and error to slip in. Acknowledgment of the Bible as a human product is the first step in undercutting its seeming authorization of the exploitation of any who are not in-group, elite males.[24]

In saying that the Bible is the human product of elite males, I do not mean to suggest that flashes of divine compassion and purpose may not be found within the Bible's covers, nor that the voice of marginalized persons is absent from its pages. The majority of those who composed and edited the Bible did so, for the most part, without any overt, explicit program of oppression. Rather, they simply did not 'see' women, children and gay or lesbian persons as true 'subjects' and, in this, they only follow the reigning world-view of the cultures to which they belonged.[25] The Bible is the *heir* of patriarchy, not its originator. Ancient Near Eastern culture had made patriarchy its response to historical and socio-economic changes long before Jews and Christians ever appeared on the historical scene, and pagan

22. So, too, with the Book of Lamentations and *Lamentations Rabbah*. For modern perspectives, see David R. Blumenthal, *Facing the Abusing God: A Theology of Protest* (Louisville, KY: Westminster/John Knox, 1993); James L. Crenshaw, *A Whirlpool of Torment: Israelite Traditions of God as an Oppressive Presence* (Overtures in Biblical Theology; Philadelphia: Fortress Press, 1984).

23. Edwin M. Good, 'Deception and Women: A Response', *Semeia* 42 (1988), p. 132.

24. Kwok Pui-Lan, 'Racism and Ethnocentrism in Feminist Biblical Interpretation', in Fiorenza (ed.), *Searching the Scriptures*, I, pp. 101-16 (102-103); Monika Fander, 'Historical Critical Methods', pp. 205-24 in the same volume.

25. Fewell and Gunn, *Gender, Power and Promise*, pp. 9-21.

communities of the Greco-Roman world were thoroughly patriarchal as well.[26]

It is common for liberation theologians to suggest that the Bible is a manifesto of divinely authorized freedom for the oppressed.[27] It can be read as such, certainly, but only by ignoring major portions of the work and burying any consideration of compositional factors. As New Testament theologian Elisabeth Schüssler Fiorenza has pointed out admirably, the Bible was written and edited by those who won the theological struggles of their day. It is the legacy of the 'winners', and shows little or no interest in promoting the perspectives of the losers.[28] One prominent black South African biblical theologian, Itumeleng Jeremiah Mosala, has stated that failure to identify the oppressor *within* the text is the single most pressing issue in biblical liberation studies. Until we understand that injustice has been coded into the very text itself as it pursues the class interests of its authors and protagonists, progressive believers will be dumbfounded by the Bible's ability to support oppression. Even when the Bible falls into liberating hands, it can still provide the catalyst for domination and submission because, as a human product, it is not free from finitude, particularized vision and sin.[29] I would add to Mosala's strictures that we must also foreground the *gender* and *race* interests of the biblical authors when we seek to construct liberating interpretations. These interpretations will naturally vary, depending on the communities making them. Some Jewish feminists may see their Christian sisters as having something of an advantage in the New Testament's (supposed) portrayal of a gospel of liberation against which all non-liberating traditions may be measured, judged and re-formed—while Jewish texts, reflecting Jewish life and practice over centuries, may lack such a unifying theme to press into feminist

26. For example, Gerda Lerner's analysis of ancient Near Eastern culture in *The Creation of Patriarchy* (New York: Oxford University Press, 1986), pp. 54-160.

27. See Susan Brooks Thistlethwaite's presuppositions in 'Every Two Minutes: Battered Women and Feminist Interpretation', in Russell (ed.), *Feminist Interpretation*, pp. 96-110; and also Elsa Tamez, *Bible of the Oppressed* (Maryknoll, NY: Orbis Books, 1982), where the author is unable to come to terms with the content of the book of Joshua and leaves it out of her survey entirely.

28. E. Schüssler Fiorenza, *In Memory of Her: A Feminist Theological Reconstruction of Christian Origins* (New York: Crossroad, 1983), pp. 3-91.

29. Itumeleng J. Mosala, 'The Use of the Bible in Black Theology', in Itumeleng J. Mosala and Buti Tlhagale (eds.), *The Unquestionable Right to Be Free: Black Theology from South Africa* (Maryknoll, NY: Orbis Books, 1986), pp. 175-99; Katie Cannon, 'Womanist Interpretation and Preaching in the Black Church', in Fiorenza (ed.), *Searching the Scriptures*, I, pp. 326-38.

service.[30] Others, like Judith Plaskow, may rightly point to subliminal and inchoate anti-Judaic propositions buried within the Christian feminist appropriation of the Hebrew Bible and understandings of Jesus that highlight his opposition to Judaism, rather than the manifold continuities which the New Testament also preserves.[31] Some Christian feminists may find Jewish feminists more empowered by the wealth of Jewish traditions about El-Shaddai, the suckling God, or God's Shekinah, the indwelling, feminine presence of God.[32] Clearly, the grass sometimes seems greener on patriarchy's other side, and each group may have something to learn from the other.[33]

To most of the Christian and Jewish scholarly world, even those seminary outposts of the scholarly guild, the Bible is in some part a human product that pursues the interests of its authors and authorizing patriarchal communities. We should not be surprised, then, when the agendas of the Bible's male authors seem to be working at cross-purposes to the establishment of a baseline of personal dignity for women, children and non-heterosexuals. Even where women or children are allowed to speak they are almost always shown as carrying out the patriarchal imperatives of their culture, and gay men are translated right out of existence.[34] The Songs of Miriam, Deborah, Hannah and even that meek and mild Virgin Mary speak glowingly of the vindicating violence of their male god and judge, simply reversing the roles of oppressor and oppressed through divine intervention.

> I will sing to the Lord, for he has triumphed gloriously;
> the horse and his rider he has thrown into the sea.
> The Lord is my strength and my song,
> and he has become my salvation;
> this is my God, and I will praise him,

30. Ellen M. Umansky, 'Creating a Jewish Feminist Theology: Possibilities and Problems', in Judith Plaskow and Carol P. Christ (eds.), *Weaving the Visions: New Patterns in Feminist Spirituality* (San Francisco: Harper, 1989), p. 189.

31. Fortune, *Faith*, p. 81.

32. For example, M.T. Winter's *Woman Prayer, Woman Song: Resources for Ritual* (Oak Park, IL: Meyer-Stone Books, 1987), pp. 5-10, 17-21, 51-57; Susan Cady, Marian Ronan and Hal Taussig, *Wisdom's Feast: Sophia in Study and Celebration* (San Francisco: Harper & Row, 1989). For a philological discussion see David Biale, 'The God with Breasts: El Shaddai in the Bible', *HR* 21 (1981–82), pp. 240-56.

33. For difficulties raised by Christian feminist appropriation of Jewish theological motifs, see the article by Katharina von Kellenbach in this volume.

34. Fewell and Gunn, *Gender, Power and Promise*, pp. 148-51.

my father's God and I will exalt him.
The Lord is a man of war;
Yahweh is his name (Exod. 15.1b-3).

Those who were full have hired themselves out for bread,
but those who were hungry have ceased to hunger.
The barren has borne seven,
but she who has many children is forlorn.
The Lord kills and brings to life;
he brings down to Sheol and raises up (1 Sam. 2.5-6).

He has put down the mighty from their thrones,
and exalted those of low degree;
he has filled the hungry with good things,
and the rich he has sent empty away (Lk. 1.52-53).

Now, even if we were to be able to prove that these psalms of thanksgiving were authored by the women to whom they are attributed—to be sure, no easy task, though research on women as authors of victory and other songs continues to inform our inquiries[35]—has very much been gained by being able to point proudly to these passages as if they were written by women? Miriam's exultation in her war-god easily glosses over the fate of the Egyptians; Hannah's joy in her pregnancy expresses itself in the gleeful observation of the wicked getting their 'just desserts'; and this same theme dominates Mary's Magnificat. Once contextualized,[36] we can see liberating reasons why the text might have been shaped in such a way—the wonder of proto-Israelite slaves escaping from the might of an imperial empire; the vindication of the humiliated barren woman (a stock character representing social failure); the acceptance

35. Jonneke Bekkenkamp and Fokkelien van Dijk, 'The Canon of the Old Testament and Women's Cultural Traditions', in A. Brenner (ed.), *A Feminist Companion to the Song of Songs* (The Feminist Companion to the Bible, 1; Sheffield: Sheffield Academic Press, 1993), pp. 67-85; Athalya Brenner and Fokkelien van Dijk-Hemmes, *On Gendering Texts: Female and Male Voices in the Hebrew Bible* (Biblical Interpretation Series, 1; Leiden: Brill, 1993).

36. Social location and literary context are powerful forces that shape our reception of any motif. To give a personal example, most middle-class white children in the United States are taught in kindergarten to identify 'our friend the policeman' as a person of safety and protection from whom they should not hesitate to seek help. As a child raised in a black ghetto in the South I was taught, both by adults and personal observation, to classify 'policemen' as sources of danger and external coercive force. However, servicemen in the Armed Forces, who might have been thought to conform to the category 'men in uniform', were *not* identified by ghetto-dwellers as dangerous, since it was our own population group that filled the lower ranks of the military: in this case, *they* were also *us*.

of the Annunciation. But, even so, are the sentiments expressed, however human and understandable, actually sentiments we want to flourish and grow? Is the answer to the violence visited on women and children to mete out the same treatment to little boys and men? An uncritical reading of these 'liberation' passages certainly leaves the answer to such questions in doubt. When the Bible (or the Midrash, or the church fathers, and so on) fails us, we should feel no hesitation in saying so. Were we to apply the same code of behavior encapsulated in these psalms to modern situations of domestic and sexual violence, we would do nothing more than contribute to the creation of another generation of abusers. Only by ending the cycle of violence once and for all, and not by perpetuating it through role reversal, can we have hope of bringing to a halt the reign of terror under which so many lives are lived.

The very nature of the Bible, then—human words in fancy divine dress—has worked to undercut critique of its violence,[37] and most Christian readers have taken the 'easy way out' of displacing objectionable material onto the 'Old' Testament with its 'God of Wrath' in order to exempt their 'New' Testament with its 'God of Love'. But there are other ways in which the believing communities' views of the Bible's divine nature has empowered the abuser as well. The male programs that guided the writing, selection and final editing of sacred texts decreed what would be of interest and what would be left out. In real terms this means that, based on these texts, we can know very little about the actual living conditions and thoughts of those who were outside the mainstream of the writer or editor's interests. Too much has been left out, and not all the power and glory of feminist biblical studies can write us back in, though many are trying. We are left arguing from silence or heretical texts, as Schüssler Fiorenza does in her *In Memory of Her*, but how binding will such arguments be to those who do not share her hermeneutic? It is a wonderful hermeneutic, this judging of the authenticity of revelation by measuring how far it goes *against* patriarchal expectations; I use it myself. But I also know from personal experience that it holds very little credibility with some of the 'old school' of biblicists and even less with conservative believers.

The Bible's assumption that male traditions and words are adequate expressions of female experience of the divine will continue to

37. For a powerful analysis of this tendency in prophetic works, see Athalya Brenner, 'Introduction', in Brenner (ed.), *A Feminist Companion to the Latter Prophets*, pp. 21-37.

mutilate women's souls as long as certain literalistic interpretations hold sway. A consideration of the Psalms will give an illustration of what is meant here. Students are often told, far too often in my opinion, that the Psalter is the prayer book of the peoples of God, that it is one of the most complete and finest expressions of all the seasons in the life of prayer. Is it really? I find no psalms that express despair over miscarriage, or seek vindication for the rape or incest survivor. My Psalter contains no thanksgiving psalms specifically aimed at the celebration of the survival of childbirth, no lyric praise for the miracle that takes place with menarche, no attention at all to the various phases of growth and biological change that mark a woman's life— unless we wish to count the royal wedding psalm, Psalm 45. This psalm addresses a few lines to the lucky bride, assuring her that her kin and the protection they offer are to be replaced by the king's desire for her (vv. 10-11) and ending with a line any abuser would cheerfully second: 'Since he is your lord, bow to him'. Despite recent admirable attempts to reconsider the possibility of women's authorship of some of the psalms,[38] the Psalter I read is about the seasons and yearnings of men's lives; and that is fine, as far as it goes. Men need poetry and prayer, too. It is only with much rewriting that women's voices and concerns are heard in these prayers. We may write ourselves in—we do and we should—but not all the femi- nine pronouns in the world, bracketed into the original text, can produce a book that cared from its inception about women and girls as central *subjects*.[39] I do not believe that the Psalmists left women out deliberately; I doubt that it ever occurred to them to put them in as anything other than bit players in the drama of the male quest for meaning, hegemony and progeny.

With such a legacy of support for the male author's unconscious tendency to place himself at the center of God's concerns, it is no wonder that the Bible can make laws that sentence a virgin who is the survivor of sexual violence to death if she was assaulted in the city, since she must have not screamed loudly enough to bring help (Deut. 22.23-29). The men who wrote those laws either did not under- stand or did not care to acknowledge all the methods of coercion and terror employed upon a woman in such circumstances. As if this law were not bad enough, its corollary is in some ways even worse: if the

---

38. Patrick D. Miller, *They Cried to the Lord: The Form and Theology of Biblical Prayer* (Minneapolis: Fortress Press, 1994), pp. 233-43.

39. There are, of course, wonderful exceptions to be found in both Hebrew and Christian Scriptures. See below.

survivor is *not* a betrothed virgin, her father receives financial compensation from the aggressor for the damage done to the woman's market value as 'untouched', and the abusee receives the unenviable compensation of being forced to marry her attacker. The New Testament presses its patriarchal vision even into the metaphysical realm: presumably, the survivor is forever joined in spirit and flesh to the one who violated her (1 Cor. 6.15-16). Those who can worship a god portrayed as authorizing such conditions for survivors are welcome to him.

These comments should not be taken to mean that the Bible is any *worse* than most of the literature of its kind from the rest of the ancient Near East, though I have found texts from Mesopotamia, Egypt, Canaan and Anatolia that are empowering in the extreme. The Bible is not as bad as some, and certainly better than many, parallel texts from the neighboring cultures—particularly in its treatment of in-group slaves, the powerful role of mothers and those not favored by being the privileged firstborn.[40] But the more or less overt exclusion of the female voice from the Bible's pages[41] was possible in part because the canonical Bible was missing an important element found in other ancient Near East religious texts: the presence of goddesses. When a culture engaged in goddess worship, women—though, to be sure, usually drawn from the elite classes—were sometimes necessary to officiate in the cult, and hence were not so easy to exclude as citizens of the moral universe.[42] It may be, however, that our usual dismissal of pagan cults containing goddesses on the basis of their presumed elitism and moral inferiority[43] must be re-evaluated. Recent evidence from the Late Bronze Age Temple of the Storm God at Emar (Tell Meskéné on the Euphrates in Syria) suggests once again how the vagaries of the survival of evidence may have skewed our

40. By 'in-group' slaves, I mean slaves who belong to the same ethnic group as their masters. The Hebrew Bible's positive treatment of the second-born is sometimes referred to as 'the success of the unsuccessful' motif.

41. But for an intriguing reassessment of the presence of the female voice in the Hebrew Bible, see Brenner and van Dijk-Hemmes, *On Gendering Texts*.

42. H.G. Güterbock, 'An Outline of the Hittite AN.TA.ÒUM Festival', *JNES* 19 (1960), pp. 80-89 (86). For an overview of the relation of women to goddess cults, see C.R. Fontaine, '"A Heifer From Thy Stable": On Goddesses and the Status of Women in the Ancient Near East', in Alice Bach (ed.), *The Pleasure of her Text: Feminist Readings of Biblical and Historical Texts* (Philadelphia: Trinity Press International, 1990), pp. 69-95.

43. For example, cultic practices in which women (allegedly) have more than one sexual partner, or a partner to whom they are not legally married.

interpretations. The ritual (Emar 369) for the installation of the Storm God's High Priestess (NIN.DINGIR), who is clearly understood as a human surrogate for and devotee of the Mother Goddess consort of the Storm God, says that the new priestess is chosen by lots from among the daughters of 'any son of Emar'. While it may be that betrothal customs caused some noble daughters to be designated for this applicant pool at birth (thereby ruling out candidates from less exalted families), we cannot ignore the fact that we may well have a sort of egalitarian cultic job opening presented here, in a ritual where kings and royal family play very limited roles in contrast to the city elders. While the NIN.DINGIR was related primarily to the Storm God, it is clear from the ritual that her relationship to his consort Hebat, the ancient Syrian mother goddess of the Hurrian–Hittite pantheon, forms a major part of the symbol system that authorizes the NIN.DINGIR's role. What is also clear from the ritual is the assumption that the enhanced status of High Priestess of the Storm God is viewed as a result of the transfer the woman in question from the sphere of control by her father to that of her divine 'husband'. The other high priestess installation text from Emar, dealing with the *maš artu* of the military goddess Aštart (Emar 370), while sharing many characteristics with the installation of the NIN.DINGIR, also contains significant differences which are possibly to be attributed to the martial character of the goddess in question.[44] Some of these goddesses whom the Bible so skillfully propagandized as some sort of an 'abomination' were thought to protect women in childbed, stand as the protector of prostitutes[45] (surely one of the most marginalized classes of women in the ancient world), and serve as the focus of prayer for real women whose words have been found on clay tablets across the Fertile Crescent.

44.   See D.E. Fleming, *The Installation of Baal's High Priestess at Emar: A Window on Ancient Syrian Religion* (Atlanta, GA: Scholars Press, 1992), pp. 49-59, 174-75, 188-92, 209-211, and 'More Help from Syria: Introducing Emar to Biblical Study', *BA* 58 (1995), pp. 139-47.

45.   This motif of 'goddess functions' needs to be contextualized, since it is clear that goddess temples benefited economically (as did private owners) from the use of female slaves hired out to brothels for prostitution: Amélie Kuhrt, 'Non-Royal Women in the Late Babylonian Period: A Survey', in Barbara S. Lesco (ed.), *Women's Earliest Records: From Ancient Egypt and Western Asia* (BJS, 166; Atlanta: Scholars Press, 1989), pp. 232-33, 235-37. In cultures where women's status and fulfillment come through legal marriage and childbearing, the closing off of these options to certain groups of women must be viewed as negatively impacting their self-esteem and life circumstances.

The words and deeds of these ancient females, human and divine, speak specifically to the matters here before us. When Inanna, the Queen of Heaven and Earth from ancient Sumer (modern Iraq), is raped by a gardener who comes across her while she sleeps beneath a tree, she hunts him into the cities of Sumer. When she cannot find him in the midst of the populace that shelters him, she turns all the wells of the land to blood—a motif repeated, with slight variation, by the Hebrew God in defense of the enslaved children of Israel (Exod. 4.9; 7.17-21). When Ninhursag, the mother-goddess, discovers that her mate Enki, the god of sweet water/wisdom, has impregnated successive generations of her daughters, she intervenes, telling the latest object of his desire how to turn the deed to her own benefit (i.e., how to become a desiring subject), and has a part in the later punishment of the god.

Moving from the cosmic to the earthly domain, when Enheduanna, a priestess of Sumer and devotee of Inanna, is ousted from her temple by a male usurper, her psalm of lament is specific and to the point: 'O my divine impetuous wild cow', she cries to her goddess, 'drive out this man, capture this man!' When a royal princess of Mari, a city on the Euphrates during the Old Babylonian period, is abused emotionally and physically by her husband and then threatened with death, she writes home, 'If he [the king] does not bring me back, I shall die; I will not live'; and again, 'If my lord does not bring me back, I will head toward Mari [and there] jump [fall] from the roof'. The determination of that one real, flesh and blood woman to reach safe haven—which she eventually did—is more of a tribute to women's will to survive than all the historicized wails for the dutiful daughter of Jephthah.[46] It may be noted from this brief citation of parallel texts that the sentiments expressed in them are *no less violent* in some respects than those mentioned above in the Bible, nor are they necessarily any more 'moral' by modern standards. But these parallel texts *do* express the depth of emotional reaction by women suffering abuse, rather than the pious words of women characters whose real-life responses have been edited out of existence, or subsumed under a nationalistic epic.[47] Such ancient Near Eastern texts point to the need

46. Fontaine, 'Heifer', p. 82. For translations of the mythological texts see *ANET*, pp. 38-41. For discussion of Inanna, see C.R. Fontaine, 'The Deceptive Goddess in Ancient Near Eastern Myth: Inanna and Inaras', *Semeia* 42 (1988), pp. 84-102.

47. Bekkenkamp and van Dijk, 'Women's Cultural Traditions', p. 69. Metaphorization of female experience into a signifier of more important *male, national* themes is a defining trait of androcentric biblical narrative.

for a divine advocate who is unambiguously ranged on the side of female sufferers and with whom women might reasonably identify. This brings us to the actual content of the Bible. As bad as the supposed 'nature' of the Bible has been and is in authorizing and perpetuating a unified view of existence which excludes the voices of woman and children and the identification of a deity who really protects them,[48] often the *content*—what the stories and laws actually *say*—is much, much worse.

The Content of the Bible

I have suggested how what has been *left out* of the Bible—the unedited voices of real women and children and a deity who saves them, regardless of their gender—works to the disadvantage of members of those groups. Now I must consider the effects of what has been *put in*. Here, I would like to address some trends in certain aspects of the patriarchal world-view that many modern readings of the Bible work to sustain.[49] I divide some of these trends into three categories and will deal with each in turn: establishment of gendered authority, role reversal, and the commodification of fertility.

Gendered Authority

The critical role that gender plays in the establishment of coercive and exclusive authority may be seen exerted in arguments from antiquity (e.g. 1 Tim. 2.11-14,) right down to present-day pronouncements by the Vatican on the fitness of womanpersons for the priesthood. Men's fear of women's power is everywhere in evidence (cf. Gen. 38.11; Est. 1.13-22; 1 Esd. 4.13-32 and many more). The almost absolute authority of the father in the patriarchal society is empowered by the choice of male pronouns to refer to the god who is the source of the father's authority. This works to create a vicious little circle in the construction of gendered authority: because God is male —not *really*, we are always told; the referential language for God just *happens* [sic] to be male—obviously the elder male in the household *ought* to be the one to hold the most authority. The contrary is then true: because the eldest male holds the most power in the household

48. All the deities and human rulers of the ANE had a special obligation to protect widows and orphans, so we cannot attribute any special concern for these groups to Yahweh (contrary to popular interpretive practice), since this is a standard motif. F. Charles Fensham, 'Widow, Orphan and the Poor in Ancient Near Eastern Legal and Wisdom Literature,' *JNES* 21 (1962), pp. 129-39.

49. Bussert, *Battered Women*, pp. 55-66.

(which is the basic unit of production in antiquity and hence usually the model for larger social units), obviously the divine being who holds the most authority *must* be the father-god. Within strict monotheism, the goddesses are officially 'disappeared'. They are polemicized out of the pages of Scripture even though they remain alive and well, though sometimes reshaped, in Aggadic legend, popular worship, the portraits of the New Testament Marys and Sophia theology.[50] This official disappearance makes the reinforcing bond between deity and maleness so much easier to view as 'normative', as does the direct transfer of the activities of goddesses to the Israelite father-god. It may be, too, that this very transfer of 'goddess functions' to the biblical god has allowed women over the centuries to find comfort and concern in a Scripture that otherwise tends to exclude them. It must be pointed out, however, that even when the protective goddesses are present, as in other ancient Near Eastern societies, we do not always see a marked improvement in the economic or power circumstances of women and children.[51] Surviving texts, while suggestive, do not usually allow for a full reconstruction of their spiritual lives.

We see now how this all works: if the divine father has absolute power over the lives of his worshippers, it must have seemed very natural that men should have similar powers over their dependents. The Bible itself sees such authority and power as good and stabilizing, and tends to view any sort of challenge to the father's authority as an attempt to rend the vary fabric of society—and rightly so. An attack on the patriarchal family wherein women and children and

50. There is currently considerable debate about whether or not Yahweh had a consort. Whatever the proper translation for 'Asherah' turns out to be, Yahweh certainly had one! See Ze'ev Meshel, 'Did Yahweh Have a Consort?', *BARev* 5 (1979), pp. 24-35; Walter A. Maier, III, *'Asherah: Extrabiblical Evidence* (HSM 37; Atlanta, GA: Scholars Press, 1986); and Saul M. Olyan, *Asherah and the Cult of Yahweh in Israel* (SBLMS 34; Atlanta, GA: Scholars Press, 1988). See also Steve Davies, 'The Canaanite-Hebrew Goddess', in Carl Olson (ed.), *The Book of the Goddess: Past and Present* (New York: Crossroad, 1985), pp. 68-79, and other articles in that volume. For a strikingly negative assessment of the presence of goddesses in ANE culture, pressed into a defense of the Hebrew Bible's monotheism, see Tikva Frymer-Kensky, *In the Wake of the Goddesses* (New York: Fawcett Columbine, 1992); and cf. the essays by Judith Hadley and Bernhard Lang in the present volume.

51. The effects of the presence of goddesses are analyzed in Gerda Lerner's *The Creation of Patriarchy* (New York: Oxford University Press, 1986), pp. 141-60; for a more textually based and methodologically nuanced discussion of the meaning of goddesses in women's religious lives, see my 'Heifer'.

the rights to their unpaid labor are viewed as the exclusive property of the father *is* an assault on the fundamental locus of patriarchal power.

Now, common sense tells us that a father who routinely sacrifices his children and murders his wives is not going to be very successful in maintaining a problem-free base of power, and so we do see limitations on the father's absolute right to do as he pleases with the lives of his 'dependents'. Still, this image of God as a patriarchal father has had a nasty, deforming effect on our theological portrait of the deity; and its legitimation of male power has had drastic and tragic effects on the lives of real women and children, even unto this very day.[52] The father-god portrayed in Hosea is an ambivalent, mean-spirited father who is jealous of the attempts of his 'son', Israel, to individuate and grow into a mature, self-directed adult; the Christian father-god who shows his 'love' by sacrificing his innocent 'son' continues this disturbing paradigm.[53] We should not be shocked then to discover that the human fathers of the Bible are as apt to sacrifice their children for the fulfillment of pious vows as they are to cradle them with tender love. One of my men students, after a course on feminist critical hermeneutics, pointed out that the gender roles decreed for men in the Bible are just as oppressive and terrorizing as the ones laid out for women—imagine being condemned to live out one's family life playing out the roles authorized by the stories of Abraham, Jephthah, David or Job! If the Bible has sometimes worked to slay women's bodies, it has also had the effect of killing men's souls.[54] If the role of the pastor, rabbi or priest has been modeled on that of the father-god or the human father, as presented by patriarchy, are we still surprised that opportunities for abuse routinely occur? If the 'root metaphor' is flawed, then the fruits of praxis drawn from it usually carry and replicate that same flaw. I personally doubt if a wholesome theology can be built using the

52. One of my women seminary students remarked that she knew an upcoming event in her life must be 'God's will', because she felt such revulsion when she thought of the dreaded and disliked duty. I commented that perhaps there might be other images of God than that of commanding father, and suggested that God was a Clown who wanted to take her to the circus, ply her with all the fat-free chocolate ice cream she could eat, and then tickle her until she collapsed in laughter.

53. Fontaine, 'Response to Hosea'.

54. The 'maleness' of God is certainly not without problems for men; see Howard Eilberg-Schwartz, *God's Phallus and Other Problems for Men and Monotheism* (Boston: Beacon Press, 1994).

models of dominance and submission that are the real 'message' carried by the structure of the patriarchal family. If we are to call humanity into greater responsibility toward the planet and those who populate it, we need models of mutuality and common respect, not gods who sacrifice their children. Rita Nakashima Brock takes the first step for Christians in reinventing the meaning of Incarnation from a feminist perspective in *Journeys by Heart: A Christology of Erotic Power*; whether this re-imagining of the faith can be tolerated, much less embraced, by the Christian Church remains to be seen.[55]

Role Reversal

That the content of the Bible can often be understood as patriarchal propaganda is attested by the number of times the text engages in overt role reversals. Powers that have to do with women's 'biological creativity' are transferred wholesale to the father-god, who is now considered to be the one who opens and closes the womb[56] and brings healthy children to birth. This may be because Israel's God bears the marks of goddess mythology and roles that have been transferred to him, but the effect has *not* been the creation of an androgynous god who is authentically 'there' for most women; at least, we have not read it that way so far. The pragmatic effect has been a lessening of women's visible role in the creation of life. Think of the Genesis narratives where the first humans are created: what a shocking reversal! Instead of the natural order of men (and women!) emerging from the bodies of women, a fact verified by simple observation, we are told as a religious datum of the highest order that the first woman emerged from the body of a male—assisted, of course, by the father-god.[57] Yes, we *can* read that first earth-creature as an androgynous, as do various Jewish traditions and many feminist biblical scholars; but this has seldom been the dominant reading in religious circles, and the reason for that is that the existing role reversal functions to privilege men over women.

55. Rita Nakashima Brock, *Journeys by Heart: A Christology of Erotic Power* (New York: Crossroad, 1991).

56. Hence, the father-god is the one who determines woman's status among her patriarchal folk group, since her evaluation as a success or failure is based on her ability to produce sons. See Jacob's reply to Rachel in Gen. 30.2.

57. This feature of the Genesis account was first pointed out to me by Judith Plaskow. For a textually-based, psychoanalytic interpretation of these reversals in the area of fertility see David Bakan, *And They Took for Themselves Wives: The Emergence of Patriarchy in Western Civilization* (New York: Harper & Row, 1979), pp. 103-34.

Another example of role reversal occurs in places where the questionable actions of men are given a new twist that conveniently allows the abusee to be blamed. Incestuous relations are usually instituted by the parent, primarily the father, not by the children; but in Gen. 19.30-38 we are told that Lot's daughters instigated the incestuous unions that resulted in the birth of the eponymous ancestors of Israel's disliked neighbors, Moab and Ammon. Of course the story serves a complex etiological function in its literary context, but the plain reading of it—which is what most people in the church are doing with the text—excuses Lot and leaves a false impression about the gender of those who usually initiate such forbidden contacts within the family unit. It is Judah who begins the questionable coupling with a supposed hierodule in Gen. 38.16, an act allowed by a fully-functioning 'double standard'; but Tamar is the one blamed for 'playing the harlot' (v. 24).[58] It is the disreputable judge, Jephthah, who makes the unnecessary vow to safeguard his victory in Judg. 11.30-31; but it is his innocent daughter who is blamed for the outcome in v. 35. The mighty hero chastises the unarmed girl with his reply to her expected greeting at his return, 'Alas, my daughter! You have brought me very low, and you have become the cause of great trouble to me; for I have opened my mouth to the Lord, and I cannot take back my vow.'[59] Samson initiates the 'dangerous liaisons' with foreign women in Judges but the text implicitly blames the foreign women (Judg. 14–16). David's lustful eye falls upon a married woman as she bathes in 2 Sam. 11.2, but it is Bathsheba and David's other children who suffer the consequences for the deaths that follow from the illicit union. When Prince Amnon sexually violates his half-sister Tamar (2 Sam. 13) we hear that, after the act, 'he hated her with a very great hate' (v. 15). Rabbinic exegetes supplied here a motivation that astonishes the modern reader: one of Tamar's pubic hairs mutilated Amnon during intercourse! Clearly, the blame is *hers*.[60] In 1 Kgs 5.13-18, Solomon exerts more coercive power over

58. This example is somewhat unusual because Judah allows that Tamar was 'more righteous' than he, since he refused to obey the law of the levirate marriage with regard to his daughter-in-law.

59. Trible, *Texts of Terror*, pp. 93-118.

60. *B. Sanh.* 21a. The passage continues by attributing a patriarchal value lesson in submission to all women onlookers: 'It was taught in the name of R. Joshua b. Kora, In that hour Tamar set up a great fence [about chastity]. They [all other women] said: If this could happen to kings' daughters, how much more to the daughters of ordinary men; if this could happen to the chaste, how much more to the wanton? (I. Epstein [ed.], *The Babylonian Talmud*. XXIII. *Tractate Sanhedrin*

his subjects than any who have gone before; but it is his foreign wives who are held responsible for any troubles in his reign in 1 Kgs 11.1-6. And so it goes on: if a woman so much as allows herself to be *seen* by the male protagonist, much less possessed by him, she can be blamed for anything that ensues, or so it would seem.[61]

The Commodification of Fertility

I have alluded to aspects of this phenomenon earlier, by suggesting the ways in which attributions of fertility to the father-god and his human stand-ins lessens the role of women in this realm. The male usurpation of the primary symbolic roles in the production of new life—otherwise known as paternity—also had concrete effects in restricting the lives of women. Once the male role in conception was properly understood, probably through contact with animal husbandry, the patriarchal control of women's sexuality was set in train. If a father was to transfer his property and power to his own offspring, he had to have some way of feeling relatively certain that the inheritor was *indeed* his son.[62] The most convenient way of safeguarding the paternity of a woman's child was to restrict her movements and, hence, the opportunity for some other male to 'poach' on the husband's private territory. Here is born the double standard: while men are permitted a variety of sexual contacts, the woman's reproductivity is to be regarded as belonging exclusively to her husband, for it is a valuable commodity to which the owner has exclusive rights.

Once a woman's body is 'owned' in such a way, rather than given freely in an atmosphere of mutual consent as in the Song of Songs (but note that the lovers there have yet to marry!), the step toward the abuse of that body has already been taken—who has the authority to

---

[trans. J. Shachter and H. Freedman; London: Soncino, 1935], p. 115). One wonders what kinds of evaluation would have been applied to Tamar, had she refused to obey an order of the king her father in order to guard a potential threat to her chastity. A traditional saying covers very well the sort of net that ensnares women trapped in patriarchal power politics: 'Damned if you do; damned if you don't'.

61. The same problems obtain in modern genres that treat women primarily as objectifications of the desiring male subject. See Ann E. Kaplan, 'Is the Gaze Male?', in Ann Snitow, Christine Stansell and Sharon Thompson (eds.), *Powers of Desire: The Politics of Sexuality* (New York: Monthly Review Press, 1983), pp. 309-27.

62. We might think here of the old joke that differentiates 'belief' from 'knowledge': a father may *believe* that his wife's child is his own, but the mother *knows* —at least, we trust that she does.

interfere in the way one man chooses to treat his own property? And if that ownership has been handed over as part of the divine plan (the typical reading of Gen. 3.16b),[63] in what court, human or divine, will the voice of the one so owned by raised with any real effect? Granted that the Bible and the traditions that interpret it try to nuance all these laws of ownership of women, children, slaves and animals so that humane treatment is the rule and not the exception, the occasions presented for abuse and betrayal out of such a way of thinking and being cannot be so easily swept away. It is no surprise that the Women's Rights Movement in the United States was born out of women's participation in the Slavery Abolition movement. Once women learned through their anti-slavery efforts where they *really* stood as persons and citizens, they realized that they must improve their own condition and achieve the vote if they were ever to be of any potential political use to slaves. It is a great sorrow to see the way white women and peoples of color in the United States today have allowed a wedge to be inserted between their struggles against racism and sexism, for the two are bound together in their real-life expressions, if not always in theory. Minorities will discover eventually that most elite white men are willing enough to give them the same kind of 'equality' that they have extended to white women, and newcomers to the power structure will learn in bitterness just how *little* such equality really means. White feminists who think no further than advancing the class interests of themselves and their sisters will also discover that unless they address issues of race and class, the freedoms and dignity they achieve will remain hollow and partial. When feminist criticism in the Christian churches and their seminaries addresses itself primarily to attaining the equality of (white, educated) women in their vocational quest to break through the 'stained glass ceiling' that keeps them from holding real power positions in the structures of authority in the church, it betrays its multicultural origins and rightly fails to interest womanist, Mujuerista and Asian women theologians in its agenda. As complex and difficult as these challenges are, they must be addressed together if progress is to be made.

We the Readers: The Function of the Bible, Revisited

I have already touched on some of the functions of the Bible in its original settings and traditional theological interpretations: preserv-

63. For a markedly different reading, see J. J. Schmitt, 'Like Eve, Like Adam: *mḥl* in Gen 3, 16', *Bib* 72 (1991), pp. 1-22.

ing a perspective on the history of the community that accepts it as its own, and serving as a template upon which new members of the communities might shape their behaviors and beliefs. Within this matrix of remembrance and education, texts could serve as many different purposes as there are genres; that is, wisdom texts teach, laws regulate community life, prophecy calls the community to account, gospels bear witness, and so on. Scholars often tend to assume implicitly that a text usually pursues and propagates the meaning intended in it by the author, but the recent flowering of literary and aesthetic theory in biblical studies has brought other analyses to bear. What I want to mention here in particular is the fact that, as religious[64] art—and since the Bible is a literary composition, it can certainly lay claim to some of what we mean when we speak of 'art'—the Bible is capable of carrying a range of meanings and interpretations *all at the same time*. This view of the Bible's multi-valence is perhaps *the* basic tenet of the literary critical approach. We are beginning to understand better *how* texts make meaning, and to press our questions into the realm of reader response. By what rules do readers select the meaning they will take away from a text? As readers, how do we do what we do and *why* do we do it? These are the sorts of questions troubling the literary branch of biblical studies these days. Another great question is waiting in the wings once the issue of reception of a text is taken up: what relationship does an artistic text bear to social reality? For instance, if a prophet raves on and on about Israel 'playing the harlot'—what inferences, if any, does that text allow us to make about harlotry in general, Israel's behavior in particular, and how society thought about women whose sexual behavior was viewed as improperly regulated by men?[65]

The issue of how the Bible functioned in ancient days and at present is not an easy one, and simple answers will fail to express the complexity embodied in our questions. Reading communities have always made interpretations with their own needs and

64. By 'religious' I do not mean the context of institutional religions, but the more broad human concern with questions of ultimate meaning.

65. Compare, for example, Robert P. Carroll, 'Desire under the Terebinths: On Pornographic Representation in the Prophets—A Response', in Brenner (ed.), *A Feminist Companion to the Latter Prophets*, pp. 275-307, with Renita J. Weems, *Battered Love: Marriage, Sex, and Violence in the Hebrew Prophets* (Overtures to Biblical Theology; Minneapolis: Fortress Press, 1995). See also Claudia V. Camp, 'Metaphor in Feminist Biblical Interpretation: Theoretical Perspectives', *Semeia* 61 (1993), pp. 3-36; and Mieke Bal, 'Metaphors He Lives By', pp. 185-207 in the same volume.

circumstances in mind: slaveholders in the nineteenth-century Southern Confederacy had no trouble in justifying their practices from biblical teachings; slaves and those who acknowledged them as persons rejected those interpretations and supplied ones more conducive to their eventual liberation.[66] African American poet Paul Dunbar (1872–1906) demonstrates the liberating power of a Scripture reinterpreted by readers in distress in his 'An Ante-Bellum Sermon' which re-reads the Exodus of the Hebrew Bible for the slaves of the American South:

> But I tell you, fellah christuns,
>   Things'll happen mighty strange;
> Now, de Lawd done dis fu' Isrul,
>   An' his ways don't nevah change,
> An' de love he showed to Isrul
>   Was n't all on Isrul spent;
> Now don't run an' tell yo' mastahs
>   Dat I's preachin' discontent.
>
> 'Cause I is n't; I'se a-judgin'
>   Bible people by deir ac's;
> I'se a-givin' you de Scriptuah,
>   I'se a-handi' you de fac's.
> Cose ole Pher'oh b'lieved in slav'ry,
>   But de Lawd he let him see,
> Dat de people he put bref in,—
>   Evah mothah's son was free.[67]

The readings presented in this essay have used the Bible in the most critical way possible, focusing on the 'plain sense' of the passages that authorize abuse and the hidden assumptions that motivate and sustain such texts and their readings. Since the principle of multivalence operates even in noxious texts, it is quite plausible that many alternative meanings might be given for the texts that I have used as examples. I stand by the readings presented here, for we have enough evidence to show that even if texts did not *set out* to marginalize women and children, such an interpretive move *did and does* take place. No one should be surprised when someone for whom the Bible's authority (and hence, the preservation of patriarchy) is the highest value affirms that, no, it doesn't mean *that* at all! There *are* many legitimate readings of a single text, but for Christians I suggest

66. Justice and full freedom for women, children, ethnic minorities, non-heterosexuals, the disabled, and others in the United States remains an unfinished program as of this writing.

67. Dudley Randall (ed.), *The Black Poets* (New York: Bantam, 1971), p. 45.

the use of Jesus' measuring stick: 'by their fruits you shall know them'. Does a way of reading produce shame, terror, helplessness and self-hatred? or does it empower survivors to action, peace, love and self-acceptance? Why have we read the Bible traditionally in such a way as to support God's and men's right to own and abuse instead of reading it as liberation, post-Holocaust Jewish, and feminist theologians now do?[68] We have done so because we have been taught to read in ways that limited our willingness or ability to challenge the *status quo*, but in some circles that is changing. If the Bible's function in past societies has been to socialize its people into an acceptance of the patriarchal world-view, for many its current function is to serve as a locus for our critique of that very system. That is as it should be: we are entering a promised land where we the readers increasingly recognize our role in the making of meaning, and refuse to submit to the old rules that made us passive receivers of the eternal 'truths' supposedly contained in the text. Denial of the widespread abuse experienced by women, children and others is still a feature of the religious communities' day-to-day existence. A Bible filled with abuse offers us a legitimate tool for foregrounding these issues that are so readily repressed by leaders and laypeople alike.

Accounting for Hope: the Four 'R's

I have come full circle back to the question raised by my title: 'The Abusive Bible'—how shall it be used in teaching for pastoral settings? Gentle Reader, you may now be wondering at this point why anyone in her or his right mind would have anything to do with the Bible at all. Good question. Fortunately, there are two solid answers: we deal with the Bible because we *must* and because it is *ours*.

First, we must take the Bible into account as long as women, children and non-heterosexuals sitting in church or synagogue are exposed to the damage that a patriarchal Scripture can wreak on their self-understanding and sense of the world. As long as government officials in the United States Senate use the Bible as a resource for denying civil rights to gay and lesbian persons, while ignoring the Bible's teachings about responsiblity toward the poor,

68. There have always been significant exceptions, even in mainstream scholarship. See, for example, C. Westermann's discussion of God's treatment of Cain in *Genesis 1–11: A Commentary* (trans. John J. Scullion; Minneapolis: Augsburg Publishing, 1984), pp. 281-320.

we must continue to be vocal and engaged *critical* readers.[69] As long as survivors of abuse turn to the Bible for comfort, or locate the God of the Bible as an actor in their history of suffering, then we must be prepared to talk openly and seriously about the nature of the Bible and the problems in its uncritical use.[70]

Secondly, we must continue to deal with the Bible because it is ours. That may sound too self-evident to be meaningful, but, restated, the Bible is part of the religious and literary heritage of Jews and Christians. To jettison it because we see it with all its pits and valleys, all its byways into oppression, is to lessen our understanding of how we got where we are and what we are up against on the paths that we now choose to travel. Give up the loving intimacy and restored paradise of the Song of Songs? Do without the active, compassionate women of the book of Exodus? Throw aside the first successful slaves' rebellion in recorded history? Live without the creation celebrated in Proverbs 8 or Job 38–42? Give up Jesus, the Jew who envisions a new humanity, demonstrating that there may be another paradigm of maleness, another way to be human, perhaps even another way to understand God than by the traditional means of structures of domination and submission?[71] Never.

The canon must be made to serve the abused instead. This can be done by attending to the 'Four 'R's': ReOpening, ReAssessing, ReSisting, and ReAppropriating. We must *reopen* the canon to include other texts that help us understand the religious experience of the text's non-subjects. We must *reassess* what is presently there within its pages. Then we must decide: content, form and function must be either *resisted* or *reaffirmed*, based on our best contextualizations and analysis. In all of this, we must covenant (as feminists do) to read

69. The so-called 'Defense of Marriage' Act of 1996.

70. In fact, those who seek to provide pastoral care for survivors of abuse from conservative religious backgrounds must be prepared to enter into that world-view of the counsellee, and manipulate it for a positive outcome (which will, ideally, include critique of that world-view and its wholesome revision in the final stages of recovery). Holocaust survivor and psychiatrist Viktor Frankl makes the same point: '...when a patient stands on the firm ground of religious belief, there can be no objection to making use of the therapeutic effect of his religious convictions and thereby drawing upon his spiritual resources. In order to do so, the psychiatrist may put himself in the place of the patient...' (*Man's Search for Meaning* [rev. and updated; New York: Pocket Books, 1984], pp. 141-42). Admittedly, this process is far more difficult when the religious system of ideas is itself permeated by abusive concepts.

71. This is, of course, a feminist liberationist reading of the 'message' of the Gospels.

together, even while fully acknowledging the manifold differences wrought by class, race, sex, nationality and religious commitments, as well as our separate and differing approaches to reading as Christians, Jews, feminists, Third World persons, neo-pagans, and so on. Only by including many points of view can we then expect to walk with integrity the fine line between a particularity that obscures and a universalism that blurs.

The Bible can be abusive, it is true. Its 'nature' masquerades as divine and universal when it is not; the content contains assumptions and prescriptions that are downright harmful to the health of some of us; the function has too often been that of keeping the abusees quiet and submissive. Students entering ministry in the United States face an epidemic of domestic and sexual abuse that their mainstream, historical-critical study of the Bible leaves them ill-equipped to address. But in the midst of all that, it is also the record of the suffering of many who never saw redemption. We must keep faith with their memory for their sake, and because we do not wish to endlessly replicate their fate. Whose side is the Bible on? It can be on *our* side, the side of hope, the side of survival, if we choose ways of reading that neither deny the truth of abuse nor seek to normatize it in order to safeguard male authority, cultural heritage, or divine innocence and prerogatives. I suggest that we read with eyes wide open. Perhaps in reading together across time, space and social location, believers can find in it a spirit of survival, and reason to give account for the hope that is in them (1 Pet. 3.15).[72]

72. I would like to thank Deborah Vickers, Gerry Braque, Cara Davis and Margaret Tabor for their technical help in the preparation of this manuscript. I would also like to thank Professor Barbara Geller of Wellesley College for her good sense and helpful comments on the manuscript in progress.

CHALLENGED BY THE TEXT: INTERPRETING TWO STORIES OF INCEST IN THE HEBREW BIBLE

Carol Smith

The title I have given this article illustrates its thesis on more than one level. I have referred to 'stories of incest', and by using the word 'incest' I have already made a statement. That word brings to mind a sexual relationship between two people who are members of the same family and probably closely related to one another. The word 'incest' is associated with a sexual relationship that is forbidden: morally forbidden and legally forbidden. Because of that association, the reader is already, at least to some extent, predisposed to deal with the stories of Lot's daughters (Gen. 19.30-38) and Tamar and Amnon (2 Sam. 13.1-22) in a particular way. However, neither of these stories includes the explicit suggestion that they are about incest in the sense I have just outlined, although they each contain suggestions that some of the behaviour described within them is to be regarded as repugnant.

I wish to discuss not so much the content of these two stories (although it will be necessary to to examine them in some detail), as the ways in which these and other biblical passages have been approached by scholars. The second half of the twentieth century is a time when the disciplines of biblical studies are being reflected upon, reassessed, and, in some instances, severely criticized. It is not necessary for me to pass judgment upon, or even describe, that debate here—except to note that I regard it as a sign of health rather than imminent catastrophe. I intend, rather, to offer some observations on two particular biblical passages and the ways in which they have been interpreted and commented upon by scholars. I do so in the hope that I can thereby make a small contribution to the wider debate.

Emotional Responses to the Text

Narratives like the stories of Lot's daughters and Amnon and Tamar arouse an emotional response in the reader. I believe that it is intended that they should do so. They are dealing with emotive topics.

However, it is often the case that commenting upon that emotional response has brought criticism upon the commentators.[1] In many cases, such criticism has been justified, especially since this kind of approach can lead to a distorted picture of what the text actually says. Problems of this kind may arise when a commentator is starting from a standpoint that says that the text is somehow normative for the behaviour of a worshipping community. This is because such a commentator may have a great deal that is personal to him or her invested in particular texts and how they are or have been used within that worshipping community.[2] But this is no excuse for dismissing such a starting point absolutely. It needs to be remembered that using the biblical text in such a way is probably the most prevalent form of biblical interpretation, and has been for many centuries. But whatever the starting point of the commentator, all uses of the biblical writings, all methods of interpretation and criticism, demand a high degree of integrity in relation to the text, and those working in an 'academic' environment have been as guilty as anyone else of using the text as a vehicle for expressing their own views and prejudices to a greater or lesser degree.

It is my belief that an emotional response to the biblical text is not necessarily a bad response, nor does it preclude a comprehensive scholarly approach. It represents an appropriate response if the content of the text demands it. Even in the context of traditional forms of scholarship, where it is often a concern to discover the 'original intention' of the writer or compiler, it is possible to argue that such an approach is valid because it may well have been one of the 'original intentions' that the reader should have a particular emotional response.[3] It is virtually self-evident to say that one cannot and should not confuse various types of biblical writing. Those who teach

1. For example, see Daphne Hampson's discussion of Phyllis Trible's work in *Theology and Feminism* (Oxford: Basil Blackwell, 1990), pp. 32-41 and Westermann's comments, cited below.

2. Some of the possible implications for women of the Bible's being seen as 'Scripture' within the context of a worshipping community are discussed in P.J. Milne, 'No Promised Land: Rejecting the Authority of the Bible', in H. Shanks (ed.), *Feminist Approaches to the Bible: Symposium at the Smithsonian Institute* (Washington, DC: Biblical Archaeology Society, 1995), pp. 47-73. See also Milne in this volume.

3. This leaves aside the questions of whether it is possible to determine a writer or compiler's 'original intention' and even if it is possible, whether it is desirable. The invalidity of this approach is discussed in D.J.A. Clines, *What Does Eve Do to Help? And Other Readerly Questions to the Old Testament* (JSOTSup, 94; Sheffield: JSOT Press, 1990), pp. 1-2.

the early chapters of Genesis point out that these are not 'scientific' texts in the way in which these are commonly understood. Those teaching about the Psalms, talk about poetry. When talking about the books of Samuel and Kings, it is appropriate to discuss the nature of history and narrative. When reading Leviticus, it is relevant to consider the forms that legal texts take and their intentions and structures. This is one way of saying that it is necessary to work out the appropriate questions to address to each type of writing. (What constitutes an 'appropriate question' may be a matter for debate between different readers, depending on their individual contexts and the context within which the text is being discussed at any given time.) Thus, while it may be productive to ask of the narratives in the books of Kings what relation they may have to verifiable historical events, such a question does not apply to, say, the account of the animals going into the ark. The question, 'does this text help us to an understanding of why God allows evil to happen?' may be appropriate for the book of Job, but not to certain chapters in Leviticus. On this level, the types of questions addressed to texts are dependent on the kinds of texts they are. On another level, the appropriateness of questions addressed may depend on the starting points of particular readers and which questions are appropriate for the contexts from which they come.[4] Different questions may be applied by different scholars to a particular text—they may even argue over which are most appropriate—but many of those who disagree on the relative merits of determining the literary origins of a text, its form, or its date, do agree on one thing: the question, 'how does this text make me feel?', cannot and should not apply in any circumstances whatever.

The particular passages I shall be considering here—Gen. 19.30-38 and 2 Sam. 13.1-22—have been selected largely because of their subject matter, which will enable me to make my point as effectively as possible. However, what follows may also be applied to other texts, as will become clear. Although the contents of these passages are

---

4.   See the discussion in the chapter 'Issues and Methodologies', in P. Dutcher-Walls, *Narrative Art and Political Rhetoric: The Case of Athaliah and Joash* (JSOTSup, 209; Sheffield: Sheffield Academic Press, 1996), pp. 11-22, esp. p. 11; see also J.E. McKinlay, *Gendering Wisdom the Host: Biblical Invitations to Eat and Drink* (JSOTSup, 216; GCT, 4; Sheffield: Sheffield Academic Press, 1996), who speaks of 'the recognition that neither texts themselves nor the act of reading and interpreting can be in any way understood as timeless or socially neutral [reinforcing] the realization that interpretation and adoption of meaning is an ever ongoing process, whereby the text that was part of the fabric of one community's construction of reality becomes in turn part of another's'.

well known, it will be worthwhile briefly to outline what they contain.

Two Stories

The story of how Lot's daughters had sexual intercourse with their father begins in Gen. 19.30 and comes after a description of the visit of the מלאכים (meaning 'messengers', but translated in NRSV as 'angels') to Sodom; the demand of the male inhabitants that the visitors be brought out 'that we may know them'; Lot's suggestion to the mob that rather than act so wickedly they should allow him to bring out his two virgin daughters to do with what they will; the refusal of this offer; the saving of Lot when his two guests pull him back inside the house and the mob is apparently struck blind 'so that they were unable to find the door' (Gen. 19.11), and, finally, the destruction of Sodom and its sister-city, Gomorrah, by fire and brimstone—or, as the NRSV prosaically phrases it—'sulphur and fire'. Lot, having been warned of the coming catastrophe, fails to convince his prospective sons-in-law of the danger, and since his wife looks back (perhaps understandably) at her former home as it goes up in flames, and is turned into a pillar of salt for so doing, his daughters find themselves alone with him in the hills after their escape, apparently convinced that there are no other men left in the world. The two daughters are then faced with the problem of how to provide themselves with children. They decide to make their father drunk and have intercourse with him on two consecutive nights. Whatever actually occurs, the biblical writer tells us that Lot did not know anything about it on either occasion. What is more, the daughters become pregnant. They each give birth to a son. Lot has fathered two sons at last. One was to become the ancestor of the Moabites and the other the ancestor of the Ammonites (Gen. 19.37-38).

The second story, that of Amnon and Tamar, is in many ways very different. It is not set in some distant time past, but in the court of a 'historical' king. It purports to be about real people—two of the king's children by different mothers. Amnon, assisted by Jonadab, pretends to be ill and lures his half-sister into his apartments, where he rapes her after she has begged him not to. (Verse 14, NRSV: 'But he would not listen to her; and being stronger than she, he forced her and lay with her'.) Having done so, he finds her disgusting and has her put out of his room. Tamar, not surprisingly, is distraught and goes into mourning. Two years later, she is revenged by her full brother, Absalom, who, in his turn, tricks Amnon into attending a sheepshearing festival at which he is brutally murdered.

Asking Questions of Texts

So, how might a commentator approach these texts? There are many possible ways of responding to Genesis 19. One could set about deciding which strand of the tradition is represented in the chapter. Is this a J, E, or P text? When this has been decided, a date for the chapter might be sought. Another approach would be to compare the chapter with other texts from the same source and then discuss the source as a whole. Thus, if it was decided that Genesis 19 belonged to J, it would be possible to focus on the theological or other viewpoint of the Yahwist. One might even decide that the Yahwist could have been a woman.[5] Some commentators might be interested in the exact location of the cities of the plain, or whether the first part of the chapter is about the conventions of hospitality, the sinfulness of homosexuality, or the blurring of the distinctions between the human and the divine. Alternatively, questions might be asked about what kind of narrative Genesis 19 is. Is it a folk story? Is it a tale, a legend, or maybe a myth? Could it be regarded as not a myth, but mythical in character? Is the second part of the chapter a genealogy of the groups which became Amnon and Moab? Other questions could be asked about why this passage appears in this particular position. What is its place in the Abraham cycle?[6] What is its place in Genesis? How does it relate to the Hebrew Bible as a whole? It is also possible that attention could be focused on more specific questions, such as whether or not sexual intercourse between father and daughter was considered immoral or illegal—particularly since there is no specific condemnation of it in the Hebrew Bible, perhaps a surprising omission from Leviticus 18 and 20, which give such detailed lists of forbidden sexual unions. It might even be that more esoteric matters are commented upon, such as whether it was possible for the daughters to be made pregnant when their father had drunk himself insensible, and quote Macbeth's porter on the subject, when he says of drink:[7]

---

5.   This suggestion is put forward in H. Bloom, *The Book of J* (trans. D. Rosenberg; London: Faber, 1991 [1990]).

6.   Kunin suggests that this text is part of a series equating Lot with Abraham; see S.D. Kunin, *The Logic of Incest: A Structuralist Analysis of Hebrew Mythology* (JSOTSup, 185: Sheffield: Sheffield Academic Press, 1995), p. 82.

7.   W. Shakespeare, *Macbeth*, Act II, scene 1, cited in this connection in J.R. Porter, 'The Daughters of Lot', *Folklore* 89 (1978), pp. 127-41. This aspect of the story is also discussed briefly by Porter in 'Genesis XIX:30-38 and the Ugaritic Text of ŠḤR and ŠLM', in *Proceedings of the Seventh World Congress of Jewish*

'Lechery, sir, it provokes, and it unprovokes; it provokes the desire, but it takes away the performance: therefore much drink may be said to be an equivocator with lechery; it makes him, and it mars him'!

Some of these questions may well provide useful and insightful answers if they are approached carefully and conscientiously. There is nothing wrong with them as such. But answering all of them could still leave the reader with an incomplete impression of the contents of Genesis 19 and of the kind of writing it contains. In any case, these questions vary in their appropriateness to the passage.

Genesis 19 is an extraordinary chapter, dealing with extraordinary and supernatural events, and it provokes many questions. Part of the task of the reader when approaching it has to be making a decision about which are most appropriate. It may or may not be helpful to discover the exact location of the cities of the plain. It may also be interesting to discover what led to their destruction.[8] However, the story in Genesis is not concerned with mundane details such as these. It is concerned with the sinfulness of Sodom and the aftermath—the action taken by Yahweh to destroy the city and its twin-city, Gomorrah. This destruction is as spectacular as it is total. That this is so can be seen not only from Genesis 19, but also from other passages describing its aftermath, such as Deut. 29.22-23 and Isa. 13.19-22. The point is reinforced by the apparent belief of the daughters of Lot that they and their father are the only people left alive in the whole area, and possibly the whole world (Gen. 19.31). So it is certainly appropriate to compare Genesis 19 with the story of the Flood (Gen. 6–9), which also tells of a total destruction and how the human race survived in the face of it.[9] Since the events described in Genesis 19, like those described in the Flood narrative, are put in a cosmic rather than a local context, it is also appropriate to speak in terms of myth, or 'mythical stories' when they are being discussed. It adds to our understanding to realize that stories of a similar type also appear within other cultures and to ponder on the significance of such stories of destruction and new beginnings.[10]

Studies: Studies in the Bible and the Ancient Near East (Jerusalem: Perry Foundation, 1981), p. 4.

8. The *Independent on Sunday*, 30 March 1997, p. 1, reports a suggestion that 'Sodom and Gomorrah may have been destroyed by debris from a comet'.

9. C. Westermann sees this as one development of the tradition in *Genesis 12–36: A Commentary* (trans. J.J. Scullion; Minneapolis: Augsburg, 1985 [1981]), p. 312.

10. For a brief summary of some other Flood narratives, see C. Westermann, *Genesis 1–11: A Commentary* (trans. J.J. Scullion; Minneapolis: Augsburg, 1984 [1974]), pp. 399-406; Westermann refers to the 'large cycle of narratives outside

Equally, the fact that someone, at some time, has decided to place this particular narrative within the context of the series of stories often referred to as the 'Abraham cycle', cannot be disregarded. Genesis 19 could be omitted from this series quite easily, without leaving the narrative unstructured or unintelligible. The chapter could be placed elsewhere and not appear irrelevant. It could, for example, with very few modifications, have been placed after the story of Noah (in Genesis), or even after Gen. 13.1-2.[11] If so placed, as a unit it would have said much of what it says in its present position—that is, it would have done if regarded as an isolated unit, although its overall impact would certainly have been different. While taking a narrative out of its context can provide new insights into its contents, failing to place it back in its context and to consider what it says when it is no longer in isolation also leads to an incomplete understanding.

Other approaches can also be productive. The question: 'why was it included?' might well lead to a consideration of the significance of the verses at the end of the chapter, telling how the sons borne by the daughters of Lot became the ancestors of the Ammonites and the Moabites. There are many genealogies in the book of Genesis and study of them is rewarding. Thus, a comparison of this account with the origins of two nations that play a major part in Israel's history with those other genealogies could be very fruitful indeed. Is this, as some have claimed, a story meant to discredit these nations, by implying that their ancestors were the product of an indecent and illegal union?[12] Or is it rather a story originating with the Moabites and Ammonites themselves, indicating something noble about their beginnings—namely that they are descended from a totally pure line without taint of foreign blood? What is more, such a story of beginnings would have divine overtones, since it is the gods who have intercourse with near relatives without condemnation, even though such unions are usually barred to humans.[13] Is the story of Lot's

---

Israel which folllow the structure of Gen. 19: crime–divine judgment–preservation of the individual' in *Genesis 12–36*, p. 298.

11. I am indebted to Athalya Brenner for this latter suggestion.

12. The law codes of many ancient Near Eastern nations specifically prohibit incestuous unions. However, Kunin suggests that incest may have been '"mythologically" acceptable' (*The Logic of Incest*, p. 192).

13. Following Gunkel, Brenner says: '[O]ne suspects that the incestuous origins of Moab and Ben Ammi are derived from an extrabiblical myth, where divine incest is the prerogative of the gods' (A. Brenner, 'On Incest' in A. Brenner [ed.], *A Feminist Companion to Exodus to Deuteronomy* [The Feminist Companion to the

daughters one which originated positively with the Moabites and Ammonites themselves and then was used against them by the people of Israel, eager to discredit their enemies?[14]

The questions asked about 2 Samuel 13 will, in some instances, be different; in some instances, the same. What is the date of this text and from where does it derive? What is its relationship to the narratives around it, or to the books of Samuel as a whole? If sexual intercourse between a brother and half-sister was forbidden (and Lev. 18.9 seems to indicate that it was forbidden at some point in Israel's history), why does Tamar suggest to Amnon that he ask their father for her? Is it the case that different standards applied in the royal household from those relevant to the rest of society, or did the law change over time? Is the story based on any kind of historical event, or is it a narrative construction?

All these approaches will be familiar. They are some of those that have traditionally been used in biblical scholarship, and they have in common that they reflect a desire on the part of scholars to make what they believe to be an objective evaluation of the text. All tend towards a view of the biblical text which implies that it may be treated impersonally and as something that does not impinge on the perceptions of the scholar except as an object for examination and clarification. All would, I believe, be approved of by Claus Westermann, who, in his commentary on Genesis, makes the following observations with regard to the story of Lot's daughters. I cite him for two reasons: because I think that his views may be considered representative of many scholars' opinions, and because they apply not simply to Genesis 19, but far more widely:[15]

> This text is particularly open to misrepresentation. When one makes evaluations such as 'incestuous' or 'incest' in its title or says at the very beginning 'This revolting story' (A. Dillmann), then one is unable to understand what it intends to say. One can do justice to the text only by taking account of the history of its growth. It goes back into a distant past on which we cannot impose our criteria. Three layers have come together in the long process of growth: the patriarchal story in the form it took in regard to the family of Lot, the primeval story under the

Bible, 6; Sheffield: Sheffield Academic Press, 1994], pp. 113-38 [p. 116]).

14. These suggestions are discussed by G. Von Rad in *Genesis: A Commentary* (OTL; trans. J.H. Marks; London: SCM Press, rev. edn, 1972), pp. 223-24. Kunin argues that it was only 'on the narrative level' that the story 'became an attack on the origins of the Moabites and the Ammonites, suggesting that they originated from sexual depravity' (*The Logic of Incest*, p. 192).

15. Westermann, *Genesis 12–36*, p. 314.

aspect of the judgment and annihilation that befell Sodom, and the
story of the people in the etiological conclusion whose goal is the peoples of Moab and Ammon, Israel's present day neighbours.

Westermann criticizes Dillmann for using the word 'revolting' about
the story of Lot's daughters. A response of this kind is simply not
permissible as far as Westermann is concerned. It is important to see
what Westermann is trying to say when he suggests that 'we cannot
impose our criteria' on the biblical text. If a text is read without
account being taken of its original context, its development as a
tradition, or the culture from which it came, the reader may not do
justice to it. However, I think it must be questioned whether it is
actually possible for a reader *not* to impose his or her own criteria
upon a text as it is read. Whoever reads a text today—and I include
those whose concerns are primarily academic—does so from within
a particular culture at a particular period in the history of that
culture. He or she also does so from a particular personal standpoint
in terms of upbringing, education and experience. It may well be that
for some texts the response of a twentieth-century scholar (particularly where scholarship carries the legacy of anti-semitism) bears
very little resemblance to that which would have been induced in
someone who encountered it when it was first written down. However, it may also bear a very close resemblance indeed. The answer
may depend on the particular nature of the text in question. Whether
it does evoke the same reaction is difficult for us to determine, but
with certain texts it maybe worthwhile to speculate on the possibility.
Claims by scholars that they are seeking, or even achieving, objectivity have only comparatively recently begun to be questioned. It is
important to ask not only whether or not they have achieved any
measure of objectivity, but also whether it is even desirable that they
should do so.

Asking Different Questions

I now wish to contrast some of the above approaches with that of
another scholar, Phyllis Trible, who represents a totally different
viewpoint. Trible has this to say about the events at Sodom:[16]

> These two stories [Genesis 19 and Judges 19] show that the rules of
> hospitality in Israel protect only males... Further, in neither of these
> stories does the male host offer himself in place of his guests. Constant

16. P. Trible, *Texts of Terror: Literary-Feminist Readings of Biblical Narratives*
(Philadelphia: Fortress Press, 1984), p. 75.

only is the use of innocent and helpless women to guard and gratify men of all sorts. Nonetheless, Lot's proposal was rejected, not out of concern for his virgin daughters but out of animosity that a sojourner should try to adjudicate the crisis. Ironically, male anger against another male spared Lot's daughters the horrors for which he had volunteered them.

For Trible, the stories of the פילגש[17] from Gibeah and Lot's daughters are 'Texts of Terror', as also is the story of Tamar and Amnon. They are 'tales of terror with women as victims'. 'Storytelling is a trinitarian act that unites writer, text, and reader in a collage of understanding', Trible writes, and goes on: 'Though distinguishable and unequal, the three participants are inseparable and interdependent'.[18] Such statements are not made by scholars who wish to distance themselves from the text in the interest of seeking objectivity. Fokkelien van Dijk-Hemmes has commented: 'Feminist research has pointed out how important it is to ask ourselves what is the effect of stories. This is especially important as regards the self-image of women. It applies even more strongly to stories in which sexual violence plays a role.'[19]

I have discussed various traditional methods of interpretation and commentary. But other methods are now coming to the fore. They are those espoused by, among others, feminist scholars,[20] liberation theologians[21] and those interested in 'reader-response' interpretation.[22]

17. Translated 'concubine' in NRSV, but the meaning of this term has been under discussion for a considerable time. See, for example, T.E. McComiskey, 'The Status of the Secondary Wife: Its Development in Ancient Near Eastern Law. A Study and Comprehensive Index' (PhD thesis, Brandeis University, 1965) and E. Neufeld, *Ancient Hebrew Marriage Laws* (London: Longmans, Green, 1944).

18. Trible, *Texts of Terror*, p. 1.

19. F. van Dijk-Hemmes, 'Tamar and the Limits of Patriarchy: Between Rape and Seduction (2 Samuel 13 and Genesis 38)', in M. Bal (ed.), *Anti-Covenant: Counter-Reading Women's Lives in the Hebrew Bible* (JSOTSup, 81; Bible and Literature Series, 22; Sheffield: Almond Press, 1989), pp. 135-56 (p. 136).

20. There is a growing number of feminist biblical scholars, but for brief introductions to feminist biblical interpretation, see the essays in H. Shanks (ed.), *Feminist Approaches to the Bible* (Washington, DC: Biblical Archaeology Society, 1995) and A. Brenner, 'On Reading the Hebrew Bible as a Feminist Woman: Introduction to the Series', in *A Feminist Companion to the Song of Songs* (The Feminist Companion to the Bible, 1; Sheffield: Sheffield Academic Press, 1993), pp. 11-27. See also the essays in L.M. Russell (ed.), *Feminist Interpretation of the Bible* (Philadelphia: Westminster Press, 1985).

21. A brief introduction to the use of the Bible by liberation theologians is given in L. Boff and C. Boff, *Introducing Liberation Theology* (trans. P. Burns; Liberation and Theology, 1; Tunbridge Wells: Burns & Oates, 1992), pp. 32-35.

22. A summary of some of the new forms of biblical criticism is to be found in

These methods are not objective and make no claim to be so. Such interpreters begin from a particular standpoint and make no secret of the fact that it informs how they view the biblical text. So, how might a feminist approach Genesis 19? A feminist scholar will probably be interested, among other things, in what a particular biblical text has to say about the situation of women in our own society, and in the society from which the text originates. A concern for the status of women in the community from which the Bible came can mean that a feminist scholar takes as a starting point the assumption that in some way or other how women were regarded in the biblical community influences how women are regarded today. This influence comes about because a worshipping community sees the Bible as somehow indicating norms for 'correct' or appropriate behaviour in socity, these norms being discoverable, both implicitly and explicitly, in the laws, stories, descriptions of women and so on which are found in the Bible.[23] Sometimes, a broader approach may be taken, which suggests that the influence of the Bible on society in those parts of the world that have been influenced by the Judeo-Christian values, even including those making no claim to be members of a worshipping community, has been so insidious and pervasive that the ideas and images it contains affect the whole culture and influence it profoundly.

Feminist interpretation of the Bible has tended to take three directions.[24] It is suggested that the Bible arises from and is steeped in a patriarchal culture that regards women as the absolute property of their fathers, husbands, or other male relatives, and as a matter of course relegates them to positions of submission and inferiority. It is further argued that it reflects such patriarchal, and even misogynistic mores throughout, and any reading of it has to take this into account.[25] Another view is that while it is true that the Bible arose out

D.J.A. Clines and J.C. Exum, 'The New Literary Criticism', in J.C. Exum and D.J.A. Clines (eds.), *The New Literary Criticism and the Hebrew Bible* (JSOTSup, 143; Sheffield: JSOT Press, 1993), pp. 11-25. See also the other essays in that volume.

23. Such an approach raises the whole question of the relationship of worshipping communities to the Bible—for instance, is the Bible to be regarded as 'Scripture', and thus having a special authority in such matters?

24. A good summary of some feminist approaches is to be found in K. Doob Sakenfeld, 'Feminist Uses of Biblical Materials', in Russell (ed.), *Feminist Interpretation of the Bible*, pp. 55-64.

25. Exum makes the following comment in her preface to *Fragmented Women*: 'This book explores the gender ideology that informs selected biblical narratives in order to reveal strategies by which patriarchal literature excludes, marginalizes,

of such a culture, it is not as irredeemably patriarchal and sexist as is frequently suggested, and, in fact, contains much that is positive and even liberating with regard to women.[26] Moreover, the fact that it can say what it does in spite of its origins, gives its message all the more power. A third view is that the Bible is absolutely and irredeemably negative in what it says about women. It thus has nothing of interest to say to our society on the subject of women and can be discounted. Daphne Hampson, for example, has this to say:[27]

> The [biblical] text is the product of a sexist, indeed misogynist, culture: the presuppositions of a patriarchal world are written into it. Moreover, such texts are the more dangerous in that they affect us at a subconscious level… There is, one must conclude, little that can be done.

So, what might a feminist scholar make of Genesis 19? She or he will possibly, like most scholars, see the first part of the chapter, which deals with the destruction of Sodom and Gomorrah, as being of more importance. Thus, the focus might well be on the fact that Lot apparently sees the protection of the male guests under his roof as a more pressing concern than the security and integrity of his daughters. His offer to give his daughters to the crowd howling at this door, so long as they do not continue to demand that he produce his guests for them, will be seen as yet another example of how women were seen as not only dispensable, but disposable, in Israelite society, and that the interests of males, whether or not they are chance-met strangers, has to come before the protection of the women of the household, even though such protection was their right. Thus, the response may be either that the text cannot be read without seeing

and otherwise operates to subjugate women'. She considers that 'the biblical text is fundamentally patriarchal', although it 'shows traces of the problematic of maintaining patriarchy' and goes on: 'Even if the Bible's authors were not all males, the world view that finds expression in the biblical literature is the dominant male world view' (J.C. Exum, *Fragmented Women: Feminist (Sub)versions of Biblical Narratives* [JSOTSup, 163; Sheffield: JSOT Press, 1993], pp. 9-10).

26. Such a view appears in, for example, J.G. Williams, *Women Recounted: Narrative Thinking and the God of Israel* (Bible and Literature Series, 6; Sheffield: Almond Press, 1982) and P. Joyce, 'Feminist Exegesis of the Old Testament: Some Critical Reflections', in J.M. Soskice (ed.), *After Eve: Women, Theology and the Christian Tradition* (London: Marshall Pickering, 1990), pp. 1-9 (see especially, pp. 2-3). I think Trible would also see herself as wishing to stress positive aspects of the biblical view of women. See, 'Eve and Miriam: From the Margins to the Centre', in Shanks (ed.), *Feminist Approaches*, pp. 5-24, especially p. 8.

27. D. Hampson, *Theology and Feminism* (Signposts in Theology; Oxford: Basil Blackwell, 1990), p. 92; see also, P.J. Milne, 'No Promised Land: Rejecting the Authority of the Bible', in Shanks (ed.), *Feminist Approaches*, pp. 47-73.

it in the context of the absolute demands of the conventions of hospitality,[28] or that it can only be dismissed, since the message it imparts
is such a negative one in relation to women.

It is actually much easier to interpret Genesis 19 in this way if the
first part of the chapter is seen in isolation from the second part, and I
shall return to this point below. First, I wish to make a more general
point about the belief that women in biblical times were absolutely at
the disposal of their near male relatives. While there is a strong
tradition in the Hebrew Bible suggesting that children are the
absolute property of their parents, this does not necessarily apply to
grown women. Thus, Hannah is able to offer her son, Samuel, for
lifelong service in the sanctuary (1 Sam. 27-28); Abraham is willing
to make a sacrifice of his son, Isaac (Gen. 22.1-3); Jephthah does
sacrifice his daughter in fulfilment of a hastily made vow (Judg.
11.29-40). On the other hand, women are not necessarily the absolute
property of their fathers or other near male relatives, although it is
frequently stated in commentaries and elsewhere that this is the case
(interestingly, while male commentators have more recently ceased
to write in this way, it is often found in the writings of women
scholars). Rebekah is apparently handed over by her brother, Laban,
and father, Bethuel, to Abraham's servant so that she can marry
Isaac (Gen. 24.51). But in vv. 57-58 it appears that she is asked
whether she is willing to go, although it is not clear whether Rebekah
had the right of refusing the marriage or only the manner or timing of
it. Jacob's wives, Rachel and Leah, appear to exercise a considerable
degree of sexual autonomy in Gen. 30.14-16, where they decide on
the basis of the ownership of a few mandrakes in whose tent Jacob is
going to spend the night. Thus, it is only if Genesis 19 is seen in
isolation from other biblical texts—and particularly texts from
Genesis itself—that the suggestion that Lot's behaviour is both to be
expected and justified in terms of the prevailing culture can be con-
templated. Moreover, the suggestion that Genesis 19 implies that Lot
had absolute rights over his daughters, and particularly over their
sexuality, is much less easy to maintain if the first thirty verses of
Genesis 19 are not seen in isolation from the last part of the chapter.

----

28. Von Rad says of the passage: 'The surprising offer of [Lot's] daughters
must not be judged simply by our Western ideas. That Lot intends under no circumstances to violate his hospitality, that his guests were for him more untouch-
able than his own daughters, must have gripped the ancient reader, who knew
whom Lot intended to protect in this way' (von Rad, *Genesis:*, p. 218). Such a
viewpoint effectively precludes any suggestion that the original intention of the
writer of this story might have been to shock its original readers.

When taken as a whole, the chapter presents a very different picture.

In Gen. 19.30-38 there appears the closest approximation possible to a female's rape of a male. Lot is not asked whether he consents to sexual intercourse, and is a passive victim of the conniving of his daughters in the events that take place. There is a parallel here to the way in which Lot intended to render his daughters passive victims when he blandly offered them to the mob to do with whatever they chose. The point about Genesis 19 is that events in the second part of the chapter are the events of the first half turned completely upside down. In the second part, the scene is set in the hills, whereas previously it has been in the plain. The noise surrounding the house when the mob is gathering outside is contrasted with the silence and emptiness around the cave where Lot and his daughters are forced to hide. The daughters, although not protected by their father, are shielded from the action of the mob by the two young men/messengers who are their father's guests. On the other hand, no one protects Lot when it is his turn to be violated. The threat of violation of the daughters comes from a nameless mob of strangers. Lot is violated by people who are members of his own family. Finally, the daughters have succeeded where the father has failed. The daughters are made pregnant and become the mothers of sons. It could be argued that it is just coincidence that the story has come out this way. Two episodes were put side by side so that they might appear in chronological order, with the parallells I have pointed out merely occurring fortuitously. This is a possibility, but it is one that makes the compiler of the final form of Genesis into a somewhat mechanical operator—someone with a literal and rather prosaic mind. One wonders, if the compiler was of such a wooden disposition, why he or she put these stories in at all. They are not the inclusions of someone seeking a 'safe option'.

I have pointed to some of the difficulties of possible feminist interpretations of Genesis 19. They do, however, have this in their favour: they acknowledge the fact that narratives such as these arouse a response in the reader which has to do with feelings and emotions. Such a response is fraught with potential pitfalls for biblical interpreters, but it is not necessarily a bad or an inappropriate response. It is to this that I now turn.

Assessing Emotional Impact

It is hard to imagine how a text such as Genesis 19 could fail to have an emotional impact on the reader and interpreter. It is certainly not

written in a gently objective way. It begins by reminding us that Lot's
guests are divine messengers—that is to say, persons worthy of
respect and even honour. Lot apparently recognizes that these are no
ordinary travellers—he 'bowed down with his face to the ground'
(Gen. 19.1), before inviting them to his home and treating them
royally. Then *all* the men of Sodom appear at Lot's door. (Emphasis
is laid on the 'all' by the addition of the phrase 'both young and old'
[v. 5].) The violence of the crowd is also emphasized. They threaten
Lot. They try to break down the door. Then they themselves are apparently struck with blindness ('so that they were unable to find the
door' [v. 11]). In an attempt to appease the crowd, Lot offers them his
daughters, together with a carte blanche to do as they please with the
young women. This is powerful writing by someone who does not
attempt to spare the reader. The intention is to shock. The writer continues to describe graphically what goes on. The reader is not simply
told that, in the absence of other males, Lot's daughters are forced to
have intercourse with their father in order to conceive. Nor is he or
she told that they discussed the matter with their father. What is said
is that the daughters make Lot so drunk that he does not know what
is happening him. They then have intercourse with him without his
consent, and apparently without his participation. What is more, it
all happens twice. Not only is all this described in great detail, but
two powerful stories are deliberately placed side by side so that their
impact on the reader can be increased. When the two halves of
Genesis 19 are looked at independently of one another, as so often
happens, part of their impact is lost. Certainly, the story of Lot's willingness to sacrifice his daughters to a mob is a shocking one, but so is
that of those daughters making a victim of their father by having
intercourse with him in such a way. The one is the more shocking to
the female reader, the other to the male one. If Genesis 19 ended at
v. 29, the picture would indeed be a hopeless, and even horrifying,
one. But vv. 30-38 leave the reader with the impression with sometimes it is the women who take the initiative and are in control. It has
to be acknowledged that the narrative which gives the power to the
women is one that does not give an unambiguously positive picture
of the women concerned, since it shows them still operating within
the context of the patriarchal concern to provide (male) heirs.[29]

29. Deborah Sawyer comments on this story: 'It is assumed that the reader will
understand that the daughters themselves do not count as offspring; only a son
could ensure the line' (D.F. Sawyer, *Women and Religion in the First Christian Centuries* [London: Routledge, 1996], p. 38).

Nevertheless it *is* there and serves as a counterbalance to the impact on the reader of the events in the first part of the chapter.

Similar observations can be made about the writer of 2 Samuel 13. The descriptions of events are equally graphic. Tamar's beauty is extolled. She is also portrayed as thoughtful and caring—willing to bake for her brother when he is ill and to wait on him. Tamar is plotted against and deceived. She begs pitifully for mercy when she discovers what Amnon intends to do to her. And Amnon is violent: 'being stronger than she, he forced her and lay with her' (v. 14). Afterwards, Amnon 'was seized with a very great loathing for her; indeed his loathing was even greater than the lust he had felt for her' (v. 15). Tamar has to suffer the added indignity of being thrown out of her brother's room by a servant. There is a further parallel with the story of Lot's daughters, as the situation in which the woman is made vulnerable is later reversed. The deceit, invitation, violation and violence of the story of Tamar becomes deceit, invitation, violation and violence in relation to Amnon when Absalom takes his revenge in 2 Sam. 13.23-33. Absalom presses the king to allow him to take Amnon to a sheep-shearing feast (notice the association with food in both stories), and, unsuspecting, Amnon relaxes over his wine and is killed at Absalom's commmand (and just as Tamar is thrown out of her brother's room by a servant, so Amnon is killed by servants). Jonadab (who appears in both incidents) makes it clear to the king that the killing is about Tamar, saying, 'This has been determined by Absalom from the day [Amnon] raped his sister Tamar' (2 Sam. 13.32, NRSV; compare v. 22b: 'for Absalom hated Amnon, because he had raped his sister Tamar' [NRSV]). Both these incidents take place within the context of the violent struggle for power and dominance among the males of the household of David that is recorded 2 Samuel 9–20 and 2 Kings 1–2. The story of the rape of Tamar is placed after the events of 2 Samuel 11 and 12, in which David wants and takes the woman Bathsheba, as a result of which occur the deaths of Uriah the Hittite, Bathsheba's husband, and David's own son. Amnon's taking of Tamar likewise precipitates a death, his own. There is also another sort of death, that of Tamar, who 'remained, a desolate woman, in her brother Absalom's house' (2 Sam. 13.20, NRSV). However, the fact of Tamar's being made such a victim does not go unacknowledged. Although the revenge carried out by Absalom reflects a patriarchal world-view, consisting as it does of violence between males with the woman on the sidelines, it *does* occur. The wrong done to Tamar cannot be put right, but it is recognized as a real wrong and dealt with accordingly. These stories are given 33 verses in the biblical narrative. They are packed with powerful, emotive language. The descriptions are vivid. What is more, when seen together, they present a slightly modified picture from what is portrayed when 2 Sam. 13.1-22 is seen in isolation. As Trible comments: 'Absalom remembers; the narrator records; and we the readers respond. If we cannot sanction the violent revenge Absalom exacted, we can appropriate the compassion he shows for his sister.'[30]

If the reader is not moved to some sort of emotion by the accounts in Genesis 19 and 2 Samuel 13—whether it is horror, sympathy, or anger—one can only feel that the biblical writer has failed in what he or she intended to do. Nevertheless, some biblical scholars continue to tell us that this aspect of the writer's intention is no concern of theirs. Doing justice to the text requires taking account of the history of its growth, its context in the culture of its time, and its place in the wider history of the Hebrew Bible, and the feelings it invokes are not relevant to scholarly enterprise.

'Objective' Scholarship: Even if it is Possible, is it Helpful?

There are two questions that now need to be addressed: the first is whether commentators actually succeed or can actually succeed in achieving the kind of scholarly objectivity for which they claim to be aiming. The second is whether the kind of detachment from the text advocated by people such as Westermann is actually a helpful or constructive way of approaching it. In fact, while claiming to deal with the story without having any personal involvement with it, scholars frequently do hint that it has an impact on another level. Thus, when interpreting Genesis 19 as a description of the origins of the Moabites and the Ammonites, scholars such as Kunin[31] discuss how such a story would have set those peoples up for ridicule because of its reference to their forebears as the products of unsavoury unions. In other words, ancient Israelites are assumed to have regarded this narrative as salacious and unsavoury, and reacted to it in those terms. Nevertheless, we are expected to believe that biblical scholars are capable of seeing a dry text that is devoid of such impact. I have already noted that the conjunction of the two stories in Genesis 19 gives a whole new perspective on the action of Lot's daughters in

---

30. Trible, *Texts of Terror*, p. 56.

31. See Kunin's comment, '[the story] therefore became an attack on the origins of the Moabites and the Ammonites, suggesting that they originated from sexual depravity' (*The Logic of Incest*, p. 192).

having intercourse with their father. It is less easy to assume that the writer of Genesis 19 believed that Lot was justified by the culture and customs of the time and place in offering his daughter to the mob, if we see in their action the message that they to some degree 'got their own back'. And yet this second part of the story is so often separated off from the Sodom incident and then played down. Could it be possible that this separation of the two parts of the chapter may have less to do with an objective evaluation of the relative merits of the texts concerned, than with a reluctance to deal with the emotional impact of the chapter as a whole? Could it be that an inability to cope with the idea that two daughters might make their father into a helpless victim of a sexual assault has led to a dismissal of the story as having little real significance, however much such a dismissal is backed up by claims of academic and intellectual objectivity? It is unlikely to escape the notice of feminists that the part of the chapter in which it is the daughters who are potentially the helpless victims is given a great deal more attention by male commentators than the section in which the father is the victim. It could be argued that, under patriarchy, women, not men, are 'appropriate victims'. J. Cheryl Exum[32] has argued that

> the biblical literature was produced by and for an androcentric community...women in the biblical literature [are] male constructs. They are the creations of androcentric (probably male) narrative, they reflect androcentric ideas about women, and they serve androcentric interests.

Exum may well be right, but if she is, then the appearance of the story of the initiative of Lot's daughters becomes all the more interesting.

It could be argued that this story is, more than anything else, about a new beginning after a terrible catastrophe,[33] but even this view is fraught with difficulty. In order to point up this interpretation it is necessary to argue that what the daughters of Lot did, whatever their motives, and however dutiful, was somehow outrageous and unprecedented, although justified by the exceptional circumstances (Westermann speaks of a 'desperate deed'[34]). Again, the reader is being asked to believe that the message is that it is intended that this account should shock and challenge him or her, but not if the reader happens to be a biblical scholar.

32. Exum, *Fragmented Women*, p. 11.
33. So Westermann, *Genesis 12–36*, p. 315: 'Central is the primeval motif of the rising again of new life, or of a new generation after an annihilation'.
34. Westermann, *Genesis 12–36*, p. 315.

Questioning Motivation

This brings me to the question of the motivation of the biblical writer. Is it possible to argue that part of the intention of the biblical writer was to provoke a particular reaction, and specifically, a particular *emotional* reaction, in the reader? If it was, how is it possible to tell? Here reference must be made again to the stories themselves. They are not written in neutral language. They do not minimize the suffering of the people involved in them. They are not talking about events that can be described as everyday occurrences. Was the original recorder of the stories of Sodom and Lot's daughters, or the rape of Tamar by her half-brother merely an uninvolved reporter of what occurred, or was he or she concerned to make the point as effectively as possible, even if it meant shocking readers into feelings as well as thought? Was the writer expecting that those who encountered these narratives would discuss them dispassionately, or would he or she have expected them to become worked up about them? This question cannot be answered just from reading the text as it now appears. Other disciplines can help readers determine the motivations of the biblical writer. For example, the question of when Genesis 19 or 2 Samuel 13 was actually written down may be very relevant, if the intention is to tease out the possible motivation of its writer, and a question that has frequently figured in traditional biblical scholarship ('what is the date of this text?') could become important for a scholar working from a different perspective. After all, those writers could only have succeeded in shocking readers with their narratives if they could be certain that the behaviour they were describing was considered unacceptable and repugnant at the time they were writing. The widespread assumption that Gen. 19.30-38 had as at least part of its purpose that the Moabites and Ammonites were of dubious origins is based on the further assumption that the behaviour of Lot's daughters would have been considered objectionable. There is no suggestion in the text that readers needed to bear in mind that there was a time when such matters were regarded differently (although such reminders do appear elsewhere within the Hebrew Bible itself, for example, in Judg. 17.6: 'In those days there was no king in Israel; all the people did what was right in their own eyes'). The perception that these were unusual and undesirable acts would have added to the power of the narrative. Equally, the intention of the writer of 2 Samuel 13, which is, after all, a narrative based within the royal household, is very much connected with when and where it was being written. It also seems legitimate to ask, if Genesis 19 and 2 Samuel 13 elicit a response from us now, what would the response have been when they were first written (and vice versa)? Is it possible to say with absolute confidence that it would have been so different that it must be discounted? Nevertheless, this is what we are often told should happen.

It has been argued, on very little evidence, that the culture and mores of biblical times were very different from those of the twentieth century, and so present-day readers must avoid the temptation to react to biblical stories as they would were they to hear them today. I should argue that the onus is rather on those who make such claims to demonstrate that this is the case. Surely the whole point of the story of Sodom and Gomorrah and its sequel is that the reader should be shocked by it. Indeed, elsewhere in the Bible, the fate of the cities of the plain is held up as a grim example.[35] If the story did not have power, that would not have been possible. A similar point may be made about the story of Tamar. Surely the reader is meant to regard the behaviour of Amnon as totally repugnant. (Certainly, Tamar's brother, Absalom, appears to have done so, as we see from his response, recorded in 2 Sam. 13.22, and subsequent behaviour.) Why else include the episode at all?

Concluding Remarks

I have used to illustrate my point two stories that have a particular impact. I have also quoted Phyllis Trible as an example of a biblical interpreter who sees an emotional response to the text as important, if not essential. However, such an approach need not be limited to particular passages, nor to a particular starting point—in this case, feminism. There is no reason why other biblical passages should not be considered in the same way. What is to be made of David's passion for Bathsheba (2 Sam. 11.2-5), or his grief over the deaths of his sons (2 Sam. 12.15b-17; 13.37; 18.33)? What, come to that, is to be made of the parable told by Nathan about the ewe lamb (2 Sam. 12.1-6)? That story, surely, was intended to move its hearers. Are the passages in the book of Lamentations that describe the devastation experienced by the people of Judah not meant to move those who read them?[36] Why should such a powerful lament move one generation and not another?

35. For example, in Isa. 13.19; Jer. 49.17-18; Amos 4.11; Zeph. 2.9.

36. It is quite reasonable to see the entire book as an appeal to the emotions, but see, for example, Lam. 1.1.; 2.10-12.

It is by no means my intention to suggest that the starting point of all biblical study should be an examination of one's own feelings about a particular passage. I simply wish to make two points. The first is that it is simply not possible for any reader to come to an 'objective' reading of a text that takes no account of his or her background or reactions to its contents. It is simply not true, as Westermann claims, that 'one is unable to understand what [a passage] has to say' if one makes evaluations of it which include statements such as 'this revolting story'.[37] It is not true because the story may itself be saying, 'I am a revolting story'. That may be its central message; if that message is not perceived, something very important will have been missed. A story may well have been written in the way it was precisely because it was intended that it should inspire disgust or revulsion. Similarly, another story might have been written with the intention of inspiring laughter, joy, sympathy, or concern.

If it is indeed the case that our feelings about a biblical passage may give us some hints as to the intentions of its writer—whatever they might have been—then there are important lessons to be learned. The reactions of the reader do indeed become part of the interpretative process. Taken in conjunction with whatever else may be learned about a text using the variety of methods and approaches available, it may well be found that the picture is made more complete rather than distorted. In fact, it could be argued that seeking a truly objective perspective, which is as comprehensive as possible, can only become possible if as many factors as possible are taken into account. Those factors must, of necessity and integrity, include an assessment of the reader's own responses and reactions to the text before him or her.

I now return to my two texts: Lot's daughters, offered by their father to a raging mob in place of his two chance-met visitors, saved by those same visitors, and then, in their turn, making their father a helpless sexual victim; and also Tamar, beautiful and affectionate, deceived and raped by her half-brother, and avenged by her full brother, but in continual mourning. I also return to the title of this article: 'Challenged by the Text: Two Stories of Incest in the Hebrew Bible', the second half being loaded with suggestions of the immoral, the repugnant and the unacceptable; and the first half asking whether there is still a great deal to be learned about the appropriate questions to put to our texts. One of the greatest contributions that feminist scholars have made to biblical study has been their insistence that we

37. Westermann, *Genesis 12–36*, p. 314.

question the motivations and presuppositions underlying those questions that have traditionally been asked of texts. It is also part of our task to ask new questions, arising from, and in full awareness of, our own starting points as feminist scholars.

IDENTIFYING THE SPEAKER-IN-THE-TEXT
AND THE READER'S LOCATION IN PROPHETIC TEXTS:
THE CASE OF ISAIAH 50

Athalya Brenner

In the [American] Society of Biblical Literature Annual Meeting in
New Orleans, November 1996, there was a panel session on 'Teaching the Prophets'. The chief speaker, David L. Petersen, pinpointed
five clusters of issues which, as he hoped, would be included in
courses on the so-called 'prophetic literature'. These are: (1) definitions of 'prophecy' and 'prophets' and 'prophetic activity'; (2) cultural contexts; (3) literary topics, including the question of 'prophecy
and poetry' as well as 'the part and the whole'; (4) social issues, as
reflected in the 'prophetic' texts and presumably fulfilling certain
roles in their production, reception and transmission; and (5) postmodern perspectives, including feminist perspectives. I find this
program attractive. It is a questioning program, as Petersen intended
it to be. Older assumptions are not taken for granted. In that spirit, I
would like to offer a preliminary analysis of Isaiah 50. This analysis
is certainly not a comprehensive analysis but one that opens up
several of the issues Petersen lists so precisely: issues of cultural
milieu, social issues, literary questions and, of course, a feminist
perspective. What I will try to do is to show that, by adopting a
feminist perspective—one of several such perspectives possible—
both reader and text are allowed another kind of existence. This
different existence neither negates nor disqualifies other perspectives-
inspired readings (for instance, those of classical *or* radical Hebrew
Bible, mainstream commentators); neither is it inferior to those simply because it is born of an admittedly biased reading. My own program agrees with Petersen to a large extent, especially on the question
of how the reader's sensitivity contributes towards another and perhaps more pluralistic understanding of a 'prophetic' text. However,
and precisely in deference to readers' sensitivities, I would like to
dwell on some problems of reading, interpreting and teaching the

'prophets' and 'prophetic literature' in general, before I proceed to exegete the specific passage Isa. 50.1-11.

Sensibilities and Offenses

From within and beyond Petersen's very sensible program the chief problem for me—the one I should like to focus on—is the following: how do I perform, how should I perform, when I find any specific so-called prophetic text that I am supposed to interpret or teach 'offensive'? In fact, I do find *many* 'prophetic' texts offensive and from several perspectives. Here is an incomplete list.

From a *feminist* perspective, be it any shade of 'feminist', many texts are problematic, such as: Hosea 1–3; Jeremiah, especially chs. 2–5 but also chs. 7 and 44; Ezekiel 13 and 16 and 23—at the very least the metaphor of the human 'wife' and the divine 'husband'; Isaiah 1–4 and especially 3.16–4.1—Jerusalem women denounced for governing their men, with a whole catalogue of female fashion attire thrown in for good measure,[1] not to mention passages in the so-called deutero- and trito-Isaiah; Amos 4.1-3 (what a lovely portrayal of urban aristocratic women as 'cows'); Zechariah 5; and there are more and similar passages. To these one might add parts of the passages dealing with Miriam (Exod. 15, Num. 12) and Deborah (Judg. 4–5), whose prophesying powers are belittled in various ways; or the narratives about Elijah and Jezebel (1 Kgs 16 onwards), where Jezebel is made a moral and religious monster over against Elijah's legitimated message and behaviour; or the dealings of Elijah and Elisha with women, be the textual women upper class (like the Shunammite, 2 Kgs 4; but cf. the report of his humane attitude to the same woman at the beginning of the chapter) or to commoners (1 Kgs 17, 2 Kgs 4.1-7).

From the perspective of *human rights*, the 'prophets' are reported as speaking against social injustice—to be sure; but slavery is accepted as a matter of fact phenomenon and as a vehicle for religious metaphors (the chief of which is the slave/servant metaphor in deutero-Isaiah). The conventional social hierarchy, god–adult male–adult women and children and slaves–other chattel, is seldom questioned.

---

1.   It is immaterial, for the present purpose, whether the list of female finery—clothes, jewels and cosmetics—which interrupts the flow of the prophecy is 'original', a later addition or a gloss. What is important is the fact that a savage attack is launched against manners perceived as peculiarly feminine, and, what is more, encouraged by the culture that makes womanhood dependent upon its attractiveness to males.

Figurations of women and children are often used symbolically and metaphorically. In our efforts to understand the text, we often forget to question this usage, which amounts to objectification of weaker societal segments.

From a *human-interaction* perspective, too many 'prophetic' texts—be they 'prose' or 'poetry'—allow the privilege of being heard to the speaker–in–the–text who delivers his statements in the first-person mode, and only to him. Inasmuch and when his self-styled adversaries are granted speech or defense, more often than not their response is embedded in his words and, formally, filtered through his ideology. Furthermore, the speaker claims divine authority for himself, not to mention self-righteousness and impeccable moral fortitude. In vain do we expect, if and when we do, an even-handed treatment: the game is solidly in favour of the textual speaker from the outset. It seems that only one side has the right for self-expression. As a result, readers—lay readers, students, scholars—tend to identify with the prophetic speaker; they are drawn into the text emotionally and they take sides. They cooperate, because if one is called upon to 'understand' a text, frequently one ends up by complying with it.

The 'oracles against the nations' are often defined as belonging to a distinct 'prophetic' genre, well attested in prophetic literature. Again, a basic fact is that this 'genre' is highly chauvinistic, xenophobic, defensive in its attacks, self-centred and cruel in its wishes for and joys concerning the downfall of foreign 'enemies'. Such prophecies, and others, are not famous for respect of the Other—be that 'other' an ethnic, geographic, gender, age, political, ideological or any other Other.

Indeed, prophetic propaganda uses threats, punishment, ridicule, contempt and scorn as some of its chief weapons. It is prescriptive and authoritarian. It claims the authority of a god who is all-knowing, omni-present and all-powerful, a just but also cruel god: less often he is merciful. This image of god, may we remind ourselves, exists also in other Hebrew Bible sources: on the other hand, in some of those (like the Torah) his image is more balanced (such as in the introduction to the commandments, Exod. 20 and Deut. 5, or Exod. 34). Prophetic literature is too often read with claims for its being didactically significant; but then, for me—a modern Jewish woman—it misses the mark because of its methods as well as many of its messages.

Prophetic literature, together with the mystique attached to 'prophecy', a mystique almost impossible to overturn even when it is partially rationalized along the lines suggested by Petersen, remains highly influential for Jews and for Christians, for Moslems and for Bahais and for adherents of other religions. And it remains influential for most readers, scholars and students included, be their religious affiliation what it may or even when they have none. We seldom manage to engage in readings that are not complicit with the text. As teachers, we scholars are careful when presenting the so-called prophets and, only in the minority of cases or in passing, pass judgment on them—which is really what 'they' deserve, being so judgmental themselves. We supply perspectives; at best, many of them. The temptation to fall in with the text that has been made seductive by centuries of readerly cooperation is seldom countered. Do we make a stand, do we commit ourselves to a balanced reading?

A balanced reading, for me, is not just a reading that takes into account all the definitions, contexts and perspectives possible. A balanced reading neither dwells only or almost exclusively, and with approval, on the granted beauty to be found in the language or the religious and ethical sentiments and ideas for which that language is the vehicle at times. A balanced reading will not *a priori* and unconditionally encourage sympathy for, justification and comprehension of the prophetic speakers and glorified tropes of the text. A balanced reading will also be taken consciously further into the shadowy zones. Yes, prophetic literature is sometimes wonderful: as literature, as ideology. For example, some consolation passages are full of compassion and breathtaking: think about Amos 9, Isaiah 66. Other passages contain shrewd political observations. It would have helped to assess their value, though, had we known whether they were composed before or after the events they refer to. But, more often than not, prophetic literature comes across as naked, abusive, cruel, even crude propaganda that allows its opponents little speech and very little choice. Such propaganda, in contemporary terms, would not be tolerated in democratic countries—neither from politicians nor from other leaders or contenders to leadership. We have certain terms to define such propaganda and such practitioners.

So What Can One Do?

The question is then, ultimately, whether we shall have the courage to go beyond 'understanding' the prophets and prophetic literature, further away from their presumed original contexts, whatever those might be, and into our own lives. To borrow a phrase from Julia O'Brien, can we learn to say 'no' to the 'prophets' and prophetic literature[2] and to go beyond this 'no'? Or, can we learn to define certain passages in the Hebrew Bible as *abusive*[3]—not only because our personal circumstances are different from the ancients' and keep changing, thus altering our readerly locations all the time but, simply, because the texts we are teaching *are wrong in our eyes*. They are wrong for our Western society as it is evolving. They are wrong for a democratic way of living. They are wrong for liberal education. They were probably wrong for their own times, whenever that might have been; there are indications in the 'prophetic' texts that the 'prophets' were not popular in 'their' own times. Perhaps we should ponder the question why, rather than assume that they were always right and their target audience always wrong. That 'prophetic' texts achieved popularity, and sanctity, and canonization long past and further away from their 'original contexts'—again, it would have been nice had we known more about those, instead of assuming too much—should not automatically confer upon them unquestioned moral, theological and social value for today or for any other time.

The challenge is, I think, not to be objective about prophetic literature but, rather, to manage to be *more* subjective about it. It has to be studied: it is very much part of the biblical text and the traditions that grew out of it. Parts of it are worthwhile not only academically but also as guidance for life. I am thinking here particularly about passages such as Isaiah 6–8 and 2.4b-c (taken out of their chauvinistic word context) and 40; Jeremiah's laments in chs. 12 or 20.7-17; the last verses of Hosea 14. I am not suggesting that we privilege only passages that suit our contemporary or personal views: that would be worse than practising revisionism. I am suggesting that we consider reading programs that are objective *not* because they present all or most of the academic, religious and emotional perspectives as *equally* valid components for understanding 'prophecy'; but, rather, that we privilege readings that allow a hearing for the voices submerged in or by the prophetic texts as much as listen to the voices overtly manifest in or by them. I suggest that we go for readings that do *not* glorify the 'prophets' for any time, precisely because our own voices need to break away from what does not suit us ethically or existentially. By resisting positivistic attitudes; by pointing to the less than savoury character of prophetic teaching about women, and

2.   In a paper entitled 'On Saying No to a Prophet', delivered, in the Israelite Prophetic Literature section, at the AAR/SBL Annual Meeting in Philadelphia, November 1995; forthcoming in *JBL*.

3.   Cf. Fontaine's article, 'The Abusive Bible', in this volume.

children, and aliens, and partners in discourse—who knows, we might even enrich the prophetic texts which, after all, are the product of author–reader interaction.

So, when I approach the task of reading Isaiah 50, I bear in mind that prophetic literature is often authoritarian, undemocratic, and one-sided, is mostly socially conservative, chauvinistic, self-righteous and monologic. If and when it is dialogic, it swallows and embeds other voices within its first-person singular mode of speech. It is imperious and imperial in tone. Its god is over-represented as 'just', and under-represented as merciful in the sense of loving unconditionally and with no demands. It very seldom allows for transformative possibilities—and, if it does, it does so through punishment and not education. But also, I bear in mind that this literature aspires to social justice, political fairness and religious wholesomeness—after its own prescribing and proscribing fashion. And, as always for me, my readerly role consists of three steps: (1) understanding the text and its possible contexts; (2) bringing my own sensibilities and sensitivities to bear on it; and (3) pointing out what seems to me, here and now, suitable for life.

Reflections on Isaiah 50

[1]Thus says the LORD. Where is your mother's bill of divorce with which I put her away? Or which of my creditors is it to whom I have sold you? No, because of your sins you were sold, and for your transgressions your mother was put away.
[2]Why was no one there when I came? Why did no one answer when I called? Is my hand shortened, that it cannot redeem? Or have I no power to deliver? By my rebuke I dry up the sea, I make the rivers a desert; their fish stink for lack of water, and die of thirst.
[3]I clothe the heavens with blackness, and make sackcloth their covering.
[4]The Lord GOD has given me the tongue of a teacher, that I may know how to sustain the weary with a word. Morning by morning he wakens—wakens my ear to listen as those who are taught.
[5]The Lord GOD has opened my ear, and I was not rebellious. I did not turn backward.
[6]I gave my back to those who struck me, and my cheeks to those who pulled out the beard; I did not hide my face from insult and spitting.
[7]The Lord GOD helps me; therefore I have not been disgraced; therefore I have set my face like flint, and I know that I shall not be put to shame;
[8]he who vindicates me is near. Who will contend with me? Let us stand up together. Who are my adversaries? Let them confront me.
[9]It is the Lord GOD who helps me; who will declare me guilty? All of them will wear out like a garment; the moth will eat them up.
[10]Who among you fears the LORD and obeys the voice of his servant,

> who walks in darkness and has no light, yet trusts in the name of the
> LORD and relies upon his God?
> [11]But all of you are kindlers of fire, lighters of firebrands. Walk in the
> flame of your fire, and among the brands that you have kindled! This is
> what you shall have from my hand. You shall lie down in torment
> (NRSV).

Commentators agree that Isaiah 50 falls into at least two asym-
metrical parts, vv. 1-3 and vv. 4-11; the second section is sometimes
further divided into two: vv. 4-9 and a third section, vv. 10-11. With
respect to content, the two parts (I shall draw the demarcation line
between vv. 3 and 4 and will return to vv. 10-11 later) ostensibly
differ in subject matter and the issues referred to. I will focus on the
second section of the chapter, while also referring to the first and to
the immediate context of so-called deutero-Isaiah.

In vv. 1-3 an old accusation crops up again—'old', for it features
regularly in 'prophetic' writings. Responsibility for their own fate—
separation (from whom or what?) and being sold out (to whom?)—is
attributed to the audience, the addressed 'you'. The metaphors for
depicting the audience's situation are two: male-initiated divorce by
means of a document; and humans being sold and thus losing their
personal freedom because of debts they have incurred. Both legal
practices are encountered in biblical literature and beyond it. Pertinent examples for male-initiated divorce outside the book of Isaiah
are passages such as Deut. 24.1-4, Jer. 3.1 (both about the hypothetical case of a sent-away woman: whether her husband should take
her back, and if so, under what circumstances) and Hosea 2 (again
with the 'husband' taking the 'wife' back). Sale of humans for debts
is recognized by different biblical genres as part of the social scene
they reflect: so in the law, Exod. 21.1-11 or Leviticus 25 for instance.
In an illuminating narrative, a woman is wailing to Elisha that her
children are being taken as slaves because of her late husband's debt;
it is clear that the only solution is to produce the necessary payment:
there is no other solution to this social practice (2 Kgs 4.1-7), no
protest on behalf of vulnerable social agents (such as women,
children and other economically disadvantaged people) is recorded.
Interestingly, the implied audience's vulnerability is conveyed by
means of metaphorizing this same audience into women and
'economic' slaves—a metaphor probably well understood, since it
refers to a well-known recurrent situation. This technique of shaming
the adversary, the implied audience, is a typical device of propa-

ganda, be it any type of propaganda. It features regularly in prophetic texts.[4]

Somewhat unexpectedly, the passage progresses into Yhwh's boasting that he can do anything, even save the implied audience, because he is omnipotent: the ending of this section assumes the format of a doxology, with creation language (water/dryness; rain). Then, in vv. 4-11 (or, more strictly speaking, vv. 4-9) the speaker–narrator claims that Yhwh has given him a message and the intellectual capacity to deliver it. Divine help has sustained, or sustains, the speaker throughout physical, social and psychological tribulations. The speaker has not given up and seems to have no intention of so doing. The opponents, the audience, the addressed 'you', the 'divorced women' and 'slaves' of the previous section—if the two sections are to be read consecutively as one passage, one composition—will surely perish. The speaker will prevail because of Yhwh's help. The imagery is varied but, unlike the previous section, does not include legal imagery. The ending (v. 11, if belonging to the section) contains a fire/light metaphor which complements by opposition the water imagery of vv. 2c-d and 3.

Stylistically, each section is a monologue delivered by a speaker–in–the–text. That speaker appears to have changed from the first to the second section. In the first, 'So says Yhwh' (v. 1a), the narrated and narrating speaker is the deity. In the second, the speaker seems to be a human 'I'. The identity of the second textual voice, the human 'I', is pivotal for the understanding of the passage as a whole.

The second section (vv. 4-11 or 4-9) is widely considered to be one of the individual 'servant' poems of Second Isaiah (together with 42.1-4, 49.2-6 and 52.13–53.13. 'Servant' is the translation of the Hebrew עבד (v. 10), literally, 'slave'. The situation of the audience as 'slaves', 'sold' because of a 'debt', is metaphorically established at the end of v. 1. The speaker–in–the–text of v. 10 is similarly identified as an individual—symbolic or metaphorical, or real—but always *male*.[5] By analogy to v. 1, where the references are to 'slaves' and a divorced wife–mother, I would like to problematize the common application of the term 'servant' instead of 'slave' to this passage, and its implications; and to question the conjectural gendering of the

4. For propaganda techniques as applied to prophetic literature see A. Brenner, 'Pornoprophetics Revisited: Some Additional Reflections', *JSOT* 70 (1996), pp. 63-86, esp. pp. 66-68.

5. For a short survey of scholarly opinions on the Isaian עבד passages, cf. R.N. Whybray, *The Second Isaiah* (OTG; Sheffield: JSOT Press, 1983), pp. 68-78.

textual voice in vv. 4-9 (or 4-11) as a metaphorical male voice instead of a female, maternal and wifely voice. If a readerly decision is made to read the passage as a unit (a literary decision adopted here), then the imagery of the first section must be allowed consideration as possibly valid for the second section as well.

But reading the passage consecutively is problematic as well: the fact that certain verses follow each other in the MT by no means indicates automatically authorial or even editorial unity. The problem is the connection, or its lack, between the two sections of the chapter. Why are these two placed next to each other? I assume that the placing is not accidental since, to begin with, I have no reason to assume otherwise. I also assume that some editorial policy was at work here: settling for a random or inexplicable policy is probably the last resort for an editor, hence should not be entertained by a reader too hastily. I would like to think that the uncovering of a link or links—compositional or editorial—between the two sections placed in sequence might provide a clue for the identity of the textual voice in the second section; and for the shift from the divine 'I' to the human 'I'.

Beyond and around Isaiah 50
It would, perhaps, be helpful to go outside Isaiah 50 in order to examine similar sections and to see the present passage against a larger backdrop.

Images of femaleness and femininity recur in the so-called Second Isaiah (chs. 40–55) and are carried over into the third part of the book (chs. 56–66). Such images metaphorize cities (like Jerusalem, 40.2, 8-9 and ch. 50; or Babylon, ch. 47), land (62.1-6), or communities, but chiefly the addressed 'Israel'. This politization of gendered images is not new.[6] The chief image among these is the image/metaphor of a mother. The metaphorical, or symbolic, mother—for 'she' is in fact Jerusalem, or Samaria, or 'Israel'—goes through a whole, if condensed, female life cycle. The figure of the wife–mother represents a variety of maternal life experiences. She is a wedded mother, at least in the beginning. In that sense, the metaphor continues the divine husband–human wife metaphor of passages in Hosea (chs. 1–3), Jeremiah (mainly in chs. 2 and 5), Ezekiel (chs. 16 and 23) and others.[7] This mother suffers. She loses her home (territory), legal hus-

---

6.   On cities/land as women, especially daughters, and Isaiah cf. J.F.A. Sawyer, 'Daughter of Zion and the Servant of the Lord in Isaiah: A Comparison', *JSOT* 44 (1989), pp. 89-107.
7.   Cf. Isa. 57.1-13.

band (Yhwh), freedom (political sovereignty), children (of Israel). She becomes a bereaved wife and mother through her own behaviour. At times Jerusalem/the land is mother, and the addressed community is the sons (not daughters, naturally); but this differentiation does not work for all passages. In Isa. 50.1, the mother and sons seem to be the two faces of the same implied 'reality' of the situation (for the textual speaker); a similar overlap between metaphorical 'mother' and 'sons' obtains in Hosea 2. Yhwh, at any rate, is the implied *pater familias*, the husband and father committed to care for his dependents, among them women, morally and also legally.[8] Finally, the image of the mother is so pronounced that it is perhaps also applied to Yhwh himself. According to Gruber, this is the case in four passages (42.13-14, 45.10, 49.15, 66.13) scattered among the other wife–mother images.[9]

Not surprisingly, these images conform to the societal mores prevalent in the Hebrew Bible: the theopolitical metaphor hardly conceals the social assumptions and allocation of gender roles underlying it. The ideal biblical woman is configured as a mother with a son or sons. This is in keeping with both the primary ideology of the 'be fruitful and multiply' propaganda, and the androcentrism of biblical literature and the society it reflects. Thus, I find it difficult to rejoice at the mother image. Employment of female imagery in biblical texts is not in and by itself any indication of female significance in society—not even in the case of the mother. Rather, the nature of the image should be questioned. It should be remembered that the metaphorical wife–mother of Isaiah 40–66 is suffering terribly. She will be restored, and this is good; however, her dependent state—she is her divine master's legally covenanted possession, to cherish and keep or to be sent away solely according to his judgment—deconstructs her. To illustrate this: there is no bill of divorce, v. 1 claims; but the wording, together with the parallels in Jer. 3.8 and Deut. 24.1-4, imply that a man divorces and a woman is divorced; a man writes the relevant document and a woman accepts it; a man stays in the household and she leaves it.[10] She, as woman or

8.   C. Pressler, *The View of Women Found in the Deuteronomic Family Laws* (BZAW, 216; Berlin: de Gruyter, 1993).

9.   M.I. Gruber, 'The Motherhood of God in Second Isaiah', in *The Motherhood of God and Other Studies* (Atlanta: Scholars Press, 1992), pp. 3-15.

10.   'The primary actor in this law [Deut. 24.1-4], as in the other Deuteronomic family laws, is the man. The man takes the wife; the man initiates the divorce; the man is prohibited from remarrying the wife' (Pressler, *Deuteronomic Family Law*, p. 62).

city/land community, has no significant autonomy, no life without the male's good will. This is a central message. In that sense, 'she' is like other biblical dependents within the household, such as minors, foreigners, inanimate possessions and slaves of both genders.[11]

'Slave' and 'Wife–Mother'

This brings me back to the issues of speaker, voice, and the function and identity of the עבד to whom the speech of vv. 4-9 or 4-11 is attributed. This עבד may indeed, at the outset, refer to a 'servant', as in many translations and as in 'Moses, servant of Yhwh/God',[12] or 'Joshua, servant of god',[13] or 'David, servant of Saul'.[14] But עבד is mostly a slave, that is, an inferior, a non-autonomous social agent whose life is *contractually* controlled by a master. If 'servant' signifies this kind of legally binding servitude, then it is a good translation for the Hebrew עבד. Otherwise, and this is what I propose to do together with numerous other scholars, the Hebrew עבד ('slave') will be retained, because the other translation sounds like an ideological downplaying of the most common denotation of the Hebrew word— a downplaying that promotes the textual speaker at the expense of understanding the social context.

The legal positions of עבד and wife respectively share a few features. Both are contractual; this indicates a relationship that entails rights as well as obligations. Both עבד and wife are subordinate, dependent and hardly autonomous legally as well as economically. In both social states, a certain mutuality of interest and ideology obtains with the superordinate partner. In both, the subordinate position is the more vulnerable, whereas the superordinate position of master (typically a male) is quite extended. Finally, both states can be terminated by the will and action of the superior partner—almost exclusively so. Perhaps significantly, the verb denoting the sending away of עבד as well as wife is שלח in the *piel* formation. A quick look at the verb's occurrences in the Hebrew Bible will illustrate that the verb's grammatical subject is nearly always the implied socially superior agent, while its grammatical object is the inferior social agent. The near equation, at least economically, of wives and chattel/slaves/minors and so on is also well documented.

11. Cf. Pressler, *Deuteronomic Family Law*.
12. Deut. 34.5; Josh. 1.1, 13, 15; and elsewhere.
13. As in Josh. 24.29; Judg. 2.8.
14. 1 Sam. 29.3.

A Female Voice in vv. 4-9 (vv. 4-11)?

Sawyer suggests that many parallels obtain between the figure of the עבד and the metaphorical figure of the wife–mother.[15] I would like to sharpen this insight and to use it for the present discussion. I shall assume that the audience in vv. 1-3 is the mother's 'sons', 'Israel'. I have already noted that the boundaries between the metaphorical 'mother' and 'sons', the city/land and the addressed community of faith, are at times blurred. 'Israel' may be the implicit mother as well as her sons. The target audience 'Israel', whatever that means histor-ically, is also defined elsewhere in Second Isaiah as Yhwh's עבד.[16] In view of the social similarity in the status of woman and עבד, and in their modes of suffering, I would like to propose—tentatively—that the textual speaker in vv. 4-9 (or 4-11) is the metaphorical Jerusalem/ Israel, in her function as bereaved wife and mother soon to be reha-bilitated. That is, I would like to entertain the notion that ch. 50 is a dialogue: between Yhwh, the implied speaker–in–the–text of vv. 1-3, and that section's implied audience, which becomes a [metaphorical] *female* speaking voice in the passage's latter part. This certainly does *not* mean that ch. 50 (or its second section) is authored by a female. It does point, however, to ways of looking at the text that account for the apparent break between its two parts.

If it is assumed that the textual voice in vv. 4 onwards, the voice of Yhwh's עבד, is the prophet's own voice or a collective prophetic voice–as do medieval Jewish commentators (RaSHI, RaDaK and Abarbanel, among others) and many modern scholars—there are serious difficulties. Who was the Second Isaiah—a historical figure, a fictive one, of what age, of what appearance and so on? All we pretend to know about 'him' (why 'him'?) is conjectural. If the pas-sage is attributed to 'him', we shall have to admit to a random editorial policy that connects the two passages of the chapter badly, if at all. Why the change of subject matter and speaker? These questions will remain without an adequate answer, unless the two sections are read as separate passages, randomly or loosely/associatively hung together. If, on the other hand, a female voice is recognized in the second passage, a female voice that—to be sure—represents a com-munity of (presumably, chiefly) male believers, then the problem of literary structure is solved. Furthermore, such a dialogic structure (Yhwh talking to the 'woman' and her embedded answer) appears

15. Sawyer, 'Daughter of Zion and the Servant of the Lord in Isaiah'.

16. For instance Isa. 41.8-13; 44.1-5, 21-22; 45.5. The '*worm* of Jacob' (Hebrew, תולעת, grammatically f.) of 41.14-16a may be added to the list.

elsewhere too; for example, Isa. 49.14 can be read as a female voice
embedded in Yhwh's words. From the perspective of contents, the
metaphorical woman's suffering is analogous to those of both
'woman' and עבד in other passages. 'Israel' is the wife/mother as
well as the עבד.

Moreover, the status of v. 10 (and 11), on which the identification of
the speaker as male hangs, is dubious. The passage can be read and
interpreted with reference to similar passages in Isaiah without
recourse to vv. 10-11: those passages contain a third-person singular
reference to the עבד, presumably the 'I' speaker of the previous verses.
Hypothetically at least, vv. 10-11 can be read as a gloss or commentary on the previous verses (4-9).

Finally, let us compare the passage to Isaiah 54. There, the speaker
(Yhwh) calls upon the community/woman to use her voice joyfully–
which, according to my interpretation, 'she' does here (although not
joyfully). The woman/sons[17] are described there as למודי יהוה, 'taught
by Yhwh'; similarly, the textual speaker claims in 50.4, 'Yhwh God
has given me the language of teaching (לשׁון למודים)...to hear as in
teaching (לשׁמע כלמודים)'. Doxological elements feature in ch. 54 too,
as indications of Yhwh's ability to save his 'woman'.[18]

Conclusions

Isaiah 50 may be read as an integral rhetorical unit of an embedded
dialogic nature. The shift from divine to human voice would then
indicate a shift in the implied signified, role and gendered voice
within the passage. In this reading the audience, passively listening
to Yhwh's 'I' voice (through a spokesperson) in the first section,
moves into agency and the activity of direct subjective speech in the
second section.

This suggestion might rationalize the issues referred to at the
beginning of my discussion of this passage. It allows the passage a
coherence otherwise absent from various interpretations. Far be it
from me to claim that my interpretation is 'right', or 'true', or the like;

17. I choose to retain the MT 'your sons' here, as against the proposed emendation to ב[ו]ניך, 'your *builders*' (BH[3], BHS). The text of 1QIsa[a] has ב[ו]ניכי, with a
supralinear [ו] of suspect provenance that looks like a later addition.

18. For a recognition of a female 'servant', albeit in a completely different
mode, see M.C.A. Korpel, 'The Female Servant of the Lord in Isaiah 54', in
B. Becking and M. Dijkstra (eds.), *On Reading Prophetic Texts: Gender–Specific and
Related Studies in Memory of Fokkelien van Dijk-Hemmes* (Leiden: Brill, 1996), pp.
153-67.

I will settle for plausibility: one attempt out of several. This interpretation is conditioned by what I am. Personal factorsinfluence my
Bible study and Bible readings, always. My own personal experience
as a feminist Bible scholar—not a good choice of vocation if one
wants a smooth career, over and apart from enormous satisfaction—
has taught me to look first, always and as a matter of course, for the
textually underprivileged. My location in life motivates my interest in
biblical voices, female and male.[19] I notice, for instance, that in
Isaiah, too, the textual woman's voice is bracketed by a male voice,
sometimes even doubly bracketed by two male voices—the textual
voices of Yhwh and of the speaker–in–the–text. I note, together with
Claudia Camp and Fokkelien van Dijk-Hemmes, that there is a possibility, however remote in the eyes of some, that wisdom and teaching is not the exclusive property of biblical male figures; a biblical
woman figure can be presented as a teacher too.[20] I look at the subtext, the stereotypical images of women that underlie the metaphor of
'Israel'/Jerusalem as bereaved woman and discarded wife, and
wonder. 'Her' story has all the relevance of a quote. Is 'she' perhaps
misquoted? Does 'she' want a comeback? Does 'she' want her children back? Freud's exasperated question, 'what does "the woman"
want', is applicable under the circumstances. The text assumes—
quite a lot. It is easy to comply with it, to the extent that we follow
unquestionably a traditional pattern. This pattern will go something
like this. Verses 1-3: the (!) prophet (questions: who? when? in what
circumstances?) images 'the people' (who? etc.) as a discarded wife–
mother whom, nevertheless, Yhwh will take back, slaves who will be
redeemed. He has the power to do so. Verses 4-11: one or two
passages, possibly unlinked to the foregoing one of the 'servant/
slave' poems. Who is the 'servant/slave'? The answer will depend, at
least up to a point, on the religious affiliation of the interpreter and on
the centrality of that affiliation to his or her thinking. But this is not
the only readerly option. At any rate, I suspect that the responses my
reading will draw will be conditioned by the measures of kinship or
distance this specific, or any other, biblical text and interpretation
experienced by any individual reader. I also expect that my own

19. Cf. A. Brenner and F. van Dijk-Hemmes (eds.), *On Gendering Texts: Female
and Male Voices in the Hebrew Bible* (Biblical Interpretation Series, 1; Leiden: Brill,
1993).

20. C. Camp, *Wisdom and the Feminine in the Book of Proverbs* (Bible and Literature Series, 11; Sheffield: Almond Press, 1985); van Dijk-Hemmes in *On Gendering Texts*.

sensibilities, those concerning social distinctions and gender distinctions and potentially offensive usage thereof—or, worse still, an interpretative ignoring of such issues—will be shared by some readers, while ignored by others for the sake of paying the 'prophets' and the texts attributed to them homage rather than questioning criticism.[21]

21. This essay is a revision and expansion of two SBL papers: a paper delivered in a panel discussion, 'Teaching the Prophets', in the Israelite Prophetic Literature section, at the AAR/SBL Annual Meeting in New Orleans, November 24 1996; and 'What Difference Does Difference Make', in the Feminist Hermeneutics Session at the AAR/SBL Annual Meeting in Chicago, October 20 1994.

RESPONSE TO BRENNER'S 'IDENTIFYING
THE SPEAKER-IN-THE-TEXT'

Carole R. Fontaine

What happens when a reader resists interpretations hallowed by the
doctrinal weight of long use and certainty of worshipping communities? For the feminist literary scholar, such resistance is often the pre-
mier hallmark of integrity, be it ever so uncomfortable personally or
dangerous professionally. The question raised in the preceding essay
was: 'What happens if we take seriously the image of the dismissed
and punished mother–slave (Hagar?) found at the beginning of a
well-known passage and use it for the interpretation of the even more
well-known, second half of the text, where the speaker must obviously be male, since we have always assumed "him" to be so?' The
gender of the embedded speaker in Isa. 50.4-9 (or 4-11) is the question raised by Brenner, and with good reason. Like the origin of
prophetic speech as divinely given and recorded without bias by the
male prophet, the sex of the so-called 'Suffering Servant' of Second
Isaiah has seldom been questioned, although the identity of this
despised, broken, yet strangely exultant figure has occasioned much
discussion in synagogue, church and scholarly circles. Do we have a
male 'Israel' speaking here as a collective entity, or a particular
individual whose 'call' sends him to the despairing exiles hoping to
hear a word of restoration? Feminist criticism turns these questions
on their heads when it starts not with the assumption of a voice of
normative maleness, but rather with the echo of the repressed and
degraded mother–wife–slave, whose imagery gives the introduction
to the whole poem (vv. 1-3) such power and pathos. Why should a
male voice suddenly, in v. 4, displace the female whose situation so
poignantly sets up the scenario for the entire passage? It does so
because we have been taught to imagine such a voice as the only
possibility. Brenner's resisting reading of Isaiah 50 offers us an
opportunity to imagine differently—but to what end?

The adoption of a sensitivity to the possibility of a repressed female
voice embedded in this text, or any text, does not, for example, lead us

to any of the sorts of certainties that an earlier historical-critical or doctrinal-theological method might have claimed in similar circumstances. We do not assume, for instance, that such an embedded female voice points to female authorship or even value for the female perspective on the matters at hand. Nor do we suggest that when one has reason to posit a female speaker, there is any obvious correspondence between what the textual speaker said and felt and what real women, then or now, say or feel on similar topics. Too many feminist essays have dealt effectively with the reality of female internalization of patriarchal expectations and affect, as well as the habitual erasure or absorption of the female voice into the more momentous, national matters that occupy 'important' male speakers in the Hebrew Bible.

One may ask, as alert readers and students are apt to do, 'so what, then?' If we abandon certainties of history and theology for the criterion of 'mere' plausibility of feminist readings, what, if anything, have we gained?

In the case of Brenner's essay, we gain a number of things. First, we find a solution that allows one to see, finally, a unifying feature between the first and second halves of Second Isaiah's song in ch. 50. A passage previously seen as disjointed and somewhat haphazard in construction gains an internal structure that should, ideally, assist one to a more coherent reading. But is coherence everything? As some have suggested elsewhere, coherence may itself be an ideological projection of patriarchy onto the very fractures, gaps and inconsistencies that may signal material of interest to feminists (of interest for the very reason that it was subject to imperfect textual repression). The search for coherence, then, may be of no particular benefit to feminist critics, though, to be sure, it is always nice to make sense of something.

More than the coherence of an apt literary solution to a textual problem, Brenner's questioning re-reading of the Suffering Servant's gender makes more space in our heads for thinking about the meaning of the gendered images and ideologies that are the Hebrew Bible's stock-in-trade, the icons of meaning out of which whole theologies are fashioned. We must ask ourselves why we prefer 'servant' to 'slave' in our translations. We challenge our imperfect historical knowledge of the educational training of women in the ancient world when we allow for a woman speaking the words: 'The Lord God has given me the tongue of those who are taught, that I may know how to sustain with a word him that is weary' (v. 4). Are such words as appropriate in a grieving, managing mother's mouth as they are to a male suffering servant? If not, why not? And does reading this speech from the perspective of a female speaker not lead us to rather different conclusions about the methods and meanings of future 'restoration'? The God who has not actually divorced the mother has still learned very little since 'she' began living apart: his will is still worked by power rather than persuasion, by command instead of consent. For a 'woman' who returns to such a 'household' tyrant (even, or perhaps, especially if he is also lord of creation as in vv. 2a-3), her future prospects of marital bliss do not seem much improved. We are left wondering if she will return, for her children's sake or for her own. After all, such a husband–father may well be able to command and receive obedience, but never love born from mutuality. This essay invites us to reconsider traditional 'salvific' images and, from a female point of view, finds them less than satisfying. One need not, after all, insist on a biblical text as warrant for identifying the 'disciplined' or abandoned mother–wife as a 'suffering slave'; personal observations of the modern world offer adequate data for making this connection.

II

DIFFERENCES AND OTHERNESS

AN APPROACH TO A CRITICAL, FEMINIST, THEOLOGICAL READING OF THE BIBLE

Sharon H. Ringe

Introduction

A critical feminist reading of the Bible entails perspective, experience and commitment. The perspective is that of the multi-faceted social location occupied by women. Perspective is largely a given of the data of one's existence: gender, race, class, ethnicity, physical condition, relationships in which one is involved, and so on. Those data are transformed into experience as one becomes aware of how the data of social location intersect with events of personal, local and global history to result in suffering or wellbeing, inclusion, or marginalization, participation as the subject of one's own life or merely as the object of others' decisions and actions. The commitment that makes a reading from such a perspective and experience specifically 'feminist' is commitment to the physical, psychological, and social wellbeing of all women through the unmasking, revisioning and transformation of the institutions, social systems and ideologies that define women's lives in 'kyriarchal' social realities—that is, those in which a small group of elite males is dominant over all women and many men.[1]

Such a feminist interpretation is neither simple nor easy. It is not simple because of the very complexity of women's realities, and because for most women that complexity results in a degree of 'status inconsistency' (for example, power or some degree of autonomy in one area of life, coupled with powerlessness or dependence in another). It is not easy because of the effort that must be expended to analyze the experience that results from one's reality, and, most of all, because commitment to the vitality of women's lives requires

---

1.   A particularly clear and challenging discussion of such a feminist project can be found in 'Transforming the Legacy of *The Woman's Bible*', Elisabeth Schüssler Fiorenza's introduction in Schüssler Fiorenza (ed.), *Searching the Scriptures. I. A Feminist Introduction* (New York: Crossroad, 1993), pp. 1-24.

living against the grain (including reading against the texts) of the dominant kyriarchal society.

The task becomes even more complex when one proposes to carry it out within a theological framework in the church or in a Christian theological seminary. There the grain against which one is moving is often that of Christian doctrine and tradition. If the challenge is to be heard in such places, the move toward a counter-reading must be carried out in the name of the same theological center that undergirds both that tradition and the commitment to a feminist interpretation. To put the matter another way, belief in a God who is at home in women's realities, who participates in women's experience and who is committed to the vitality and wholeness of all women and men, is challenged by the institutions and systems within which people live. But that is just the beginning of the challenge. Such belief is also contradicted by the dominant interpretations of the Scriptures that are said to bear witness to God and to the divine intent for human-kind. At times belief in such a God even seems to stretch the bound-aries of those Scriptures themselves.

Negotiating the challenges of the vocation of critical, feminist, theological interpretation of the Bible is a constant fact of my life. I was thus delighted with the opportunity to explore what that process might mean relative to Phil. 2.5-11.[2] My intention in this study is to offer a constructive analysis of the text, not to engage the specific arguments of other scholars or of other interpreters of this much-studied passage, and hence the absence of references to commen-taries or other scholarly literature about it. I conclude this study with reflections on its implications for learning the art of critical, feminist, theological interpretation.

A Case Study: Reading Philippians 2.5-11

Identification of Questions and Concerns

Instead of following the precise instructions given for this assign-ment—to interpret the assigned text, then discuss how my own multi-contextuality shaped that interpretation—I found I must begin at the opposite end, with an acknowledgment of those aspects of my identity and context that are engaged as I read through the assigned

2.   The opportunity came in the invitation to participate in a panel on multi-contextuality and feminist readings of the Bible that was convened by the Feminist Theological Hermeneutics of the Bible Group of the Society of Biblical Literature at its meeting in 1994. This article is a reworking of the paper I presented on that occasion.

text, and that influence the questions that shape my investigation. Indeed, motifs of power, exaltation, humility and obedience in the text touch on the status inconsistency that marks my own life. As a woman I find my defenses going up when I encounter themes of humility and obedience in the Bible, given the way such attitudes and conduct have been imposed on me and other women. As a white, middle-class, North American professor, I also find my defenses going up when the Bible talks about humility and obedience, but my nervousness then comes because I have learned that such texts frequently take aim at the place of privilege I have come to enjoy.

When I read this text from the two contexts of solidarity that also define my life—that of survivors of domestic violence, and that of marginalized people of Central America—I find myself similarly pulled in different directions. The process of *kenosis* or emptying is one that has reinforced the pain for persons already lacking power, especially when it is urged prescriptively upon them. On the other hand, I am drawn to explore the implications of this hymn that celebrates God's own move into history at the side and on the side of these same persons on the margins.

In addition to these aspects of my context, several moments of my past history with this text also shape my reading. This text is deep in my unconscious in the form of the hymn 'At the Name of Jesus', which is a much-loved hymn in my church. (In fact, the melody of that hymn was running through my head the whole time I worked on this project, and I found myself typing to its rhythm.) I am an ordained minister, and this passage was the text assigned for exegesis as part of my ordination process. That previous encounter has predisposed me to read the text with a spin toward questions of 'vocation', both in the professional sense and in the sense of the call common to all people to live out their full humanity.[3]

The hymn in Philippians 2 is also a text that was thrown in my face repeatedly during my years as an assistant pastor. It was cited by a senior pastor who intended its words to shame me into obedience and into the effacing of my own will in favor of his, as part of a syndrome of emotional battering that nearly succeeded in putting a permanent end, not only to my wilfulness, but also to my life. As a result, I have had to fight against using the distancing effects of abstraction, generalization and professional *artificio*—skill, cunning and deceit—as insulation in this reading.

___

3.   This human calling is how I understand the Christian expression, 'to live in Christ'.

Occasion of the Letter

Contexts of suffering that in my experience cluster around this text as if around a magnet echo what I understand to be Paul's own situation in prison at the time of writing, and that of the community to which he wrote. It is not clear what was happening to them, but the letter itself portrays a part and consequence of their suffering as anxiety that the partnership in ministry they shared with Paul would be terminated should he not survive his imprisonment (Phil. 1.18b-25).

I am struck by Paul's way of addressing that suffering by an accent on 'joy' and 'rejoicing' throughout the letter, and by his incorporation of a hymn into the letter in ch. 2, and perhaps in a paraphrase in the very singable 'Rejoice in the Lord always' (4.4-7). Perhaps they were indeed hymns sung in worship by the congregation at Philippi. Paul may have cited them here much as African American preachers incorporate into their preaching hymns that retell and celebrate the principal truths and stories of the faith, and thus tap into a reservoir of strength and courage that they can then develop in the specific analysis of the sermon.

Literary Context

The hymn in 2.5-11 functions as the sharp midpoint of a three-part ring structure in the first two chapters of Paul's letter. Following the greeting and thanksgiving (1.1-11), the first section of the chiasmus (1.12–2.4) acknowledges the realities of his context and theirs and of the anxieties that haunt them. Paul thus presents his own solidarity with them in their suffering, as well as the solidarity of Christ, as the reason they can rejoice regardless of what befalls them or him. The hymn (2.5-11) then sketches in the spare language of poetry the theological key that will empower them to survive the present sufferings, namely Christ as the one in whom they are to find encouragement—παράκλησις. The remainder of ch. 2 then identifies specific steps they can take as a community to see them through.

Close Reading of the Text

The clue of how to sing the hymn is given in v. 5. Just as ch. 1 and the beginning of ch. 2 pointed to the intertwining of the Philippians' story with Paul's story in a pattern of community wellbeing and unity for the sake of Christ, so now they are urged to share in Christ's own stance toward life. Τοῦτο φρονεῖτε ἐν ὑμιν ὃ καὶ ἐν Χριστῷ Ἰησοῦ ('Let the same mind be in you that was in Christ Jesus' [NRSV]) is not an invitation to abstraction and the intellectual escapism to which I found myself fleeing. Instead, the etymology of the verb draws us not to the head alone, but to head and heart together as the organizing center of the human person, where thought, attitude, and concern come together. The point is not that one should think about or understand the world the way Jesus did, but rather that one should come as an integrated whole to life as Jesus did. The hymn explores that center.

In brief, the formative center or 'mindedness' is the story of the movement of Christ Jesus:

  A. from primordial identity in the form of God (2.6)
      B. through appropriate actions to live out that identity (2.7a-b)
          C. to incarnation as truly human (2.7c-d)
      B´. through appropriate actions to live out that identity (2.8)
  A´. to the result (διὸ καί) of realizing God's purpose:
      God exalts and gives the name above all names so that
      (ἵνα) humanity, in turn, bows and confesses (2.9-11).

Scholarly debate about this hymn centers on its provenance, assuming that Paul himself was not 'moonlighting' as a hymn-writer. Is it principally Jewish Christian or gentile Christian in the imagery by which it speaks of Jesus? The debate remains unresolved. The principal lexical discussion turns on the words ὁμοίωμα ('likeness') and σχῆμα ('shape' or 'outward form'[4]). The debate is whether these words place the hymn writer in a gnostic or docetic context, saying that Jesus only *seemed* to be human (or as I put it in introductory classes, the divine ducking into a phone booth to zip on a human suit that only covers but does not change the real super-hero identity), or whether they should be understood in Paul's usage as affirming Jesus' full humanity—without, of course, the sinfulness of the rest of us. Strangely enough, a similar debate does not surround the meaning of the word μορφή ('form'), despite the paradoxical affirmation of Jesus as being in the 'form' of God, then taking the 'form' of a slave. Or perhaps the silence on a matter related to slavery is not surprising among interpreters who come in large majority from the dominant culture, whose wont is to spiritualize such references instead of examining their potential social implications.

Engaging the Text
My close reading of the text suggests that the extant lexical discussions and debates about the hymn's provenance are red herrings

---

4. The NRSV's use of 'form' to translate both σχῆμα (found only in the last phrase of v. 7) and μορφή (found in v. 6 and earlier in v. 7) obscures the fact that two distinct words are used in the Greek.

diverting us both from the conformity of the hymn to the gospel encountered elsewhere in Paul's letters and in the canonical Gospels, and from a social reading of the language (which in fact might be enhanced by further work on the implications of the word μορφή). The pursuit of that reading involves both literary and theological analyses of the hymn itself and the exploration of what might be called a 'dynamic intertextuality' that entails, not direct citation, but theological transposition into the christological 'key' of this hymn.

The hymn begins with the affirmation that Jesus (like other human beings?) bears the divine image. The route from that primordial formal identity with God to incarnation in full humanity is what is encompassed in the double step of self-emptying and identification with the most marginalized of people, one who is enslaved. This dynamic mirrors God's engagement with Israel, as seen in the Exodus traditions that portray a God who met God's people, not when they were riding the crest of power and national prestige, but when they were enslaved in Egypt. The new key of the hymn, however, marks a shift from the community's history to Jesus, the Anointed One, as the locus of divine presence among humankind, or what might be called God's historical project.

From that central fact (κήρυγμα or הגדה) of incarnation follows the vocation or הלבה of life in conformity with God's historical project. That vocation is not humiliation and subjection (as v. 8 has often been read prescriptively), but rather a life in solidarity with people who are most lacking in honor and prestige. In terms of the narratives of the canonical Gospels, that same vocation is unfolded in a life of commitment to God's βασιλεία—the sort of historical project that would lead to Jesus' crucifixion by forces operating out of a different value structure. In the hymn as in the Gospels, God is affirmed not to allow death to carry the last word, which belongs instead to the life that overcomes death. In the hymn the proclamation of resurrection comes not through the narratives of the empty tomb and appearances of the risen one, but in the form of a liturgical celebration echoed throughout the cosmos (Phil. 2.9-11).

The movement or dynamic of the hymn, from its beginning in v. 6 to the glorious confession in v. 11, suggests that the Philippians to whom the letter was addressed may well have been persons of power and prestige, whom Paul was calling to recognize a different model of human life than the one that prevailed among them. Their old model appears to have equated success and wellbeing with the sort of financial security and social honor that they apparently enjoyed prior to the troubles that recently beset them. The new model does not

appeal to evidence of worldly security and comfort, but rather
reminds the Philippians that the way and truth of God are sufficient
to see them through their present sufferings.

Engaged by the Text
As a theological key, the hymn offers not an abstract, universalizing
Christology but a celebration of Jesus' incarnation into a life clearly
centered on—'minded' toward, if you will—the logic of divine identity and commitment central to the Hebrew Bible and the New Testament alike. According to this hymn, Jesus is portrayed as in no way
the innocent victim forced to accept humiliation and abasement as
somehow good for him, or denoting the mark of a holy life. Rather,
Jesus acts at the acme of power, from an integrative center of his life
that makes him a trustworthy companion especially for those who
suffer.

The drama sketched in the hymn is not that of human achievement
striving toward God, but rather that of the Christ as God's full
identification with humanity, leaving the safety of divine identity to
join the most vulnerable of human beings. Being humble and obedient does not mean groveling, but moving in deliberate solidarity and
commitment with God's own logic, called elsewhere God's βασιλεία.
At work within the text read in this way is what Rita Nakashima
Brock calls the 'hermeneutics of wisdom', which recovers the tales
that have sustained one's culture, rejects innocence in favor of survival skills that benefit the whole community, and requires preservation of a multi-layered self that keeps its options open.[5]

In short, the text conveys a summons to commitment to a vocation
of full humanity that will not compromise even to cheat death. According to this hymn, the result of such a life is not a personal reward
for good behavior, but God's emphatic 'yes!' to, and celebration of,
life; and God's 'no!' to death's claim to speak the final word.

Reading this again from the multiple contexts I identified at the
outset, I continue to rage at the misuse of this text by persons with
power to abuse and intimidate persons without it. I am struck by the
common note in this account of the life of Jesus as the Christ and in
the synoptic Gospels—a note which sounds the clear tone of solidarity with, and commitment to, persons pushed to the margins of life
and of society as the human echo of God's presence. It is Exod. 3.17—
God who hears the cry of God's people—transposed into a new key,

5.   Rita Nakashima Brock, 'Dusting the Bible on the Floor: A Hermeneutics of
Wisdom', in Schüssler Fiorenza (ed.), *Searching the Scriptures*, I, pp. 64-75.

or a new tune discovered for a beloved hymn text.

Where the threat appropriately comes in singing this hymn is when I sing it in the taffeta and velvet robes of academia or other trappings of power and prestige, for its melody of a 'mindedness' that is the product not of a PhD, but of solidarity and identification with those on the margins, strains the heart if not the throat.

Conclusion

Insofar as the above study takes into account the multifaceted reality of women's lives experienced in the light of particular events and circumstances, in commitment to the physical, psychological and social well-being of all women and men, and in the framework of confession of and response to a divine reality sharing that commitment, it does represent one critical, feminist, theological reading of Phil. 2.5-11. It is clearly not the *only* possible reading that would merit such a label. Those controlling principles, however, as well as the limits defined by the language, literary form and social context of the text itself, prevent the likely plurality of readings from dissolving into the relativism that considers any and every reading acceptable. In particular, the commitment to the life and wellbeing of all women and men, and the affirmation of the theological significance of that commitment, mandate that those who engage in a reading conformed to those values do so in a community of critical engagement one with another about the interpretations each would offer.

The communal dialogical context, the critical reflection on the interpreter's social location and experience, and the commitment or engagement needed for such interpretation represent factors not usually recognized as essential dimensions of the introduction to biblical studies. In fact, despite the contextual hermeneutical challenges brought to the discipline of biblical studies from many quarters in recent years, such factors are often explicitly disallowed—particularly in introductory courses and discussions—in favor of a critical methodology that incorporates ideals of objectivity and value-neutrality, and tools supposedly able to support such ideals.

Perhaps the most significant challenge brought to biblical studies by critical, feminist, theological interpretation is that it is not a single methodology that can be described or learned, and then applied in all circumstances. Rather, it is an art which, while it may be encouraged by a book or article, can only be appropriated in a process of accompaniment and mutual engagement of teacher–learner and learner–teacher with the texts of life and the life of texts.

A TRIPLE HERMENEUTIC: SCRIPTURE AND REVISIONIST WOMEN'S POETRY

Alicia Suskin Ostriker

The Bible is an ancient Volume—
Written by faded Men—[1]

So wrote the poet Emily Dickinson, tongue firmly in cheek, probably around 1882, a decade and a half before the publication of Elizabeth Cady Stanton's *Woman's Bible*. In the century since Dickinson's and Cady Stanton's time, increasing numbers of women have taken note, usually with little amusement, of the Bible's male authorship and its privileging of divine and human male authority. Not without reason, the typical feminist reader of the last century has seen the Bible as the very foundation of women's oppression, and biblical texts as exemplifying the process whereby patriarchy constitutes itself through the rejection of female power. Like Cady Stanton, with her no-nonsense Enlightenment rationalism, we argue against whatever principalities and powers 'make a fetish' of male-written texts 'inspired by the natural love of dominion', we deplore the subjection of women taught by such texts, and we insist that religious reform is necessary for social reform. I have argued elsewhere that the text of the covenant itself depends upon a subtext of female erasure, and that the process by which female power is erased is imperfect, so that the erasure has to be obsessively repeated and is never quite finished.[2]

Yet if a feminist's stance toward Scripture is inevitably adversarial, it can also be more than that. For to diagnose is not to heal. If our object is to retrieve from the palimpsest of patriarchal narrative what

---

1.   Emily Dickinson, *Complete Poems* (Thomas H. Johnson ed.; Boston: Little, Brown, 1955), no. 1545. Subsequent Dickinson poems are quoted from this edition and cited by number.

2.   Alicia Suskin Ostriker, 'Out of My Sight: The Buried woman in Biblical Narrative', in Ostriker, *Feminist Revision and the Bible* (Oxford: Basil Blackwell, 1993), pp. 27-55. The present article has been adapted from a second essay in this volume, 'A Word Made Flesh: the Bible and Women's Poetry', pp. 56-91.

the narrative attempts to bury and deny, we may seek for traces or tracks of the female story. Reading with the eyes of desire, we may peer between the lines for a lost past, and we may discover fresh and transforming meanings within supposedly familiar stories. Further, remembering that the Bible was—whether inspired from above or not—written down here below, by human beings over a period of millennia in acts of composition not so very different from our own, we may want to recognize how filled it is with gaps and fractures, and take advantage of its contradictions. When we do so, we cease to posit a simple polarity or adversarial relationship between male text and female re-writers. Instead, we begin to discover that our revisionist interpretations of the Bible are not simply forbidden by the text and tradition we are challenging. They are also invited and supported.

In this essay I will first survey, briefly, those elements within the Hebrew Bible and the New Testament that most clearly encourage transgressive and subversive attitudes toward sacred authority, including the authority of Scripture itself. Then I will look at the biblical appropriations by English and American women poets, including Emily Dickinson, Elizabeth Barrett Browning and Christina Rossetti in the nineteenth century, then H.D., as representing high modernism, and, finally, the work of contemporary American women poets. I suggest that biblical revisionism takes three sometimes overlapping forms: a hermeneutics of suspicion, a hermeneutics of desire, and a hermeneutics of indeterminacy. With the first of these we are, as I have already indicated, quite familiar; sceptical critique is the feminist's stock in trade. Its opposite, the hermeneutics of desire—the discovery in a text of what we need to discover, the citing of what we love and wish to find sacred, the bending a text to our will—is equally important for the woman writer. It needs to be recognized, of course, that the hermeneutics of desire is what all theologians, scholars and exegetes from Rabbi Akiba and St Paul to the present time have practised, although they do not call it by that name. Lastly, the hermeneutics of indeterminacy depends on the recognition that, as the rabbis say, 'there is always another interpretation'. Although I will not press this point, it seems to me that the ways women writers deal with biblical texts are paradigmatic for the ways we deal with male texts and traditions in general. Indeed, this triple model of (re)interpetive modes might well serve to describe how writers of any marginalized group come ultimately to deal with a dominant culture that both inspires and repels them. I would encourage my readers to consider whether they find this to be the case. [3]

I

The questioning of authority, including divine authority, has been built into Judaism in several different ways. From the moment God

---

3.   Contemporary feminist theology, as I read it, makes ample use of the hermeneutics of suspicion and the hermeneutics of desire; that is, feminist theology has occupied itself on the one hand with demonstrating biblical misogyny, on the other with finding in the biblical texts narrative and other material supportive of women and of femaleness. The idea that the scriptural text can (must?) always be plurally interpreted has not yet become popular among feminist scholars, although the principle is well enough understood in modern biblical scholarship. Important exceptions are Mary Callaway, *Sing, O Barren One: a Study in Comparative Midrash* (Atlanta: Scholars Press, 1986); Elaine Pagels, *Adam, Eve and the Serpent* (New York: Random House, 1988); Marina Warner, *Alone of All Her Sex: The Myth and the Cult of the Virgin Mary* (New York: Knopf, 1983); and above all Mieke Bal, in *Lethal Love: Feminist Literary Readings of Biblical Love Stories* (Bloomington: Indiana University Press, 1987); *Murder and Difference: Genre, Gender and Scholarship on Sisera's Death* (Indiana Studies in Biblical Literature; Bloomington: Indiana University Press, 1988); *Death and Dissymetry: the Politics of Coherence in the Book of Judges* (Chicago: University of Chicago Press, 1988). Bal's recurrent point is that her own readings 'present an alternative to other readings, not a "correct", let alone the "only possible" intereation of what the texts "really say". Texts trigger readings; that is what they are: the occasion of a reaction. The feeling that there is a text in support of one's view makes texts such efficient ideological weapons'. Nevertheless, 'every reading is different from, and in contact with, the text' (p. 132). My own view strongly concurs. We have all been taught to assume that the Bible is consistent and monolithic. As feminists we should find ourselves urging that the scriptural text is, on the contrary, *not* necessarily monolithic, *not* necessarily coherent, *not* necessarily unified, but riddled with gaps and contradictions and textual ambivalences allowing for plural readings of which *none can ever be definitive*. An insistent heterodoxy is, it seems to me, one of the great strengths of feminist thinking. Such a view intersects with multiculturalism in Elisabeth Schüssler Fiorenza's anthology *Searching for the Scriptures* (2 vols.; New York: Crossroad, 1993), particularly in several essays by women of color, e.g., Anna Julia Cooper's view of the gospels as gradually unfolding their truth over millennia, during which no interpretation is complete, and misunderstanding is part of an inevitable process of discovery. A beautiful example of how biblical texts yield varying meanings to varying communities is offered by Kwok Pui-Lan, who observes of the story of Hagar that 'African-American women focus on Hagar as a slave woman, the Latin Americans stress that she was poor, the Africans underscore the fate of Hagar in polygamy, and Asians emphasize the loss of cultural identity' (Kwok Pui-Lan, 'Racism and Ethnocentrism in Feminist Biblical Interpretation', in Schüssler Fiorenza [ed.], *Searching the Scriptures*, I, pp. 101-16 [106]).

confides to Abraham his intention of destroying Sodom and Gomorrah, and Abraham is appalled and replies 'Shall the Judge of all
the earth not do justly'?—making clear that he, Abraham, thinks God
has no right to harm innocent people—the right and even the duty of
God's children to interrogate their father becomes a recurrent biblical
theme. 'That be far from thee', cries Abraham, 'to do after this manner, to slay the righteous with the wicked: and that the righteous
should be as the wicked.'

> And the Lord said, If I find in Sodom fifty righteous within the city,
> then I will spare all the place for their sakes. And Abraham answered
> and said, behold now, I have taken upon me to speak unto the Lord,
> which am but dust and ashes: Peradventure there shall lack five of the
> fifty righteous: wilt thou destroy all the city for the lack of five? And he
> said, if I find there forty and five, I will not destroy it. And he spake
> unto him yet again, and said, Peradventure there shall be forty found
> there (Gen. 18.25-29).[4]

And so on, until Abraham bargains God down to ten. In this rather
comedic scene we see the origins of Jewish *chutzpah*. Jacob's wres-
tling with the angel and Job's challenge to God are similar episodes
in different tones: one heroic, one lyric or rhapsodic. But these are
hardly unique episodes within Judaism. 'Wherefore doth the way of
the wicked prosper'? asks Jeremiah, inaugurating the tradition of
interrogating God's goodness that still reverberates in contemporary
Jewish writers. In Elie Wiesel's *The Gates of the Forest*, a rabbi in a
concentration camp announces to his fellows, 'I intend to convict
God of murder, for he is destroying his people and the Law he gave
them from Mount Sinai. I have irrefutable proof in my hands.' In I.B.
Singer's autobiographical *In My Father's Court*, the boy Isaac asks
himself, 'What did the Emperor of everything, the Creator of heaven
and Earth require? That he could go on watching soldiers fall on
battlefields?' In Malamud's *The Fixer* occurs this dialogue: '"Yakov",
said Shmuel passionately, "Don't forget your God". "Who forgets
who?" the fixer said angrily. "What do I get from him but a bang on
the head and a stream of piss in my face?"' Thus the woman poet
who challenges what Sylvia Plath calls 'Herr God, Herr Lucifer' continues a tradition of challenge and interrogation of divinity that has
been a core theme within Jewish writing.

As to earthly authority, here too the scriptural tradition supports its
questioners. The Jews as a nation originate in a slave rebellion; the

---

4.   I use the King James Version of the Bible throughout this essay because it is
the translation most influential in English poetry.

Exodus story continues to resound in the aspirations and rhetoric of oppressed populations throughout the world, as Michael Walzer observes in *Exodus and Revolution;*[5] the story has inspired generations of Afro-Americans, from spirituals such as 'Let My People Go' to Martin Luther King Jr's 'I've been to the mountain', in which the soon-to-be assassinated leader identifies himself with the aged Moses. Prophetic texts freely attack Israelite ruling classes, kings and priests alike. Notwithstanding the centrality of ritual in the Israelite community, it is Isaiah who is the mouthpiece of a God who says 'Your new moons and your appointed feasts my soul hateth' (Isa. 2.14) and demands that his people feed the hungry, clothe the naked, and help the oppressed. 'I hate, I despise your feasts', exclaims the God of Amos, 'but let justice roll down like waters' (Amos 5.21-24). Social justice as opposed to whatever authority resists it becomes a core motivation in Jewish history, in ways obviously resonant with the consciousness of feminism, as numerous feminist theologians have noted.

Rosemary Radford Ruether argues that 'the prophetic-messianic tradition' in which God speaks 'as critic, rather than sanctifier, of the status quo' implies 'a rejection of every elevation of one social group against others as image and agent of God, every use of God to justify social domination and subjugation'.[6]

Like Judaism, Christianity has been from its inception a self-revising tradition, in which the letter of the law killeth while the spirit giveth life, the letter signifying a fixed canon and a privileged set of clerics and theologians to interpret it, while the spirit represents the unmediated truth directly available to the believer. From Christ's repeated defiance of religious law and his mockery of pharisees and saducees, from his announcement that he is himself the fulfillment of Law and its virtual antidote, from the powerful conception of social

---

5.   Michael Walzer, *Exodus and Revolution* (New York: Basic Books, 1985).

6.   Rosemary Ruether, *Sexism and God-Talk: Toward a Feminist Theology* (Boston: Beacon Press, 1983), pp. 117-19. Mary K. Wakeman argues in 'Biblical Prophecy and Modern Feminism' that the Bible in general and the prophets in particular may be read as a paradigm for cultural transformation. Prophecy involves '(1) an inner convulsion (2) under pressure of historical circumstances which results in (3) a radical break with prevailing beliefs; that inner convulsion depends on (4) the resurrection of suppressed values (that have in fact underpinned the dominant ethos), and the radical break then results in (5) subversion of the dominating institutional forms (6) including language' (Rita Gross [ed.], *Beyond Andro-centrism: New Essays on Women and Religion* [Missoula, MT: Scholars Press, 1977], p. 67).

reversal that structures the sermon on the mount, from Christ's promise to provide the faithful with the interior guidance of the Holy Spirit, and above all from his insistence that the kingdom of heaven is within us, Christianity throughout its history has produced wave after wave of anti-institutional protestant reform. As often as a church has strengthened its absolute hold over its community, just so often have dissenters guided by one or other version of inner light challenged both dogma and power—appealing always to the high tribunal of the scriptural text itself. The history of Christianity is a history of periodic schisms that are ultimately reinterpretations of the meaning of the New Testament. Nor is feminist rebellion against fathers, husbands and political authorities on Christian grounds confined to the twentieth century. Rather, it is a key theme in Christian martyrology, in the lives of the female saints, in women's conversion narratives. Indeed, wherever women's spirituality has arisen as an independent force, there we are typically reminded that we are to call no man father, master or Lord, and that 'whosoever shall exalt himself shall be abased; and he that humbleth himself shall be exalted' (Mt. 23.1-12).[7]

Regarding textual canonicity and authority, modern biblical scholarship informs us that the notion of Scripture as a unitary Word dictated or directly inspired by God, a Word presumed to be One like its author, and therefore fixed, changeless and eternal, has always been a myth. At no single moment in its history has the Bible been a unified, monolithic text. Rather, it has has ever been a radically layered, plurally authored, multiply motivated composite, full of fascinating mysteries, gaps and inconsistencies, a garden of delight to the exegete. If traditional exegesis attempts to maintain the view of a unified Scripture despite apparent contradictions, contemporary critics find in Scripture a kind of paradise of polysemy. 'The really significant elements in biblical narrative are the contradictions', claim the structuralists Leach and Aycock.[8] John Barthes remarks: 'What interests me most...is...the abrasive frictions, the breaks, the discontinuities of readability, the juxtaposition of narrative entities

---

7. See Stevan Davies, *The Revolt of the Widows: the Social World of the Apocryphal Acts* (Carbondale, IL: Southern Illinois Press; London: Feffer and Simons, 1980); Rosemary R. Ruether and Eleanor McLaughlin (eds.), *Women of Spirit: Female Leadership in the Jewish and Christian Traditions* (New York: Simon & Schuster, 1979); Carolyn Bynum, *Holy Feast and Holy Fast* (Berkeley: University of California Press, 1986).

8. Edmund Leach and Alan Aycock, *Structuralist Interpretations of Biblical Myth* (Cambridge: Cambridge University Press, 1983).

which to some extent run free from an explicit logical articulation'.[9] Geoffrey Hartman enjoys 'the fault lines of a text, the evidence of a narrative sediment that has not entirely settled', and proposes that biblical writing is 'a fusion of heterogeneous stories...layered' like Lévi-Strauss's bricolage in myth, or Bakhtin's heteroglossia in novels. Robert Alter stresses the contradictions and debates within biblical texts as well as their unities.[10] But the reader for whom the text is genuinely sacred may be at least as engaged with its radical indeterminacies as the secular critic:

> For what is at issue with respect to the Scriptures is not what lies behind the text in the form of an (always elusive) original meaning but what lies in front of it where the interpreter stands. The Bible always addresses itself to the time of interpretation... If the text does not apply to us it is an empty text... We take the text in relation to ourselves, understanding ourselves in its light, even as our situation throws its light upon the text, allowing it to disclose itself differently, perhaps in unheard-of ways.[11]

Within the very temple of fixity, then, lives the invisible daimon of flux: 'Revelation is not something that occurs once for all and is now over and done with'.[12] The feminist reader, whether committed to secular or religious readings of the Bible, should find the in the text's wild variety a fascinating asset.

9.   John Barthes, 'The Struggle with the Angel', in *Image, Music, Text* (ed. and trans. Stephen Heath; New York: Hill & Wang, 1977), p. 140.

10.   Geoffrey Hartman, 'The Struggle for the Text', in Geoffrey Hartman and Sanford Budick (eds.), *Midrash and Literature* (New Haven: Yale University Press, 1986), pp. 11-13. Robert Alter, 'Introduction', in Robert Alter and Frank Kermode (eds.), *The Literary Guide to the Bible* (Cambridge, MA: Harvard University Press, 1987), pp. 12-13.

11.   Gerald L. Bruns, 'Midrash and Allegory: The Beginning of Scriptural Interpretation', in Alter and Kermode (eds.), *The Literary Guide*, pp. 627-33. Compare Elizabeth Schüssler Fiorenza's politically oriented concept of the *ecclesia gynaikon* or 'woman-church' as 'the locus or place of divine revelation' which must both 'challenge the scriptural authority of patriarchal texts and explore how the Bible is used as a weapon against women in our struggles...it also must explore whether and how the Bible can become a resource in this struggle' and it must claim the authority 'to choose or to reject' biblical texts; E. Schüssler Fiorenza, 'The Will to Choose or to Reject: Continuing Our Critical Work', in Letty Russell (ed.), *Feminist Interpretation of the Bible* (Philadelphia: Westminster Press, 1985), pp. 128-31.

12.   Bruns, 'Midrash and Allegory', p. 633.

II

In her second letter to the well-known man of letters, Thomas Wentworth Higginson, written in April 1862, Emily Dickinson describes her family: 'They are religious, except me, and address an eclipse, every morning, whom they call their Father'. Dickinson here is testing the waters of Higginson's tolerance for verbal mischief. As a critique of conventional religiousness she may mean that Christians routinely lack any real notion of God; or that the God they worship remains (deliberately?) remote, invisible to them; or that they are actually worshiping their own shadows; or that there is no God. In her poems Dickinson is no less bold, no less impudent. If 'the Bible is an antique Volume/ Written by faded Men', she feels quite free as a woman to rewrite it, and to use it for her own purposes.

One purpose is critique: the God Dickinson has been taught to propitiate is, in her judgment, manipulative, brutal, and indifferent to human suffering. 'Of course—I prayed—/ And did God care?' (no. 376). Omnipotence extorts worship in a divinely monopolistic economy where we are beggars and he is the 'Burglar! Banker—Father'(no. 49), the 'mighty Merchant' (no. 621) who meanly withholds his goods from the would-be purchaser. He is 'Inquisitor', 'mastiff', a 'God of flint'. Can we know if he is real? His inaccessibility—'I know that He exists/ Somewhere—in Silence'—is perhaps but 'an instant's play' designed to make immortality a more blissful surprise. But then again, perhaps not: 'Should the play/ Prove piercing earnest', the joke would have 'crawled too far' (no. 338). Dickinson's portrait of the biblical bully who,

> On Moses seemed to fasten
> With tantalizing play
> As Boy should deal with lesser Boy
> To prove Ability (no. 597),

leads her again to an epistemological paradox. Although she readily acknowledges that the story is fiction, since 'in soberer moments/ No Moses can there be', the cruelty of this 'Romance' continues to torment her:

> Old Man on Nebo—late as this—
> My justice bleeds—for Thee!

Whatever awe Emily Dickinson experiences for the God of her Fathers is more than balanced by rage at his power and distance, not to mention fury at his possible non-existence.

Yet anyone who reads Dickinson at all recognizes that her poetry is saturated with biblical allusions that represent desire at its most intense, blissful and playful. Fantasies of heaven and paradise stream through her work, not merely as a figure for the transcendent and unattainable ('"Heaven" is what I cannot reach', no. 239) but precisely as a figure for earthly and immanent joy. Staying home from church to hear the birds preach, Emily finds that instead of getting to heaven later, she's 'going all the time' (no. 324). Inebriate of air and debauchee of dew, she imagines herself admired by the saints and angels as the 'little Tippler/ Leaning against the Sun' (no. 214), presumably replacing the woman clothed with the sun of Revelation. The palpable eroticism of 'Come slowly—Eden—' (no. 211), and the orgasmic and possibly lesbian fantasy of 'Rowing in Eden—/Ah, the Sea!' in 'Wild Nights—Wild Nights!' (no. 249), make paradise regained a locus of gratified sexuality. Pursuing her erotic dramas Dickinson is 'Empress of Calvary' (no. 1072) and usurps a lover's crucifix (no. 1736) in an exhibitionistic demonstration of her own superior pain.[13] She archly questions Paul's condemnation of the flesh as 'sown in dishonour' by her own reading of both Bible and body: 'Not so fast!/ Apostle is askew' (no. 62). She likes, unsurprisingly, the story of Jacob who 'Found he had worsted God'! (no. 59). She identifies at times with the Satan who walks to and fro on the earth, at times with the Eve whose burial place is unknown ('and why am I not Eve'?), at times with David fighting Goliath. She feminizes God as a mother bird who notices when her sparrows fall (no. 164), and as the Typic Mother in whose Book June and Autumn are Genesis and Revelation (no. 1115). She incarnates and eroticizes language itself in 'A Word made Flesh' (no. 1651), a poem that crosses the boundaries dividing spirit and flesh, the transcendant and the immanent:

> A Word made Flesh is seldom
> And tremblingly partook
> Nor then perhaps reported
> But have I not mistook
> Each one of us has tasted
> With ecstasies of stealth
> the very food debated
> To our specific strength—
> A Word that breathes distinctly

13. Additional Dickinson poems that appropriate the figure of Calvary to describe her own suffering, are nos. 313, 322, 348, 364, 549, 553, 561, 577, 620, 725. Fair copies of all were made in the early 1860s; most are clearly love poems.

Has not the power to die
Cohesive as the Spirit
It may expire if He—
'Made Flesh and dwelt among us'
Could condescension be
Like this consent of Language
This loved Philology.

Let me suggest just a few of the outrageous ideas that seem incorporated here. First, the incarnate Christ who in this poem is eaten with ecstasies of stealth (spiritual ecstasy being indivisible from sensual) is distinguished from the publicly consumed Christ of the churches, and may even be distinguished from the publicly 'reported' Christ of Scripture. He is dangerous; he is also multiple, a food that varies with the eater. In the poem's second half he becomes, moreover, fused with, or infused into, a poetic Word whose immortality consists paradoxically in the fleshly embodying that makes it a 'loved Philology'. Indeed, the poem's close hints that Christ's descent to dwell among us—and/or the sentence in the Fourth Gospel which describes that descent—may imitate the process whereby language consents to incorporate itself in and for us. Like the loaded gun of one of Dickinson's most elliptical poems, 'My Life had stood—a Loaded Gun' (no. 754), the living Word 'Has not the power to die'. The incarnate Christ is thus something like a poem; and if we recall that Emily's 'life' was the loaded gun, it looks as if Christ, the Word incarnate, is also something like Emily.

In this apparently bewildering array of Dickinson's biblical appropriations, can be located the triple hermeneutics of my title. First, there is obviously here a hermeneutics of suspicion that concentrates on issues of power and powerlessness. Insofar as she identifies herself as powerless, the poet mistrusts, resists, and attacks the embodiment of patriarchal power—both the being and the text. Yet at other moments she lets the text stand for pleasure, eroticizing it by inserting herself into the story, by identifying its spiritualities with her own sensualities, and by feminizings of the divine. In contrast with the hermeneutics of suspicion, the hermeneutics of desire finds in the text what it desires to find; the text shapes itself to the author's wish. But there is also in Dickinson a studied indeterminacy that may be her most radical characteristic. 'Alas, that Wisdom is so large/ And Truth—so manifold' (no. 568). Dickinson anticipates modernist linguistics in her understanding that a signifier may not correlate in any direct way with a thing signified. '"Heaven" has different Signs—to me' (no. 575), she begins one poem, going on to explain that the word may mean different things at different times. 'A pen has so many inflections and a Voice but one', she explains in a letter, implying that anything *written* is plurally interpretable. We are aware, when reading any of Dickinson's readings of a biblical text, that an act of interpretation is occurring that may be immediately persuasive yet retains an irreducible element of the wilful, the made thing, the playful poetic fiction. Just as she habitually foregrounds the humanly composed and therefore contingent aspect of Scripture, so her interpretation never makes what the philosophers call 'truth claims'. Further, when we read Dickinson's poetry at large, we see something larger: that she never worries about contradicting herself, that terms such as 'God', 'Jesus', 'heaven' and so forth have an abundant variety of meanings, some of them highly ambiguous, many of them mutually incompatible, yet each convincing within the local perimeters of the poem. Just as she brackets Scripture as a man-made and therefore non-absolute thing, so she allows her own stances to it to vary. As a recent critic observes, 'Whether Dickinson believed in an afterlife or not will ever be open to question. Readers can select poems and letters and construct compelling arguments to prove that she did or did not, as well as to demonstrate that she believed in God or not.'[14] To read Dickinson on God (etc.), then, is to divest oneself of the desire for a fixed and unitary eternal truth and to accept willy-nilly a plurality of contingent truths. Putting this another way: to the powerless Dickinson daughter, Scripture is an antagonist, to the passionate woman, Emily, it is a lover, to the powerful poet, Emily Dickinson, it is a poem out of which one makes, of course, further poems.

Dickinson is the boldest of nineteenth-century women poets, perhaps because she is the shyest. Since she did not write for publication, she wrote only what passion and intellect dictated. Her nineteenth-century sisters, on the other hand, labored in a vineyard that required (and inspired) heavy doses of piety and right-thinking, especially in women poets. Outside of Dickinson there is little of the hermeneutics of suspicion or of the dancing indeterminacies. These are *earnest* poets. Still, if we lift a veil or two we find some rather startling erotic revisionism, for example, in Elizabeth Barrett Browning and Christina Rossetti, for whom Victorian ideas about women's superior morality lead to feminized versions of sacred narratives.

14. Martha Nell Smith, *Rowing in Eden: Rereading Emily Dickinson* (Austin: University of Texas Press, 1992), p. 312.

Consider the complicated subversiveness of Barrett Browning's 'novel in verse', *Aurora Leigh*. Despite the fact that this is a poem in which high-minded appeals to God seem to lurk beyond every second caesura, Browning's poet-heroine, Aurora, begins by rejecting Eve's role of 'helpmeet' to her suitor Romney, claiming the higher vocation of poetry. Rejecting her conventional education, the autodidactic (and very didactic) Aurora describes the soul as 'A palimpsest—a prophet's holograph/Defiled, erased and covered by a monk's', and culture itself as palimpsestic—an obscene text beneath which we may yet discern the 'Upstroke of an alpha and omega/ Expressing the old scripture'.[15] The implication is that by searching her own soul, the woman poet will discover something equivalent to a sacred writing, beneath layers of cultural accretions.

Successful as a poet, Aurora fails as a woman, for the usual nineteenth-century reason that she has not found true love. Reunited, however, with a worshipful and physically disabled Romney at the narrative's inspirational close, Aurora assumes the stance of a warrior-prophet. Fusing Joshua and Isaiah, pressing the clarion to her 'woman's lip' now consecrated by connubial love, her vocation is to 'blow all class walls level as Jericho' (389). Meanwhile, Aurora's lower-class alter ego, the 'sweet holy Marion' (262) of the sub-plot, is a combination Virgin and Magdalene. Abducted and raped, mother of a child whose father is unknown, Marion's 'holiness' is at first doubted by Aurora just as Mary's purity is doubted by Joseph in Christian legend. Nor is this second heroine merely a Madonna. Browning is at pains to repeat the point that Marion has suffered a symbolic death from which she can never recover. 'I was...murdered', she says; 'I told you that I waked up in the grave'. She recounts throwing away a medallion of the Virgin: 'How heavy it seemed!... A woman has been strangled with less weight'. Recovering from madness she sees a sunset as 'The great red stone upon my sepulchre/ Which angels were too weak to roll away' (276-77). Marion is here a Christ lacking the consolations of resurrection. Her inconsolability in Browning's scheme makes her not less Christlike, but more. In the poem's final trinity of Aurora, Romney and Marion, the slippery Marion is something like a holy ghost.

Veiled in a conventional romance-plot as Browning's conception may be, it represents a radical female usurpation of scriptural

15. Elizabeth Barret Browning, *Aurora Leigh and Other Poems* (intr. Cora Kaplan; London: The Women's Press, 1978), p. 64. Subsequent passages are quoted from this edition.

authority. *Aurora Leigh* feminizes and eroticizes Old Testament prophetic tradition and hints at the divinization of a woman who suffers for society's sins, yet refuses to identify female divinity either with sexual purity or with suffering. Perhaps most interestingly, the poem serves to relocate sacred history in a 'realistic' secular context. One of *Aurora Leigh*'s critics worries that 'Milton's organ is put by Mrs. Browning to play polkas in Mayfair drawing rooms'.[16] In the context of nineteenth-century feminism, with its concern for social reform, that most patriarchal of literary instruments—Milton's organ—could not have been put to better use.

Christina Rossetti's 'Goblin Market', a poem whose surface is some degrees more pious than Browning's, is also perhaps some degrees more subversive. Exploiting the conventions of ballad as *Aurora Leigh* exploits those of blank verse narrative, 'Goblin Market' bites off the whole plot of the Bible: it is a feminized version of temptation, fall and redemption. Instead of Adam and Eve, the poem's allegory gives us two sisters in a pastoral. Instead of a snake, there is a mysterious troop of goblin men haunting a genitalized glen, who appear and disappear into the landscape like animalcules or free-floating phalli, bearing a wicked excess of temptingly exotic fruits. Their refrain, 'Come buy, come buy', shrewdly brings the Christian trope of selling one's soul into juxtaposition with the marriage market and the unspeakable Victorian fact of female sexuality as commodity. When the adventurous sister Laura gorges herself on fruits paid for with a lock of golden hair the goblin men, having had their way with her, appear no more, and she falls into a deathly decline for want of another taste. Virtuous sister Lizzie goes to help and is subjected to a kind of attempted gang rape by the goblins who attack her and smear her with juices while she 'would not open lip from lip/ Lest they should cram a mouthful in'. One does not at first reading think of this as a crucifixion. But at the poem's climax Lizzie offers herself to Laura:

> She cried, 'Laura' up the garden,
> 'Did you miss me?
> Come and kiss me.
> Never mind my bruises,
> Hug me, kiss me, suck my juices
> Squeezed from goblin fruits for you,

16. Henry Chorley, *Atheneum* (22 November 1856), p. 1425. Quoted by Dorothy Mermin, *Elizabeth Barrett Browning: The Origins of a New Poetry* (Chicago: University of Chicago Press, 1989), p. 223.

Goblin pulp and goblin dew.
Eat me, drink me, love me,
Laura, make much of me;
For your sake I have braved the glen
And had to do with goblin merchant men.'[17]

Laura obediently 'kissed and kissed her with a hungry mouth' in a communion feast that portrays a full-scale female and even quasi-lesbian Christ. In the poem's moralizing epilogue, wherein Lizzie and Laura years later instruct 'children of their own' (perhaps produced parthenogenetically, since there is no sign of any male in this poem's idyllic female universe, save the invasive goblins), it is Laura who retells the tale, suggesting, as with the very similar conclusion of 'The Ancient Mariner', that the poetic voice finds its best habitation in the throats of fortunately-fallen and reformed sinners. While 'Goblin Market' shows no symptom of being a protest poem, it appropriates the Christian scheme of good and evil, sin and salvation, with a theological exactness that far exceeds Browning's relatively loose religiosity. Sandra Gilbert and Susan Gubar have argued that 'Victorian women, identifying at their most rebellious with Satan, at their least with rebellious Eve, and almost all the time with the Romantic poets, were...obsessed with the apocalyptic...transformations a revision of Milton might bring about'.[18]

Still more, one might add, a revision of the Bible itself.

III

In her autobiographical meditation 'The Gift', H.D. (the pen name of the modernist poet, Hilda Doolittle) writes: 'There is, beneath the carved superstructure of every temple to God-the-Father, the dark cave or inner hall or cellar to Mary, mere, mut, mutter, pray for us'.[19]

17. Christina Rossetti, *The Poetical Works of Christina Rossetti* (ed. William Michael Rossetti; repr.; London: Macmillan, 1911 [1904]), I, pp. 3-22.

18. Sandra M. Gilbert and Susan Gubar (eds.), *The Madwoman in the Attic: The Woman Writer and the Nineteenth Century Literary Imagination* (New Haven: Yale University Press, 1979), p. 205. Two important nineteenth-century pieces of radical biblical revisionism by American poetesses now forgotten are Maria Brooks, *Zophiel, or the Bride of Seven*, a highly eroticized retelling of the Book of Tobit, complete with comparative-religion footnotes anticipating those of *The Waste Land*; and Elizabeth Oakes Smith, *The Sinless Child*, in which the heroine is both a second Eve and a female Christ figure. See A. Ostriker, *Stealing the Language* (Boston: Beacon Press, 1986), p. 214.

19. H.D., 'The Gift', Beinecke Library, MS chapter 4, p. 10. Quoted in Susan

The sentence exhibits H.D.'s characteristic compression and wit: the image of the fixed, superior, patriarchal structure juxtaposed with an indeterminate inner-or-under feminine space halfway between nature and artifact, the utterance itself gliding seductively from the rationally symbolic to the playfully semiotic. Beneath or within the law of the father, the love of the mother is the spiritual and etymological object of H.D.'s quest in *Trilogy* as well.

The first of her great late poem-cycles, H.D.'s *Trilogy* was written in London during and just after World War II, and takes as its initial condition the bombing of that city. Like T.S. Eliot in *Four Quartets*, H.D. urges a spiritual response to the devastations of personal and political history, though her saving faith is virtually antipodal to Eliot's. For, where Eliot espouses a conservative *via negativa* of self-denial centered on a Christ who is a 'wounded surgeon', she seeks Christ as Lover. And where Eliot's Christianity is indistinguishable from the church, H.D. combines intense spirituality with an insouciant resistance to religious authority. Buttressed by her Moravian heritage and a lifetime steeped in the study of myth, comparative religion and the occult, H.D. insists on the continuity of Egyptian, Greek and Christian divinities. Her Christ will cease to represent 'pain-worship and death-symbol' and be recovered as resurrected avatar of Osiris; her Virgin is one with Aphrodite and Isis; and her Magdalen will be a figure for the poet herself, 'unseemly', 'an unbalanced, neurotic woman' who, in an illustration of the promise that the last shall be first, was 'the first actually to witness His life-after-death'.[20] The three poems of *Trilogy* form an ascendingly feminized and eroticized rewriting of scriptural themes, co-ordinated with an increasingly subversive and playful treatment of scriptural texts and traditions. Each poem is an extended meditation interrupted by a dream-vision of which the poet is herself exegete; each dream reimagines a biblical subject, retrieving it from dogma and cultural fixity, and relocating it within an economy of desire. Their trajectory moves from war and doubt within civilizations and souls, to birth and revelation for both. Dialogic not only with past texts but with a despairing self, with twentieth century materialism and

Friedman, *Penelope's Web: Gender, Modernity, H.D.'s Fiction* (Cambridge: Cambridge University Press, 1990), p. 329.

20. H.D., *Trilogy* (New York: New Directions, 1973), section 12. Further quotations are from this edition; numbers refer to the numbered sections of the poem. The major work on H.D. as a revisionist poet of the sacred remains Susan Stanford Friedman, *Psyche Reborn: The Emergence of H.D.* (Bloomington: Indiana University Press, 1975).

death-worship, with father-figures who alternately support and condescend, the poem from its outset is dialogic as well with the reader. We are directly addressed, made intimate with the poet's struggles, invited to share her visions as she reopens the closed Book, reconceives a story we thought was finished.

'The Walls Do Not Fall' (1942–43) begins with an effort to reconstruct the poet's position as sacred scribe, preserver of spiritual truths through eons of successively destroyed civilizations, despite the murderous and cynical materialism by which she is surrounded:

> Thoth, Hermes, the stylus,
> the palette, the pen, the quill endure,
>
> though our books are a floor
> of smouldering ash under our feet (9).

Like Dickinson, H.D. seizes on the opening of the Fourth Gospel, 'In the beginning/ was the Word' (10), urging the priority of Word over Sword. But in a radical swerve from modernism's usual privileging of language and the consciousness of an intellectual elite, she further asserts the deeper priority of 'their begetter,/Dream/Vision...open to everyone' (11, 20). Dream needs no institutional mediator, no authority; it is the Holy Ghost within the self. Language in the poet's imagery is feminized, uterized, organicized, as shells and pearls; what words contain is more important than what they reveal; they are 'anagrams, cryptograms/ little boxes conditioned/ to hatch butterflies' (39). Torn by self-doubt, H.D. argues that 'my mind (yours),/ your way of thought (mine),/ each has its peculiar intricate map' of 'the eternal realities' (38). Thus H.D.'s redemptive strategy overtly fuses a hermeneutics of desire with a hermeneutics of indeterminacy. At the center of 'The Walls Do Not Fall' the poet's dream of a youthful Osiris–Christ precipitates a series of playful yet serious puns on 'Osiris/ Sirius/ O sire is' which resolve in the 'zrr-hiss' of the bombs still falling and the awareness that

> *we know no rule*
> *of procedure,*
>
> *we are voyagers, discoverers*
> *of the not-known,*
>
> *the unrecorded;*
> *we have no map;*
>
> *possibly we will reach haven,*
>
> *heaven* (43).

The play of textual desire accelerates in 'Tribute to the Angels' (1944). At the same time, the poet in this second sequence begins gently to deploy a hermeneutics of suspicion, which until this point she has suppressed. The suspicion addresses itself to the issue of patriarchal power and its capacity to make cruelty and orthodoxy mutually supportive principles. Quoting John of Patmos, the poet juxtaposes his assertion of authority and dogma with the divinely anti-authoritarian utterance of Christ:

> *I John saw. I testify;*
> *if any man shall add*
>
> *God shall add unto him the plagues,*
> *but he that sat upon the throne* said,
>
> *I make all things new.*
> *I John saw. I testify*
>
> but *I make all things new,*
> said He of the seven stars
>
> he of the seventy-times-seven
>
> passionate, bitter wrongs (3).

Seizing this textual permission, the poet becomes not merely scribe but alchemist. She transforms language, distilling 'a word most bitter, *marah*,/ a word bitterer still, *mar*', in a crucible and flame which represent female and male principles, until the terms for seabrine and bitterness 'are melted, fuse and join/ and change and alter,/ mer, mere, mere, mater, Maia, Mary,// Star of the Sea,/ Mother' (8). Spliced with this narrative, the poet describes seeing a burnt-out apple tree flowering as by miracle in London 1944. In a gesture that restores the authority of interpretation and revelation from author to reader, she confesses her inability to define the resurrection she has witnessed in conventional terms, but reminds us 'You have seen for yourself/ that burnt-out wood crumbling.../ you have seen for yourself' (21). In yet another splicing she alters John's apocalyptic plague-dealing angels into a new set of angelic messengers who balance destruction and war with creation and peace, and whom she honors by giving 'thanks that we rise again from death and live'. In each of the poem's strands, H.D. transforms suffering to rebirth.

At the center of 'Tribute', the poet's ritual invocation of an already revisionist set of angels is interrupted by a dream of the white-clad 'Lady' who is and is not a compound of pagan and Christian goddesses, is and is not her iconography. A nameless companion in dialogue with the poet attempts to label the vision, but the poet half-mockingly begs to differ:

> ...she wasn't hieratic, she wasn't frozen,
> she wasn't very tall;
>
> she is the Vestal
> from the days of Numa,
>
> she carries over the cult
> of the *Bona Dea*,
>
> she carries a book but it is not
> the tome of the ancient wisdom,
>
> the pages, I imagine, are the blank pages
> of the unwritten volume of the new...
>
> but she is not shut up in a cave
> like a Sibyl; she is not
>
> imprisoned in leaden bars
> in a coloured window;
>
> she is Psyche, the butterfly,
> out of the cocoon (38).

The poet pointedly observes that the Lady 'as I saw her' had none of her usual attributes: 'The Lamb was not with her,/ either as Bridegroom or Child'. Instead, 'We are her bridegroom and lamb/ her book is our book' (39). Re-empowering the female as psyche, the soul, the poet locates her as well in the world of natural rebirth: for the Lady is also the flowering tree. It is important throughout this sequence to be aware not only of the radically feminist quality of the poet's vision, but of its insistent avoidance of an authoritarian stance. What the poet sees is real, and she refuses to have an interpretation imposed upon her, but by the same token she will not impose upon others. What 'I imagine' is vividly poetic, with a ripple of levity beneath it, but with none of the hieratic and didactic solemnities of Eliot's poem.

In 'The Flowering of the Rod' (December 1944) H.D. writes in a spirit of joy and confidence her own Gnostic Gospel, re-telling the story of the woman of Bethany who anoints Christ with precious ointment. Not coincidentally, she has chosen a tale that varies slightly in each Gospel. In H.D.'s version, the woman is the Magdalen; she obtains her ointment from the Magus Kaspar, rigorously trained in a centuries-old hermetic tradition, who surrenders to her both his mystic myrrh and his worldly misogyny. The poet tenderly parodies and reproduces on her own terms the discourses of esoteric learning. 'What she did, everyone knows,/ but it is not on record/ exactly where and how she found the alabaster jar', she explains (12). 'Some said this distillation...lasted literally forever' (14).

> Some say he was masquerading,
> some say it never happened,
> some say it happens over and over...
> some say he was an old lover
> some say he was Abraham
> some say he was God (20).

Through the 'unseemly' Magdalen, whom he initially attempts to dismiss, the representative of patriarchal wisdom experiences a vision of the ancient goddesses and of the 'scope and plan' of paradise. H.D. mocks as well the prudery of the conventionally pious, in the figure of the shocked Simon who expresses his irritation at the erotic scene of the uninvited woman at his party 'actually kissing the feet' of his guest.

Yet more startling is the play of indeterminacy around the jar of myrrh which the Magdalen both obtains and is, and which becomes the poem's final focus:

> I am Mary, she said, of Magdala,
> I am Mary, a great tower;
>
> through my will and my power,
> Mary shall be myrrh;
>
> I am Mary—O there are Marys a-plenty,
> (though I am Mara, bitter) I shall be Mary-myrrh (16).

Myrrh was for H.D. a figure for poetry, and by the time she writes *Trilogy*, its significance is cross-culturally implicate with love, death, resurrection. 'A bundle of myrrh is my well-beloved unto me' in the Song of Songs; 'he shall lie all night between my breasts' (1.13). Myrrh in Egypt was used to embalm the dead in preparation for the afterlife. The Greek Myrrha was the mother of Dionysius. According to certain occult traditions, the Tree of Life was a myrrh tree. Then in the poem's final words, at the Nativity, when the Virgin speaks in response to Kaspar's gift, their encounter adds a final meaning:

> she said, Sir, it is a most beautiful fragrance
> as of all flowering things together;
>
> but Kaspar knew the seal of the jar was unbroken,
> he did not know whether she knew

the fragrance came from the bundle of myrrh
she held in her arms (43).

The repetition of the pun Mary-myrrh joins Magdalen, Virgin, the child in the virgin's arms, and the poem we are completing. Thus H.D. in 'Flowering' implies an ultimate fusion of the virgin–whore with the Christ and with poetry itself. It is an ending curiously similar to the ending of Dickinson's 'A Word made flesh'. In another sense, however, it is no ending at all, but a beginning, a nativity, in which we feel not the satisfactions of achieved closure, but the alternative pleasure of mystery. It is appropriate that *Trilogy* closes with a statement about something that is not known. For H.D. wishes to privilege experience above knowledge. At no point does she offer her readings as 'authoritative' or herself as a scriptural 'authority'. Rather, she does what the woman poet must do when confronted with centuries of exegesis: bypassing authority, implying that what 'some say' can never equal sacred truth, she offers the divinely playful alternative of poetry.

IV

Among the major Anglo-American women poets of the twentieth century, H.D. is the most profoundly religious, the most seriously engaged in spiritual quest, and the most determined to rescue poetry from secularism.[21] By the same token, she is also the most radically transgressive in her interpretation of the Gospels. For her explicit goal is to recover, in a moment of apocalyptic revelation, as the blasting open of cities in war becomes the blasting open of intellectual and spiritual paradigms, at the heart of the worship of the Father and Son, an older worship of the Mother.

To a woman writing in the last decade of the twentieth century, it is an open question whether the work of H.D. will become part of a larger movement to resurrect the goddess whose presence was denied and whose worship was forbidden at the advent of patriarchal monotheism. H.D. has influenced numerous poets concerned with matters intellectual and spiritual, including Robert Duncan, Denise Levertov, Adrienne Rich and Judy Grahn, and may ultimately be

21. For a discussion of her deliberate undertaking of these projects, as well as her autobiographical account of visionary experiences at Corfu, see H.D., *Tribute to Freud* (New York: New Directions, 1956). H.D. makes clear in this volume her quarrel with secular rationalism. The figure of the Magus Kaspar in 'Flowering' is based on Freud, with whom H.D. undertook analysis in 1933–34.

credited with serving as a midwife for the return of the goddess to women's imaginations.

Meanwhile, however, it will be useful to summarize what is most characteristic in the revisionist biblical poetry women have been writing in the postwar period, and especially since the sixties. To begin with, it is important to indicate that such work exists in bulk, including not simply countless individual poems, but book-length collections.[22] Secondly, as one would expect from the synchronicity of second-wave feminism and this period in women's writing, much of it involves an outpouring of explicit anger, including indictments of God the Father that go far beyond the subtle critiques of earlier poets. Poems from the point of view of the insulted and injured, the abused and abandoned women in the Bible have multiplied: Eve, Sarah, Lot's wife and daughters, Dinah, Miriam, Zipporah, Jephthah's daughter, the Levite's concubine, Tamar the daughter of David who was raped by Amnon, and so on. There are as well some icy poems from the point of view of Jael and Judith. 'How cruel is the story of Eve', as Stevie Smith says:

> What responsibility
> It has in history
> For cruelty.

Maurya Simon's dialogue between Adam and Eve begins

EVE	ADAM
She said	He said
couldn't we	why can't you
just one more time	for once
dance like the crabs	be a lady wear
at midnight	flowers of silk
on the western shores	cover yourself

and proceeds to delineate a relationship in which female sensuousness triggers male disgust and blame: 'why can't you/ remember/ remember your crime?' asks Adam. Sylvia Plath overhears the Father and the Son, jealous of nature and women's rotundity, deciding to 'flatten and launder the grossness from these souls'. Her Virgin Mary, recognizing the three wise men as enemies, is terrified by 'the ethereal blankness of their face-ovals'. Her 'Lady Lazarus' sneers at the exploitive savior she calls 'Herr God, Herr Lucifer', who represents the source and rationale for all male condescension, authority,

---

22. An excellent anthology is Marilyn Sewall (ed.), *Cries of the Spirit: A Celebration of Women's Spirituality* (Boston: Beacon Press, 1991).

righteousness and control. Ann Sexton in her mordant retelling of the Gospels, 'The Jesus Papers', depicts the Son as half a performing artist, half an Oedipal cripple obsessed by a loathing for sexuality. She describes the Angel of the Annunciation looking at Mary 'with executioner's eyes', and her God explains how when the Christ is born 'we all must eat beautiful women'. Marge Piercy describes 'the God of the Puritans playing war games on computers'. Celia Gilbert parallels the destruction of Sodom with that of Hiroshima, in a poem that chillingly condemns God the Father through the mouth of Lot's wife as a 'behemoth in love with death'. Eleanor Wilner's Sarah, in the title poem of *Sarah's Choice*, instructs Isaac not to go with Abraham; her Miriam—as horrified at the murder of first-born Egyptians as at that of first-born Hebrews—must leave 'one ruler/ for another, one Egypt for the next'.[23] Like Dickinson, women writers today commonly recognize the God of patriarchy as an enemy, but the bitterness of their writing belongs specifically to a century that has learned the horror of world war and totalitarianism, and to a feminist analysis which can claim, with Mary Daly, that the religion of patriarchy is a projection of masculine ego, masculine will to power, masculine death-worship.

A second recent development in women's biblical revisionism is a cascade of comedy, shameless sexuality, an insistence on sensual immediacy and the details belonging to the flesh as holy, an insistence that the flesh is not incompatible with the intellect. In Diana George's 'The Fall', the poet lets us know that the fruit in question 'was no apple, people', but the banana, 'sidekick and brother/ of the snake', and that Adam and Eve 'fell into metaphor'. Linda Pastan's Eve deftly suggests that the story of the rib makes her exemplary of what is 'chosen/ To grow into something quite differ-ent', thus appropriating the idea of the covenant and of historical process as female. Naming becomes a female act in many women's poems; or, as in Ursula LeGuin's counter-parable 'She Un-Names Them', women reject the categories that obscure animal reality. Exile becomes not a punishment but an escape from a paradise and an

23. Stevie Smith, *Collected Poems* (New York: Oxford University Press, 1976), p. 481; Maurya Simon, 'Adam Eve', *Grove Magazine* 1.6 (Spring 1982), p. 44; Anne Sexton, *Complete Poems* (Boston: Houghton Mifflin, 1981), pp. 344-45; Sylvia Plath, *Collected Poems* (ed. Ted Hughes; New York: Harper & Row, 1981), pp. 129-30, 148, 246; Marge Piercy, 'The Emperor', in *Circles on the Water: Selected Poems* (New York: Knopf, 1982), pp. 99-101; Celia Gilbert, 'Lot's Wife', in *Bonfire* (Boston: Alice James Press, 1983), pp. 65-71; Eleanor Wilner, *Sarah's Choice* (Chicago: University of Chicago Press, 1989), pp. 21-24, 8.

Adam whom women poets with startling frequency describe as 'boring'. The embrace of adventure as well as knowledge governs many women's poems. Thus, Kathleen Norris invokes Eve as 'Mother of fictions/ and of irony... Mother of science/ and the critical method... Come with us, Muse of exile,/ Mother of the road'. Leda Whitman's Eve 'laughed at his tree, his keep out/ sign and electrical fence'. Enid Dame's raunchy and philosophical Lilith, in *Lilith and her Demons*, 'stormed out of Eden/ into history', where 'the names they call me/ haven't changed/ in 4,000 years'. Madeline Tiger's Magdalene, in her *Mary of Migdal* sequence, sexually abused, abused by Donatello's image of her, posessed by demons ('He tells my story, revealing my scars/ It is he, in my mouth, calling me whore'), neglected by history, maintains 'the true Eucharist' of her erotic connection with God. Anne Sexton, often criticized as merely neurotic, was in fact a religious poet of extraordinary power and range, anguish and exaltation. Sexton's psalm sequence, 'O Ye Tongues', is fiercely spiritual as well as sensual; and her last book, *The Awful Rowing Toward God*, deserves to stand among the major works of spiritual longing in our language.

Maternity as well as sexuality is redefined in women's revisionist work. Repossessing the maternal language appropriated by the gospels, it is a nursing mother who, in Robin Morgan's 'Network of the Imaginary Mother', says to her infant son, and by implication all infants suffering from hunger and poverty:

> Take. Eat. This is my body,
> this real milk, thin, sweet, bluish,
> which I give for the life of the world.

To insert the female self into Scripture, into history, would mean a transvaluation of values, as Miriam Kessler suggests:

> Where at that Last Supper was a woman?
> Someone to pour the wine,
> a cautionary voice that might have said
> *Take it easy, boys.*
> *This kind of thing could get a fellow killed.*
> A *Seder* without women, kids?
> I'd edit the entire script.[24]

24. Diana George, 'The Fall', in *The Evolution of Love* (Grenada, MS: Salt-Works Press, 1977), p. 2; Linda Pastan, 'Aspects of Eve', in *Aspects of Eve* (New York: Norton, 1975); Ursula LeGuin, 'She Un-Names Them', in *Buffalo Gals and Other Animal Presences* (Santa Barbara: Capra Press, 1987); Kathleen Norris, 'A Prayer to Eve', *Paris Review* 115 (Summer 1990); Leda Whitman, 'Overheard in the Garden

The motifs and motivations of women's contemporary hermeneutics of desire include the return of immanence and nature, the reconnection of body to spirit, the rejection of dogma and the embrace of syncretism, and an insistence on the unmediated personal experience of the divine. Among living poets, the finest representative of all these impulses is the African-American, Lucille Clifton. In one of her earliest published poems, Clifton defines an outrageously female holiness, deploying a tone that fuses celebration, defiance, and humorous sympathy for 'the man' whose gods deprive him of grace:

if i stand in the window
naked in my own house
and press my breasts
against my windowpane
like black birds pushing against glass

and if the man come to stop me
in my own house
naked in my own window
saying i have offended him
i have offended his

gods

let him watch my black body
push against my own glass
let him discover self
let him run naked through the streets
crying
praying in tongues.[25]

To reveal oneself enables the other to 'discover self', perhaps to suffer, perhaps to be delivered. If 'all flesh is kin and kin', as Clifton later writes, her black body might well serve as Pentecostal miracle to an antagonistic white man. Clifton has written a sequence of poems to the black Hindu Goddess, Kali, in which an assertion of terrifying, dark female power is initially resisted, ultimately accepted. One may

and Elsewhere' (unpublished MS); Enid Dame, 'Lilith', 'Lilith Talks About Men', in *Lilith and Her Demons* (Merrick, NY: Cross-Cultural Communications, 1986) pp. 4, 10; Madeline Tiger, *Mary of Migdal* (Galloway, NJ: Still Waters Press, 1991); A. Sexton, *The Awful Rowing Toward God* (London: Chatto and Windus, 1992). Robin Morgan, 'Network of the Imaginary Mother', in *Lady of the Beasts* (New York: Random House, 1976), pp. 63-88; Miriam Kessler, 'Last Supper', in *Someone to Pour the Wine* (Shippensburg, PA: Ragged Edge Press, 1996), p. 47.

25. Lucille Clifton, *Good Woman: Poems and a Memoir 1969–1980* (Brockport, NY: Boa Editions, 1987), p. 25. Subsequent poems are quoted from this edition, except where noted.

hear Kali behind a sequence of miniature lyrics entitled 'some Jesus', in which Clifton's voice as a black woman blends with the major figures of both testaments, male and female. In 'good friday',

> i rise up above my self
> like a fish flying
>
> men will be gods
> if they want it (104).

In 'to a dark moses',

> you are the one
> i am lit for.
> come with your rod
> that twists
> and is a serpent.
> i am the bush
> i am burning
> i am not consumed (127).

In 'the making of poems',

> the reason why i do it
> though i fail and fail
> in the giving of true names
> is i am adam and his mother
> and these failures are my job (186).

In another sequence, Clifton tells the story of the Mother of God as a tale of anticipated suffering: 'at a certain time when she see something/ it will break her eye' ('the astrologer predicts at mary's birth', 196). Suffering becomes an almost terrifying bliss in 'holy night',

> joseph, i afraid of stars,
> their brilliant seeing
>
> joseph, is wind burning from east
> joseph, i shine, oh joseph, oh
> illuminated night (200).

Ecstasy becomes normalcy, and, at last, Mary in old age wondering 'could i have fought these thing...could i have walk away?' (202), and the poet speaking for a chorale of women praying for their sister woman 'split by sanctified seed' (203). Like the spirituality of H.D., that of Lucille Clifton is intensified rather than dissipated by its independence of dogma, its sycretism, and its ability to represent women as central to sacred drama. In a later book, *Next: New Poems*, 'at creation',

...i and my body rise
with the dusky beasts
with eve and her brother
to gasp in
the unsubstantial air
and evenly begin the long
slide out of paradise.
all life is life.
all clay is kin and kin.[26]

Finally, in a poem called 'my dream about God':

He is wearing my grandfather's hat
He is taller than my last uncle...
when i whisper He strains to hear me and
He does whatever i say.

It is a common dream, sprung from an old promise. For the Moses of Exodus exclaims 'Would God that all the Lord's people were prophets' (Num. 11.29). If the Bible is a flaming sword forbidding our entrance to the garden, it is also a burning bush urging us toward freedom. It is what we wrestle with all night and from which we may, if we demand it, wrest a blessing.

26. Lucille Clifton, *Next: New Poems* (Brockport, NY: Boa Editions, 1987), p. 22. The following poem is quoted from this volume as well.

OVERCOMING THE TEACHING OF CONTEMPT*

Katharina von Kellenbach

During the past decade feminist Christian and post-Christian theologians have been alerted to the fact that some portrayals of Judaism as patriarchal reinstate traditional anti-Jewish patterns of arguments.[1] This essay will briefly summarize how feminists have

---

* This article is based on my book, *Anti-Judaism in Feminist Religious Writings* (Atlanta: Scholars Press, 1994). I want to thank my colleagues at St Mary's College of Maryland for their careful reading and supportive questioning in preparing this summary essay.

1. J. Plaskow, 'Blaming Jews for Inventing Patriarchy', and A. Daum, 'Blaming the Jews for the Death of the Goddess', in Evelyn Torton Beck (ed.), *Nice Jewish Girls* (Trumansburg: Crossing Press, 1982), pp. 255-65; J. Plaskow, 'Anti-Semitism: The Unacknowledged Racism', in J. Kalven and M. Buckley (eds.), *Womanspirit Bonding* (New York: Pilgrim Press, 1984), pp. 89-95; J. Plaskow, 'Feminist Anti-Judaism and the Christian God', *Journal of Feminist Studies* 7.2 (1991), pp. 99-109; B. Brooten, 'Jüdinnen zur Zeit Jesu', in B. Brooten and N. Greinacher (eds.), *Frauen in der Männerkirche* (Münich: Chr. Kaiser Verlag, 1982), pp. 141-49; B. Brooten, 'Early Christian Women and Their Cultural Context: Issues of Method in Historical Reconstruction', in A. Yarbro Collins (ed.), *Feminist Perspectives on Biblical Scholarship* (Chico, CA: Scholars Press, 1985), pp. 63-93; A. Daum and D. McCauley, 'Jewish-Christian Feminist Dialogue: A Wholistic Vision', *USQR* 38.2 (1983), pp. 147-89; S.Heschel, 'Altes Gift in neuen Schläuchen: Anti-Judaismus und Antipharisäismus in der christlich-feministischen Theologie', in Frauenforschungsprojekt zur Geschichte der Theologinnen Göttingen (ed.), *Querdenken: Beiträge zur feministisch-befreiungs theologischen Diskussion* (Pfaffenweiler: Centaurus Verlagsgesellschaft, 1992), pp. 65-77; J. Plaskow, 'Anti-Judaism in Feminist Christian interpretation', in E. Schüssler Fiorenza (ed.), *Searching the Scriptures. I. A Feminist Introduction* (New York: Crossroad, 1993), pp. 117-30. Three collections on feminist theological anti-Judaism have appeared in German: C. Kohn Ley and I. Korotin (eds.), *Der Feministische 'Sündenfall': Antisemitische Vorurteile in der Frauenbewegung* (Wien: Picus Verlag, 1994); L. Siegele-Wenschkewitz (ed.), *Verdrängte Vergangenheit, die uns bedrängt* (Munich: Chr. Kaiser Verlag, 1988). C. Schaumberger (ed.), *Weil wir nicht vergessen wollen...zu einer Theologie im deutschen Kontext* (Münster: Morgana Verlag, 1988).

transformed the 'teaching of contempt'[2] and examine the attitudes and arguments that perpetuate the continuation of anti-Judaism. In conclusion I suggest the development of a teaching of respect that actively confronts and neutralizes anti-Jewish conventions in feminist writings.

The teaching of contempt has its roots in Christian theology and refers to a systematically distorted portrayal of Judaism that is designed to discredit, defame and disinherit the older faith. The teaching of contempt presents Judaism as *antithesis* by portraying Jewish ideas and practices as the negative foil of Christianity. It *scapegoats* Jews and Judaism by casting them as powerful conspiratorial enemies and Christ-killers, and it disguises the continuing viability of Judaism by presenting it as a defunct predecessor and *prologue* to Christianity. Theological anti-Judaism was developed during the first four centuries of the Christian era,[3] and has shaped Western culture from art to music, philosophy and literature. It has been secularized in the nineteenth century into political and racist anti-Semitism. Because we are heirs to both theological anti-Judaism and racial anti-Semitism, and because the resulting Jew-hatred remains the same, I use anti-Judaism and anti-Semitism interchangeably.

Feminist authors have added a new reason for Jew-hating: Jews invented patriarchal religion, 'killed' the Goddess and instituted patriarchal laws and customs that shaped subsequent patriarchal cultures. In *Anti-Judaism in Feminist Religious Writings* I identify numerous descriptions of Judaism in Christian and post-Christian, pagan, German, US American, feminist and womanist publications that reinstate perceptions of Judaism as an inferior Other (antithesis), evil (scapegoat) or superseded (prologue). Mostly, these anti-Jewish arguments are not central to the feminist theological agenda. They are usually subtle, incidental and marginal, and only become conspicuous when taken out of their original context and analyzed separately. Their anti-Jewish implication is often unintended by the individual author. However, the resulting message remains the same: Judaism is irredeemably patriarchal and sexist, the antithesis of feminist politics and spirituality.

2.   J. Isaac, *The Teaching of Contempt* (trans. Helen Heaver; New York: Holt, Rinehart & Winston, 1964).

3.   D.P. Efroymson, 'The Patristic Connection', in A. Davies (ed.), *Anti-Semitism and the Foundations of Christianity* (New York: Paulist Press, 1979), pp. 98-118; J. Gager, *The Origins of Anti-Semitism: Attitudes Towards Judaism in Pagan and Christian Antiquity* (New York: Oxford University Press, 1985); R. Radford Ruether, *Faith and Fratricide* (New York: Seabury Press, 1974).

Judaism as Antithesis

Of the many antithetical constructions, I want to focus on portrayals of the biblical God that depict Yahweh as the enemy of feminist values. Several feminist theologians highlight Yahweh's role as patriarchal lawgiver, as opposed to the feminist ideal of relationality and mutuality.[4] Others emphasize the bodiless, otherworldly nature of biblical monotheism as conflicting with feminist calls for greater affirmation of nature and the body.[5] Biblical monotheism is also characterized as male monotheism; and rejected because a feminist spirituality must include female imagery for the divine.[6] In each case, selective and reductionist interpretations of the Hebrew Bible make Jewish monotheism the negative foil of feminist spirituality. The cumulative effect of these accounts renders Judaism inferior to Christianity and paganism, because only the latter seem to contain the seeds for feminist theological revisions. The argument that frames Yahweh as a warrior God is a case in point. In discussing this specific example I will quote individual scholars but, as mentioned earlier, my concern is with the general pattern, not the particular authors.

Some feminists reject the Hebrew God as a male militaristic warrior God and, instead, draw on Near Eastern goddesses whose gender seems to preclude military involvement and whose anger is understood as empowering.[7] In *Womanguides*, Rosemary Radford Ruether presents the Mesopotamian prayer to the goddess Ishtar under the heading: 'Ishtar, Shepherdess of the People'.[8] This prayer

4.   For this argument see P. Wilson-Kastner, *Faith, Feminism and the Christ* (Philadelphia: Fortress Press, 1983); E. Moltmann-Wendel, *Land, wo Milch und Honig fließt* (Gütersloh: Gütersloher Verlagshaus, 1985; ET: *A Land Flowing with Milk and Honey* (trans. J. Bowden; New York: Crossroad, 1986); E. Sorge, *Religion und Frau*, (Stuttgart: Kohlhammer Verlag, 1985).

5.   For this argument see R. Radford Ruether, 'Motherearth and the Megamachine', in C. Christ and J. Plaskow (eds.), *Womanspirit Rising* (San Francisco: Harper & Row, 1979), pp. 43-53; S. Collins, *A Different Heaven and Earth* (Valley Forge, PA: Judson Press, 1974); C. Ochs, *Behind the Sex of God* (Boston: Beacon Press, 1977); J. Ochshorn, 'Ishtar and Her Cult', in C. Olson (ed.), *The Book of the Goddess* (New York: Crossroad Publishing Company, 1985), pp. 16-29.

6.   Kellenbach, *Anti-Judaism in Feminist Religious Writings*, pp. 5-105.

7.   For this argument see C. Christ, *Laughter of Aphrodite* (San Francisco: Harper & Row, 1987); C. Mulack, *Die Weiblichkeit Gottes* (Stuttgart: Kreuz Verlag, 1983); R. Radford Ruether, *Womanguides* (Boston: Beacon Press, 1985); G. Weiler, *Ich verwerfe im Lände die Kriege* (Munich: Frauenoffensive, 1984).

8.   Ruether, *Womanguides*, p. 10.

invokes the goddess as 'star of lamentation, who causes peaceable brothers to fight', 'strong one in battle', and 'firebrand' which 'brings about the destruction of the furious'. Similarly, the 'Song of Anat' is titled 'Anat, Savior of Baal, Restores the World', and opens with an enumeration of her heroic deeds and the many enemies whom she previously 'crushed, destroyed, muzzled, cut off, fought, drove out, chased away'.[9] In her commentary Ruether notes that 'we feel immediately the enormous power and authority of Anat. She commands the center of stage with her swift, decisive actions on behalf of Baal and in confrontation with any power'.[10] Ruether's choice of words shifts the focus away from Anat's violence. By calling the goddesses' violence 'power', 'authority' and describing it as 'decisive', Ruether turns their angry actions into virtues that women are trying to emulate.

In contrast, Ruether's passage from the Hebrew Bible, entitled 'the Male Warrior God of Israel and His Son, the Anointed One (Messiah), the King of Israel', emphasizes the soldier-like qualities of Yahweh. While Ruether reinterprets Anat's violence as empowering for women, she finds no redeeming qualities in Zechariah's messianism. In introducing her selection from Zechariah she points out that the text shows 'some of the dreams of power and vengeance of Israelite messianism',[11] and that it illustrates the notion of the messiah as one who will come to restore the kingdom and establish Israel 'as the overlord of the world (the Middle East)'.[12] While military actions of the 'shepherdess' Ishtar or the female 'savior' Anat are portrayed as incidental to their role, the anger of the 'male warrior god of Israel' appears to be essential to the biblical vision. Hebrew monotheism becomes the paradigm for patriarchal militarism, and is repudiated as antithetical to feminism.

Judaism as Scapegoat

Traditional Christian anti-Judaism has portrayed Israel's history as a succession of crimes and failures that climaxes in the rejection and murder of God's only son. The Jews become paradigmatic sinners and enemies of God whose history, faith and practice are presented as examples of depravity, obstinacy and infidelity. By attacking the

9. Ruether, *Womanguides*, pp. 113-14.
10. Ruether, *Womanguides*, p. 106.
11. Ruether, *Womanguides*, p. 107.
12. Ruether, *Womanguides*, p. 107.

Jewish people as evil, savage persecutors of the prophets and Christ-killers, the teaching of contempt legitimizes the replacement of Israel as the covenantal community by the gentile church. Feminist theologians perpetuate this anti-Jewish reconstruction of Jewish history by depicting the proponents of monotheism as oppressive invading forces that persecuted and destroyed peaceful 'matriarchal' communities.[13] The Jewish feminist Annette Daum was among the first to denounce the argument that Hebrew monotheism annihilated woman-affirming goddess religions. She warned that this thesis resurrected the old Christian charge of deicide.[14] Since then, numerous Jewish and non-Jewish feminists have pointed to the parallels between traditional portrayals of Jews as Christ-killers and feminist (as well as non-feminist)[15] religio-historical narratives of the downfall of goddess religions and 'matriarchal' cultures. Historically, the notion that Jewish monotheism is uniquely responsible for the creation of patriarchy is untenable because patriarchy was established equally successfully in polytheistic cultures.[16] Theologically, the accusatory focus on Hebrew monotheism is objectionable because it confirms gentile prejudices about Judaism as a hostile and destructive force in the world.

As the alleged originators of patriarchy, Jews are seen as uniquely responsible for various social ills. Based on the paradigm of fall and redemption, which projects the blame for humanity's current sinful condition onto the original sin committed by the first couple, the origin of patriarchy is of crucial importance. Most current social evils, such as militarism, intolerance, sex, class and racial oppression, are

13. For this argument see Weiler, *Kriege*, p. 81; C. Spretnak, *Lost Goddesses of Early Greece* (Berkeley: Moon Books, 1978), p. 29; M. Stone, *When God was a Woman* (New York: Harcourt Brace Jovanovich, 1978), pp. 68-128; L. Swidler, *Biblical Affirmations of Woman* (Philadelphia, Fortress Press, 1979), p. 23.

14. A. Daum, 'Blaming the Jews'; J. Goldstein, 'Antisemitism, Sexism and the Death of the Goddess', in M. Curtis (ed.), *Antisemitism in the Contemporary World* (Boulder: Westview Press, 1986), pp. 251-57; M.T. Wacker and B. Wacker, 'Matriarchale Bibelkritik: ein antijudaistisches Konzept?', in Siegele-Wenschkewitz (ed.), *Verdrängte Vergangenheit, die uns bedrängt*, pp. 181-243; M. T. Wacker, 'Die Göttin kehrt zurück: Kritische Sichtung neuerer Entwürfe', in M.T. Wacker (ed.), *Der Gott der Männer und die Frauen* (Düsseldorf: Patmos, 1987), pp. 11-38.

15. For this argument see R. Graves, *The White Goddess* (New York: Octagon Books, 1978), p. 475; Ilse Korotin, 'Die mythische Wirklichkeit eines Volkes: J.J. Bachofen, das Mutterrecht und der Nationalsozialismus', in Kohn-Ley and Korotin (eds.), *Der feministische 'Sündenfall '*, pp. 84-131.

16. T.S. Frymer-Kensky, *In the Wake of the Goddesses: Women, Culture, and the Biblical Transformation of Pagan Myth* (New York: Free Press, 1992).

said to have arisen out of the advent of patriarchy and to have defined human beings (specifically males) ever since. The origin of evil seems to coincide with the origin of patriarchal religion. Carol Christ, for instance, maintains that a

> passage in Amos contains an example of the pervasive prophetic intolerance toward other religions that *has produced, among other horrors,* a climate in which witches could be put to death in Europe, in which the genocide of Native Americans could be attempted by Europeans, and in which genocide of Jews could be attempted by the Nazis[17]

Following her logic, the biblical prophets must be blamed for having created the climate of violence which ultimately led to the Holocaust. Although Carol Christ would deny any such imputation, the impression that the Jews are somehow responsible for the Holocaust is irresistible. As the alleged origin of patriarchy, the Hebrew Bible assumes the burden of responsibility for patriarchal evil. Since the prophets produced the ideological framework for violence and intolerance, subsequent perpetrators are exonerated as mere products of patriarchy.

This is spelled out explicitly by German feminist Christa Mulack, who, in an often quoted passage, maintains that patriarchal religion 'becomes necessarily authoritarian' and that 'the last consequence of this process...presents itself in the Nazi system, which trained "German sons" to harass and kill Jewish mothers, children and fathers'.[18] In describing Germans as children trained by a system, she absolves Germans and shifts responsibility for the Holocaust towards the inventors of 'the system', namely, the Jews. Again, Jewish religion becomes the scapegoat for modern horrors.[19]

Judaism as Prologue

The teaching of contempt disguises the continuing existence of Judaism as a separate and equally valid religion by reducing it to the prologue of Christianity. Traditional anti-Judaism conceals Judaism

17. Christ, *Laughter*, p. 78 (emphasis added).

18. Mulack, *Weiblichkeit*, p. 248. For a critique of Mulack see Susanne Heschel, 'Konfigurationen des Patriarchats, des Judentums und des Nazismus in deutschen feministischen denken', in Kohn-Ley and Korotin (eds.), *Der feministische 'Sündenfall'*, pp. 168-70.

19. For similar argumentation, see Weiler, *Kriege*, pp. 84-85; Sorge, *Religion und Frau*, p. 42; Mulack, *Weiblichkeit*, pp. 310, 159. For a critique of these theologians, see Anita Natmessnig, 'Antisemitismus und feministische Theologie', in Korotin and Kohn-Ley (eds.), *Der feministische 'Sündenfall'*, pp. 185-209.

as a competing religious tradition, based on some of the same sacred texts and challenges that triumphalist Christian truth claims. Christian theologians have actively ignored Judaism by referring to it as 'late Judaism' (when contemporaneous with the early church) or to the 'Judeo-Christian tradition' (which reduces Judaism to the Old Testament), and have presupposed that Judaism became obsolete and ceased to exist with the onset of Christianity. Feminist theologians exhibit a similar tendency to subsume Judaism in their critique of 'patriarchal religion' without drawing attention to Jewish religion, history and culture as a distinct and independent actuality.

Sometimes Jewish concepts are expropriated and assimilated into feminist thought without discussion of their *Sitz im Leben* in a distinctly Jewish interpretive practice. Christian feminists sometimes embrace feminine Hebrew concepts, such as God's wisdom (*ḥokmâ*) and God's spirit (*rûaḥ*), as possible starting points for inclusive God-imagery without properly appreciating their Hebrew–Jewish origins. For instance, V. Mollenkott incorporates the concept of God's *šᵉkîāh* as God's immanent and relational presence into her interpretation of the New Testament. She traces the concept of the *šᵉkîāh* through the Hebrew Bible and concludes:

> The Shekinah glory of God, that 'feminine' Presence, dwelt in the temple of Jerusalem; but John 1:14 together with John 2:21 asserts that the body of Christ has now become the temple and is the perfect dwelling place of the Shekinah glory… In other words, in the presence of Christ the Shekinah within the worshiping congregation is expected to expose the absurdity of all classist, racist, or sexist prejudices.[20]

This appropriation fails to respect the *šᵉkîāh* concept as a distinctly Jewish notion of God, and reasserts traditional replacement theology by dispossessing a Jewish concept for Christian purposes. It renders Judaism the prologue of Christianity whose theological integrity and distinctiveness need not be honored.

The silencing of Jewish voices also occurs when a universal feminist vision of egalitarian sisterhood is used to deny and suppress the particularities and differences among women. Jewish women are often overlooked even when differences of race, class and culture are asserted. Since Jews are neither fully white nor of color, neither exclusively a religious nor a separate national commmunity, neither rich nor poor, their ambiguous situation defies easy political categorization and is easily subsumed and neglected. The appropriation of Jewish concepts and the silencing of Jewish feminism leads to the

20. V. Mollenkott, *The Divine Feminine* (New York: Crossroad, 1983), p. 40.

denial of Judaism as a separate and important religious and cultural voice.

Obstacles on the Way to Respect

The first step towards combating anti-Semitism is education, since the teaching of contempt is often repeated by people who are not personally prejudiced and who do not intend to disparage Judaism. Knowledge of the history, form and function of anti-Judaism enables the scholar who unconsciously participates in this cultural and religious convention to extricate herself from it. However, despite a vague awareness and general goodwill, few theologians and exegetes are willing to institute radical changes. Often, theological responses to anti-Judaism remain on the surface and involve linguistic and cosmetic adjustments only, because the importance of anti-Judaism is underestimated. There are four dismissive attitudes that prevent a thorough analysis of anti-Judaism: trivialization, particularization, spiritualization and universalization.[21]

Anti-Judaism is *trivialized* when it is treated as a less than urgent concern in comparison to seemingly larger problems such as sexism, racism, poverty, war or the environment. Jews, one is told, are white, affluent, powerful and in no imminent danger. Hence, anti-Semitism is not a serious topic. Mary Daly, for instance, dismisses the study of the Holocaust in favor of an examination of sexism as the more ultimate context of oppression. The 'roots of the evil of genocide', according to her, are not found 'in the kind of research which shrinks/localizes perspectives on oppression so that they can be contained strictly within ethnic and "religious group" dimensions'.[22] The Holocaust as the singular culmination of centuries of violence against Jews and unique incident of industrialized mass murder is trivialized in comparison to 'the sado-rituals of patriarchy [which] are perpetually perpetrated'.[23] Having belittled the Holocaust to 'trite, everyday banalized gynocide', Daly then denounces the investigation of anti-Semitism as a reactionary and unfeminist undertaking that detracts from a serious analysis of patriarchy.[24]

21. These four categories were first developed by M. Daly, who used them to describe the denial of sexism in *Gyn/Ecology* (Boston: Beacon Press, 1978).

22. Daly, *Gyn/Ecology*, p. 311-12.

23. Daly, *Gyn/Ecology*, p. 311-12.

24. For an extensive critique see E. Bulkien, 'Hard Ground: Jewish Identity, Racism and Anti-Semitism', in E. Bulkien, M.B. Pratt and B. Smith (eds.), *Yours in Struggle* (New York: Long Haul Press, 1984), pp. 126-29.

The teaching of contempt is *particularized* when it is reduced to being somebody else's problem. This argument holds that anti-Semitism is a problem for Germans, or right-wing conservatives, or the Black community, but not for society in general, nor for politically aware feminists. However, the teaching of contempt has infiltrated all movements in Christian theology, as well as post-Christian religious and secular world views. By particularizing the problem, one is pushing it into somebody else's backyard in order to avoid a serious confrontation with one's own anti-Jewish patterns of thought.

Anti-Judaism is *spiritualized* when people insist that their condemnation of the Jews is meant religiously, and that their theological statements about the pharisees or ancient Israelites have nothing to do with their attitudes towards contemporary Jews. It is quite possible, one is told, to denounce the Jews theologically without being biased against the actual Jewish community. Such a position, however, cannot account for the persistence of anti-Semitism through the ages. Theological images of the 'evil Jew' operate on the unconcious level and provide religious justification for violence. They validate the oppression of this minority and approve of Jews as a socially and religiously acceptable target for violence.

Lastly, anti-Judaism is *universalized* and employed as a metaphor to exemplify patriarchal oppression. A universal concern for the victims of patriarchal injustice and cruelty deflects attention from the particular (male and female) victims of anti-Semitism. Anti-Semitic violence and, especially, the Holocaust are used as mere symbols to highlight the situation of battered women or the epidemic of racist and sexist violence, as I pointed out in my previous quote by Mary Daly. The universalization of the 'lessons of the Holocaust' thwarts a systematic and sustained investigation of the specific contours of theological and political anti-Judaism.

These dismissive arguments prevent a sincere discussion of anti-Judaism, and downplay anti-Semitism as a minor prejudice among the ignorant few. However, anti-Judaism is not a relic of an ancient past overcome by enlightenment and goodwill; on the contrary, it continues to be a formidable force in the modern world. It is re-establishing itself in the political arenas of many European countries, not to mention the Middle East. We cannot afford to misjudge its power as a political and religious force. In order to counter the teaching of contempt we need more than verbal condemnations and well-intentioned dialogues. Half-hearted attempts at education will not enable us to confront anti-Semitism effectively, because it is a force that involves more than the rational mind. We must also understand the affective basis of anti-Semitism, the emotional passion that accompanies stereotypes and ideologies. As Deborah Lipstadt warns in *Denying the Holocaust*,

> Reasoned dialogue has a limited ability to withstand an assault by the mythic power of falsehood, especially when that falsehood is rooted in an age-old social and cultural phenomenon. There was no rational basis for the Nazi atrocities... Mythical thinking and the force of the irrational have a strange and compelling allure for the educated and uneducated alike.[25]

Anti-Semitism has always had the uncanny ability to mobilize and unite opposing social groups and to serve as social glue between rich and poor, educated and uneducated, left and right. It taps into feelings of discontent and resentment, and directs them towards a socially approved target. Liberal forms of 'enlightenment' and dialogue alone do not have the power to address these emotional issues. Instead, we have to understand anti-Semitism as a religious symbol system that 'does not depend on rational assent, for a symbol also functions on levels of the psyche other than the rational. Religion fulfills deep psychic needs by providing symbols and rituals that enable people to cope with crisis situations.'[26] The emergence of women's consciousness was such a crisis situation. In forging new religious identities feminists reached back into familiar thought patterns, thereby adopting anti-Judaism and integrating it into a new feminist theological discourse. As Carol Christ has pointed out, symbol systems cannot simply be rejected, 'they must be replaced. Where there is no replacement, the mind will revert to familiar structures at times of crisis, bafflement or defeat.'[27] Anti-Judaism is such a symbol system that has, at times, been rejected but has always re-emerged in times of crisis. It is therefore critical to move beyond mere rejections of anti-Semitism. The teaching of contempt must be replaced by a 'teaching of respect'.[28]

25. D. Lipstadt, *Denying the Holocaust: The Growing Assault on Truth and Memory* (New York: Free Press, 1993), p. 25.

26. Christ, *Laughter*, p. 118.

27. Christ, *Laughter*, p. 118.

28. This term has been coined by C. Williamson, *A Guest in the House of Israel: Post-Holocaust Church Theology* (Louisville, KY: Westminster/John Knox Press, 1993), p. 245.

The Teaching of Respect

The teaching of respect foils traditional representations of Judaism as antithesis, scapegoat and prologue. It challenges the reader on intellectual as well as emotional levels, because it demands a shift from the traditional feeling of contempt to the unfamiliar attitude of respect. The long history of symbolizing Jews as evil must be substituted with a teaching of acclaim and commendation. Specifically, the teaching of respect demands that the Jewish tradition of monotheism (God), community (Israel) and practice (Torah) be portrayed positively in its distinctiveness and integrity. The teaching of respect requires that gentile feminist writings describe Judaism in a manner to which a Jewish-identified feminist can assent. It holds Jewish women's 'no' to Christian superiority and conversion attempts in esteem. It makes explicit that Jews and Christians share the Hebrew Bible as a common text but disagree in perspective, method and interpretation. Although feminism has forged bonds between Jewish and Christian women, and has led to a significant sharing of exegetical and theological work, feminism must not be used to deny the differences among Jews and Christians. Jewish approaches to biblical studies are patently different from Christian exegetical ways, and should be studied alongside Christian exegesis. Christians have long read the 'Old' Testament in light of the 'New', ignored priestly and legal texts and emphasized the prophetic tradition. Feminist 'Old Testament' scholars need to develop a feminist critique of traditional anti-Jewish appropriations of the Hebrew Bible as Old Testament, and must begin to appreciate the Hebrew Bible as a Jewish text with a different interpretative tradition. For Christians (and particularly Protestants), the Bible is a battleground where issues of authority, ethics and theology are resolved. For Jewish feminists 'it is not biblical authority, but rabbinic interpretation of male Jewish experience as embodied in halakhah that is both the starting point and the nexus of struggle'.[29] While religious feminists are committed to a shared vision of justice and gender equality, the paths towards this vision may differ substantially. But the shared goal gives feminists a unique opportunity to foster respect across our religious communities despite, or better, because of, our differences.

The teaching of respect explains the peculiar mechanisms of Jewish oppression and alerts the reader to the history of Christian

29. Daum and McCauley, 'Jewish-Christian Feminist Dialogue', pp. 147-89.

violence against Jews. Jewish contributions to the struggle against oppressions based on gender, race and class need to be valued and the times when Jews have extended their commitment to prophetic justice to include other groups must be noted. The teaching of respect emphasizes that Jews have contributed to the common good of their cultures in and through their distinct and particular communities. Jewish women have made gains (or lost ground) in their communities at about the same time and at the same rate as their sisters of the majority religions, whether in Egypt, Canaan, Alexandria, Cordoba, Baghdad, Prague, Berlin or New York. The teaching of respect frustrates attempts to paint Jewish women's situation as inherently inferior (or superior) to that of women in surrounding cultures.

The teaching of respect is not equivalent to uncritical philo-Semitism and romantic idealization of Jews and Judaism. Rather, it calls for a 'theological theory of Jews and Judaism in which Jews can recognize themselves'.[30] It is not a rule of unconditional approval, but remains committed to and vigilant for the wellbeing of this religious minority. It maintains respect and appreciation even in periods of disagreement. Above all, it is alert to the impulse and suspicious of the tendency to criticize Jews and Judaism. Any criticism of Judaism must be reflected in the context of century-old Jew-hatred and must account for its own place in that history: does it reinforce the tradition of Jew-hating or does it break with it? By way of analogy, we may look at legitimate criticisms of feminist theology. An author who has no vested interest in the survival and flourishing of feminist theology, and launches into criticism of it, needs to be questioned as to his or her motivation. Since feminists and Jews are besieged minorities, attacks from the powerful (patriarchal, gentile-Christian) majorities are usually intended to negate our communities. Criticism can only be accepted as legitimate and helpful if there is a commitment to the survival of our communities, and if attention is given to the structures of oppression that deny our wellbeing.

> Those who offer criticisms of a group that has been the target of racism for long periods in history must carefully and systematically show that they are aware of the dangers of playing into the history of racism, that they are consciously aware of how that racism functions, and that they are taking systematic steps in all their statements and writings simultaneously to confront and disavow that racism or anti-Semitism even as they make their specific and limited criticism.[31]

30. Williamson, *Guest*, p. 245.
31. M. Lerner, *The Socialism of Fools: Anti-Semitism on the Left* (Escondido, CA:

Constructive criticism is not a sign of disrespect but an integral part of any respectful relation. Respectful criticism presupposes the existence of relationship, a precondition often not met by those who criticize Judaism. To this day, Christian theologians fault Judaism for a variety of theological and ethical shortcomings, complaints not made for the benefit of Jews and Judaism but for the self-aggrandizement of Christians. The negative feminist commentaries collected in *Anti-Judaism in Feminist Religious Writings* occurred almost always as asides and marginal remarks. They were not intended as constructive criticism of Judaism, but were uttered in pursuit of another theological agenda. The work of Jewish feminists, though also profoundly critical of Judaism, is usually not anti-Jewish. Jewish feminists are not distinguished from non-Jewish feminists by the severity of their denunciation of patriarchy, but by their willingness to allow for reinterpretation and change within the tradition. Anti-Judaism means the rejection of Judaism and the refusal to enter into relationship with an evolving and dynamic community. Legitimate criticism of Judaism is concerned with the continuing vitality of the Jewish faith community. It is well-balanced, aware of the motivation, mindful of the context and willing to engage in dialogue. It maintains a basic level of respect and explicitly resists being used to justify hatred and injustice against this oppressed group.

The growing awareness of anti-Judaism in feminist thinking creates the possibility for exchange and dialogue among Jews and Christians. The *Feminist Companion* series is one such project, bringing together Jewish and Christian feminist voices, in the hope that our religious differences may become places for learning respect rather than for teaching contempt.

Publisher's Group West, 1992), p. 99.

OVERLAPPING COMMUNITIES AND MULTICULTURAL HERMENEUTICS

Kwok Pui-lan

Where are the overlapping communities? In Boston where I currently live, there are different communities, such as Chinatown, where immigrants from Hong Kong and China live; Roxbury, an African-American neighborhood; Beacon Hill, where many state politicians and officials reside, and Jamaica Plain, with its ethnic and class diversity. There are people who live in Boston but seldom go to Chinatown except when they have to accompany their tourist guests. Many Bostonians are reluctant to go to Roxbury or Dorchester because the media have often portrayed these neighborhoods stereotypically as full of drugs and street violence. Some time ago *The Boston Globe*, a leading local newspaper, reported that some taxi drivers did not want to take passengers to certain neighborhoods. The article created quite a controversy in this city, one of oldest in the United States, where students of different races have been able to study in the same classroom only since the Civil Rights movement in the 1960s. Where is the overlapping between America's chocolate inner cities, where poor people of color struggle to survive, and the vanilla suburbs, where middle-class white people build their homes?

Where are the overlapping communities in the academy? As I look over the landscape of the field of biblical studies in the past decade or so, I notice two significant changes. One is the renaissance of Jesus studies. As one scholar has put it: 'the historical quest for the historical Jesus has ended; the interdisciplinary quest for the historical Jesus has just begun'.[1] Why has the resurgence of Jesus studies captured such attention in both the academy and the popular media? Is this newest Quest for Jesus a refined form of positivism, a new cult

---

1. A remark made by Bernard Brandon Scott at the annual meeting of the Historical Jesus Section of the Society of Biblical Literature in Chicago in December 1984, quoted in Marcus J. Borg, *Jesus in Contemporary Scholarship* (Valley Forge, PA: Trinity Press International, 1994), p. 7.

of objectivity, or a masked reification of the male hero, Jesus? Can we be good New Testament scholars without reading the works of Crossan, Borg, Sanders, Mack, and Horsley? It seems not.

At the same time, a new body of literature in biblical studies has emerged, challenging the Eurocentric nature of the discipline and creating an alternative interpretive space. I am referring to the publication of the *Semeia* volume on 'Interpretation for Liberation', *Stony the Road we Trod, Voices from the Margin, Biblical Hermeneutics and Black Theology in South Africa*, and *Cultural Interpretation.*[2] My own book, *Discovering the Bible in the Non-Biblical World*, also belongs to this genre.[3] From Africa, Asia, Latin America, and minority communities in the United States emerges a new generation of biblical scholars and theologians who are reading the Bible through a new lens. Can we be good biblical scholars without reading Mercy Amba Oduyoye, Itumeleng Mosala, Renita Weems, Clarice Martin, Hisako Kinukawa, R.S. Sugirtharajah, and Elsa Tamez?[4] I cannot tell for sure. I asked my students to read many of these authors in my course on 'Feminist Biblical Interpretation', co-taught with Elisabeth Schüssler Fiorenza. Some students were advised not to take the class because, according to some of their peers, 'it's not real science, so why bother studying it!' Where is the overlapping if the communities of discourse do not interact with one another?

If overlapping does not refer to geographical proximity or to an

2. 'Interpretation for Liberation', *Semeia* 47 (1989); Cain Hope Felder (ed.), *Stony the Road we Trod: African American Biblical Interpretation* (Minneapolis: Fortress Press, 1991); R.S. Sugirtharajah (ed.), *Voices from the Margin: Interpreting the Bible in the Third World* (new edn; Maryknoll, NY: Orbis Books, 1995); Itumeleng J. Mosala, *Biblical Hermeneutics and Black Theology in South Africa* (Grand Rapids: Eerdmans, 1989); Brian K. Blount, *Cultural Interpretation: Reorienting New Testament Criticism* (Minneapolis: Fortress Press, 1995).

3. Kwok Pui-lan, *Discovering the Bible in the Non-Biblical World* (Maryknoll, NY: Orbis Books, 1995).

4. Mercy Amba Oduyoye, *Daughters of Anowa: African Women and Patriarchy* (Maryknoll, NY: Orbis Books, 1995); Mosala, *Biblical Hermeneutics*; Renita J. Weems, *Battered Love: Marriage, Sex, and Violence in the Hebrew Prophets* (Minneapolis: Fortress Press, 1995); Clarice J. Martin, 'The Haustafeln (Household Code) in African American Biblical Interpretation: "Free Slaves" and "Subordinate Women"', in Felder (ed.), *Stony the Road we Trod*, pp. 206-31. Hisako Kinukawa, *Women and Jesus in Mark: A Japanese Feminist Perspective* (Maryknoll, NY: Orbis Books, 1994); R.S. Sugirtharajah, 'The Bible and its Asian Readers', *Biblical Interpretation* 1.1 (1993), pp. 54-66; Elsa Tamez, *The Amnesty of Grace: Justification by Faith from a Latin American Perspective* (trans. Sharon H. Ringe; Nashville: Abingdon Press, 1993).

integrated discourse, it may signify the intersection of different worlds experienced by people with multiple identities. Many of us are busy serving as 'translators' for the different communities to which we simultaneously belong. I find myself doing translation endlessly: translating European theologies for my predominantly Euro-American students, translating feminism for my male colleagues and students, translating the biblical message for people in my Chinese congregation, translating Crossan, Borg, and Horsley[5] for students with 'hyphenated' identities, including African-Americans, Asian-Americans, and Hispanic/Latino-Americans.

If the question of 'overlapping' is unsettling, so is the issue of 'multicultural'. Why do we need to talk about multiculturalism at our professional gatherings? Is it because people like me, who have often been consigned to the role of the Other, suddenly begin to speak? I do not think so. There are still so few of us and our voices are so small. At the annual meeting of the Society of Biblical Literature held at Chicago in 1994, I went to listen to the presidential address by Phyllis Trible, the second female president of the Society. I was surprised to see that the overwhelming majority of the people there were middle-aged white men. There were some women and very few people of color. What does this tell us about the field of biblical studies in general and the perpetuation of Eurocentrism in particular?

Another reason we need to talk about multiculturalism may be that the student bodies in seminaries, divinity schools, and at proper universities have become much more diverse than before. At the Episcopal Divinity School where I am teaching, about one-quarter of the students are international students and racial minorities in the United States. We have engaged in serious conversations about racial diversity and cultural sensitivity in the classroom and in our community life. I assume my colleagues teaching in liberal arts colleges must face similar challenges. Yet, I have not seen many changes in our curriculum, pedagogy and standard of excellence as a result of the diversity of the students and teachers. Our higher education is still dominated by the ideology of Eurocentric monoculturalism.

A third reason for talking about multiculturalism is because it is politically correct to do so. While Harold Bloom, Henry Louis Gates,

5.   John Dominic Crossan, *The Historical Jesus: The Life of a Mediterranean Jewish Peasant* (San Francisco: HarperSanFrancisco, 1991); Marcus J. Borg, *Meeting Jesus again for the First Time: The Historical Jesus and the Heart of Contemporary Faith* (San Francisco: HarperSanFrancisco, 1994); Richard A. Horsley, *Jesus and the Spiral of Violence: Popular Jewish Resistance in Roman Palestine* (Minneapolis: Fortress Press, 1993).

Patricia Williams, and Sandra Harding[6] are debating about multi-culturalism in their respective disciplines, those of us in biblical studies must demonstrate that we are not oblivious to the current intellectual debate. In his introduction to the book *Multiculturalism*, David Theo Goldberg[7] observes that commitments to cultural diversity in the United States have their genealogies. They have often emerged out of a 'conflictual history of resistance, accommodation, integration, and transformation'.[8] The emergence of multiculturalism must be understood in relation to the twentieth-century dominance of monoculturalism, as he says sarcastically:

> This universe of knowledge, and knowledge of the universe, imagined in and by the unicultural university, began to rupture under its self-imposed constrictions because it was unable to accommodate—unable to assimilate or placate—the insights, vision, and demands of those whose subjectivities it had acknowledged only as barbarian. Unable to speak, let alone write, the barbarians uttered unrecognizable sounds. Eventually, those sounds came to be named multiculturalism.[9]

It is, therefore, understandable that minority scholars do not embrace multiculturalism without reservations, for we need to clarify the question, 'multiculturalism on whose terms?'

I would like to use a few Chinese dishes to illustrate the different paradigms of multiculturalism. The first example is the roasted chicken with a piece of beautifully carved carrot on the side. Everyone knows the roasted chicken is the main dish, and the carrot is for decoration. In case the reader is not familiar with Chinese custom, let me hasten to say that one is not supposed to touch or eat the piece of carrot. Sometimes it will be recycled and used again on another dish. In this example there is no mixing between the center and the margin. Furthermore, the margin must be kept strictly as it is because its function is to decorate, to amuse, and to entertain. In the first paradigm of multiculturalism, Europe is the center and other cultures are merely decorations. No wonder popular myths still portray

6.   Harold Bloom, *The Western Canon: The Books and School of the Ages* (New York: Harcourt Brace, & Company, 1994); Henry Louis Gates, Jr (ed.), *'Race', Writing, and Difference* (Chicago: University of Chicago Press, 1986); Patricia J. Williams, *The Alchemy of Race and Rights* (Cambridge, MA: Harvard University Press, 1991); Sandra Harding (ed.), *The 'Racial' Economy of Science: Toward a Democratic Future* (Bloomington: Indiana University Press, 1993).

7.   David Theo Goldberg (ed.), *Multiculturalism: A Critical Reader* (Cambridge, MA: Basil Blackwell, 1994).

8.   Goldberg, *Multiculturalism*, p. 7.

9.   Goldberg, *Multiculturalism*, p. 11.

the Chinese people with their pigtails and Native American people as wearing feathers. We just need to look at the image of the Native American people on the flag of the Commonwealth of Massachusetts to know what I mean.[10]

The other favorite Chinese dish in America is chop suey. Originally it was the mixing of different left-over food in the restaurant. Now it has become a popular dish of sliced vegetables with meat in America's Chinese restaurants. One will be surprised to know that restaurants in Hong Kong or China do not serve chop suey, just as they do not serve 'fortune cookies'. As far as I know, both of these are ingenuous creations from the Chinatown in San Francisco. I have never ordered chop suey in Chinese restaurants, and if I order it, the waiter probably will advise me that this dish is mainly for foreigners. I understand that cultural elements change when they are transplanted elsewhere and have to adapt to the dominant culture. What bothers me is that the availability of ethnic food does not mean genuine cultural pluralism, because these chop sueys and ethnic dishes are not prepared and cooked in their home-made style, but in a way primarily for white consumption. While the chicken and the carved carrot maintain a clear boundary, chop suey sometimes masks the hidden power dynamics in the marketplace, no matter whether it is a marketplace of food or ideas.

What will a dish look like that can signify genuine respect for cultures, willingness to embrace differences, courage of transgressing boundaries, and fun and joy in the company of Others? I invite you to try this dish in your kitchen and let me know. Until we are taught not only about footbinding in China, but also about the continuous tradition of Chinese female poets,[11] a tradition unparalleled in most other civilizations, I cannot think of the name of that dish. Until students are taught not only about the pain of slavery, but also the perseverance and humanness of black people in a world that daily denies their dignity, I cannot imagine the beauty of that dish. Until we all learn to speak some Spanish, which is fast becoming the second language in the United States, I can hardly dream of that dish.

One may begin to wonder what the chicken and the carrot, the chop suey, and the fortune cookies have to do with hermeneutics. For some, these images are simply irrelevant. For others, they are at the

10. The Native American man on the flag is shown wearing feathers on his head-dress and carrying a spear.

11. See for example Kenneth Rexroth and Ling Chung (trans. and eds.), *The Orchid Boat: Women Poets of China* (New York: Seabury, 1972).

heart of the matter. For what is multiculturalism if we do not talk about the ways we eat, dress, and live. It is no coincidence that the acronym for the Ecumenical Association of Third World Theologians is EATWOT: eat what.

I would like to use a concrete example to discuss the challenges of multiculturalism in biblical interpretation. The example I have chosen is the story of the Syro-Phoenician woman in Mk 7.25-30 and Mt. 15.21-28. In the history of interpretation of this story among European and American scholars, there are three major models: the salvation history model, the socio-cultural model, and the feminist model.

The oldest model is the salvation history model, which argues that the gentile woman's story is included in the Gospels to justify the admission of gentiles into the Christian community. The story has been interpreted as the beginning of mission to the gentiles, because even Jesus allegedly went to the foreign land of Tyre and Sidon and spoke to a gentile woman. Although at first Jesus emphasized that salvation was only for the Jews, he later changed his mind and healed the gentile woman's daughter, showing that gentiles could partake in God's salvation.

The admission of the gentiles was full of tensions and difficulties, as the story attests. According to a form-critical study of the Markan passage, the order of motifs is: petition, difficulty, overcoming of difficulty, and assurance.[12] In Matthew, the pattern is repeated several times to heighten the difficulty and introduce greater dramatic tension in the story.[13] Even the disciples, who were supposed to be the faithful ones, became part of the barrier when they asked Jesus to send the woman away. Furthermore, as Antoinette Wire has suggested, the difficulty was more dramatic when the healer himself became the obstacle.[14] Jesus either refused to answer the woman or gave her a less than sympathetic answer, which has puzzled many readers of the text.

The climax of the story comes when the gentile woman makes the critical statement: 'Yes, Lord, even the dogs under the table eat the

12. Gerd Theissen, *The Miracle Stories of the Early Christian Tradition* (trans. Francis McDonagh; Philadelphia: Fortress Press, 1983), pp. 181-83. Theissen says the order is repeated four times in Matthew.

13. Elaine Mary Wainwright notes that the woman makes only three petitions and modifies Theissen's scheme. See *Towards a Feminist Critical Reading of the Gospel according to Matthew* (New York: de Gruyter, 1991), p. 219.

14. Antoinette Wire, 'The Structure of the Gospel Miracle Stories and their Tellers', *Semeia* 11 (1978), pp. 83-113 (103).

children's crumbs'. This statement has largely been interpreted to signify both the women's faith and her humility.[15] Jesus' harsh or rude answer has been taken as a challenge and a test of faith for the woman. Although she was publicly humiliated when Jesus likened her to a dog, she did not refuse to be a dog in God's house so that she could at least share the crumbs from the table. Furthermore, her humility and self-abasement have been hailed as Christian virtues. According to the salvation history scheme, salvation is first offered to the Jews and since they have rejected it, the blessing is offered to the gentiles. The salvation history scheme is clearly anti-Jewish and has been used to persecute the Jews.

The second model is the socio-cultural model proposed by Gerd Theissen, one of the pioneers in the sociological study of the New Testament. Instead of situating the story in the early Christian debates about the legitimation of gentile mission, Theissen places it in the ethnic, cultural, economic and political relationships of peoples living on the border regions of Tyre and Galilee.[16] Wary of making assumptions about the faith and virtue of the the Syro-Phoenician woman, he investigates the social and cultural forces shaping the interchange between the woman and Jesus.

According to his study, the woman is a Hellenized Phoenician from the border of Tyre and Sidon. Her knowledge of Greek language and culture indicates that she is educated and from the upper class. Relatively affluent, she belongs to the urban dwellers who were oppressing the people in the Galilee hinterland. Theissen uses socio-cultural conflict between the two groups of people to explain the seemingly offensive remark of Jesus. Jesus' statement, 'It is not fair to take the children's food and throw it to the dogs', may not be purely metaphorical, but may be rooted in the material condition of the region. It might have implied that it is not good to take the food of the poor Jewish people and throw it to the rich gentiles.[17]

Theissen's model may be helpful in generating socio-cultural data for explaining Jesus' remark, but falls short in providing a persuasive interpretation for the response of the woman. In fact, he displays inconsistency in his own thinking on the subject. In *The Gospels in Context*, he analyzes how the woman 'restructures' the cynical image

15. See Elisabeth Schüssler Fiorenza, *But She Said: Feminist Practices of Biblical Interpretation* (Boston: Beacon, 1992), p. 161.

16. Gerd Theissen, *The Gospels in Context: Social and Political History in the Synoptic Tradition* (Minneapolis: Fortress Press, 1991), pp. 61-80.

17. Theissen, *The Gospels*, p. 75.

of a 'dog' to overcome the barrier between Jesus and herself. Portraying the woman as persistent and loyal, he writes: 'The woman
not only evokes the image of the faithful dog in her clever reply, she
behaves like a "devoted dog"'.[18] But in a sermon based on this story,
Theissen presents the woman as actively challenging Jesus' own
prejudice. Thus, he asks rhetorically: 'If even Jesus depends on someone else to rid him of prejudices, who couldn't also be ready to help
themselves get rid of prejudices?'[19]

Theissen's inconsistency points to some of the limits of applying
social sciences to explain biblical narratives. The use of social sciences cannot claim to be 'objective' or 'neutral', because the synthesis
and interpretation of data depend on the horizon of the researcher.
Very often conjectures and guesses have to be made because of
insufficient or fragmented data. Theissen follows the traditional theological position when he describes the woman as a 'devoted dog',
but suggests that she is iconoclastic and daring in his sermon. The
inconsistency may result from Theissen's wavering position on
gender issues.

The last model to be considered is the feminist model, which consists of a multiplicity of voices. Instead of focusing on Jesus, feminist
scholars are more interested in the woman, whom they consider the
protagonist of the story. In a much quoted essay, Sharon H. Ringe
cheers the woman for 'her gutsiness, wit, and self-possession'.[20] She
says the church has trouble with such uppity women. 'Such women
are co-opted, ridiculed, ignored, condemned'.[21] Ringe contends that
the story would not have been created by the early church because of
the negative portrayal of Jesus. Ringe suggests that the woman may
be widowed, divorced, or never married. Alone and isolated, she has
no male relative to intercede on her behalf. Refusing to be bound by
social norms, she comes to Jesus and brings about the healing of her
daughter. Ringe says her story has christological significance because of her gifts and ministries to Jesus. First, she bears witness to
Jesus as a miracle worker and as one who can be won by persistence.
Secondly, her sharp retort enables Jesus to see the situation differently and to enlarge his ministry. Jesus is helped by the least

18. Theissen, *The Gospels*, p. 80.

19. Gerd Theissen, 'Dealing with Religious Prejudices: The Example of the
Canaanite Woman', in *The Open Door: Variations on Biblical Themes* (Minneapolis:
Fortress Press, 1991), p. 42.

20. Sharon H. Ringe, 'A Gentile Woman's Story', in Letty Russell (ed.), *Feminist
Interpretation of the Bible* (Philadelphia: Westminster Press, 1985), p. 65.

21. Ringe, 'Gentile Woman', p. 65.

expected person: a gentile, a woman, a social outcast.[22]

While Ringe points to the contribution of the female subject within the christological context, Elisabeth Schüssler Fiorenza credits her as a speaking subject and reconstructs her story within women's historical leadership in a transitional period of the early church. For Schüssler Fiorenza, the woman 'represents the biblical-theological voice of women, which has been excluded, repressed, or marginalized in Christian discourse'.[23] In the story she 'wins' the contest, for her argument prevails over that of Jesus.[24] She serves as the prototype of those courageous women who dare to speak out, although the church and academy want to silence them.

Calling the woman the apostolic foremother of gentile Christians, Schüssler Fiorenza points to the roles women played in enlarging the vision of the Jesus movement. She writes:

> Although the Syro-Phoenician respects the primacy of the 'children of Israel', she nevertheless makes a theological argument against limiting the Jesuanic inclusive table-community and discipleship of equals to Israel alone. That such a theological argument is placed in the mouth of a woman gives us a clue to the historical leadership of women in opening up the Jesus movement to 'Gentile sinners' (Gal. 2:15). The story of the Syro-Phoenician makes women's contribution to one of the most crucial transitions in early Christian beginnings historically visible.[25]

While European and American scholars have constructed various interpretations, Asian Christian women and men have also looked at the passage through their darker eyes. I would cite several examples to show the ways Asian readers both challenge and build on Western biblical scholarship in their cross-cultural interpretation. In order to highlight the diversity and complexity of multicultural Asia, my examples are selected from different socio-cultural contexts.

In a dramatization of the story, several Indian women retell the story as follows. In the episode, Sister Kranti, Frances and Judith have come to see the Bishop to request his support for a shelter for battered women. The Bishop dismisses their request, saying that they have exaggerated the problem and battering of women does not exist in the Christian community. The end of the episode takes a different turn from the original story:

22. Ringe, 'Gentile Woman', pp. 70-72.

23. Schüssler Fiorenza, *But She Said*, p. 11.

24. Elisabeth Schüssler Fiorenza, *In Memory of Her: A Feminist Theological Reconstruction of Christian Origins* (New York: Crossroad, 1983), p. 137.

25. Schüssler Fiorenza, *But She Said*, p. 97.

> *Kranti*:   We are prepared to give our professional skills and energies to
> begin the shelter, but we need money—you should understand that!
> *Bishop*:   It's an administrative problem, for me, you must understand!
> If I help you, I must help others—it's opening the door to a flood I can't
> cope with. I will be accused of favoring some...
> *Frances*:   It seems as though the Church is not interest[ed] in helping us
> to free ourselves [from] the demons of violence that are throttling us.
> *Judith*:   Looks like we have to do things on our own to free ourselves.
> *Bishop*:   Women, you have great faith. Your wish will come to pass
> (blesses them).
> *Kranti*:   With the crumbs of your blessing we will make living bread.
>
> (The women rise and leave and when their backs are turned, the Bishop
> makes the deliberate gesture of washing his hands of them.)[26]

In this retelling, Jesus' granting the request of the Syro-Phoenician
woman contrasts sharply with the Bishop's dismissal of the women.
The story is presented in *double-voiced* form: one hears the original
story and the new story at the same time.[27] The episode frames the
story in a new way, using the tension created by the original story
and the new construction as a radical critique of the patriarchal
church and society.

Employing the techniques of oral hermeneutics that are predominant in Asian religious life, these Indian women do not feel bound by
the text and feel free to reappropriate it in their context.[28] By setting a
new context to frame the story, by playing with the borders and by
creating stylizing variants, the retelling raises the questions of the
boundary of the text, the elitist emphasis on textuality and the relationship between Scripture and its interpretive communities.

Another example is a multifaith reading by R.S. Sugirtharajah of
Sri Lanka, who has cautioned that Asians live in a multiscriptural
world and biblical interpreters should bear in mind that their
prospective audiences would likely include Buddhist and Hindu
friends and colleagues.[29] Sugirtharajah laments that the story of the
Syro-Phoenician woman has long been read from a missiological
point of view. The church has seen this gentile woman, just as any

26. Rita Monteiro, Judith Sequeira, and Frances Yasas, 'Living Bread from
Crumbs', *In God's Image* (September 1988), pp. 50-51 (51).

27. The concept of double-voicedness is from Henry Louis Gates, Jr, *The Signifying Monkey: A Theory of African-American Literary Criticism* (New York: Oxford
University Press, 1988), pp. 48-50.

28. For a more detailed discussion of oral hermeneutics, see Kwok, *Discovering
the Bible*, pp. 44-56.

29. R.S. Sugirtharajah, 'Inter-faith Hermeneutics: An Example and Some Implications', in *Voices from the Margin*, p. 307.

Hindu, Muslim, Buddhist or Sikh, as a target for evangelization, and this deters any meaningful dialogues with people of other faiths.[30]

Sugirtharajah stresses that in the Markan version, the faith of the woman is not mentioned. In the Matthean version, Jesus praises the woman's faith, but there is no hint that she becomes a follower of Jesus. In his article he appreciates Ringe's interpretation of the woman's faith as trust in another human being and willingness to take a risk. He agrees with Ringe, who interprets the story as 'the woman's ministry *to* Jesus by her "faith"—a faith that is no doctrinal confession of his messianic identity, and no flattery of his apparently miraculous power, but rather an act of trust, of engagement, risking everything'.[31] Sugirtharajah turns the salvation history model on its head when he comments that, in the story, 'it is the evangelizer who is evangelized now'.[32]

The third example is a Japanese feminist perspective presented by Hisako Kinukawa. Although she borrows insights from social sciences, especially the anthropological framework by Bruce Malina, her research interests are fundamentally different from those of Theissen's. She reads the Syro-Phoenician woman's story within the framework of cultic purity and the tension within Mark's cross-racial community. She notices the common experiences of shame and honor within boundaries of power, sexual status and respect for others in a group-oriented society found in both the first-century Palestinian people and contemporary Japanese society.[33]

Instead of simply focusing on the socio-cultural boundaries of ethnicity, economic status and political relationships in Jesus' time, as Theissen has done, Kinukawa is more interested in the lessons that can be drawn to address ethnocentrism and imperialism in the present Japanese context. Transposing the Syro-Phoenician woman's story to modern Japan, she condemns parallel ethnic exclusive attitudes in Japanese society, and lifts up the struggles of the Koreans living in Japan.[34] While one may argue whether the honor and shame system in the ancient Mediterranean world can be compared

30. R.S. Sugirtharajah, 'The Syrophoenician Woman', *ExpTim* 98 (October 1986), p. 14.

31. Ringe, 'A Gentile Woman's Story', p. 71 as quoted in R.S. Sugirtharajah, 'Jesus and Mission: Some Redefinitions', in Wendy S. Robins and Gillian Hawney (eds.), *The Scandal of the Cross: Evangelism and Mission Today* (London: United Society for the Propagation of the Gospel, 1992), p. 3.

32. Sugirtharajah, 'Jesus and Mission', p. 3.

33. Kinukawa, *Women*, p. 16.

34. Kinukawa, *Women*, pp. 61-65.

to her Japanese system, Kinukawa clearly combines her training in Western biblical scholarship with her sensitivity to struggles for justice in her society.

Kinukawa also differs from some of the Western feminist scholars in her construction of the subjectivity of the Syro-Phoenician woman. Both Ringe and Schüssler Fiorenza praise the woman's wit and courage, and give her credit for winning the argument. In Kinukawa's Japanese context, these qualities do not necessarily characterize a strong feminist woman, and Kinukawa flatly rejects that these qualities are at issue here. Instead, she appreciates the woman's persever-ance, her remaining hopeful even in a hopeless situation, and her risking herself for her daughter in a society not only defined by patriarchy but also by group identity:

> Though many scholars, including women scholars, admire her wit or uppityness, I do not think these qualities are at issue here. Rather, a woman who is oppressed and held to be worthless, living in such a patriarchal society and caring for her suffering daughter, is driven to an impossible situation and cannot find any other solution than to forget tradition, neglect social custom, and rush ahead recklessly to Jesus. She can no longer turn back. She risks everything on Jesus. This is her last resort.[35]

The last example is taken from a postcolonial reading from my recent book, which differs from the above interpretations in three ways.[36] First, using literary criticism, especially narratological theories, I investigate the way the woman is presented in the canonical Gospels. I am inspired by the works of Gayatri Chakravorty Spivak, who challenges the power dynamics underlying how colonized people are inscribed in texts and how they are often consigned to signify the Other in history.[37] Both the woman's action (bowing down) and her speech, as presented in the story, point to the unequal subject posi-tion between her and Jesus. She is the one who begs, and Jesus is the one granting the request. She is the passive spectator witnessing a miracle, and Jesus is the healer.

Secondly, a postcolonial interpretation makes the connection be-tween anti-Judaism and the condemning of the religions of colonized people. In the long history of interpreting the story, the gentiles have

---

35. Kinukawa, *Women*, p. 59.

36. Kwok, *Discovering the Bible*, pp. 71-83.

37. See her books, *In Other Worlds: Essays in Cultural Politics* (New York: Methuen, 1987) and *The Post-Colonial Critic: Interviews, Strategies, Dialogues* (New York: Routledge, 1990).

been regarded as the ones who will inherit God's kingdom, while the Jews have been portrayed as giving up their promise from God. In a fateful twist of events, the colonizers used this story as a pretext to justify their mission to the 'uncivilized', their mission to the 'heathen'. In one broad stroke, the missionaries linked their anti-Judaism with their ethnocentrism, displayed toward people of other faiths.

Thirdly, a postcolonial interpretation takes full account of the multiple identities of the woman. As a gentile woman with a daughter with an unspeakable disease, the woman is despised by Jews and oppressed as a woman in a patriarchal society. But as a member of the elite urban class speaking the Greek language, she also has the potential of being an oppressor exploiting the Galilean hinterland. Her multiple identities remind us to analyze marginalization in its myriad ways, and cautions us that there is always the Other within the Other.[38] A postcolonial reading insists that a woman should not be treated solely as a sexualized subject, because her identity is also shaped by her class, language, ethnicity and so on. Thus, a feminist reading should not simply emphasize the sex–gender system that is at work in the story, but also pay attention to the intersection of class, race, ethnicity and other factors.

The multicultural readings of the story by Asian women and men challenge the established models of reading the text. Together with Christians from other parts of the world, Asian Christians de-center the readings of European and American scholars. The questions they have posed to biblical hermeneutics are many: What decides which reading is valid and true? Who decides which questions are good questions? Who serves as the gatekeeper to keep certain voices out from the church and classroom? What is the majority discourse in biblical studies? Why should the tiny minority of biblical scholars in the academy define, dictate, and set the agenda for reading the Bible? To use the metaphor of the chicken and the carrot once again: who are the chickens and who are the carrots?

38. Kwok, *Discovering the Bible*, p. 82.

III

OTHER WORLDS

FEMINIST RESEARCH AND ANCIENT MESOPOTAMIA: PROBLEMS AND PROSPECTS

Julia M. Asher-Greve

> Making women visible was not simply a matter
> of unearthing new facts; it was a matter of
> advancing new interpretations.
>
> —*Joan Wallach Scott*

1. *Introduction*

It is still premature to analyse and evaluate feminist scholarship in ancient Near Eastern studies,[1] which is in the initial phase of *engendering*. No history of women in Ancient Mesopotamia has been published,[2] and only one book and a handful of articles utilize feminist theory.[3] However, feminist scholars from other disciplines

---

1. For the terms 'Mesopotamia' and 'ancient Near East' see below, section 4.1. The terms 'science' and 'scientist' refer not only to the sciences but to the humanities as well; and the total community of scholars, comparable to the more general German words *Wissenschaft* and *Wissenschaftler/in*.

2. A bibliography on women in the ancient Near East is in preparation by this author, and will be published in *NIN: Journal of Ancient Near Eastern Gender Studies*, 2 (Groningen, NL: Styx).

3. T. Frymer-Kensky, *In the Wake of the Goddesses: Women, Culture, and the Biblical Transformation of Pagan Myth* (New York: Free Press, 1992); M.I. Marcus, 'Dressed to Kill: Women and Pins in Early Iran', in *The Oxford Art Journal* 17 (1994), pp. 3-15; *idem*, 'Incorporating the Body: Adornment, Gender, and Social Identity in Ancient Iran', in *Cambridge Archaeological Journal* 3 (1993), pp. 157-78; *idem*, 'Geography and Visual Ideology: Landscape, Knowledge, and Power in Neo-Assyrian Art', in M. Liverani (ed.), *Neo-Assyrian Geography*, Quaderni di Geografia Storia 5 (Roma: Università di Roma 'La Sapienza', 1995), pp. 193-202; *idem*, 'Sex and the Politics of Female Adornment in Pre-Achaemenid Iran (1000–800 B.C.E.)', in N.B. Kampen (ed.), *Sexuality in Ancient Art: Near East, Egypt, Greece, and Italy* (Cambridge: Cambridge University Press, 1996), pp. 41-54; S. Pollock, 'Women in a Men's World: Images of Sumerian Women', in J.M. Gero and M.W. Conkey (eds.), *Engendering Archaeology: Women and Prehistory* (Oxford: Basil Blackwell, 1991), pp. 366-87.

exploit Mesopotamian sources in building theories: most prominently the advocates of 'matriarchy', 'great goddess theory', and the
theory of origin and development of patriarchy. Such studies reflect
an agenda about women and gender to which antiquity is supposed
to give legitimacy. But the evidence is inaccurate, or else the sources
are quoted out of context.[4] Using data from ancient Mesopotamia
involves in-depth knowledge of the discipline, its methodology and
historiography. Reading and interpreting cuneiform texts is not like
reading Greek or Latin. There is no complete Sumerian dictionary,
and the use of Akkadian dictionaries is difficult for the non-special-
ist.[5] Any 'outsider' studying two or more translations of the same text
would be puzzled by the differences.[6] It is therefore not surprising
that non-specialized feminists, writing on ancient Mesopotamia, mis-
read and misinterpret the sources and, thus, are not taken seriously
by scholars in this discipline.[7] The feminist approach encounters

4.   Cf. A. Barstow, 'The Uses of Archaeology for Women's History: James
Mellaart's Work on the Neolithic Goddess at Çatal Hüyük', in *Feminist Studies* 4,
1978, pp. 7-18; G. Lerner, *The Creation of Patriarchy* (Oxford: Oxford University
Press, 1986); F.I. Strika, 'Prehistoric Roots: Continuity in the Images and Rituals of
the Great Goddess Cult in the Near East', *RSO* 57 (1983), pp. 1-41; S. Brown,
'Feminist Research in Archaeology: What Does it Mean? Why Is it Taking so
Long?', in N.S. Rabinowitz and A. Richlin (eds.), *Feminist Theory and the Classics*
(London: Routledge, 1993), pp. 238-71; pp. 185-91, 197-98; S.B. Pomeroy, 'A
Classical Scholar's Perspective on Matriarchy', in B.A. Carroll (ed.), *Liberating
Women's History: Theoretical and Critical Essays* (Chicago: University of Illinois
Press, 1976), pp. 217-23; L.E. Talalay, 'A Feminist Boomerang: The Great God-
dess of Greek Prehistory', in *Gender and History* 6 (1994), pp. 165-83; B. Röder,
J. Hummel and B. Kunz, *Göttinnen Dämmerung: Das Matriarchat aus archäologischer
Sicht* (München: Droemer Knaur, 1996). For a more detailed analysis, see my forthcoming article 'Women, Gender and Scholarship', in *NIN: Journal of Ancient Near
Eastern Gender Studies* 1 (forthcoming, 1997).
5.   Since 1984 three volumes have been published: Å. Sjöberg (ed.), *The Sumerian Dictionary*, Volumes A.I and A.II (from 'a' to 'ab'), and Volume B (Philadelphia: The University Museum, University of Pennsylvania); The *Chicago Assyrian
Dictionary* (*CAD*) approaches completion.
6.   Compare, e.g., S. Dalley, *Myths From Mesopotamia* (Oxford: Oxford University Press, 1989); B.R. Foster, *From Distant Days* (Bethesda, MD: CDL Press,
1995); T. Jacobsen's translations in *The Harp That Once... Sumerian Poetry in
Translation* (New Haven: Yale University Press, 1987), used by many non-special-
ists, are 're-creations' which fill in much of the missing text. But, without being
familiar with the original text editions containing transliterations and translation,
it is nearly impossible to evaluate Jacobsen's work.
7.   In addition to works listed in n. 4 above, see R. Bleier, *Science and Gender*
(New York: Pergamon Press, 1984): 138-61; J. O'Brien, 'Nammu, Mami, Eve and
Pandora: What's in a Name?', *The Classical Journal* 79 (1983), pp. 35-45;

several additional hurdles:[8]

- Sexual dissymmetry in teaching, excavating and research, which has an impact on the choice of topics,
  and as some feminists claim, on theory, methodology,
  and interpretation as well.[9] Although there were always

R. Rohrlich, 'State Formation and the Subjugation of Women', *Feminist Studies* 6 (1980), pp. 76-102; R. Rohrlich-Leavitt, 'Women in Transition: Crete and Sumer', in R. Bridenthal and C. Koonz (eds.), *Becoming Visible: Women in European History* (Boston, Atlanta: Houghton Mifflin, 1977), pp. 16-59; M. Wakeman, 'Ancient Sumer and the Women's Movement: The Process of Reaching Behind, Encompassing and Going Beyond', *JFSR* 1.2 (1985), pp. 27-38; W. Dumont du Voitel, *Macht und Entmachtung der Frau: Eine ethnologisch-historische Analyse* (Frankfurt and New York: Campus, 1994), pp. 94-149.

    8.   Cf. J. Blok, 'Sexual Asymmetry: A Historiographical Essay', in J. Blok and P. Mason (eds.), *Sexual Asymmetry: Studies in Ancient Society* (Amsterdam: Gieben, 1987), pp. 1-58; Brown, 'Feminist Research in Archaeology'; S.B. Pomeroy, 'The Study of Women in Antiquity: Past, Present, and Future', *AJP* 112 (1991), pp. 263-68; A. Richlin, 'Zeus and Metis: Foucault, Feminism, Classics', *Helios* 18 (1991), pp. 160-80; C. Claassen (ed.), *Exploring Gender Through Archaeology: Selected Papers From the 1991 Boone Conference* (Monographs in World Archaeology, 11; Madison, WI: Prehistoric Press, 1992); E. Engelstad, 'Images of Power and Contradiction: Feminist Theory and Post-processual Archaeology', *Antiquity* 65 (1991), pp. 502-14; Gero and Conkey, *Engendering Archaeology*; R. Gilchrist, 'Women's Archaeology? Political Feminism, Gender Theory and Historical Revision', *Antiquity* 65 (1991), pp. 495-501; V. Pinsky and A. Wylie (eds.), *Critical Traditions in Contemporary Archaeology: Essays in the Philosophy, History and Socio-Politics of Archaeology* (Cambridge: Cambridge University Press, 1990); D. Walde and N.D. Willows (eds.), *The Archaeology of Gender: Proceedings of the 22nd Annual Conference of the Archaeological Association of the University of Calgary* (Calgary: University of Calgary Archaeological Association, 1991); A.Wylie, 'Feminist Theories of Social Power: Some Implications for Processual Archaeology', *Norwegian Archaeological Review* 25 (1992), pp. 51-68; *idem*, 'The Interplay of Evidential Constraints and Political Interests: Recent Archaeological Research on Gender', *American Antiquity* 57 (1992) pp. 15-35; *idem*, 'A Proliferation of New Archaeologies: "Beyond Objectivism and Relativism"', in N. Yoffee and A. Sherratt (eds.), *Archaeological Theory: Who Sets the Agenda?* (Cambridge: Cambridge University Press, 1993), pp. 20-26. For ancient Mesopotamia, cf. J.G. Westenholz, 'Towards a New Conceptualization of the Female Role in Mesopotamian Society', *JAOS* 110 (1990), pp. 510-21.

    9.   E.g. Blok, 'Sexual Asymmetry'; Brown, 'Feminist Research'. For surveys of feminist theory see, e.g., R. Tong, *Feminist Thought: A Comprehensive Introduction* (Boulder and San Francisco: Westview Press, 1989); S.J. Hekman, *Gender and Knowledge: Elements of a Postmodern Feminism* (Boston: Northeastern University Press, 1990), pp. 94-104; J. Lorber, *Paradoxes of Gender* (New Haven: Yale University Press, 1994).

some women in the field, even some who conducted excavations, as a rule women were excluded from excavations and academic scholarship.[10]

- Androcentrism evident in the exclusion, or at least neglect, of women and gender as research topics and categories.[11] This is definitely the case in ancient Near Eastern studies which still lack a comprehensive scholarly book on women, although there is ample source material.[12]
- Scholars who are unaware of, or are not prepared to evaluate, feminist publications.
- The perception that feminist research is primarily concerned with women and women's issues and therefore relevant to special interest groups only.
- The perception that feminist research is partial.
- Reluctance to criticize the androcentric bias in the work of colleagues.
- Widespread disinterest of editors and professional organizations in this topic.[13]
- Tradition of scholarship that is obsessed with typology, form, style, dating rather than hermeneutics.

According to Shelby Brown, 'as a result, archaeology has had difficulty defining and criticising its goals and sharing new ideas internally';[14] this, of course, applies equally to philology. The purpose of

10. C. Claassen (ed,), *Women in Archaeology* (Philadelphia: University of Pennsylvania Press, 1994). A publication in preparation that documents the situation of women in classics, Egyptology and Near Eastern studies is: G.M. Cohen and M.S. Joukowsky (eds.), *Women in Archaeology: The Classical World and the Near East*.

11. E.g. Hekman, *Gender and Knowledge*, pp. 30-47 and from p. 94.

12. As will be evident from my forthcoming bibliography on women (*NIN: Journal of Ancient Near Eastern Gender Studies* 2); for examples of bias and androcentrism in ancient Near East scholarship, see Asher-Greve, 'Women, Gender and Scholarship'. Examples of studies of women in the ancient Near East include: A. Cameron and A. Kuhrt (eds.), *Images of Women in Antiquity* (London: Routledge, 2nd rev. edn, 1993); J.-M. Durand (ed.), *La Femme dans le Proche-Orient Antique: XXXIIIe Rencontre Assyriologique Internationale* (Paris: erc, 1987); B.S. Lesko (ed.), *Women's Earliest Records: From Ancient Egypt and Western Asia* (BJS, 166; Atlanta: Scholars Press, 1989).

13. Cf. Pomeroy, 'The Study of Women'.

14. Brown, 'Feminist Research'; Richlin, 'Zeus and Metis'; H. Smith, 'Feminism and the Methodology of Women's History', in B. Carroll (ed.), *Liberating Women's History*, pp. 369-84. According to I. Hodder, 'it may be archaeology's recent positivist history coupled with its increasing resource base in the science that has

this article is to outline what a feminist approach can contribute and how it will change our understanding of ancient Mesopotamian societies and cultures.

2. *Methodology and Ancient Near Eastern Studies*

Theory and methodology have never been a favourite subject in ancient Near East studies and scholars have relied largely on established, conventional theory and method adapted to the particular needs of ancient Near East archaeology, art and cuneiform texts. The result is that the discipline lacks a comprehensive treatment of its methodology.[15] Uncovering and reconstructing ancient Mesopotamian civilization is a multi-methodological task, ranging from excavating to studying texts written in various scripts and languages. Specialization has divided ancient Near East archaeologists, art historians and philologists into different departments or institutes.[16] The historiography of ancient Mesopotamia reflects these differences: archaeologists have traditionally emphasized the interpretation of material culture, philologists the interpretation of written evidence.[17]

impeded the development of feminist archaeology for so long' ('Gender Representation and Social Reality', in Walde and Willows [eds.], *Archaeology of Gender*, pp. 11-16 [15]).

15. It is necessary to consult a variety of books and articles, ranging from field archaeology to introductions to Sumerian and Akkadian; such as, B. Hrouda (ed.), *Methoden der Archäologie: Eine Einführung in ihre naturwissenschaftlichen Techniken* (Munich: Beck, 1978); M. Joukowsky, *A Complete Manual of Field Archaeology: Tools and Techniques of Field Work for Archaeologists* (Englewood Cliffs, NJ: Prentice Hall, 1980); W.H.P. Römer, *Einführung in die Sumeriologie* (Nijmegen: Katholieke Universiteit, 9th rev. edn, 1986); R. Caplice, *Introduction to Akkadian* (Studia Pohl, SM; Rome: Biblical Institute Press, 1983). W. von Soden's *Einführung in die Altorientalistik* (Darmstadt: Wissenschaftliche Buchgesellschaft, 1985) focuses on written records and is not concerned with methodology. For a feminist critique see my forthcoming article, 'Women, Gender and Scholarship'.

16. See section 4.1 below.

17. A selection of widely read histories from the last 75 years, augmented by recently written articles for a dictionary, demonstrates the different approaches: B. Meissner, *Babylonien und Assyrien* (Heidelberg: Carl Winter, 1920 and 1925); A. Scharff and A. Moortgat, *Ägypten und Vorderasien im Altertum* (Munich: Bruckmann, 1950); S.N. Kramer, *The Sumerians: Their History, Culture, and Character* (Chicago: University of Chicago Press, 1963); A.L. Oppenheim, *Ancient Mesopotamia: Portrait of a Dead Civilization*, (2nd rev. edn; Chicago: University of Chicago Press, 1977); J. Oates, *Babylon* (London: Thames & Hudson, 1979); H.J. Nissen, *The Early History of the Ancient Near East: 9000–2000 B.C.* (Chicago: University of Chicago Press, 1988); J.N. Postgate, *Early Mesopotamia: Society and Economy at the*

In 1960 A. Leo Oppenheim warned his colleagues that Assyriology would remain stagnant unless it opened itself to current intellectual discourse, a warning that was heard by few.[18] Although Oppenheim favoured a more anthropological approach, the trend moved in the direction of social and economic history.[19] Research in ancient Near East cultures and languages seems to share its anti-theory and anti-feminist bias with classical studies and Egyptology.[20] Ancient Near East studies is one of the few disciplines that has not yet embraced the postmodern era. In a volume dedicated to methodology in ancient Near East study, Giorgio Buccellati describes the discipline as a 'developing field'.[21] Scholars of the ancient Near East rarely use their data to formulate new theory. The prevailing research model is positivistic and empiricistic, purporting to be value-free because it is based on presumably neutral archaeological observations and neutral philological analyses.[22] There is a strong belief that 'facts', that is,

Dawn of History (London and New York: Routledge, 1992); see also the articles by A.B. Knapp, 'History of Mesopotamia: Mesopotamian Chronology', in D.N. Freedman (ed.), *The Anchor Bible Dictionary*, IV, pp. 714-21; H.T. Wright, 'History of Mesopotamia: Prehistory of Mesopotamia', in Freedman (ed.), *Anchor Bible Dictionary*, IV, pp. 720-24; P. Steinkeller, 'History of Mesopotamia: Mesopotamia in the Third Millennium B.C.', in Freedman (ed.), *Anchor Bible Dictionary*, IV, pp. 724-32; A.K. Grayson, 'History of Mesopotamia: History and Culture of Assyria; History and Culture of Babylonia', in Freedman (ed.), *Anchor Bible Dictionary*, IV, pp. 732-77. Cf. also B.G. Trigger, *A History of Archaeological Thought* (Cambridge: Cambridge University Press, 1989).

18. A.L. Oppenheim, 'Assyriology: Why and How?', *Current Anthropology* 1 (1960), pp. 409-23. This article was incorporated in Oppenheim's book *Ancient Mesopotamia*. Oppenheim favoured a more anthropological approach; anthropological theory and method have only recently elicited attention from archaeologists and a few philologists.

19. Cf., I.J. Gelb, 'Approaches to the Study of Ancient Society, *JAOS* 87 (1967), pp. 1-8; G. Buccellati, 'Methodological Concerns and the Progress of Ancient Near Eastern Studies', *Or NS* 42 (1973), pp. 9-20. In the same volume of *Orientalia*—dedicated to I.J. Gelb and methodology—R. Renger published an article, 'Who Are All Those People?', in which he uses an anthropological approach with, as he remarks, 'a surprisingly coherent picture which I had not originally anticipated' (pp. 259-73 [273]). How trends in thought and theory have influenced archaeology has been analysed in B.G. Trigger, *Archaeological Thought*; Trigger, however, did not include feminist thought and theory in his work.

20. Cf. Rabinowitz in N.S. Rabinowitz and A. Richlin (eds.), *Feminist Theory and the Classics* (Thinking Gender, NY: Routledge, 1993), pp. xxx; G. Robins, *Women of Ancient Egypt* (London: British Museum Press, 1993), pp. 11-20.

21. Buccellati, 'Methodological Concerns'.

22. For a similar attitude in the classics see Rabinowitz in Rabinowitz and Richlin (eds.), *Feminist Theory and the Classics*, pp. 4-5; Richlin, 'Zeus and Metis'.

excavated material and cuneiform texts, speak for themselves. The antiquity of the objects strengthens the belief in the objectivity of the observer. Archaeologists using scientific techniques assume that such methods guarantee objectivity, and many see themselves more as scientists than historians. The realization that interpretation may also depend on the scholar's viewpoint or ideology is rare.[23]

Ancient Near East scholarship is also burdened by the ascription of a higher value to philology than to archaeology.[24] Synthesizing both is rare; the interdisciplinary approach remains predominantly biblical.[25] A nascent tendency towards a more integrated 'contextual' approach has taken little notice of postmodern and feminist critiques of the validity of theories of 'objectivity' and the 'truth' of knowledge.[26]

23. E.g. Oppenheim, 'Assyriology'; Renger, 'Who Are All Those People', p. 264; Trigger, *Archaeological Thought*. This is perhaps 'the' central issue of feminist critique; cf. Westenholz, 'Towards a New Conceptualization', and my forthcoming article, 'Women, Gender and Scholarship'.

24. This is also the case in the classics: cf. Oppenheim, *Ancient Mesopotamia*, pp. 4-5; V. French, 'What is Central for the Study of Women in Antiquity?', *Helios* 17 (1990), pp. 213-19. For the ancient Near East, see J.S. Cooper and G.M. Schwartz (eds.), *The Study of the Ancient Near East in the 21st Century: The William Foxwell Albright Centennial Conference* (Winona Lake, IN: Eisenbrauns, 1996).

25. The discipline was developed by biblical scholars; European interest in ancient Mesopotamia results from the biblical accounts; cf., e.g., G. Sievernich and H. Budde (eds.), *Europa und der Orient*, 800–1900 (Gütersloh: Bertelsmann, 1989); articles by J.M. Lundquist, P.T. Daniels, M.T. Larsen and J. Maier, in J.M. Sasson (ed.), *Civilizations of the Ancient Near East* (New York: Charles Scribner's Sons, 1995), I, pp. 67-122. For the development in the USA, cf. B. Kuklick, *Puritans in Babylon: The Ancient Near East and American Intellectual Life*, 1880–1930 (Princeton, NJ: Princeton University Press, 1996).

26. Cf., e.g., E.C. Stone, 'Texts, Architecture and Ethnographic Analogy', *Iraq* 43 (1981), pp. 24-33; *idem*, *Nippur Neighbourhoods* (SOAC, 14; Chicago: The Oriental Institute, 1987); B.N. Porter, *Images, Power, Politics: Figurative Aspects of Esarhaddon's Babylonian Policy* (Philadelphia: American Philosophical Society, 1993); J.N. Postgate, *Early Mesopotamia*; cf. also Cooper and Schwartz, *Study of the Ancient Near East*.

For feminist critique and epistemology, see, e.g., L. Alcoff and E. Potter (eds.), *Feminist Epistemologies* (London: Routledge, 1993); L.M. Antony and C. Witt (eds.), *A Mind of One's Own: Feminist Essays on Reason and Objectivity* (Boulder and San Francisco: Westview Press, 1993); Hekman, *Gender and Knowledge*; L.J. Nicholson (ed.), *Feminism/Postmodernism* (London: Routledge, 1990); J.McC. Nielsen (ed.), *Feminist Research Methods: Exemplary Readings in the Social Sciences* (Boulder and San Francisco: Westview Press, 1990). See also the forthcoming article by J.M. Asher-Greve and A.L. Asher, 'From Thales to Foucault...and Back to Sumer', in *Intellectual Life of the Ancient Near East: Proceedings of the 43. Rencontre Assyriologique*

3. Feminist Methodology

In analysing what feminist methods have to contribute to the study of antiquity, it is obvious that feminist scholarly literature is either too theoretical or very pragmatic.[27] Feminist science is still preoccupied with a primarily philosophical, theoretical discourse. Historically, philosophy has succeeded in evolving methodology in concert with its application to a problem, rather than in placing excessive emphasis on *a priori* development of methodology. The question of interrelation between method and androcentric bias was first raised by feminist philosophers. Understandably, critique of science became one focal point of feminist methodology, and critique of epistemology

Internationale, Prague, 1-5 July 1996 (forthcoming).

27. Feminist scholars are still in the process of developing feminist research methods; cf. Nielsen, *Feminist Research Methods*. I could not find feminist methods that are applicable to the analysis of ancient culture. Some methods that are propagated as 'feminist'—for example interviewing (women), studying women's environment, women's spoken language, taping, keeping diaries, being a participant and writing about the women's movement, etc.—are neither specifically feminist nor relevant to ancient historians. Data such as women's diaries, biographies, art works and treatises about women are extremely rare (only one women poet is known from Mesopotamia) or non-existent in ancient Mesopotamia. Neither sociology nor psychology offers more than a theoretical approach for the historian of the Old World. Even anthropology has its limitations because it is, to a large degree, ahistorical. Cf. T. De Laurentis (ed.), *Feminist Studies Critical Studies* (Bloomington: Indiana University Press, 1986); Hekman, *Gender and Knowledge*, pp. 124-25; Nielsen, *Feminist Research Methods*; A. Diezinger *et al.* (eds.), *Erfahrung mit Methode: Wege sozialwissenschaftlicher Frauenforschung* (Forum Frauenforschung, 8; Freiburg: Kore, 1994).

For a widely employed historical approach, see J.W. Scott, 'Gender: A Useful Category of Historical Analysis', *American Historical Review* 91 (1986), pp. 1053-75; *idem, Gender and the Politics of History* (New York: Columbia University Press, 1988), esp. pp. 1-27; J.W. Scott (ed.), *Feminism and History* (Oxford: Oxford University Press, 1996), pp. 1-13.; cf. P. Schmitt Pantel, 'Women and Ancient History Today', in P. Schmitt Pantel (ed.), *A History of Women*. I. *From Ancient Goddesses to Christian Saints* (Cambridge, MA: Harvard University Press; London: Belknap Press, 1992), pp. 464-69. Cf. also, L.J. Nicholson, *Gender and History: The Limits of Social Theory in the Age of the Family* (New York: Columbia University Press, 1986), esp. pp. 69-104.

For feminist perspectives on ancient history, see S.B. Pomeroy (ed.), *Women's History and Ancient History* (Chapel Hill: University of North Carolina Press, 1991); M. Skinner (ed.), *Rescuing Creusa: New Methodological Approaches to Women in Antiquity* (Special Issue of *Helios*, NS 13; Lubbock, TX: 1987), pp. 9-30; and for archaeology, see I. Hodder, *Reading the Past: Current Approaches to Interpretation in Archaeology* (Cambridge: Cambridge University Press, 2nd edn, 1991), pp. 168-72.

another. Diverse feminist theories and epistemologies have been developed.[28] The problems with these are substantial, not the least because the notion of 'feminine' has been defined by the (androcentric) thought system that is criticized.[29]

Joyce McCarl Nielsen, basing her work on Paul Ricoeur, argues that social action and written text are objective in the sense that once performed or written, they are 'outside' of the actor, creator or initiator, which makes them available to the world. According to Nielsen this 'shared empirical evidence is part of the "fusion of horizons"[30] that seems to be the beginning or the basis of a viable postempirical epistemology'.[31] Scholars confronted with these problems, having no training in philosophy but wishing to research women and gender, seek comprehensible criteria on which to decide the validity of a viewpoint. Postmodern and feminist scholars agree that knowledge is socially constructed—that everyone, including the scientist, is socially and historically situated, and this influences the production of knowledge. This is a fundamental, but still not widely accepted criterion. The claim of an objective, neutral, disinterested perspective is an artificial concept not grounded in the reality of research.[32]

What can be said *in favour* of the feminist viewpoint and the feminist approach to science? If past research and the underlying scientific methodology have been flawed by androcentrism—for which

28. For summaries see, e.g., Hekman, *Gender and Knowledge*; Tong, *Feminist Thought*.

29. E.g. R. Bleier, *Science and Gender: A Critique of Biology and its Theories on Women* (New York: Pergamon Press, 1986); S. Harding, *The Science Question in Feminism* (Ithaca, NY: Cornell University Press, 1986); H. Longino, 'Science, Objectivity, and Feminist Values (A Review Essay)', *Feminist Studies* 14 (1988), pp. 561-74; E.F. Keller, *Reflections on Gender and Science* (New Haven: Yale University Press, 1985); E.F. Keller and H.E. Longino (eds.), *Feminism and Science* (Oxford: Oxford University Press, 1996); cf. also Hekman, *Gender and Knowledge*; Nicholson, *Gender and History*.

30. Nielsen, *Feminist Research Methods*, p. 29, borrows this term from Gadamer and defines 'horizon' as 'the full range of one's standpoint', including 'the particulars of one's situation (historical time, place, culture, class, any number of contextual variables are appropriate here)'. 'Fusion', according to Nielsen, 'results from seeking knowledge while grounded in a perspective (in this case, *feminism*) that cannot be bracketed or held aside during the inquiry process'. Nielsen claims that although one's 'horizon' is 'limited and finite...it is open to relating and connecting with horizons other than one's own (for example, feminist work does not ignore men the way androcentric work ignores women)'.

31. Nielsen, *Feminist Research Methods*, p. 31.

32. E.g. Nielsen, *Feminist Research Methods*.

there is ample proof—then it cannot be considered 'objective'. Feminists claim that their approach produces *more* 'objective' results, because it is *more* complete and inclusive than the positivistic approaches that did not prevent male-biased science. That is indeed an argument *for* feminist science.[33]

Feminist critique is of relevance to all scholars, including ancient historians. It forces scholars to rethink and re-evaluate their individual standpoints, as well as their discipline's approach to data. Increased proof of the validity of feminist approaches has already reduced male opposition, and men begin to use feminist research models.[34] The world of male scholars is not a Berlin Wall; the history of science has had several heretics responsible for major scientific paradigm shifts—like Socrates, Newton, Marx and Einstein—who attacked the dominant mode of thought. Despite massive resistance this ultimately led to the acceptance of new theories. The same will probably apply to feminist theory.[35]

In feminist studies it is not uncommon for authors to state explicitly a subjective viewpoint by interweaving into a study 'biographical' data such as ethnic background, religious affiliations, private and professional stages and situations.[36] However, the relevance of biography to research is not always convincing. I am certain that my choice of discipline has less to do with my background than with

33. For a comprehensive summary and analysis see Hekman, *Gender and Knowledge*.

34. E.g. G. Duby, *History Continues* (Chicago: University of Chicago Press, 1994), pp. 127-28; J.S. Cooper, 'Gendered Sexuality in Sumerian Love Poetry', in I.L Finkel and M.J. Geller (eds.), *Sumerian Gods and their Representation* (Cuneiform Monographs, 7; Groningen, NL: Styx, 1996), pp. 85-97; T. Laqueur, *Making Sex: Body and Gender from the Greeks to Freud* (Cambridge, MA: Harvard University Press, 1990).

35. Nielsen, *Feminist Research Methods*, sees in feminist theory a Kuhnian paradigm shift (a scientific revolution). What impact feminism will eventually have, for instance, on medicine, biology, genetics etc., is impossible to evaluate for a 'scientist of ancient civilizations'. By comparison to Marxist theory, which had a major impact on the social sciences, but did not change nature sciences, feminism might change nature science as well. At least, that is one of the goals of feminist scientists (e.g., Bleier, *Feminist Approaches*; Harding, *Science Question*; Keller, *Reflections*; Keller and Longino [eds.], *Feminism and Science*). Should this happen, there will be a Kuhnian paradigm shift.

36. E.g. S.P. Haley, 'Black Feminist Thought and Classics: Re-membering, Re-claiming, Re-empowering', in Rabinowitz and Richlin (eds.), *Feminist Theory*, pp. 23-43; T. Passman, 'Out of the Closet and into the Field: Matriculture, the Lesbian Perspective and Feminist Classics', in Rabinowitz and Richlin (eds.), *Feminist Theory*, pp. 181-208.

intellectual curiosity, and the reasons for my engagement in feminist research are the same as those repeated by others over and over again. I therefore cannot think of any plausible reason for inserting a personal account. I do, however, advocate the scrutiny of theories, methods and terminology usually taken for granted—since Mesopotamian research tends to avoid consideration of 'tacit knowledge' and precise definitions of terminology, such as the terms 'civilization', 'culture', 'class', 'status organization', 'structure', 'bureaucracy' and 'patriarchy'.[37]

4. The 'Interdisciplinary' Approach

Many feminist scholars advocate an 'interdisciplinary' approach in their analysis of women and gender.[38] But quite often 'interdisciplinary' refers not to methodology but to 'cross-cultural' analysis and comparisons postulating universal norms, such as the presence of patriarchy and gender asymmetry in nearly all known civilizations and cultures. These sweeping generalizations rarely include precise definitions of terminology, and cannot be distinguished from positivistic and essentialistic metanarratives.

4.1 Civilization and Culture

In a recently published multi-volume survey of Egyptian, Mesopotamian, Syrian, Anatolian, Iranian and ancient biblical cultures, titled *Civilizations of the Ancient Near East*,[39] the editor and authors do not define 'civilization', and differentiations are loosely based on geography, language, duration, religion, uniformity, coherence or style.[40] Distinction between civilization and culture remains blurred. This is not surprising because there is little scholarly consensus on the criteria for defining civilizations and culture and for distinguishing the one from the other.[41] Most scholars seem to agree that Egypt and

37. Cf. M. Polanyi, *The Tacit Dimension* (London: Routledge and Kegan Paul, 1967).

38. Scott, *Gender and the Politics of History*, pp. 8-9; Rabinowitz, xxx, in Rabinowitz and Richlin (eds.), *Feminist Theory and the Classics*, pp. 1-20; E. Fantham, H.P. Foley, N.B. Kampen, S.B. Pomeroy and H.A. Shapiro, *Women in the Classical World: Image and Text* (Oxford: Oxford University Press, 1994).

39. Sasson (ed.), *Civilizations*. Women and gender were not included in these volumes!

40. For these criteria see M. Melko and L.R. Scott (eds.), *The Boundaries of Civilizations in Space and Time* (Lanham, MD: University Press of America, 1987), pp. 5-10, 29-31, 371-378.

41. Melko and Scott (eds.), *Boundaries*, esp. pp. 1-58; H. Frankfort, *The Birth of*

Mesopotamia represent two distinct civilizations, but some regard the Levantine (Anatolia, Syria, Lebanon, ancient Israel) as a separate civilization; yet others separate a Levantine from a Judaic civilization, or see the Levantine as part of the Mesopotamian civilization.[42] David Wilkinson even proposes a theory of 'central civilization', which started with the 'coupling of Egyptian and Mesopotamian civilizations' around 1250 BC into a 'Near Eastern civilization'.[43]

Qualities considered essential for classification as 'civilization' are: the existence of cities, writing and monumental architecture. Civilizationists, however, disagree about the importance of further criteria such as world-view (*Weltanschauung*); religion; language; coherence; uniformity; political, social and technological development; value system; or style.[44] Gender is never mentioned in this context. The categorization of civilizations is a complex (and dubious) pursuit if certain criteria are excluded. These criteria, possibly including gender systems, fundamentally determine a civilization's special nature. In postmodern discourse, Western civilization is equated with a specific thought system whose central values (rationalism, dualism, objectivity, universality, absolute values) have come under attack.

Civilization and culture are often used indiscriminately as synonyms.[45] In anthropology and archaeology, culture is commonly understood as opposition to nature. For Clifford Geertz, 'the concept of culture...is essentially a semiotic one', constructed of webs of significance in which man is suspended.[46] Michael Carrithers understands culture as a product of human sociability, as a pattern of life.[47] Carrithers's theory that cultures are not coherent, autonomous wholes, but open to infusion from other cultures, corresponds to the situation in the ancient Near East, where various cultures were in

Civilization in the Near East (Garden City, NY: Doubleday, 1956), p. v; C.K. Maisels, *The Emergence of Civilization* (London: Routledge, 1990), pp. xv-xx; Michael Mann, *The Sources of Social Power.* I. *A History of Power from the Beginning to A.D. 1760* (Cambridge: Cambridge University Press, 1986), pp. 63-104; J. Oates and D. Oates, *The Rise of Civilization*, (Oxford: Phaidon, 1976).

42. Melko and Scott (eds.), *Boundaries.*

43. D. Wilkinson, 'The Connectedness Criterion and Central Civilization', in Melko and Scott (eds.), *Boundaries*, pp. 25-28. It is noteworthy that no Egyptologists or scholars of the ancient Near East participated in the discussion.

44. Melko and Scott (eds.), *Boundaries.*

45. Cf. Frankfort, *Birth of Civilization.*

46. C. Geertz, *The Interpretation of Cultures* (New York: Basic Books, 1973), p. 5.

47. M. Carrithers, *Why Humans Have Cultures: Explaining Anthropology and Social Diversity* (Oxford: Oxford University Press, 1992), esp. pp. 15-18, 34-36.

contact with each other. Culture, although a precondition for the formation of civilization, may or may not lead to civilization.

The complex issues of civilization and culture cannot be pursued here, although it is necessary to be aware of the diverse concepts concerning ancient Mesopotamia. The boundaries of ancient Mesopotamia fluctuate not only in and by time and geography but also according to the viewpoints of scholars who may see it as one, two or three distinct civilizations. Mesopotamian 'civilization' is characterized by heterogeneous, simultaneous as well as successive, 'cultures', if we use 'culture' as referring to different ethnic groups, religions, languages and styles. Feminists use 'Western civilization' when referring to a particular androcentric world-view, but more often use 'culture' when comparing different ethnic, religious or social groups.

The 'ancient Near East', apart from a descriptive historical-geographical term, is used as a general term for multiple sub-disciplines (Sumeriology, Assyriology, Hittitology, Iranology, Ugarit and Hurrian languages, ancient Near East archaeology and art history), and in order to circumvent the ambiguity of the nation concept inherent in terms such as 'ancient Anatolia', 'ancient Iran', 'ancient Iraq', 'ancient Syria', 'ancient Israel' or 'Palestinian' archaeology.

4.2 Definitions of 'Interdisciplinary'

The 'interdisciplinary' approach is often portrayed as possibly the most promising method for overcoming the confinements of specialization, as well as for bridging the three scientific cultures (nature science, social science and culture science).[48] Interdisciplinary methods are practised in all three scientific cultures; in the humanities (culture science), 'interdisciplinary' describes the following approaches:

1. Synthesizing the analysis of different types of material (texts, architecture, visual art, artefacts, tools, etc.) from the same civilization/culture, sometimes separated into disciplines that use different methodologies (e.g. anthropology, archaeology, art history, philology, feminist theory, semiotics, deconstruction).

2. Employing theory and methodology from another scientific culture, that is, combining methods from nature

48. These are translations of the German *Naturwissenschaften, Sozialwissenschaften, Kulturwissenschaften*; cf. U. Felt, H. Nowotny and K. Taschwer, *Wissenschaftsforschung: Eine Einführung* (Frankfurt and New York: Campus, 1995), pp. 170-79.

or social science and culture science (e.g. archaeometry, psychohistory, sociolinguistics, psycholinguistics, sociobiology), or using theories from nature or social science in culture science (e.g. critical theory, systems theory, chaos theory).

3.   Comparative analysis of distinctly different civilizations and/or cultures: for instance, urbanism or kinship structures in Mesopotamia and Egypt, or Mesoamerica, or India.

These three approaches are based on the constellation of the subject matter and methodology of academic disciplines. Thus 'interdisciplinary' in Egyptology or anthropology would mean something different than in ancient Near East studies.[49] More precise terms would help to distinguish the different meanings of 'interdisciplinary':

1.   An *inter*disciplinary or *contextual* approach, depending on the definition of a discipline. (In Europe, the division into archaeology and philology in Egyptology is practically unknown. Egyptologists work with texts and images without considering this an interdisciplinary approach; scholars of the ancient Near East often call text and image studies a contextual approach; anthropologists and feminists speak of an interdisciplinary approach when using methods from different disciplines).[50]

2.   A *trans*disciplinary approach, going beyond and transcending the limits of one scientific culture.[51]

3.   A cross-civilizational or cross-cultural approach.

These different approaches are not mutually exclusive. They are, however, neither specifically feminist nor new to archaeologists, historians and philologists studying ancient Mesopotamia. The feminist approach is more inclusive in paying attention to women and to the dimension of gender in its analyses.

49. Cf. Cooper and Schwartz (eds.), *Study of the Ancient Near East.*
50. Cooper and Schwartz (eds.), *Study of the Ancient Near East.*
51. Cf. Felt, Nowotny and Taschwer, *Wissenschaftsforschung.*

5. *The Feminist Approach*

5.1 *The Concept of Patriarchy*

Central to an understanding of the diverse and partly overlapping schools of feminist thought is the concept of patriarchy, though variously conceptualized:[52] patriarchy is simultaneously process, structure and ideology. All these are used to subordinate women. Patriarchy is viewed as a global system that has existed in nearly every known society, and originates in the authority of the father. The assumption, however, that patriarchy is always the primary source of male authority is questionable. Male dominance and authority does not seek justification exclusively in man's part in procreation, or in his role as father: neither Jesus Christ nor his disciples or the pope depend on 'fatherhood' to establish authority. Clarissa Atkinson observed that in early medieval France, royal power was based upon the king's strength and physical courage, his family possessions, his treasury and his ability to attract and pay warriors. In the sixteenth century a change took place, whereby royal authority was presented in terms of patriarchy.[53] Considering this change in the European ideology of kingship, it seems unlikely that similar concepts of patriarchy and royal ideology can easily be applied to ancient Mesopotamia.

However, Sumerian and Akkadian royal epithets do suggest that fatherhood was *not* central to royal ideology. Authority derived primarily from heroic deeds and military prowess. The epithet 'father' is rare.[54] Epithets referring to masculine qualities, such as force and strength, are more common than 'father'.[55] By far the most common epithet is 'shepherd', emphasizing the notion of guardianship of men and women, perhaps even the notions of care and nurture that are usually considered 'feminine' qualities.[56] How masculinity and femininity are defined, and how these definitions translate into societal norms, structures and ideology has yet to be researched. But the

52. E.g. Tong, *Feminist Thought* (Index).

53. C.W. Atkinson, *The Oldest Vocation: Christian Motherhood in the Middle Ages* (Ithaca, NY: Cornell University Press, 1991), pp. 90, 198-99.

54. M.-J. Seux, *Epithètes royales Akkadiennes et Sumériennes* (Paris: Letouzey et Ané, 1967), pp. 383, 384.

55. Seux, *Epithètes*, pp. 383-84 (*á*), 415 (*kala*), 429-30 (*nita-kala-ga*); cf. J.M. Asher-Greve, 'The Essential Body', in E. Hall and M. Wyke (eds.), *Gender and the Body in Antiquity* (special issue of *Gender and History*; Oxford: Oxford University Press, 1997).

56. Seux, *Epithètes*, pp. 441-46 (*sipa*).

term 'patriarchy' can be misleading when used indiscriminately because it implies that 'fatherhood', and its female correlate, 'motherhood', are fundamental to the definitions of gender.

5.2 *Gender Matters*

We have been trained to believe that asking the right question already provides half the answer, and that theories aid in formulating questions.[57] But what is considered a 'right' question has been, and still is, largely determined by the community of predominantly male scholars which exhibits little or no interest in women and gender. Feminist inquiry into the processes of theory-construction resulted in assailing the philosophical foundations and paradigms of science and the humanities because they are 'corrupted by patriarchy'.[58] According to feminist philosophers, 'gender matters—even in very abstract theories in which one might not suspect that it would'.[59] For example, feminist philosophers attack paradigmatic dualism and either/or categorization, claiming that those are neither normative nor universal. Because such paradigms and categorizations are used by most scholarly colleagues, including myself, I began to systematically re-examine my own work. I realized that I had relied on tacit knowledge, such as bipolar gender theory, which I had never questioned.

My study of women in ancient Sumer was based on the either/or model, that is, if it is not male then it must be female.[60] Depictions of persons whose dress and features were apparently ambiguous were still pressed into a two-gendered system, or the visual object was interpreted as of low artistic quality, perhaps of provincial origin. The implication that (provincial) artists were gender blind never occurred. But feminist theory asks different questions. Is this gender ambiguity perhaps intentional? What other forms of gender ambiguity are known either in Mesopotamia or in other civilizations? In what contexts is gender either important or unimportant? Gender ambiguity is not rare; genderless angels and saints, as well as androgynous figures, are depicted in European art. These European

57. Buccellati, 'Methodological Concerns', p. 9.

58. So Antony and Witt, in their introduction to *Mind of One's Own*, pp. xiii-xiv; cf. also Hekman, *Gender and Knowledge*; A. Garry and M. Pearsall (eds.), *Women, Knowledge, and Reality: Explorations in Feminist Philosophy* (New York and London: Routledge, 1992); Keller and Longino (eds.), *Feminism and Science*.

59. Garry and Pearsall (eds.), *Women, Knowledge, and Reality*, p. xiii.

60. J.M. Asher-Greve, *Frauen in altsumerischer Zeit* (Bibliotheca Mesopotamica, 18; Malibu, CA: Undena Publications, 1985).

representations are relatively easy to decipher; but the meaning in Mesopotamian art is far more difficult to uncover. Combining an interdisciplinary–contextual approach with a feminist viewpoint, I began to re-examine visual material, texts, individual words, narrative contexts and socio-cultural contexts. The evidence led to new interpretations. An analysis of gender in mass produced seals in the late Uruk period (c. 3100–2900 BCE) revealed that, although there is a division of gender and work or tasks, this gender division is not very rigid; women occasionally do men's work, like herding, and occupy positions as overseers of groups. But it was not always important to the Sumerians to specify gender. The tasks or roles of a group (and, occasionally, of an individual) are sometimes more important than gender differentiation. In some instances a task like weaving, herding or fishing is sufficient to indicate which gender was associated with that work.[61]

In another study on gender and the body I present evidence of a multiple gender system. Castrates and people without any sexual organs were assigned specific social tasks.[62] In early Mesopotamia (c. 2500–1500 BCE) neither gender nor mind–body were dualistic concepts: gender taxonomy tolerated ambiguity beyond the 'normative' masculine–feminine; body and mind were an inseparable unity, denoted by the same Sumerian word.[63]

A feminist model such as gender theory will lead to new questions, but not necessarily to a new methodological approach. My own approach (interdisciplinary and contextual) might include iconology, hermeneutics, critical analysis of texts and words, and what is now termed *trans*disciplinary analysis (such as archaeometry) in one article; and cross-civilizational comparisons in another. These are 'conventional' methods in our discipline. Re-examining visual material, texts and words is not specifically feminist; it has a long tradition in a discipline that is continuously confronted with new archaeological discoveries, and experiences a growing understanding of cuneiform languages. The feminist aspect of my approach, however, is the standpoint that women and gender are equally important as ideological, religious and social concepts; that gender is a fundamental concept in socio-historical theory and important in the structure of

61. Cf. J.M. Asher-Greve and W.B. Stern, 'A New Analytical Method and its Application to Cylinder Seals', *Iraq* 45 (1986), pp. 157-62; J.M. Asher-Greve, 'Where are the Missing Men? A Gendered Analysis of Simple Pattern Seals' (in preparation).
62. Asher-Greve, 'The Essential Body'.
63. Asher-Greve, 'The Essential Body'.

religion and economic, social and cultural life; and that gender concepts have undergone historical and cultural changes.

Philologists would profit from feminist theories that pursue questions such as how language encodes 'male' meanings; how cultures differentiate the masculine from the feminine; and how the process of gender socialization relates to language socialization.[64] These questions would lead to questions about how Sumerian or Akkadian differentiates women from men, whether women are addressed or described in a different manner than men, whether there is a specific female voice.[65]

6. Towards a Feminist Ancient History

No specifically feminist methodology has been developed for the study of ancient societies like Mesopotamia. Uncritical adaptation of theory and methodology developed in other disciplines does not address problems specific to the study of ancient societies. A pressing concern for us as historians who try to understand and explain the past and to make it meaningful for the present, is the relevance of the study of ancient Mesopotamia in today's world. This concern is influenced also by contemporary policy.[66] The history we present is remote, and the available evidence often makes it difficult to address current topics of debate. We must face the challenge of postmodern critiques by demonstrating the significance of our field to current scientific dialogue, thus justifying continuation of public support.

The anthropological models to which many archaeologists turn

64. E.g. D. Cameron, *Feminism and Linguistic Theory* (London: Macmillan, 2nd rev. edn, 1992); K. Hall and M. Bucholtz (eds.), *Gender Articulated: Language and the Socially Constructed Self* (London: Routledge, 1995); D. Tannen (ed.), *Gender and Conversational Interaction* (Oxford: Oxford University Press, 1993).

65. Cf. Cooper, 'Gendered Sexuality'. For *emesal* and other women's languages and dialects, cf. M.K. Schretter, *Emesal-Studien: Sprach- und literatur-geschichtliche Untersuchungen zur sogenannten Frauensprache des Sumerischen* (Innsbrucker Beiträge zur Kulturwissenschaft, 69; Innsbruck, 1990), pp. 105-20. An analysis of *'emesal'* from a feminist linguistic perspective could lead to new insights and new interpretation.

66. In the current economic and social climate, small 'exotic' disciplines face severe cuts and closing of departments. To justify their existence these disciplines have to participate in, and change their attitude towards, the broader theoretical and methodological academic debate. Standing apart isolates these disciplines and makes them vulnerable to easy elimination. For a discussion of the justification of humanities in today's academy, see Felt, Nowotny and Taschwer, *Wissenschaftsforschung*, pp. 158-69.

often lack the historical dimension crucial in the study of ancient
literate societies where processes, changes and continuities have to be
taken into account.[67] Although the *annales* school's model of *longues
durées* emphasizes analysis of processes and change, it has not
included gender in its model.[68] Anthropologists study relatively
homogenous (contemporary) societies, whereas scholars of the ancient Near East study multiple cultures extending horizontally (in
space) and vertically (in time). Some feminist anthropologists and
historians assert that there is no historically coherent and singular
identity to 'women'; therefore the analytical category of 'difference'
should to be added to that of 'gender'. Therefore, in several recent
studies the focus has shifted to *difference* as an analytical category
referring to race, ethnicity, class, religion and even age.[69]

Mesopotamian social organization might reveal systems rather
different from sociological models used in the past. Preliminary
analysis shows that social concepts have to be redefined and refined
for ancient Mesopotamia; that social stratification might have been
more varied than previously thought—depending not only on power
and economic privileges, but also on knowledge, skills, occupation,
gender and 'difference'. We can adopt a feminist position by focusing
on women and gender as socio-cultural concepts, not as biologically
determined persons assumed to have had a marginal effect on
history. 'Feminine', 'masculine' and 'gender' in ancient Mesopotamian art, texts and artefacts are endowed with semiotic significance
transcending biological sex. As Ian Hodder states, what gender
analysis offers for antiquity will lead 'to a re-evaluation of other
apparently unrelated issues, such as meaning, representation, power
and general archaeological theory';[70] and, it should be added, new

67. Cf. Claassen, *Exploring Gender*; Gero and Conkey (eds.), *Engendering
Archaeology*; Pinsky and Wylie (eds.), *Critical Traditions*; Walde and Willows
(eds.), *Archaeology of Gender*; Wylie, 'Feminist Theories'. This trend can also be
observed in the classics, e.g. L.J. Archer, S. Fischler, and M. Wyle (eds.), *Women in
Ancient Societies: An Illusion of the Night* (London: Macmillan, 1994); French, 'What
is Central for the Study of Women in Antiquity?'; Rabinowitz, in Rabinowitz and
Richlin (eds.), *Feminist Theory and the Classics*.

68. E.g. B.A. Knapp, *Archaeology, Annales and Ethnohistory* (Cambridge:
Cambridge University Press, 1992); *idem, Society and Polity at Bronze Age Pella: An
Annales Perspective* (Sheffield: Sheffield Academic Press, 1993); P. Michalowski,
'Third Millennium Contacts: Observations on the Relationship between Mari and
Ebla', *JAOS* 105 (1985), pp. 293-302.

69. Cf. J.W. Scott, 'Introduction', in J.W. Scott (ed.), *Feminism and History*
(Oxford and New York: Oxford University Press, 1996), pp. 1-13.

70. I. Hodder, 'Gender Representation', p. 11.

models in ancient Near East studies as well. In order to *engender* ancient Near East studies, attention has to be given to the basic principles of a feminist approach: continuous and reflective consideration of women and gender, which includes testing a variety of old and new theories, explicit assumptions and implicit tacit knowledge. By considering all variants, it should be possible to elucidate 'gender' as a principle in socio-cultural organization, and women as historical beings who participated in the creation and development of ancient Mesopotamian civilization. With the shift of historiography away from events, personalities and metanarratives towards in-depth analyses of societal and cultural processes and change, women and gender can no longer be considered irrelevant or marginal analytical categories. Scholars of ancient Mesopotamia should realize that this is not just a passing feminist trend but, possibly, a sign of a 'scientific revolution'.

ENGENDERING CREATION IN ANCIENT EGYPT: STILL AND FLOWING WATERS*

Lana Troy

The Beginning described in the book of Genesis consisted of existence as a formless dark void, above which hovered the spirit of God. Gender as a concept, or actualized in any form, had no place in this pre-creation world.[1] In the biblical narrative, male and female become relevant concepts first when humankind, as the dual earthly images of God, appear. The divine creation of the world and its

---

*   A number of challenging discussions with Professor Fekri A. Hassan have precipitated this article and encouraged me to present these hypotheses with a more well defined line than would otherwise have been the case. His support and influence is hereby acknowledged. Whatever flaws may be found in the argument presented in the text remain, however, the author's. See F.A. Hassan, 'Primeval Goddess to Divine King: The Mythogenesis of Power in the Early Egyptian State', in R. Friedman and B. Adams (eds.), *The Followers of Horus: Studies Dedicated to Michael Allen Hoffman, 1944–1990* (Egyptian Studies Association Publication, 2, Oxbow Monograph, 20; Oxford: Oxbow Publications, 1992), pp. 307-21, for a discussion of 'the mythogenetic process by which the sacred powers of female deities were absorbed by male leaders' in the formative period leading up to the Egyptian state.
   1.   See, e.g., C. Meyers, *Discovering Eve: Ancient Israelite Women in Context* (Oxford: Oxford University Press, 1988), pp. 84-86 for a discussion of Adam and Eve as representing the first manifestation of biological gender. P. Trible's classic work (*God and the Rhetoric of Sexuality* [London: SCM Press, 1978, pp. 31-59]), which attributes feminine (uterine) qualities to Yahweh by showing the philological and philosophical interrelationship between the concept 'womb' (*reḥem*) and compassion and mercy, does not, however, attribute sexual characteristics to the deity. On the contrary, she states (p. 15) that sexuality was treated as a human quality, not even shared by the animals. Cf. also H. Schüngel-Straumann, 'On the Creation of Man and Woman in Genesis 1–3: The History and Reception of the Text Reconsidered', in A. Brenner (ed.), *A Feminist Companion to the Book of Genesis* (The Feminist Companion to the Bible, 2; Sheffield: Sheffield Academic Press, 1993), pp. 53-76; and P. Bird, 'Sexual Differentiation and Divine Image', in K.E. Børresen (ed.), *The Image of God: Gender Models in Judaeo-Christian Tradition* (Minneapolis: Fortress Press, 1995), pp. 5-28, for treatments of this subject.

creatures, and human procreation after the fall from grace in the garden, are dissimilar in kind.

For the ancient Egyptians, however, creation on all levels was firmly linked to reproductive sexuality. The imagery of the 'First Time' (*sp tpy*), the moment when the life contained within the primeval waters began a process of transformation from potential to manifest, was patterned on female and male reproductive modes, on the mechanisms of conception and birth. The means whereby a single source could develop into the multiplicity of the ordered world emanated from the presence of both female and male in that source.[2] Thus, the origin of all life, the source of both creators and creation, was not asexual, nor presexual, but androgynous, incorporating both genders equally. Gender both predated and presupposed creation itself.[3]

Two modes, associated with female and male reproductive roles, are reiterated in the different creation myths of ancient Egypt. These have different regional origins and the sources that preserve them vary widely in their chronology, ranging from c. 2400 BCE with the Pyramid Texts[4] to the second century CE. One myth complex in particular stands out in its association with the kingship and the early development of the Egyptian state. It is known as the Heliopolitan

2. The importance of the question of the derivation of many from one is reflected in the title of the classic work on Egyptian religion by E. Hornung, *Der Eine und die Vielen* (Darmstadt: Wissenschaftliche Buchgesellschaft, 1971); ET: Hornung, *Conceptions of God in Ancient Egypt: The One and the Many* (London: Routledge & Kegan Paul, 1982). J.P. Allen, *Genesis in Egypt: The Philosophy of Ancient Egyptian Creation Accounts* (Yale Egyptological Studies, 2; New Haven: Yale Egyptological Seminar, 1988), p. 14, expresses the Egyptians' obsession with this problem as a question, 'how could a lone parent produce an offspring?'. This formulation reflects the biological frame of reference used by the Egyptians in relation to the creation.

3. The discussion of sexual imagery in the Heliopolitan creation myth has been treated at length, with reference to the development of the ancient Egyptian queenship, in the first part of L. Troy, *Patterns of Queenship in Ancient Egyptian Myth and History* (BOREAS, 14; Uppsala: Acta Universitatus Upsaliensis, 1986), pp. 5-51. The reader is also referred to S.-A. Naguib, *Le clérge féminin d'Amon thébain à la 21e dynastie* (Orientalia Lovaniensia Analecta, 38; Leuven: Peeters and Departement Oriëntalistiek, 1990), which deals with the interrelationship between the mythic role of the feminine and that of the priestess as the female counterpart of the god. Cf. also Troy, *Patterns of Queenship*, pp. 73-91 on this subject.

4. Cf. R.O. Faulkner, *The Ancient Egyptian Pyramid Texts Translated into English* (Oxford: Clarendon Press, 1969) for an English translation; and K. Sethe, *Die altägyptischen Pyramidtexten* (Leipzig: Hinrichs, 1908–1910) for the currently standard text. These texts are cited according to the Egyptological convention, using the paragraph number (§) assigned to each line in Sethe's edition.

Cosmology, and is documented in the earliest corpus of religious texts. This cosmology incorporates images of both female and male versions of the androgynous creator.

This paper begins by examining the gender imagery of the Heliopolitan cosmology. It then turns to the texts of Esna and Thebes in order to delineate the two structural variations found in the Heliopolitan complex, which alternatively highlight female and male reproductive modes as the primary characteristics of the creator. The first of these, from Esna, formulates a mother–son paradigm, giving the mother the role of sole creator. The Theban model focuses on the ithyphallic creator god, who regenerates himself as his own son. This is accomplished through the medium of a physical attribute which is identified as feminine, and termed his daughter.

In both versions creation, from the watery void to the ordered world of Egyptian kingship, is framed by the reproductive powers of the female and the male as the means of the transformation of the aging father into the rejuvenated son. Although source material cited here for the most definitive female and male creator gods comes from the last centuries of ancient Egyptian civilization, the deities and iconographic images refer back to Egypt's earliest period; and can be regarded as formative elements in the royal ideology of the young nation.

Still and Flowing Waters: The Heliopolitan Cosmology

Nun: Before the Beginning[5]

The limitless waters of the beginning, personified as Nun, 'the Father of the Gods' (*it nṯrw*), is an element common to all ancient Egyptian cosmologies. These waters contained all life as latent and unmanifested, in a state of total darkness.

The essence of this pre-creation state is described as four pairs of deities, male and female. In the earliest references, found in the Coffin Texts of the early Middle Kingdom (c. 2000 BCE),[6] these gods are

5.   Cf. Allen, *Genesis in Egypt*, p. 4; S. Bickel, *La cosmogonie égyptienne: Avant le Nouvel Empire* (OBO, 134; Fribourg: Editions Universitaires; Göttingen: Vandenhoeck & Ruprecht, 1994, pp. 23-31, with references for further discussion of this god's role.

6.   Cf. R.O. Faulkner, *The Ancient Egyptian Coffin Texts* (3 vols.; Warminster: Aris & Philips, 1973–1978), for an English translation. These texts are cited as CT, according to the volume number of the text edition as published by A. deBuck (*The Egyptian Coffin Texts*. IV. *Texts of Spells 268-354* [University of Chicago Oriental Institute Publications, 67; Chicago: University of Chicago Press, 1961]), and

known collectively as the *Ḥḥw* gods. Sometimes translated as 'chaos-gods', the term can be understood as derived from the verb *ḥḥy*, 'to search', referring to the purpose of these waters as they spread out and making these gods, embodied in the waters, 'the seekers'. In later texts these gods are called the *ḥmnyw*, 'the Eight', which is also a pun on the name of the native city of these gods, Hermopolis (*Ḥmnw*). The literature commonly refers to them with the Greek term, Ogdoad.

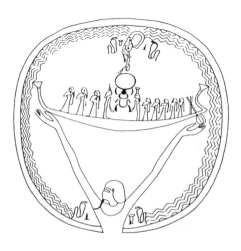

Figure 1. Nun Papyrus of Khonsu-mes.
Bibliothèque Nationale, Paris.

The four pairs of male and female deities describe Nun as a watery state (*nnw*), with a limitless expanse of flood waters (*ḥḥw*); it is dark (*kkw*); and, finally, lacks order or is in a state of confusion (*tnmw*). The last attribute varies, and can be replaced by either the concept of negation 'that which is not' (*niw*), or the mystery of becoming, 'that which is hidden' (*imn*). In addition, the eight gods are given the forms of aquatic snakes (male) and frogs (females), as well as the epithet 'the fathers and the mothers'.

Although identified as a male deity, Nun, as the motionless and limitless waters that contain all the potential of life, is a prefiguration

followed by a reference to the page and line. For the Ogdoad see the classic work by K. Sethe (*Amun und die acht Urgötter von Hermopolis* [Leipzig: Verlag der Akademie der Wissenschaften, 1929]; as well as the discussions in Allen, *Genesis in Egypt*, pp. 18-21 and Bickel, *La cosmogonie*, pp. 26-29.

of uterine birth, and thus the first manifestation of the feminine generative mode. His androgyny is confirmed by the male–female pairs that comprise his nature, giving him the potential of procreation. Nun is an eternal element. He is neither created nor self-generated and is, in this manner, the universal precondition for all existence.

Atum: The Self-created[7]

The god Atum appears spontaneously in the waters of Nun. Distinguished by his self-creation, he is 'the one who came into being by himself' (*ḫpr ḏs.f*). The name Atum is derived from *tm*, a verb which means 'to complete' but which also functions as a verbal negation. Thus Atum comprises non-existence as well as existence as 'he who is complete' and 'he who is not'.

Atum is an anthropomorphic male deity. The manner in which he creates emphasizes male fertility as a creative principle. The description of Atum's creative act is sexually explicit. He grasps his phallus in his hand, masturbates, swallows his own seed and spits it out as the brother–sister pair, Shu and Tefnut.[8]

> When I came into being, Being came into being,
> And all beings came into being after I came into being.
> Many were the forms of existence which came forth from my mouth,
> Before the sky had come into being
> Before the earth had come into being
> Before land and serpents had been created in this place
> I knitted them together in Nun as inert beings when I could find no place to stand.
> I contemplated with my heart, I planned with my sight
> And I alone made every shape
> Before I had spat out Shu,
> Before I had expectorated Tefnut
> Before any other had come into being who could create with me.
> I planned with my own heart
> And many forms of being came into being,
> Consisting of the forms of children and the forms of their children.
> I am the one who masturbated with my fist, I stimulated with my hand

7. For discussions of Atum, cf. W. Barta, *Untersuchungen zum Götterkreis der Neunheit* (Münchener agyptologische Studien, 28; Munich: Deutschen Kunstverlag, 1973), pp. 78-85 and Bickel, *La cosmogonie*, pp. 33-53.

8. Cf. PT §1246 for the earliest reference to the masturbation on the mound. Papyrus Bremner-Rhind (R.O. Faulkner, *The Papyrus Bremner-Rhind [British Museum No. 10188]* (Bibliotheca Aegyptiaca, 3; Brussels: Fondation egyptologique reine Elisabeth, 1933) which is cited here, although dated to the early fourth century BCE, repeats a tradition reiterated throughout ancient Egyptian history.

> My seed fell in my own mouth.
> I spat out Shu and I expectorated Tefnut
> And my father Nun brought them up
> (Bremner-Rhind, 26.21-27.1; Faulkner, *The Papyrus Bremner-Rhind*,
> p. 60)

> I united my members,
> And they issued from me myself.
> After I had masturbated with my grasp,
> My desire came into my hand
> And seed fell in my mouth.
> I spat out Shu, I expectorated Tefnut
> (Bremner-Rhind 29.2-3; Faulkner, *The Papyrus Bremner-Rhind*, p. 71).

Although Atum gives birth to the twins without a partner, the feminine element is not absent from their creation, as the god incorporates a number of feminine attributes. The texts relate Atum's arousal to his hand. The word 'hand', *ḏrt* is feminine in Egyptian and the hand of the god is interpreted as his consort.[9] The Eye of the god, traditionally identified as the daughter of the god and personified by such goddesses as Hathor, plays an important role in 'locating' the twins in Nun before they are born.

> I am this Eye of Horus, the messenger of the Sole Lord who has no equal
> I am truly she who made his name
> I have sprouted that which has grown, I have transformed that which is transformed
> Before the heaven was born, and she could give me praise
> Before the earth rose up, and he could exalted me
> Lo, I seek your saliva and your spittle, they are Shu and Tefnut
> I have searched
> I have sought out
> Behold, I have fetched'. (CT IV 173f-174j; de Buck, *The Egyptian Coffin Texts*).

> It was my Eye that brought them to me after aeons when they were far from me
> (Bremner-Rhind 29:1-2; Faulkner, *The Papyrus Bremner-Rhind*, p. 71)

The Eye of the god is the active element that brings the children to the father.

---

9.   Cf. Troy, *Patterns of Queenship*, p. 16. In a ritual context, the title 'Hand of the God' (*ḏrt nṯr*) is given to the divine consorts of the god in Heliopolis, the goddesses Iousaas and Nebethetepet. For a discussion of these goddesses see J. Vandier, 'Iousaas et (Hathor)-Nebet-Hetepet', *Revue d'egyptologie* 16-18, 20 (1964–66), pp. 55-146, 89-176, 67-143, 135-48. It is also a title of the royal priestesses of the cult of Amun, the 'Wife of the God' (*ḥmt nṯr*); cf. Troy, *Patterns of Queenship*, pp. 97-99.

Nun and Atum exist in a pre-creation environment as two phases of the pre-creation process. Nun is a limitless and diffuse expanse, and Atum is the coalesced manifestation of both existence and non-existence. The two male deities also represent the sequence of female and male reproductive roles while functioning as androgynous creators. They share a number of attributes with deities found in other mythic complexes. The manner in which these attributes cluster around the concept of creation as a biological process, homologous with pregnancy and ejaculation, suggests that the descriptions of Nun and Atum are composed in reference to two creator types, a 'mother' and a 'father'.

Shu and Tefnut: Son and Daughter, Brother and Sister[10]

The children who are spat out by Atum are the twins Shu and Tefnut. They are the first manifestation of life as two beings of differentiated gender. They are male and female, son and daughter, brother and sister.

The names given to the twins indicate their identification with the bodily fluids of their father, functioning as puns for 'saliva' (*išs*) and 'spittle' (*tftf*).[11] They are traditionally associated with the first manifestations of creation as air and moisture.

Geb and Nut: Father and Mother[12]

The completion of the creation of the natural world comes about with the next generation. Earth and sky come into being with Geb and Nut, the children of Shu and Tefnut. The common iconographic image of the New Kingdom (c. 1550–1090 BCE) shows the two deities as separated by their father, Shu. According to a later explanation of this image, the two are forced apart when their father comes upon them in the act of intercourse.[13] Shu, as 'air', lifts his daughter's arched body above that of the limp Geb, thus creating the heavenly vault above the earth.

10. For discussions of Shu and Tefnut, see Barta, *Untersuchungen*, pp. 85-94; Bickel, *La cosmogonie*, pp. 128-36, also pp. 168-76.

11. Cf. Barta, *Untersuchungen*, pp. 86-87 and 89-90 for a discussion of these gods' names.

12. For Geb and Nut see Barta, *Untersuchungen*, pp. 94-104. A discussion of these gods as gender representatives is found in T. Martinelli, 'Geb et Nout dans les Textes des Pyramides: Essai de compréhension du caractère masculine de Geb et de la Terre ainsi que du caractère féminin de Nout et du Ciel', *Bulletin de Société d'Egyptologie, Genève* 18 (1994), pp. 61-77.

13. Cf. H. te Velde, 'The Theme of the Separation of Heaven and Earth in Egyptian Mythology and Religion', *Studia Aegyptiaca* 3 (1977), pp. 161-70.

Figure 2. Geb and Nut (taken from Troy 1986: 30, Papyrus of Nisti-ta-Nebet-Taui. Cairo Museum).

The position of Shu and Tefnut in the Heliopolitan cosmology is that of the children of the Atum, with almost no explicit reference to their role as parents of the next generation. Geb and Nut are, on the other hand, closely identified with their status as mother and father of the next generation. Thus—just as Nun and Atum function as the sequential introduction of female and male modes of procreation— the pairs, Shu and Tefnut and Geb and Nut, represent not only the physical landscape of the ordered world, but also the establishment of the generational roles of son and daughter, father and mother.

Nut and Geb reiterate the attributes of 'female' and 'male' found in the first two manifestations of the reproductive modes, Nun and Atum. Nut's identification as the sky, particularly the night sky, mirrors the role of Nun; numerous scholars have argued that her name indicates that she is a feminine variation of that god. Geb's name does not allow any elaborate interpretation but, representing the earth, he is—on another level—of the same essence as the mound which appeared in the primeval waters and is associated with Atum. Like Atum, Geb can be represented as ithyphallic (Fig. 3) and even as curled around with the phallus in his mouth.

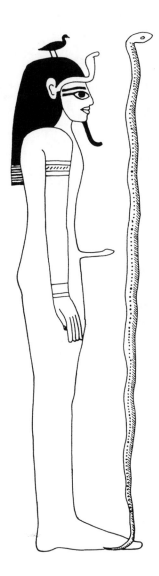

Figure 3. Geb and the Primeval Serpent (Tomb of Ramses VI)

With the birth of Geb and Nut, the physical world is complete. The next generation of gods are no longer concerned with the physical properties of the earth, but introduce the themes of kingship and inheritance.

Osiris and Isis, Seth and Nephthys[14]

In the Heliopolitan version of the myth the children of Geb and Nut number four, creating two pairs: Osiris and Isis, Seth and Nephthys. The Egyptian kingship, according to myth, dates back to the creator Atum(-Re), and was passed down from father to son. Osiris, the eldest son, inherited the office from his father, Geb. No information is given about the reign of Osiris; instead, he enters the narrative as the victim of fratricide.[15] Seth, jealous of his brother's power, murders him either by striking him down or by drowning him. Osiris's body is cut up into forty-two parts, one per each Egyptian province, which are scattered about the land. His sisters Isis and Nephthys change themselves into birds of prey and, shrieking their mourning cries, search for the remains of their brother. Once these are found, the goddesses create the first mummy by joining together the pieces of the god's body. Isis, known for her wisdom and magic, brings the king back to life in order to conceive his heir Horus. Concealing herself from Seth in the delta marshlands, she gives birth to Horus, who is born as a falcon (Fig. 4).

Figure 4. Horus in the Marshes the Temple of Karnak.

14. Cf. Troy, *Patterns of Queenship*, pp. 32-43; *idem*, 'The First Time: Homology and Complementarity as Structural Forces in Ancient Egyptian Cosmology', *Cosmos: Journal of the Traditional Cosmology Society* 10.1 (1994), pp. 3-51 (from p. 9), for other discussions of this group of gods. For their role in the Ennead see Barta, *Untersuchungen*, pp. 105-32.

15. For a thorough review of the Osirian myth see J.G. Griffiths, *The Origins of Osiris and the Cult* (Studies in the History of Religion, 40; Leiden: Brill, 1980).

Although the gender identification of these four gods and goddesses appears to lack any ambiguity, the imagery associated with them indicates that the myth goes into another phase here when it come to defining the interrelationship of male and female elements. In the royal pair Osiris and Isis there are several indications that they represent a form of functional gender inversion. The name of Osiris is written with the signs of the feminine images of the eye and throne, and philological analyses of the name suggest that it is composed of two feminine elements. Some scholars have gone so far as to suggest that Osiris was originally a mother-goddess whose gender was transformed to fit into this narrative.[16] On the other hand, his consort, Isis, displays powers that indicate male characteristics, compensating for the passivity of her dead husband. These are referred to explicitly in several texts.

> There is no god nor goddess who has done what I have done, for I have played the part of the husband, though I am a wife (*nn wn nṯr iry n.i nṯrt r-pw ir.n.i tȝy iw.i m ḥmt*) (Louvre I. 3079.10[17]).

In some variations of the myth, the phallus of the god is never found and must be replaced by a wooden replica provided by the goddess. One suggested etymology for her name associates it with the verb meaning to 'pour' or 'ejaculate'.

While implications of inverted gender characteristics can be attributed to Osiris and Isis, Seth and Nephthys appear instead to reflect male and female characteristics in their most absolute form. Seth is known for his uncontrollable male force.[18] This makes him a natural ally with the powers of chaos, personified by the demon-like figures functioning as the enemies of the kingship. The name Nephthys, in Egyptian *Nbt-Ḥwt*, 'Mistress of the House', suggests a personification of the womb, leaving no room for any other form of association.[19] But, whereas the gender inversion of Osiris and Isis

16. For a discussion of the names Osiris and Isis see Troy, *Patterns of Queenship*, pp. 32-35, with special reference to J. Osing, 'Isis und Osiris', *Mitteilungen des deutschen Instituts für ägyptische Altertumskunde in Kairo* 30 (1974), pp. 91-113. For Osiris as an expression of feminine procreation cf. Barta, *Untersuchungen*, pp. 105-108.

17. J.-C. Goyon, 'Le céremonial de glorification d'Osiris du papyrus du Louvre I. 3079 (colomnes 110 a 112)', *Bulletin de l'institut français d'archéologie orientale du Caire* 64 (1966), pp. 89-156.

18. See H. te Velde's classical study of Seth, *Seth, God of Confusion: A Study of his Role in Egyptian Mythology and Religion* (Probleme der Ägyptologie; Leiden: Brill, 1967).

19. Cf. the common analysis of the name of Hathor *Ḥwt-Ḥr*, House of Horus,

conquers death in the conception of the heir Horus, the relationship of Seth and Nephthys is sterile.

The children of Geb and Nut rework the idea of gender. One pair displays inverted sexual symbolism and, as such, once again mirrors the feminine (Osiris) and masculine (Isis) modes of generation. The other pair, in contrast, is absolute in its gender identification. The myth makes clear which variation is regarded as the most potent when it comes to reproduction.

The Ennead[20]

The generations leading to the birth of Horus consist of nine gods. The number three was used by the Egyptians to signify plurality and, thus, three times three can be said to stand for absolute plurality. In fact, the Egyptian numerical system is decimal: the numbers one to nine can be written by adding individual strokes to one another; but with ten, a new sign is introduced. The Nine Gods, beginning with Atum and concluding with the children of Geb and Nut, comprise a group called the *psḏt*, 'the nine'—or, to use the common Greek term, the Ennead.

The Ennead occurs in a personified form as a goddess, or pair of goddesses, and is cited in the texts as the mother of the gods, in much the same way as Nun is the father. The term *psḏt* may also be read as the 'shining one' (feminine), thus creating a binary relationship between the two uterine entities of the 'father' (waters/darkness) and the 'mother' (solar entity/light), marking the boundaries of the beginning and completion of creation.

Horus and Seth: Eye and Testicles[21]

Horus is the tenth god. The multiplicity that developed from the Being–non-Being of Atum comes around to another form of Oneness, Horus the rightful king of Egypt, with whom every historical king is identified.

The reconstructed narrative continues with the conflict between Horus and his uncle, Seth. Once grown, Horus leaves the marshes to seek revenge on his uncle and claim his rightful inheritance, the

---

as referring to her role as his mother, e.g. Troy, *Patterns of Queenship*, p. 29.

20. See L. Troy, 'The Ennead: The Collective as Goddess. A Commentary on Textual Personification', in G. Englund (ed.), *The Religion of the Ancient Egyptians: Cognitive Structures and Popular Expressions* (BOREAS, 20; Uppsala: Acta Universitatis Upsaliensis, 1989), pp. 59-69, for a more complete version of this discussion.

21. See Troy, *Patterns of Queenship*, p. 40.

kingship of Egypt. The two engage in a struggle in which both are wounded, Horus in the eye and Seth in the testicles. The Eye of Horus, a powerful image in all contexts, is the objective of Seth's attacks and the wounded eye is eventually abducted by Seth. It is later rescued and returned in a healed state to Horus, becoming the sound (*wḏꜣt*) eye. Upon Horus's coronation as King of the Living it is offered to Osiris, giving him the power of resurrection as the King of the Dead in the Netherworld.

The Eye and the Testicle indicate in clear terms which gender characteristics are assigned the two gods. The Eye appears in a number of contexts as a goddess, and has been cited above as the feminine attribute of Atum that functions in an active role in the birth of Shu and Tefnut. A grammatically feminine word in Egyptian, *irt*, it is the form taken by the daughter of the solar god, Re, and, consistently, represents feminine generative power as an attribute of the male creator. The conflict between Horus and Seth becomes a conflict between female and male generative powers, implying violent sexual encounters. This aspect of the symbolism comes through implicitly in the texts that describe Seth sticking his fingers in the eye of Horus.[22] It is also explicitly described in the various texts that tell of the rape of Horus by Seth, or in the episode in which Horus tricks Seth into drinking Horus's semen.[23]

Horus Crowned King: Osiris Resurrected

The triumphant ending of the story brings the myth into the realm of contemporaneous Egyptian kingship. A court, presided over by Geb himself, confirms Horus's claim to the kingship, making him King of the Black Land (*Kmt* = Egypt) while giving Seth the Red Land (*Dsrt* = the desert) beyond its borders. The Eye of Horus, rescued from Seth, is given to Osiris as the first funerary offering and the dead king grows round like the primeval ocean, reiterating the feminine reproductive mode, and achieving resurrection and eternal life as the King of the Netherworld.[24]

22. te Velde, *Seth, God of Confusion*, p. 36, draws the same conclusion as to the sexual connotations of Seth's finger.

23. Different versions of this story are known from the Pyramid Texts and a Middle Kingdom literary papyrus. Its most well-known variant is found in a text known as 'The Contendings of Horus and Seth', found in English translation in M. Lichtheim, *Ancient Egyptian Literature: A Book of Readings.* I. *The Old and Middle Kingdoms* (Berkeley: University of California Press, 1976), pp. 214-33.

24. The implications of the god's pregnancy are clear in the text, cf. PT §188-

The Heliopolitan theology is replete with commentary on the inter-action of male and female reproductive powers as the generative forces in creation. During the first stages, Nun and Atum establish the female and male generative modes. The following generations of Shu and Tefnut, Geb and Nut, bring into play parent–child relation-ships, with Shu and Tefnut functioning as the first son–daughter pair and Geb and Nut as the first father–mother pair. These character-istics established, the generations of Osiris, Isis, Seth and Nephthys point to two alternatives for the further evolution of the interaction between female and male reproductive properties. The symbolism associated with Osiris and Isis suggests a pattern of inverted roles, while that of Seth and Nephthys tends to present absolute identifi-cation with either male or female reproduction. The sterility of the latter pair confirms the view of the Egyptians that totality must be reflected in the part for the process of creation–generation to continue.

In the conflict between Horus and Seth the theme of feminine versus masculine generative modes is once again taken up, with the eye and the testicles serving as signs for what is, in this context, an opposition of conflict. Horus is triumphant and the eye is given as a funerary offering to his dead father, who uses it to overcome death and achieve resurrection as the King of the Netherworld.

In this interpretation of the myth, the structural framework con-sists of interplay between feminine and masculine elements in a sequential relationship (Nun and Atum), in a relationship of equiva-lency (Shu and Tefnut), in complementary opposition (Geb and Nut), in inversion (Osiris and Isis) and in conflict (Horus and Seth). There is a conscious exploration of the ways the most primary expression of life's power, in its two gendered forms, can interact.

The Mother of All: Enclosing Waters

In the Heliopolitan cosmology Nun is the source of all life. Although the deity is given a male identity, he has a female function. The primeval waters provide a prototype for all life-giving 'containers' and is thus the first womb. The sky goddess, Nut, shares many of Nun's attributes as a watery womb and, in her function as regener-ative place, is comparable to Nun.

For the Egyptians the sky was a body of water which, like the Nile, provided a means of transportation from east to west. This was used

192 and discussion in Troy, *Patterns of Queenship*, pp. 41-43 and 'The First Time', pp. 31-32.

by the solar god who sailed through the sky in his barge day and night. Like the waters of Nun, the waters of the heaven also had a creative function. This is seen in the role played by Nut in the resurrection of Osiris and the regeneration of the solar god, Re.

In the Heliopolitan myth complex Nut is the mother of Osiris, the resurrected king of the Netherworld. The rebirth–resurrection of the son necessitates a return to the mother,[25] and the Pyramid Texts contain numerous passages describing the various ways in which Osiris ascends to the sky.

Nut is also the mother of the solar deity, Re. The god travelled by boat through the night sky, within the body of the goddess. Re had three aspects: that of a child born at sunrise (Khepri), a youth at the height of his powers at noon (Re-Harakhty), and the weakening father at sunset (Atum-Re). The father aspect of the god entered the body of the goddess through her mouth in the west and during the night underwent a transformation into his own child. At dawn the god was reborn from between the thighs of the goddess in the east. The goddess, as a medium of transformation, provided the means whereby the god could overcome death and achieve rebirth every day at sunrise.

These two elements of Nut's role, as mother of both Osiris and Re, may have had independent origins. They are joined together, however, no later than the New Kingdom and comprise an important theological thesis of cosmic regeneration.[26]

In the Heliopolitan version of the creation myth, the first form of the feminine reproductive mode is reserved for the masculine deity as a personification of the primeval waters. The feminine identity of the waters is actualized, however, with the function of the heavens as the mother within whom the continual regeneration of the solar god takes place. Often associated with the figure of the cow, this type of goddess is found under a number of different names, of which Hathor is the best known. The relationship between the heavenly cow as the divine mother and the creative waters is implicit in the texts, although the first survival of a complete creation myth in which she plays the main role belongs to the final years of ancient Egyptian

25. The coffin lid was traditionally decorated with the image of the sky goddess, Nut.

26. Cf. Troy, 'The First Time', pp. 33-37 for an outline of the relationship of Re and Osiris as representing cyclical contra durative time, in Egyptian terms *nḥḥ* and *ḏt*, with references. *Nḥḥ* and *ḏt* have also been analysed as representing male and female elements, and the union of the two deities as they meet in the Netherworld or night sky has been compared to intercourse.

culture. It is found in the Upper Egyptian temple at Esna.

The texts from the temple of Neith and Khnum at Esna date to c. 100 CE thus are among the last religious texts inscribed in the temples of ancient Egypt. Written in the Middle Egyptian of the second millennium BCE, the language of the myth is relatively simple. The hieroglyphic writing, employing a system of signs devised specifically for this temple, is nevertheless not simple. Therefore, this body of material has had some difficulty reaching an audience outside a small group of specialists in Graeco-Roman temple texts.

The history of the goddess Neith goes back to Early Dynastic times (c. 3100 BCE) when, as the patron goddess of the west Delta centre at Sais, her name recurs repeatedly in the documentation of the period.[27] She is closely associated with the Red Crown of Lower Egypt which is one of her characteristic symbols, as are the bow and arrow that mark her role as huntress and mistress of the marshlands. Her cult, together with that of Hathor, was among the most popular during the Old Kingdom at Memphis.[28] Evidence for this goddess declines during the Middle and New Kingdom, only to re-emerge in the Late Period when the status of her native centre at Sais was re-asserted as a national capital.

Neith is consistently identified, like Nut, as the mother of the solar god, Re. At Esna this aspect of her role is assigned to her form as Mehetweret, 'the Great Flood'. Like Nut, she is often depicted as a cow. Mehetweret is not, however, a regenerative mother, but the primeval creator of the solar god and his divine realm.

Although reference to Mehetweret occurs only sporadically in the earliest text collections, it is possible to pinpoint her functions and web of associations in the creation myth. The name of the goddess, *Mḥt wrt*, indicates that she is a personification of the flood waters, both those that engulf all life potential and those that submerge the fields during the inundation. She is found within Nun as an aspect of his being.

Mehetweret, as the flooded landscape of the fields, makes her connection with the goddess Neith a natural one. Another aspect of

27. This includes repeated reference to the name of the goddess in theophoric name formations, as well as references to her shrines in the labels accompanying offering gifts from the tombs of the aristocracy. This material dates c. 3100–2800 BCE.

28. Cf. B.L. Begelsbacher-Fischer (*Untersuchungen zur Götterwelt des Alten Reiches im Spiegel der Privatgräber der IV. und V. Dynastie* (OBO, 37; Fribourg: Editions Universitaires; Göttingen: Vandenhoeck & Ruprecht, 1981), pp. 119-20, for the documentation of this goddess's cult during the Old Kingdom.

the mythological status of Neith links her with the Faiyum, where she is identified as the mother of the solar crocodile, Sobek-Re, and, as such, with the marshy waters from which he emerges.

The temple of Esna has preserved a creation myth in which Neith, as Mehetweret, is the creator, preparing the world of the gods for the arrival of her son Re. It is used to explain the origin of a ritual which celebrates the completion of an annual re-enactment of the creation, culminating with the appearance of Neith and Re in Esna and its sister-city Sais. Although this is the only Egyptian text known to this author that contains a complete narrative featuring a female creator, the only published translation is, to my knowledge, the one that accompanies the text edition. The most relevant parts of the texts are given below. The text headings, marked by square brackets ([ ]), have been added for the reader's convenience.

Esna Text no. 206[29]
[A Description of the Origin and Transformations of Neith, 206.1-2]

> The father of the fathers, the mother of the mothers, the deity who began the transformation at the beginning when she was residing in Nun, who came forth from her [own] body when the earth was still in darkness and the land had not come forth nor had any vegetation sprouted.
>
> It was into a cow, unknown by any god or anyone else, that she transformed herself. It was into a Lates-fish that she transformed herself again when she went forth by herself. She made the rays of her eyes bright and light came into being.

[Esna, Sais and all of Egypt is Created, 206.2-3]

> And then she said: 'I have gone forth to this place from the mound in Nun after I had supported myself on it. This place is on the soil ($s\underline{t}$) which is in Nun.' And just like she had said, Esna (Sny), which is also Sais ($S\jmath w$), came into being. She flew up on this mound which became Pi-Neter which is also Buto.[30] She said: 'I am happy on this mound'. It is Dep which came into being, the sweet, sweet land which is also called Sais. All that her heart desired happened immediately, and she went to work ($B\jmath\underline{h}w$) on this mound and Egypt ($B\jmath k$) came into being in joy.

29. The text is published in S. Sauneron, *Le temple d'Esna* (Esna, 3; Cairo: Institut français d'archéologie orientale, 1968), as text no. 206; for the translation of that author see Sauneron, *Les fêtes religieuses d'Esna aux derniers siècles du paganisme* (Esna, 5; Cairo: Institut français d'archéologie orientale, 1962), pp. 257-71.

30. Pe, Dep and Buto were all names of an important cult site, located not far from Sais in the western delta. The statement 'I am happy on this mound' is a pun on the name of Dep.

[*The Gods Are Created, 206.3-4*]

> She created the thirty gods[31] by saying their names one by one, and she rejoiced when she saw them. They said: 'Greetings to you, Mistress of the Gods, our mother who brought about our existence, the one who made our names, even though we did not know them ourselves. You have separated light and darkness. You have made the land on which we support ourselves. You have divided night from day. How very useful is all that comes forth from your heart. O Unique One, who came into being in the beginning. Cyclical time (*nḥḥ*) and enduring time (*ḏt*) pass before your face.'[32]
>
> Then she said to her children: 'Come, let us lift ourselves on this place on earth. It is a place where we can stand to repel our weariness. Let us sail to this place Esna-Sais, this land which is in Nun. This very pleasant mound on which we will live.' She put an expanse of land in Nun to which she gave the name of 'High Ground'.

[*The Gods Question Neith about the Future, 206.4-5*]

> And then they said to the Great and Powerful One: 'O you who have given birth to us, O you from whom we came, Reveal for us that which has not yet happened, for lo there is only this one thing and we do not know what is to be.'
>
> Then Neith said: 'I will tell you what will happen. We will invent the four glorification spells.[33] Let us give form to that which is in our bellies and let us say what is on our lips so that we shall know it today.' They did everything that she had said, and eight hours passed.

[*The Akhet Cow Predicts the Birth of Re, 206.5-7*]

> The Akhet-cow[34] began to think about what would happen. She said: 'A noble god shall be born today, and when he opens his eye light will come into being, and when he closes it darkness will spread out. The common people will be born from the tears of his eye and the gods from the saliva of his lips.[35] And I will make him strong with my strength,

31. Thirty is another indication of plurality, relating to the number of days in an Egyptian month.

32. For a discussion of *ḏt* and *nḥḥ* cf. Troy, 'The First Time', pp. 33-37.

33. The glorification spells or *sꜣḥw* were instrumental in transforming the dead into an effective and immortal spirit. Here their powers are used in order to transform thought into reality.

34. The term Akhet (*ꜣḫt*) is related to *sꜣḥw*, 'to make akh', and refers to the transformatory powers of the goddess. Note below, where the uraeus is referred to as the Akhet-serpent. Cf. G. Englund, *Akh: une notion religieuse dans l'égypte pharaonique* (BOREAS, 11; Uppsala: Acta Universitatis Upsaliensis, 1978), for a study of the concept *Akh*.

35. The creation of humankind (*rmṯ*) is related by wordplay to the tears (*rmi*) of the god.

and I will make him active with my activity, and I will make him powerful with my power. Although his children will rebel against him, they will be defeated in his name and then they will fight for him, my son who came forth from my flesh and who will be king in this land forever. I will protect him in my arms so that no evil will touch him. I will tell you his name, Khepri in the morning and Atum in the evening; and he will be the radiant one forever in this his name of Re, every day.'

Then these gods said: 'You speak of things of which we are ignorant (ḥm)'. Thus the Eight (ḫmnw) became the name of these gods, and the name of this town.

[*Re is Born, 206.7-8*]

And then this god was born from the fluids which came forth from her flesh, which she had placed in the body of this egg. When she removed the waters, the Nile rose at one single place and semen fell on the egg. And when the shell which was around this noble god broke it was Re, who had hidden himself inside Nun in this his name of Amun—the Ancient, the one who unites the gods and goddesses with his rays in this name of Khnum.

[*Mother and Son, 206.8-9*]

His mother the Akhet-cow called out in a loud voice: 'Come, come you whom I have created! Come, come you whom I have brought into being. I am your mother, the Akhet cow!' Then this god came, smiling and with arms open to this goddess. He threw himself into her embrace, for this is that which a son does when he sees his mother. Thus that day became a good day for the beginning of the year.

Then he cried in Nun when he could no longer see his mother, the Akhet cow, and humankind was born out of his tears. He drooled when he saw her again and the gods were born out of the saliva of his lips.

[*The Other Gods Worship Re, 206.10*]

The gods who were created [earlier] rested in their chapels, they were chanting when this goddess saw them, protecting Re inside their chapels and adoring this god saying: 'Welcome, welcome, the heir of Neith, who was made with her hands, who was created with her heart. You are king in this land forever, just as your mother predicted.'

The text continues with the description of the creation of other elements important for the mythology of the period. It includes the creation of the chaos serpent, Apophis, as well as the birth of Thoth, the god of wisdom and writing. The text concludes with a description of the journey taken by Neith and her son to Esna-Sais, with the cow goddess placing her child between her horns and swimming to the site. This event is said to explain her name, which is read here as the

'Great Swimmer'. They finally arrive at their palace in time for the festival celebrated in their honour, which is the starting point of the text.

Mehetweret is identified as the 'first cause' of creation. She is the active element of the primeval waters and as such she is, like Atum, self-created and the source of light and earth and the multiplicity of the gods. Her creative activity is, like that of Atum's—as described in Bremner-Rhind and dated some four hundred years earlier—intellectual as much as physical. She plans and considers, which results in the physical act of creation–birth.

There is little doubt as to the physicality of her creation, since Re is born when she takes fluids that flood from her body and puts them in an egg. Fertilization of the egg occurs with the semen associated with the rising of the Nile. The birth of Re creates the first female–male duality, not the duality of son and daughter but that of mother and son.

While the late date of this text (c. 100 BCE) should be kept in mind when drawing conclusions as to the influence of this myth—or other versions of it—on earlier material, it does indicate the conceptualization of a female creator associated with the primeval waters. Given the form of the favourite Egyptian icon of female fertility, the cow, this myth provides a frame of reference for the regenerative relationship between Re and his mother. An earlier text, dated to the late 18th dynasty (c. 1300 BCE) and known as the *Book of the Heavenly Cow*,[36] also takes up this theme: the ageing god Re returns to heaven after his period of reign, leaving humankind on the back of his mother the cow.

The mother–son relationship posited by the structure of the Esna myth is visible on two levels in the Heliopolitan cosmology. It is found in the female–male sequence of reproductive modes in Nun and Atum. The regenerative aspect of this relationship is taken up in the role of Nut. As mother of Osiris, she mediates the Osiris–Horus cycle of regeneration; and as the mother of the sun god, Re, she provides the environment in which the declining powers of Atum are reborn each morning as Khepri. It is worth noting that this paradigm gives precedence to the feminine as a precondition for birth and rebirth.

36. See E. Hornung, *Der ägyptische Mythos von der Himmelskuh: Eine Ätiologie des Unvolkommenen* (OBO, 46; Fribourg: Universitätsverlag; Göttingen: Vandenhoeck & Ruprecht, 1982), for the definitive edition of this text.

Father of Multitudes: Flowing Streams

Masculine sexuality is the primary creative force in the Heliopolitan cosmology, in the form of Atum. The masculine reproductive mode, with phallus in hand and ejaculation, creates the first division into male and female in the twins Shu and Tefnut.

Other traditions also attribute creation of the divine world to masculine fertility. The image of the ithyphallic god is well known in ancient Egypt and is most commonly identified with the Coptite god, Min. Statues of colossal size, depicting the masturbating god, are dated as early as the beginning of dynastic period (c. 3100 BCE).[37] The concept of the male as self-renewing, as well as self-generating, is incorporated in the ideology of the kingship. It is summarized in the epithet Kamutef (*k₃ mwt.f*), 'bull of his mother',[38] which hypothesizes the kingship as a continual self-regeneration through the agency of a mother-deity, interfacing with the mother–son paradigm described above.

Just as the cow provides an icon for female fertility, male fertility is associated with the bull as well as the ram. The primeval male god can also take serpent form, such as that of Atum as Nehebkaw (the provider of *kas*) and, as seen below, in the two first generations of the Theban cosmology.

In a text from the Theban temple of Khonsu at Karnak, dated to c. 200 BCE, the imagery of the male creator dominates. Just as male fertility is incidental in the Esna version of creation, at Thebes the feminine reproductive mode is largely subsumed as an attribute of the male creator.

In Theban myth, Khonsu is the child of the god Amun and his consort, Mut. Often depicted in a mummified form with a crescent moon on his head he is, in this context, the regenerated form of his

---

37. The remains of three colossal statues in an ithyphallic pose, hand clasping the missing phallus, were discovered at Coptos in Middle Egypt by Petrie. Now in the Cairo (JE 30770) and Ashmolean Museums (Ashm. 1894.105), these statues are dated c. 3250–3100 BCE. Cf. B. Williams, 'Narmer and the Coptos Colossi', *Journal of the American Research Center in Egypt* 25 (1988), pp. 35-59 and G. Dreyer, 'Die Datierung der Min-Statuen aus Koptos', *Kunst des Alten Reiches* 28 (1995), pp. 49-56 for this discussion.

38. Cf. the classic study of H. Jacobsohn, *Die dogmatische Stellung des Königs in der Theologie der alten Ägypter* (Agyptologische Forschungen, 8; New York: J.J. Augustin, 1939); and a brief resumé in Jacobsohn, 'Kamutef', in *Lexikon der Ägyptologie* (Wiesbaden: Otto Harrassowitz, 1981), III, pp. 308-309.

father. In the myth related in the temple inscription, the waters of creation are conceptualized as the flowing semen of the god, which, as in the Heliopolitan myth, lead to self-insemination and birth.

The explication of the four generations of Amun is at the core of this text. The first two generations of creators are serpents, Kematef and Iryta. The first is associated with the moment of becoming (*km-ɜt.f*, 'the one who completes his moment') which initiates creation, while the second is the creator of land (*iry-tɜ*, 'the one who makes land'). In the third generation, Amun is identified as the head of the Ogdoad, of which he is, in other contexts, one of its eight gods. The text contains numerous references to the Hermopolitan myth, in which the Ogdoad create the solar egg by swimming together in Nun. The final generation of Amun, known as 'Amun in the Harem' (*Imn-m-ipt*) in some texts, is associated with the youthful and vigorous solar god mentioned in the last section of the text. That is the role played by Khonsu as the child of Amun. Along the way there are brief references to several phases of creation, such as the appearance of heaven and earth, the birth of the Ogdoad and the creation of the egg from which the solar god emerges. These are, however, all subordinate to the power attributed to the semen of the god as repeatedly self-generating.

The text is built around recurring puns on the name of the Karnak temple in which the inscription is found. It is called *Bnnt* ('Temple of Abundance') and traces numerous associations to sexual creation: *bnn* can mean 'to overflow', 'erection' and *bnnt* is 'seed'. As this text contains a coherent narrative, and like the text of Esna is not to be found outside specialist literature, a translation is given here.[39]

[*Introduction: Amun is Described as the Primeval God, the First Serpent, The-One-who-Completes-his-Moment (kmɜ-ɜt.f)*]

The noble Ba of the Kematef-serpent
Father of the Semen, Mother of the Egg
The One who engendered every living thing
The Concealed Ba who made the gods
The One who formed the land with his semen
Father of the fathers of the Ogdoad

39. A copy of the text is given in Sethe, *Amun und die acht Urgötter*. A new study of the text with a translation is found in R. Parker and L. Lesko, 'The Khonsu Cosmology', in *Pyramid Studies and Other Essays presented to I.E.S. Edwards* (Occasional Papers, 7; London: Egyptian Exploration Society, 1988), pp. 168-75. The translation given here is a reworking of that found in Parker and Lesko.

The One who is in the burial chamber in the necropolis in Medinet Habu[40]
The One who begat this place [i.e. the temple of Khonsu] in Nun [which is called]
Abundant of Semen of the First Time.

[Heaven and Earth are Created, and the Second Snake Earth-Maker (iry-tȝ) Comes into Being]

The First Snake made heaven because of his desire…
…earth
The sky spit out an egg like the egg of a falcon
Its face was like the face of…
The Second Snake came into being, being spit out with the face of a beetle[41] too.

[Amun Appears as Ptah]

The cow[42] was before the first one who came forth
In his name of Amun Father of the Ogdoad in the burial chamber of the necropolis of Medinet Habu
Amun was first in this his name of Ptah
The one who is called Ptah, the one who created the egg which came forth from Nun,
     …as Ptah of the Hehu-gods and the Nenu-goddesses
The One who created heaven and earth.

[Amun Ejaculates and Fertilizes the Egg, the Ogdoad Come into Being]

He ejaculated and he made the semen into the lake which was created in Tjenenet.[43]
It flowed under him like that which came into being in its name of seed of grain.
He ejaculated onto the egg.[44]
The Eight came into being in it in the regions of the Ogdoad.

[Amun Swallows the Eight]

He languished in Nun, in the Great Flood
He swallowed them and his throat conceived.

40. Traditionally the Theban temple, Medinet Habu, was regarded as the burial place of the Ogdoad.
41. Both falcon and beetle refer to the rising phase of the sun.
42. There is a possible reference to Mehetweret here, as well as below where the 'Great Flood' is named.
43. This was a shrine of Ptah in Thebes.
44. Cf. the Esna text, where the egg is fertilized in connection with the rising waters of the Nile.

He travelled to Thebes in his crocodile-form of Khonsu
He cleared his throat from the water which was in the seed of grain
The Noble One in the Great Flood.

[*Maat/Naunet/Thebes/Hathor Is Born from the God's Semen*]

He stared at the semen.
It was his Maat, the Great One who raised herself as Sakhmet, as an amulet on his breast,
Conceived like that which was brought from the...high earth in Nun
Naunet / City [Thebes] came into being in her name of Valley
Hathor the Great who is in the [temple called] 'Seed of Grain' came into being in her name of Nut.

[*The Ogdoad is Born Again as the People of the Shrine of Ptah*]

He put his body on top of her and he opened her as Ptah, Father of the Gods
The Ogdoad came into being...with its four males, and one wife for each
This is the spittle [?] which the City made together with the four drops which
were in her
They are the men and the ladies of Tanenen
The land of the City rejoiced because of Tanenen, who gave birth to the Ogdoad in Thebes.

[*Amun himself Comes into Being*]

They floated to the Island of Flames
His form, the first primeval one of the Great Flood came into being
They worship the eldest one among the gods in the portal of Upper Egypt
The Great God who came into being in the First Time,
Being praised in his presence, rejoicing in Nun
Darkness circling around them
He says: 'Your son brightens the earth in darkness
And his companion will be seen'.
They give praise...they give praise to Re at [his] coming forth
(Temple of Khonsu, KM 583, west wall).[45]

The Theban myth interprets the waters of Nun as masculine in origin, the semen of the god. As a creative, life-giving element it can form land as well as make up the holy lake of the Tjenenet shrine of Ptah. Falling to the ground, it is the source of grain. It also fertilizes

---

45. Parker and Lesko, 'The Khonsu Cosmology', pp. 169-74, plates 35 and 36.

the egg that produces the Ogdoad. The Ogdoad itself which, as seen in the Heliopolitan cosmology, is a manifestation of the primeval waters, functions as semen. They are swallowed and inseminate the throat of the god.

In spite of the masculine context given the primeval water–semen here, the waters themselves remain bound to a feminine reference point. The most common Egyptian word for male seed is the grammatically feminine, *mtwt*.[46] In the Theban myth, the semen becomes an independent attribute of the god, personified as a goddess.[47]

When the god spits out the semen he finds that it has the form of Maat, the goddess of justice. Although the text is somewhat fragmentary at this point, it would appear that this goddess is also somehow associated with two others. The name of the first of these is written with a sign commonly read *niwt*, 'city'. This provides a pun on at least two levels. On one level it is a reference to Naunet, the feminine counterpart of Nun; on another it may be read 'city', thus referring to Thebes itself, often represented as the goddess 'Thebes' (*Wȝst*). The latter interpretation is most consonant with the recurring sense of relationship between the god and his city. The goddess is also related in this text to Hathor and to Nut, encompassing the most important goddesses in one manifestation.

It is at this point in the narrative that insemination and birth are related to a feminine rather than masculine personification, and where male and female are found in independent forms. Amun, in the form of the craftsman god Ptah, copulates with the goddess, creating, once more, the Ogdoad; but, this time, the multiplicity that this image represents is translated into the many servants of the shrine of Ptah.

Thus the semen of the god, on the final level, is associated with those goddesses most closely identified with the roles of daughter and mother of the creator god. This theme is reiterated in the speeches of the gods and the kings which accompany the representations found with the inscription. Ptah says of Khonsu that he 'is the *ba* in the midst of his semen...he united himself with the body of his father, that he might make earth in the midst of the water. The heart of his father went forth into his body in order to beget him,

---

46. This term can also mean 'poison'. This pun is employed in a number of magic spells. See Troy, *Patterns of Queenship*, pp. 68-69.

47. Cf. T. DuQuesne, ' "Semen of the Bull": Reflexions on the Symbolism of Ma'et with Reference to Recent Studies', *Discussions in Egyptology* 32 (1995), pp. 107-16.

and thus his words came into existence...and earth likewise...He is the heart of Amun.'[48]

This text places the son in the father's semen which functions—in the same sense as the waters of the womb—as the child's 'mother'. Similarly, a description of Hathor from the same text refers to her as 'semen of the Bull which came forth from him, she who flowed from him on the occasion of the First Time'.[49] This text also makes explicit the association of sexual excitement (*sty*) and intellectual activity of the heart (*ib*) as a generative combination.[50]

The Theban myth, with its focus on masculine fertility as the source of life and self-renewal, reflects a paradigm in which there are three main elements: the ithyphallic father, a feminine element identified as a physical attribute of the god, and the regenerated form of the father as his own son. This is parallel to the structure of the mother–son paradigm—with the exception that the role assigned to the feminine element, the creative waters, is interpreted not as a pre-existent mother but as an aspect of the father. By returning to the Heliopolitan myth complex, it is possible to discern the consistency with which this structural relationship is employed as an expression of the male creator.

The daughter of the god, as an active assistant of the father, is a common feature of Egyptian mythology. Her most common manifestation is as the Eye of the God, met with above as the active feminine element in the creative act of Atum, as she seeks out the twins Shu and Tefnut. The Eye, as a 'container' of water, is also evident as that part of the god responsible for the creation of humankind, said to come from the tears of the god (employing the pun on *rmi*, 'cry' and *rmṯ*, 'humankind' or 'people'). The Hand of Atum, which stimulates the god, can also be identified as his daughter and is likewise a feminine attribute of the god. The incestuous implications are confirmed as, in fact, the generative male–female pair in this paradigm consists of the male god and a secondary characteristic which, placed

---

48. Parker and Lesko, 'The Khonsu Cosmology', p. 170, plate 35.
49. Parker and Lesko, 'The Khonsu Cosmology', p. 170, plate 35.
50. There is a tendency to see 'intellectual' creation by mind (e.g. heart, *ib*) and word as apart from the sexual creation of Atum. The textual sources make it clear, however, that the two acts are linked, with an insistence that speech and ejaculation are parallel. See, for example, Lichtheim's translation of the Memphite Theology in *Ancient Egyptian Literature*, I, p. 51; and discussions in D. Müller, 'Die Zeugung durch das Herz', *Or* NS 35 (1966), pp. 247-74.

on a subordinate level to the masculine manifestation of the deity, is termed his daughter.[51]

The Theban myth exemplifies the pattern employed in the father–daughter relationship. The feminine attribute of the father—be it semen, hand or eye—'contains', or mediates, the transformation into the regenerated son. Just as the semen contains the child Khonsu, the Eye has within the pupil an image which is said to be the child[52] (Fig. 5).

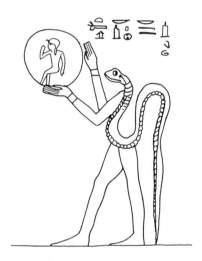

Figure 5. The child in the Eye, Held up by the Serpent Form of Atum
(Brooklyn Magic Papyrus 47.218.156).

Thus the female element is both daughter (of the father) and mother (of the child), while remaining a physical part of the androgynous god who repeats his act of self-generation.[53]

51. Incestuous marriages between father and daughter are a distinctive feature of the late 18th and early 19th dynasties. This is a pattern that recurs in the mythological formulation of the relationship between male and female powers. An example that can be cited is the imagery of the god's daughter, which is combined with that of the wife in the formulation of the role of the Theban priestess, known as the Wife of the God. The Kamutef, 'Bull of his Mother' paradigm also assumes an incestuous relationship between the mother and the son.

52. For this discussion see Troy, *Patterns of Queenship*, pp. 21-23.

53. Note the association of Shu and Tefnut, the children of Atum, with the semen/spittle of the god. Tefnut is often identified as the Eye of the God, playing this part in the well-known demotic fable.

Although the daughter as goddess and physical attribute can be subordinated to the self-generation of the father, there are indications that she/it also has an independent existence in Egyptian religious thought. There is a set of myths that feature this goddess in a central role. It is evident that the Eye of the God, as a mythological concept, comprises the active and transformatory ability of the creator. In the narrative from the New Kingdom royal tombs known as the Destruction of Humankind,[54] Re is said to call forth his Eye, his daughter, to destroy rebellious humankind. She appears as a ferocious lion and, being over-zealous, must be drugged into passivity when it becomes clear that humankind will be annihilated.[55] The text of the Bremner-Rhind papyrus outlines a conflict between father and daughter too:

> My eye planned and humankind came into being. Then I replaced her with the Akhet-serpent and she was enraged with me when she returned, for another had grown in her place. Her rage fell away when I restored her and she was calm, having indeed been promoted to her place in my face so that she ruled the entire land. (Bremner-Rhind, 29.4-5).[56]

In the description of the Eye's role in the birth of Shu and Tefnut, she must leave the father and wander in the waters of Nun to find the twins. On her return she finds that the Akhet-cobra, a rival, has taken her place. Famous for her temper, she must be soothed and induced to return to her father. Once given her rightful place on his brow she is recognized as the ruler of Egypt, in the guise of the uraeus that guards the God–king from his enemies.

The flight motif found in these myths is the basis for a ritual, performed in a number of variants, which induces goddesses identified with the Eye to return to Egypt from beyond the borders in Nubia or Libya. A drinking festival celebrates the goddesses' return.

The transformatory powers of the feminine element called the Eye are employed as part of the denouement of the myth, the resurrection of Osiris and the triumph of Horus. Here the Eye, as an attribute of Horus, is, after having been returned to her owner, offered to Osiris. The Pyramid Texts refer to the Eye—which, as an offering, is actually

54. For an easily accessible translation see Lichtheim, *Ancient Egyptian Literature*, II, pp. 197-99.

55. The two sides of this goddess, ferocious and mild, are central to the conceptualization of the feminine role. See L. Troy, 'Good and Bad Women: Maxim 18/284-288 of the Instructions of Ptahhotep', *Göttinger Miszellen* 80 (1984), pp. 77-82 for this discussion.

56. See Faulkner, *The Papyrus Bremner-Rhind*, p. 71.

a cake—as the daughter of Osiris.[57] Having consumed the cake, the god is self-'inseminated' and grows round in imitation of both Nun and pregnancy, then is transformed into the King of the Netherworld.

The offering—cake or jewellery, clothing or incense—has a double identity. It is both the Eye of Horus, offered to Osiris, as well as Maat, who, as noted above, is also the Daughter of the God, identified at Thebes as the god's semen. Indeed, the speech addressed by the King to Amun in the Theban inscription ties together all these themes.

> I give you Maat in my left hand
> While my right hand protects her
> So that you may eat with her eyes
> And swallow with her sight
> And anoint the skin with her sight
> And that you may stand in front of her manifestation.
>
> Live on her limbs
> Gild [yourself] with her body
> Gleam with her skin
> May your heart come with the semen of your father.
> That you may unite with it.

For the Theban priests, the male creator was the precondition for creation. The waters of life, otherwise thought to be around him, were in fact in him. His semen was equated with the waters of Nun, thus his fertility was the source of all life. The creative waters of the god are interpreted, however, as his feminine attribute, that which carries the child, just as do uterine waters. The capacity of the god to regenerate himself is interpreted, in the Theban context, as a function of the relationship between the father god and his feminine 'part' as daughter— be it semen, eye or hand. Here, although there is an obsessive need to image creation as the product of male sexuality, there is an equal insistence on the necessity of incorporating the transformatory power of feminine sexuality into the physical being of the male creator.

The figure of the ithyphallic father, just like that of the celestial mother cow, is one that is documented earlier than the inscriptional evidence of the Heliopolitan cosmology. Its inclusion in the Old Kingdom formulation of the Heliopolitan cosmology suggests that this paradigm, like that where the feminine creator is given precedence, was adapted in an attempt to create an all-inclusive creation myth which could promote a homogenous ideology in the widespread provinces of the developing nation.

---

57. PT §§185-92; cf. Troy, *Patterns of Queenship*, p. 41.

Conclusions

The questions that the Egyptians posed concerning 'the beginning' were formulated in reference to their knowledge of procreation. The prevalent image of creation entailed a single parent with access to the reproductive properties of the opposite sex. Even in those instances when creation is brought about through thought transformed into word, the metaphor of ejaculation is included as an explanatory component. In speculating as to the identify and character of this single parent, two very obvious options were available: the mother or the father. If the analysis presented above is correct, it would appear that while the Egyptians could conceptualize the mother, sans partner, as a first cause, it was more difficult to present the father as totally independent of feminine assistance. In one paradigm it is the mother who independently gives birth and then continuously renews the son. In the other, the father is equipped with a feminine element that enables him to reproduce himself. In one instance the mother provides an environment, equated with the primeval waters, in which the transformation of the masculine element can take place. In the other, the creative process is self-contained within a male deity who, since feminine reproductive capabilities are ascribed to his physical attributes, is able to accomplish continual self-regeneration.

Although one model gives precedence to the female creator and the other to the male, both display a consonant pattern. Both feature a feminine element that functions as a medium whereby the father is transformed into his own son. Both allude to the ideology of the *Kamutef*, whereby there is an unquestioned continuity in the male succession. The inclusion of both paradigms and their successful integration, which involves the creation of a continuum between the mother and the daughter as two aspects of the same element,[58] testifies to the genius of the Heliopolitan cosmology as a tool of ideological integration.

For the Egyptians, the creative process that brought the ordered world out of the original void emanated from a tangible physical reality. The employment of the imagery of female and male reproduction as a means of conceptualizing the first cause of creation established an indissoluble link between the divine and mortal worlds. The powers which brought about the first manifestation of divine life were still at work, creating the miracle of birth from palace

58. Cf. Troy, *Patterns of Queenship*, p. 45.

to mud-brick dwelling. This connection between human and divine reproduction may be interpreted as a devaluation of the creation of humankind as man and women, which in Genesis was the culmination of the creator's labours. However, it can also be seen as elevating gender, since that part of the human condition most closely connected with sexuality, birth and death, is related to the level of the divine—thus foregrounding it as an object of speculation in the religious philosophy of the ancient Egyptians.

IV

OTHER CLOSE CONTEXTS

RECOVERING OBJECTS, RE-VISIONING SUBJECTS:
ARCHAEOLOGY AND FEMINIST BIBLICAL STUDY

Carol Meyers

Almost no one does it. Almost no one attempts to integrate the results of archaeological research into the various projects of biblical study that might be called feminist.[1] Virtually no one concerned with the social location of texts dealing with women or of the texts' producers looks at data recovered from the material record of the biblical world.

The notion of archaeology as 'Recovering Objects', to call attention to the language of the title of this essay, is really meant to be a cipher for a much larger enterprise—archaeology as recovery of objects, the realia discovered or unearthed by surveys and excavations, to be sure, but also archaeology as the analysis of objects and the reconstruction of their cultural meanings. I intend to explain this recent expansion of the archaeological enterprise and the promise it holds for feminist biblical archaeology. In the process, I will touch upon aspects of traditional archaeology that may have made feminist biblical scholars turn aside from it. My underlying assumption is that, although very few feminist biblical scholars attend to artifacts from the biblical world and their meanings, it is worthwhile if not mandatory for them to do so. Recovering the biblical world, to the limited extent possible to modern investigators, is essential, in my estimation, for bridging the enormous chasm between biblical antiquity with its cultural products, both epigraphic and anepigraphic, and the world in which we live today. The fact that the Bible has been read during the millennia that separate our present from the biblical past does not constitute a sufficient bridge. It must not be forgotten that the biblical past is dead, extinct, gone forever. So too are its ways of

---

1. For a discussion of the history and goals of feminist biblical interpretation, see Alice Ogden Bellis's essay, 'Feminist Biblical Interpretation', in Carol Meyers, Toni Craven and Ross Kraemer (eds.), *Women in Scripture: A Dictionary of Named and Unnamed Women in the Hebrew Bible, Apocrypha, and New Testament* (Boston: Houghton Mifflin, forthcoming).

thinking, doing, living.[2] It is incumbent upon us to try to discern the differences.

The recovery of ancient objects—and the process of reconstructing the material and ultimately the social contexts in which they were used—provides, I am convinced, a necessary angle of vision on the women who inhabited the ancient landscape. To refer to the title of this essay once again, by 'Subjects' I mean women as the explicit theme or focus of study: female inhabitants of the biblical world. I do not here invoke the meaning of 'subject' as referring to someone under the control or authority of another, but I do invoke the grammatical sense of subject, as denoting the doer of an action, in order to suggest the presence of female agency. It is my contention that archaeologically informed theories of social forms and cultural productions in the biblical world can provide a new critical perspective. As such, they offer the possibility of re-visioning and revising our notions of gender in that world, and ultimately, on how we read texts that have survived from it. I use 'Re-visioning' in the sense in which Adrienne Rich uses it in her 1971 essay, 'When We Dead Awaken: Writing a Re-Vision'. She declares that re-visioning is 'the act of looking back, of seeing, with fresh eyes, or entering an old text with a new critical direction'. That new critical direction would be the one informed by the insights into the gendered life of female subjects that can be provided by analysis of objects, of material culture.

Archaeology: Old, 'New', Now

Looking at artifacts discovered in ancient Palestine or other lands of the Bible, in the hopes of providing some connection between that world and the world represented in the biblical text, is hardly a new enterprise. Indeed, as any handbook of, or introduction to, biblical archaeology will tell you,[3] archaeological research in the Holy Land

2.   A brief and eloquent statement of how the biblical world-view is radically different from our own is found in Victor H. Matthews and Don C. Benjamin, 'Social Sciences and Biblical Studies', in Victor H. Matthews, Don C. Benjamin and Claudia Camp (eds.), *Honor and Shame in the World of the Bible* (Semeia, 68; Atlanta: Scholars Press, 1994), pp. 7-21 (10-11).

3.   See, for example, the 'History of Archaeology' section (pp. 43-158) of Henry Thompson, *Biblical Archaeology: The World, the Mediterranean, the Bible* (New York: Paragon House, 1987) and Philip J. King, *American Archaeology in the Mideast: A History of the American Schools of Oriental Research* (Philadelphia: American Schools of Oriental Research, 1983). For more specialized treatment of the history of archaeology in the Near East, see the entries dealing with 'History of the Field'

goes back to the mid-nineteenth century and coincides with the emergence of modern critical biblical scholarship. The expanding intellectual horizons of Europe and America probably contributed to the opening of theological doctrine to the discoveries of 'scientific' literary and historical analysis of Scripture. At the same time, it enticed intrepid travelers and explorers, epitomized by the American Edward Robinson (1794–1863), to travel in the Near East. Robinson was remarkably successful in identifying the known places that he and his traveling companion Eli Smith visited, as well as the previously unknown sites that they discovered, with biblical toponyms. Today we might put a disciplinary label of 'historical geography' on Robinson's enterprise; he called his work 'Biblical Researches'.[4]

From the earliest days, therefore, archaeology in lands and locales mentioned in biblical texts was inextricably affected by the possibility of a biblical connection. Indeed, it is fair to claim that the disproportionately intense level of exploration and excavation of the Near East, compared to that of field projects in most other parts of the world, is a function of interest generated by attention to the biblical text rather than by concern for recovery of past civilizations.

Given its close association with biblical studies, it is inevitable that the archaeology of Syria-Palestine was not only touched by biblical interests but also tainted by them. In making that statement, I am trying to move towards understanding the relative paucity of the use of archaeological data in studies that can be listed under the rubric of feminist biblical scholarship. The fact that scholars dealing with gender in biblical texts and in the social location of those texts rarely consider archaeological evidence may be rooted to some extent in the perception of 'biblical archaeology'[5] as a pietistic and biased enter-

(archaeology in Syria, Israel, Jordan, Mesopotamia, Persia, the Anatolian Plateau, Egypt, Cyprus, the Aegean Islands, the Arabian Peninsula) in *The Oxford Encyclopedia of Archaeology in the Near East* (5 vols.; New York: Oxford University Press, 1997).

4.   Robinson's survey was published in a monumental three-volume work called *Biblical Research in Palestine, Mount Sinai and Arabia Petraea* (New York: Ayer, 1977 [1841]), and another volume called *Later Biblical Researches in Palestine and in Adjacent Regions* (New York: Ayer, 1977 [1856]).

5.   This term is used for convenience as a way of indicating archaeological excavation and interpretation that pertain in any way to biblical studies. The location-specific term, Syro-Palestinian archaeology, is more accurate and less tendentious, but also less familiar. For discussion of these terms and what they signify, the work of William G. Dever is especially helpful. A summary of his views along with relevant bibliography appear in two recent articles in reference works: 'Archaeology, Syro-Palestinian and Biblical', in *Anchor Bible Dictionary* (New York:

prise. That perception reflects rather accurately, unfortunately, the motivations that have driven all too many archaeological projects and studies focusing on the biblical world. Many archaeologists have believed, some consciously and others without being quite aware of it, that the recovery of objects from the periods and places represented in the Bible might address the issue of the historicity of the biblical record. In its most crass form, it was expected by a fair number of practitioners and also by a vast population of believers that archaeology might somehow 'prove' the Bible.[6] In any case, the conservative attitudes surrounding the emergence and growth of biblical archaeology bespoke an adherence to the 'truth' and authority of Scripture that would have precluded the kind of distancing from, if not critique of, Scripture that characterizes much feminist biblical scholarship.

It is certainly the case that realia mentioned in the Bible can often be rather securely related to materials recovered in archaeological excavations. Such is to be expected for a document emerging from an ancient cultural milieu, a literary production characterized by concrete images more than by abstract language. But do those links between artifacts (objects made by human craft) and logo-facts (words made by human expression) have any significance for the 'veracity' of Scripture? Hardly. Nor does the next level of archaeological analysis, a level that has held sway in Palestinian archaeology ever since the launching of major field projects early in the twentieth century and especially immediately following each of the world wars, provide validation of biblical texts.

This next level deals with events. It holds that certain events mentioned in various biblical passages can be held up for archaeological scrutiny; and it assumes that if archaeological evidence—the destruction of a city, for example—can be related to the biblical account of a city's demise, then archaeology authenticates the texts. This use of archaeology to establish political history has dominated biblical archaeology until this very day—even though, for the last few decades, some archaeologists have conceded that it is difficult, if not impossible, to make secure links between written sources describing an event and information discernible in the material culture of the city or people involved in that event. But even if such links could be drawn,

Doubleday, 1992), I, pp. 354-67; and 'Biblical Archaeology', in *Oxford Encyclopedia of Archaeology in the Near East* (New York: Oxford University Press, 1997), I, pp. 315-19.

6.   One thinks of Werner Keller's *Und die Bibel hat doch Recht in Bildern*, which became something of a best-seller in its English translation, *The Bible as History: Archaeology Confirms the Book of Books* (London: Hodder & Stoughton, 1980 [1956]).

the most such connections could accomplish, most archaeologists admit—some happily, some reluctantly—is that archaeology provides an independent witness indicating that an event related in a biblical text in fact took place. But archaeology can never authenticate the foundational biblical claim that the event took place because of divine action or intervention in human affairs.[7]

Thus, the silent agenda behind much field work that looks towards establishing the political history of ancient Israel becomes repugnant to feminist critics on two counts. First, the tendency for demonstrable links between archaeological and historical epochs to be viewed as indicators of scriptural veracity and at least by some, ultimately, as evidence for scriptural authority, would be contested by feminist refusal to accept such authority without a hermeneutic that circumvents or subverts its androcentrism.[8] Secondly, the very focus on political history represents a privileging of the area of the biblical past in which the actors were for the most part males. Archaeology interested in ancient political history, as marked by military conflicts and monarchies, tends to look at the material remains of a biblical site as if they were deposited only by its male inhabitants—its warriors and its royal bureaucrats. Such archaeology is thus blind to the human dynamics of cities and villages populated by women and children as well as by men.[9] The 'great men' perspective of the Hebrew Bible has fitted all too well into the dominant modes of Western political history and of traditional biblical archaeology.

But in recent decades, the impetus to do political history has been

7.   A classic statement about how archaeology is misused to claim it can 'prove' the Bible is found in Roland de Vaux's 'On Right and Wrong Uses of Archaeology', in James A. Sanders (ed.), *Near Eastern Archaeology in the Twentieth Century: Essays in Honor of Nelson Glueck* (Garden City, NY: Doubleday, 1970), pp. 64-80. Many similar critiques have followed, but the notion that the Bible will be authenticated by archaeology dies hard. Even such a severe critic of biblical archaeology as William Dever, in a recent interview, found himself saying, 'the Bible was right after all!', and that some biblical texts could find confirmation in archaeological discoveries. See W. Dever, 'Is the Bible Right After All?', *BARev* 22 (1996), pp. 30-37, 74-77.

8.   I resist using the term 'patriarchal' in reference to either the Hebrew Bible or ancient Israelite society. That term implies judgments that, given the alterity of the biblical world, may not be legitimate. See my chapter on 'The Problem of Patriarchy', pp. 24-46 in *Discovering Eve: Ancient Israelite Women in Context* (New York: Oxford University Press, 1988).

9.   See my critique of this male bias in archaeology in *Discovering Eve*, pp. 16-18. See also William G. Dever, '"Will the Real Israel Please Stand Up?". II. Archaeology and the Religion of Ancient Israel', *BASOR* 298 (1995), p. 45.

supplemented or even replaced by the concern, often provoked by feminist historians, to look at the social history of human communities. Joan Kelly-Gadol's programmatic essay, 'Did Women Have a Renaissance?',[10] was among the first examples of feminist historical research that challenged traditional periodization and in so doing emphasized that women's experiences, and their own evaluations of their social reality, could differ quite substantially from the way men experienced and represented their social environment.

At about the same time that feminist critics were assessing and revising the methods by which scholarship reconstructed past historic eras, archaeologists themselves were in the midst of revolutionary changes, especially in their approach to prehistoric or ahistoric epochs. The 'New Archaeology' emerged in the 1960s in Americanist anthropological circles.[11] Although this New Archaeology was concerned with prehistoric societies, its attention to full data recovery and to establishing the potentials and constraints of the ecological context in which any human community exists led to dramatic changes in both the scope and the methods used for data collection at Palestinian sites.[12]

With respect to scope, it led, in a fortuitous turn that was to benefit feminist interests in archaeology, to a more egalitarian agenda. Instead of being inexorably drawn to major cities with their elite male

10. First published in the 1976 edition of Renate Bridenthal, Claudia Koonz and Susan Stuard (eds.), *Becoming Visible: Women in European History* (Boston: Houghton Mifflin), and republished unchanged in the second (1987) edition.

11. The term 'New Archaeology', narrowly construed, indicates the work of people such as Lewis Binford (beginning with his influential article, 'A Consideration of Archaeological Research Design, *American Antiquity* 29 [1964], pp. 425-41 and in the book he published with Sally R. Binford in 1968, *New Perspectives in Archaeology* [Chicago: Aldine]) and his followers, as they struggled to redefine the methods and goals of archaeology. That struggle is now over, and New Archaeology now more generally indicates the methodological and theoretical advances that emerged from Binford's critiques.

12. For analysis of the nature of the New Archaeology and its influence on Syro-Palestinian or biblical archaeology, see, *inter alia*, William G. Dever, 'The Impact of the "New Archaeology" on Syro-Palestinian Archaeology', *BASOR* 242 (1981), pp. 14-29, and Lawrence E. Toombs, 'A Perspective on the New Archaeology', in Leo G. Perdue, Lawrence E. Toombs and G.L. Johnson (eds.), *Archaeology and Biblical Interpretation* (Atlanta: Scholars Press, 1987), pp. 41-52. Perhaps the first explicit acknowledgment that the goals and processes of the New Archaeology should be brought into archaeology as relevant to biblical studies came from the man often called the 'father' (I would now say 'parent') of traditional biblical archaeology, G. Ernest Wright, in his article on 'The New Archaeology', *BA* 38 (1974), pp. 104-15.

buildings—palaces, fortifications, temples—reflecting societal domains controlled by males, archaeologists increasingly recognized
the need to examine the living spaces and implements of populations
inhabiting villages or even isolated farmsteads. Investigating these
smaller settlements, with reconstructed socio-economic hierarchies
that seem less pronounced than in the urban settlements long the
favored objects of Western archaeologists, meant uncovering the material remains of the daily lives of both women and men.

A similar development could be seen in the new ideas about data
collection. Earlier emphasis on ceramic evidence, which was—and
still is—critical for establishing chronology and thus inevitably for
making judgments about political history, gave way to, or at least
became accompanied by, the realization that *everything* recovered in
excavation was important evidence for some or other aspect of an
ancient community. A multi-disciplinary approach gradually accompanied or replaced the traditional preoccupation with architecture
and pottery. With the realization that recovering subsistence patterns
was essential for understanding ancient cultures and the changes
that took place in them, *all* aspects of the material record, both
organic and inorganic, as well as of a site's natural environment and
resources became salient for field projects. It became as important to
assemble ecofacts as it was to recover artifacts. Digs took on a multi-
disciplinary cast, as experts from the natural and social sciences
complemented the stratigraphers and ceramists of traditional expedition staffs. Paleobotanists, geologists and cultural anthropologists,
for example, are now involved in the collection and analysis of data
from Palestinian sites. Again, this significant shift favors feminist
interests. It has led to the recovery of data that inform us about the
processes of daily life necessary for survival in the precarious environment in which early Israelite settlements were located. Those processes were carried out by all members—young and old, female and
male—of the residential units that comprised Israelite settlements.

Even more important than the shift in the scope and data collection
aspects of biblical archaeology as a result of the impact of the New
Archaeology was the shift in—or, more accurately, the introduction
of—theoretical models for the interpretation of data. Archaeological
remains, as has often been noted, are mute. They are virtually mean-
ingless unless we say what they are, how they were used, why their
use was sustained or discontinued, how their use relates to other
elements of the material culture. Most of this interpretive information
is provided through analogic reasoning, sometimes used intuitively

and unconsciously, sometimes explicitly and intentionally.[13] If a ceramic vessel that is large and thick-walled is found, it can be said with some assurance that it is a storage jar because we know, from first-hand observation or from ethnographic reports, that such vessels generally function in that way. In other words, archaeology, 'New' or old, relies to a certain extent on analogy from known or existing functions of items of material culture. Analogy allows us to deal with the paradox of dealing with an inanimate archaeological record that exists in the present, in order to view animated lives that existed in the past and performed the operations of daily living that created that record.[14]

As problematic as it sometimes is to use analogy to understand the direct functions of various aspects of material culture, it is even more difficult—and at the same time more essential—to turn to information gleaned from ethnographic or ethno-historical sources in order to reconstruct behavior and thus the dynamics of past social existence. All the theoretical models generated in the decades since the emergence of the New Archaeology have, in some way or other, relied upon data about human behavior from observable communities in order to formulate explanatory hypotheses about non-observable ones.[15] That formation of these models has been concerned with the significance of the lives of ordinary individuals as well as of governing elites and corporate social forms, is another aspect of theory-building in recent archaeology that is congenial to feminist interests.

Current archaeological interpretation is inevitably ethnoarchaeological and, therefore, comparativist in its approach. Those features must be kept in mind in considering feminist archaeology. Invoking the broad range of ethnoarchaeological materials and interpretations provides a powerful new way to use material culture for the study of gender. We must break out of the perception of archaeology as a

13. An excellent examination of the problems and benefits of analogy in archaeological interpretation can be found in Charles E. Carter, 'Ethnoarchaeology', *The Oxford Encyclopedia of Archaeology in the Near East*, II, pp. 280-84.

14. Introductory archaeological handbooks invariably emphasize this paradox and the way analogy resolves it. See, e.g., Wendy Ashmore and Robert Shaver, *Discovering Our Past: A Brief Introduction to Archaeology* (Mountain View, CA: Mayfield, 1988), pp. 137-46.

15. Ian Hodder's *Reading the Past: Current Approaches to Interpretation in Archaeology* (Cambridge: Cambridge University Press, 1991) provides a cogent summary of the development of theory in archaeology. Hodder examines structuralism, neo-Marxism and critical theory; he also sets forth an original 'post-processual' contextual approach.

discipline devoted solely to 'objects', to observable archaeological remains. Rather, ethnoarchaeolgy, or social archaeology as it is sometimes called, affirms the notion that organizational schemes and social structures can be determined by examining the full range of artifactual and ecofactual data recovered by field projects. I also deem it philosophically appropriate to turn to methodologies that look across cultures and bring the observable details of life and group processes in existing societies to bear upon the analysis of extinct ones. The most appropriate comparative material for the world of the Hebrew Bible comes from examining observable societies that are most like ancient Israel, or at least are most like it in aspects salient to the comparative intents, rather than from considering biblical modalities in relation to our own contemporary Western experience.

Archaeology, Gendered and Feminist

The title of this essay suggests that by recovering 'objects', that is, as I have now explained, by engaging in the broad ethnoarchaeological enterprise, one may be able to 're-vision subjects'—to study the lives of women in the biblical past, and thus to understand better the social location of biblical texts mentioning, or in some cases being silent about, women. This process is essentially one that involves gendered archaeology/ethnoarchaeology. That enterprise properly focuses on the study of gendered systems in past societies, meaning the study of both women and men as categories of individuals comprising social systems. However, because the traditional interest of historical and ethnographic as well as ethnoarchaeological research has been on male behavior, the notion of gendered archaeology has come to indicate a central concern with women. Women are the ones who have been notoriously neglected, or subsumed under a male norm, in Western scholarship. The second wave of American feminism in the 1960s and subsequent decades, however, has brought about a critique of traditional approaches that has deeply influenced virtually every discipline in the social sciences and humanities.

In this sense, gendered archaeology (also called 'gender archaeology') becomes a feminist project. It must grapple with the biases in the contemporary world and in the academy that have led to ignoring women or to misrepresenting them. I have already pointed out that the elitist character of traditional biblical archaeology precluded the recovery of data that could lead to gender balance in the interpretation of material culture. But, as I have also suggested, recent developments in field projects in Israel and Jordan have begun to redress the elitist bias and thus, concomitantly, the androcentric one.

Let me consider, then, two other kinds of biases that have concerned feminist archaeologists.[16] Although those biases have been critiqued mainly by anthropological archaeologists working largely in prehistoric or ahistoric cultures, the critiques are relevant to the study of gender in all pre-modern societies. The first bias is the inappropriate use of analogy; it is the tendency to view the division of labor by gender in the past as somehow similar to what we are familiar with in the present. Because artifacts are not 'gender noisy'— because the problem of the silence of material objects about how they functioned is especially acute with respect to who used them— archaeologists have repeatedly made assumptions linking female pursuits of the past with those of the present. To do so not only may erroneously represent the kind of things women did or did not do in the past; it also subtly reinforces essentialist notions about female (and male) behavior that impede current feminist goals for equality.

The other kind of bias is that which foregrounds and favors male activities. This tendency, which relates to the preoccupation with political history already noted in discussing biblical archaeology, is manifest in the way history or prehistory is written. The past is construed from the perspective of what males did in terms of leadership, allocation of resources, establishment of marital ties and so on. It ignores the possibility of female agency, direct or indirect, in such areas of social behavior. For historic periods we now know that the relative invisibility of women's activities, because of the bias of verbal informants and written sources alike, is not a legitimate indicator of female subordination in the dynamics of day-to-day gender relations.[17]

Gendered archaeology can thus be meaningful and successful only

16. See Margaret W. Conkey and Janet Spector, 'Archaeology and the Study of Gender', in Michael Schiffer (ed.), *Advances in Archaeological Method and Theory* (New York: Academic Press, 1984), vol. 7, pp. 1-38. The ground-breaking work of Conkey and Spector is summarized in Hodder, *Reading the Past*, pp. 168-69.

17. A good example, from an observable society, is presented in Ernestine Friedl's pioneering study of Greek villages, 'The Position of Women: Appearance and Reality', *Anthropological Quarterly* 40 (1967), pp. 47-108. A compelling example from the ancient record is found in the work of Elizabeth M. Brumfiel, 'Weaving and Cooking: Women's Cooking in Aztec Mexico', in Joan M. Gero and Margaret W. Conkey (eds.), *Engendering Archaeology: Women and Prehistory* (Oxford: Basil Blackwell, 1991), pp. 224-54. See also Judith A. McGaw, 'Recovering Technology: Why Female Technologies Matter', in Rita P. Wright (ed.), *Gender and Archaeology* (Philadelphia: University of Pennsylvania Press, 1996), pp. 52-75.

if it operates with methodological advances and interests that are shaped by feminist perspectives. Indeed, it is arguable that gendered archaeology cannot proceed independently of feminist critiques. It must expose gender bias in all aspects of archaeological investigation, in what it deems to be relevant evidence, in how it creates or uses interpretive models, and in what kinds of concepts or assumptions about gender and difference surround its processes. Only then can women and their experiences be located amidst the physical and social structures that sophisticated archaeological excavation and ethnoarchaeological analysis can reconstruct. Only then can the gender roles, relations and even ideologies in which women participated be identified, at least as hypotheses to be examined further and otherwise tested.[18]

Toward a Feminist Biblical Archaeology

Clearly, the time has come for the recent developments in archaeological method and theory and in feminist and gendered archaeology to be integrated into biblical studies.[19] The multidisciplinary and social science orientation needed for such integration may be daunting in a field in which the existing challenges of acquiring the tools to study an ancient text are already formidable (and which may constitute a simple and too easy reason for the fact that most feminist biblical scholarship does not attend to archaeological data or theory).

18. Margaret W. Conkey and Joan M. Gero make this point in 'Tensions, Pluralities, and Engendering Archaeology: An Introduction to Women and Prehistory', in Gero and Conkey (eds.), *Engendering Archaeology*, pp. 3-54. See also the other introductory essay (Alisin Wylie, 'Gender Theory and the Archaeological Record: Why is There No Archaeology of Gender?', pp. 31-56) in that anthology of studies about how archaeological data can help reveal how gender systems operated in the past.

19. Several new historiographies and historiographical critiques dealing with ancient Israel, such as those of Thomas L. Thompson (*Early History of the Israelite People from the Written and Archaeological Sources* [Leiden: Brill, 1992]); Gösta W. Ahlström (*The History of Ancient Palestine from the Paleolithic Period to Alexander's Conquest* [JSOTSup, 146; Sheffield: Sheffield Academic Press, 1993]) and Philip R. Davies (*In Search of 'Ancient Israel'* [JSOTSup, 148; Sheffield: Sheffield Academic Press, 1992]), claim that archaeological data are critical in biblical studies. Yet they have not successfully integrated such data and the essential interpretive models (see W.G. Dever, '"Will the Real Israel Please Stand Up?" Archaeology and Israelite Historiography, Part I', *BASOR* 297 [1995], pp. 61-80), nor have they enlarged the focus on national political and social history to include an examination of family dynamics and women's lives.

Yet that should be no excuse for ignoring the important if not essential insights that archaeology, as now broadly construed, can contribute to feminist concerns in biblical studies. Indeed, the recent renewal of interest in social science method in our discipline in general[20] should be read as a sign that social science approaches, many of which can be classified as ethnoarchaeological, are becoming more accessible to scholars who would involve them in feminist projects.

The resurgence of attention to social science method and potential in biblical studies involves a set of goals and sensitivities that overlap in striking ways with those of feminist archaeology. Perhaps most noteworthy of those convergences is the attempt, as more and more information about pre-industrial societies becomes available, to appreciate ancient societies as complex social systems that acquired particular characteristics in order to adapt to the environmental and political challenges they faced. The past tendency of scholars to evaluate products or producers of premodern culture in terms of present Western norms is obviously being redressed, as it is when modes of ancient behaviors called 'primitive' or 'ritualistic' by earlier generations of researchers are no longer so labeled. The tendency to judge ancient gender behavior by current feminist standards must likewise be resisted.

To put it another way, effective gender study of a past society and its cultural products should invoke the emic rather than the etic approach; that is, it must evaluate culture from the perspective of its members rather than from the perspective of the observer.[21] I respect the sensibilities that move biblical scholars to critique the texts they are investigating, especially with respect to gender; but I vigorously protest the materials being compared in such critiques.

It is compelling and important to suggest, for example, that

---

20. A book by Thomas W. Overholt on *Cultural Anthropology and the Old Testament* has just been added to the Guides to Biblical Scholarship Series (Minneapolis: Fortress Press, 1996). Another series, Sources for Biblical and Theological Study, also has a new volume (Charles E. Carter and Carol Meyers [eds.], *Community, Identity, and Ideology: Social-Science Approaches to the Hebrew Bible* [Winona Lake, IN: Eisenbrauns, 1996]) on the subject. The introductory essay in that volume (Charles E. Carter, 'A Discipline in Transition: The Contributions of the Social Sciences to the Study of the Hebrew Bible', pp. 3-36) is exceptionally frank in critiquing social science approaches while advocating their value. Note that, in addition to the new books on social science and the Bible, there is also a flurry of retrospective interest in some of the pioneers, such as William Robertson Smith, in this enterprise.

21. The emic/etic distinction is set forth in Marvin Harris, *Cultural Materialism: The Struggle for a Science of Culture* (New York: Vintage, 1980), pp. 32-45.

women today should control their bodies and make choices about their lives and the kinds of families they want. But it is a misplaced and misguided critique that condemns biblical texts that suggest that such was not the case for the women they present. Consider the biological world of those women, as ethnoarchaeology along with the paleopathological analysis of human skeletal remains now reveals. Woman barely lived beyond thirty, and probably half of all infants died before reaching the age of five. Yet the cropping patterns and climatic constraints of the agrarian inhabitants of the highland villages of Iron Age (biblical) Palestine required that women have enough pregnancies to achieve demographic stability (if not growth), to provide an adequate labor force for household survival, and to ensure care for the occasional male or female that survived into old age. Cultural codes controlling female sexuality and encouraging female fecundity can be construed as laudable survival techniques, when considered from an emic perspective, rather than oppressive patriarchy when evaluated as an etic operation. A hypothetical 'native' informant should be the judge of the value, and morality, of whatever phenomenon is being described and analyzed.

Archaeology broadly construed is indeed comparative. The use of analogy, as indicated above, involves inferential functions. It involves the examination of an aggregate of artifacts and ecofacts from an extinct community in light of the way observable communities with similar artifacts and ecofacts and, if possible, with comparable diachronic trajectories, have constructed themselves as social systems. Using rigorous criteria for inferring human behavior through analogic analysis of material culture constitutes a comparative method that respects the past culture it investigates.

The portrayal of biblical texts as hopelessly patriarchal risks being an act of cultural hubris, if not academic orientalism. I do not mean to suggest that one can never critique another culture; all human cultures have flaws and failures, some more than others. But I urge caution in leaping from the twentieth-century CE West and modern urban comfort to ancient village misery. Rather, the passion in our response to biblical images that attract the label 'patriarchal' and evoke negative evaluations should be directed towards the patriarchal structures of traditional Judeo-Christian religion that have ossified those images into authoritative models, and have refused to let them be replaced by new images that better represent or address the needs of subsequent generations. The patriarchal control of the texts, rather than the texts themselves, deserves the critique of contemporary scholarship.

Let me close with one concrete example of how a biblical text dealing with gender is often evaluated without regard for its social and material location and, hence, with misplaced assumptions about female worth. I am referring to the passage in Leviticus (27.1-8) dealing with the commutation of vows. The payment of differential amounts of shekels to release females and males in various age categories from a commitment to help fund the religio-cultic establishment is often viewed as an indicator that, although women are not worthless, they are not worth as much as men.[22] But such claims fail to ask, not worth as much for what?

The table of commutation of vows in Leviticus, as in other similar texts known from ancient cultic archives, relates to labor value—the amount of productive labor females and males of various ages could theoretically contribute to the tasks of maintaining a sanctuary and its holdings. If one takes a female–male pair of a given age as representing a full complement of labor potential, then the contribution of females comes close to 40 per cent of the whole (the male supplying the other 60 per cent). When evaluated from the perspective of ethnoarchaeology that figure represents a high, not a low, status for women. That is, when women are perceived as contributing nearly half of the productive labor in agrarian societies in addition to their reproductive roles, they occupy a position of esteem in society.[23]

Re-visioning the female subject of the Leviticus passage from a new, ethnoarchaeological perspective allows us to understand that gender relations are not static; they shift over time and are shaped by the exigencies of their own time. To recognize this means that we must radically realign traditional categories that tend to trivialize, minimize, ignore or otherwise degrade women's roles in production, reproduction and the construction of cultures.[24] We have no contemporary category of 'women's work', typically degraded in the West, which is the equivalent to the constellation of tasks and roles that characterized women's lives in highland Palestinian villages of the Iron Age. Consequently, we must remain open to the possibility that

22. Such is the assumption of, for example, David J.A. Clines's *What Does Eve Do to Help? and Other Readerly Questions of the Old Testament* (JSOTSup, 94; Sheffield: Sheffield Academic Press, 1990), p. 45.

23. See the correlations presented by Peggy R. Sanday, 'Female Status in the Public Domain', in Michelle Z. Rosaldo and Louise Lamphere (eds.), *Women, Culture, and Society* (Stanford: Stanford University Press, 1974), pp. 189-206 and also my analysis of the Leviticus passage in 'Procreation, Production, and Protection: Male–Female Balance in Early Israel', *JAAR* 51 (1983), pp. 569-93.

24. See Conkey and Gero, 'Tensions, Pluralities', p. 9.

when we perceive with horror the way women appear in literary productions emerging from that specific spatial and temporal location, we may be reacting in a way that is unfair to that location, its inhabitants and its cultural expressions.

It is time for us to appreciate and utilize the way in which archaeology, broadly construed, can liberate the biblical past from the patriarchal control of traditional interpretations. Ethnoarchaeology can provide a new vision of gender in the biblical world and, thus, a new understanding of female images in the biblical word. Liberating the biblical past in this way is a feminist project that will surely serve present concerns as well. The social knowledge thereby obtained will be more open, contingent and humanistic than traditional social knowledge.[25] Donna Haraway has it right: 'The open future rests on a new past'.[26]

25. Marcia Westkott, 'Feminist Criticism of the Social Sciences', *Harvard Educational Review* 49 (1979), pp. 422-30.

26. Donna Haraway, 'Animal Sociology and a Natural Economy of the Body Politic. II. The Past is the Contested Zone: Human Nature and Theories of Production and Reproduction in Primate Behavior Studies', *Signs* 4 (1978), p. 59.

AN ICONOGRAPHIC APPROACH TO GENESIS 38*

Eleanor Ferris Beach

Pre-view

The undergraduates in my 'Women and the Bible' course usually assume that we will be studying the women *in* the Bible, because their starting point is the question, 'what does the Bible say about women?' That is a good question from which to explore how feminist readers use existing methods to open new perspectives on women as literary characters in narrative; on the gleaning of women's history from biblical and nonbiblical depictions; and on the appropriation of female imagery both to symbolize divine attributes and to critique religious practices disapproved by the writers. From these studies, however, another level of analysis emerges: what and whose experiences and ideas are privileged, and what materials are privileged to convey them? Such questions draw attention as much to the absence of certain elements as to the presence of those being examined. They also provoke students to examine issues of gender and power in their own lives.

In my experience, ancient Near Eastern iconographic materials are among those underrepresented elements that can be used as effective, if non-traditional, resources for exegeting texts and investigating dynamics of gender and power in biblical literature. 'Visual exegesis'

* I thank the conveners of two occasions where earlier versions of this work were presented. Karen King and Karen Torjesen cochaired the Conference on 'Women and Goddess Traditions', Claremont Graduate School, May 1992. My revised paper, 'Transforming Goddess Iconography in Hebrew Narrative', appears in the forthcoming conference proceedings: Karen L. King (ed.), *Women and Goddess Traditions: Studies from Asia, the Ancient Mediterranean, and Contemporary Goddess Thealogy* (intr. K.J. Torjesen; Studies in Antiquity and Christianity; Minneapolis: Fortress Press, 1997). Pamela Thimmes and Richard Weis organized the Feminist Theological Hermeneutics of the Bible Group for the Society of Biblical Literature annual meeting in Washington, DC, November 1993, where the theme was, 'What makes a feminist reading feminist?'

is my term for this approach,[1] a method whose application to Genesis 38 may be supported by a brief autobiographical note and a selective survey of research.

My intuition that the religious environment described in the Bible had a visual component, undervalued in modern studies of biblical texts, arose when I traveled to Israel and the West Bank (then Jordan) as a college student in 1966. The mosaic floor of the sixth-century synagogue at Beth Alpha surprised me, with its Graeco-Roman zodiac centered around Helios in his chariot, sharing sanctuary space with the biblical scene of Abraham's interrupted sacrifice of Isaac. That experience created a discrepancy between what I saw before me and what I thought I knew about the biblical prohibition of images in Judaism. My investigations that summer found the problem had already been addressed by Goodenough's *Jewish Symbols of the Greco-Roman Period*.[2] Goodenough's response was to posit that rabbinic literary prohibitions of visual representation may have been considered prescriptive by their authors, but that the diversity within formative Judaism included Torah-loving Jews who created or borrowed the images found in their tombs and sanctuaries for legitimate religious expression, not pure decor. While Goodenough's specific analyses have been challenged, his ideas encouraged me to wonder whether the artifacts and designs of the biblical period being unearthed by archaeologists were not also valid religious expressions from Yahwistic contexts, despite biblical injunctions and condemnations.

Although by the mid-1970s I was a woman graduate student applying visual evidence, much of it with female subjects, to form-critical analyses of Hebrew Bible texts, I did not yet consider myself a feminist—I just did not have anyone to talk to. When, after a professional and personal time-out, I returned to investigating historical connections between art and text in the mid-1980s, the limitations of text-based reconstructions of Yahwistic religion, even when pluralism was acknowledged, became obvious. The remnants of religious iconography, of goddess traditions and women's religious practice in the material culture had become undeniable. Biblical studies lacked adequate methods for relating visual and verbal arts to each other and to gender, but the concepts were available in women's studies,

1. I acknowledge that this term is influenced by Jo Milgrom's quite different technique of 'visual midrash'.

2. Erwin Ramsdell Goodenough, *Jewish Symbols of the Greco-Roman Period* (Bollingen series, 37; 12 vols., New York: Pantheon, 1953–1968).

psychology, philosophy of art, literary criticism and semiotics. The discrepancy between my experience and what was 'supposed to be' became a willingness to take seriously visual evidence that was generally not privileged by Euro-American Christian and Jewish (male) textual scholarship, and an increasing recognition of the social and gendered constructions of power and their symbols in antiquity as well as the present.[3]

Any attempt to chronicle the uses and abuses of visual evidence in biblical interpretation would exceed the bounds of this essay, but I shall make some observations pertinent to feminist concerns.[4] First, a biblical interpreter who wants to incorporate visual evidence into exegesis of a particular text confronts an area where there is little 'raw' material, since oppositional dichotomies already mark the evidence. Secondly, the methods of applying material culture to biblical interpretation are often weakened either by separating both text and artifact from their context or by overgeneralizing potential connections.

First, feminists will not be surprised to find that the set of dualisms that opposes man, mind and culture to woman, body and nature can be extended to include word and image respectively, especially in biblical study. To those for whom the god of biblical literature is (metaphorically, of course) male, singular and solitary, invisible and revealed by word and deed as preserved in text, religious artifacts (and texts) that represent the divine as female, sometimes paired with another, corporeal and visual are self-evidently incompatible and antithetical to their theological premise, for which they claim ancient historical orthodoxy. These occurrences can be explained away as 'other' in a variety of ways—as foreign, or Canaanite, or 'popular'

3.   I find it ironic that the current interest in Israelite goddesses was sparked for logocentric scholars not by the long-known visual evidence, but by texts being published in the 1970s. These extrabiblical votive inscriptions from the ninth and eight centuries that apparently mention 'Yahweh and his Asherah' gave text-based interpreters license to ask new questions of the canon and of archaeological evidence. Raphael Patai's 1967 book, *The Hebrew Goddess*, was an early synthesis that gained a new audience in the shift (repr.; New York: Avon Books, 1978). For studies with differing conclusions about Asherah's place in Yahwism, see Saul M. Olyan, *Asherah and the Cult of Yahweh* (SBLMS, 34; Atlanta: Scholars Press, 1988), and Mark S. Smith, *The Early History of God: Yahweh and the Other Deities in Ancient Israel* (San Francisco: Harper & Row, 1990), pp. 80-114.

4.   A much more fully detailed and nuanced treatment is given in my Claremont Graduate School doctoral dissertation. See Eleanor Ferris Beach, *Image and Word: Iconology in the Interpretation of Hebrew Scriptures* (Ann Arbor, MI: University Microfilms, 1991). The following section is based on chapters 2 and 3.

(meaning 'local', or women's practices supposedly not endorsed by the official establishment), or apostate, or not depictions of deity. Such implicit judgments underlie the descriptions in some biblical encyclopaedias where visual images are discussed only as idols or decoration; where art is not a legitimate Yahwistic production; and where photographs of such artifacts are used routinely to illustrate aspects of material culture without receiving any explanation of their own. If one seeks more direct access to artifacts through archaeological reports, one sometimes finds similar prejudices and accompanying caveats to distance the objects from the religion described in the Bible. For example, a mixed fascination with female anthropomorphic figurines as indicative of sexual and (apostate) religious values leads to their being described and illustrated in special studies[5] and out of proportion to their number among the finds, while the more numerous animal figures from the same site receives cursory treatment[6] or are devalued as 'crude playthings'.[7] But these are the modern commentators' sexual and religious interests; can we ever know what the ancients thought?

On the other hand, interpreters who credit material culture as reasonable evidence of pluralistic or complementary religious views may be criticized for trying to establish connections that are too inferential, or too broad, or for dislocating artifact and text from their respective contexts to the detriment of the argument. The collections of illustrations designed to give ancient Near Eastern background to the Bible may arrange the entries thematically (Gressmann, Pritchard) or conceptually (Keel). Where there is reference to a specific biblical passage (Keel, Mazar), a meaningful chronological and historical association may be lacking, and the connection remains effectively conceptual.[8]

5. For an early example, see G. Contenau, *La déesse nue babylonienne: Etude d'iconographie comparé* (Paris: Paul Geuthner, 1914).

6. Only 20 per cent of the 180 published finds at Israelite Samaria were female anthropomorphic pieces. The rest were zoomorphic, except for two male figures. J.W. Crowfoot, G.M. Crowfoot and K.M. Kenyon, *The Objects from Samaria* (London: Palestine Exploration Fund, 1957).

7. Olga Tufnell, *Lachish III: The Iron Age* (London: Oxford University Press, 1953), p. 374.

8. Hugo Gressmann, *Altorientalische Texte und Bilder zum Alten Testament* (Tübingen: Mohr [Paul Siebeck], 1909); H. Gressmann, *Altorientalische Bilder zum Alten Testament* (Berlin: de Gruyter, 1927); *ANEP*; Othmar Keel, *The Symbolism of the Biblical World: Ancient Near Eastern Iconography and the Book of Psalms* (trans. T.J. Hallett; New York: Seabury, 1978); Benjamin Mazar (ed.), *Views of the Biblical World* (Ramat Gan, Israel: International Publishing, 1958–1961).

A steady stream of iconographic studies by Keel and his student-colleagues at the University of Freiburg (Switzerland) has made it very clear that, as one title declares, there were images in Israel (Schroer, *In Israel gab es Bilder*). The connections between image and text are more persuasive in their small-scale works, where image and text share a limited historical venue. In Keel's *Jahwes Entgegnung an Ijob*, for example, the motifs he cites from Egyptian and Mesopotamian monuments were also found on Iron Age Palestinian scarabs and seals. Winter's *Frau und Göttin* presents a valuable compilation of (520!) images, but is open to the criticism of constructing a comprehensive deity from disparate artistic forms and claiming that this goddess was an attractive option for Israelite women. To her discussion of visual motifs and thematically related biblical passages, Schroer prefaces two cautionary notes worth repeating: about the androcentric interests evident in the selection and redaction of biblical literature, and about the logocentric interests of Western exegetes.[9]

If the image does not illustrate what one already 'knows' from a text, how does one bring the multiple visual associations to the words, or how can one discern if an image was the generative impetus around which words were gathered? The dichotomy that opposes image to word implies an inherent and essential incomparability, but this, like other dichotomies, can be dismantled by several strategies: by recognition of the historically and socially conditioned nature of symbolic expressions; or by philosophical and literary criticisms; or by psychological approaches. Visual exegesis approaches the intersection of image and word not as an a priori boundary between opposites but as a compositional device in which the elements have potentially complementary roles. If an opposition

---

9.   Comments on these few examples are not intended to cover the full range and depth of this growing corpus, much of which appears in Orbis Biblicus et Orientalis volumes. Othmar Keel, *Jahwes Entgegnung an Ijob* (Göttingen: Vandenhoeck & Ruprecht, 1978); Urs Winter, *Frau und Göttin: Exegetische und ikonographische Studien zum weiblichen Gottesbild im alten Israel und in dessen Umwelt* (OBO, 53; Göttingen: Vandenhoeck & Ruprecht, 1983); Edward Lipinski, 'The Syro-Palestinian Iconography of Woman and Goddess' (Review of *Frau und Göttin* by U. Winter) *IEJ* 36 (1986), pp. 87-96; Silvia Schroer, *In Israel gab es Bilder: Nachrichten von darstellender Kunst im Alten Testament* (OBO, 74; Göttingen: Vandenhoeck & Ruprecht, 1987). A chronologically systematic study of local iconography and its implications for the history of Israelite religion is undertaken with feminist interests in Othmar Keel and Christoph Mehlinger, *Göttingen, Götte und Gottessymbole: Neue Erkenntnisse zur Religionsgeschichte Kanaans und Israels aufgrund bislang unerschlossener iconographischer Quellen* (Freiburg: Herder, 1995).

emerges, it is treated as symptomatic of an ideological boundary constructed by the authors and thereby open to further study.[10]

Re-view

Genesis 38 is one of several family stories in Genesis 12–50 to have attracted feminist study because of its depiction of women working to achieve patriarchal priorities, by means that run counter to patriarchal control. The themes familiar from these stories are abundant in Genesis 38: that the desired male lineage is in jeopardy creates the narrative tension, heightened through a dramatic encounter activated by a woman, to a dénouement beyond the control of the male protagonist (and contrary to primogeniture) but apparently congruent with the divine covenant program. In this instance, Tamar—widowed and childless by Judah's two sons and promised to a third whom he keeps from her—takes the initiative to conceive offspring for her father-in-law's line by making herself available to him in the guise of a prostitute. Her unborn children, threatened by Judah's death sentence for her harlotry, are spared and legitimated when he acknowledges the pledge of ring, cord and staff that he left with the 'prostitute'. One of her sons is King David's ancestor Perez, who emerged first from the womb after his twin Zerah's false start.

Several of the elements one associates with feminist interpretation have been examined in pre-feminist studies of Genesis 38: literary characterization of women's roles, resources for women's history, and the influence of ancient Near Eastern traditions, especially about goddesses.

The observation that King David's lineage is carried by the stories of women with unconventional matings was first made not by twentieth-century feminists, but by the author of Matthew's gospel (1.1-17). Tamar of Genesis 38 is mentioned with Rahab the mother of Boaz, Ruth and Uriah's wife (unnamed in the gospel, but we know her as Bathsheba) among Solomon's foremothers in the genealogy leading to Joseph, whose wife Mary bore Jesus also in exceptional circumstances. Such intertextual mirroring within the Hebrew Scriptures has been examined by structuralists who point out the parallels between the Genesis 38 women—Judah's wife Bath-shua and his

---

10. For discussion of methods of dealing with image–word dichotomies, see Terry Eagleton, *Literary Theory: An Introduction* (Minneapolis: University of Minnesota Press, 1983), especially p. 133 and W.J.T. Mitchell, *Iconology: Image, Text, Ideology* (Chicago: University of Chicago Press, 1986), especially p. 44.

daughter-in-law Tamar—and David's wife Bathsheba and his daughter Tamar in 2 Samuel 11 and 13.[11]

Bal and van Dijk-Hemmes make explicitly feminist studies of Tamar's literary characterization.[12] Bal does not attempt to discover what the 'original' audience might have understood, but uses Genesis 38 to illustrate the reading fallacy by which 'love' is lethal and woman is to be feared. She demonstrates that, according to 'the heterogeneous ideology of the text' (p. 131), the Tamar character is not fatal, but is used positively 'as the sidestep that restores broken chronology' and as one who will 'teach man insight into his own paralyzing neuroses' (p. 102). Van Dijk-Hemmes sees Tamar's literary role both as a corrective to her father-in-law Judah's over-cautious and life-denying behavior; and as a pre-emptive critique of David's careless sending of the second Tamar to the sickbed of her half-brother Amnon, who rapes her (2 Sam. 13) without any disciplinary consequences from David. This interpretation takes more interest in the texts' history, seeing Genesis 38 as a critical commentary composed after the 2 Samuel account but placed as its precursor in the canonical order.

Genesis 38 has been used as a source for information about ancient women's history and social roles: about the practice of levirate marriage, customs of widowhood, father's control of offspring's marriage, procreation, inheritance and prostitution in conventional and 'cultic' forms.[13]

Feminist research outside biblical studies has identified how such social institutions work to the advantage of privileged males and of women who benefit by association with them.[14] Tamar's bold plan,

11. Edmund Leach, 'The Legitimacy of Solomon', in *Genesis as Myth and Other Essays* (London: Jonathan Cape, 1969), pp. 25-83.

12. Mieke Bal, 'One Woman, Many Men, and the Dialectic of Chronology', in *Lethal Love: Feminist Literary Readings of Biblical Love Stories* (Bloomington: Indiana University Press, 1986), pp. 89-103. Fokkelien van Dijk-Hemmes, 'Tamar and the Limits of Patriarchy: Between Rape and Seduction', in M. Bal (ed.), *Anti-Covenant: Counter-Reading Women's Lives in the Hebrew Bible*, (Sheffield: Almond Press, 1989), pp. 135-56.

13. T. Thompson and D. Thompson, 'Some Legal Problems in the Book of Ruth', *VT* 18 (1968), pp. 79-99; George W. Coats, 'Widow's Rights: A Crux in the Structure of Genesis 38', *CBQ* 34 (1972), pp. 461-66; U. Cassuto, 'The Story of Tamar and Judah', in *Biblical and Oriental Studies,*. I. *Bible* (Jerusalem: Magnes, 1973), pp. 29-40.

14. For an analysis of these practices in the ancient Near East, see Gerda Lerner, *The Creation of Patriarchy* (New York: Oxford University Press, 1986), especially chapters 3 and 5.

acting outside Judah's control, may be appreciated as a woman's initiative within the restrictive society; yet, one must remember that she is approved for having supported patriarchal goals, even if her means were unusual. Interpreters of this passage who do not share Tamar's position in relation to patriarchal institutions may have different evaluations of her efforts to produce an heir. Not all men share privilege, either. Paul has looked carefully at Onan's place in the story and concluded that this second son is even less privileged than Tamar.[15] He is exploited solely as a stud animal in a system of male primogeniture, a function from which he intentionally 'withdraws'. His resistance costs him his life at the hands of the deity. So, one must be aware of interpreting from gender and class location in relation to 'privilege by association' even when dealing with historical reconstruction of social aspects of the text.

Recognition of the chapter's ancient Near Eastern mythic themes and visual elements has long called into question its value as a historical source.

(1) The woman who brings death is also known in Sarah from the apocryphal book of Tobit. Skinner relates both Tamar in Genesis and this Sarah to Ishtar and thereby to the goddess who slays her lovers.[16] Gunn and Blenkinsopp posit a special interest in this 'folk motif' among Davidic authors—the 'J writer' and Davidic chroniclers.[17] The narrative of Genesis 38 makes clear, however, that although Judah may suspect Tamar of such death-dealing influence, Yahweh has the killing role of goddess or demon competitor.

(2) Father–daughter unions are known from the account of Lot's daughters (Gen. 19) and from extrabiblical tales. In the myth of Adonis, as told by Panyasis, a father who had unknowingly slept with his daughter tried to kill her with a sword, but was thwarted by divine intervention that transformed her into a myrtle tree. Their son, Adonis, burst from the tree at birth and was saved by Aphrodite. Similar mythological vestiges in the biblical story may include the

15. Garrett Paul, chapel talk printed in *Gustavus Adolphus College Faculty Notes* 42.3 (1993), pp. 6-7.

16. John Skinner, *A Critical and Exegetical Commentary on Genesis* (ICC; Edinburgh: T. & T. Clark, 2nd edn, 1930), p. 452.

17. D.M. Gunn, 'Traditional Composition in the "Succession Narrative"', *VT* 26 (1976), pp. 214-29, and J. Blenkinsopp, 'Theme and Motif in the Succession History (2 Sam XI 2ff) and the Yahwistic Corpus', (VTSup, 15; Leiden: Brill, 1966), pp. 44-57.

Judah–Tamar union, the tree motif (Tamar means 'palm') and breach at birth (Perez means 'breach').[18]

(3) The birth and conflict of twins is also credited as an originally extrabiblical mythical theme, that included redness for the firstborn and supremacy for the younger.[19] Within Genesis, the resemblance to Esau and Jacob's birth story is also unmistakable (Gen. 25.19-26).

(4) Tamar's ruse of prostitution evokes much comment on her costume,[20] the fertility implications of sheep-shearing festivities,[21] and legislation governing the marriages and childbearing of hierodules.[22]

For the most part, these scholars are not explicit in speculating how these elements of cultural background, including goddesses' roles, were historically integrated into ancient Israelite culture and Yahwism. Emerton, however, locates the story's origin among Canaanites who had intermarried with Judahites and who circulated a tale with a somewhat humorous critique of Judah that was adopted by the tribe and by the J-writer.[23] As early as 1913, Hartmann linked Tamar's name and Enaim, the place of Judah and Tamar's meeting, to worship of a female 'nature god' in the sacred palm oasis of Ein Gedi.[24]

Visual hints of a mythic background have also been observed. Gray noted the frequent identification of palm tree and goat with 'fertility goddesses' in ancient Near Eastern art, hence the cleverness of Tamar's name and the fee of a kid for services rendered,[25] again without saying what role such art may have played in Israelite practice.

The application of my visual exegesis of Genesis 38 begins with a similar observation—the resemblance of Judah's ring, cord and staff to ancient Near Eastern iconography—and pursues the implications

18. Michael Astour, 'Tamar the Hierodule: An Essay in the Method of Vestigial Motifs', *JBL* 85 (1966), pp. 185-96, especially pp. 195-96, and G.R.H. Wright, 'The Positioning of Genesis 38', *ZAW* 94 (1982), pp. 523-29.

19. Skinner, *Commentary on Genesis*, pp. 455-56.

20. Bernhard Luther, 'Die Nouvelle von Juda und Tamar und andere israelitische Novellen', in E. Meyer (ed.), *Die Israeliten und ihre Nachbarstämme* (Halle: Max Niemeyer, 1906), pp. 175-206, especially pp. 179-80.

21. Menahem Haran, '*zebah hayyamim*', *VT* 19 (1969), pp. 11-22, especially p. 22.

22. Astour, 'Tamar the Hierodule'.

23. J.A. Emerton, 'Some Problems in Genesis XXXVIII', *VT* 25 (1975), pp. 338-61.

24. Richard Hartmann, 'Zu Genesis 38', *ZAW* 33 (1913), pp. 76-77.

25. John Gray, *I and II Kings: A Commentary* (Philadelphia: Westminster Press, 2nd rev. edn, 1970), p. 350.

of art historical study back to literary, historical and theological levels in the text.

Iconographic Resources

The plot's dramatic turn of events hinges upon Tamar's being able to prove that her partner in 'harlotry' was none other than Judah himself. The 'harlot' had specifically requested Judah's pledge of ring, cord and staff, which his emissary the Adullamite fails to retrieve with the payment of a kid. Judah's insignia join the other markers of male identity in Genesis used to change a relationship (Esau's clothes on Jacob, Joseph's coat retained by Potiphar's wife, Joseph's cup hidden in Benjamin's baggage).[26] When Tamar sends them back to Judah to stay her execution, he acknowledges his ownership, his accumulated errors and his new offspring.

A frequently cited comment on the ancient function of these objects is Herodotus' report that Babylonians carried a seal ring and carved wooden staff as instruments of personal identification and authority in transactions.[27] They would thus appear to be fairly common but distinctive items for heads of household such as Judah. In the iconographic repertoire of the ancient Near East, however, a ring (sometimes with cord) and staff are frequently royal symbols, appearing as early as the late third millennium in the Egyptian Old Kingdom and the Sumero-Akkadian period in Mesopotamia. The ring is not a metal finger ring but a large, often bound, circlet, from which a longer cord is looped. The staff is rendered from walking-stick size to a much shorter rod. As an artistic motif, the design is often called the rod and ring. The four illustrations at the end of this chapter highlight some common features from among dozens of examples.

The stone stele commemorating Ur-Nammu's role in temple construction (c. 2050 BCE) features several registers of carved relief (figure 1).[28] Near the top, the king is shown standing before a seated god (Nanna, moon god) whose extended hand holds ring, cord and staff while the king pours a libation into an altar vase from which a palm frond or similar emblem protrudes. The king's libation is repeated on

26. Nelly Furman, 'His Story versus Her Story: Male Genealogy and Female Strategy in the Jacob Cycle', in Adela Yarbro Collins (ed.), *Feminist Perspectives on Biblical Scholarship* (Chico, CA: Scholars Press, 1985), pp. 107-16.

27. Noted in Hermann Gunkel, *The Legends of Genesis* (trans. W.H. Carruth; Chicago: Open Court, 1907), p. 416, and in subsequent commentaries.

28. This is a limestone stele found at Ur, now at the University Museum of the University of Pennsylvania, Philadelphia. See *ANEP*, ill. 306 and p. 285.

the same register before a seated goddess (Nirgal), perhaps to signify a single action before the divine couple seated side by side. In the building scenes of the lower registers, the king himself ceremonially carries and lays the temple bricks. In this context, the apparatus may be construed as surveying tools with which the divine architect commissions the king to be his earthly contractor. The only biblical occurrence of a rod and cord outside Genesis 38 appears in Ezek. 40.3, where the instruments are used by a figure in Ezekiel's vision to measure the new temple. The prophet is explicitly commissioned to report the dimensions to the house of Israel as an architectural plan.[29]

The 'meting out of justice' as a figure of speech in English ('mete' = 'measure') has its visual antecedent in the sun god Shamash's commission to the Babylonian Hammurabi (1728–1686 BCE) preserved on another stone stele on which the king is directed 'to promote the welfare of the people,...to cause justice to prevail in the land'.[30] Again, the enthroned deity holds extended rod and ring at the king's investiture, memorialized on the stele inscribed with Hammurabi's law code (figure 2).

Actual use of rod, bound circlet and cord as surveying tools is documented in scenes from several Eighteenth Dynasty Theban tombs.[31] However, in a major survey of the rod and ring motif Pierre Bikai presents an alternative interpretation, that 'the origin of the rod and the ring can be found in the taming stick and the nose rope with a ring at the end. Thus the later meaning of victory [and] divine power had its roots in early animal domestication.' Bikai concludes, 'Ultimately, in representational art, these symbols came to demonstrate that the recipient of them is a true king'.[32] The pastoral connection may be supported on Hammurabi's stele, where 'shepherd' is a royal epithet in the text as well.

Although neither surveying nor pastoral motifs figure in most investiture scenes, the rod and ring persist as emblems of royal

29. The Hebrew for cord is the same word as in Genesis 38; a different word is used for staff.

30. Prologue of 'The Code of Hammurabi', translated by T.J. Meek, in *ANET*, pp. 163-80. The diorite stele was discovered at Susa in 1901–1902 and is now in the Louvre. See *ANEP*, p. 277 and ill. 246, 515.

31. Suzanne Berger, 'A Note on Some Scenes of Land-Measurement', *JEA* 20 (1934), pp. 54-56 and pl. X.

32. Pierre M. Bikai, 'The Rod and the Ring', a paper presented at the 1990 Society of Biblical Literature annual meeting; *Society of Biblical Literature Abstracts* (Atlanta: Scholars Press, 1990), p. 329, S136.

commissioning, often in temple settings. An example contemporary with Hammurabi's stele early in the second millennium was found in a wall painting at Mari.[33] The temple scene is framed with stylized palms, appropriate for the goddess Ishtar who stands upon a lion and holds rod and ring before the king (figure 3).

Almost a thousand years later the tradition, which has continued in a variety of media and contexts, produces a striking Neo-Babylonian example on an inscribed tablet from Nabuapaliddin's report of rebuilding a temple (885–850 BCE). The enthroned Shamash extends rod and ring toward three approaching figures—priest leading king, with goddess as escort (figure 4). Shamash is seated beneath a canopy which is supported by a palm tree/column, topped in turn by two gods captioned 'the twins', Kittu and Misharu, Justice and Righteousness.[34] The astral symbols of moon, sun and star are also labelled—Sin, Shamash and Ishtar. The stone tablet was preserved with a clay envelope 250 years later in another restoration of the temple by Nabopolassar, the father of the Nebuchandezzar who captured Jerusalem.[35]

Popularity of the auspicious motif led to its westward migration. Already in the second millennium Syrian glyptic art miniaturized Babylonian monumental images, and Western cylinder seals reproduced scenes of rod and ring as symbols of authority.[36] In the first millennium, the Assyrians likewise adopted as wall decor the now standing god with rod and ring receiving homage from the king.[37]

33. The wall painting was excavated in the 1935–36 season at the Palace Court 106. See *ANEP*, ill. 610 and pp. 322-23. This setting has been investigated by Jack Sasson, who noted the exceptional role of the goddess and women in this setting in his paper, 'Queens and Goddesses at Mari', for the Gender and Cultural Criticism Consultation, Society of Biblical Literature annual meeting, November 1993.

34. For discussion of the twins, see Roy Rosenberg, 'The God Sedeq', *HUCA* 36 (1965), pp. 161-77, especially pp. 161-63.

35. The stone tablet and two clay impressions of the relief were preserved in a clay box found at Abu Habbah in 1881, now in the British Museum. See *ANEP*, ill. 529 and p. 313.

36. For the artistic influence of Hammurabi's dynasty, see Henri Frankfort, *Cylinder Seals: A Documentary Essay on the Art and Religion of the Ancient Near East* (London: Gregg Press, 1965 [1939]), p. 155. For examples of Western cylinder seals with this motif, see Andre Parrot (ed.), *Studia Mariana* (Leiden: Brill, 1950), pp. 17-19 and fig. 5.

37. For example, the scene appears on glazed bricks at Assur and on a wall painting at Khorsabad; Andre Parrot, *The Arts of Assyria* (trans. S. Gilbert and

One can be confident that the Jerusalem court and many others in the kingdom were well aware of the significance not only of the rod and ring, but also of its accompanying motifs.

The word translated 'ring' in Genesis 38 may serve as an internal footnote to the motif's presence on western seals. As a verb, the root *ḥtm* has the sense 'to seal, confirm', reflecting the surface imprint rather than the shape of the stamp seal or cylinder or ring that bears it. 'Signet' or 'seal' is thus a more literal translation of the nouns in Gen. 38.15, 25. In both Egyptian and Semitic usage, however, the meaning expanded from the earlier stamps and cylinders to include seal rings. Wearing such a ring on a cord around the neck may be the referent of the poetic image in Song 8.6: 'set me as a seal upon your heart' in parallel to 'a seal upon your arm', that is, 'hand'.[38] It would be a masterful artistic device to have the narrative become a symbolic enlargement of the image on Judah's seal ring.

Visual Exegesis

The surface of Genesis 38 seems to show Judah as a family head equipped with a special staff, wearing his signet ring on a cord. These objects, mentioned as a set nowhere else in the Bible, raise the issue of an allusion that is partly linguistic (to a finger ring), partly visual (to the image of a ring on a seal or monument), largely connotative. To build a solid case for visual–verbal correspondence, there must be more than one look-alike feature.

In other work I have proposed a four-level analysis to identify essential aspects for congruency: representation, denotation, connotation, and abstract form.[39] At the representational level of this design, the scenes of royal investiture share a cluster of elements: the king, the inaugurating deity with rod and ring (and cord), often a palm emblem and/or symbol of Ishtar. The specific denotation of investiture probably acquired a more generalized connotation of official authorization (the emblems appear in the hands of gods and goddesses in other contexts), while the king's temple building and law giving were especially likely occasions for invoking the inaugural commission. In the formal sense, the reduction of the scene to

J. Emmons; New York: Golden Press, 1961), p. 71 fig. 79, and p. 99 fig. 108 respectively.

38. Otzen, '*ḥatam, ḥotam*', in *TDOT* IV, pp. 263-69.

39. Beach, *Image and Word*, especially pp. 142-49, and chapters 5 and 6. The method is applied without identifying the separate levels in Beach, 'The Samaria Ivories, *Marzeaḥ*, and Biblical Text', *BA* 56 (1993), pp. 94-104.

its most abstracted shapes and lines still conveys a sense of transaction, an exchange observed in profile by a third party. Even though
the king is never shown actually receiving the material objects extended toward him, the sense of his being a recipient of their power is
clear in the barest visual structure and its affective quality. When
these aspects are shared by art and text with a reasonable historical
connection, I believe the likelihood of the text's making an intentional
visual allusion is quite high.

One can make a strong case that the visual allusion suggested by
the Genesis 38 representation of ring, staff, and cord can be sustained
through these other elements as well. There is a god, although he
seems quite removed after killing Onan. The central transaction is
initiated by the chief female character, symbolically named 'palm';
she is euphemistically referred to as $q^ed^e\check{s}\bar{a}h$, 'sacred/holy one', by
those in the story who have not seen her, a witticism that reinforces
the knowing reader's suspicions of a goddess. The male protagonist
fathers twins, one of which produces the Judahite royal line.[40] At
least two in this lineage were especially remembered for the adminis-
tration of justice and temple (re)building—Solomon and Josiah—and
perhaps all boasted of those roles. Within the story itself, Judah is
shown trying to adjudicate Tamar's case in an appeal of a death
sentence that may also reflect royal prerogative. Thus the denotative
and connotative aspects of the art are also present in the text. And
clearly, the chapter depicts a transaction, a transformative one that
depends on the ring, cord, and staff for its completion.

If one lets the visual cues of the narrative crux guide one's thinking, they focus attention on the issues of royal investiture and legitimation. A reader might get this message at the very end of the chapter
upon realizing that Perez was David's ancestor. A viewer familiar
with the symbols picks up the cues much earlier. The visual allusion
to ring, cord, and staff, around which the text's central exchange
is shaped, directs the interpreter's eye to the story's significance:
through Tamar's mediation, Judah's patriarchal insignia and lineage, both of which appeared to be lost, are restored and transformed
into the inaugural symbols and ancestry of a Davidic king.

But which one? It may be perilous to seek an exact historical correspondence to these mythic dimensions, but parallels noted by the
structuralists between Genesis 38 and the Davidic succession are

---

40. A later Jewish version made the royal symbols explicit without the benefit
of archaeology. In *T. Jud.* 15.3, 'Judah is presented as designated king and the seal
has been transformed into a royal diadem'. Otzen, *TDOT*, IV, p. 266.

suggestive. Solomon was the second son of Bathsheba, who was also once an illegitimately pregnant widow. He gained power after the deaths of several older half-brothers and heirs, including one who lay with (the other) Tamar, in a contested race after his half-brother Adonijah had made a bid for the birthright–throne. He was celebrated for law-giving and temple building. If the allusion was not to Solomon directly, it could have referred to a descendent still claiming Solomon's credentials as typical of all Judahite kings.

This story's symbolic inauguration of the Judahite monarchy in the earliest generations would also help to explain the chapter's position as a disruptive digression in the middle of the Joseph story. Just when Joseph, soon-to-be savior of the whole Israelite family and later patronymic head of the northern kingdom,[41] is enslaved and carried to Egypt, dynastic kingship is being designated for the southern tribe of Judah. Joseph will regain temporary prominence in the Genesis storyline, but the rule of Judah's heirs is already authorized. This would be an apt subject in the royal rivalries between north and south and in disputes within Jerusalem's court.

How does an iconographically directed interpretation open new perspectives for feminist readings, for investigating the dynamics of gender and power?

Examination of Tamar as a 'woman in the Bible' must be reoriented if her literary role is an adaptation, even a parody, of a goddess's legitimating function. The origin of Judahite kingship is described in apparently realistic terms as a family story, yet by renewing the visual vocabulary, one perceives that the highly symbolic elements have been transformed into narrative props—a woman/palm and goat, ring-cord-staff, perhaps the twins. I believe this is an intentional artistic strategy, one that 'naturalizes' divine and royal symbols into realistic settings.[42] This is the opposite of the demythologizing or historicizing tendencies often credited to biblical writers; if anything, the origins of monarchy are being remythologized. For the encoded symbolism to be effective, the denotation and connotations of that transaction had to be still active, recognizable to an audience from

41. 'House of Joseph' refers to the north as a whole in Josh. 18.5; 2 Sam. 19.20; Amos 5.6, among others.

42. It may be worth investigating this artistic strategy across several media in the region. On the Phoenician ivory carvings, the cow and calf figures appear to have been naturalized from the more explicit Egyptian representations of a Hathor cow and a pharaoh calf, yet I believe the 'realistic' version still had recognizable religious significance without the figures' divine or royal trappings.

their knowledge of contemporary art and, perhaps, royal Judahite practice.

This reorientation to the symbolic realm affects literary, historical and theological readings. In literary terms, Tamar no longer appears only as a 'real woman' disguised as widow/prostitute—surely a powerless social role—but also as a goddess hidden in those robes. The double disguise is a virtuoso display of Hebrew literary wit which delights in irony, paradox, comic reversals and double entendre. And such humor is an effective instrument for critiquing power.

But if Tamar is not a real woman, even as a literary character, one may have to re-evaluate the reliability of her depicted social setting as a historical resource. The focus shifts from the rural family situation on the text's surface to royal succession in the complex allusion. At this level, one may ask questions about the relation of a Judahite queen mother to a goddess and about her/their ceremonial role in legitimating royal succession. The minority deuteronomic school's repeated condemnation of the religious and political activities of royal women (and of visual representations) must have been responding to actual practices, probably those endorsed by other Yahwists at the royal court. I take the allusion in Genesis 38 to be further evidence for goddess imagery and women's participation in the legitimating ideology and iconography of Judahite monarchy.[43]

Whether at the level of family ancestor or royal progenitor, Judah is not given a complimentary portrayal. He works hard to arrange his marriage, to control his sons' marriages and procreation, to respond to Tamar's apparent violation of family order—but in each instance the reader is made aware of Judah's misjudgments. Onan's attempt at control even has fatal consequences. In the theological context of Genesis 12–50, kingship is a divine prerogative, delegated to Judah's line by Yahweh's covenant loyalty to Abram and not awarded for merit. This implicit theological critique of (men's) institutional attempts to control situations is present outside Genesis as well, for example in the military accounts in Joshua and Judges where God's power brings the victory with token assistance from inadequate armies (Joshua at Jericho, Gideon against Midian) or, worse yet, from

43. See, for example, Susan Ackerman, 'The Queen Mother and the Cult in Ancient Israel', *JBL* 112 (1993), pp. 385-401. Ishtar is also a major figure in her article. Jo Ann Hackett described goddesses' activity in legitimating and blessing contemporary Phoenician kings in her paper, 'Phoenician and Punic Goddesses', delivered to the Gender and Cultural Criticism Consultation at the Society of Biblical Literature annual meeting, November 1993.

unarmed women (Jael and Abimelech's unnamed assailant).[44]

To balance these theological observations, I introduce a *theagraphical* perspective. Yahweh's only explicit role in this chapter is as slayer; the 'happy ending' is not credited to him. Tamar is the one who perceives the dead end of Judah's decisions, and her actions in narrative and symbol mediate new life and a new dynastic line. As the supposedly unproductive female—childless widow, prostitute, or goddess—she does move the lifeflow forward by unconventional means. The marginalized woman and the disguised, if not repressed, goddess exercise more imaginative and effective life power than men and male institutions. Where is Yahweh in this?

Reflections

A final exegetical step is a hermeneutical stage seeking meaning for the present audience. To this use of the term 'hermeneutic', I preface some remarks about meaning in a wider sense.

Philosophically, an exegesis that understands a visual referent as a formative element in literary composition, and therefore in interpretation, opens a broad field for multivalent readings. An audience aware of the visual allusions in Genesis 38 has to deal simultaneously with royal symbols and tribal storyline, with implied goddess and depicted widow. But the apparent intersection between the urban high culture of the visual and the pastoral family setting of the verbal a boundary of playful juggling as well as critique. Tending sheep is as much a royal image in biblical and extrabiblical references as building temples. The interaction between these inferred social locations and their media may be complementary rather than antithetical.

In trying to identify visual or verbal as background or foreground, one's attention cannot rest for long on one without shifting to the other, once both are discerned. Like the image of a vase—or is it the space between two faces?—the visual/verbal dynamic keeps the experience and the reading in motion. That is an interesting effect for a medium—the visual arts—accused by some biblical authors and interpreters of creating a static image, capable of being fixed and made captive to manipulative control, an idol. I believe, rather, that visual exegesis may be an effective antidote to a too rigid (idolatrous?) reading of the word.

For an applied exegesis, what may a feminist reading highlight

---

44. Josh. 6; Judg. 7; Judg. 4–5; Judg. 9.50-57.

about the depictions of power in this chapter? We should be sensitive to the fact that while this text canonically serves royal interests by locating Judahite authority in the patriarch's generation, it simultaneously pokes fun at them. A Judahite king whose legitimacy depended on a report of the monarchy's origin might prefer the foundation story of Samuel's anointing David (1 Sam. 16) to Tamar's waylaying of Judah. Could this be a farcical critique of Davidic succession, and if so, who is telling it? Is it women's humor about men's incompetence[45] or men's use of female images to demean other men?

Imagine Genesis 38 redrawn as a Mari wall painting. Framed by palms, the profile of a pregnant woman in widow's robes stands upon a lion[46] and extends ring, cord, and staff to a shame-faced king. This is a political cartoon! It mimicks conventional royal art by creating a verbal picture to deflate the institutional rhetoric about divinely ordained dynastic succession and to release the tension of those outside that order, who get others to laugh at the sordid realities behind royal power. No character escapes this parody—not Yahweh, not Judah/king, not the goddess/widow/queen mother.

Feminists may well disagree on how much of this cartoon is retrievable, as the visual–verbal dynamic constantly changes the image. Does one find positive values in the resourceful widow, the legitimating goddess, the implied queen mother, the institutional critique? Does one admire or deplore the author's manipulation of stock female literary and visual roles as tools of wit and denigration?

At the very least, one retrieves a greater appreciation for the power of visual allusion to have kept the options open over time. As current research reveals more of the iconographic environment of biblical writing, modern interpreters have a chance once more to be engaged by the complex artistic visions created for ancient audiences. Although visual exegesis is not a uniquely feminist method in its application, re-vision of exegesis may disclose other materials for feminist examination of literary strategies, women's history, theology and

45. Some recent interpreters suggest the author may have been a woman. David Rosenberg and Harold Bloom, *The Book of J* (New York: Grove Weidenfeld, 1990). Adrien Janis Bledstein argues for a woman storyteller in Genesis and the Davidic Court History in 'Binder, Trickster, Heel and Hairy-Man: Rereading Genesis 27 as a Trickster Tale Told by a Woman', in Athalya Brenner (ed.), *A Feminist Companion to Genesis* (The Feminist Companion to the Bible, 2; Sheffield: Sheffield Academic Press, 1993), pp. 282-95.

46. The lion is not an explicit narrative prop in Gen. 38 but, as Adrien Bledstein notes, Judah is the lion. I thank Adrien for sharing a 1993 draft of her paper 'Judah, the Lion, and Tamar, the Tree of Life: Excavating Genesis 38'.

theagraphy. The fears of those who think the image is subversive may be well-founded; it may challenge, if not turn upside down, too simplistic understandings of the word and the authority claimed for it. Genesis 38 once functioned that way and, ironically, it was valued enough to become Torah.

All illustrations are line drawings from
Othmar Keel, *The Symbolism of the Biblical World: Ancient Near Eastern Iconography and the Book of Psalms* (New York: Seabury, 1978).

Figure 1
Caption: Detail from Ur-Nammu's stele

Source: Keel, p. 135, ill. 180
Keel's description, p. 396
180. Section of a limestone stele (height of section, 32 cm.): Ur, Urnammu (ca. 2050 BC); Philadelphia, University Museum, *ANEP*, no. 306. A. Parrot, *Sumer*, figs. 279-282. H. Schmökel, *Ur, Assur*, pl. 54.**

Figure 2
Caption: Relief from Hammurabi's stele

Source: Keel, p. 288, ill. 390
Keel's description, p. 405
390. Relief, diorite stele, h. ca. 65 cm.: Susa: Hammurabi (1728–1686 BC); Louvre.
AOB, no. 318. *ANEP*, nos. 515, 246. H. Schmökel, *Ur, Assur*, pl. 64.**

Figure 3
Caption: Wall painting from court 106, Mari

Source: Keel, p. 143, ill. 191
Keel's description, p. 396
191. Wall painting, 1. 2.5 m., h. 1.75 m.: Mari: period of Hammurabi (1728–1686
BC); copy (after the original) in the Louvre. A. Parrot, *Sumer*, pp. 279f., fig. 346.
M.T. Barrelet, 'Une peinture de la cour 106', pl. 1. Cf. A. Moortgar, *Kunst*, p. 74.**

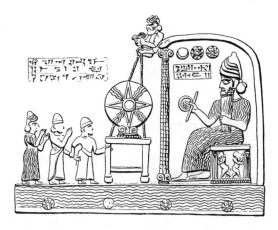

Figure 4
Caption: Nabuapaliddin's inscribed stone tablet

Source: Keel, p. 174, ill. 239
Keel's description, p. 398
239. Stone tablet with inscription, 18 × 30 cm. (scene, 18 × 10 cm.): Sippar (40 km.
southwest of Baghdad): Nabuapaliddin (885–850 BC); BM 91000. *AOB*, no. 322.
ANEP, no. 529. A. Parrot, *Assur*, fig. 215. M.A. Beek, *Atlas of Mesopotamia*, fig. 37.
Cf. M. Metzger, 'Himmlische und irdische Wohnstatt', pp. 141-44.**

FAMILY VIOLENCE IN CROSS-CULTURAL PERSPECTIVE:
AN APPROACH FOR FEMINIST INTERPRETERS OF THE BIBLE*

John J. Pilch

The Mideast Bureau of The Dallas Morning News filed this story in
the Sunday Edition of 12 March, 1989 regarding an incident in Jaba,
in the Occupied West Bank. Mahmud Assasa's 36-year-old, unmarried daughter returned home with her mother after a medical examination that determined she was six months pregnant. That evening,
Mahmud and his daughter and all the family's women went to a
back room where the father strangled his daughter to death, pulling a
cord placed around her neck while he held her head in position on
the floor with his foot. He had intended to cut her head off but yielded
to her pleas to strangle her instead.

After the slaying, Mahmud walked out of the house and shouted to
his kin near the village. 'I have killed her. I have washed the stain
from my family.' The 300 villagers rushed to Mahmud's house and
saw the body. The men shook Mahmud's hand and congratulated
him. The women filed slowly past the corpse. The next day Nura's
body was dumped into an unmarked grave. No one washed it, or
provided a shroud, or recited any prayers. Everything she owned and
all pictures of her were burned. All traces of her existence were totally
eradicated.

Mahmud is sheik of his clan of 300 persons who live near the
village. He explained: 'For us, the honor of the woman is sacred. If a
woman violates the honor of the family, then a man must act to
restore that honor. If he does not, he is not a man.'

Though the father turned himself over to the Israeli police, he was
to be tried in a local Arab court that deals with issues involving
'family honor'.

---

* Dedicated to my wife, Jean Peters Pilch, who, while battling with the violence of ovarian cancer, urges me daily to return to the study and complete my
projects. 'Many women have done excellently, but you surpass them all.' Jean died
April 14, 1997.

The 'honor defense' permits full or partial excuse for homicide or bodily injury inflicted on a woman by her husband (or any direct male relative) who surprises her in the act of illicit sexual relations. The concept still exists in the penal codes of several Middle Eastern and Mediterranean countries and is used even where there are no provisions for it in law.[1]

Moshe Sharon, of the Hebrew University, explains,

When a crime is committed, most of us feel guilt, and we are punished in accordance with the law. But Arab society is a shame-oriented society. Anything an individual does is in relation to the group. If an individual dishonors himself, he dishonors the group, he brings shame on the group, and the only way to erase this shame is to carry out some kind of revenge.

As reported in the newspaper, this factual incident carries three interpretations: of the Arab villagers; of Moshe Sharon; and of the Westerner(s) in the Mideast Bureau of the Dallas newspaper who wrote the report. In technical anthropological terms, presuming all the quotations are exact, there is the 'emic', or native, or 'insider', report of the event and its meaning for that community, and the 'etic', or 'outsider', reports and interpretations.

In similar fashion, the report about Jephthah and his daughter (Judg. 11), the story of Tamar (2 Sam. 13) and the prescriptions of Deut. 22.13-21, are native or 'emic' reports. Even if they are interpretations, they have to accord with the values of their cultural context in order to be intelligible to the original audience or readers. Non-native interpreters, including feminist scholars who review texts such as these, offer 'etic' or outsider interpretations. Anthropologists believe that it is possible to begin with an 'imposed etic' interpretation and ultimately, in dialogue with the target culture, arrive at a 'derived etic' interpretation that would fairly represent the 'emic' view.[2]

In this article, I encourage feminists to recognize the cross-cultural challenges of interpreting ancient texts from the Mediterranean world and to adopt concepts, approaches, methods and models from the social sciences, notably cultural anthropology and related disciplines

1.   M. Schuler in Schuler (ed.), *Freedom from Violence: Women's Strategies from Around the World* (Washington, DC: OEF International, 1992), p. 298; referring to L. Moghaizel, 'The Arab and Mediterranean World: Legislation Towards Crimes of Honour', in M. Schuler (ed.), *Empowerment and the Law: Strategies of Third World Women* (Washington, DC: OEF International, 1986), pp. 174-80.

2.   M.H. Segall, P.R. Dasen, J.W. Berry and Y.H. Poortinga (eds.), *Human Behavior in Global Perspective: An Introduction to Cross-Cultural Psychology* (Boston: Allyn & Bacon, 1990), pp. 54-56.

such as Mediterranean anthropology. Such tools would ensure a more accurate understanding of the 'native' point of view; and contribute to the building of reliable bridges toward honest and respectful feminist interpretation that would be neither anachronistic nor ethnocentric. I select family violence as the general topic, and will draw upon my previous and ongoing research into its various dimensions (violence toward children,[3] the elderly[4] and spouses[5]).

Cross-Cultural Studies

With regard to the modern and biblical examples of family violence mentioned above, Levinson's comment is relevant:

> It is important to remember that there is a long list of human behaviors that can be classified as types of family violence, with virtually each type considered abuse in some societies but legitimate behavior in others.[6]

The repeated advice of Proverbs to use physical means for disciplining young boys (13.24; 19.18; 22.15; 23.13-14; 29.15, 17) is legitimate behavior in the ancient Near Eastern world but considered 'abuse', deserving legal punishment, in the contemporary United States. Inclusive language translations like the NRSV, which render the Hebrew words for 'son' and 'lad' inconsistently but inclusively, distort and misrepresent the emic position. For people who use the Bible as a warrant for behavior, such a translation actually promotes the very problem feminism seeks to redress in understanding and interpreting these biblical texts. It represents the Bible as encouraging physical punishment of girls, something neither the Bible nor Mediterranean culture would permit.

Contemporary feminist methodology will fare best by recognizing its task as basically cross-cultural. Broadly defined, 'cross-cultural studies' include 'any information collection and analysis approach that involves either the implicit or explicit comparison of two or more

3.   J.J. Pilch, 'Beat His Ribs While He is Young (Sirach 30:12): A Window on the Mediterranean World', *BTB* 23 (1993), pp. 101-13; *idem, Introducing the Cultural Context of the Old Testament* (New York: Paulist Press, 1991), pp. 71-94.

4.   J.J. Pilch, 'Death with Honor: The Mediterranean Style Death of Jesus in Mark', *BTB* 25 (1995), pp. 65-70.

5.   J.J. Pilch, 'Violence toward Spouses' (in progress).

6.   D. Levinson, 'Family Violence in Cross-Cultural Perspective', in V.B. Van Hasselt, R.L. Morrison, A.S. Bellack and M. Hersen (eds.), *Handbook of Family Violence* (New York: Plenum Press, 1988), p. 452.

cultural groups'.[7] The results will be more reliable if the comparisons are explicit, with assumptions and guiding principles clearly identified and enunciated. Generally speaking, anthropology and its sub-disciplines (e.g. psychological anthropology, Mediterranean anthropology, medical anthropology, etc.) engage in cross-cultural studies, making *explicit* comparisons with the aid of clear definitions and carefully designed models.

As Levinson notes,[8] a comparative approach is helpful for many reasons. First, it expands our knowledge of the range of human actions that constitute family violence and factors relating to this violence—including types of families, types of family relationships and methods of interpersonal conflict resolution. I shall return to this consideration in more detail below. Secondly, as the opening example demonstrates, there is a need to analyze family violence in its cultural context and to recognize exactly what this means to participants and to the cultural group as a whole.[9] Mediterranean anthropologists recognize the agonistic nature of Mediterranean culture: that is, it is prone to arguments, fights and violence.[10] As one might expect from the analogous nature of God-talk, the God of Israel readily commands the use of violence, even among the deity's chosen people, to maintain, defend or restore the *status quo*. Hence, establishment violence or vigilantism is a cultural given.[11]

Thirdly, worldwide studies allow for testing theories of family violence as they are operationalized at the societal level.[12] Instead of projecting, imposing or attributing motives and explanations that would most likely be anachronistic or ethnocentric, the available worldwide studies force the feminist researcher to raise questions about the relationship of wife-beating to sexual inequality; the existence of wife-and-child beating to a cultural acceptance of violence;

7.   Levinson, 'Family Violence', p. 435.

8.   Levinson, 'Family Violence', p. 435; Levinson, *Family Violence in Cross-Cultural Perspective* (Frontiers of Anthropology, 1; Newbury Park, CA: Sage, 1989), p. 10.

9.   See J.E. Korbin, 'Anthropological Contributions to the Study of Child Abuse', *Child Abuse and Neglect* 1 (1977), pp. 7-24; and *Child Abuse and Neglect: Cross-cultural Perspectives* (Berkeley: University of California Press, 1981).

10.   D.D. Gilmore, *Manhood in the Making: Cultural Concepts of Masculinity* (New Haven: Yale University Press, 1990); and *Aggression and Community: Paradoxes of Andalusian Culture* (New Haven: Yale University Press, 1987).

11.   B.J. Malina, 'Establishment Violence in the New Testament World' *Scriptura* 5 (1994), pp. 51-78 (61).

12.   G.R. Lee, 'The Utility Of Cross-Cultural Data', *Journal of Family Issues* 5 (1984), pp. 519-41.

and the relationship of various forms of family violence to various forms of social organization, and so on.

Fourthly, comparative worldwide studies allow the researcher to study the effect of social change on family relationships, including violent ones. Longitudinal studies are especially helpful in this regard, and comparative studies from the circum-Mediterranean regions are eminently useful in research on the Hebrew Bible. Finally, such worldwide comparative studies allow us to compare low-violence with high-violence cultures in order to identify factors or processes that may help control or prevent family violence. While this last item is the contemporary synchronic benefit of comparative studies, it can contribute valuable insights to those who look to the Hebrew Bible as warrant for desirable contemporary behaviors—or scapegoat for contemporary behaviors that should be discarded.[13]

Definitions

Too many researchers, including biblical scholars, neglect to define terms. Such an omission is especially damaging in cross-cultural investigations, since the understanding of the researcher's culture inevitably tends to be imposed on the culture under study. Here, then, are some basic definitions relative to family violence, drawn from cross-cultural research, that would serve biblical scholars well. 'Cultural groups', which form the focus of cross-cultural study, include 'nations, political subdivisions within nations, ethnic groups, small-scale (primitive, non-literate) societies, peasant societies, and so on'.[14] Since 'nation' is a very modern idea,[15] the cultural groups of interest to biblical research could be peasant groups, or the elite, and the like. 'The family' in cross-cultural studies is 'a social group characterized by common residence, economic cooperation, and reproduction'.[16] 'Family violence' is 'the action of a family member that will very likely cause physical pain to another family member'.[17]

---

13. B.J. Malina, 'The Bible: Witness or Warrant? Reflections on Daniel Patte's *Ethics of Biblical Interpretation*', *BTB* 26 (1996), pp. 82-87.

14. Levinson, 'Family Violence', p. 435.

15. Pilch, 'People (ethnos)', in S.M. Tomasi (ed.), *The Pastoral Dictionary on Migration and Human Mobility* (New York: Center for Migration Studies of New York and the G.B. Scalabrini Federation of Centres for Migration Studies, forthcoming); *idem*, 'Citizen', in Tomasi (ed.) *The Pastoral Dictionary*.

16. G.P. Murdock, *Social Structure* (New York: Macmillan, 1949), p. 1.

17. R.J. Gelles and M.A. Straus, 'Determinants of Violence in the Family: Toward a Theoretical Integration', in Wesley R. Burr, Reuben Hill, F. Ivan Nye, and

Levinson has subsequently sharpened this definition of 'family violence' to 'an act carried out with the intention or perceived intention of physically hurting another person'.[18]

The seeming exclusive emphasis on 'physical' elements in Levinson's definitions illustrate how difficult it is to grasp the complex concepts of violence and aggression. Gelles notes that 'family violence' now is a 'broader concept of maltreatment that include[s] harmful, but not necessarily physically violent, acts'.[19] This broader definition would seem to include David's reaction to Michal's complaints about his dancing (2 Sam. 6.16-23). Indeed, cross-cultural psychology views aggression as a broader concept and understands it as 'any behavior by a person that inflicts harm on an other'.[20] Beyond this, the researcher can zero in on one or another specific type of family violence (like wife-beating or husband-battering), define it on the basis of cross-cultural data, then use such concepts as a lens through which to read the biblical data.

Types of Family Violence

Levinson[21] presents the following list of forms of family violence according to state of life.

Infancy

> Infanticide
> Sale of infants for sacrifice
> Binding body parts for shaping (head, feet, etc.)
> Force feeding
> Harsh disciplinary techniques, such as cold baths

Childhood

> Organized fighting promoted by adults
> Ritual defloration
> Harsh socialization techniques (beating, kicking, slapping, burning, twisting ears, etc.)

Ira L. Reiss (eds.), *Contemporary Theories About the Family*. I. *Research Based Theories* (New York: Free Press, 1979), pp. 549-81.

    18. Levinson, 'Family Violence', p. 11.

    19. R.J. Gelles, 'Family Violence', in Robert L. Hampton, Thomas P. Gullotta, Gerard R. Adams, Earl H. Potter, III, and Roger P. Weissberg (eds.), *Family Violence: Prevention and Treatment*. I. *Issues in Children's and Families' Lives* (Newbury Park, CA: Sage, 1993), p. 4.

    20. Segall *et al.*, *Human Behavior*, p. 265; the entire chapter on aggression (pp. 262-85) is pertinent.

    21. Levinson, 'Family Violence', p. 442.

Child marriage
Child slavery
Child prostitution
Drugging with hallucinogens
Parent–child homicide/suicide
Child labor
Sibling fighting
Nutritional deprivation
Corporal punishment in schools
Mutilation for begging

Adolescence (Puberty)
Painful initiation rites (circumcision, supercision, clitoridect-
omy, scarification, cold baths, piercings, sleep deprivation,
whippings, bloodletting, forced vomiting)
Forced homosexual relations
Harsh socialization techniques
Gang rape of girls

Adulthood
Killing young brides
Forced suicides by young brides
Wife-beating
Husband-beating
Husband–wife brawling
Matricide
Patricide
Forced suicide of wives
Wife-raiding
Marital rape
Parent beating

Old Age
Forsaking the aged
Abandonment of the aged
Beating the aged
Killing the aged
Forcing the aged to commit suicide

In this list, compiled from HRAF data (about which see below) and
other sources, both the aggressor and the victim are family members;
and events (initiation rites, child marriages) allow one family member to place another in a situation where the other will very likely be
harmed. Most of these types occur in only a few societies around the
world. Selling infants for sacrifice, child marriage, forced homosexual relationships for adolescents and forced suicide by wives are
quite rare. Others, like scarification, are rapidly disappearing. When
they do occur they are often infrequent, like infanticide.

Levinson concludes,

> Although the data to measure the relative frequency of these types of family violence is not yet available, my review of the literature suggests that wife beating, punishment of children, sibling violence, infanticide, and harsh initiation rites at puberty are the ones that occur in the greatest number of societies.[22]

Is Levinson's listing also reflected in the biblical record? Finally, in this long list of human behaviors reflecting family violence, 'virtually each type [is] considered abuse in some societies but legitimate behavior in others'.[23] It is advisable not to use the word 'abuse' at all in cross-cultural studies.

Cross-Cultural Approaches

Specialists identify six different strategies that can be adopted in cross-cultural studies: case studies; longitudinal comparisons; regional comparisons; intrasocietal comparisons; small scale comparisons; and hologeistic or worldwide studies.[24] No one approach alone is perfect. But, used in various combinations, the approaches can provide much information.

Case Studies

The major value of case studies is the descriptive information they provide about the nature and meaning of family violence in different cultural contexts. Few reliable studies of this nature exist. The rape of Tamar, or the story of Jephthah's daugther, are two biblical episodes that could serve as case studies. To conduct an adequate case study, the researcher must gather related case studies from other cultures to highlight similarities and differences. Unfortunately, few such studies exist.

Longitudinal Comparisons

Longitudinal comparisons of individuals or families or entire societies with themselves at two or more points in time could be a powerful tool to test the causes and, in modern times, prevention of family violence. A longitudinal study of family violence or one aspect of it in ancient Israel, performed in the best tradition of historical

22. Levinson, 'Family Violence', p. 443.
23. Levinson, 'Family Violence, p. 452.
24. Levinson, 'Family Violence', pp. 436-38.

critical research, would be a significant contribution to the field. Though not directly about family violence, Paul Hanson's study of community in the Bible could be considered a longitudinal comparison of this reality in ancient Israel at various points of its history.[25]

Regional Comparisons

Regional comparisons are perhaps some of the most enlightening studies for identifying similarities in family violence patterns among cultures in a particular geographical region. Samples are entire cultural groups rather than individuals or families. 'Regional comparisons operate on the belief that regional similarities can be attributed to historical contact between the neighboring cultures, which has led them to be similar on a number of basic cultural dimensions.'[26] Lozios's study of wife-beating in rural Mediterranean cultures is a good example of this approach.[27] He traces the high frequency of wife-beating in Greece, Portugal, Sicily and Cyprus to a basic value orientation that emphasizes male control and male honor, sometimes expressed in a form called compensatory masculinity.[28] Much of the research conducted and published by members of The Context Group[29] utilizes data of this nature—in the conviction that the circum-Mediterranean world is a distinct culture continent; that the social institutions and values of this world have perdured here relatively unchanged over 4,000 years; and that the insights derived from such research are very helpful and relevant for reading and understanding ancient texts from this region.

Intrasocietal Comparisons

Intrasocietal comparisons compare family violence in subcultural groups in one society. The research is available in two forms: cross-state comparisons,[30] in which cultural differences from one state to

25. P.D. Hanson, *The People Called: The Growth of Community in the Bible* (San Francisco: Harper & Row, 1986).

26. Levinson, 'Family Violence', p. 437.

27. P. Lozios, 'Violence and the Family: Some Mediterranean Examples', in J.P. Martin (ed.), *Violence and the Family* (Chichester: Wiley, 1978), pp. 183-96.

28. Segall *et al.*, *Human Behavior*, pp. 281-82.

29. See J.H. Elliott, *What is Social Scientific Criticism?* (Minneapolis: Fortress Press, 1993).

30. See K. Yllö, 'Political and Methodological Debates in Wife Abuse Research', in K. Yllö and M. Bograd (eds.), *Feminist Perspectives on Wife Abuse* (Newbury Park, CA: Sage, 1988), pp. 28-50; and 'Sexual Equality and Violence against Wives in American States', *Journal of Comparative Family Studies* 14 (1983), pp. 67-86.

another may be important with an emphasis on economic and political aspects; and cross-ethnic comparisons (such as in former Yugoslavia: Bosnians, Macedonians, Serbs, and others[31]). The value of such an approach is that it helps ideas about motives of family violence to surface, and offers a means of testing those ideas in a pluralistic society context. Relative to the Hebrew bible, the researcher could explore relationships between family violence in Israelite life, and the changing context of its various conquerors or occupying forces: the Babylonians, Persians, Greeks, and so on.[32]

Small-Scale Comparisons
Small-scale comparisons usually compare a small number of societies (usually two or three) to relate differences in family violence to differences in legal, economic or cultural factors from one society to the others. A study of the strategies for disciplining boys and girls, as reflected in the book of Proverbs and in the contemporary United States, could be conducted using this approach.[33]

Hologeistic or Worldwide Comparative Studies
Finally, hologeistic or worldwide comparative studies test general theories of family violence with either worldwide samples of small-scale societies (holocultural studies) or worldwide samples of nations (holonational studies). In such studies, it is essential to use 50 to 100 societies or nations to represent all major geographical and cultural regions of the world.

Levinson and his team have conducted their holocultural study of family violence in 90 small-scale and peasant non-Western societies. The data was drawn from the ethnographic reports in the Human Relations Area Files (HRAF), which contain more than 6,000 reports on the way of life of 330 different cultural groups around the world, gathered by cultural anthropologists who lived with and observed these societies. Ten Middle-East societies form part of the data base. I have utilized studies based on the HRAF in previous research[34] to great advantage and am currently using Levinson's research on

31. See V.S. Erlich, *Families in Transition: A Study of 300 Yugoslav Villages* (Princeton, NJ: Princeton University Press, 1966).
32. See J.L. Berquist, *Judaism in Persia's Shadow: A Social and Historical Approach* (Minneapolis: Fortress Press, 1996).
33. Pilch, *Introducing the Cultural Context*, pp. 71-94.
34. J.J. Pilch, 'The Transfiguration of Jesus: An experience of Alternate Reality', in Philip F. Esler (ed.), *Modeling Early Christianity: Social Scientific Studies of the New Testament in its Context* (London: Routledge, 1995), pp. 47-64.

family violence, which continues to produce excellent results relative to my work-in-progress on the Hebrew Bible.

As sensate skeptics and critics of the value of such social scientific strategies recognize, this kind of global (holocultural) study sacrifices variation *within* society to identify variations *between* societies.[35] The advantage of this broader focus, however, is that it controls the intrusion of ethnocentric bias into the research. Besides, sensate scholars will never fail—appropriately and correctly—to insert the distinctive details and variations where they are appropriate. Other admitted shortcomings of the HRAF data base is that the secondary literature is of widely diverse quality, and some variables are missing or poorly described. All this notwithstanding, HRAF-based publications are a marked improvement over 'close and careful reading of the [biblical] text' as a tool for critical analysis.

Types of Families[36]

It is possible to identify five different types of families: matrifocal, nuclear, polygynous, polyandrous and extended. In each family type, the family members occupy different kinship roles.[37] Hence, each family type faces different interpersonal problems and has different organizational potentials. Obviously, the presence of different categories of kin and the different roles they fill create the potential for forms of family violence that differ from one society to another. Thus, in polygynous societies, aggression and violence between co-wives or rival wives is not uncommon (1 Sam. 1.2-7; Gen. 29.31–30.24; Sir. 25.8; 26.6; 37.11; and more).

The matrifocal (mother and her children) family type is not dominant in any society, but has been very strong in Polish culture. It appears as a distinct family type only in very specific circumstances. In the Western hemisphere, this type occurs only in lower socio-economic groups where men have very little economic security.

The nuclear family type (wife–mother, husband–father and their children) is the most common among all societies. Also known as 'conjugal' or 'elementary', the nuclear family type is a small social group whose members—through birth, marriage or adoption—stand in a relation of parent, child, spouse or sibling to other members of the group. Murdock seems correct in his observation:

---

35. Levinson, *Family Violence*, p. 10.
36. Levinson, 'Family Violence', p. 438.
37. On status and roles see Pilch, *Introducing the Cultural Context*, pp.117-52.

The nuclear family is a universal social grouping. Either as the sole prevailing form of the family or as the basic unit from which more complex familiar forms are compounded, it exists as a distinct and strongly functional group in every known society.[38]

Malina observes that such a mode of integration is not natural, but has to be learned and attended to after it has disappeared as the central organizing principle of a group. The proverb 'Blood is thicker than water' dates only to the early seventeenth century. For this reason he suggests that 'nucleated' is preferable to 'nuclear' in describing this type of family.[39]

The polygynous family type (husband–father, two or more wives–mothers and their children) is perhaps not as easy to identify as it might seem. This type could also be viewed as a cluster of nuclear families with a common father, or a group of matrifocal families with a common father. Nevertheless, there are three sets of *relations* in polygynous families that are not present in nuclear ones: co-wives (shared sexuality with one husband); siblings (limited shared descent); and children and wives who are not their mothers.

Each type of relationship may lead to feelings of rivalry, jealousy, hostility and antagonism that each polygynous family must control in order to function and survive. Certain factors may help maintain order: clearly defined roles, equitable distribution of tasks, sororal polygyny (co-wives are sisters) and equitable treatment of co-wives by the husband. The stories of the biblical patriarchs illustrate the kinds of aggression, hostility and violence that this family type engenders.

The most rare type is the polyandrous family (one wife–mother, her children, and two or more husband–fathers). In order to be classified as polyandrous, each husband must be eligible to be considered the legal father of at least one of the women's children. One explanation is that this family type was needed to keep real property together. Or perhaps this family type was linked to female infanticide.

Finally, the extended family type is a group in which individuals are recognized as both husband–father and son–brother or wife–mother and sister–daughter at the same time. This family type offers relationships not found in others, particularly parents-, children-, and siblings-in-law. These in-law relationships are often difficult

38. Murdock, *Social Structure*, p. 2.

39. B.J. Malina, 'Religion in the Imagined New Testament World: More Social Science Lenses', *Scriptura* 5 (1994), pp. 1-26 (5).

and disruptive, and frequently handled through institutionalized rules of behavior, like jokes and avoidance. Though seemingly free of family violence, life in extended families can be and often is quite stressful.

Though not explicitly devoted to family violence, K.C. Hanson's trilogy of articles on the Herodians and Mediterranean kinship is a model social scientific study worthy of emulation by all serious researchers.[40] It would not be difficult to pursue further research into the violence of the Herodian family with these articles as a basis. In addition, Malina's longitudinal view of kinship and marriage-types, as diverse ways of fusing families together during the entire sweep of the biblical period, is yet another useful tool for analyzing family violence in its appropriate cultural context.[41]

Method

One final consideration remains before I present a model for exploring family violence in a holocultural perspective. Levinson writes,

> To the extent possible, I have followed a behavioral approach throughout the study and have focused on the *actual behaviors of the people as described in the ethnographic literature*. Thus unless otherwise noted, I have not been concerned with whether the behavior is condoned or not. I have been mainly concerned with whether or not it occurs and how often it occurs in each society.[42]

This is essentially what a biblical investigator attempts when analyzing a narrative text. But what about prescriptive texts like Leviticus or Proverbs? I think it is legitimate to read these as indicators of what is really happening in society. Thus, the Bible records divine commandments to honor father and mother, not to kill, and so on; yet the repetition of this advice in Proverbs suggests that it was honored more in the breach than in the observance. To illustrate the point: the HRAF ethnographic literature concerning the Cagaba of Colombia notes that aggression is prohibited, but in reality much happens.

Finally, in discussing the word 'abuse', Levinson observes,

---

40. K.C. Hanson, 'The Herodians and Mediterranean Kinship. I. Genealogy and Descent', *BTB* 19 (1989), pp. 75-84; 'The Herodians and Mediterranean Kinship. II. Marriage and Divorce', *BTB* 19 (1989), pp. 142-51; 'The Herodians and Mediterranean Kinship. III. Economics', *BTB* 20 (1990), pp. 10-21.

41. B.J. Malina, *The New Testament World: Insights from Cultural Anthropology* (Louisville, KY: Westminster/John Knox, rev. edn, 1993), pp. 117-48.

42. Levinson, *Family Violence*, p. 12 (my emphasis).

> I am not especially interested in cultural definitions of spouse abuse,
> child abuse, or elder abuse, since the concept of abuse is so bound by
> the cultural context in which the behavior occurs that it is not an espe-
> cially useful heuristic device for ordering data for cross-cultural com-
> parative purposes. So I am interested in behavior, not in cultural defini-
> tions of abuse or in whether the behavior is proscribed or not. [43]

Biblical interpreters would do well to adopt this same position in
their research reports. As noted previously, what one culture considers abuse another culture accepts as legitimate behavior.

7. A Holocultural Model

The specific model that I propose for investigating family violence or
aspects of it in the Hebrew bible was designed by Straus in his
research on wife-abuse.[44] At the 1990 annual meeting of the Society
of Biblical Literature, I presented a modified version of this model to
illustrate the systemic elements of violence toward elders as reflected
in biblical texts, particularly Proverbs and Sirach. While I continue to
develop and refine the model, the essential elements can be presented
here for use by others. See figure overleaf.

This is a systems model, that is, the model accepts the
anthropologists' contention that:

> no cultural manifestation is an isolated, independent occurrence. Each
> culture forms an integrated whole, in which all elements are closely
> interrelated and interdependent and in which each element is an
> expression of the whole. Social, religious, economic and moral
> manifestations in the life of a people can be understood only in their
> relationship to each other.[45]

The numbered boxes on this model identify and cluster under seven
different categories the cultural factors conducive to family violence.

This is also a holocultural model, that is, it was constructed from
the HRAF data containing worldwide samples of small-scale societies, including ten from the Middle East. Thus, the content of the
'boxes' represents general elements found in all these societies. These
elements may or may not be present in the Hebrew Bible. A highly
recommended strategy for 'filling in the blanks' of Mediterranean

43. Levinson, *Family Violence*, p. 12.

44. M.A. Straus, 'Wife-beating: How Common and Why?', in M.A. Straus and
G.T. Hotaling (eds.), *The Social Causes of Husband–Wife Violence* (Minneapolis: University of Minnesota Press, 1980), pp. 23-36.

45. M. Zborowski, *People in Pain* (San Francisco: Jossey-Bass, 1969), p. 43.

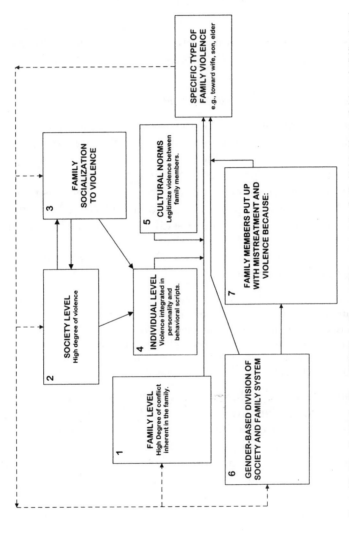

General Systems Model (after Straus 1980) illustrating some factors accounting for the high incidence of violence (solid lines) and positive feedback loops maintaining the system (dashed lines). Adapted to the Mediterranean world by J.J. Pilch.

Inside the figure:

SPECIFIC TYPE OF FAMILY VIOLENCE e.g., toward wife, son, elder

3 **FAMILY SOCIALIZATION TO VIOLENCE**

5 **CULTURAL NORMS** Legitimize violence between family members.

2 **SOCIETY LEVEL** High degree of violence

4 **INDIVIDUAL LEVEL** Violence integrated in personality and behavioral scripts.

7 **FAMILY MEMBERS PUT UP WITH MISTREATMENT AND VIOLENCE BECAUSE:**

1 **FAMILY LEVEL** High Degree of conflict inherent in the family.

6 **GENDER-BASED DIVISION OF SOCIETY AND FAMILY SYSTEM**

culture, a strategy that helps understand the high-context literature of the Bible, is reliance on the enormous amount of information provided by Mediterranean anthropology.[46]

As it stands, the model can indeed be viewed as a structural functional model. It assumes that a society wishes to remain stable and functional, and does all in its power to do that. With regard to Mediterranean society, we know that its basically agonistic characteristics makes it more amenable to analysis with a conflict model.[47] Nevertheless, this structural model is a good starting point for gathering data from the Bible and its culture, and for interrelating various pieces of cultural information. The lines on this model help the researcher to co-ordinate the data. The solid lines connecting the various boxes seek to illustrate some of the factors that account for a high degree of violence in ancient Israel. The dashed lines constitute 'positive feedback loops' that maintain the system or, as modern researchers would phrase it, continue the cycle of violence.

The Family Level
In ancient Mediterranean society there is a high level of conflict inherent in the family, especially in the polygynous type. Many impinging activities cause friction between women and men, older and younger generations (Prov. 17.1). Family members are more intensively involved in each other's activities, so that injury experienced inside the family is greater than the same injury outside the family. This is equally true for fictive kin (Job 19.13-19; Ps. 55.12-14). The right of some family members to influence the behavior of other family members—such as the young and the elderly (Sir. 32.3-4)—is another source of conflict and aggression. In the system of arranged—cross-cousin—marriages, such involuntary membership in the family creates still other sources of hostility (Sir. 42.9). Ultimately, a high level of stress within the family leads to violence: for example, the stress between what is expected of children and what results (Sir. 16.1-4). Guijarro Oporto's insights are particularly relevant here.[48]

46. See D.D. Gilmore, *Manhood in the Making: Cultural Concepts of Masculinity* (New Haven: Yale University Press, 1990); *Aggression and Community: Paradoxes of Andalusian Culture* (New Haven: Yale University Press, 1987); and D.D. Gilmore (ed.), *Honor and Shame and the Unity of the Mediterranean* (Washington, DC: American Anthropological Association, 1987).

47. See B.J. Malina, 'Dealing with Biblical (Mediterranean) Characters: A Guide for U.S. Consumers', *BTB* 19 (1989), pp. 127-41.

48. Santiago Guijarro Oporto, 'La Familia en la Galilea del siglo primero', *Estudios Biblicos* 53 (1995), pp. 461-88.

Society Level
Mediterranean society itself is characterized by a high level of violence: blood-feuds (Num. 35.9-34), wars,[49] riots, murder, assault, rape.

Family Socialization in Violence
Spousal violence toward each other (e.g. Rebekah toward elderly Isaac [Gen. 27]), the violent discipline of sons by fathers [Proverbs and Sirach] provides ready models for imitation (Mic. 7.6). Tolerance of sibling violence (Cain and Abel; Jacob and Esau; Joseph's brothers toward him; David's children: Amnon and Tamar, Absalom and Amnon) continues the cycle of violence. Pro-violence values, especially as taught to young boys (exaggerated masculinity in relationship to honor), prepare them for an adult life of violence: war, rape, the honor of suffering pain and suffering without flinching (e.g. the Servant of Yahweh in Deutero-Isaiah; Eleazar in 2 Macc.).

Individual Level
In the Mediterranean world, violence is integrated into personal and behavior scripts.[50] Particularly significant here is the Mediterranean cultural fusion of love and violence (Prov. 3.11-12; 13.23).

Cultural Norms
Cultural norms legitimize violence between family members (Prov. 3.11; 13.24; 19.18; 22.15; 23.13-14; 29.15, 17), or expect God to behave in a similar way (Prov. 3.11-12).

Gender-Based Division of Society and Family Systems
Care of young boys prior to the age of puberty—together with the girls, exclusively by the women, without the presence of adult male models—leads to the development of hypermasculinity in adulthood as a male virtue, with significant consequences for family violence.[51]

49. T.R. Hobbs, '*BTB* Readers Guide: Aspects of Warfare in the First Testament World', *BTB* 25 (1995), pp. 79-90.

50. Malina, 'Dealing with Biblical (Mediterranean) Characters'; B.J. Malina and J.H. Neyrey, 'First-Century Personality: Dyadic, Not Individualistic', in Jerome H. Neyrey (ed.), *The Social World of Luke–Acts: Models for Interpretation* (Peabody, MA: Hendrickson, 1991), pp. 67-96; Pilch, 'Beat His Ribs'; Pilch, 'Death with Honor'.

51. Gilmore, *Manhood in the Making* and *Aggression and Community*; Segall, *Cross-Cultural Psychology*, and 'Psychological Antecedents of Male Aggression: Some Implications Involving Gender, Parenting and Adolescence', in P.R. Dasen and J.W. Berry (eds.), *Health and Cross-Cultural Psychology: Toward Applications*

On this topic I have found immensely enlightening the work of trained, female, cultural anthropologists of Middle Eastern descent such as Lila Abu-Lughod, Soraya Altorki and Camilla Fawzy el-Solh, among others.[52]

Family Members Putting Up with Mistreatment and Violence
Family members put up with mistreatment and violence because this is the way the culture works. The rules are clear; the consequences of keeping or breaking the rules are equally clear.

I have filled the boxes many times over with data and continue to gather, correlate and interpret new information. The model works superbly well for specialists in cross-cultural studies. There is no reason why it cannot serve biblical scholars equally well.

Conclusion
At a national meeting of biblical scholars some years ago, a world-renowned feminist scholar listened impatiently to a discussion of social scientific approaches to interpreting biblical texts and an explanation of models for conducting such research. At the end of the discussion, she stormed out of the room while observing aloud: 'They are still like little boys. They love to play with their models.'

It is the hope of this social science investigator that serious feminist researchers, even those who admire the famous scholar who made the above remark, will recognize the enormous contributions social scientific methods and models can make to the feminist enterprise. This sketch of a social scientific approach to investigating family violence is offered as a small contribution to that enterprise.

(Cross-Cultural Research and Methodology Series; Newbury Park, CA: Sage Publications, 1988), pp. 71-92.

52. See Pilch, *Introducing the Cultural Context*, p. 152.

V

OTHERNESS AND TRANSLATION

SEPTUAGINT AND GENDER STUDIES:
THE VERY BEGINNING OF A PROMISING LIAISON

Kristin De Troyer

A Most Burlesque Barbarous Experiment

I love Rilke's poetry. Rilke wrote some beautiful texts on the cemetery of Ragaz. The collection of his poems written from 1913 to 1926 was translated from German into Dutch, introduced and commented on by W. Blok and C.O. Jellema.[1] The German text is printed on the left hand side of the book, and the translations on the right hand side. Translating these texts must have been a tremendous challenge. And sometimes a burden too! For example, how does one translate *in das unbedingte Bemühen* ('in conditionless caring')? The translator chose not to translate the aspect 'care', but looked at the result of caring: being able to grow without difficulties.[2] Sometimes the original language appears in the translated text. Instead of translating *Also bist du, bein den Toten, immer in ein ausgespartes Licht gestellt, langsam schwankend...*('so you have, among the dead, always been put in an outlined light, slowly moving back and forward'), the translator used for *schwankend* ('slowly moving back and forward') another German (!) word in the Dutch (!) text: *wankend* ('moving back and forward'). This word, *wankend*, does not exist at all in Dutch, but resembles another Dutch word.[3] I would not have noticed these minor problems, of course, if the original text and its translation had not been printed opposite each other, and if I did not understand German. What I feel when reading the German text is different from what I feel when reading the Dutch text. Although the words have more or less the same meaning in their own language system, they seem to be different; and I associate different aspects, different emotions, different colours with the words in each language. Translators—like all

---

1. R.M. Rilke, *Gedichten uit de jaren 1913–1926* (trans., ed. and annotated W. Blok and C.O. Jellema; Baarn: Ambo, 1993).
2. Rilke, *Gedichten uit de jaren 1913–1926*, pp. 72-73.
3. Rilke, *Gedichten uit de jaren 1913–1926*, pp. 76-77.

readers—make choices between different words, and between different levels of meaning of words and the concepts they signify. In so doing, translators offer their interpretations of texts. Can we object and state that translators should not give an interpretation of a text, but offer a 'real, strict' translation. Not really. I believe that language is related to a translating subject and therefore, subjective. All translations, and all texts, are therefore (subjective) interpretations.[4]

Translation problems increase when the language of the text which is to be translated (source language) is totally remote from the language into which the text should be translated (target language). As Alfred Lord Tennyson wrote in 'On translations of Homer: Hexameters and Pentameters':

> These lame hexameters the strong-wing'd music of Homer!
> No—but a most burlesque barbarous experiment.
> When was a harsher sound ever heard, ye Muses, in England?
> When did a frog coarser croak upon our Helicon?
> Hexameters no worse than daring Germany gave us,
> Barbarous experiment, barbarous hexameters.[5]

And what happens if one is to translate the ancient languages of the Bible? How can one transfer meanings from one language system to another, totally remote language system?

In her book on the Alpha-Text of Esther, K.H. Jobes uses—in a slightly modified form—the criteria formulated by E. Tov for determining the character of a Greek translation of the Hebrew Bible.[6] These criteria are:

1. lexical consistency;
2. equivalence between units;
3. preservation of word order in the Greek;
4. extent of correspondence between individual elements of the units in the Hebrew and Greek texts;
5. linguistic adequacy of the corresponding Greek expression.

These criteria can indicate whether a translation is free or literal.[7]

---

4. Moreover, language only exists in subjects.

5. A. Lord Tennyson, *Poetry* (Everyman's Library, 626; London and New York: Dent, 1949), II, p. 229.

6. E. Tov, *The Text-Critical Use of the Septuagint* (Jerusalem: Simor, 1981), pp. 54-60.

7. K.H. Jobes, *The Alpha-Text of Esther: Its Character and Relationship to the Masoretic Text* (SBLDS, 153; Atlanta, 1996), pp. 53-94. See also my review of Jobes's book in *BO* 54 (1997), pp. 459-63, forthcoming.

These criteria also give an idea of how complex translating from one language system into another is, and how many factors affect the process and the end product.

A Fool or a Reviler and Blasphemer?

Translating biblical texts seems more challenging than translating Rilke. At least this is what 'it looks like'. But is translating biblical texts indeed that different from translating 'secular', 'non-religious' texts? If one states that there is a difference, then this might be a reference to the Bible's canonical status and origin in divine inspiration: the text of the Bible was written by God, many say. It is written by God, with his own finger![8] Therefore, one has to develop a special sense for translating these very special divine texts.

This approach to the biblical text is, of course, not new. As long as there has been a Bible, people have considered it to have been written by God. And this seemed and still seems to make translating it more complicated. Even Jerome changed his style of translating when confronted with the word of God. Translating or correcting a translation is taking a big risk, as Jerome points out clearly:

> Is there a man, learned or unlearned, who will not, when he takes the volume in his hands, and sees that what he reads does not suit his settled tastes, break out immediately into violent language and call me a forger and a profane person for having had the audacity to add anything to the ancient books, or to make any changes or corrections in them.[9]

Jerome's self-defence has a remarkable parallel in a talmudic statement attributed to Rabbi Yehuda:

> Whoever translates a biblical verse literally is a fool, while one who adds [to it] is a reviler and a blasphemer.[10]

Jerome made a distinction between translation techniques one can use for ordinary texts, and translation techniques for biblical texts. Rules, strict rules of translation techniques are put forward in the latter case. In his letter to Pammochius, Jerome defended the translation

8.   By the way, which finger was it?

9.   D. Brown, *Vir Trilinguis: A Study in the Biblical Exegesis of Saint Jerome* (Kampen: Kok, 1992), p. 97; quotation from Jerome, *Preface to the Four Gospels*.

10.   Quotation from *b. Qid.* 49a and *t.b. Meg.* 4.41 in M.J. Bernstein, 'Translation Technique in the Targum to Psalms. Two Test Cases: Psalms 2 and 137', in E.H. Lovering (ed.), *SBL 1994 Seminar Papers* (Atlanta: Scholars Press, 1994), pp. 326-45 (330).

techniques he used and stated his major argument:

> I not only admit but proclaim freely that when translating from Greek (except in the case of the holy scripture, where even the order of the words is a mystery) I translate sense for sense and not word for word.[11]

In this argument Jerome follows Cicero, who says,

> I have translated the noblest speeches of the two most eloquent of the Attic orators...but I have rendered them not as a translator, but as an orator, keeping the sense but altering the form...adapting both the metaphors and the words to suit our language.[12]

Why did Jerome change his attitude when confronted with 'holy scripture'? Because the texts were considered holy, because a whole ecclesio-theological debate was based upon the Bible.[13] But, what exactly has changed? Did Jerome in fact offer a word-for-word translation? Brown answers this question in the negative. In his opinion Jerome disregarded, in many cases, his declared principles about translating holy Scripture word for word. Jerome was confronted with the fact that the languages from which and into which he translated did not allow for a strict literal translation. Jerome's rhetorical education inclined him against literal translations. Finally, Jerome was influenced by various theological considerations that made it impossible to adhere totally to his own principles.[14] The result (the Vulgate) was 'a most gratifying compromise'.[15] Translating the Bible by word-for-word principles is difficult and, sometimes, strict rules have to be abandoned.

The same remarks apply to the Aramaic translations, the Targumim. Some of them, in various places, seem literal, because of their word (target) for word (source) reproduction; but they are not 'literal',

11. Brown, *Vir Trilinguis*, p. 105, quotation of Jerome, *Ep.* 57.5 (CSEL 54, 508).

12. Brown, *Vir Trilinguis*, p. 105, quotation of Jerome, *Ep.* 57.5 (CSEL 54, 509).

13. Although I have the impression that a word-for-word translation offers more problems for the biblical arguments used in ecclesiologial–traditional debates, than a sense-for-sense translation.

14. Brown, *Vir Trilinguis*, p. 111. This could be seen as contra A. Kamesar, who argues that Jerome always—at least since his conversion to the *Hebraica Veritas*—preferred the Hebrew text to the Greek text. Cf. A. Kamesar, *Jerome, Greek Scholarship and the Hebrew Bible: A Study of the Quaestiones Hebraicae in Genesim* (Oxford: Clarendon Press, 1993). However, Kamesar's book only appeared in 1993, whereas Brown's study was published in 1992.

15. Brown, *Vir Trilinguis*, p. 120, quotation from B. Keder-Kopfstein, *The Vulgate as a Translation: Some Semantic and Syntactical Aspects of Jerome's Version of the Hebrew Bible* (PhD dissertation, Jerusalem, 1968), pp. 284-85.

because of the significations of their own words in their own target language.[16]

Modern Translations on the Trail of Old Translations

In contemporary translations we are confronted with similar dilemmas. Should one allow priority to the Hebrew or Greek text of the Bible or to the target language, whatever it is? Korsak's translation of Genesis can be classified as an extremely literal modern translation. She gives full priority to the source language—the Hebrew text—without offending the English language.[17] An example:

MT Gen.1.26: ויאמר אלהים נעשה אדם

Korsak: Elohim said: we will make a groundling (Adam)[18]

The translation of אדם into 'groundling' is extremely literal, but remarkably beautiful. Compare with the NRSV, Catholic Edition: 'Then God said, "Let us make humankind..."',[19] which may be considered gender-neutral, but is not beautiful at all. Korsak's translation is one of the few literal translations that is also very poetic; but what Korsak manages is a rare exception.

However, focusing on the target language entails some very special problems. I will give an example from the discussion which arose when—already some time ago—the Dutch translation of the New Testament was to be revised. As in many European languages, Dutch has two forms of the second person singular. When the people are very polite they will use *u*, 'thee', (and, in some cases, also *gij*, 'thou'); when they are less polite they use *jij*, 'you'. Addressing a German professor with *Du, jij*, 'you', is not correct, unless he or she has given permission for use of the popular second person. Now, how polite are the angels of the New Testament? Do they use the popular second form or do they not? I will never forget the title in one of the Dutch newspapers: 'angels say "thee", not "you"' (*engeltjes tutoyeren niet*). What does this signify? It does certainly signify something about the critical reviewer and his or her theology (or, more appropriately, his

16. Bernstein, 'Translation Technique', pp. 326-31 and *passim*.

17. M.P. Korsak, *At the Start: Genesis Made New* (Leuven: Poetry Centre; Garden City, NY: Doubleday, 1994).

18. Korsak, *At the Start*, p. 3. Cf. also M.P. Korsak, 'Genesis: A New Look', in A. Brenner (ed.), *A Feminist Companion to Genesis* (The Feminist Companion to the Bible, 2), Sheffield: Sheffield Academic Press, 1993), pp. 39-52.

19. *Holy Bible: The New Revised Standard Version, Catholic Edition* (Nashville: Thomas Nelson, 1993).

or her angelology) rather than about the translation!

Echoes and traces of a similar discussion can be found in all layers of the Greek translation. The central debate of the second century BCE was, Do the Greek translations require revising?[20] Brock distinguishes between five stages of development:[21]

1. The earliest translators worked in an *ad hoc* fashion, producing a text simply because there was a need for a text.

2. Subsequent translators usually aimed at a more even rendering—and a more literal translated product.

3. By the end of the second century BCE at the latest, the need was recognized in some circles to 'correct' the earlier versions, bringing them closer into line with the Hebrew. The culmination of this process of 'correction' is Aquila's edition in the second century CE.

4. Contemporaneous with the developments of stage 3 were the reactions of diaspora Judaism, which had no interest in revision of the original translations.

5. The course taken by the literalist revisers was carried to its logical conclusion: no translation at all could do justice to the original language of revelation. Once the Hebrew text has been sacralized the translations perforce became interpretations and commentaries.

These stages are found in Judaism. One should realize that Christians regarded the LXX as a real 'sister' of the Hebrew text, a text which was also considered to be divinely inspired and holy. The same process of revisions and correction can also be found in Christian circles.

It may by now be apparent that, among other things, the art of translating is dependent on the function and use of the translation.[22] The Aramaic Targumim were not 'just' translations: they provided exegetical explanations to the text of the Hebrew Bible. 'It [the targum] translates the text, but simultaneously produces notes on the translation or a primitive form of commentary'.[23] First the Hebrew text was read, then the Aramaic translation and interpretation were

20. Cf. S. Brock, 'To Revise or not to Revise: Attitudes to Jewish Biblical Translation', in G.J. Brooke and B. Lindars (eds.), *Septuagint, Scrolls and Cognate Writings* (Septuagint and Cognate Studies, 33; Atlanta: Scholars Press, 1992), p. 305.

21. Brock, 'To Revise', pp. 325-27.

22. If art can be dependent on anything.

23. Bernstein, 'Translation Technique', p. 329.

offered. The important clue is that the Aramaic translation was never read without the Hebrew original.[24] The same could be true for the Old Latin translations. The biblical text would be read in Greek (LXX for the Old Testament) and then repeated in the vernacular. As time went by, the originally oral renderings were written down for continued use in the liturgy. However, the (oral) reading in Greek died out; what was left was only the vernacular Latin translation.[25] It is still a point of discussion whether the origin of the LXX should be seen in the same line. Was the translation made for liturgical purposes? Was it read alongside the Hebrew text? Another problem in this area is that some Greek translations could more or less be considered as 'Targumic translations'. I am thinking especially of the work of Aquila and the interpretation given of it by Veltri. Aquila translated into Greek, but was closer to the Aramaic targumim than one would think. 'Aquila's translation is a targum, because it is unthinkable without the presence of the MT'.[26] Veltrie goes on to write: 'The LXX, on the other hand, is not a Targum, for it has replaced—even according to rabbinical understanding—the Hebrew text'.[27]

Perhaps the LXX is best viewed as an artefact from the Hellenistic–Jewish tradition, situated along the lines of Jewish translations and interpretations such as the targumim.[28] Or was the LXX taken over by Christians, thus becoming a Christian Bible, serving as a necessary translation for the Greek-speaking community, whether for liturgical services or for apologetical treatises?[29] Perhaps it would be better to read the opposition between Greek translation techniques and Jewish translation techniques as a false opposition?[30] Does the history of the

24. G. Stemberger, *Introduction to the Talmud and Midrash* (trans. and ed. M. Bockmühl: Edinburgh: T. & T. Clark, 1996 [1991]), p. 236.

25. Brown, *Vir Trilinguis*, pp. 98-99.

26. G. Veltri, 'Der griechischen Targum Aquilas: Ein Beitrag zum rabbinischen übersetzungsverständnis', in M. Hengel and A.M. Schwemer (eds.), *Die Septuaginta zwischen Judentum und Christentum* (WUNT, 72; Tübingen: Mohr [Paul Siebeck], 1994), pp. 92-115 (108).

27. Veltri, 'Der griechischen Targum Aquilas', p. 108.

28. Or such as the Jewish–Greek translation of Aquila, who translated into Greek, using Jewish translation techniques; cf. Veltri, 'Der griechischen Targum Aquilas'.

29. M. Hengel, 'Die Septuaginta als "christliche Sammlung": ihre Vorgeschichte und das Problem ihres Kanons', in Hengel and Schwemer (eds.), *Die Septuaginta zwischen Judentum und Christentum*, pp. 182-284.

30. J. Barr, *The Semantics of Biblical Language* (Oxford: Oxford University Press, 1961; London: SCM Press, 1991 [1983]; Philadelphia: Trinity Press International, 1991).

Jewish translations prove such an opposition to be false? Does the history of the Greek translations prove such an opposition to be false? What if all translations just try to explain the 'deeper' meaning of a text? What if translating *is* interpreting? If so, what are we left with? How can biblical translations be characterized? Probably only by their use and functions: when are translations used, how, and why? If we accept that the characters of the translations are dependent on their function, we have to forget the other (false) opposition between literal, sometimes characterized as 'formal' and free, 'functional' translations. In this case the word 'functional' receives a new sense: the character of a translation is dependent upon its function. This emphasizes the importance of the audience, the aim and the purpose of a translation.

What if a 'She' is Involved?

And what if the audience consists of either men or of women? Does it make a difference when translators write for a male audience or for a female audience, or for a mixed-gender community? Are or were the translators always 'men'? What would happen to a translation if at least the implied reader is a she?

Much research has been done on female voices in the Hebrew text. The *Feminist Companion* series and the sessions on the Gendered Body at the International SBL meeting in Dublin, July 1996, are examples of the ongoing research on female authorship, female audience, female voices, female input and output in the Hebrew Bible. To speak broadly, these are discussions of issues relating to the gender contexts of texts. Much research has been done in arts and literature on gender and translation techniques. But, for biblical translations, hardly anything has been done in this gender research. Therefore, I shall limit my contribution to the asking of questions. What if the reader is a she? How does this affect translation techniques, and translations?

I would like to point at this stage to a limitation of my contribution to this topic. The limitation is my own limited area of research. As I am working on the MT, the LXX (and the Second Greek text) of the book of Esther,[31] I will only focus on the LXX translation; and leave the Vulgate, the Itala, the Aramaic, the Syriac, the Armenian, the Slavic and other translations to other specialists.

---

31. K. De Troyer, 'The End of the Alpha-Text of Esther: Translation Techniques and Narrative Techniques in MT 8.1-17, LXX 8.1-17 and AT 7.14-41' (Leuven: Peeters, forthcoming, 1997 [Dutch]).

Methods in Septuagint Research

When comparing the MT and the LXX, one can develop and follow different methods and have different goals in mind. Most of the comparative research starts from a synopsis. The Hebrew text is placed in line with the Greek text. As an immediate result, the pluses and minuses of the Hebrew and the Greek vis-à-vis one another become clear. Pluses and minuses are, at this stage, terms and concepts without any theoretical value. They are used in order to indicate where the Hebrew text has more or less text (words) than the Greek, and where the Greek text has more or less text than the Hebrew. In this kind of synopsis one can also see the differences between the texts. In such synopses there may be a Greek as well as a Hebrew text available, but these respective texts are different from one another. I will use the term 'variant readings' for these differences. If one is looking for an explanation for these differences, these pluses and minuses, one should also be aware of and explain the similarities. This last aspect of similarities is often forgotten.

A synopsis is a very basic tool; but, all synopses and text-alignments are *already* interpretations. The simple fact that two texts should be placed next to each other in order to see pluses and minuses, differences and similarities, implies that the author or translator has to decide upon the correlation of the texts. Of course, this choice can be corrected and changed later, but a first alignment of the text already gives a certain impression and a certain direction to the research.[32] Some scholars do not start by offering a synopsis simply

---

32. Day gives the following text alignment:

    MT 8.4//AT VIII 16a
    MT 8.5//ATVIII 16b
    MT 8.6//ATVIII 18

Jobes puts AT 7.16-17 (which is Day's VIII, 16-17) before MT 8.2 and after MT 8.1, so giving no parallel. I incline to put AT 7.17//to MT 8.1-2 and AT 7.18//to 8.3(.7). Cf. L. Day. *Three Faces of a Queen: Characterization in the Books of Esther* (JSOTSup, 186; Sheffield: Sheffield Academic Press, 1995), pp. 136-37 (for text) and pp. 137-51 (for notes and commentary); Jobes, *The Alpha-Text of Esther*, Appendix 1. Even the choice for a Greek critical edition could lead towards an interpretation. See my comment on the difference between Hanhart's edition and Rahlfs' on LXX 2.13, in K. De Troyer, 'An Oriental Beauty Parlour: An Analysis of Esther 2.8-18 in the Hebrew, the Septuagint and the Second Greek Text', in A. Brenner (ed.), *A Feminist Companion to Esther, Judith and Susanna* (The Feminist Companion to the Bible, 7; Sheffield: Sheffield Academic Press, 1995), pp. 47-70, esp. 60-61, and n. 4.

because they do not want to compare the texts in this way.

An evaluation of the pluses, minuses and variant readings can serve different goals. The LXX can, for example, be used to reconstruct the Hebrew text, especially in cases where the Hebrew makes no sense, or at least when all possible solutions offered by the Hebrew text itself prove to be insufficient. A glance at the text-critical apparatus of the *BHS* makes this clear.[33] The text-critical apparatus of Est. 1.14 proposes another reading: וְהַקְרֵב ('to come near') instead of וְהַקְרֹב ('the friend'), and refers to the LXX, which has καὶ προσῆλθεν. The Hebrew is understood better when following the Greek text. The Greek helps to reconstruct the original Hebrew text and is, therefore, mentioned in the text-critical apparatus of the Hebrew text in the *BHS*. The suggested (reconstructed) Hebrew text is then the result of a retroversion from the Greek word into Hebrew. But, one has to take care with retroversions. The Greek sometimes explains the Hebrew and furnishes a primary exegesis. In some cases the Greek text cannot be retroverted and cannot help with the reconstruction of the Hebrew text. An example of rigorous retroversion into Hebrew can be found in G. Jahn, *Das Buch Ester nach der Septuaginta hergestellt, übersetzt und kritisch erklärt*.[34] Jahn actually retroverted the whole Greek text of Esther into Hebrew. But this work is not only the result of an extremely careless and uncritical retroverting into Hebrew, but also the outcome caused by non-scholarly and non-academic political motivation. Tov devotes part of a chapter to the analysis of reliable and doubtful retroversions.[35]

One should also realize that the LXX text could be a translation from a Hebrew text that is different from the Masoretic text. The Qumran scrolls can prove very useful in this area. G. Brooke has carefully compared the LXX of Exodus and the Temple scroll, and concludes that the LXX is based on a text that is close to the MT but not exactly the MT. Moreover, parts of the Temple Scroll reveal a Hebrew text that is close to the *Vorlage* of the LXX.[36]

Of course, not all Septuagint research aims at reconstructing the

33. All my examples are taken from the book of Esther. As a consequence, this contribution is a limited one. All conclusions are valid only for the book of Esther, and if one is to make a general conclusion, then the non-quoted texts should be checked throughout the rest of the Bible.

34. G. Jahn, *Das Buch Ester nach der Septuaginta hergestellt, übersetzt und kritisch erklart* (Leiden: Brill, 1901).

35. Tov, *The Text-Critical Use of the Septuagint*, pp. 131-41.

36. G.J. Brooke, 'The Temple Scroll and LXX Exodus 35–40', in Brooke and Lindars (eds.), *Septuagint, Scrolls and Cognate Writings*, pp. 81-106.

Hebrew text and its history. The reconstruction of the Greek text itself and its history is as important as the former praxis.

Is it not a luxury and pure scholarly excitement to be able to look at passages from Origen in which he added a Greek translation of a Hebrew passage that he did not find in the Greek text he had in front of him? Or where he indicated that some Greek passages were not in the original Hebrew text, and added them to the Greek translation? In Est. 8.11, for example, Origen indicated with the common critical symbols that he had not found this passage in his Greek text, but that this was indeed the translation of the Hebrew text that was in front of him. This asterisk–and other diacritical symbols–can nowadays be found in the text-critical apparatus of the LXX text. This correcting of Origen is the result of a process of recensional activity that started from the very moment there was a Greek text. Again and again in the history of translation translators and other critical minds have looked back at the original text, and tried to correct the given translation towards the original text or to revise the text.

Another related question is the one concerned with the *Sitz im Leben* of the different Greek texts. Where and for which audience was a translation made? In the case of Esther the history is even more complex, due to the existence of a second Greek version. Scholarly views are wide-ranging: is the Hebrew *Vorlage* of the second Greek version (the AT) older than the Hebrew (Masoretic) text, or younger than the LXX version? Thus, is the oldest Hebrew text from the Esther scroll from the third or second century or even younger? And where was it written: Palestine? Egypt? Persia?

All these questions are worth studying. And, independently of the goals, most LXX researchers will be confronted with questions concerning the translations techniques and the narrative techniques used in the different LXX books. How far was the translator a translator and how far was he or she an author, an editor who carefully shaped the text into a different text: a different text with a different meaning, or for—at least—a different audience? For Hanhart, the LXX can be seen as an interpretation and as an actualization. But, interpretation must be seen as 'the explanation of possible understandings which are already inherent in the formulation of the Hebrew *Vorlage*'.[37] Insofar as the interpretation is the translation of one aspect of the Hebrew text, it is 'pure translation'. Actualization, on the other hand, goes beyond this first step, and adapts a text to a new context. The terms 'interpretation' and 'adaptation' can function as eye-openers.

---

37. Hanhart, 'Septuagint', pp. 342-43.

What we would call 'translation' Hanhart calls 'interpretation' (from whichever meaning is possibly given in the Hebrew text), leaving hereby more space for what we call 'interpretation'.

These concepts lead me to the following question. Can one really separate pure translation from additional interpretation—our concepts, not Hanhart's? Or from interpretation and actualization—concepts from Hanhart not ours? And is all translation not interpretation, whether it is given in the *Vorlage* as a possibility or not? And is actualization not an extended form of interpretation? Is not even the rabbinical exegesis a sort of etymology from the Hebrew text, a method of reading, with occasional ignoring of morphology and syntax, in order to explain the Hebrew text (and, in so doing, moving from explaining what 'is' in the Hebrew text to ignoring and omitting the Hebrew text)?[38]

Gender-Specific Questions

After having indicated the different methods and goals in LXX research, I now come to the task of asking critical gender-specific questions. Let me start with a clear example.

A Clear Example
A very famous translation and interpretation problem is Isa. 7.14. Is the woman mentioned merely 'a young woman' or 'a virgin'?

> In 'the Dialogue' JS 7.14 is cited nine times in its LXX version ἡ παρθένος, and four times Justin sets this reading which he defends strongly, against the reading that is defended by the Jews and that Justin is rejecting: Ἰδοὺ ἡ νεᾶνις ἐν γαστρὶ λήψεται.[39]

The translation of the LXX was hardly welcomed by the Christian community. It is, of course, no wonder that this text is found in an apologetical context: with this translation the Christians were able to defend the virginity of the mother of Christ: 'The Virgin Mother was born'.[40] This could serve as an argument in the Irenaen typology. The link between God–Adam–Christ on the one hand, and the Eve–Mary–Church line on the other hand clearly made 'man/men' Godlike. 'Man' became the *imago dei*...only 'men'. Of course, women

38. Whether it is Targum or Midrash, cf. Stemberger, *Introduction to the Talmud and Midrash*, p. 236.

39. Hengel, 'Septuaginta', p. 192.

40. Cf. M. Rösel, 'Die Jungfraugeburt des endzeitlichen Immanuel: Jesaja 7 in der übersetzung der Septuaginta', *JBTh* 6 (1991), pp. 135-51.

could still obtain salvation through becoming male in Christ.[41] The translation from the LXX was possible on the basis of the MT.[42] But, how unfortunate that this translation was chosen. And how even more unfortunate that people do not realize that this translation was but one out of several possibilities. This examples does not necessarily prove that the LXX translator made a 'gender-specific' choice,[43] but that at least the first readers and interpretators of this Greek text deliberately chose one meaning, be it a conscious apologetical choice or unconscious gender-specific choice.

The interpretations of translations, the differences in choice can become clear when there are different translations of the same text, or when translation techniques can be distinguished from interpretation and narrative techniques. Most LXX researchers develop a list of translation techniques first, and then establish a list of 'editorial' or 'interpretative' reworkings and reshapings of the text. Only in a few cases is there 'external evidence', such as the Temple Scroll for comparing the LXX and MT of Exodus or the asterisked passages from Origen. Another unique possibility for comparing texts are the two Greek texts of the book of Esther. For Esther, indeed, we are fortunate in having two different Greek texts deriving from one or two Hebrew texts of Esther.[44]

Research Done So Far
The title of Day's book, *The Three Faces of a Queen*, clearly points towards the problem. In the three different texts (MT, LXX and the second Greek text commonly indicated as AT), Esther has three different faces. And although I do not agree with Day's (and others') underlining hypothesis that the AT is an original translation of a Hebrew text different from the MT, I do see the differences in char-

41. Cf. K.E. Børresen, *Subordination and Equivalence: The Nature and Role of Woman in Augustine and Thomas Aquinas* (Lanham, MD: University Press of America, 1981; Kampen: Kok, 1995).

42. It was probably an adaptation to a new context: 'Das bedeutet, dass Unterschiede zwischen LXX Jes und MT Jes immer auch Resultate einer solchen Aktualisierung sien können und deshalb nicht ohne weiteres andere Lesungen in der Vorlage erschliessen lassen'; cf. A. van der Kooij, *Die alten Textzeugen des Jesajabuches: Ein Beitrag zur Textgeschichte des Alten Testaments* (OBO, 35; Göttingen: Vandenhoeck & Ruprecht, 1981), p. 65.

43. Van der Kooij has made clear that this interpretation of the text could be seen as an adaptation to a new and different political context, cf. A. van der Kooij, *Textzeugen*, p. 65.

44. Hebrew texts that could be called 'sisters' texts. However, I am not convinced of the existence of a Hebrew text other than the one we have.

acterization of Esther in each of the three texts. In the LXX queen Esther is a beauty queen, faithful to her Jewish faith and obedient toward her uncle Mordecai. She solves problems in a gentle, 'female' way. The AT omits the so-called 'irrational' elements of the story, and turns Esther first into a necessary tool for the plot and then into a revenge-seeking person. Even in her role as revenge-seeking queen, Esther is a necessary tool for the development of the plot in the AT.

A similar conclusion has been reached by Standhartinger in dealing with similar texts. She compared the different Greek recensions of the Jewish–Hellenistic *Joseph and Aseneth* story and discovered that, precisely concerning the image of the woman, there are many differences between the different Greek recensions.[45]

Suggestions for Research

We will now suggest some gender-specific questions for the different areas of Septuagint research.[46]

Reconstructing the Hebrew text, one should be very critical of what exactly is proposed and why. Is the new reading, the retroversion, a really adequate and reliable retroversion from a variant reading? Or is the suggestion made in order to avoid a certain kind of text, or to avoid a possible interpretation? Did the text suggest *too much*? What is too much? And for whom is it too much? Respecting the Hebrew text could also lead to avoidance of unnecessary omissions.

Reconstructing the Greek text, one should note very carefully what exactly is *removed* from the translation. What is not accepted by revisers? What is the norm for correcting, for adapting? Is it a 'male' or a 'female' norm? Which standard is set out? Who set this out and why? What were and are the motivating strategies, be they literary or gender-political?

Distinguishing between translation techniques and narrative techniques, one should be aware of the following questions. For translation techniques: who was the author and what kind of audience did he or she write for? For narrative techniques: what kinds of interpretations are given, what kinds of actualizations, aiming at which kind of audience? Who is included in the audience? Who is excluded? For

---

45. A. Standhartinger, *Das Frauenbild in jüdisch–hellenistischer Zeit: Ein Beitrag anhand von 'Joseph und Aseneth'* (Leiden: Brill, 1995).

46. It is worth noting that Bernstein has similar, but not gender-specific, questions for Targum research: 'Can we learn anything from the targum about the targumist's audience, about the assumptions which he could make about their knowledge, about the body of information on which he drew in composing his version?'. Cf. Bernstein, 'Translation Technique', pp. 326-45, esp. p. 327.

which purpose was the actualization made? Was it a male apologia?

Asking these kinds of questions may perhaps seem strange or, at least, a little unusual. Rabbi Yehuda had a point when he described translators as fools. Evaluating and asking critical questions of translations could be seen as following naturally from this line of argument; or maybe not? Anyhow, asking gender-specific questions about translation of biblical texts looks like the very beginning of a promising liaison.

An Example from the Hebrew and Greek Texts of Esther[47]

In the MT Vashti and Esther are made queens and called 'queen'. We read in MT 2.4: והנערה אשר תיטב בעיני המלך תמלך תחת ושתי, and in MT 2.17: וימליכה תחת ושתי. Haman and Mordecai—the other two main characters in the book of Esther—are promoted to high ranks. Haman's seat is set above all the other officials; MT 3.1: גדל המלך אחשורוש את־המן...וישם את־כסאו מעל כל־השרים; and Mordecai is made next in rank to king Ahasuerus, MT 10.2-3: כי מרדכי...אשר גדלו המלך. היהודי משנה למלך אחשורוש וגדול ליהודים.

In the Greek text Vashti and Esther are queens, as they are in the MT. When Vashti refuses to come at the king's command, Memucan proposes to give the royal position to another who is better than she (LXX 2.4: καὶ ἡ γυνὴ, ᾗ ἂν ἀρέτῃ τῷ βασιλεῖ, βασιλεύσει ἀντὶ Ἀστιν), and Esther is made queen. Mordecai refers to this in LXX 4.14: καὶ τίς εἶδεν εἰ εἰς τὸν καιρὸν τοῦτον ἐβασίλευσας, 'perhaps you have come to royal dignity for just such a time as this?' Haman is called in LXX App. B.3: δεύτερον τῶν βασιλείων, and in LXX App. E. 11 τὸ δεύτερον τοῦ βασιλικοῦ θρόνου. Mordecai is described as follows in LXX 10.3: ὁ δὲ Μαρδοχαῖος διεδέχετο τὸν βασιλέα Ἀρταξέρξην.

At first sight the LXX seems to translate the Hebrew text very strictly. Esther is indeed queen. But, we wonder, what does this really mean for the translator of the LXX? Haman and later on Mordecai seem to be second to the king. Again, we wonder, what does this mean for the LXX?

We can also look at the different descriptions of the main characters' bodies. What do they wear? Which attires and ornaments do they have? Esther puts on her royal dress in MT 5.1: ותלבש אסתר מלכות. Mordecai is dressed in royal clothing in MT 6.8: לבוש מלכות אשר לבש־בו המלך. After this event Mordecai returns to the king's gate.

---

47. This example is taken from my paper, presented at the SBL International Meeting in Dublin 1996, entitled, 'The Gendered Body as a Criterion for Evaluating Translations'.

What happens to the royal clothes? It seems that Mordecai is still dressed in royal clothes in MT 8.15: ‏ומרדכי יצא מלפני המלך בלבוש מלכות‎.

What is said in the LXX about royal clothes? Esther took off the garments in which she had worshipped and arrayed herself in splendid attire in LXX App. D.1: ἐξεδύσατο τὰ ἱμάτια τῆς θεραπείας καὶ περιεβάλετο τὴν δόξαν αὐτῆς. The royal clothes of the king are also described in LXX App. D.6: καὶ πᾶσαν στολὴν τῆς ἐπιφανείας αὐτοῦ ἐνδεδύκει, ὅλος διὰ χρυσοῦ καὶ λίθων πολυτελῶν—the king is clothed in the full array of his majesty, all covered with gold and precious stones. Mordecai has to wear the fine linen robe that the king has worn in LXX 6.8: στολὴν βυσσίνην ἣν ὁ βασιλεὺς περιβάλλεται; and Mordecai goes out dressed in the royal robe in LXX 8.15: ὁ δὲ Μαρδοχαῖος ἐξῆλθεν ἐστολισμένος τὴν βασιλικὴν στολήν.

The question is now, what does the LXX mean with the περιεβάλετο τὴν δόξαν αὐτῆς of the LXX App. D.1? Is this the translation of MT 5.1, ‏ותלבש אסתר מלכות‎? The word δόξα is also found in LXX 1.4 and LXX 10.2, and is used in the context of the glory and the splendour of the kingdom. Esther's clothes in LXX App. D.1 should be seen in this context, the context of the glory and the splendour of the kingdom. The verb is used when the king honours Haman in LXX 3.1: μετὰ δὲ ταῦτα ἐδόξασεν ὁ βασιλεὺς Ἀρταξέρξης Ἀμάν; and later Mordecai (LXX 6.6): τί ποιήσω τῷ ἀνθρώπῳ ὃν ἐγὼ θέλω δοξάσαι.

Strictly speaking, the LXX allows proper royal clothes only to Mordecai. The king does honour Haman and Mordecai. Esther only wears splendid attire, if—at least—one can read LXX App. D.1 (καὶ περιεβάλετο τὴν δόξαν αὐτῆς) as putting on some clothes. To conclude: Mordecai and Haman have come close to the royal throne. They even wear royal clothes. Esther has even become queen. But she is, in the LXX, kept away from real royal clothing. That makes her different from at least Mordecai. Mordecai and Haman are—not both at the same time—honoured by the king. Esther has to put on her 'dress of honour' herself. And that is exactly the whole point. It is not the king who honours Esther, but it is Esther who puts on her dress of honour. Esther is made queen, but royal attire and royal honour are given only to men. For the LXX translator men can come closer to the throne than women, even if the women are called 'queen'. Translations are *indeed* interpretations!

The proof of the pudding is in the eating, so I shall now look at the second Greek text of the book of Esther (AT) and see whether this text is also an interpretation. Mordecai leaves the royal palace in AT 7.39: ἐστολισμένος τὴν βασιλικὴν ἐσθῆτα. He probably receives this royal garment in AT 6.11: Ληφθήτω στολὴ βασιλική, where the king orders Haman to honour Mordecai and Haman gives the royal clothes to Mordecai. The king wanted to honour Mordecai by giving him these clothes, as in AT 6.9: Τί ποιήσωμεν τῷ ἀνδρὶ τῷ τὸν βασιλέα τιμῶντι, ὃν ὁ βασιλεὺς βούλεται δοξάσαι ('what shall we do to the man who fears the king, whom the king wishes to honour?'). Someone who fears the king seems to receive royal clothes. That is good to know. Esther wears in AT 5.1 approximately the same thing as in App. D.1: καὶ περιεβάλετο τὰ ἱματια τῆω δόξῆς. It is at least very clear in the AT that these are indeed garments, clothes.[48] And the king wears in AT 5.4 almost the same things as in LXX App. D.6: καὶ πᾶσαν στολὴν ἐπιφανείας ἐνδεδύκει, ὅλος διάχρυσος καὶ λίθοι πολυτελεῖς ἐπ᾽ αὐτῷ. To conclude: it seems that Mordecai and the king wear similar clothes. The clothes of Mordecai can be seen as royal clothes, intended to honour a man who fears the king. Esther only wears a dress of honour. The AT is an interpretation too, and follows the ideas set forth in the LXX.

Finally, let us go one step further. Who or what is Esther in the second Greek text? Is she a queen? Is she someone who is to be honoured? When Vashti refused to come before the king and his friends, the eunuch proposed making a law that would prevent women from refusing (LXX 1.20): καὶ οὕτω πᾶσαι αἱ γυναῖκες περιθήσουσιη τιμὴν τοῖς ἀνδράσιν ἑαυτῶν. Women should respect their husbands. The AT alters this statement only a little, but significantly enough. It does so in AT 1.20: καὶ πᾶσαι αἱ γυναῖκες δώσουσι τιμὴν καὶ δόξαν τοῖς ἀνδράσιν αὐτῶν. What will be required from Esther is now clear: she has to honour her husband! She is the one who shall stand as an example. The LXX already had the element of 'honour'. The AT clarifies by adding: καὶ δόξαν. This is different from another example that has already been shown: Mordecai honoured the king and, therefore, he was honoured by the king. Esther is the one who has to honour, but she will not be honoured even if she eventually honours her husband and even if two verbs are used to indicate her duty of honouring him. Whereas the male body is minimally promoted, the female is reduced to the lowest level of respect. It is to be honoured, she is not to be honoured. But, although the female (body) is underestimated, it looks like a very threatening thing, for the eunuchs who look after Esther are—in the Alpha-text—certainly castrated men. It should be of no surprise that Esther is not

---

48. The AT here uses a phrase that the LXX uses earlier in App. D.1 for Esther: τὰ ἱμάτια τῆς θεραπείας.

writing letters to people in the Alpha-text, not even requesting to withdraw royal decrees. The only thing she is allowed to ask is permission for revenge, for killing and for hanging people. If it had been possible, the author of the second Greek text of Esther would have created an Esther scroll with only men, certainly without Esther.[49] And would that not be the work of a fool, a reviler and a blasphemer?

49. For a similar analysis, but focusing on the relation of the texts, see K. De Troyer, 'On Crowns and Diadems of Kings, Queens, Horses and Men', in B.A. Taylor (ed.), *Proceedings of the IOSCS Conference in Cambridge 1995* (Septuagint and Cognate Studies; Atlanta: Scholars Press, forthcoming).

At the SBL International meeting in Dublin the theme of 'women's laws' and 'women's guardians' were developed further.

SURVIVING LAMENTATIONS*

Tod Linafelt

Surviving Lamentations is no easy task. With its barrage of violent images, the reader is not so much engaged by the book of Lamentations as assaulted by it. But the book itself is less concerned for the survival of the *reader* than for the suffering, perishing *children* that haunt its pages. This holds true particularly in Lamentations 1 and 2, where the personified figure of Zion refuses to let the reader's—or God's—attention stray far from the children. After my reading of these chapters below, I will consider how the Targum to Lamentations (its translation into Aramaic) and portions of Isaiah 40–66 can themselves be construed as 'survivals' of Lamentations, keeping alive as they do the concern for children that goes unmet in Lamentations.

It will become obvious that the theoretical underpinnings of this article are reliant on Walter Benjamin's understanding of translation in terms of survival, and by Jacques Derrida's subsequent commentary on Benjamin's essay, 'The Task of the Translator'.[1] Robert Detweiler's brief reflections in his article, 'Overliving', have also proven quite important for this study.[2] Extending Benjamin's metaphor, Detweiler utilizes the term 'survival' as a way of construing not only *translation*, but the nature of *interpretation* as well. Interpretation is for Detweiler 'an act of survival' for, by its very nature, it is concerned with the survival of the interpreted text. This is achieved by the 'piling on' of more texts. Survival, then, becomes 'excessive' or 'life in excess'.[3] Detweiler ruminates on the possible literal render-

---

* Reprinted, with permission, from *HBT* 17.1 (1995), pp. 45-61.

1. Benjamin's article, 'The Task of the Translator', can be found in the collection *Illuminations* (London: Fontana, 1973), pp. 70-82. Derrida's treatment of Benjamin in relation to the Tower of Babel first appeared as 'Des Tours de Babel' in *Difference in Translation* (trans. and ed. J. Graham; Ithaca, NY: Cornell University Press, 1985). It is reprinted in *Semeia* 54 (1991), pp. 3-34, from which the citations that follow are taken.

2. R. Detweiler, 'Overliving', *Semeia* 54 (1991), pp. 239-55.

3. Detweiler, 'Overliving', p. 241.

ings of the word survival (*überleben*): 'overliving, to live above, and to live again'.[4] To these may be added Derrida's sense of survival (*survie*) as 'afterlife' or 'more life'. All of these senses will be important, in varying degrees, for my reading of Lamentations and those texts that survive it.

As a final introductory comment, I must note that it is no accident that both the theoretical reflections and my reading of Lamentations take place after the Holocaust. Survival has become perhaps the dominant metaphor of our century, albeit a survival that seems random and precarious. After Auschwitz, questions of survival take on an urgency even—or particularly—for the biblical God. Has God survived Auschwitz? The question looms large for theologians. But for biblical scholars the question is, rather, have these texts survived? If so, how do we read them differently? This article offers no definitive answers, but it does raise the possibilty of a 'hermeneutics of survival' in which we read the Bible so that it might survive, even as we read for our own survival.[5]

'None Survived or Escaped': A Reading of Lamentations 1 and 2

The book of Lamentations opens with the voice of the poet elaborating the state of fallen Jerusalem, citing Yahweh as the source of the destruction (v. 5) and justifying the destruction as punishment (vv. 5 and 8). Verse 9 of chapter 1 begins as if to carry on this general sentiment. But there occurs a radical shift in v. 9c, when what is unmistakably the voice of Zion interrupts the poet:

> See, Yahweh, my affliction;
> how the enemy magnifies himself.

This interruption is short, only two colons, but nonetheless compelling. The poet's monopoly on the reader is momentarily broken; the one spoken about now becomes the one who speaks. Likewise, while the poet has spoken *about* Yahweh, it is Zion who first speaks *to* Yahweh. Theology is put on hold, as Zion challenges Yahweh (and the reader) to look upon her affliction rather than explain the reasons

---

4. Detweiler, 'Overliving', p. 240.
5. For more on the implications of the Holocaust for biblical studies, see T. Linafelt, 'Reading the Hebrew Bible After the Holocaust: Toward an Ethics of Interpretation', in *The Holocaust: Progress and Prognosis, 1934–1994* (Lawrenceville, NJ: Holocaust Resource Center of Rider College, 1994), pp. 627-41; also T.K. Beal and T. Linafelt, 'Sifting for Cinders: Strange Fires in Leviticus 10:1-5', in *Semeia* 69-70 (1995), pp. 19-32.

for it. No sooner has the reader realized that Zion is speaking than she is silent once more. But it is not Yahweh who answers her, for the speaking voice reverts again to the poet.

Verse 11 is the final verse of the first half of the poem, and represents a climax and a transition:

> They have given their precious things for food,
> in order to restore their lives (1.11b).

The sense of 'precious things' here is debatable, but the bitter irony of the line is better exploited by emphasizing the connotation of *children* as the 'precious ones'.[6] Read thusly it anticipates 2.20 and 4.10, where children themselves are said to be eaten by their mothers.

This, it seems, is too much for Zion. The poet is once again interrupted by the voice of Zion, with the same imperative as verse 9c: 'See, Oh Lord!' The transition is a major one, with the voice of Zion dominating for the remainder of the chapter. 'What has been a personification becomes more like a person';[7] and faced with the testimony of a woman raped and tortured, questions of just punishment are ludicrous. So, for the moment at least, the reader (and the poet) are forced to consider only the lived pain of the widow Zion.

In v. 16 there is the climax to Zion's first speech. In response to the terrifying situation she has just described, Zion cries out:

> For these things I weep... My eyes, my eyes!
> They pour out tears.
> How far from me is one to comfort,
> one to restore my life.
> My children are ravaged;
> O, how the enemy has triumphed.

The section culminates, then, with a mother wailing over the loss of her children. She is alone—with no one to offer comfort, no one to share the pain. With Zion momentarily overcome by grief the poet interjects in v. 17, repeating the by now familiar refrain, 'there is no one to comfort her'.

Zion regains her voice in v. 18, taking a different tack this time to elicit a response from Yahweh. She begins by acknowledging

6.   Both N. Gottwald, *Studies in the Book of Lamentations* (Chicago: Alec R. Allenson, 1954), p. 8, and T. Meek, *The Book of Lamentations* (Nashville: Abingdon Press, 1956), p. 11, take it to mean 'possessions'. D. Hillers, *Lamentations* (AB; Garden City, NY: Doubleday, 1992), p. 87, argues that it refers to children. I. Provan, *Lamentations* (Grand Rapids: Eerdmans, 1991), p. 47, allows either.

7.   A. Mintz, *Hurban: Responses to Catastrophe in Hebrew Literature* (New York: Columbia University Press, 1984), p. 26.

Yahweh's justice and her own rebelliousness. It should be noted that the character of Zion, for all her challenging of Yahweh, never claims complete innocence. But she does shift the rhetoric to the experience and extent of pain; and in this final section of ch. 1 she does not let up, despite her admission of rebelliousness.

The voice of the poet begins ch. 2 and, picking up the cue from Zion, portrays God in line after line as an enemy warrior. The reader of 2.1-4 is confronted by a poetic whirlwind of wrath and fire. Verse 1: the Lord in 'his wrath' (אף) has shamed Zion; has forgotten his footstool on 'the day of his wrath' (יום אפו   ). Verse 2: 'In his fury' (עברה) the Lord has razed Judah's defenses. Verse 3: The Lord has cut down 'in blazing wrath' (בחרי־אף   ) the horn of Israel; the Lord has 'burned (בער) against Israel like a blazing fire (אש להבה), consuming (אכל) on all sides'. Verse 4: The Lord pours out against Zion 'his wrath (אף) like raging fire' (אש חמה). The English language is exhausted in an attempt to describe the destructive inferno unleashed by God's anger.

After recounting the state of the vanquished city in vv. 5-10, v. 11 brings us to the halfway point of the second poem. Like the first poem, this halfway point marks a climax and a transition. In light of the suffering figure of Zion, the poet finally breaks down:

> My eyes are spent with tears, my stomach churns;
> my bile is poured out on the ground,
> at the destruction of the daughter of my people;
> as the children and the infants collapsed
> in the squares of the city.
>
> They kept saying to their mothers,
> 'Where is bread and wine?'
> as they collapsed as if wounded
> in the squares of the city,
> as their lives ran out in the bosoms of their mothers.

The poet again echoes the words of Zion. Even as Zion's eyes have flowed with tears, so the poet's eyes are spent with tears. And the poet employs the same phrase Zion has used in 1.20, 'my stomach churns', to describe his physical and/or emotional state. But most significantly, it is the *children perishing in the street* that finally prove too much for the poet, even as they did for mother Zion in 1.16.

Reading of the poet's inability to continue, I cannot help but recall Theodor Adorno's famous remark that poetry is impossible after Auschwitz; and think that perhaps he was anticipated in this judgment by the book of Lamentations. Irving Greenberg offers the following as a 'working principle' for discourse after the Holocaust: 'No statement, theological or otherwise, should be made that would not be credible in the presence of the burning children'.[8] Given this criteria, there is no speech adequate. Perhaps Greenberg too was anticipated by Lamentations, as we read in 2.13:

> What can I say for you, to what can I compare you,
> daughter Jerusalem?
> To what can I liken you, that I may comfort you,
> daughter Zion?
> For your breach is as vast as the sea—
> who could heal you?

The questions are rhetorical. Nothing can be said; there is no comparison; for no one can heal a breach as vast as the sea. The poet is caught in the survivor's dilemma: to speak is to betray the memory of the dead, for no metaphors are adequate, but to remain silent is a worse betrayal. So the poet continues, as even Adorno conceded must be done.[9]

With verses 18 and 19 we come to the end of the poet's speech, and a final intensification of rhetoric. Having taken up the cause of Zion, but able neither to find a comforter nor to comfort Zion adequately himself, the poet urges Zion to cry out once again to Yahweh.

> Cry out to the Lord from the heart,
> wall of daughter Zion.
> Shed tears like a torrent, day and night!
> Give yourself no rest, and do not let your
> eyes be still.
>
> Arise! Wail in the night, at the beginning of the watches.
> Pour out your heart like water in front of the Lord.
> Lift your hands to him, for lives of your children,
> who collapse from hunger at the corner
> of every street!

The rhetorical move imagined by the poet is for Zion to affront Yahweh with the intolerable suffering of children. It is exactly this, we may recall, that led to Zion's breaking down into tears in 1.16. It

8.   I. Greenberg, 'Cloud of Smoke, Pillar of Fire: Judaism, Christianity, and Modernity after the Holocaust', in E. Fleischner (ed.), *Auschwitz: Beginning of a New Era?* (New York: Ktav, 1977), p. 26.

9.   Adorno's famous remark, 'To write a poem after Auschwitz is barbaric', was written in 1949. But he later wrote in *Negative Dialectics* (trans. E.B. Ashton; New York: Continuum, 1973), p. 362, 'Perennial suffering has as much right to expression as a tortured man has to scream; hence it may have been wrong to say that after Auschwitz you could no longer write poems. But it is not wrong to ask the less cultural question whether after Auschwitz you can go on living.'

is also the perishing children that led to the poet's own breakdown in 2.11. Perhaps, then, the 'lives of the children' will be enough to move Yahweh.[10]

Zion responds to the urging of the poet, beginning with the most accusatory passage in the book (2.20):

> See, Yahweh, and consider who it is
> you have so ruthlessly afflicted!
> Alas! Women are eating their offspring,
> the children they have born!

Zion employs the same imperative that she did in 1.9 and 1.11 in an attempt to command the attention of Yahweh. The verb עלל ('afflict') is sardonically placed here in a parallel position with עולל ('child'), contrasting the *ruthlessness* of Yahweh with the *suffering* of children, and making clear that these are whom Yahweh is afflicting.

Zion continues in this final section to elaborate on the suffering of the population, and employs ironically the language of the cult. But it is a gruesome perversion of the cult that affronts the reader in the last line of v. 22: 'those whom I bore and reared, the enemy has consumed!' Zion's final speech of 2.20-22—bounded at beginning and end by the cannabalizing of children—is the last we hear from her in the book of Lamentations. Her penultimate line (22b) rings fitting as a summary: 'none survived or escaped'.

There is no response from Yahweh. The book goes on, of course, employing a number of rhetorical strategies to express the grief and anger of the community and to elicit a response from the Lord. In the final chapter the community speaks in a first-person plural voice, addressing God directly. Lamentations ends with their plaintive appeal:

> Why have you forgotten us utterly,
> forsaken us for all time?
> Take us back, O Lord, to yourself, and let us come back;
> renew our days as of old!

---

10. The rhetoric is forceful, but it is not without its more subtle artistry. The occurrence of שפך, 'pour out', at this critical point in the poem represents a nexus of inter-relations between the characters. Indeed, we may say that each character is defined by what s/he is said to 'pour out'. Mother Zion is told here to 'pour out your heart like water…for the lives (נפש) of your children'. In 2.12 it is precisely the 'lives (נפש) of the children' which are being 'poured out (שפך) in the bosoms of their mothers'. Moreover, in that same passage it is the pouring out of the children's lives that move the poet to 'pour out' (שפך) his grief. In sharp contrast, when the word שפך is used to describe Yahweh in 2.4, it describes the 'pouring out' of Yahweh's 'raging fire'.

> for truly you have rejected us,
> bitterly raged against us (5.20-22, JPSV).

This appeal, like the earlier appeals of Zion and the poet, remains unanswered. The voice of Yahweh never sounds in the book of Lamentations. There seems little hope of surviving Lamentations, either for the children or for the community as a whole. Indeed, even the reader may feel that she or he can barely endure the tenor of grief that pervades its five chapters. For survival, then, we must turn elsewhere—to the 'afterlife' of this biblical text in other texts.

'Survival in Translation': The Targum to Lamentations

Ostensibly a translation of Lamentations from Hebrew to Aramaic, the Targum is less concerned with preserving the biblical text verbatim than with ensuring its survival among a later generation of readers. Survival is, as mentioned above, a primary metaphor for translation in Walter Benjamin's article, 'The Task of the Translator'. Benjamin's reflections are strikingly appropriate to the nature of the Targum. He writes:

> For in its survival, which would not merit the name if it were not mutation and renewal of something living, the original is modified.[11]

The Targum is surely a parade example of a text's survival, both in the sense of 'living on' (Benjamin's 'renewal') and of 'overliving' (Benjamin's 'mutation').

Commenting on Benjamin's essay on translation, Derrida writes:

> The translation will truly be a moment in the growth of the original, which will complete itself *in* enlarging itself. Now, it has indeed to be…that growth not give rise to just any form in just any direction.[12]

If what Derrida writes is true for the Targum (that its excesses come about because 'the original calls for a complement'),[13] and if my reading of the 'original' Lamentations is correct (that it is driven by a concern for the suffering of children), then a confluence of the two claims may be presumed. To put it simply, does the Targum exhibit 'growth' along the trajectory of 'concern for children?' The answer is 'yes', as the following examples will show.

---

11. Cited and translated in J. Derrida, 'Des Tours de Babel', p. 16.
12. Derrida, 'Des Tours de Babel', p. 20.
13. Derrida, 'Des Tours de Babel', p. 20.

Lamentations 1.16

Consider, first of all, Lam. 1.16. This is a crucial verse, for it is here that Zion is first overcome with emotion on behalf of her ravaged children, as well as the first time that a response is elicited from the poet. The Targumic version of 1.16 reads as follows:

> *Because of the babes who were smashed and the pregnant women whose wombs were torn open*, the Congregation of Israel says, 'I weep, and my eyes pour tears like a spring of waters. For far from me is any comforter to revive me and speak comforting things to my spirit. My children are forlorn, for the foe has prevailed over them.'[14]

While the Targum makes some typical minor changes, the most significant change is the addition of the opening phrase. The cause of Zion's breakdown, which I identified as the fate of the children, is here picked up by the Targum as a point of supplementarity. By presenting the children as 'smashed' and 'torn' from their mothers' wombs, the Targum intensifies the emotional level. And by placing the fate of the children at the beginning *and* the end of the verse, it emphasizes their importance as the cause of Zion's weeping.

Lamentations 2.20

Another crucial passage for my reading of MT Lamentations is Zion's final speech of 2.20-22, in which she responds to the poet's exhortation to affront God with the suffering of her children in order to elicit a response. I have suggested that those whom Yahweh has 'so ruthlessly afflicted' are the children of the line immediately following. Taking it this way implies that the final line of v. 20, 'Priest and prophet are slain in the sanctuary of the Lord', is less connected with what comes before than with what follows. That is, it begins the description of the inhabitants of the city which then continues through v. 21.

Now consider 2.20 in the Targum to Lamentations:

> See, O Yahweh and behold from heaven: against whom have you been as angered as against these? Is it right that *from starvation* the daughters of Israel should eat the fruit of their wombs, delicate children wrapped in linen swaddling cloths? *The Attribute of Justice replied, and said*, 'Is it right to kill priest and prophet in the Temple of Yahweh, *as you killed Zechariah son of Iddo the High Priest and faithful prophet, in the Temple of Yahweh on the Day of Atonement, because he reproached you, that you refrain from evil before Yahweh?*'

14. All quotes from the Targum are from E. Levine's edition, *The Aramaic Version of Lamentations* (New York: Hermon, 1976). Italics are my addition.

The Targum reads this verse as though it were a dialogue, with the
second half of the verse expanded and placed in the mouth of the
divine 'Attribute of Justice'. The importance of this is twofold. First, it
shows that the Targum recognizes the focus of Zion's concern in
Lamentations to be the children. It is indeed these to whom God has
been so ruthless. The last line of the verse, concerning priest and
prophet, are effectively separated off by attributing it to another
speaker. Secondly, the Targum acknowledges the unfulfilled need for
a response from God to the charges of Zion. According to my reading,
the rhetoric of Lamentations was geared toward getting a response
from God, with the fate of the children utilized here because that is
what earlier achieved the desired result for the poet. The Targum
supplements the MT with an answer from the divine at the moment
when the absence of God's voice is most prominent.

The answer given is, of course, largely unsatisfactory. The Attribute
of Justice presents the stoning of the prophet Zechariah (2 Chron.
24.15-22) by the people of Israel as a justification for the punishment
now meted out on Jerusalem. Zion, however, is little concerned with
why the punishment is taking place and makes no claims for the
sinlessness of the people. She is more concerned with the survival of
the children, the barbarous treatment of whom precludes any theodic
settlement.

Lamentations 2.22
The next major supplement in the Targum grows out of just this need
in Lamentations for the children's survival to be addressed. As has
been noted, the MT of 2.22—the final verse of Zion's speech—ends on
a very somber note: there are no survivors among Zion's children.
The Targum to 2.22, however, reads:

> You will proclaim freedom to your people the House of Israel, through
> the Messiah king, as you did through Moses and Aaron on the day that
> you brought forth Israel from Egypt. And my youths will gather together
> from every place where they were scattered on the day of your fierce
> anger, O Yahweh, when there was no escapee or survivor among them.
> Those whom I had wrapped in fine linen, and those whom I had nour-
> ished with regal dainties, my enemies consumed.

The supplement of the Targum—in which the youths are gathered
together—is generated by the text's inherent (but frustrated) drive for
the survival of the children. As Derrida writes,

if the original calls for a complement, it is because at the origin it was not there without fault, full, complete, total, identical to itself. From the origin of the original to be translated there is fall and exile.[15]

The Targumist (consciously or not) apprehends this lack and supplies the midrashic complement for which 'the original calls'.[16]

The move is all the more bold in placing the return of the children alongside the 'original' statement that 'there was no escapee or survivor among them'. How can children *return* when there was no survivor in the first place? The Targum is not bothered by the logical inconsistency. Survival for the Targum is imagined—to borrow a phrase from Detweiler—'*as if* we had a future'. Survival is 'to live *again*'.[17]

While the Targum, on this reading, is concerned to complete the lack (what Derrida appropriately calls 'the fall and exile') of the original, it too is frustrated. This is most obvious, I think, in the clash between what is said by the Attribute of Justice in v. 22, and what is said by Zion in v. 22. Both address a lacuna in the original, but the gap between them produces another. For Benjamin, this is to be expected: 'both the original and the translation [are] recognizable as fragments of a greater language'.[18] Fragments engender their survival in other fragments, whose existence is just as incomplete and precarious.

Living Beyond Lamentations: Second Isaiah

In *Lamentations Rabbah* (the midrash on Lamentations) it is stated that 'all the severe prophecies that Jeremiah prophesied against Israel were anticipated and healed by Isaiah'.[19] For the Rabbis, of course, Jeremiah was the author of Lamentations, and so they are often concerned to show how responses to the book of Lamentations may be found in the book of Isaiah.

Modern interpreters have likewise noted a similarity of language and theme between Lamentations and Second Isaiah, but have only

15. Derrida, 'Des Tours de Babel', p. 20.

16. This is similar to the understanding of midrash offered by Daniel Boyarin, *Intertextuality and the Reading of Midrash* (Bloomington: Indiana University Press, 1990), p. 15, in which 'the dialogue and dialectic of the midrashic rabbis [are] understood as readings of the dialogue and dialectic of the biblical text'.

17. Detweiler, 'Overliving', p. 240.

18. Benjamin, 'Task of the Translator', p. 78.

19. *Lamentations Rabbah*, trans. A. Cohen, in *Midrash Rabbah* (London: Soncino, 1939), VII, p. 57.

rarely posited a direct relationship. For example, Claus Westermann speculates that the prophet used נחם ('comfort, help') in the opening verses, 'perhaps on the basis of the lament common in Lamentations, "There is no helper"'.[20] But, he does not pursue the implications of this 'perhaps'. Norman Gottwald reproduces in a footnote a list of verbal linkages provided by Lohr, and goes so far as to say that Second Isaiah 'knew the Book of Lamentations', but offers no sustained reflection on the significance of this.[21] Carol Newsom, however, has recently articulated a more immediate relationship between the two books, writing that 'when Second Isaiah [writing for the exiles] takes up aspects of Lamentations, he engages dialogically the voice of the Judahite community'.[22] Newsom focuses particularly on the figure of Zion and the mention of the populace to show that Second Isaiah uses the language of Lamentations in order to prepare for the reintegration of exiles into the Judahite community.

Taking the intimations of these scholars one step further, I suggest that Isa. 49.14-26 is in fact a direct answer to Lamentations, and that it is generated by the same concern for survival identified above.[23] Moreover, unlike the Targum, Isaiah 49 is able to hold together the divine response and the survival of the children. (Which is not to say that it does not have wants of its own.)

Most strikingly, Isa. 49.14 opens with what is nearly a direct quotation of Lam. 5.20:[24] 'Zion said, "The Lord has forsaken me, my

20. C. Westermann, *Isaiah 40–66: A Commentary* (Philadelphia: Westminster Press, 1969 [1966]), p. 34.

21. Gottwald, *Studies*, p. 44. See also M. Lohr, 'Der Sprachgebrauch des Buches der Klagelieder', *ZAW* 14 (1894), pp. 31-50 (41).

22. C. Newsom. 'Response to Norman K. Gottwald, "Social Class and Ideology in Isaiah 40–55"', *Semeia* 59 (1992), pp. 73-78 (75).

23. While I cannot deal with this here, I am also of the opinion that Isaiah 47 is a response to Lamentations. Here, 'daughter Babylon' is portayed in much the same terms as 'daughter Zion' was in Lamentations. We may note in particular that Babylon is presented as thinking 'I shall not become a widow, or know the loss of children' (v. 8). Yet the poet says that 'these two things will come upon you...loss of children and widowhood' (v. 9). Such a reversal is exactly what is imagined by Zion in 1.22 and by the 'man of affliction' in Lam. 3.60-63.

24. This was first suggested to me by Walter Brueggemann in a conversation. The only other mention of it I have found is in the footnote in Gottwald, *Studies*, p. 44, mentioned above. See now also Patricia Willey, '"Remember the Former Things": The Recollection of Previous Texts in Isaiah 40–55' (PhD dissertation, Emory University, 1996), and Tod Linafelt, 'Margins of Lamentation, or, The Unbearable Whiteness of Reading', in T.K. Beal and D.M. Gunn (eds.), *Reading Bibles, Writing Bodies: Identity and the Book* (London: Routledge, 1996), pp. 219-31.

Lord has forgotten me"'. The same word-pair placed in the mouth of Zion, עזב and שכח, is picked up by the poet of Second Isaiah and used as a starting point for a new section. We may recall that when this word-pair occurred at the end of Lamentations it was utilized in the form of an unanswered question. It is appropriate, then, that in the text's survival in Isaiah the exegesis of it comes in the form of an extended response by Yahweh. But what is most striking, in light of my reading of Lamentations, is the *content* of this response. For what follows are eleven verses pertaining nearly exclusively to *the return of the children which Zion had lost*!

The response begins with Yahweh assuming the persona of a mother (49.15, NRSV).

> Can a woman forget her nursing child,
> or show no compassion for the child of her womb?
> Even these may forget, yet I will not forget you.

The poet chooses here the one metaphor for Yahweh that can begin to answer the rhetoric of Lamentations: Yahweh as a mother who also laments and hopes for the return of her children.

The poem quickly switches to the question of Zion's children in 49.17 (JPSV): 'Swiftly your children are coming; those who ravaged and ruined you shall leave you'. Here, as in Lam. 1.5 and 1.16, there is the juxtaposition of children and enemies. But while in Lamentations it was the children who went into exile at the coming of the enemies (1.5), here the children return and the former destroyers are the ones to 'go out'. 'Look up', Zion is told, 'they are all assembled, are come to you' (v. 18). The ruins, desolate places and devastated land (v. 19) will become crowded with inhabitants; a complete reversal of the opening verses of Lamentations, where Zion the widow sat alone, her roads empty.

A certain rhetorical giddiness sets in, as the poet compounds the image of restoration to the point where the beloved children say in the hearing of the long-abandoned mother Zion, 'The place is too crowded for me, make room for me to settle' (49.20, JPSV). Zion can only repeat to herself in stunned amazement,

> Who bore these for me?
> I was bereaved and barren.[25]
> Who brought these up?

25. I leave out here the phrase 'גלה וסורה', as suggested by BHS. It is not clear to whom it refers since Zion is not portrayed here as exiled, but rather abandoned in Judah. Without the phrase the verse is nicely parallel.

See how I was left alone.
These—where were they?

This is indeed survival in the sense of 'afterlife', or 'overliving', for the children were truly 'dead' to Zion. They are identified in v. 20 as 'children of your bereavement' (בני שכליך). Translations typically elide the fundamental meaning of שכל, which is to suffer the death of one's children. This accounts for Zion's stunned disbelief at the news of their return; such a thing is unimaginable.

But the rhetoric of survival is strong in Second Isaiah, for it must attempt to succeed the equally strong rhetoric of destruction in Lamentations.[26] On the heels of Zion's questions comes the phrase, אדני כה יהוה אמר (49.22). 'Thus says the Lord God': I have only to raise my hand to the nations and they will bring back 'your sons in their bosoms, and carry your daughters on their shoulders'. The children who once collapsed in the street from hunger will now have kings to support them and queens to nurse them (49.23). Those whose life was once poured out will now have life in excess (or, 'survival').

At stake in this poem, from beginning to end, is the survival of children. Yet on another level, the poem is concerned with survival of a different sort. I noted above Newsom's argument that Second Isaiah utilizes the language and symbols of Lamentations as a means of imagining the return of the Babylonian exiles to Judah.[27] The exiles are cast as the lost children, with Judah given the role of mother Zion, who is to welcome back the children. If Newsom is correct, then the poet of Second Isaiah is extraordinarily skillful. Not only does the poet discern and address the need for a *rhetoric* of survival generated by the literary form of Lamentations, but the poet also utilizes this to articulate an *ideology* of survival generated by the social context of exile. While what is at stake at the level of rhetoric remains the survival of children, at the level of ideology it is the survival of a community.

The Afterlife of Lamentations

Surviving Lamentations is a complex affair. We have seen that the supplements generated by Lamentations enable the children lost therein to live again. We have also seen that these texts may carry the

26. I am indebted to Mintz, *Hurban*, pp. 40-46, for his trenchant discussion of the 'rhetoric of destruction' and the 'rhetoric of survival' in Lamentations and Second Isaiah, respectively.

27. Newsom, 'Response to Gottwald', p. 75.

larger burden of the survival of whole communities. And how do we, as readers, survive the unremitting pain of Lamentations if it is not by turning to other texts?

In the long run, however, it is no less than the survival of the book of Lamentations *itself*, its 'afterlife', that is procured by these subsequent texts. Can we imagine Lamentations being admitted to the canon without its answer in Isaiah? Can we imagine diaspora Judaism including the book of Lamentations in its liturgy (even on the ninth of Av) without the hope of restoration offered by the Targum? No, it is through its supplements that Lamentations is enabled to live on.

There is, of course, a final irony in that the fundamental (unmet) drive for a response—which generated these supplements—remains in the book of Lamentations, thereby denying the very texts that have guaranteed its survival. The unrelenting absence at the center that defines the book of Lamentations continues to demand that the suffering of children be addressed, even as it stands as a constant critique of every attempt to do so. How could it be otherwise? For how can one say anything in the presence of burning children? And how can one be silent?

VI

GODDESSES AND WISDOM

FROM GODDESS TO LITERARY CONSTRUCT: THE TRANSFORMATION OF ASHERAH INTO ḤOKMAH*

Judith M. Hadley

The worship of deities other than Yahweh in Israel and Judah has long been a matter of interest. Recent archaeological discoveries have reopened the debate on the worship of various goddesses in ancient Israel and Judah. Ever since the discovery of the Kuntillet 'Ajrud and Khirbet el-Qom material interest in the worship of Asherah in particular has been building. On the basis of these finds, together with other supporting evidence, such as the Taanach cultic stands and the numerous female pillar figurines from eighth century BCE Judah, and especially the discovery of the Ugaritic material, many scholars now agree that the goddess Asherah was worshipped as the consort of Yahweh in both Israel and Judah during the period of the Israelite monarchy. However, the picture derived from the biblical text is that the worship of Asherah was condemned, as well as the worship of other deities such as Astarte. Finally, in some of the postexilic wisdom literature the figure of Lady Wisdom emerges, portrayed as a

---

*   Parts of this article are taken as excerpts from longer, fuller treatments to be found in J.M. Hadley, 'Yahweh and "His Asherah": Archaeological and Textual Evidence for the Cult of the Goddess', in W. Dietrich and M.A. Klopfenstein (eds.), *Ein Gott allein?: JHWH-Verehrung und biblischer Monotheismus im Kontext der israelitischen und altorientalischen Religionsgeschichte* (OBO, 139; Fribourg: Editions universitaires; Göttingen: Vandenhoeck & Ruprecht, 1994), pp. 235-68; Hadley, 'Wisdom and the goddess', in J. Day, R.P. Gordon and H.G.M. Williamson (eds.), *Wisdom in Ancient Israel: Essays in Honour of J.A. Emerton* (Cambridge: Cambridge University Press, 1995), pp. 234-43; Hadley, 'The Fertility of the Flock?: The Depersonalization of Astarte in the Old Testament', in B. Becking and M. Dijkstra (eds.), *On Reading Prophetic Texts: Gender-Specific and Related Studies in Memory of Fokkelien van Dijk-Hemmes* (Biblical Interpretation, 10; Leiden: Brill, 1996), pp. 115-33; and Hadley, 'Chasing Shadows? The Quest for the Historical Goddess', in J.A. Emerton (ed.), *Congress Volume, IOSOT 1995* (Leiden: Brill, in press). I wish to express my thanks to E.J. Brill; Othmar Keel, editor of OBO; and Chris Scarles of Cambridge University Press for permission to reproduce parts of those articles here.

'virtual' goddess. This study will examine the evidence that establishes the worship of the goddess Asherah during the monarchy
period, together with the gradual 'evolution' of the term *asherah* in the
biblical text into representing merely a wooden object. Next, the
similar 'evolution' of Astarte from denoting a goddess to becoming
an idiom of fertility will briefly be considered, followed by a cursory
examination of the personification of the figure of Lady Wisdom, perhaps as literary compensation for the eradication of the worship of
goddesses such as Asherah and Astarte.

   The first new evidence in recent times concerning the worship of
Asherah came from excavations at Ras Shamra in north-western
Syria (ancient Ugarit).[1] Before the discovery of this Ugaritic material,
the general consensus was that *asherah* in the Hebrew Bible referred
merely to an object.[2] Admittedly, in most of the verses in the Hebrew

---

   1.   For the Ugaritic texts themselves, see the various volumes in the Publica-
tions de la Mission de Ras Shamra series, including A. Herdner, *Corpus des tablettes
en cunéiformes alphabétiques découvertes à Ras Shamra–Ugarit de 1929 à 1939*
(CTA) (Publications de la Mission de Ras Shamra, 10; Paris: Geuthner, 1963) and
C. Virolleaud, *Le Palais Royal d'Ugarit* 2 (PRU) (Publications de la Mission de Ras
Shamra, 7; Paris: Geuthner, 1957); C.H. Gordon, *Ugaritic Textbook* (UT) (AnOr,
38; Rome: Pontifical Biblical Institute, 1965) and M. Dietrich, O. Loretz, and
J. Sanmartín, *Die Keilalphabetischen Texte aus Ugarit. I. Transkription* (KTU) (AOAT,
24.1; Kevelaer: Butzon & Bercker; Neukirchen–Vluyn: Neukirchener Verlag, 1976);
for an English translation and commentary see J.C.L. Gibson, *Canaanite Myths and
Legends* (Edinburgh: T. & T. Clark, 2nd edn, 1978) (originally edited and translated by G.R. Driver in G.R. Driver, *Canaanite Myths and Legends* [Old Testament
Series, 3; Edinburgh: T. & T. Clark, 1956]). For a discussion of the Ugaritic material with specific reference to Athirat, see T. Yamashita, 'The Goddess Asherah'
(PhD dissertation, Yale University, 1963); K.-H. Bernhardt, 'Aschera in Ugarit
und im Alten Testament', *Mitteilungen des Instituts für Orientforschung* 13 (1967),
pp. 163-74; E. Lipiński, 'The Goddess Aṯirat in Ancient Arabia, in Babylon, and
in Ugarit', *OLP* 3 (1972), pp. 101-19; A.L. Perlman, 'Asherah and Astarte in the
Old Testament and Ugaritic Literatures' (PhD dissertation, Graduate Theological
Union and University of California, Berkeley, 1978); W.A. Maier, III, *'Ašerah:
Extrabiblical Evidence* (HSM, 37; Atlanta: Scholars Press, 1986); O. Loretz, *Ugarit
und die Bibel: Kanaanäische Götter und Religion im Alten Testament* (Darmstadt:
Wissenschaftliche Buchgesellschaft, 1990); M. Dietrich and O. Loretz, *'Jahwe und
seine Aschera': Anthropomorphes Kultbild in Mesopotamien, Ugarit und Israel: das bib-
lische Bilderverbot* (Münster: Ugarit-Verlag, 1992); and S.A. Wiggins, *A Reassessment
of 'Asherah': A Study According to the Textual Sources of the First Two Millennia
B.C.E.* (AOAT, 235; Kevelaer: Butzon & Bercker; Neukirchen–Vluyn: Neukirchener
Verlag, 1993), among others.

   2.   See, for example, F.-M. Lagrange, 'Etudes sur les religions sémitiques: Les
déesses: Achéra et Astarté', *RB* 10 (1901), pp. 546-66; P. Torge, *Aschera und
Astarte: Ein Beitrag zur semitischen Religionsgeschichte* (Leipzig: Hinrichs, 1902);

Bible that mention *asherah* it is clear that some sort of wooden object is meant (see below). In those few verses that appear to indicate a goddess, most scholars assumed that the goddess was Astarte, as a goddess Asherah was unknown at that time (although a few scholars, notably Kuenen and his followers, believed that the word *asherah* could indicate a specific goddess as well as a wooden object).[3] W. Robertson Smith, on the other hand, believed that *asherah* always referred to a wooden pole that had no divine associations whatsoever.[4]

The discovery of the Ugaritic material has established the existence of a goddess Asherah at Ugarit without any doubt.[5] Although in Ugaritic her name appears as *'aṯrt (athirat)*, this is etymologically equivalent to Hebrew *'šrh (asherah)*.[6] Therefore, most scholars now believe that the Hebrew term *asherah* can mean both a goddess and her image or symbol.[7] However, a few scholars in recent times,

W.R. Smith, *Religion of the Semites* (London: A. and C. Black, 2nd edn, 1907), and especially W.L. Reed, *The Asherah in the Old Testament* (Fort Worth, TX: Texas Christian University Press, 1949) for a discussion of this position.

3.   Cf. A. Kuenen, *The Religion of Israel to the Fall of the Jewish State*, I (trans. A.H. May; London: Williams & Norgate, 1874).

4.   W.R. Smith, *Semites*, and see J.M. Hadley, 'William Robertson Smith and the asherah', in W. Johnstone (ed.), *William Robertson Smith: Essays in Reassessment* (JSOTSup, 189; Sheffield: Sheffield Academic Press, 1995), pp. 164-79 for a full discussion of Smith's views on the asherah.

5.   See, for example, *UT* 19.428 and the references 1.6; 3.40; 49.I.12, 16, 199, 25; V.1; 51.I.15, 22; III.25, 27; IV.49; V.64, etc.

6.   The transformation of the early 'th' (*ṯ*) to the later 'sh' (*š*) is a well attested change (cf., e.g., F.M. Cross, *Canaanite Myth and Hebrew Epic: Essays in the History of the Religion of Israel* [Cambridge, MA: Harvard University Press, 1973], pp. 52-53 n. 36). Similarly, the final *h* is a typical Hebrew feminine singular suffix, and is to be considered a normal adaptation of the Ugaritic feminine name.

7.   Most modern scholars hold this view, albeit with some differences. See, for example, Cross, *Canaanite Myth*; J. Day, 'Asherah in the Hebrew Bible and Northwest Semitic Literature', *JBL* 105 (1986), pp. 385-408; W.G. Dever, 'Recent Archaeological Confirmation of the Cult of Asherah in Ancient Israel', *Hebrew Studies* 23 (1982), pp. 37-44; W.G. Dever, 'Asherah, Consort of Yahweh? New Evidence from Kuntillet 'Ajrûd', *BASOR* 255 (1984), pp. 21-37; J.A. Emerton, 'New Light on Israelite Religion: The Implications of the Inscriptions from Kuntillet 'Ajrud', *ZAW* 94 (1982), pp. 2-20; D.N. Freedman, 'Yahweh of Samaria and His Asherah', *BA* 50 (1987), pp. 241-49; J.M. Hadley, 'Some Drawings and Inscriptions on Two Pithoi from Kuntillet 'Ajrud', *VT* 37 (1987), pp. 180-213; Z. Meshel, *Kuntillet 'Ajrud: A Religious Centre from the Time of the Judaean Monarchy on the Border of Sinai* (Israel Museum Catalogue, 175; Jerusalem: The Israel Museum, 1978); Z. Meshel, 'Did Yahweh Have a Consort?', *BARev* 5.2 (1979), pp. 24-35; S.M. Olyan, *Asherah and the Cult of Yahweh in Israel* (SBLMS, 34; Atlanta: Scholars

notably Lipiński and Lemaire, believe that *asherah* in the Hebrew Bible was not a goddess at all but solely an object (either some type of wooden image, sanctuary, grove or living tree).[8]

Evidence from Khirbet el-Qom and Kuntillet ʿAjrud

The discovery within the last 25 years of the inscriptions from Khirbet el-Qom and Kuntillet ʿAjrud has raised new questions concerning the role that the *asherah* played in Israelite religion. I will examine the finds from these two sites first, together with the ornate cult stand from Taanach, before turning to the biblical material.

Khirbet el-Qom is located about 13 kilometers west of Hebron, and lies in the foothills between the Judaean mountains and the coastal plain (grid ref. 1465-1045).[9] The inscription (see Fig. 1) was found in

Press, 1988); R. Patai, 'The Goddess Asherah', *JNES* 24 (1965), pp. 37-52; R. Patai, *The Hebrew Goddess* (New York: Ktav, 1967); Reed, *The Asherah*; and M.S. Smith, *The Early History of God: Yahweh and the Other Deities in Ancient Israel* (San Francisco: Harper & Row, 1990), to mention but a few.

8.   Reed, *The Asherah*, includes an excellent summary of this position up to the time of his writing. For recent scholars who hold this view see Lipiński, 'The Goddess Aṯirat', pp. 101-19; and A. Lemaire, 'Les inscriptions de Khirbet el-Qôm et l'Ashérah de YHWH', *RB* 84 (1977), pp. 595-608; A. Lemaire, 'Date et origine des inscriptions Hébraïques et Phéniciennes de Kuntillet ʿAjrud', *Studi epigrafici e linguistici* 1 (1984), pp. 131-43 and A. Lemaire, 'Who or What Was Yahweh's Asherah?', *BARev* 10.6 (1984), pp. 42-51.

9.   For discussions of the site and inscription at Khirbet el-Qom, see S. Ahituv, *Handbook of Ancient Hebrew Inscriptions from the Period of the First Commonwealth and the Beginning of the Second Commonwealth* (Jerusalem: Keter, 1992 [Hebrew]); G.I. Davies, *Ancient Hebrew Inscriptions: Corpus and Concordance* (Cambridge: Cambridge University Press, 1991); W.G. Dever, 'Iron Age Epigraphic Material from the Area of Khirbet el-Kôm', *HUCA* 40-41 (1970), pp. 139-204; W.G. Dever, 'Inscriptions from Khirbet el-Kom', *Qadmoniot* 4 (1971), pp. 90-92 (Hebrew); W.G. Dever, 'el-Qôm, Khirbet', in M. Avi-Yonah and E. Stern (eds.), *Encyclopedia of Archaeological Excavations in the Holy Land* (4 vols.; Jerusalem: Israel Exploration Society and Massada Press, 1978), IV, pp. 976-77; W.G. Dever, 'Qôm, Khirbet el-', in E. Stern (ed.), *The New Encyclopedia of Archaeological Excavations in the Holy Land* (Jerusalem: Israel Exploration Society, 1993), IV, pp. 1233-35; G. Garbini, 'Su un'iscrizione ebraica da Khirbet el-Kom', *AION* NS 38 (1978), pp. 191-93; J.M. Hadley, 'The Khirbet el-Qom Inscription', *VT* 37 (1987), pp. 50-62; R. Hestrin, 'First Temple and Persian Periods', in E. Carmon (ed.), *Inscriptions Reveal* (Israel Museum Catalogue, 100; Jerusalem: The Israel Museum, 1972 [Hebrew]); K. Jaroš, *Hundert Inschriften aus Kanaan und Israel: Für den Hebräischunterricht bearbeitet* (Fribourg: Verlag Schweizerisches Katholisches Bibelwerk, 1982); K. Jaroš, 'Zur Inschrift Nr. 3 von Ḥirbet el-Qôm', *Biblische Notizen* 19 (1982), pp. 31-40; O. Kaiser *et al.*, *Texte aus der Umwelt des alten Testaments* (*TUAT*;

364   *Reading the Bible*

a burial cave near the site, and has been dated to around 750 BCE.[10]
Because of the poor quality of the rock upon which it was engraved,
the inscription is quite difficult to read. It consists of four main lines,
with two fragmentary lines at the bottom. The inscription appears to
read:

1. אריהו. העשר. כתבה
2. ברכ. אריהו. ליהוה
3. ומצריה לאשרתה הושעלה
4. לאניהו
5. לאשרתה
6. ולא??רהה

1.   Uriyahu the rich wrote it.
2.   Blessed be Uriyahu by Yahweh
3.   (and) by his *asherah*, for from his enemies he has saved him.[11]

Gütersloh: Gerd Mohn, 1982–); O. Keel, (ed.), *Monotheismus im Alten Israel und seiner Umwelt* (BibB, 14; Fribourg: Verlag Schweizerisches Katholisches Bibelwerk, 1980); Lemaire, 'Les inscriptions'; A. Lemaire, *Les écoles et la formation de la Bible dans l'ancien Israël* (OBO, 39; Fribourg: Editions universitaires; Göttingen: Vandenhoeck & Ruprecht, 1981); B. Margalit, 'Some Observations on the Inscription and Drawing from Khirbet el-Qôm', *VT* 39 (1989), pp. 371-78; P.D. Miller, Jr, 'Psalms and Inscriptions', in J.A. Emerton (ed.), *Congress Volume: Vienna 1980* (VTSup, 32; Leiden: Brill, 1981), pp. 311-32; S. Mittmann, 'Die Grabinschrift des Sängers Uriahu', *ZDPV* 97 (1981), pp. 139-52; J. Naveh, 'Graffiti and Dedications', *BASOR* 235 (1979), pp. 27-30; R. North, 'Yahweh's Asherah', in M.P. Horgan and P.J. Kobelski (eds.), *To Touch the Text: Biblical and Related Studies in Honor of Joseph A. Fitzmyer* (New York: Crossroad, 1989), pp. 118-37; M. O'Connor, 'The Poetic Inscription from Khirbet el-Qôm', *VT* 37 (1987), pp. 224-30; Olyan, *Asherah*; F. Scagliavini, 'Osservazioni sulle Iscrizioni di Kuntillet 'Ağrud', *RSO* 63 (1989), pp. 199-212; S. Schroer, 'Zur Deutung der Hand unter der Grabinschrift von Chirbet el Qôm', *UF* 15 (1983), pp. 191-99; W.H. Shea, 'The Khirbet el-Qom Tomb Inscription Again', *VT* 40 (1990), pp. 110-16; K.A.D. Smelik, *Behouden Schrift: historische documenten uit het oude Israël* (Baarn: Ten Have, 1984); *Writings from Ancient Israel: A Handbook of Historical and Religious Documents* (trans. G.I. Davies; Louisville: Westminster/John Knox Press, 1991); J.H. Tigay, *You Shall Have No Other Gods: Israelite Religion in the Light of Hebrew Inscriptions* (Harvard Semitic Studies, 31; Atlanta: Scholars Press, 1986) and Z. Zevit, 'The Khirbet el-Qôm Inscription Mentioning a Goddess', *BASOR* 255 (1984), pp. 39-47, among others.

  10.   Lemaire, 'Les inscriptions', p. 603 and Dever, 'Iron Age', p. 165; however, Dever states in n. 53 that Cross prefers a date closer to 700 BCE; and see also Olyan, *Asherah*, p. 23, who follows Cross.

  11.   Literally 'for from his enemies by his (YHWH's) *asherah* he (YHWH) has saved him'. Shea, 'Khirbet el-Qom', p. 112; and R.S. Hess, 'Yahweh and His Asherah? Epigraphic Evidence for Religious Pluralism in Old Testament Times', in A. Clarke and B.W. Winter (eds.), *One God, One Lord in a World of Religious Pluralism* (Cambridge: Tyndale House, 1991), pp. 5-33 (24-25) prefer to translate

4.   by Oniyahu
5.   by his *asherah*
6.   and by his a[she]rah

Figure 1. Khirbet el-Qom inscription no. 3. The author's own copy.

As can be seen, the fourth line bears the name Oniyahu, which may indicate the engraver. Lines 5 and 6 may contain further references to *asherah*, but only a few letters have been preserved. Also engraved into the rock, below the main part of the inscription, is something that appears to be a hand. It is approximately the size of a small human hand, probably indicating the right hand pointing downwards with the palm facing outward from the surface of the rock. The thumb is poorly carved, but that may be a result of the

ומצריה as pertaining to 'Egyptian'; see a similar tentative suggestion in Hadley, 'Khirbet el-Qom'; cf. also the bibliography in n. 9. For a full discussion of this inscription including this view see J.M. Hadley, *Evidence for a Hebrew Goddess: The Cult of Asherah in Ancient Israel and Judah* (Oriental Publications Series; Cambridge: Cambridge University Press, forthcoming).

fractured state of the soft, chalky stone. It may be that the hand is indicative of some sort of memorial, serving as an everlasting remembrance before God.[12] The practice of carving hands on steles or standing stones, in gestures of adoration, is not unknown in the ancient Near East.[13] This symbol would be especially appropriate to tomb inscriptions, as the supplicant would want to be remembered before the God of his or her salvation. An alternative, or perhaps additional, interpretation could be that the hand served some sort of apotropaic function. Often amulets are found with depictions of hands, intended to ward evil away from the wearer.[14] Therefore, the hand may have also been intended to 'guard' the tomb of the deceased.[15]

There is thus in this inscription a reference to Yahweh and his *asherah*. But what does *asherah* mean here? Does it refer to the goddess or to her wooden symbol? From the context it could be either. The main issue is the Hebrew word that is translated 'by his *asherah*'. The possessive pronoun 'his' is affixed directly to the noun *'asherah'*. The fact that pronominal suffixes are not attested affixed to personal names in biblical Hebrew is the strongest objection to considering *asherah* as the name of the goddess.[16] It therefore appears that the

12.   יד is sometimes used in the Hebrew Bible in the sense of a monument (1 Sam. 15.12; 2 Sam. 18.18; 1 Chron. 18.3; Isa. 56.5). 1 Sam. 15.12 states יד והנה מציב לו. This may be a figurative expression for a monument or stele. Or could this mean that Saul actually carved a hand on the stele?

13.   Cf., for example, the stele found at Hazor; Y. Yadin *et al.*, *Hazor I: An Account of the First Season of Excavations, 1955* (Jerusalem: Magnes, 1958), p. 89 and pl. 29.1.2.

14.   A. Grenfell, 'The Iconography of Bes and of Phoenician Bes-hand Scarabs', *Proceedings of the Society of Biblical Archaeology* 24 (1902), pp. 21-40, fig. 26 cites a porcelain scarab from the Ashmolean Museum of a sacred hand being worshipped by a monkey. She states (p. 38) that this form passed into an amulet with apotropaic force at an early date.

15.   This is the interpretation that Keel, *Monotheismus*, gives to the hand, citing the use of the hand on scarabs and magic texts from Egypt (caption, p. 172). Although the article is by F. Stolz ('Monotheismus in Israel', in Keel (ed.), *Monotheismus*, pp. 143-89), the captions were written by Keel. For additional discussions and interpretations of the engraved hand see Mittmann, 'Die Grabinschrift'; Schroer, 'Zur Deutung'; and Shea, 'Khirbet el-Qom'.

16.   This case does occur, however, in Ugaritic. *PRU* II, R.S. 16.394 line 39 reads *l.'aṯrty* 'for my Athirat' (cf. *UT* 1002:39). Presumably it is El who is speaking but, unfortunately, this occurs in a damaged part of the tablet, and it is difficult to follow the context of the story. The phrase may be repeated again in line 60, but there only *'aṯr* is preserved. Some scholars believe that *'aṯrt* can be used of a goddess in general terms (cf. Gibson's [1978] translation of *CTA* 3.A.i.15; and

wooden image or symbol of the goddess is meant.[17] There is thus an inscription that connects the symbol of Asherah with Yahweh worship. This supports the prohibition found in Deut. 16.21 that forbids the planting of an *asherah* of any type of wood beside the altar of Yahweh. Evidently it was common to find *asherah* poles in sanctuaries dedicated to Yahweh. In fact, because of its association with the altar of Yahweh, the *asherah* could be regarded as 'his *asherah*'. In the case of this inscription Yahweh remains the subject of the blessing

---

B. Margalit, 'The Meaning and Significance of Asherah', *VT* 40 [1990], pp. 264-97), just as *'il* can be used generally for a god. This passage may help to support that view. However, it is known that other Semitic languages have suffixes on proper nouns. Cf., for example, Dietrich and Loretz, *'Jahwe und seine Aschera'*, pp. 98-101, where they note that *KTU* 1.43:13; *KTU* 2.31:41 and *KTU* 1.17 I 26.44 have pronominal suffixes attached to (presumably) personal names; and G.R. Driver, 'Reflections on Recent Articles', *JBL* 73 (1954), pp. 125-36 (125) where he refers to 'our Keret' in *KTU* 1.16 I 39 (his K II.i.39), as well as pronominal suffixes on proper names in Akkadian, Arabic and Ethiopic (and cf. G.R. Driver, 'Supposed Arabisms in the Old Testament', *JBL* 55 [1936], pp. 101-20). Nevertheless, the mere fact that this use is attested in Ugaritic does not mean that it will occur in Hebrew. Emerton ('New Light') notes that this fact 'is not altered by G.R. Driver's evidence for such a use of a suffix in other Semitic languages…the use of a suffix with a personal name is not in accordance with Hebrew idiom as far as we know it, and it is unwise to interpret the newly-found inscriptions in such a way unless there is no satisfactory alternative' (pp. 14-15). See also A. Angerstorfer, 'Ašerah als "consort of Jahwe" oder Aširtah?', *Biblische Notizen* 17 (1982), pp. 7-16; Zevit, 'Khirbet el-Qôm' and Hess, 'Yahweh and His Asherah?', who all read *'šrth* as only the name of the goddess, without any pronominal suffix, and vocalize it as Aširtah (Angerstorfer) or Asherata (Zevit and Hess). This vocalization is also suggested as a possibility in North, 'Yahweh's Asherah'. For opposition to this vocalization, see H.P. Müller, 'Kolloquialsprache und Volksreligion in den Inschriften von *Kuntillet 'Aǧrūd* und *Ḥirbet el-Qōm'*, *ZAH* 5 (1992), pp. 15-51.

17.   Lipiński, 'The Goddess Aṭirat'; Perlman, 'Asherah and Astarte' and others prefer to interpret *asherah* here and in the Hebrew Bible as a shrine. This interpretation is possible, as the term is known to mean 'sanctuary' in other Semitic languages and, indeed, may even be the appropriate translation of the recently discovered inscriptions at Tel Miqne (cf. Anonymous, 'Cultic Inscriptions Found in Ekron', in 'Arti-facts: News, Notes, and Reports from the Institutes', *BA* 53 [1990], p. 232), although S. Gitin ('Seventh Century B.C.E. Cultic Elements at Ekron', in A. Biran and J. Aviram [eds.], *Biblical Archaeology Today 1990: Proceedings of the Second International Congress on Biblical Archaeology: Jerusalem, June–July 1990* [Jerusalem: Israel Exploration Society, 1993], pp. 248-58) interprets this inscription as referring to the goddess Asherah. It is also possible that *asherah* here may be a Phoenician loan word (see the discussion on the 'Ajrud inscriptions in Hadley, *Hebrew Goddess*). However, to date this usage is nowhere attested in Hebrew, and it is better to use an attested meaning if there is one.

and salvation, but this is carried out by his *asherah*; perhaps the supplicant prayed to Yahweh before the *asherah* in the shrine, or by offering prayers to Yahweh by means of the *asherah* which is therefore mentioned in the inscription. Alternatively, the *asherah* may have been the hypostasis of Yahweh's benevolence and succor, and so represented the desired help.[18] Whichever interpretation is accepted, evidently at this time (mid-eighth century BCE) Yahweh and *asherah* were considered a 'paired set' and appear in poetic inscriptions in parallel as such.

Some additional inscriptions that mention Yahweh and *asherah* have been discovered at Kuntillet 'Ajrud, in northern Sinai, about 50 kilometers south of Kadesh-barnea (grid ref. 0940-9560).[19] These

18.   Angerstorfer, 'Ašerah', notes that a translation of the inscriptions with 'by his holy tree' makes the *asherah* into a hypostasis through which Yahweh blesses (p. 10). See also P.K. McCarter, Jr, 'Aspects of the Religion of the Israelite Monarchy: Biblical and Epigraphic Data', in P.D. Miller, Jr, P.D. Hanson, and S.D. McBride (eds.), *Ancient Israelite Religion* (Philadelphia: Fortress Press, 1987), pp. 137-55 (147-49).

19.   For the site and inscriptions at Kuntillet 'Ajrud see Ahituv, *Handbook*; B. Bayer, 'The Finds That Could Not Be', *BARev* 8.1 (1982), pp. 20-33; P. Beck, 'The Drawings from Ḥorvat Teiman (Kuntillet 'Ajrud)', *Tel Aviv* 9 (1982), pp. 3-68; A. Catastini, 'Le inscrizioni di Kuntillet 'Ajrud e il profetismo', *AION NS* 42 (1982), pp. 127-34; A. Catastini, 'Note di epigrafia ebraica I–II', *Henoch* 6 (1984), pp. 129-38; A. Catastini, 'Profeti tra epigrafia ed epistolografia', *Egitto e Vicino Oriente* 13 (1990), pp. 143-47; D.A. Chase, 'A Note on an Inscription from Kuntillet 'Ajrud', *BASOR* 246 (1982), pp. 63-67; Davies, *Ancient Hebrew Inscriptions*; Dever, 'Asherah'; Emerton, 'New Light'; G.G. Garner, 'Kuntillet 'Ajrud: An Intriguing Site in Sinai', *Buried History* 14.2 (1978), pp. 1-16; M. Gilula, 'To Yahweh Shomron and his Asherah', *Shnaton* 3 (1978–79), pp. 129-37 (Hebrew); J. Gunneweg, I. Perlman, and Z. Meshel, 'The Origin of the Pottery of Kuntillet 'Ajrud', *IEJ* 35 (1985), pp. 270-83; Hadley, 'Some Drawings'; J.M. Hadley, 'Kuntillet 'Ajrud: Religious Centre or Desert Way Station?', *PEQ* 125 (1993), pp. 115-24; Hess, 'Yahweh and His Asherah?'; Jaroš, *Hundert Inschriften*; Kaiser *et al.*, *Texte aus der Umwelt*; Keel, *Monotheismus*; O. Keel and C. Uehlinger, *Göttinnen, Götter und Gottessymbole* (Freiburg: Herder, 1992); Lemaire, 'Date et origine'; Margalit, 'The Meaning and Significance'; McCarter, 'Aspects of the Religion'; Z. Meshel, 'Kuntillat 'Ajrud: An Israelite Site on the Sinai Border', *Qadmoniot* 9 (1976), pp. 119-24 (Hebrew); Z. Meshel, 'A Lyre Player Drawing from Ajrud in Sinai', *Tatzlil* 17 (1977), pp. 109-10 (Hebrew); Z. Meshel, 'Kuntilet-Ajrud', *RB* 84 (1977), pp. 270-73; Z. Meshel, 'Kuntilat 'Ajrud, 1975–1976', *IEJ* 27 (1977), pp. 52-53; Z Meshel, *Kuntillet 'Ajrud: A Religious Centre*; Z. Meshel, 'Kuntillet 'Ajrûd: An Israelite Religious Center in Northern Sinai', *Expedition* 20 (1978), pp. 50-54; Z. Meshel, 'Consort?'; Z. Meshel, 'Kuntillat-Ajrud', *Le Monde de la Bible* 10 (1979), pp. 32-36; Z. Meshel, 'A Religious Center at Kuntillet 'Ajrud, Sinai', in A. Biran (ed.), *Temples and High Places in Biblical Times* (Jerusalem: Nelson Glueck School of Biblical

inscriptions were painted on large storage jars, together with many drawings of animals:[20] a cow and calf; two caprids flanking a stylized tree; a procession of worshippers; and a seated lyre player and two standing figures (see Fig. 2). The inscription of most interest here is the one that is written above the standing figures. Most of this inscription can be seen on Fig. 2. This inscription, as far as it has been preserved, reads:

אמר. א...ה...כ. אמר. ליהל[לאל] וליועשה. ו...ברכת. אתכמ. ליהוה. ליהוה. שמרנ. ולאשרתה.

'X says: say to Yehal[lel'el] and to Yo'asah and [to Z]: I bless you by Yahweh of Samaria and by his *asherah*.'[21]

Archaeology of Hebrew Union College, 1981), p. 161; Z. Meshel, 'The Israelite Religious Centre of Kuntillet 'Ajrud', *Bulletin of the Anglo-Israel Archaeological Society* (1982–83), pp. 52-55; Z. Meshel, 'The Inscriptions of Kuntillet 'Ajrud', communication given at the 12th Congress of the International Organization for the Study of the Old Testament in Jerusalem, 1986; Z. Meshel, 'The Israelite Religious Centre of Ajrud, Sinai', in A. Bonanno (ed.), *Archaeology and Fertility Cult in the Ancient Mediterranean* (Amsterdam: Grüner, 1986), pp. 237-40; Z. Meshel, 'Teman, Horvat', in E. Stern (ed.), *The New Encyclopedia of Archaeological Excavations in the Holy Land* (Jerusalem: Israel Exploration Society, 1993), IV, pp. 1458-64; Z. Meshel and C. Meyers, 'The Name of God in the Wilderness of Zin', *BA* 39 (1976), pp. 6-10; Naveh, 'Graffiti and Dedications'; North, 'Yahweh's Asherah'; B. Otzen, 'Indskrifterne fra Kuntillet Ajrud: Tekst—Form—Funktion', *SEÅ* 54 (1989), pp. 151-64; S. Singer, 'Cache of Hebrew and Phoenician Inscriptions Found in the Desert', *BARev* 2.1 (1976), pp. 33-34; Smelik, *Behouden Schrift*; M. Weinfeld, 'A Sacred Site of the Monarchic Period', *Shnaton* 4 (1980), pp. 280-84 (Hebrew); M. Weinfeld, 'Additions to the Inscriptions of 'Ajrud', *Shnaton* 5–6 (1982), pp. 237-39 (Hebrew); M. Weinfeld, 'Kuntillet 'Ajrud Inscriptions and their Significance', *Studi epigrafici e linguistici* 1 (1984), pp. 121-30 and G. Wilhelm, 'Kuntilet 'Ağrud', *AfO* 26 (1978–79), p. 213, among others.

20. Many other inscriptions were discovered at 'Ajrud as well. Most of these are letters incised on the pottery, some before and some after firing; inscriptions incised on stone vessels; or inscriptions written in black or red ink on plaster. For these inscriptions see Meshel, *Kuntillet 'Ajrud: A Religious Centre*; Meshel, 'Teman, Horvat'; Catastini, 'Le inscrizioni'; Catastini, 'Profeti'; Weinfeld, 'Kuntillet 'Ajrud Inscriptions'; Davies, *Ancient Hebrew Inscriptions*; Ahituv, *Handbook*; Keel and Uehlinger, *Göttinnen*; Hadley, 'Kuntillet 'Ajrud' and Hadley, *Hebrew Goddess*. For the drawings see Beck, 'The Drawings from Horvat Teiman'; Hadley, 'Some Drawings'; Keel and Uehlinger, *Göttinnen* and Hadley, *Hebrew Goddess*.

21. For this and other readings see Ahituv, *Handbook*; Davies, *Ancient Hebrew Inscriptions*; Emerton, 'New Light'; Gilula, 'To Yahweh Shomron'; Hadley, 'Some Drawings'; Keel and Uehlinger, *Göttinnen*; Lemaire, 'Date et origine'; Meshel, 'Inscriptions'; Weinfeld, 'A Sacred Site' and Weinfeld, 'Kuntillet 'Ajrud Inscriptions', among others.

Figure 2.   Pithos A from Kuntillet ʻAjrud. A close-up view of the two Bes
             figures and lyre player, showing the overlap with inscription
             no. 1 (cf. Meshel, Israel Museum Catalogue, 175; [1978]).

The inscription appears to date to the mid-ninth to mid-eighth century BCE.[22] The fact that this inscription is found with these other figures has tantalized scholars. Many scholars have taken the inscriptions to be a commentary on the drawings, and so have sought to identify Yahweh and Asherah with the standing figures.[23] Gilula believes that the left figure is Yahweh and the right one is Asherah, mainly because of the depiction of the breasts.[24] He then has a problem with the appendage between the legs of this figure, which he

22.   Meshel, 'Consort?', p. 34; and see Olyan, *Asherah*, p. 32, who favors a date ca. 800 BCE on the basis of a similarity to the Samaria ostraca. McCarter, 'Aspects of the Religion', p. 138, assigns a date of ca. 790 BCE.

23.   For this view see Gilula, 'To Yahweh Shomron'; M.D. Coogan, 'Canaanite Origins and Lineage: Reflections on the Religion of Ancient Israel', in P.D. Miller, Jr, P.D. Hanson and S.D. McBride (eds.), *Ancient Israelite Religion* (Philadelphia: Fortress Press, 1987), pp. 115-24 (119) and McCarter, 'Aspects of the Religion', pp. 146-47, among others.

24.   Gilula, 'To Yahweh Shomron', pp. 130-33.

takes to be a later addition. However, most scholars identify both standing figures with the god Bes, who is well known from Egyptian iconography.[25] Bes has leonine features, often a beard and occasionally is shown with breasts (there is even a female Beset, with pendulous breasts). Bes often wears a lion skin, and is shown with either a phallus or the tail of the lion skin between his legs. He is usually depicted in an apotropaic function, and multiple figures of him can easily be found in the same place.[26] It is therefore best to identify both the standing figures with the god Bes.

Other scholars, notably Dever, have suggested that the standing figures are Bes figures, but that the seated lyre player is Asherah.[27] There are several difficulties with this view.[28] First, the lyre player is turned away from the other figures, and is painted on a different level. This is most uncommon in iconography of the period, which usually places all figures on the same plane and with the same general orientation to the scene.[29] Secondly, the hairstyle of the seated figure, which to twentieth-century eyes looks like a female hairstyle, is a common Egyptian male wig.[30] Thirdly, the lyre player's garments could be male garments as easily as female ones.[31] Thus it is not even proved that the lyre player is female. However, even if it be female, there are still problems with this identification. If the lyre player were Asherah, why is she depicted with Bes and not Yahweh? Asherah also has no known connection with music and, even if she did, why would she, as a major goddess, be playing for a minor deity such as Bes? Bes, on the other hand, *is* associated with music and dancing;[32] and so, if the lyre player is to be included in the scene, it is more likely

25. Stolz, 'Monotheismus in Israel', p. 170; Beck, 'The Drawings from Ḥorvat Teiman', p. 29; Dever, 'Asherah', p. 25; Lemaire, 'Who or What?', p. 46 and Hadley, 'Some Drawings', among others.

26. For a comprehensive study of the iconography of Bes see V. Wilson, 'The Iconography of Bes with Particular Reference to the Cypriot Evidence', *Levant* 7 (1975), pp. 77-103, as well as H. Altenmüller, 'Bes', in W. Helck and E. Otto (eds.), *Lexikon der Ägyptologie* (Wiesbaden: Otto Harrassowitz, 1975), I, cols. 720-24. For the female Beset, see H. Altenmüller, 'Beset', in W. Helck and E. Otto (eds.), *Lexikon der Ägyptologie* (Wiesbaden: Otto Harrassowitz, 1975), I, col. 731.

27. Dever, 'Asherah'.

28. Cf. Hadley, 'Some Drawings'.

29. I owe this information to Mr John Ray of Cambridge University. I wish to thank him for discussing Egyptian art and iconography with me, especially in reference to the lyre player.

30. I owe this information to Mr John Ray of Cambridge University.

31. Cf. Hadley, 'Some Drawings'.

32. Wilson, 'The Iconography of Bes', p. 80.

that it is a young prince or court musician who is accompanying Bes. Finally, there are three figures in the drawings and only two agents of blessing mentioned in the inscription, which overlaps one of the figures.[33] If the inscription was intended to be a commentary on the drawing, it is unlikely that the author would allow the text to be distorted by writing over the drawing, or that the artist would obliterate part of the commentary with the drawing. If the inscription and the drawing were unrelated, however, such an overlap would not be worrisome.

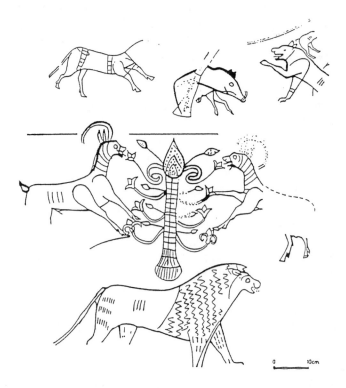

Figure 3.   Pithos A from Kuntillet 'Ajrud. The stylized tree is flanked by two caprids, with a striding lion beneath. Four other animal figures are shown along the shoulder of the vessel (cf. Beck, *Tel Aviv 9* [1982]).

33.   Beck, 'The Drawings from Ḥorvat Teiman', believes that the second Bes figure with the headdress that overlaps the inscription was added at a later time. This would leave two figures to go with the inscription, but it is clear that the one figure is a representation of Bes and the other figure cannot be Asherah on the basis of the argument outlined above and discussed more fully in Hadley, 'Some Drawings'.

And so it appears that the drawings are not related to the inscription. The inscription is a standard letter formula, and so the author may have been merely practising his or her letter writing skills.[34] Moreover, there is the same problem in this inscription as in the Khirbet el-Qom one: that the pronominal suffix is directly attached to the noun *asherah*.[35] Therefore, the inscription probably refers to the wooden symbol of the goddess.

Having said that, it is possible that Asherah is depicted on the pithos after all, not in the scene just examined, but rather on the other side of the vessel (see Fig. 3). Depicted here is a tree flanked by caprids. As will be seen below, the symbol of Asherah in the Hebrew Bible is some sort of tree or pole. Furthermore, the tree in some ancient Near Eastern depictions is often found interchanged with a naked woman, which seems to indicate that the tree equals the woman (presumably the goddess) and vice versa.[36] This grouping of

34.   Cf. A. Dupont-Sommer, 'Le syncretisme religieux des Juifs d'Éléphantine d'après un ostracon Araméen inédit', *RHR* 130 (1945), pp. 17-28; Müller, 'Kolloquialsprache'; and A. Lemaire, 'Abécédaires et exercices d'écolier en épigraphie nord-ouest sémitique', *JA* 266 (1978), pp. 221-35 (233), who cites many of these greeting and blessing formulae and discusses them at length.

35.   See the discussion above as well as Emerton, 'New Light' and Hadley, 'Khirbet el-Qom'.

36.   Cf. U. Winter, *Frau und Göttin: Exegetische und ikonographische Studien zum weiblichen Gottesbild im Alten Israel und in dessen Umwelt* (OBO, 53; Fribourg: Editions universitaires; Göttingen: Vandenhoeck & Ruprecht, 1983), Abb. 143, where a naked goddess is depicted with a tree flanked by two caprids; and Abb. 144, where a tree is depicted with a naked goddess flanked by two caprids. Also, Hartmann (B. Hartmann, 'Monotheismus in Mesopotamien?', in Keel, *Monotheismus*, pp. 49-81, Abb. 1; and cf. Winter, *Frau und Göttin*, Abb. 458-59) presents a cylinder seal on which a vegetation goddess is portrayed with a stylized tree behind her, representing her image. That this shows the goddess and her image is made clear by the fact that they both have the same style of branches. Several other Egyptian seals depict the personification of the tree as a goddess. Winter, *Frau und Göttin*, presents many of these examples of trees as goddesses (Abb. 460-66). In fact, one can clearly see this idea in the depictions. The first example portrays the goddess Nut standing in front of a tree, with the word 'Nut' written above the head of the goddess and on the trunk of the tree (and see O. Keel, *Die Welt der altorientalischen Bildsymbolik und das Alte Testament: Am Beispiel der Psalmen* [Zürich: Benziger Verlag; Neukirchen–Vluyn: Neukirchener Verlag]; ET: *The Symbolism of the Biblical World* [trans. T.J. Hallett; New York: Seabury, 1978], fig. 255; and Winter, *Frau und Göttin*, Abb. 466). The second example is that of the goddess forming the trunk of a tree (Keel, *Die Welt der altorientalischen Bildsymbolik*, fig. 254; and Winter, *Frau und Göttin*, Abb. 462; cf. also Abb. 463). The third example is that of the goddess in the form of a tree, nurturing pharaoh. The only 'female' attributes of the tree at all are the arm that cradles pharaoh and the breast that

naked goddess and caprids or tree and caprids is often depicted above a striding lion which appears to be Asherah's animal.[37] Here on the storage jar the tree and caprids are drawn above a striding lion that is facing to the right, usually the way that Asherah's lion faces.[38]

nurtures him; otherwise the form is totally that of a tree (Keel, *Die Welt der altorientalischen Bildsymbolik*, fig. 253, and Winter, *Frau und Göttin*, Abb. 460; cf. Abb. 464). The final example of this personification is that of a tree alone, with no evident sign of divinity except that it is flanked by cherubim whose task it is to 'guard' the god (Keel, *Die Welt der altorientalischen Bildsymbolik*, fig. 190). Another interesting depiction is found in Keel, *Die Welt der altorientalischen Bildsymbolik* (fig. 180), who presents a picture of a tree in a vase on an altar, indicating an embodiment of the deity. See also the ewer discovered at Lachish (Tell ed-Duweir), which has an inscription mentioning 'the goddess' (*'lt*) written directly above a stylized tree (cf. J.J. Obermann, *The Archaic Inscriptions from Lachish* [JAOS Supplement, 2; Baltimore: The American Oriental Society, 1938], pp. 8-17; T.H. Gaster, 'The Archaic Inscriptions', in O. Tufnell, C.H. Inge, and L. Harding [eds.], *Lachish II: The Fosse Temple* [London: Oxford University Press, 1940], pp. 49-54; D. Diringer, 'Duweir Ewer', in O. Tufnell [ed.], *Lachish IV: Text* [London: Oxford University Press, 1958], p. 130; E. Puech, 'The Canaanite Inscriptions of Lachish and Their Religious Background', *Tel Aviv* 13 [1986], pp. 13-25; R. Hestrin, 'The Lachish Ewer and the 'Asherah', *IEJ* 37 [1987], pp. 212-23 and Hadley, *Hebrew Goddess*).

37.   This association of Asherah with a lion would be strengthened if Asherah were to be identified with Qudshu, as many scholars believe. Cross, *Canaanite Myth*, p. 33 (among others) believes that *qdš* in CTA 14.iv.197 (as well as 16.i.11 and 22) is an epithet for Athirat at Ugarit. He cites the 'Winchester stele' published by I.E.S. Edwards, 'A Relief of Qudshu–Astarte–Anath in the Winchester College Collection', *JNES* 14 (1955), pp. 49-51 as support for this view. This stele depicts a naked goddess wearing a 'Hathor-type' wig and standing on a lion, while holding serpents. An inscription in hieroglyphs reads 'Qudshu–Astarte–Anath'. Cross believes that Qudshu is here the equivalent of Hebrew Asherah and Canaanite Athirat (*Canaanite Myth*, p. 34; and cf., e.g., W.F. Albright, *Yahweh and the Gods of Canaan* [London: Athlone Press, 1968], p. 106). In this he is enthusiastically followed by R.J. Pettey, *Asherah: Goddess of Israel* (American University Studies, Series VII [Theology and Religion], 74; New York: Peter Lang, 1990), p. 29; and Maier, *'Ašerah: Extrabiblical Evidence*, pp. 82-96, who includes a discussion on representations of naked female figurines that have been discovered both in Canaan and Egypt. Maier presents a strong case for the identification of Qudshu with Hebrew Asherah (Canaanite Athirat), if only for the sheer volume of comparisons. Yamashita, on the other hand, believes that the goddess represented on the Egyptian stele 'is a deity into which three goddesses have been fused, but who shows 'Anat's characteristics predominantly' ('The Goddess Asherah', p. 118). See also S.A. Wiggins, 'The Myth of Asherah: Lion Lady and Serpent Goddess', *UF* 23 (1991), pp. 383-94 and Wiggins, *A Reassessment of "Asherah"*, who agrees with Yamashita that Asherah is not necessarily to be identified with Qudshu (or represented by lions) on the Winchester stele or elsewhere.

38.   Cf. also Hestrin, 'The Lachish Ewer', who independently came to the same

It is possible that Israelite iconography in the eighth century BCE did not allow anthropomorphic portrayals of major gods, only minor ones, especially in terms of Yahweh. Mettinger has shown that Israelite Yahweh worship was basically aniconic.[39]

The Taanach Cult Stand

The final archaeological find to be examined here is an amazing discovery from Taanach, on the southern side of the Jezreel Valley. Here Lapp discovered in 1968 an ornate cultic stand, dated to the tenth century BCE (see Fig. 4).[40] Unfortunately the stand was discovered in

conclusion that this grouping represents the goddess Asherah.

    39.   Cf., for example, T.N.D. Mettinger, 'The Veto on Images and the Aniconic God in Ancient Israel', in H. Biezais (ed.), *Religious Symbols and their Functions* (Scripta Instituti Donneriani Aboensis, 10; Stockholm: Almqvist & Wiksell, 1979), pp. 15-29 and T.N.D. Mettinger, 'YHWH SABAOTH: The Heavenly King on the Cherubim Throne', in T. Ishida (ed.), *Studies in the Period of David and Solomon and Other Essays* (Winona Lake, IN: Eisenbrauns; Tokyo: Yamakawa-Shuppansha, 1982), pp. 109-38. This may explain in part the paucity of male figurines from Judah, as opposed to the hundreds of female figurines discovered. It is also not clear whether or not these female figurines are meant to portray a goddess or merely represent some aspect (perhaps fertility?) of a deity, either male or female. For discussions of these and other female figurines see W.F. Albright, 'Astarte Plaques and Figurines from Tell Beit Mirsim', in *Mélanges syriens offerts à Monsieur René Dussaud* (Paris: Geuthner, 1939), I, pp. 107-20; J.B. Pritchard, *Palestinian Figurines in Relation to Certain Goddesses Known through Literature* (American Oriental Series, 24; New York: Kraus, 1943); M.-T. Barrelet, *Figurines et reliefs en terre cuite de la Mésopotamie antique* (Bibliothèque Archéologique et Historique, 85; Paris: Geuthner, 1968), I; T.A. Holland, 'A Typological and Archaeological Study of Human and Animal Representations in the Plastic Art of Palestine During the Iron Age' (2 vols; DPhil. thesis, Oxford University, 1975); J.R. Engle, 'Pillar Figurines of Iron Age Israel and Asherah/Asherim' (PhD dissertation, University of Pittsburgh, 1979); M. Tadmor, 'Female Relief Figurines of Late Bronze Age Canaan', *Eretz-Israel* 15 (1981), pp. 79-83 (Hebrew); M. Tadmor, 'Female Cult Figurines in Late Canaan and Early Israel: Archaeological Evidence', in Ishida (ed.), *Studies*, pp. 139-73; M. Tadmor, 'Female Figurines in Canaan in the Late Bronze Age', *Qadmoniot* 57 (1982), pp. 2-10 (Hebrew); M.D. Fowler, 'Excavated Figurines: A Case for Identifying a Site as Sacred?', *ZAW* 97 (1985), pp. 333-44; S. Schroer, 'Die Zweiggöttin in Palästina/Israel', in M. Küchler and C. Uehlinger (eds.), *Jerusalem* (Novum Testamentum et Orbis Antiquus, 6; Freiburg: Universitats Verlag; Göttingen: Vandenhoeck & Ruprecht, 1987), pp. 201-25; and Hadley, *Hebrew Goddess*.

    40.   P.W. Lapp, 'The 1968 Excavations at Tell Taʻannek', *BASOR* 195 (1969), pp. 2-49; P.W. Lapp, 'A Ritual Incense Stand from Taanak', *Qadmoniot* 5 (1969), pp. 16-17 (Hebrew); and see Fig. 4; for color photographs of the stand cf., for

a cistern, and so it is impossible to know if it was actually used in a cultic context or not. However, the beings depicted on it are most extraordinary.

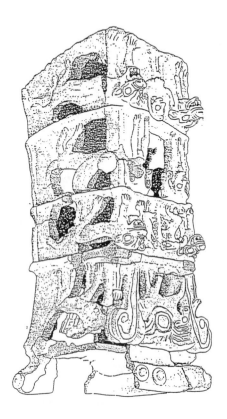

Figure 4.   Taanach cultic stand discovered by Lapp;
(cf. Lapp, *Qadmoniot* 5 [1969]).

example, Lapp, 'A Ritual Incense Stand', pl. 3; A.E. Glock, 'Taanach', in M. Avi-Yonah and E. Stern (eds.), *Encyclopedia of Archaeological Excavations in the Holy Land* (Jerusalem: Israel Exploration Society and Massada Press, 1978), IV, pp. 1138-47 (1142); C.H.J. de Geus, 'The Profile of an Israelite City', *BA* 49 (1986), pp. 224-27 (224); and L.F. DeVries, 'Cult Stands: A Bewildering Variety of Shapes and Sizes', *BARev* 13.4 (1987), pp. 26-37 (32), among others. For a full description of the remains from the tenth century BCE stratum see P.W. Lapp, 'The 1963 Excavation at Ta'annek', *BASOR* 173 (1964), pp. 4-44; P.W. Lapp, 'Taanach by the Waters of Megiddo', *BA* 30 (1967), pp. 2-27 and Lapp, 'The 1968 Excavations at Tell Ta'annek'; cf. also Glock, 'Taanach' (1978), and A.E. Glock, 'Taanach', in E. Stern (ed.), *The New Encyclopedia of Archaeological Excavations in the Holy Land* (Jerusalem: Israel Exploration Society, 1993), IV, pp. 1428-33.

The stand is made up of four tiers with human and animal representations.[41] On the lowest tier a naked female is standing *en face*, flanked by two lions. She appears to be grasping the lions by the ears.[42] In the next tier are two sphinxes with wings. No symbol of divinity has been preserved between them. It appears that the edges of the clay around this hole have been smoothed, and so it may be that a hole was intended to be in this position, with no other symbol. The next highest level again portrays two lions, identical to those on the bottom tier. However, in this case, a tree between two caprids is depicted instead of the naked female figure. The caprids are standing on their hind legs and eating (blossoms?) at the top of the tree. The top scene depicts a pair of voluted columns flanking a quadruped that is supporting a sun disk on its back. At the bases of the two columns are two smaller objects which may depict cultic stands. The sides of the vessel show the sides of the creatures (either lions or sphinxes) that are begun on the façade. On the top tier, on the sides behind the voluted columns, are winged sphinxes similar to those on

41. For discussions of the Taanach stand and descriptions of the site, see P. Beck, 'The Cult-Stands from Taanach: Aspects of the Iconographic Tradition of Early Iron Age Cult Objects in Palestine', in I. Finkelstein and N. Na'aman (eds.), *From Nomadism to Monarchy: Archaeological and Historical Aspects of Early Israel* (Jerusalem: Yad Izhak Ben-Zvi and Israel Exploration Society, 1994; Hebrew original [1990, pp. 417-46]), pp. 352-81; M. Dayagi-Mendels, 'Canaanite Cult Stand', in J.P. O'Neill (ed.), *Treasures of the Holy Land: Ancient Art from the Israel Museum* (New York: Metropolitan Museum of Art, 1986), pp. 161-63; DeVries, 'Cult Stands'; M.D. Fowler, 'Excavated Incense Burners: A Case for Identifying a Site as Sacred?', *PEQ* 117 (1985), pp. 25-29; Glock, 'Taanach' (1978) and Glock, 'Taanach' (1993); Hadley, *Hebrew Goddess*; R. Hestrin, 'The Cult Stand from Ta'anach and its Religious Background', in E. Lipiński (ed.), *Studia Phoenicia* 5 (Leuven: Peeters, 1987), pp. 61-77; Keel and Uehlinger, *Göttinnen*; Lapp, 'The 1963 Excavation'; Lapp, 'Taanach by the Waters of Megiddo'; Lapp, 'The 1968 Excavations'; Lapp, 'A Ritual Incense Stand'; S. Schroer, *In Israel gab es Bilder: Nachrichten von darstellender Kunst im Alten Testament* (OBO, 74; Fribourg: Editions universitaires; Göttingen: Vandenhoeck & Ruprecht, 1987); E. Sellin, *Tell Ta'annek* (Vienna: C. Gerold's Sohn, 1904); J.G. Taylor, 'Another Cult of Yahweh and Asherah?', communication given at the Annual Meeting of the Society of Biblical Literature in Boston, MA, 1987; J.G. Taylor, 'Yahweh and Asherah at Tenth Century Taanach', *Newsletter for Ugaritic Studies* 37 (1987), pp. 16-18 and J.G. Taylor, 'The Two Earliest Known Representations of Yahweh', in L. Eslinger and G. Taylor (eds.), *Ascribe to the Lord: Biblical and Other Studies in Memory of Peter C. Craigie* (JSOTSup, 67; Sheffield: JSOT Press, 1988), pp. 557-66.

42. However, Carole Fontaine, in a private communication, has expressed the opinion that the figure is not holding the lions' ears but is, rather, intended to be holding up a skirt—similar to depictions of the Hittite Shaushga.

the second level. The back of the stand is smooth and contains no depictions, merely two roughly square-shaped holes.[43]

Taylor[44] agrees with Yadin's suggestion[45] that the tiers represent temple scenes, and that the creatures on the sides of the registers resemble the large animal orthostats associated with Syro-Palestinian temple architecture.[46] Taylor believes that 'the pillars, lions and cherubim on these tiers thus "house" the deities represented by the winged sun above the quadruped (tier one), the sacred tree (tier two) and the nude female (tier four)'.[47] There is general agreement that the naked female figure and the tree flanked by caprids on the second and lowest levels are depictions of Asherah.[48] Asherah can be represented by a tree or pole (see below). Furthermore, if she is to be identified with Qudshu,[49] this would provide parallels for the lion as her special accompanying animal. Taylor believes that the fact that the lions on the Taanach stand in levels two and four are identical makes it clear that Asherah, and not any other goddess, is indicated.

> Thus, though the sacred tree and nude female might independently represent different deities (in the case of the nude female, Astarte, for example), the only deity likely to be represented as *both* nude female and sacred tree, in each case flanked by identical pairs of lions, is Asherah.[50]

43.   Dayagi-Mendels, 'Canaanite Cult Stand', p. 161. Taylor, 'Earliest Known Representations', attributes to Hestrin the article I have cited by Dayagi-Mendels. This may be on the basis of Taylor's personal discussions with Hestrin. There is nothing in the book, however, to indicate that the article is not by Dayagi-Mendels.

44.   Taylor, 'Earliest Known Representations', p. 559.

45.   Lapp, 'The 1968 Excavations', p. 44.

46.   Cf. Dayagi-Mendels, 'Canaanite Cult Stand', p. 163.

47.   Taylor, 'Earliest Known Representations', pp. 559-60; cf. Taylor, 'Yahweh and Asherah', p. 16. But see also Keel and Uehlinger, *Göttinnen*, pp. 175-84; and Beck, 'The Cult-Stands from Taanach', who argue that the stand is a collection of ancient Near Eastern motifs, and therefore interpret it differently.

48.   W.G. Dever, 'Material Remains and the Cult in Ancient Israel', in C.L. Meyers and M. O'Connor (eds.), *The Word of the Lord Shall Go Forth: Essays in Honor of David Noel Freedman in Celebration of his Sixtieth Birthday* (Winona Lake, IN: Eisenbrauns, 1983), pp. 571-87 (573); Dayagi-Mendels, 'Canaanite Cult Stand', p. 163; Hestrin, 'The Cult Stand from Ta'anach'; Hestrin, 'The Lachish Ewer', p. 220; Taylor, 'Another Cult of Yahweh'; Taylor, 'Yahweh and Asherah'; Taylor, 'Earliest Known Representations', p. 560 and S. Ackerman, *Under Every Green Tree: Popular Religion in Sixth-Century Judah* (HSM, 46; Atlanta: Scholars Press, 1992), pp. 190-91; cf. also Olyan, *Asherah*; and M.S. Smith, *The Early History of God*, among others, but see also n. 47.

49.   See n. 37.

50.   Taylor, 'Earliest Known Representations', p. 560.

On the basis of this double representation of the goddess Asherah, it makes sense that the other two levels represent a second deity. The identification of this deity, however, is more difficult. As mentioned above, the third register does not appear to have a portrayal of any deity or divine symbol. In the top level the sun disk is clearly represented, although there is a difference of opinion on its interpretation and the type of quadruped beneath it. Keel and Uehlinger believe that the sun disk is not representative of a deity, but of the sky in general.[51] Lapp thinks that the 'winged disk' symbolizes a deity, and that the quadruped beneath it is a calf serving as a pedestal for this deity. However, he states that this symbol is too fluid in its use to enable a certain identification with any deity.[52] Dayagi-Mendels[53] and Hestrin[54] also believe that the animal is a calf, and that therefore (in their opinion) it represents Baal-Hadad. Glock[55] and Taylor,[56] on the other hand, believe that it is an equid. To test his theory Taylor consulted two experts in zoology, one of whom was well acquainted with the iconography of the ancient Near East. They both expressed the opinion independently that the animal in question was equine, on the basis of the hairy tail (not roped like a cow's), the attitude of the ears, the long muzzle and prominent hooves.[57] Taylor thus identifies the deity so represented as Yahweh and draws the obvious comparison with 2 Kgs 23.11, which describes Josiah's removal of the 'horses of the sun' from the temple in Jerusalem. A further comparison is that of the discovery of many clay figurines of horses that Kenyon excavated from Jerusalem Cave 1. Several of these horses bore clay disks between their ears, which led Kenyon to speculate whether these were reminiscent of the 'horses of the sun'.[58]

Taylor's arguments are convincing.[59] After a close examination the

51. Keel and Uehlinger, *Göttinnen*, p. 181.
52. Lapp, 'The 1968 Excavations', p. 44.
53. Dayagi-Mendels, 'Canaanite Cult Stand', pp. 161-63.
54. Hestrin, 'The Cult Stand from Taʻanach', pp. 67, 74-77.
55. Glock, 'Taanach' (1978), p. 1147.
56. Taylor, 'Another Cult of Yahweh'; Taylor, 'Yahweh and Asherah' and Taylor, 'Earliest Known Representations'.
57. Taylor, 'Earliest Known Representations', p. 563 n. 15.
58. K. Kenyon, *Royal Cities of the Old Testament* (London: Barrie and Jenkins, 1971), p. 120; and cf. T.A. Holland, 'A Study of Palestinian Iron Age Baked Clay Figurines, with Special Reference to Jerusalem: Cave 1', *Levant* 9 (1977), pp. 121-55, where these finds are published. See also the discussion in Hadley, *Hebrew Goddess*.
59. Although I must confess to a certain degree of skepticism when I first heard them at the 1987 Society of Biblical Literature conference in Boston, USA;

quadruped does look more like a horse than a calf, although it must be noted that a calf (or bull) could be associated with Yahweh as well. However, the connection between calves or bulls and sun disks is not well attested whereas there are numerous examples of horses and sun disks, often with chariots as well.[60] A sun disk would also be an odd symbol for Baal, who is primarily a storm god. Furthermore, as seen from the Ugaritic evidence, Asherah was not a consort of Baal but openly antagonistic towards him. Additionally, there is not much evidence from the Hebrew Bible to show that the goddess Asherah had any connection with Baal, apart from the desire of the deuteronomists to discredit her worship (see below). The inscriptions from Khirbet el-Qom and Kuntillet 'Ajrud definitely mention *asherah* in connection with Yahweh, and so it would seem reasonable to assume that the other deity on the Taanach stand is Yahweh.[61]

This still leaves the problem of the lack of representation of a deity on the third register. There never was anything in the place where there is a hole. The moulded sides of the hole have been preserved, and nothing has been broken out.[62] So who is the deity that can best be represented by non-representation, flanked by two sphinxes? As noted above, Mettinger has shown that the official Yahweh cult was aniconic (though not without symbols) from early times; and that over the cherub throne and the ark Yahweh sat in invisible majesty, for the place where the deity was usually represented was empty.[63] Therefore Taylor suggests that the deity 'portrayed' by the empty space is Yahweh.[64] The following pattern on the stand would thus be

cf. Taylor, 'Another Cult of Yahweh'.

60.   Holland, 'Iron Age Baked Clay Figurines', and also his 'Human and Animal Representations'; cf. also Keel and Uehlinger, *Göttinnen*.

61.   A full discussion of possible solar connections with Yahweh is beyond the scope of this study; see Taylor, 'Earliest Known Representations'; J.G. Taylor, *Yahweh and the Sun: Biblical and Archaeological Evidence for Sun Worship in Ancient Israel* (JSOTSup, 111; Sheffield: JSOT Press, 1993); and M.S. Smith, *The Early History of God*, among others.

62.   See the description in Dayagi-Mendels, 'Canaanite Cult Stand'; and Taylor, 'Earliest Known Representations', pp. 560-61. I was also able to confirm this for myself in 1991, when I visited the Israel Museum in Jerusalem where the stand is displayed, and was able to closely examine it. The only part of the sides of the hole that has been reconstructed is a small part at the top. Theoretically, something very long and thin could have hung down into the opening from this point, but that is highly unlikely.

63.   Mettinger, 'The Veto on Images'; and Mettinger, 'YHWH SABAOTH'; and cf. Taylor, 'Earliest Known Representations', p. 561 n. 11.

64.   Taylor, 'Earliest Known Representations', p. 561.

noted: a scene evoking the recollection of Yahweh was on the top tier,[65] followed by a scene evoking the recollection of Asherah. On the third register was an open space, meant to portray Yahweh, followed by a depiction of Asherah on the bottom.[66] Thus, this stand shows a concrete association between Yahweh and the goddess Asherah. From the portrayal of the goddess herself, and not merely her wooden symbol, it can be inferred that the two deities were linked in a consort relationship, at least in the tenth century BCE.[67]

From the Khirbet el-Qom and Kuntillet 'Ajrud inscriptions, it can be seen that Yahweh and Asherah are still linked; only in the ninth–eighth century BCE it appears that the cultic object is indicated, although still connected with the goddess. The Taanach stand shows, however, that earlier Yahweh and Asherah, the god and goddess, were linked together in a consort relationship. Later it appears that Asherah's cultic pole is being taken over by Yahweh as 'his *asherah*'. It may be becoming a symbol of Yahweh's fertility aspects. I shall now turn to the biblical text to see if this change is indicated there as well.

Asherah in the Hebrew Bible

In the Hebrew Bible, the word *asherah* occurs 40 times in nine different books. In eighteen occurrences the word is in its feminine singular form אֲשֵׁרָה.[68] The masculine plural occurs in nineteen verses: thirteen times in its pure form אֲשֵׁרִים[69] and six times with suffixes.[70]

---

65. It is not necessary to identify Yahweh specifically with the horse and sun disk. Indeed, it is possible that the deity represented by the horse and sun disk was a solar deity in Yahweh's pantheon. All that is needed for the top tier is a scene that would cause the viewer to think of Yahweh in the temple.

66. Cf. Taylor, 'Yahweh and Asherah', p. 18.

67. See Hadley, *Hebrew Goddess* for a discussion of a second cultic stand from Taanach discovered by Sellin, which also depicts alternating sphinxes and lions on the sides as well as two caprids flanking a tree at the base of the stand; and cf. Sellin, *Tell Ta'annek*, p. 75 fig. 102 and pls. 12-13; Lapp, 'A Ritual Incense Stand from Taanak', p. 16; Glock, 'Taanach' (1978), p. 1144 and Glock, 'Taanach' (1993), p. 1431; Keel and Uehlinger, *Göttinnen*, p. 176; and Beck, 'The Cult-Stands from Taanach'.

68. Deut. 16.21; Judg. 6.25, 26, 28 and 30; 1 Kgs 15.13; 16.33; 18.19; 2 Kgs 13.6; 17.16 [spelled אֲשֵׁירָה]; 18.4; 21.3 and 7; 23.4, 6, 7 and 15; and 2 Chron. 15.16 [=1 Kgs 15.13].

69. 1 Kgs 14.23; 2 Kgs 17.10; 23.14; 2 Chron. 14.2 [ET v. 3]; 17.6; 24.18; 31.1; 33.19; 34.3, 4 and 7; Isa. 17.8; 27.9.

70. Exod. 34.13; Deut. 7.5 [אֲשֵׁירֵהֶם]; 12.3; 1 Kgs 14.15; Jer. 17.2; and Mic. 5.13 [ET v. 14; אֲשֵׁירֶיךָ].

Reading the Bible

In some manuscripts and versions, the plural occurs at times where the MT has the singular.[71] The remaining three verses use the feminine plural אשרות.[72]

As can be seen, eleven of the references come from the books of Chronicles. All but one are in the plural.[73] Many of the references have no parallel in Kings; and all the references to asherah/asherim in the Northern Kingdom of Israel found in Kings are omitted in Chronicles. It therefore may be that the Chronicler had a different idea of what the asherim were (see below).

The general consensus amongst scholars is that all the references to asherah in the Hebrew Bible are by the hand of the deuteronomist or later[74] (with the possible exceptions of the passages in Isa. 17.8; 27.9; Mic. 5.13; and Exod. 34.13). Isa. 17.8 is generally considered an addition, while the origin and dating of Isa. 27.9 and Mic. 5.13 are disputed.[75] According to Noth, Exod. 34.13 appears to be part of the expansion in the style of the deuteronomist.[76] A comparison of Deut. 7.5 and 12.3 with Exod. 34.13 shows a stereotyping in the formula for altars and מצבות, but no standard phraseology for the destruction of the asherim (and in two examples of פסילים, 'images').[77]

71. For example 2 Kgs 21.3, versions; and 18.4 Ms and versions.

72. Judg. 3.7; 2 Chron. 19.3, 33.3.

73. The one is virtually a direct citation of the Kings parallel; cf. the discussion in Hadley, *Hebrew Goddess*.

74. See for example Reed, *The Asherah*, pp. 59-68; Yamashita, 'The Goddess Asherah', p. 125; Olyan, *Asherah*; and Pettey, *Asherah*, pp. 85-171 *passim*, among others.

75. Cf. Pettey, *Asherah*, pp. 163, 165.

76. M. Noth, *Überlieferungsgeschichtliche Studien* (Halle: Niemeyer, 1943); ET: *The Deuteronomistic History* (JSOTSup, 15; Sheffield: JSOT Press, 1981); and *The Chronicler's History* (JSOTSup, 50; Sheffield: JSOT Press, 1987), p. 13 n. 2.

77. For summaries of the various scholarly opinions on the dating of Dtr see H. Gressmann, 'Josia und das Deuteronomium', *ZAW* 42 (1924), pp. 313-37; H.H. Rowley, *From Moses to Qumran* (London: Lutterworth, 1963), pp. 187-208; J. Gray, *I & II Kings: A Commentary* (OTL; London: SCM Press, 2nd rev. edn, 1970), pp. 6-9; M. Weinfeld, *Deuteronomy and the Deuteronomic School* (Oxford: Clarendon Press, 1972); H. Weippert, 'Die "deuteronomistischen" Beurteilungen der Könige von Israel und Juda und das Problem der Redaktion der Königsbücher', *Bib* 53 (1972), pp. 301-39; Cross, *Canaanite Myth*, pp. 274-89; R.D. Nelson, *The Double Redaction of the Deuteronomistic History* (JSOTSup, 18; Sheffield: JSOT Press, 1981), pp. 13-28; A.D.H. Mayes, *The Story of Israel between Settlement and Exile* (London: SCM Press, 1983), pp. 1-21; N. Lohfink, 'The Cult Reform of Josiah of Judah: 2 Kings 22–23 as a Source for the History of Israelite Religion', in P.D. Miller, Jr, P.D. Hanson and S.D. McBride (eds.), *Ancient Israelite Religion* (Philadelphia: Fortress Press, 1987), pp. 459-75; L.K. Handy, 'Hezekiah's Unlikely Reform', *ZAW*

An examination of the verbs used with *asherah* seems to support the theory that in most cases it is some sort of humanly-made, carved wooden object.[78]

In addition, there are some verses in which *asherah* does not seem to be an object—especially 1 Kgs 15.13, 18.19; 2 Kgs 21.7, 23.4 and perhaps v. 7; 2 Chron. 15.16 and possibly Judg. 3.7 (see below where some of these are discussed in more detail). This has led most scholars today to conclude that the goddess Asherah is mentioned in the Hebrew Bible in addition to the wooden cultic object.

The idea that a cultic object can bear the same name as the deity it represents would not be a foreign concept to the people of the ancient Near East, who recognized that there was some type of 'magical' connection between the symbol and the symbolized. This could lead to the hypostatization of certain attributes of the deity, attributes which in their turn became deified.[79] As noted above, an example of a fertility goddess depicted with her symbol is given by Hartmann.[80] An Egyptian seal shows the goddess Nut together with a tree that symbolizes her. That the tree represents the goddess is clear from the fact that the word 'Nut' is written above the head of the goddess as well as on the trunk of the tree.[81] It is therefore not unreasonable to argue that the same term (*asherah*) can be used to describe both the goddess and the symbol of the goddess.

100 (1988), pp. 111-15 and I.W. Provan, *Hezekiah and the Books of Kings* (BZAW, 172; Berlin: de Gruyter, 1988), pp. 1-31, among others.

78.   These verbs are כרת, 'to cut' (Exod. 34.13; Judg. 6.25, 26, 28 and 30; 2 Kgs 18.4 and 23.14); גדע, 'to cut down' (*piel*: Deut. 7.5; 2 Chron. 14.2 and 31.1); שרף, 'to burn' (Deut. 12.3; implied in Judg. 6.26; 2 Kgs 23.6 and 23.15); נטע, 'to plant' or 'to establish' (Deut. 16.21); עשׂה, 'to make' (1 Kgs 14.15, 16.33; 2 Kgs 17.16, 21.3 and 7 [although in v. 7 it is unclear whether the *asherah* or the פסל of the Asherah is meant]; and 2 Chron. 33.3); בנה, 'to build' (1 Kgs 14.23); עמד, 'to stand' (2 Kgs 13.6); עמד, 'to set up' (*hiphil*: 2 Chron. 33.19); נצב, 'to set up' (*hiphil*: 2 Kgs 17.10); יצא, 'to bring out' (*hiphil*: 2 Kgs 23.6); דקק, 'to make into dust' (*hiphil*: 2 Kgs 23.6; and 2 Chron. 34.4); סור, 'to take away' (*hiphil*: 2 Chron. 17.6); בער, 'to consume, burn, remove' (*piel*: 2 Chron. 19.3); טהר, 'to purge' (*piel*: 2 Chron. 34.3); שׁבר, 'to break into pieces' (*piel*: 2 Chron. 34.4); נתץ, 'to pull or break down' (2 Chron. 34.7); and נתשׁ, 'to pluck up' (Mic. 5.13). The verbs in Isa. 17.8 (ראה, 'to look upon'), Isa. 27.9 (קום, 'to arise' [after being cast down]), and Jer. 17.2 (זכר, 'to remember') appear neutral. However, here the *asherim* are paired with altars or idols, and thus the implication is that the *asherim* are objects.

79.   Cf., for example, the examples in Olyan, *Asherah*, p. 40 and pp. 55-56.

80.   Hartmann, 'Monotheismus in Mesopotamien?', Abb. 1.

81.   Keel, *Die Welt der altorientalischen Bildsymbolik*, fig. 255 and Winter, *Frau und Göttin*, Abb. 466; cf. also above, and Hadley, *Hebrew Goddess*.

Therefore *asherah* in the Hebrew Bible can be understood to mean, in most cases, some type of wooden object which appears to represent the goddess Asherah, who may be mentioned herself in some of the remaining passages.[82] Furthermore, most of the earlier Hebrew Bible passages that mention *asherah* can be attributed to the hand of the deuteronomistic historian. For the most part these inferences are condemnatory, showing *asherah* in a negative light. It is clear, then, that the religious reformers in the late Judaean monarchy period (perhaps during the reign of Josiah[83]) wished to eradicate the worship of *asherah*, whether it was the wooden cultic symbol or the goddess herself. But was this attitude necessarily prevalent *before* the period of the reformers? In other words, is it possible to determine whether or not the worship of *asherah* was ever an integral part of the religion, rather than a mere syncretistic weakness on the part of the ancient Israelites?

The prophets are surprisingly silent when it comes to Asherah. Out of a total of 40 occurrences of *asherah* in the Hebrew Bible, only four occur in prophetic writings: two in Isaiah (17.8 and 27.9), one in Micah (5.13 [ET v. 14]) and one in Jeremiah (17.2)—but the two references in Isaiah and that in Micah may be additions, while the reference in Jeremiah is considered a prose gloss.[84] It is interesting to note that Hosea, who was so concerned with the purity of Yahweh worship, never condemns Asherah by name although he *does* condemn Baal worship.[85] It may be that the worship of Asherah (and indeed

82.   See Hadley, *Hebrew Goddess*, for a full discussion of the identification of the term *asherah* with both the goddess and her cultic object or symbol. See also the discussions below of 2 Kgs 23.4, 1 Kgs 18.19 and 2 Kgs 21.7.

83.   A full discussion of the dating of Dtr and the deuteronomistic reform is beyond the scope of this article. Many scholars, however, acknowledge some degree of reform activity during the reign of Josiah. For discussions of this reform and dating, see the works mentioned in n. 77, among others.

84.   Cf., e.g., W. Thiel, *Die deuteronomistische Redaktion von Jeremia 1–25* (WMANT, 41; Neukirchen–Vluyn: Neukirchener Verlag, 1973), pp. 202-203 and R.P. Carroll, *Jeremiah* (OTL; Philadelphia: Westminster Press, 1986), p. 349.

85.   See B. Halpern, '"Brisker Pipes than Poetry": The Development of Israelite Monotheism', in J. Neusner, B.A. Levine and E.S. Frerichs (eds.), *Judaic Perspectives on Ancient Israel* (Philadelphia: Fortress Press, 1987), p. 93; and cf., for example, Hos. 9.10, 11.2 and 13.1. See also Hadley, *Hebrew Goddess*, for a discussion of Hos. 14.9 [ET v. 8] in which some scholars, beginning with J. Wellhausen, *Die kleinen Propheten* (Berlin: Georg Reimer, 3rd edn, 1898), emend the text to obtain a reference to Asherah and Anat. Whereas most scholars now disagree with Wellhausen's proposed emendation, many scholars still identify a 'word play' on Asherah in this passage (cf. Day, 'Asherah in the Hebrew Bible', p. 405 and A.A. Macintosh,

other deities as well) was totally acceptable to all segments of society *before* the deuteronomistic reform movement gained momentum in the seventh century BCE. But since the text of the Bible was significantly composed or edited by the deuteronomistic school, this fact is not immediately apparent. It may also be that Asherah worship was a legitimate part of Yahweh worship.

On the surface (e.g. Judg. 3.7 and 6.25), however, the picture in the Bible seems to suggest that Asherah was paired with Baal and not Yahweh.[86] That is presumably the picture that the deuteronomists want to portray. But was it really the case? It has been seen that the contemporary prophets do not widely condemn Asherah worship, as they condemn Baal[87] (although it must be noted that Amos never condemns Baal worship). It may be that Asherah was never associated with Baal, and that the pairing of her name with his was a later attempt on the part of the deuteronomists to discredit her cult.[88]

At Ugarit Athirat was the consort of the chief deity El. She was opposed to Baal and was often openly antagonistic towards him.[89] Baal, in turn, slew the sons of Athirat.[90] There was evidently not much love lost between them. Many scholars presume that, by the time of the monarchy, Asherah had forsaken her consort El and paired up with Baal.[91] However, most of the verses in the Hebrew Bible that mention *asherah* occur in deuteronomistic polemics against undesirable cults and cultic practices. Of the seven verses in the Hebrew Bible that may refer to the goddess, only three mention Baal with the Asherah.[92] Of these, Judg. 3.7 probably should read 'Ashtaroth'. It is a summary passage, describing how the children of Israel do evil in the sight of God by forsaking Yahweh and following

---

Hosea [ICC; Edinburgh: T. and T. Clark, 1997]. I am grateful to Mr Andrew A. Macintosh for providing me with a draft copy of his commentary on this passage in Hosea.

86. Many modern scholars appear to accept this pairing of Baal and Asherah at face value; cf., for example, Weinfeld, *Deuteronomy*, p. 320 and Freedman, 'Yahweh of Samaria', among many others.

87. See the references to Hosea, above.

88. Cf. Olyan, *Asherah*.

89. See the Ugaritic tablets *passim* and also *CTA* 4.ii, where Athirat is afraid for her safety at the approach of Baal and Anat but rejoices when she sees the gifts of gold and silver that they bring to her to gain her favor.

90. *CTA* 6.v.1-3.

91. Cf., for example, M.H. Pope, *El in the Ugaritic Texts* (VTSup, 2; Leiden: Brill, 1955), who believes that even at Ugarit Athirat was losing interest in her (impotent?) partner El, and gravitating toward the more virile Baal.

92. Judg. 3.7; 1 Kgs 18.19; 2 Kgs 23.4.

after other gods. In many of these summary passages the gods in question are 'the Baalim and the Ashtaroth', not the Asherah.[93] In fact, the Syriac and the Vulgate both imply Ashtaroth for this verse, and so it is not certain that Asherah is to be paired with Baal here.[94]

2 Kings 23.4 describes how Josiah had all the vessels that were made for the Baal and the Asherah[95] and all the hosts of heaven brought out of the temple and burned in the Kidron. Here Asherah is mentioned with Baal, but not specifically in a consort type of relationship. Josiah was simply clearing out of the temple all the cultic paraphernalia that belonged to any deity other than Yahweh. Verse 5 mentions the priests of Baal, the sun, the moon, the planets and all the host of heaven (omitting the Asherah). If Asherah was the consort of Baal, one might expect her to be mentioned in this verse along with him. But if Asherah was associated with the worship of Yahweh, perhaps her priests (or priestesses?) were not mentioned because they were part of the same temple personnel as those that served the Yahweh cult.

1 Kings 18.19 may be the most instructive passage of all. This verse mentions the contest that Elijah had on Mount Carmel with the priests of Baal. Verse 19 mentions the four hundred and fifty prophets of Baal and the four hundred prophets of Asherah. Throughout the rest of the contest, the prophets of Asherah are not mentioned again. This has led scholars to believe that this part of the verse is an addition.[96] If the reference to Asherah is a later addition, it would show evidence of an attempt (presumably deuteronomistic) to discredit the worship of Asherah by associating her with Baal. If, on the other hand, it is *not* an addition, some attempt must be made to explain the subsequent silence about the prophets of Asherah. It may be that the prophets of Asherah are not mentioned again because Elijah had no quarrel with them; he was concerned only with Baal.[97]

93.   Judg. 2.13; 10.6; 1 Sam. 7.4 and 12.10.

94.   See Hadley, *Hebrew Goddess*, for a fuller discussion of this and the following biblical passages, as well as for a discussion on the use of the definite article with *asherah*.

95.   The definite article with Baal and Asherah here in 2 Kgs 23.4 is a matter of Masoretic vocalization only.

96.   The LXX, however, mentions the prophets of Asherah again in v. 22. This has led Reed, *The Asherah*, p. 55, to conclude that the original Hebrew text may have included Asherah in both verses, and that it is just as likely that the phrase 'the prophets of Asherah' was omitted from v. 22 as it is that it was added to v. 19.

97.   Patai, *The Hebrew Goddess*, pp. 40-41 and Pettey, *Asherah*, p. 118, among

Asherah worship might then be considered a legitimate part of Yahwism. Furthermore, the biblical texts do *not* mention the destruction of the *asherah* which, according to the deuteronomist, stood in the sanctuary in Samaria. No mention of the destruction of the *asherah* in Samaria is made by the historian during the succeeding reigns of Ahaziah, Joram, Jehu and Joahaz; and so the cult object, if it existed, may have remained standing and the prophets of Asherah, if genuine, continued their service.[98] Admittedly, this is an argument from silence, but it may prove instructive.

Therefore, it may be that the deuteronomistic reformers were attempting to eradicate the worship of the goddess Asherah. If so, some sort of compensation needed to be made. The book of Hosea may have the very beginnings of this idea, where the prophet speaks of Yahweh as a luxurious cypress tree, although Hosea never explicitly condemns Asherah. It may thus be possible to trace an 'evolution' of the meaning of 'asherah': from that denoting a goddess in her own right during the Monarchy period, to referring to solely an object by the time of the exile.

The 'Demotion' of Asherah

The biblical passages that best illustrate the 'demotion' of the goddess Asherah to solely an object can be seen in those passages in the books of Kings in which Asherah is referred to in the singular, together with the parallel accounts in Chronicles where the term appears in the plural. For example, in 1 Kgs 15.13 and its parallel account in 2 Chron. 15.16, Asa removes Maacah his (grand?)mother from the position of Queen Mother because she made a מפלצת, 'horrid thing' for the asherah.[99] It is then this מפלצת which Asa cuts down (כרת), beats into dust (דקק, Chronicles only) and burns (שׂרף) in the Kidron. As there is no mention of the removal of the asherah, scholars have interpreted Asherah here to refer to the goddess.

The word מפלצת occurs in the Hebrew Bible only in these two verses. What exactly it is remains open to speculation, especially since the word denotes a feeling of abhorrence to an unspecified object and not necessarily the object itself. But since the object here is cut down and burned, which is the same treatment often afforded to

others. See also Freedman, 'Yahweh of Samaria', who believes that as a result of the contest on Mt Carmel Yahweh won the 'hand' of Asherah as his bride.

98. Cf. Patai, 'The Goddess Asherah', p. 46 and Pettey, *Asherah*, p. 118.

99. BDB, p. 814a.

the wooden cultic object of the goddess, it is reasonable to assume that מפלצת in this instance referred to something similar to an asherah and may in fact have been an (explicit?) image of the goddess.

The parallel account in 2 Chron. 15.16 mentions asherah in the singular, against all other places where the Chronicler uses the plural. The Chronicler has also changed the word order here, from מפלצת לאשרה to לאשרה מפלצת (in pause). Perhaps we are intended to read 'because she made a *mip̄leṣet* in the function of an asherah'. To add to the confusion, the LXX has a variant reading here which mentions Astarte instead of Asherah. This may indicate that by the time of the Chronicler[100] the term 'asherah' had ceased to mean either the goddess or the cult symbol associated with the goddess, and the distinction between the two ideas had become obscured. Therefore, when the Chronicler envisioned an asherah, the image brought to mind was only a wooden object. This may be the reason the Chronicler had a tendency to speak of the asherah in the plural. In the Kings passage, however, the combination of asherah and מפלצת was baffling, especially if the Chronicler was not acquainted with the goddess Asherah in whose image the original מפלצת was made. The LXX writer, as well, evidently did not immediately recognize the term asherah as referring to a deity, since the variant reading in the LXX refers to Astarte.[101]

Perhaps a clearer example is to be found in 2 Kgs 21.7 and its parallel account in 2 Chron. 33.7. Here, Manasseh places an image (פסל) of the Asherah in the temple. The first part of v. 7 reads וישם את פסל האשרה אשר עשה בבית('and he put the image of the Asherah that he had made in the house [of God]'). The parallel account in 2 Chron. 33.7 states that Manasseh set up את פסל הסמל, replacing הסמל for האשרה. The etymology of סמל is uncertain; but, as the only places outside the Hebrew Bible in which it occurs are several Phoenician and Punic inscriptions,[102] many recent scholars believe that it came into Hebrew from the Phoenician.[103] It is evidently some type of

100. Around the mid-fourth century BCE; cf. H.G.M. Williamson, *1 and 2 Chronicles* (New Century Bible Commentary; Grand Rapids: Eerdmans; London: Marshall, Morgan & Scott, 1982), p. 16.

101. For more on these and the following passages see Hadley, *Hebrew Goddess*.

102. *KAI* 26, 41, and 33, which has *smlt*).

103. Cf. J.W. McKay, *Religion in Judah Under the Assyrians: 732–609 B.C.* (London: SCM Press, 1973), pp. 22-23 and Schroer, *In Israel gab es Bilder*, pp. 25-27, both of whom include discussions on the various interpretations of *semel*, and cf. also C. Dohmen, 'Heisst Semel "Bild, Statue"?', *ZAW* 96 (1984), pp. 263-66.

image, perhaps anthropomorphic, and may be related to the הקנאה סמל in Ezek. 8.3, 5.[104] If so, it is interesting that the term *asherah* is no longer used, almost as if the goddess (or at least her connection with the statue) had been forgotten.[105] Thus it is not proven that the Chronicler knew that סמל stood for a representation of an actual deity; it may have been considered as simply another 'idol'. Furthermore, in the summary of Manasseh's rule in 2 Chron. 33.19 the Chronicler relates that Manasseh set up *asherim* as well as פסלים. It may be that the writer understood the asherah to be an 'idolatrous' object like the פסל and not a goddess. Therefore, when considering the comment in 2 Kgs 21.7 that Manasseh made a פסל for the Asherah, the Chronicler could not understand how an idol could be made for another type of idol, and so changed the text to read that Manasseh made *asherim and* פסלים.[106]

The Goddess Astarte

A similar shift can be seen in the treatment of Astarte in the biblical text. Astarte is a well-known North-west Semitic goddess, known from Ugarit[107] and elsewhere throughout the Levant, Egypt and Cyprus.[108] Scholars are agreed that the goddess is mentioned in the

104. Cf. McKay, *Religion in Judah*, p. 22 and Ackerman, *Under Every Green Tree*, pp. 60-61. Schroer believes that the סמל mentioned both here in 2 Chron. 33.7 and in Ezek. 8.3, 5 may be a statue of Asherah in the form of a suckling cow (*In Israel gab es Bilder*, p. 41).

105. McKay believes that the Chronicler may have referred to Manasseh's idol in this verse as a סמל precisely because it represented some Phoenician goddess, probably Asherah, especially in the light of Dtr's reference to the asherah which Ahab set up (*Religion in Judah*, p. 23). Williamson is of the opinion that if this is correct, then 'the change probably already stood in the text of Kings that the Chronicler was following, since it is unlikely that he himself would have still known the precise significance of the word' (*1 and 2 Chronicles*, p. 391).

106. And cf. S. Japhet, *I & II Chronicles* (London: SCM Press; Louisville: Westminster/John Knox, 1993), p. 1007.

107. Cf. *ʿttrt* in *KTU*; *CTA*; *UT*; H.P. Müller, עשתרת, *ʿštrt* (*ʿaštoreṯ)*', in G.J. Botterweck and H. Ringgren (eds.), *Theologisches Wörterbuch zum Alten Testament* (Stuttgart: Kohlhammer, 1989), VI, pp. 453-63; M.H. Pope, '''Aṭtart, ʿAštart, Astarte', in H.W. Haussig (ed.), *Wörterbuch der Mythologie* (Stuttgart: Ernst Klett, 1965), pp. 250-52; Perlman, *Asherah and Astarte*; J. Day, 'Ashtoreth', in D.N. Freedman (ed.), *The Anchor Bible Dictionary* (Garden City, NY: Doubleday, 1992), I, pp. 491-94, among others.

108. *CAD*; Botterweck and Ringgren (eds.), *Theologisches Wörterbuch*; *KAI*; S.R. Driver, *Notes on the Hebrew Text and the Topography of the Books of Samuel* (Oxford: Clarendon Press, 2nd rev. edn, 1913), pp. 62-63; C.F. Burney, *The Book of Judges*

Hebrew Bible but in the altered form of Ashtoreth (plural Ashtaroth). The term Ashtoreth appears nine times in the Hebrew Bible as a goddess: three times in the singular עַשְׁתֹּרֶת,[109] the other six times in the plural עַשְׁתָּרוֹת.[110] A further four times the term appears in Deuteronomy in the context of an idiom.[111] A full examination of this passage is beyond the scope of this article;[112] however, it is to be noted that *all* the references to the goddess Astarte in the Hebrew Bible are to be found in the books of the deuteronomistic history, and all of them identify her as a 'foreign' deity and are polemical in nature. It may furthermore be instructive that 1 Chron. 10.10, the parallel passage in Chronicles to 1 Sam. 31.10, omits any reference to Astarte and instead reads 'the temple of their gods'. Chronicles does, however, refer to a temple of Dagon that is lacking in the 1 Samuel account.

It may be that the Chronicler does not know of the existence of a goddess Astarte, at least in Israel. That the cult of Astarte continued into Greco-Roman times in the ancient Near East is not in question; but the Chronicler may not have felt that the goddess was relevant to any account of the history of Israel and Judah. Nowhere in the books of Chronicles is the goddess mentioned. Admittedly, this is an argument from silence; but even in two accounts where the goddess Astarte is mentioned in what may be a parallel account in Dtr (the first in the Solomon narratives, the second in 1 Sam. 31.10//1 Chron. 10.10), the goddess is notably absent from the Chronicler's account. Of course, this may in part depend on the Chronicler's use of Dtr as a source, which is not proved for either passage, especially for the Solomon narratives. Even so, if any reference to Astarte were lacking in the narrative material that the Chronicler was using for the account, then that might further indicate the polemical nature of Dtr's

(London: Rivingtons, 1920), n. on pp. 58-59; R. Stadelmann, *Syrisch-Palästinensische Gottheiten in Ägypten* (Leiden: Brill, 1967), pp. 96-110; R. Giveon, 'Ptah and Astarte on a Seal from Accho', in G. Buccellati (ed.), *Studi sull 'Oriente e la Bibbia offerti a P Giovani Rinaldi* (Gênes: Editrice Studio e Vita, 1967), pp. 147-53; Gray, *I & II Kings*, pp. 275-76; M. Delcor, 'Astarté et la fécondité des troupeaux en Deut. 7,13 et paralleles', *UF* 6 (1974), pp. 7-14; M. Delcor, 'Le personnel du temple d'Astarté à Kition d'après une tablette phénicienne (cis 86 A et B)', *UF* 11 (1979), pp. 147-64; W. Helck, 'Zur Herkunft der Erzählung des sog. "Astartepapyrus"', in M. Görg (ed.), *Fontes atque pontes* (Wiesbaden: Otto Harrassowitz, 1983), pp. 215-23.

    109. 1 Kgs 11.5, 33; 2 Kgs 23.13.
    110. Judg. 2.13, 10.6; 1 Sam. 7.3, 4; 12.10; 31.10.
    111. Deut. 7.13; 28.4, 18, 51.
    112. But see Hadley, 'The Fertility of the Flock?'.

views. The question thus remains: did the Chronicler omit reference to Astarte, or did Dtr add it?

So again we appear to have a case where a goddess is treated polemically and in a negative fashion in Dtr, but it is nevertheless still possible to identify a deity behind the references. And yet, by the time of the Chronicler, all reference to that deity appears to be lost or deliberately omitted. And, as in the case of Asherah but even more clearly, in between these two positions lies the treatment of the term in the book of Deuteronomy.

Astarte is mentioned only four times in the book of Deuteronomy (apart from a fifth time where it denotes a place name): where the word appears in the idiom עַשְׁתְּרֹת צֹאנֶךָ in 28.4 and 18, and spelled defectively in 7.13 and 28.51. All four instances are in the context of blessings (7.13, 28.4) or parallel curses (28.18, 51).[113]

It may be that Astarte's connection with fertility of the land and animals has led to the development of the Deuteronomy idiom, 'the Astartes of the flock'. This idiom, עַשְׁתְּרֹת צֹאנֶךָ, 'issue of your flock', seems to be a 'fixed idiom' which appears together with the idiom שְׁגַר אֲלָפֶיךָ, 'the increase of your cattle'. The two terms are in parallel in all four passages in Deuteronomy and do not occur elsewhere in the Hebrew Bible (although שְׁגַר as 'firstborn of your flock' appears in Exod. 13.12; though this interpretation is slightly more nuanced, the basic interpretation remains that of fertility and increase of herds). שְׁגַר (*šgr*) is known from the Ugaritic texts also as a fertility deity.[114] Astarte and Sheger are listed together in *KTU* 1.148.31, where both are allocated a sheep as an offering.[115] The use of shegar and ash-taroth here as common nouns is parallel to the use of dagan in these verses as 'grain'. Dagon is a Canaanite deity, mentioned in the Hebrew Bible in 1 Chron. 10.10 noted above, as well as elsewhere and at Ugarit (indeed, Dagon also appears in *KTU* 1.148, in line 26).

In this way both deities, Astarte and Sheger, are reduced to merely

113. For a full discussion of these verses see Hadley, 'The Fertility of the Flock?', and cf. Delcor, 'Astarté'.

114. *KTU* 1.5.3.16, 17 = *UT* 67:111:16, 17; *KTU* 1.148.31; some scholars, however, contest Sheger as a deity, especially at Deir Alla; see C. Frevel, *Aschera und der Ausschließlichkeitsanspruch YHWHs* (2 vols; Bonner Biblische Beiträge, 94; Weinheim: Beltz Athenäum Verlag, 1995), p. 459 n. 1557 for some of these.

115. Cf. T. Nougayrol, E. Laroche, C. Virolleaud and C.F.A. Schaeffer, *Ugaritica V* (Mission de Ras Shamra, 16; Paris: Geuthner, 1968), p. 584; L. Fisher, *Ras Shamra Parallels* (2 vols; Rome: Pontificum Institutum Biblicum, 1975), p. 305; Gibson, *Canaanite Myths* , p. 70.

their functions and distanced from any divine identification.[116] Delcor asks the question if perhaps the idiom started first and then the deity grew out of that, in a manner similar to that of a hypostasis. He agrees, however, that the chronology of the attestations of deity and idiom necessitates that the deity came first, before the idiom.[117] This still leaves us with the de-personalized use of these names in Deuteronomy, despite the presumption that the deities are known within the larger Palestinian area.

This apparent 'de-personalization' or 'de-deification' of deities is evidently common to Deuteronomy, which does not (as far as I know) list a single 'foreign' deity by name in the whole book (with the possible exception of 'Baal of Peor' in 4.3, although even in that context Baal probably refers to 'foreign deity' in general). 'Foreign' deities are instead called 'other gods' or some similar general notation. On the other hand deities such as Shegar, Astarte, Dagon and Asherah are treated as common nouns. This may be an attempt by the author(s) of Deuteronomy to eradicate the worship of other deities by 'reducing' them to merely their roles, and to then grant the control of these roles to Yahweh. In this way the power of the other deities is severely curtailed, and Yahweh is given dominion over them and ultimate control over their previous jobs as well.

Evidently this attempt worked, for by the late exilic period and later our Hebrew sources seem to ignore or be unaware of even the names of some of these deities. Thus we read in Jeremiah that the Israelites made cakes for and worshipped the 'Queen of Heaven'.[118] Much has been written on this deity in recent years.[119] Many scholars identify

116. For both sides of the issue, see Botterweck and Ringgren (eds.), *Theologisches Wörterbuch*, pp. 461-62; Loretz, *Ugarit*, p. 87; Keel and Uehlinger, *Göttinnen*, pp. 166-68; Frevel, *Aschera*, pp. 457-58.

117. Delcor, 'Astarté', p. 14.

118. Jer. 7.16-20; 44.15-19, 25.

119. Cf. S. Ackerman, '"And the Women Knead Dough": the Worship of the Queen of Heaven in Sixth-century Judah', in P.L. Day (ed.), *Gender and Difference in Ancient Israel* (Minneapolis: Augsburg–Fortress, 1989), pp. 109-24; K. Koch, 'Aschera als Himmelskoenigin in Jerusalem', *UF* 20 (1988), pp. 97-120; S.M. Olyan, 'Some Observations Concerning the Identity of the Queen of Heaven', *UF* 19 (1987), pp. 161-74; M. Delcor, 'Le culte de la "Reine du Ciel" selon Jer 7,18; 44,17-19, 25 et ses survivances', in W.C. Delsman, *et al.* (eds.), *Von Kanaan bis Kerala* (Kevelaer: Butzon & Bercker; Neukirchen–Vluyn: Neukirchener Verlag, 1982), pp. 101-22; W.E. Rast, 'Cakes for the Queen of Heaven', in A.L. Merrill and T.W. Overholt (eds.), *Scripture in History and Theology: Essays in Honor of J. Coert Rylaarsdam* (Pittsburgh: Pickwick Press, 1977), pp. 167-80; W. Culican, 'A Votive Model from the Sea', *PEQ* 108 (1976), pp. 119-23; R. Patai, 'The Goddess

the 'Queen of Heaven' with West Semitic Astarte, although others have made their case for other deities such as Babylonian Ishtar, Asherah and Anat, among others.[120] However, it may be that the author or editor of Jeremiah knew of worship of some 'foreign' goddess in Israel, but had no idea of her name apart from a more general designation 'Queen of Heaven'. Furthermore, since the 'head' goddess at a particular place was often called 'Queen of Heaven',[121] then it may be that the designation refers more to a general role than to any specific goddess.

By the time of the Chronicler, this distancing of the deity and the job description has evidently worked well enough that, although the Chronicler knows that the Philistines worship a god called Dagon, perhaps the Chronicler is unaware that the deity Astarte was ever worshipped in Israel or Judah. And so in 1 Chron. 10.10 we read that Saul's armor was placed in the temple to 'their gods', no longer associated with Astarte. Thus the de-personalization of Astarte is complete: she has moved from being a well-known and presumably widely worshipped deity in Palestine to becoming an abstraction of fertility in a Hebrew idiom, and then to total silence on the part of the latest biblical writers.

Lady Wisdom in Proverbs

So where have all the goddesses gone? If Asherah and Astarte are no longer known as deities, and even the worship of the 'Queen of Heaven' appears to be little understood, what has happened to the goddess in ancient Israel and Judah?

Cult in the Hebrew–Jewish Religion', in A. Bharati (ed.), *Realm of the Extra-Human: Agents and Audiences* (The Hague: Mouton, 1976), pp. 197-210, among others.

120. See the sources above and the references there.

121. Cf. the designation on the stele dedicated to Antit (=Anat?) at Beth-Shan in A. Rowe, *The Topography and History of Beth-Shan* (Publications of the Palestine Section of the Museum of the University of Pennsylvania, 1; Philadelphia: University Press, 1930), pp. 32-33 and pl. 50.2; A. Rowe, *The Four Canaanite Temples of Beth-Shan. I. The Temples and Cult Objects* (Publications of the Palestine Section of the University Museum, University of Pennsylvania, 2; Philadelphia: University of Pennsylvania Press, 1940), pp. 33-34 and pl. LXVI.1; A. Kempinski, 'Beth-Shean: Late Bronze and Iron Age Temples', in M. Avi-Yonah (ed.), *Encyclopedia of Archaeological Excavations in the Holy Land* (London and Jerusalem: Israel Exploration Society and Massada Press, 1975), I, pp. 213-15 (215); A. Mazar, 'Beth-Shean', in E. Stern (ed.), *The New Encyclopedia of Archaeological Excavations in the Holy Land* (Jerusalem: Israel Exploration Society, 1993), I, pp. 214-23 (218, 220); and also Asherah as 'Mistress of the Gods' at Ugarit, etc.

I believe that the answer may lie in some curious way with the figure of Lady Wisdom in the book of Proverbs, as well as in the deuterocanonical books of Sirach, Baruch and the Wisdom of Solomon. The personification of Wisdom as a woman is a much discussed topic, but a few comments are in order.[122]

The main texts which appear to give divine status to Lady Wisdom are Proverbs 1, 8 and 9; Job 28 (although Wisdom is not explicitly personified there); Sir. 1.1-10 and 24.1-22; Bar. 3.9–4.4; and Wisdom of Solomon 7–9—although other more isolated passages in Proverbs 1–9, Sirach and Wisdom also appear to give Lady Wisdom divine status. The consensus is that these texts in their present form are all relatively late, although the dating of Proverbs 1–9 and Job 28 are disputed.[123]

Many suggestions have been made for the origin of the portrait of Lady Wisdom. Some look to goddesses: for example Egyptian Ma'at or Isis, Canaanite Astarte, Mesopotamian Inanna, or even to a Persian provenance.[124] Others see her as a hypostasis of God's Wisdom.[125] Conzelmann sees her not only as a hypostasis, but also as a

---

122. For a discussion of possible divine connections to wisdom see Hadley, 'Wisdom' and the references there, and also B. Lang, *Wisdom and the Book of Proverbs: A Hebrew Goddess Redefined* (New York: Pilgrim Press, 1986), who perhaps amongst modern scholars advocates most strongly the divinity of חכמה (wisdom) in the Hebrew Bible. Cf. also Lang in this volume.

123. Cf. J.A. Emerton, 'Wisdom', in G.W. Anderson (ed.), *Tradition and Interpretation: Essays by Members of the Society for Old Testament Study* (Oxford: Clarendon Press; New York: Oxford University Press, 1979), pp. 214-37 (229).

124. Cf. H. Conzelmann, 'The Mother of Wisdom', in J.M. Robinson (ed.), *The Future of Our Religious Past: Essays in Honor of Rudolf Bultmann* (New York: Harper & Row, 1971), pp. 230-43 (230-31) and the references there including, H. Ringgren, *Word and Wisdom: Studies in the Hypostatization of Divine Qualities and Functions in the Ancient Near East* (Lund: Hakan Ohlssons Boktryckeri, 1947); cf. also Lang, *Wisdom*, G. Hölscher, *Das Buch Hiob* (Tübingen: Mohr [Paul Siebeck], 1937); O.S. Rankin, *Israel's Wisdom Literature* (Edinburgh: T. & T. Clark, 1936); G. Boström, *Proverbia Studien: Die Weisheit und das fremde Weib in Spr. 1–9* (Lund: Gleerup, 1935).

125. Cf. for example, R. Marcus, 'On Biblical Hypostases of Wisdom', *HUCA* 23 (1950–51), pp. 57-171, who follows the definition of hypostasis as given by Ringgren in *Word and Wisdom*; and R.N. Whybray, *The Book of Proverbs* (Cambridge: Cambridge University Press, 1972), p. 50. It should be noted, however, that the term 'hypostasis' has no agreed definition; cf. H. Cazelles, 'La Sagesse de Proverbes 8, 22: Peut-elle être considérée comme une hypostase?', in A.M. Triacca and A. Pistoia (eds.), *Trinité et Liturgie* (Rome: C L V Edizioni liturgiche, 1984), pp. 51-57 (53). It apparently comes from Christology, in an attempt to provide some degree of individuality while still maintaining a monotheistic theology.

Person.[126] Still others prefer to explain the apparent divine imagery as a literary device.[127] In a much different vein C.V. Camp, while admitting some echoes of goddesses, sees the image as an abstraction from women sages and counsellors (and biblical stories about them).[128] Fontaine considers each of these positions, and concludes that the best understanding of the personification of wisdom would combine aspects of each.[129] Another recent suggestion has been proposed by M.D. Coogan, that the divine attributes given to Lady Wisdom in Proverbs 1–9 and especially Job 28 (as elsewhere in the deuterocanonical books) is a legitimization of the worship in Israel and Judah of more 'established' goddesses, such as Asherah.[130] It is my opinion that the apparent apotheosis of Lady Wisdom in the

126. Conzelmann, 'The Mother of Wisdom', p. 232.

127. Murphy, who believes that wisdom cannot be a hypostasis or distinct person because of the strict monotheism of the post-exilic period, may be the most vocal advocate of this view; see, for example, R.E. Murphy, 'Wisdom: Theses and Hypotheses', in J.G. Gammie *et al.* (eds.), *Israelite Wisdom: Theological and Literary Essays in Honor of Samuel Terrien* (Missoula, MT: Scholars Press for Union Theological Seminary, 1978), pp. 35-42; R.E. Murphy, 'Hebrew Wisdom', *JAOS* 101 (1981), pp. 21-34; R.E. Murphy, 'Proverbs and Theological Exegesis', in D.G. Miller (ed.), *The Hermeneutical Quest* (Allison Park, PA: Pickwick Publications, 1986), pp. 87-95; R.E. Murphy, *The Tree of Life: An Exploration of Biblical Wisdom Literature* (Garden City, NY: Doubleday, 1990), pp. 133-49; etc.

128. Cf. C.V. Camp, *Wisdom and the Feminine in the Book of Proverbs* (Bible and Literature Series, 11; Sheffield: Almond Press, 1985); C.V. Camp, 'Woman Wisdom as Root Metaphor: A Theological Consideration', in K.G. Hoglund, *et al.* (eds.), *The Listening Heart: Essays in Wisdom and the Psalms in Honor of Roland E. Murphy* (JSOTSup, 58; Sheffield: JSOT Press, 1987), pp. 45-76; C.V. Camp, 'The Female Sage in Ancient Israel and in the Biblical Wisdom Literature', in J.G. Gammie and L.G. Perdue (eds.), *The Sage in Israel and the Ancient Near East* (Winona Lake, IN: Eisenbrauns, 1990), pp. 185-203; and S. Schroer, 'Weise Frauen und Ratgeberinnen in Israel', *Biblische Notizen* 51 (1990), pp. 41-60; rev. and trans. as, 'Wise and Counselling Women in Ancient Israel: Literary and Historical Ideals of the Personified Ḥokmâ', in A. Brenner (ed.), *A Feminist Companion to Wisdom Literature* (The Feminist Companion to the Bible, 9; Sheffield: Sheffield Academic Press, 1995), pp. 67-84; cf. also C.R. Fontaine, 'The Social Roles of Women in the World of Wisdom', in Brenner (ed.), *A Feminist Companion to Wisdom Literature*, pp. 24-49.

129. C.R. Fontaine, 'Proverbs', in J.L. Mays (ed.), *Harper's Bible Commentary* (San Francisco: Harper & Row, 1988), pp. 495-517 (501-503); cf. C.R. Fontaine, 'Proverbs', in C.A. Newsom and S.H. Ringe (eds.), *The Women's Bible Commentary* (Louisville: Westminster/John Knox, 1992), pp. 145-52 (147-48).

130. M.D. Coogan, 'The Goddess Wisdom—"Where can she be found?": Literary Reflexes of Popular Religion', communication given at the Society of Biblical Literature Meetings in Washington DC, 1993; I wish to thank Professor Coogan for furnishing me with a rough draft of this communication.

biblical literature is not a legitimization of the worship of 'established' goddesses, but rather is a literary compensation for the eradication of the worship of these goddesses.

The passage in Proverbs which might give the best support to viewing חכמה as a deity is Prov. 8.22-31, where Wisdom declares herself to
be the first of all of Yahweh's creations/ acquisitions/children, and
to have been present when Yahweh established the heavens and set
the boundaries of the sea.[131] Additionally, Prov. 3.19 indicates that
Yahweh 'by wisdom founded the earth; by understanding he established the heavens'. Since Yahweh obviously needs Wisdom in order
to create the heavens and the earth, then Yahweh must have been
acquainted with Wisdom before the acts of creation could be performed. Although some scholars see this passage as poetic imagery,[132] others believe the passage identifies Wisdom as a divine or at
least personified figure.[133]

Job 28

However, the question still remains: is this apparent apotheosis of
Lady Wisdom a result of her actually being (or having been) a deity
as such, or is it a literary device of some sort? To try to answer this
question, I will now briefly turn to Job 28.

The uniqueness of the book of Job and its lack of historical allusions have created difficulties for scholars in determining a date for
it. Nevertheless, most scholars date it to some time between 700 and
200 BCE, with perhaps the majority of scholars placing the book in
the early post-exilic period.[134] As far as ch. 28 is concerned, some

131. For a full analysis of this passage see Fontaine, 'Proverbs' (1988), pp.
507-508, as well as Hadley, 'Wisdom' and the references there.

132. Cf. for example, Whybray, *The Book of Proverbs*, p. 51, among others.

133. See above, and Sir. 1.1-9.

134. For example, M.H. Pope, *Job* (AB; Garden City, NY: Doubleday, 1965),
after an extended discussion on the previous suggestions for the date of the Book
of Job (pp. xxx-xxxvii), declines to give it a more precise dating apart from the
seventh century BCE for the dialogue. R. Gordis, *The Book of God and Man: A Study
of Job* (Chicago: University of Chicago Press, 1965), pp. 216-18 places it between
500 and 300 BCE, with probabilities favouring the fifth rather than the fourth
century (and see also the relevant notes on p. 361). J.C.L. Gibson, *Job* (Philadelphia: Westminster Press, 1985), p. 3 dates the book to around 600 BCE, but he
'would not object if it were dated a little later'. J.G. Janzen, *Job* (Atlanta: John
Knox, 1985), p. 5 believes that it was 'written in the exile', and N.C. Habel, *The
Book of Job* (OTL; London: SCM Press, 1985), p. 42, tentatively suggests a date

scholars believe that it is an independent poem or 'Hymn to Wisdom', whereas others believe that the poem was still written by the author of Job.[135]

Verses 1-11 describe the activities of humanity in the search for precious metals and stones; but the question 'But where shall wisdom be found?' in v. 12, and the answer in vv. 13-19, lead one to realize that the most precious acquisition of all is inaccessible to humans and cannot be bought for any price. Even Abaddon (Sheol) and Death (who are personified here) have only heard rumours of it (vv. 20-22). Only God knows the way to Wisdom and noted Wisdom's presence in creation (vv. 23-27).

Verses 23-27 are perhaps the most instructive. Especially, the verbs יביט, 'looks to' and יראה, 'sees' in v. 24 may indicate that God is seeking for Wisdom, which has her own independent existence and origin. Verse 23 may also suggest that Wisdom lies elsewhere, and that even God must 'find' Wisdom by following a path that leads to her own special abode. Nevertheless, most commentators are reluctant to attribute divine status to Lady Wisdom.

So how, then, are we to view this personified figure, with seemingly divine attributes, re-emerging in the late exilic period? Perhaps the best interpretation of the apparent apotheosis of חכמה in Israelite wisdom literature is that the gradual eradication (or assimilation into Yahweh) of legitimate goddesses such as Asherah and Astarte has prompted a counter-reaction (perhaps even subconsciously) where the feminine needs to be expressed. Georgi follows a similar view, seeing a shift in Wisdom from an abstraction to a person to a heavenly character taking her place at the side of Yahweh, which in pre-exilic times was filled by other female figures such as Asherah (at Kuntillet 'Ajrud) and Anat (at Elephantine). He further notes, however, that now Wisdom is not the wife of Yahweh but rather the

somewhere in the post-exilic era. See the commentaries and the discussions there for more opinions.

135. So Gibson, *Job*, pp. 188-89, who also notes that F.I. Andersen, *Job* (London: Inter-Varsity Press, 1976) and C. Westermann, *The Structure of the Book of Job* (Philadelphia: Fortress Press, 1981) hold similar positions; Gordis, *The Book of God and Man*, p. 278 and repeated in R. Gordis, *The Book of Job: Commentary, New Translation and Special Studies* (New York: Jewish Theological Seminary, 1978), p. 298; Janzen, *Job*, p. 187, etc.; one notable exception being Pope, *Job*, p. xviii. For a good survey of the various positions see Habel, *The Book of Job*, pp. 391-92, who himself believes that this chapter is the poet's 'personal reflection on the debate thus far'.

daughter.[136] Similar situations to this may be seen in the Hosean imagery of Israel as the bride of Yahweh, and the 'demotion' of Asherah into a hypostasis of Yahweh and the 'reduction' of Astarte into a common idiom meaning fertility. Now, here in the wisdom literature, can be seen a female figure of Lady Wisdom with seemingly divine attributes, but still very much 'under the thumb' of Yahweh, which may be an attempt at satisfying this apparent need for the feminine to be represented in the deity.[137]

Summary and Conclusions

It is therefore possible to trace a process by which deities other than Yahweh, here specifically Asherah (as well as Astarte), have 'devolved' to the extent that their names no longer refer to goddesses but rather, and solely, to objects. First, I examined how the term *asherah* changed from denoting a goddess and her image to merely an object.[138] It has been seen that the Hebrew Bible passages that mention *asherah* are largely condemnatory and can be attributed to Dtr or later. It may be, then, that for whatever reason, religious reformers in the time of Josiah and later wanted to eradicate the worship of Asherah, whether it was the wooden cultic symbol or the goddess herself. But during the centuries before this, as shown by the finds from Taanach, Kuntillet 'Ajrud and Khirbet el-Qom, Asherah has appeared paired with Yahweh in most positive ways. Furthermore, the early eighth century BCE prophets do not condemn Asherah worship. The worship of Asherah was evidently totally acceptable before the deuteronomistic reform movement gained momentum in the seventh century BCE. But since the biblical text was significantly com-

136. D. Georgi, 'Frau Weisheit oder das Recht auf Freiheit als schöpferische Kraft', in L. Siegele-Wenschkewitz (ed.), *Verdrängte Vergangenheit, die uns bedrängt: Feministische Theologie in der Verantwortung für die Geschichte* (Munich: Chr. Kaiser Verlag, 1988), pp. 243-76 (246); cf. A. Brenner, 'Some Observations on the Figurations of Woman in Wisdom Literature', in Brenner (ed.), *A Feminist Companion to Wisdom Literature*, pp. 50-66 (55).

137. Cf. Fontaine, 'Proverbs' (1988), p. 502, and B. Lang in this volume.

138. For an opposing interpretation, see P.D. Miller, Jr, 'The Absence of the Goddess in Israelite Religion', *HAR* 10 (1986), pp. 239-48, who states: 'Either the feminine deity was implicitly absorbed in Yahweh from the beginning along with all other divine powers and so had no independent existence or character, or the radical integration of divine powers in the male deity Yahweh effectively excluded the goddess(es)... In Israelite religion, of course, this was not a slow process that can be traced. The feminine dimension of deity is absorbed or absent from the beginning' (p. 245).

posed or edited by the deuteronomistic school or even later, this positive attitude toward either Asherah the deity or asherah the cultic symbol is not immediately apparent. Part of this discrediting can be seen in the deuteronomistic attempt to pair Asherah with Baal instead of her real partner, Yahweh. Furthermore, the author of Deuteronomy goes to great pains to point out in 16.21 that the asherah standing next to the altar of Yahweh is an object, and nothing more. The use of נטע 'plant' (used with asherah only in this verse) and of כל עץ, 'any kind of tree' helps to underscore the physical nature of the object. Evidently this attempt to de-personalize the term worked, for a gradual shift in the understanding of *asherah* can be seen. At first, in the tenth century BCE as shown by the Taanach stand, Yahweh and Asherah were linked together as god and goddess in a consort relationship. Then, from the mid-ninth to the mid-eighth century BCE Khirbet el-Qom and Kuntillet ʿAjrud inscriptions, it is clear that Yahweh and Asherah are still positively linked but now her cultic symbol is indicated. Although still associated with the goddess, the cultic pole appears to be being taken over by Yahweh, since it can now be designated 'his *asherah*'. It may have become a symbol of Yahweh's developing fertility aspects. Then, by the time of the Chronicler, it appears that the distinction between Asherah the goddess and *asherah* the cultic pole has become totally obscured—with the term asherah denoting merely some type of object, as the goddess Asherah and her worship were gradually eradicated. A similar shift can be seen for Astarte—from the recognition of her cult (albeit portrayed as a foreign one) during the monarchy period, to the use of her name as merely an idiom denoting fertility in the book of Deuteronomy. By the time of the Chronicler she is not even mentioned. Finally, as a literary compensation for this 'eradication' of the worship of these goddesses, the figure of Lady Wisdom emerges in the late post-exilic period, complete with goddess-like imagery but very much acting on behalf of Yahweh as one of Yahweh's co-workers. As Fontaine notes, 'it may be that by "co-option" of surrounding goddesses to create the Yahwistically subordinated figure of Woman Wisdom, Israel met its own psychological need for female imagery of the divine without serious compromise of patriarchal monotheism'.[139] The former goddesses are thus absorbed into the cult of Yahweh, and become attributes of Yahweh which are expressed in the figure of Lady Wisdom.

139. Fontaine, 'Proverbs' (1988), p. 502.

LADY WISDOM: A POLYTHEISTIC AND PSYCHOLOGICAL INTERPRETATION OF A BIBLICAL GODDESS

Bernhard Lang

In the eleventh century, the Hispano-Arabic scholar Ibn Hazm observed that Wisdom, in Proverbs 8, is not simply the wisdom of the only God—an interpretation, he argued, which violates the canons of sound textual exegesis. He felt that here the Bible refers to a goddess.[1] At the beginning of our century, Hermann Gunkel wrote: 'The sages had a kind of female patron deity of whom they sometimes spoke; Hebrew tradition calls her "Wisdom". For Israel's sages, this figure was perhaps a mere personification. Some of her features, however, betray her former divine nature.'[2] Gunkel is certainly correct in arguing that, in monotheistic times, some of the sages considered Lady Wisdom—as she appears in the book of Proverbs—a 'mere' personification, not a goddess with an abstract name. However, this paper deals with the entity Gunkel calls the patroness of the sages and her divine nature. For, today, we see more clearly than in Gunkel's days that ancient Israel's religion was not committed to the exclusive worship of one single deity right from the beginning of its history; the 'alone-ist' movement came later, presumably in the eighth century BCE, when the prophet Hosea appears as one of its early promoters.

'You shall have no other gods before me' (Exod. 20.3) says the biblical God, but the Bible itself suggests that not all ancient Israelites followed this precept, as does archaeological evidence. Along with their national god, they venerated a host of other gods and goddesses. The list of goddesses is particularly impressive: it includes the Queen of Heaven (Jer. 44.17), Astarte (1 Sam. 7.4), the (to us, anonymous) Naked Goddess,[3] Asherah (2 Kgs 21.7) and Lady Wisdom. While

1. M. Asín Palacios, *Abenházam de Córdoba y su Historia crítica de las ideas religiosas* (Madrid: Real Academia de la Historia, 1928), II, p. 367.
2. H. Gunkel, *Zum religionsgeschichtlichen Verständnis des Neuen Testaments* (Göttingen: Vandenhoeck & Ruprecht, 1903), p. 26.
3. Iconographic material in U. Winter, *Frau und Göttin: Exegetische und ikonographische Studien zum weiblichen Gottesbild in Alten Israel und in dessen Umwelt*

scholars disagree about the identity and even existence of some of these—especially about Asherah, who might be a sacred tree rather than a goddess; and Lady Wisdom, whom some consider a mere personification—most of them recognize the fact of polytheistic worship. So, if we wish to gain insight into what it meant for some of the ancient Hebrews to believe in and worship a goddess, we must study the first nine chapters of the book of Proverbs. We know more about Lady Wisdom, the ancient Hebrew goddess who figures prominently in Proverbs 1–9, than about any other goddess mentioned in the Bible or known through archaeological finds.[4]

The Main Biographical Source: Proverbs 1–9

The first nine chapters of the book of Proverbs seem to have been an independent, self-contained sapiential book, used in the scribal school.[5] Like ancient Egyptian school miscellanies, its textual units— exhortatory discourses and poems—served as texts to be copied or written to dictation and presumably to be memorized by the pupil. We must think therefore of the book as meant for the advanced student who has already mastered the alphabet as well as the writing of individual words and sentences, for it was in such a sequence that the ancient scribal curriculum proceeded throughout the ancient world. One began with learning how to trace individual letters but, eventually, worked on longer textual units of the kind collected in Proverbs 1–9. While the school background of these chapters seems to be fairly straightforward, the date is more difficult to fix. The reference to the monarchy, the urban milieu,[6] and the allusion to the

(OBO, 53; Fribourg: Universitätsverlag, 1983), figs. 11-69.

4.   For earlier studies, here supplemented, see B. Lang, *Wisdom and the Book of Proverbs: A Hebrew Goddess Redefined* (New York: Pilgrim Press, 1986); *idem*, 'Figure ancienne, figure nouvelle de la Sagesse en Pr 1 à 9', in J. Trublet (ed.), *La Sagesse biblique de l'Ancien au Nouveau Testament* (Paris: Cerf, 1995), pp. 61-97; *idem*, 'Wisdom', in K. van der Toorn *et al.* (eds.), *Dictionary of Deities and Demons in the Bible* (Leiden: Brill, 1995), cols. 1692-702. See further M.D. Coogan, 'The Goddess Wisdom—Where can she be found?' (forthcoming in L. Schiffman *et al.* [eds.], *Baruch A. Levine Festschrift*).

5.   On the ancient scribal school and its curriculum, see B. Lang, 'Schule und Uterricht im alten Israel', in Lang, *Wie wird man Prophet in Israel?* (Düsseldorf: Patmos, 1980), pp. 104-19; also in M. Gilbert (ed.), *La Sagesse de l'Ancien Testament* (Leuven: Peeters, 2nd edn, 1990), pp. 186-201, 412-14.

6.   For the urban milieu of Prov. 1–9 see R.N. Whybray, *Wealth and Poverty in the Book of Proverbs* (JSOTSup, 99; Sheffield: JSOT Press, 1990), pp. 101-104.

typical domestic architecture of the Iron Age[7] all point to a pre-exilic
date, but it seems to be difficult to be more precise than this. Since the
anonymous teacher who composed or compiled the text was not
affected by the Yahweh-alone idea, which may have emerged not
earlier than the mid-eighth century, it seems reasonable to assume a
ninth- or eighth-century BCE date. The biblical author's polytheism is
most vivid in his presentation of Lady Wisdom as a goddess whose
sphere of competence includes scribal learning and royal adminis-
tration. She may be compared with the goddess Nisaba, whom the
Sumerians called 'Mistress of Science'; or Seshat, whom the Egyptians gave the titles 'foremost in the library' and 'she who directs the
house of books'.[8]

In order to sketch a portrait, and indeed a 'biography' of the Wisdom goddess, Proverbs 1–9 has to be read as carefully as possible.
For this, two (in this context, rarely used) analytical tools will be of
particular help: Jungian psychology and the comparative study of
the role and function ancient Semitic deities had for those who venerated them. These tools enable us to explore certain aspects of the
goddess and to sketch her biography from her birth and origins to her
active professional life and, eventually, to her disappearance.

Origins: The Wise Old Woman Tells Her Myth

At an unknown date, Lady Wisdom was conceived, elaborated and
born in the mind of an ancient scribe. With the help of Jungian psychology we can understand why and how she emerged out of the
unconscious mind. In Proverbs 8 Wisdom is presented as the Creator's daughter. For the psychologist, it matters little whether we consider Lady Wisdom to be a poetic figure or a goddess. The psychologist's major distinction is between elaborations (poetical, mythical)
and primary experience, and so the question is: which experience
forms the basis of the assertion that Wisdom is the Creator's daughter? According to the the school of Freud the primary experience is
that of the parents, so that Lady Wisdom and the Creator are echoes
and figurations of mother and father. In listening to Lady Wisdom's
voice, the student actually listens to his own mother who has become

Whybray points to the reference to walls, streets and city gates; see esp. the urban
setting of sexual seduction, Prov. 7.

7.   Prov. 9.1, see B. Lang, 'Die sieben Säulen der Weisheit (Sprüche IX 1) im
Licht israelitischer Architektur', *VT* 33 (1983), pp. 488-91; *idem, Wisdom and the
Book of Proverbs*, pp. 90-93.

8.   On these goddesses see the references given in Lang, 'Wisdom', col. 1694.

his superego. If we follow the school of Jung things are somewhat more complex but, also, closer to the world of myth. The primary experience happens when male and female figures appear spontaneously in dreams and fantasies, and try to influence the ego. Jung himself had a primary experience as he began to confront and explore his unconscious mind. His *Memories, Dreams, Reflections* include a description of how, transported into an other world, he 'caught sight of two figures, an old man with a white beard and a beautiful young girl'.[9] Jung calls the male figure the Wise Old Man and the young female the Anima, the primary figuration of the feminine in a man's soul. Typically, the Anima appears in tandem with the Wise Old Man, and Jung considers it normal that her relationship to him is that of a daughter.[10]

Jung felt that the Anima in men and the Animus in women (that is, the contrasexual archetype) both attract and irritate the ego. For men, the ambivalence of the Anima is particularly annoying. When, for instance, a professor in his seventies abandons his family and runs off with a young redheaded actress, we suspect that the Anima has claimed another victim.[11] However, there is another side to the Anima:

> Although she may be the chaotic urge to life, something strangely meaningful clings to her, a secret knowledge or hidden wisdom, which contrasts most curiously with her irrational elfin nature... The first encounter with her usually leads one to infer anything rather than wisdom. This aspect appears only to the person who gets to grips with her seriously.[12]

Jungian analysts have consistently emphasized this double nature of the Anima. 'The commonest guise in which the Anima is encountered', writes Anthony Stevens,

---

9. C.G. Jung, *Memories, Dreams, Reflections* (London: Fontana, 1983), p. 205.

10. C.G. Jung, *Symbols of Transformation* (Collected Works, 5; New York: Pantheon, 1956), no. 515.

11. C.G. Jung, *The Archetypes and the Collective Unconscious* (Collected Works, 9.1; New York: Pantheon, 1959), no. 62. A. Stevens, *Archetype: A Natural History of the Self* (London: Routledge & Kegan Paul, 1982), pp. 67-68 explains: 'Enormous power seems to be possessed by the woman on to whom the archetype is projected, and the man who does the projecting is quite unable to use his critical faculties, because the archetype, once constellated, has him in its grip. Whatever conscious reasons he may advance in explanation of his choice, they are in fact secondary—rationalizations merely: the primary motivation lies in the numinous quality of the activated archetype.'

12. Jung, *The Archetypes and the Collective Unconscious*, no. 64.

is in dreams, where she frequently appears as an unknown young
woman. Although she looks young, there is about her a timeless quality
and often a suggestion that she has years of experience behind her. She
may be connected with earth or water and is often endowed with great
power. Like the mother archetype she has positive and negative aspects:
on the one hand she is a loving, helpful figure, on the other a seductress
or witch. Anima dreams can be extremely vivid and their numinosity
may live on in the imagination long after most dreams are forgotten.[13]

The Anima figure has two sides; she is wise and maternal, but also
irrational and seductive. How will men react when confronted with
this figure? Jung did not like the Anima figure that appeared in his
dreams; he felt more comfortable with the Old Man. He advises men
to withstand the Anima's seductions and to eliminate her godlike
quality, so that she cannot control and 'possess' their egos and make
them behave in unmanly, emotional, feminine or irrational ways.
Jung could even speak of the dethronement of the Anima as the
repetition of a primordial, mythical scene: men had had a female
deity originally but, growing tired of being governed by her, they had
overthrown this deity.[14] But once Jung had eliminated the irritating
presence of the Anima, other figures appeared in his dreams and fantasies. Eventually, a male character by the name of Philemon emerged
as a friend and *guru* who accompanied and guided Jung for many
years.[15] Stage 1, with Wise Old Man and Anima, has given way to
stage 2, with the Wise Old Man. By elimination, Jung had resolved
the irritating duality of Wise Old Man and Anima. No longer subject
to the rule of two (or more) inner voices, but just to one, he had made
progress toward spiritual maturity.

In his attempt to deal theoretically, not just practically, with his
inner experience, Jung came to distinguish three levels of the human
psyche: the level of the unconscious, the semi-conscious level of
dreams and fantasies, and the conscious level of the ego. Figures
such as the Anima and the Wise Old Man manifest themselves in
dreams and fantasies as messengers through whom the unconscious
mind sends messages, deeper knowledge or psychological power to
consciousness and thus helps the ego to stay in touch with its
unconscious roots. Jung feels that the Anima, for all her potential for

13. Stevens, *Archetype*, p. 68.

14. C.G. Jung, *Analytical Psychology : Notes of the Seminar Given in 1925* (Princeton, NJ: Princeton University Press, 1989), p. 46.

15. Jung, *Memories, Dreams, Reflections*, pp. 207-208. For the 'Wise Old Man',
see Jung, *The Archetypes and the Collective Unconscious*, pp. 207-54: 'The Phenom-
enology of the Spirit in Fairy Tales'.

wisdom, should be pushed aside; only *one* inner figure should remain. Of the same sex as the ego, this figure is a 'mana-personality', that is, a personality full of numinous power and endowed with superior knowledge and a strong will. It is this figure and its counsel that the ego can trust.[16]

Despite the avowal of his esteem for the Anima and this figure's positive—maternal and sapiential—side, Jung does not seem to have envisaged a positive relationship with her. But not all men reject the Anima, and Goethe could actually indulge in quite amusing fantasies about her. In a poem he entitled 'My Goddess' (1780), he extols Lady Fantasy as his lover and spouse, while also acknowledging the more sobering, restraining influence of 'the old mother-in-law, Wisdom'.[17] Split into the two figures of imagination and wisdom (in the roles of daughter and mother), the Anima is allowed to rule the poet's heart. In the book of Proverbs there is another, and quite appealing, way of integrating the Anima into the spiritual life of a man.

From a Jungian perspective, the two figures that appear in Proverbs 8—the Creator and Lady Wisdom—are more than the private fantasy of an individual; associated to form a myth, they represent common notions or 'archetypes'. It is easy to recognize the archetypal conjunction of the Wise Old Man with a young woman, here presented as Daughter Wisdom[18] (because she is presented as the Wise Old Man's daughter). The Wise Old Man is the one who 'gives wisdom; from his mouth come knowledge and understanding' (Prov. 2.6). We also recognize Daughter Wisdom's association with earth and water, for she is present when the Creator dealt with earth and waters (Prov. 8.27-30). Moreover, the biblical text does a thorough job in coming to grips with the two archetypal figures. The ambivalence of Daughter Wisdom as a being with both negative and positive attributes is eliminated. Her negative part is split off and survives, even textually, as Lady Folly, the seductress of Proverbs 9. Freed from her shadow, only the Wise Woman remains. The second, and more visible elimination is that of the Creator. He is pushed into the background, so that only one 'mana-personality' is actively present in the

16. C.G. Jung, *Two Essays on Analytical Psychology* (Collected Works, 7; New York: Pantheon, 1953), nos. 374-406: 'The mana-personality'.

17. 'Meine Göttin', in *J.W. von Goethes Werke* (ed. E. Trunz; Munich: Beck, 1981), I, p. 145.

18. Expression coined by A. Brenner, 'Some Observations on the Figurations of Woman in Wisdom Literature' in A. Brenner (ed.), *A Feminist Companion to Wisdom Literature* (The Feminist Companion to the Bible, 9; Sheffield: Sheffield Academic Press, 1995), p. 55.

student's mind. Lady Wisdom alone addresses the student, and she refers to the Creator (the Wise Old Man) only when telling her story. For the present, the Creator stays in heaven while Lady Wisdom acts on earth. Stage 1, with the Creator and Daughter Wisdom, has given way to stage 2, with Lady Wisdom. The Jungian model here does not quite fit, for it makes us expect the elimination of the Anima and not of the Wise Old Man. Unlike Jung, the biblical text does not eliminate the female figure but the Wise Old Man. Perhaps one can say that in the biblical text Lady Wisdom is the fusion of Daughter Wisdom and Creator. She is the Wise Old Woman. She has the characteristics of a conjunction of opposites, for as the Wise Old Woman she unites wisdom and womanhood but still remains erotic and seductive. A wise, friendly, loving and maternal spirit, she is the scribe's guide, lover and protectress—mother and companion at the same time. Viewed from the perspective of Goethe's poem, one might say that Lady Wisdom is both mother and daughter, Wisdom and Fantasy at the same time.

Before we study Lady Wisdom's divine roles, we have to take a closer look at her relationship with her father, the Creator. And in so doing we will no longer be dependent on Jungian analysis only, for ancient sources provide adequate materials for studying her position in the ancient Semitic pantheon.

Lady Wisdom's Promotion: The Creator's Daughter and Her Place within the Pantheon

For the early career of the goddess we must turn from the biblical text to an extra-biblical source: the Aramaic Aḥiqar papyri. They tell about the young lady's promotion to a high position within the pantheon. In 1904–1906, during their excavations on the Nile island of Elephantine in Egypt, German archaeologists found ancient papyri. On close study those were shown to carry Aramaic texts dating from the fifth century BCE. The papyri had belonged to the Jewish diaspora community living on this island. Of particular importance is the so-called 'Aḥiqar novel', a sapiential writing that combines a story with a collection of wise sayings. By joining two papyrus leaves, Arthur Ungnad was able to reconstruct a passage of this book that refers to a goddess. She bears the same name as the book of Proverbs' Lady Wisdom. The Aḥiqar passage extols those who behave wisely by not drinking without libating to the gods, by storing wisdom in their heart, and by guarding secrets. The Aḥiqar author underlines his praise of wisdom by adding that the gods also appreciate her. In fact, he treats wisdom as a goddess. A recent rendering of the relevant passage reads:

> From heaven humankind is favored: the gods have [made known their wisdom]. Among the gods, too, she is honored; [she shares with her lord] the rulership. In heaven she is established; yea, the lord of the holy ones has exalted her.[19]

The context implies that the gods have favored humankind by granting wisdom: specifically, by sending Lady Wisdom to teach them knowledge and wise behavior. Lady Wisdom appears here as a goddess belonging to the 'holy ones', that is, to the children of the creator god El. However, El has exalted her to co-rulership with himself. Whatever the precise implications of the exaltation, there can be no doubt about her prominent position in Ahiqar's pantheon.[20]

While the book of Ahiqar gives us no more than a glimpse of the divine world, the gaps from the texts of Ugarit may be tentatively filled in. While these texts date from a much earlier period and do not mention a wisdom deity, they provide information about the presumably unchanging structure of the ancient Semitic pantheon. This pantheon is led by El and Asherah, the divine couple owning the universe and giving birth to all the gods and goddesses. Below El and Asherah stand, in descending rank, the 'active deities', the 'artisan deities' and the 'messenger deities'. Lady Wisdom is one of El's children, presumably his favorite daughter. She belongs to the 'active deities' such as Baal, Mot (Death, the god of the hot desert wind), Yamm (the Sea) and Shapash (the Sun) who, while responsible to El and Asherah, rely on their own power to administer and control the universe.[21]

It does not seem to be too difficult to imagine that Lady Wisdom, before she appears in the book of Proverbs, started her career in a polytheistic world resembling the one found in the Ahiqar text and in Ugaritic mythology. At that stage her divine father must have been

19. Ahiqar 94-95. Admittedly, the text is badly broken and reconstructed; I give the trans. of I. Kottsieper, in O. Kaiser (ed.), *Texte aus der Umwelt des Alten Testaments* (3 vols; Gütersloh: Gütersloher Verlagshaus, 1990–), III, pp. 335-36.

20. In a Mesopotamian hymn, the goddess Inanna is boasting that she has received lordship over heaven, earth, ocean and war, for the god Enlil has 'exalted' her; see *ANET*, pp. 578-79. 'Exaltation' in the sense of a promotion to a suprior rank among the gods is a standard motif of Mesopotamian mythology and, certainly, supports the idea that the book of Ahiqar refers to a wisdom goddess; see Lang, *Wisdom and the Book of Proverbs*, p. 172.

21. L.K. Handy, *Among the Host of Heaven: The Syro-Palestinian Pantheon as Bureaucracy* (Winona Lake, IN: Eisenbrauns, 1994).

known under the name of El or Elohim, not under the name of
Yahweh. The Massoretic text of Proverbs 8 identifies Lady Wisdom's
father as Yahweh who is then characterized as the creator god, the
god who established heaven and earth. But behind Yahweh stands
the ancient Semitic creator god El, whom the biblical authors have
identified with their own national deity Yahweh. This identification
seems of relatively recent date within biblical history; it does not
seem to antedate the early sixth century BCE.[22] Before that date,
polytheistic Israel distinguished between the creator god El and the
national deity Yahweh, and the latter was never spoken of as the
creator. Yahweh led the people out of Egypt, gave the land, protected
the royal dynasty, inspired prophets, and granted victory in war; he
was Israel's tutelary and perhaps was the creator of Israel, but not
the creator of the universe. Our assumption that Proverbs 1–9 originated in a pre-monotheistic times therefore implies another assumption, namely that Lady Wisdom's father is, originally, El or Elohim
and not Yahweh.

That El's daughter should be called Wisdom is not surprising at
all, for El, in the texts of Ugarit, is closely associated with the idea of
wisdom and intelligence. 'Your decree, O El, is wise, your wisdom is
everlasting', says the goddess Anat in the story of Baal's Palace, one
of the myths from Ugarit.[23] It has been pointed out that when El's
wisdom is here acknowledged, this implies more than an empty
compliment; El, the sage, is the Ugaritic equivalent of the Mesopotamian god Enki (Ea) who knows the laws of creation and hence incarnates wisdom.[24] Wisdom is the divine artisan's skill in the making of
the universe. Proverbs 3.19-20 refers to the Creator's practical wisdom: 'Yahweh by wisdom founded the earth, by understanding he
established the heavens; by his knowledge the deeps broke forth,
and the clouds drop down the dew.' (Here, as in Proverbs 8, the
original reference to 'El' or 'Elohim' seems to have been replaced by
'Yahweh'.) Wisdom may here stand for a blend of the architect's
expertise with manual dexterity and, presumably, magical power. It
is with these capabilities that Lady Wisdom is associated. A close

22. B. Lang, 'Ein babylonisches Motiv in Israels Schöpfungsmythologie (Jer
27,5-6)', *BZ* 27 (1983), pp. 236-37; W. Herrmann, 'Wann wurde Jahwe zum
Schöpfer der Welt?' *UF* 23 (1991), pp. 165-80.

23. J.C.L. Gibson, *Canaanite Myths and Legends* (Edinburgh: T & T Clark, 1977),
p. 54.

24. M. Dietrich and O. Loretz, 'Die Weisheit des ugaritischen Gottes El im
Kontext der altorientalischen Weisheit', *UF* 24 (1992), pp. 31-38, esp. p. 35. On
El's wisdom see further Handy, *Among the Host of Heaven*, pp. 79-83.

reading of Proverbs 1–9 reveals, however, that we should be very cautious in using the rhetoric of power when speaking of wisdom, for the sages themselves avoided such reference. For them wisdom is always and predominantly associated with intellectual capabilities. There is only one explicit reference to strength, presumably military prowess (*gᵉbûrāh*), in all of Proverbs 1–9. 'I have good advice and sound wisdom; I have insight, I have strength (*gᵉbûrāh*)', Lady Wisdom says (Prov. 8.14) and the context suggests that this is what she gives to kings, rulers and civil servants. Here there is the typical attitude of the sages, who tend to see everything from the intellectual point of view. God's act of creation depends on intellectual skills, not on power; and when reference to military prowess seems unavoidable, the sages use the typically Semitic way of accumulating nouns to present a 'stereometric' view of the reality they describe. Speaking of 'advice, wisdom, insight and strength', they blend three parts of wisdom (advice, wisdom, insight) with one part of power (strength).[25] Even today, intellectuals rarely exert any direct power; they act more behind the scenes and wield their authority indirectly, that is, through others whom they advise. Though often having considerable influence over others, intellectuals seldom have much formal authority. They are like ministers without portfolio, experts without the power to translate their ideas into public policy.[26] The ancient sages felt more at home with the almost imperceptible, calm rulership of El and Lady Wisdom than with Baal, the boisterous warrior and weather god who manifests his presence in thunderstorms, rain and lightning.[27] In his very first discourse in the book of Proverbs, the teacher challenges the student to renounce the violent ways of those who waylay, rob and kill others (Prov. 1.8-19). The basic choice is one between wisdom and violence. Only those who prefer wisdom can become true students of Lady Wisdom and, indeed, her lovers. As we

25. The same attitude is expressed in Isa. 11.2, when the king's wisdom and strength are referred to, and in Job 12.13, when God's wisdom and strength are mentioned. On the accumulation of expressions and their presentation in the form of rhetorical parallelism to achieve a 'stereometric' image of reality, see G. von Rad, *Wisdom in Israel* (trans. J.D. Martin; London: SCM Press, 1972), p. 27.

26. G.E. Lenski, *Power and Privilege: A Theory of Social Stratification* (New York: McGraw–Hill, 1966), p. 365.

27. See A. Caquot, 'Israelite Perceptions of Wisdom and Strength in the Light of the Ras Shamra Texts', in J.G. Gammie *et al.* (eds.), *Israelite Wisdom: Theological and Literary Essays in Honor of Samuel Terrien* (Missoula, MT: Scholars Press, 1978), pp. 25-33.

shall see, love of wisdom implies the love for Lady Wisdom and her adoption as a 'personal goddess'.

Her Professional Life (1): The Scribe's Personal Goddess

The scribal training echoed in the book of Proverbs aimed at more than the teaching of writing skills. The exhortations aim to inculcate traditional morality, and recommend a special kind of scribal spirituality built on the relationship between the apprentice scribe and Lady Wisdom. This relationship is that between a scribe and his 'personal goddess'. As an active goddess, Lady Wisdom supports and cares for the scribes.

A typical function of an ancient Semitic god or goddess is to serve as someone's 'personal deity'.[28] According to ancient Mesopotamian and Hebrew thought, each human person has a 'personal god'. This expression does *not* refer to a god or a goddess who has a personality (for this applies to all deities, however vague their personal traits may be). Instead, the personal god or goddess forms the human being in the mother's womb, protects the infant during pregnancy and birth, and serves as a person's tutelary deity during all of his or her life. The ancient Mesopotamians, according to Leo Oppenheim, attributed their feeling of strength and security to the presence of one or more personal deities charged with their protection. When feeling at their best, in full vigour, enjoying economic prosperity and spiritual peace, individuals ascribe this enviable state of body and mind to the presence of supernatural powers that either fill their bodies or guard them. 'To experience a lucky stroke, to escape a danger, to have an easy and complete success, is expressed in Akkadian by saying that such a person has a "spirit"', that is, a personal god who is responsible for physical well-being, success, and luck in all dealings.[29] Both men and women enjoyed the presence of personal gods

28. For the Mesopotamian notion of the personal god, see H. Vorländer, *Mein Gott: Die Vorstellung vom persönlichen Gott im Alten Orient und im Alten Testament* (Kevelaer: Butzon & Bercker,1975); T. Jacobsen, *The Treasures of Darkness: A History of Mesopotamian Religion* (New Haven: Yale University Press, 1976), pp. 155-160; L. Boström, *The God of the Sages* (Stockholm: Almqvist & Wiksell, 1990), pp. 193-96; R.A. Di Vito, *Studies in Third Millennium Sumerian and Akkadian Personal Names* (Rome: Pontifical Biblical Institute, 1993), pp. 1-15, with review by W.G. Lambert, *Or* 64 (1995), pp. 131-36. Vorländer has demonstrated that the notion of the 'personal God' is well attested in the Bible, but his work seems to have had little impact on Anglo-Saxon biblical scholarship.

29. A.L. Oppenheim, *Ancient Mesopotamia: Portrait of a Dead Civilization*

whose protection they acquired by choice. Only free women apparently had no choice in the matter: they were first under the protection of their father's and later under the protection of their husband's tutelary deity.[30] When in the biblical story Ruth says to Naomi that 'your God is my God' (Ruth 1.16), she either states the fact that the two women share a personal god or she adopts her mother-in-law's tutelary deity, for 'my god' is the standard way of referring to one's personal deity. At times, the personal god's protection does not seem to be available. People readily blame their misfortunes, illnesses and failures on the deity's absence, for once the tutelary deity has left the protégé he or she is an easy prey for hostile forces, be they human or demonic. Psalm 22 not only asks the desperate question: 'My God, my God, why have you forsaken me?' (v. 22), but also refers to the dogs and the company of evildoers—presumably to be identified as demons—encircling the unfortunate individual. As soon as personal deities abandon their protégés, these fall prey to evil spirits. Once the personal deity has withdrawn from someone demons 'cover him like a cloak', as one Mesopotamian source states.[31]

The Hebrew Bible is full of texts that express or echo belief and trust in a personal god. The language of protection and care is familiar to all who have ever read the book of Psalms; just think of 'The Lord is my shepherd' (23.1). The book of Proverbs includes a passage that tells us how a young Hebrew boy came into contact with Lady Wisdom whom he adopts as his personal goddess. In Proverbs 4 the teacher reports how, as a boy, he had received the relevant instruction from his own master:

> When I was a son with my father, tender, the only one in the sight of my mother, he taught me, and said to me, 'Let your heart hold fast my words, keep my commandments, and live; do not forget, and do not

(Chicago: University of Chicago Press, rev. edn, 1977), p. 200.

30. J.J. Stamm, *Die akkadische Namengebung* (Leipzig: Hinrichs, 1939), p. 309. Some of the logic involved can be gleaned from Plutarch, *Moralia: Advice to Bride and Groom* 19 (140D): 'A wife ought not to make friends of her own, but to enjoy her husband's friends in common with him. Therefore it is becoming for a wife to worship and to know only the gods that her husband believes in.' Marcus Cato gave similar instructions concerning the female housekeeper (*vilica*): 'She [the *vilica*] must not engage in religious worship herself or get others to engage in it for her without the orders of the master or the mistress; let her remember that the master attends to the devotions for the whole household' (*De agricultura* 153).

31. 'They [demons] have encountered the man from whom his god has withdrawn and covered him like a cloak', Shurpu VII, 19-20; see E. Reiner, *Šurpu: A Collection of Sumeran and Akkadian Incantations* (Graz: E. Weidner, 1958), p. 36.

> turn away from the words of my mouth. Get wisdom; get insight. Do
> not forsake her, and she will keep you; love her, and she will guard you.
> The beginning of wisdom is this: Get Wisdom, and whatever you get, get
> insight. Prize her highly, and she will exalt you; she will honor you if
> you embrace her. She will place on your head a fair garland; she will
> bestow on you a beautiful crown' (Prov. 4.3-9).

Lady Wisdom is here recommended by the father to the son, which
means, in the language of the ancient scribal school, by the teacher to
the young student. The student is told that the acquisition of knowledge must be accompanied by another acquisition. He must acquire
both certain technical skills *and a personal goddess*—Lady Wisdom.
She will be his tutelary; she will grant protection and ensure his
success in life. In the exhortation, Wisdom and wisdom alternate and
are mutually inclusive. Whoever wants to become a true sage must
adopt Lady Wisdom as his personal goddess. In this function Lady
Wisdom has a fairly close Egyptian equivalent; it is not goddess Maat
(as has often been suggested[32]) but the divine scribe, Thoth. According to Bernard Couroyer the ancient Egyptian 'instruction' texts,
which often refer to 'god' (*ntr*) in the singular without giving a name,
consistently envision one particular deity, Thoth, and none other.
This god, who is the scribe, bookkeeper and secretary of the gods,
serves as the patron deity of the Egyptian scribes and civil servants.

> Throughout his career, from his appointment [his calling] to his old age,
> Thoth is the scribe's providence. This calling is higher than any other
> calling, and Thoth ensures good luck and success. He loves those who
> are competent and sees to their promotion.[33]

This is exactly what the biblical scribes expect from Lady Wisdom.

To expect from one's personal deity help and support in one's
occupational life was for the ancient Israelites a matter of course.
Since the profession of most Israelites was that of farming the land,
they hoped their personal god would help them with their agricul-
tural work. The peasant knows his business, says the prophet Isaiah,
'for he is instructed aright; his god teaches him' (Isa. 28.26). Peasants
learned their trade in the family: usually their fathers would have
instructed them how to plow, how to level the ground, how to sow
dill, cumin, wheat, barley and spelt—all examples given by Isaiah. In
the age of Sigmund Freud it does not sound strange at all that the

---

32. See M. Fox, 'World Order and Ma'at: A Crooked Parallel', *JANESCU* 23
(1995), pp. 37-48. Fox has finally put the Maat error to rest.

33. B. Couroyer, 'Le "Dieu des sages" en Égypte. II', *RB* 95 (1988), pp. 70-91,
quotation on p. 88.

peasant should somehow confuse his father's voice with the voice of the personal god, just as young Samuel had to learn how to distinguish between the almost identical voices of his human and his divine masters (1 Sam. 3).[34]

Lady Wisdom is 'acquired' in the same way a man 'acquires' a woman whom he marries. In Prov. 7.4, the teacher supplements this legal terminology by using erotic language in his exhortation: 'Say to Wisdom, You are my sister, and call Insight your intimate friend'. The erotic meaning of calling a female friend or spouse one's 'sister' is well known from the Song of Songs: the expression stands for 'darling' or 'sweetheart' and belongs to the language used by lovers. It denotes tenderness and intimacy. The young man, then, establishes a kind of marriage relationship with Lady Wisdom. In the history of religions mystical marriage is, of course, well known: the shaman's marriage with a female spirit, the voodoo marriage with a deity of the opposite sex, mystical marriage between Christ and the believer's soul. In ancient Judaism, the book of Wisdom develops the theme and prepares the way for what in medieval Christianity becomes the basis of a major current of elite spirituality. In the middle ages (and beyond) some Christian mystics followed Henry Suso[35] in thinking of Wisdom as their actual spouse. For our purposes, it may suffice to point out the basic meaning of such a spiritual alliance. It is simply the expression of the human wish to belong to the world of the gods, to be related to them as closely and as permanently as possible. In traditional Siberia a community gave one man, the shaman, to the gods; once the marriage bond between the shaman and a female deity was established the shaman could be considered a 'relative' or 'affine' of the gods, and it is through this relative that the entire community could approach the gods.[36] In many cultures mystical marriage allows individuals, and sometimes entire groups, to establish a close and permanent relationship with the divine world and to consider themselves as belonging to the gods' kin. Like humans, the gods care for their kin and feel obliged to do so.

Lady Wisdom was not the only deity functioning as a personal tutelary of Israelites. Yahweh, the national god, seems to have been the personal God of the members of the Davidic dynasty and of all

---

34. R.W.L. Moberly, 'To Hear the Master's Voice: Revelation and Spiritual Discernment in the Call of Samuel', *SJT* 48 (1995), pp. 443-68.

35. Henry Suso, *The Exemplar, with Two German Sermons* (trans. F. Tobin; New York: Paulist Press, 1989), pp. 67-70. In this chapter of his autobiography Suso recounts 'how he entered into a spiritual marriage with Eternal Wisdom'.

36. R. Hamayon, *La Chasse à l'âme* (Nanterre: Société d'Ethnologie, 1990).

the prophets who spoke in Yahweh's name. Unfortunately, the scarcity of ancient sources from pre-monotheistic times does not allow much to be said about the names and ideas associated with the 'normal' Israelite peasant's or artisan's personal deities. It is tempting to think of them as minor spirits who serve as intermediaries with the higher and more powerful gods of the pantheon. In the ancient world popular devotion was often directed to gods and goddesses of quite inferior status. The ordinary Israelites, it seems, devoted their prayers and personal requests to a group of minor gods and goddesses whom scholars call 'household deities', for they possessed no temples and enjoyed no regular priestly cult; instead, they were worshipped at small domestic shrines. These deities could be approached for help and guidance in everyday matters and were, presumably, worshipped widely throughout most levels of society. Popular devotion seems to have favored a (to us, anonymous) goddess whose terracotta plaques and small figurines have been found in large quantities throughout the land of Israel; represented in the nude, she often holds her breasts and sometimes wears a wig echoing the iconography of the Egyptian goddess Hathor.[37] A kind of demon reminiscent of the Egyptian god Bes is also known, both from objects placed in the tombs and two rough drawings found on an eighth-century BCE pot found in Kuntillet 'Ajrud in the Negev.[38] Presumably, ancient Israelite devotion to these two deities was not very different from that of the ancient Egyptians, among whom Bes and Toweret were quite popular minor demons. In Egypt as well as in the land of Israel, Bes is represented with the body of a grotesque dwarf; Egyptians considered him the god of love, marriage, dancing and jolly entertainment. Toweret (Tauert, Toëris)—who appears as an upstanding, pregnant hippopotamus—was the goddess of fecundity and childbirth. She gave assistance to Egyptian women of all classes at the birth of their children. In polytheistic times, many Israelites may have thought of their personal gods or goddesses along similar lines. It is tempting to understand Bes-amulets and the Naked Goddess, as found in the tombs of ancient Palestine, as images of the personal deity venerated by the buried individual. The personal god or goddess accompanied their protégés wherever they went, even into

37. See the iconographic material in Winter, *Frau und Göttin*, figs. 11-69.

38. See the iconographic material in D.N. Freedman (ed.), *The Anchor Bible Dictionary* (Garden City, NY: Doubleday, 1992), IV, p. 108 ('Kuntillet 'Ajrud'); E. Bloch-Smith, *Judahite Burial Practices and Beliefs about the Dead* (JSOTSup, 123; Sheffield: Sheffield Academic Press, 1992), p. 252 (fig. 13B).

the grave, where they may have been thought to help with the passage from the grave to the nether world. One ancient Israelite book, the book of Job, even echoes the singular hope that the personal deity will restore the life of the deceased (Job 19.25[39]). Ultimately, even the traditional Catholic veneration of the 'patron saint' and the 'guardian angel' can serve as illustrations of what a personal god or goddess meant for the ancient Israelites.[40]

Lady Wisdom's Professional Life (2): Cosmic Initiation and the Patroness of Nature Wisdom

The activity of Lady Wisdom is not exhausted by being the scribes' personal goddess. Recounting her myth to the students, Lady Wisdom makes them participate in the training that she received from her father as he created the universe. As we have seen, it is through mystical marriage with her that the sage—or scribe—belongs to and has access to the world of the gods. Of great importance is his link of affinity with Wisdom's father, that is, in legal terms, his father-in-law. Lady Wisdom's father is the wise Creator. Through both their learning and their love for Lady Wisdom, the sages participate in divine wisdom and therefore also in the Creator's wise rulership. This is what they are proud of. Proverbs 8 reveals the whole mythological dimension of this complex of ideas: Elohim (and not Yahweh, as the Masoretic text has it) begat the Wisdom goddess and then created the universe in her presence.

Three levels of meaning can be distinguished in the myth told in Proverbs 8. First, the myth obviously serves to present Lady Wisdom's charter of nobility, as commentators have pointed out.[41] The goddess praises herself and invokes her noble birth, to impress the students whom she addresses. I am a great goddess, she says, and

39. Note that in Job 19.25 the protagonist refers to 'my Redeemer', which is an equivalent of the expression 'my god', denoting the personal god. The biblical passage can be compare to an Akkadian text from Nippur (IM 58424, line 17) which refers to the personal god as 'my redeemer' (*šaṭipi*, from *šaṭâpu*, 'to preserve life, to save'); see B. Groneberg, 'Eine Einführungsszene in der altbabylonischen Literatur', in K. Hecker *et al.* (eds.), *Keilschriftiche Literaturen* (Berlin: Georg Reimer, 1986), pp. 93-108, on pp. 101-102.

40. For an attractive account of the early history of the Christians' 'invisible companions' see P. Brown, *The Cult of the Saints: Its Rise and Function in Latin Christianity* (London: SCM Press, 1981), pp. 50-68.

41. B. Gemser, *Sprüche Salomos* (HAT; Tübingen: Mohr, 1963), p. 49, who also cites G. Wildeboer and H.-J. Kraus.

this is why you have to listen to me. Behind the goddess stands the human teacher who asserts his authority: this is the second, and equally obvious, level of meaning. The ancient Hebrew schoolmaster, in addressing his students, claims the goddess's authority. Whenever I speak, he says, it is not merely I who am teaching and exhorting; Lady Wisdom herself is using me to speak to you. The teacher's words are backed up by divine authority. These two levels of meaning in no way exhaust the message of Proverbs 8. A look at what both Lady Wisdom and, by implication, the schoolmaster teaches, reveals a third and more profound level. Far from serving merely to support the teacher's authority, the myth has its own, distinctive and noble, message.

The key to understanding the third level of the myth is what scholars have termed 'nature wisdom'. According to the Bible, King Solomon

> uttered a thousand proverbs, and his songs were a thousand and five. He spoke of trees, from the cedar that is in Lebanon to the hyssop that grows out of the wall; he spoke also of beasts, and of birds, and of reptiles, and of fish (1 Kgs. 5.12-13 [ET 4.32-33]).

Sayings commenting on the scorpion's preference for foul food, the sexual appetite and practices of asses (Aḥiqar[42]) or the insatiable nature of the leech (Prov. 30.15) provide good examples of the kinds of sayings attributed to King Solomon. Not only sayings, but also lists of words, were the stock in trade of ancient scribal education. In both Egypt and Mesopotamia the apprentice scribes copied long lists of words. Systematically arranged, the words list gods, plants, animals, cities and so on, and served as dictionaries or vocabularies. At the same time, they can be considered encyclopedic inventories of the entire universe, inventories that served scientific and theological purposes. The ancients seem to have believed that the lists manifested the order of the world and the working of the gods.[43] The legend of King Solomon seems to presuppose the existence of such lists, but nothing of this material has been preserved in ancient Jewish literature.[44] Certain texts, however, stand close to lists and can give us an

---

42. The Aḥiqar texts can be found in J.H. Charlesworth (ed.), *The Old Testament Pseudepigrapha* (London: Darton, Longman & Todd, 1983-85), II, p. 499.

43. W. von Soden, *The Ancient Orient* (trans. D.G. Schley; Grand Rapids: Eerdmans, 1994), p. 146.

44. The classic papers on Israelite 'nature wisdom' by A. Alt ('Solomonic Wisdom') and G. von Rad ('Job XXXVIII and Ancient Egyptian Wisdom') are included in J.L. Crenshaw (ed.), *Studies in Ancient Israelite Wisdom* (New York: Ktav,

idea what they may have looked like. The book of Genesis and the non-canonical book of *Jubilees* give lists of nations (Gen. 10, *Jub.* 8–9), while the *Song of the Three Young Men* lists some forty 'works of the Lord'—the heavens, the angels, heavenly bodies, natural elements such as rain, wind and snow, the earth and earthly bodies, and human beings (Greek additions to Dan. 3). Apparently, the students copied such lists and the teacher based his 'geography' or 'science' lesson on them. Particularly relevant for understanding Proverbs 8 is the universal, all-inclusive character of nature wisdom. The study of this chapter can be seen as a grand initiation into the created world in its entirety. The process of the scribe's initiation culminated, I suggest, in the study of the creation myth that traced everything back to its ultimate origins in the act of creation.

The myth implies a threefold message. First, that El (or, as in the present text, Yahweh) is the creator and owner of the universe; ultimately, all power and all wisdom have their roots in him. Secondly, that Lady Wisdom was the original witness of the acts of creation. Older than all things, she was a little child when her father fashioned the world. She delighted in watching the Creator's activities, just as our children delight in watching how trash is collected, a wall built, a fence painted, a tree planted or a bicycle repaired. By watching, Lady Wisdom acquired superior and, indeed, superhuman knowledge of the entire world, of all 'nature wisdom', some of which the sages have tried to codify in their lists. In the first century BCE or CE, the Greek book of Wisdom's author was still aware of this dimension of the myth's message: 'Wisdom is with you [God], she knows your works, for she was present when you made the world; she understands what is pleasing in your eyes' (Wis. 9.9). The third message implied in the myth of Lady Wisdom relates to the apprentice scribe. When Lady Wisdom reports that as an infant[45] she took 'delight in

---

1976), pp. 102-12, 267-77. Von Rad thought of Job 38 as a possible echo of ancient Israelite nature wisdom that was originally transmitted in the form of word lists. However, the existence of Egyptian-and Mesopotamian-style 'onomastica' in Israel has been challenged by M. Fox, 'Egyptian Onomastica and Biblical Wisdom', *VT* 36 (1986), pp. 302-10. For ancient Israelite sayings on animals see I. Kottsieper, 'Die alttestamentliche Weisheit im Licht aramäischer Weisheitstraditionen', in B. Janowski (ed.), *Weisheit außerhalb der kanonischen Weisheitsschriften* (Gütersloh: Kaiser, 1996), pp. 128-62.

45. While some translations, including the NRSV, give 'I was beside him, like a *master worker*', Prov. 8.30 is to be rendered 'I was at his side as an *infant*'—see Lang, *Wisdom and the Book of Proverbs*, pp. 65-67. Prov. 9.1, by contrast, may be understood to present Lady Wisdom as an architect. According to Prov. 1–9,

the sons of man' (Prov. 8.31), this apparently means that humans were also there at the dawn of creation. The context suggests that the apprentice scribes somehow identify with these 'sons of men' and thus are present at creation and at Lady Wisdom's side as she watches the Creator.

Presumably, these 'sons of men' have to be thought of as children, for it would make little sense to associate Lady Wisdom, the child, with adults. At the dawn of creation human children were the playmates of Wisdom. Whenever the Bible speaks of creation, or of the renewal of creation, reference is made to children. In Psalm 8 the Creator uses the voices of children as a bulwark against the powers of chaos whom he pushes to the periphery of creation; these children, it seems, are also given dominion over the world.[46] In Isaiah's great vision of the pacified world a little child dominates wolf and lamb, leopard and kid, calf and lion, that is to say, the entire animal kingdom (11.1-9). Moreover, 'the nursing child shall play over the hole of the asp, and the weaned child shall put its hand on the adder's den' without being harmed (Isa. 11.8). It seems that the apprentice scribe, when being initiated into the cosmic dimensions of his learning, somehow regresses to being a little child and to being present at creation. Thus he comes into close contact with Lady Wisdom, acquires superior knowledge, and participates in the undiminished forces characteristic of the Beginning. The young sage 'regresses' to childhood and to the mythical Beginning of the world.

We have no knowledge of how exactly the ancient sages experienced the process of mythical regression to Childhood, that is, to their own infancy, Lady Wisdom's childhood and the childhood of creation. From the history of religions we know, however, that sensitive individuals may have visions of the Beginning. In his autobiography, Ignatius of Loyola refers to one such experience. He writes,

> At another time, it was made present to his understanding, with great spiritual joy, the manner in which God had created the world. It seemed that he saw something white, out of which some rays were coming, and that from this God was making light. But he did not know how to explain these things, nor did he remember well the spiritual illumination which God impressed on his soul at that time.[47]

Wisdom is an architect *in* the world, but not the architect *of* the world.

46. M. Görg, *Aegyptiaca Biblica: Notizen und Beiträge zu den Beziehungen zwischen Ägypten und Israel* (Wiesbaden: Otto Harrassowitz, 1991), pp. 309-15: 'Der Mensch als göttliches Kind'.

47. 'Ignatius of Loyola, Autobiography', in A.T. de Nicolas, *Powers of Imagin-*

Ignatius felt 'great spiritual joy', without remembering much of the Beginning that he experienced. His vague description can be compared with an equally vague, yet somewhat more explicit twentieth-century report. In his book *Le Tout, l'Esprit et la Matière* (1987), the French physicist Jean Charon tells of one of his most extraordinary experiences. During a vacation he spent in Brittany he walked by the sea and played with his two dogs. All of a sudden he felt deeply moved:

> Compared with the preceding days, there was nothing special about this morning. Nothing had changed. And yet, all of a sudden I was seized by an abrupt, inexplicable emotion, as if I were present at a new birth of the world. A marvelous, unforgettable feeling. Everything combined to form an image that came from nowhere, and it filled me completely... This emotion had a taste of freedom. I was transported to where I never had been, but where something or someone had decided to go and to take me with him. Today I know that this experience, this primordial feeling came from my Spirit who offered me a moment of communion with the Universe.[48]

The ancient Hebrew scribes, when being initiated into the cosmic dimensions of Wisdom, must have had similar feelings of being guided, being present at the Beginning and being filled with delight and insight and knowledge. They must have gone through an experience very much akin to what the American psychologist Abraham Maslow calls the 'peak-experience', the mystical moment of creativity, of encounter with the transcendent, with a loved person or a work of art. This kind of experience transports us to a realm outside time and space and 'is reacted to with awe, wonder, amazement, humility and even reverence, exaltation and piety'; typically, in peak experience the nature of reality itself is 'seen more clearly and its essence penetrated more profoundly'.[49] Initiated into cosmic wisdom, the scribes saw the world in a new light: in the light of the Creator and Lady Wisdom. Refreshed, empowered and instructed by this experience, they were enabled and entitled to assume political and administrative responsibilities of cosmic dimensions.

ing: Ignatius de Loyola (Albany: State University of New York Press, 1986), p. 260. The date of the vision is 1522–23.

48. J. Charon, *Le Tout, l'Esprit et la Matière* (Paris: Albin Michel, 1987), pp. 213-14.

49. A.H. Maslow, *Toward a Psychology of Being* (New York: Van Nostrand, 2nd edn, 1968), p. 81.

Monotheism and Latest News about Lady Wisdom

The foregoing interpretation has attempted to read Proverbs 1–9 as an ancient Semitic polytheistic believer would have read it. Taking the myth of Wisdom seriously, I have told her story from birth to professional activities. But the story does not end at this point. The advent of Jewish monotheism in the sixth century BCE opens another chapter of her biography.

Promoting belief in only one God, Yahweh, Jewish leaders transformed or eliminated earlier polytheistic notions. It was difficult for Lady Wisdom to survive under monotheistic circumstances. Ancient Jewish sources dating from Hellenistic and Roman times allow us to discern two different interpretations of Lady Wisdom: one mythological and one poetical.

In the mythological reading which we have developed in the present essay, Lady Wisdom is a 'real' goddess of the ancient Israelite pantheon. For some Jewish thinkers who opted for the exclusive worship of Yahweh, Lady Wisdom did not have to be eliminated from tradition. Subordinated to Yahweh, she could enter into a 'duotheistic' constellation comparable to the constellation of the 'Ancient of Days' and the (angelic) 'Son of Man' of the book of Daniel.[50] As in the Danielic myth, the subordinate being acts upon the world for the benefit of Israel while Yahweh remains in the background. In a 'duotheistic' system Lady Wisdom filled the position of a second deity above whom only the Creator stood. In that position she survived all the other ancient Hebrew deities whom the monotheistic reform had abolished. Even on monotheistic premises Lady Wisdom could survive. This interpretation can be seen in the Greek book of Wisdom, where Sophia seems to have been patterned after the Hellenistic goddess Isis.[51] However, the book of Wisdom also uses different language to describe Sophia. At times she is spoken of as an impersonal power emanating from God and pervading his creation. She also resides in the souls of prophets and leaders, inspiring their divine utterances or guiding their deeds (Wis. 7.27, 10.16). This mixture of personal and mythological language with impersonal and

---

50. See B. Lang, 'Monotheismus', in M. Görg *et al.* (eds.), *Neues Bibel-Lexikon* (Düsseldorf: Patmos, 1995), II, cols. 834-44, esp. from col. 838. See also M. Barker, *The Great Angel: A Study of Israel's Second God* (London: SPCK, 1992); R. Scroggs, 'Christ the Cosmocrator and the Experience of Believers', in A.J. Malherbe *et al.* (eds.), *The Future of Christology* (Minneapolis: Fortress Press, 1993), pp. 160-75.

51. S. Kloppenborg, 'Isis and Sophia in the Book of Wisdom', *HTR* 75 (1982), pp. 57-84.

philosophical notions makes the book of Wisdom an attractive piece of literature. It allows for two interpretations of Sophia: a more mythological one (for the common people, presumably) and a more philosophical one (for the elite). Philosophers can look beyond traditional mythology and give it a new, more abstract and sophisticated meaning, one that comes close to the poetical reading to which I will now turn.

The poetical reading has often been defended by commentators of Proverbs 1–9, including the present writer in an earlier study.[52] In this interpretation Lady Wisdom is not a goddess but a purely literary figure, created by poetic imagination to support sapiential teaching. Monotheism would not allow for another divine being. The poet or poets who devised Lady Wisdom borrowed her various characteristics from the goddesses of ancient Israel's polytheistic milieu, but also gave her the characteristics of 'real' women who were influential as counselors and bearers of folk wisdom, or even had the official role of 'king's mother' at the royal court.[53] There can be little doubt that in monotheistic times, the poetical reading of the Lady Wisdom texts was adopted by Jewish literati. There is an echo of this reading in the book of Ben Sira, who identified Lady Wisdom with God's Torah. For Ben Sira Wisdom was Law personified—a book to be loved and studied, not a person. When Scripture was read in the synagogue, her voice could be heard (Sir. 24.2); but the goddess had disappeared.

It is attractive to end Lady Wisdom's story with recounting a myth included in the first book of Enoch. The Jewish author draws upon Greek mythology when he relates how Wisdom, not finding a place to stay among humans, returns to her heavenly home.

> Wisdom went out to dwell among the children of men, but she found no dwelling place. So Wisdom returned to her place and settled permanently among the angels.[54]

The angels gain Wisdom, while humankind receives Iniquity to dwell among them. So the biography of Lady Wisdom has a happy ending for the goddess (who settles among the angels), but a tragic one for humankind.

---

52. B. Lang, *Frau Weisheit* (Düsseldorf: Patmos, 1975).

53. C. Camp, *Wisdom and the Feminine in the Book of Proverbs* (Bible and Literature Series, 11; Sheffield: Almond Press, 1985); G. Baumann, *Die Weisheitsgestalt in Proverbien 1–9* (Forschungen zum Alten Testament, 16; Tübingen: Mohr, 1996).

54. *1 Enoch* 42, in Charlesworth (ed.), *The Old Testament Pseudepigrapha*, I, p. 33. For the Greek model of this myth see Lang, 'Wisdom', cols. 1700-1701.

Summary

By way of conclusion I shall repeat that in Proverbs 1–9, a polytheistic book of uncertain date, there is clear evidence of a Wisdom Goddess. Mythologically, she was Elohim's daughter but later, when Elohim and Israel's god became identified, she was styled as Yahweh's daughter. It is hard to assume that the poems and exhortatory discourses in which Lady Wisdom figures prominently should have served only as texts for scribal exercises. Their vivid style and mythological substance suggest a deeper message. The apprentice scribe was exhorted to adopt Lady Wisdom as his personal goddess and to let himself be guided by her to the dawn of Creation. A double movement—erotic love, and regression to childhood—marks this singular sapiential spirituality, whose specific form I have tried to reconstruct and to appreciate. Psychologically, Lady Wisdom can be considered a culturally specific elaboration of the Anima, the female figure inhabiting the male soul. Unlike Jung, the ancient Israelites did not eliminate the Anima figure from their minds; instead, they made her into a personal goddess. From a poetical point of view Wisdom is a mere figure of speech, and this was no doubt how some of the strict monotheists felt about her in early Judaism. Lady Wisdom started her career in the human soul, came to be considered the scribe's personal goddess and, finally, was retired from active life as a poetic figure. But, even today, she continues to fascinate us.

Appendix: A Note on Method

I have presented two different readings of the Lady Wisdom texts, one psychological and one mythological. A third, poetical reading was mentioned only briefly. From the perspective of Jungian psychology, Lady Wisdom can be identified as a figuration that appears within individual consciousness and gives voice to the unconscious mind. Mythologically, she is a goddess. Poetically—or rather, prosaically—she is an artificial device of poetry, representing the Jewish Law. How do these three readings relate to each other?

In the foregoing article I have arranged the three readings chronologically: Lady Wisdom's life starts in a scribe's soul; she is then mythologically elaborated, but eventually loses her divine power in an era of monotheism and demythologizing. However, a second approach is possible. It seems that mythological texts generally invite these three interpretations. The demythologized reading appeals to our monotheistic, historical and rational, modern mentality. We are prepared to accept it and to locate it within space (the ancient land of Israel) and time (the Persian or Hellenistic period). The mythological reading, while still somehow located in space and time, is more vague. It appeals to what the Emperor Julian called 'the myth-loving, childlike, unreasonable part of the soul' of men and women living in the ancient world.[55] The goddess appealed to the mythological mentality not only of the ancient Israelites (of the pre-canonical, pre-monotheistic period), but also of the Arameans who were scattered throughout the ancient Near East, from Mesopotamia (where the Aḥiqar text originated) to Egypt (where this text was found in a fifth-century BCE Jewish archive). While the 'poetic' reading is specifically Jewish, the mythological one is specifically Middle-Eastern and could be understood by a much larger group of people. The depth-psychological, Jungian reading is again of a much wider appeal. It can be understood by everyone, for it relies on archetypal structures common, it seems, to humankind as a whole.

When moving away from the surface of the biblical text and descending into its depth dimension, we move first from history to mythology and then from mythology to psychology. The reading moves from the surface of the text down to ever deeper levels that concern an increasing number of persons. The first level, which may be termed the historical or surface level, concerns just one culture: early Judaism. The second level, symbolically located below the surface, concerns ancient Near Eastern people in general, for the myth is much less specific than historically defined poetry. The third level, again located below the previous one, concerns or may concern everyone. We move from history to myth and from myth to psychological reality and, thus, to the timeless world of human experience.

As I have shown elsewhere, the analysis of biblical texts often fits into the same general pattern of three levels: a historical surface level, a mythical level and a psychological level.[56] They may be represented as three superimposed layers of meaning:

> A. History
> B. Myth
> C. Human Existence.

The three levels thus distinguished can serve as a guide to understanding and describing the relationship between various ways of reading the biblical text. Autobiographically, I may add that as a young scholar I saw only the first, 'historical' level when writing my PhD thesis on Lady Wisdom (1975). Later I came to realize that there is one more dimension to the Lady; and made it a point of honor to recant my earlier, narrow view when republishing my thesis in 1986. In recent years (1990s) I have become increasingly aware of the third or depth-level. Lady Wisdom still appeals to me, and she may reveal to me ever-new sides of her (and my own) complex personality.

---

55. I borrow the expression from the Emperor Julian, *Against the Galileans*, bk 1, Introduction.

56. B. Lang, *Drewermann, interprète de la Bible* (Paris: Cerf, 1994) and *Die Bibel neu entdecken* (Munich: Kösel, 1995).

VII

INTERTEXTUALITY

INTERTEXTUALITY: RUTH IN DIALOGUE WITH TAMAR*

Ellen van Wolde

A text can be read as an autonomous structure or as a complex result of an ideologically shaped culture; it can be read as a collection of language signs that in interaction with a reader becomes a network of meaning, or as a product of an intentional writing process of an author. A text might also be read as a piece of work that is causally influenced by other works, or as a work in dialogue with other texts. All these approaches, as well as many others, function as windows that enable us to look at the text from different angles or perspectives; they make a special perception of the text possible. Construing new windows, and looking through the old and new ones, we might discover over and over again in the familiar textual forms new aspects of meaning. This article is primarily concerned with intertextuality, or the dialogue between texts. Consideration will be given to various views of intertextuality and to a procedure for studying the dialogue between biblical texts. In conclusion, a study of the intertextual relationships between the Ruth and Tamar narratives will be presented.

Intertextuality in a General Sense

The history of the concept of intertextuality begins with Michael Bakhtin.[1] In the 1920s this Russian literary critic, in contrast to his contemporaries who were occupied purely with text-immanent

---

* Reprint of 'Texts in Dialogue with Texts: Intertextuality in the Ruth and Tamar Narratives', *Biblical Interpretation* 5.1 (1997), pp. 1-28.

1. Translations of M. Bakhtin's work, which was written in Russian, include: *The Formal Method in Literary Scholarship* (trans. A. Wehrle; Baltimore; The Johns Hopkins University Press, 1978); *The Dialogic Imagination* (ed. M. Holquist; trans. C. Emerson and M. Holquist; Austin, TX: University of Texas Press, 1981); *Problems of Dostoevsky's Poetics* (ed. and trans. C. Emerson; Minneapolis: University of Minnesota, 1963, rewritten 1984); *The Bakhtin Reader: Selected Writings of Bakhtin, Medvedev and Voloshinov* (ed. P. Morris; London: Edward Arnold, 1994).

matters, posed the question of the connection of literary texts with each other and with society. He introduced the notion of *dialogičnost* or dialogicity, by which he meant that someone who writes is not only led by text internal considerations but also enters into dialogue with other texts and with reality. This understanding of dialogicity is to be situated within Bakhtin's general theory of language, in which linguistic expression and context are inextricably linked. Bakhtin regards context as a social, communicative situation, which is shared among people, and in which each utterance is in dialogue with previous utterances. This dialogue gives rise to a text that forms a microcosm of polyphony or multivalency and is a reflection of earlier texts and of reality.

Forty years later Julia Kristeva introduced Bakhtin's ideas in France.[2] She evaluated him positively, because he was the first to replace a static view of the text with a dynamic one, since he did not study a text as something that stood on its own but as something that came about in relation to other texts. Kristeva, following Bakhtin, is of the opinion that a text stands in dialogue with other texts. She created the term 'intertextuality' in order to indicate that a text intersects with other texts. Words have no longer to be considered as points or fixed meanings, but as intersections of textual surfaces: 'every text is constructed like a mosaic of quotations, every text is an absorption and a transformation of another text'.[3] Major differences are evident between Bakhtin and Kristeva, however. Bakhtin is not only concerned with the relationship between texts but also with the relationship between text and reality, while Kristeva restricts intertextuality to the relationship between texts. At the same time, Kristeva extends the concept of text further and further so that reality becomes a text too. A second difference is that Bakhtin looks from the perspective of one text to other texts, while Kristeva does not look from the text but from the intertext or 'the book of the culture' of which a text forms a small part.

These differences have become gradually bigger, because in the course of time the theories concerning intertextuality have been developed further into an ever vaguer concept by French (post) structuralists such as J. Kristeva, L. Jenny, R. Barthes and J. Derrida, and American postmodernists such as S. Fish, H. Bloom and P. De Man

---

2. J. Kristeva, *Semeiotik: Recherché pour une semanalyse* (Paris: Seuil, 1969); English translations of Kristeva's work are collected in *The Kristeva Reader* (ed. Toril Moi; Oxford: Basil Blackwell, 1986).

3. J. Kristeva, 'Word, Dialogue and Novel', in *The Kristeva Reader*, pp. 35-36.

into an ever vaguer concept.[4] Their perspective might be compared to a river: elements from other texts are incorporated in a text like drops of water in a river. In addition, they find that it is not the writer who is determinative of the intertext, but the reader. This can be expressed in the images of metaphor: it is not the writer who determines where the drop ends and the river begins, but the reader who distinguishes particular drops within the unfathomable quantity of water. In their view, furthermore, it is not only the author's particular subject that disappears, but also the work itself. For it is culture (the flowing river of the metaphor) that determines everything and forms the universal, intersubjective or collective text. Finally these authors see a text as an unending universe, from which no escape is possible. Everything is text and everything has become intertext: the intertextual space shows the impossibility of living outside the unending text. Within this unending universe only the reader can make distinctions and give meaning. Little by little, then, the phenomenon of intertextuality has become more and more general and more and more absolute. Bakhtin's emphasis on text production in interaction with other texts and with reality has become completely displaced in favour of an all-embracing view of text.

So far, two points of criticism can be made.[5] Kristeva's definition, 'every text is absorption and transformation of other texts', is very much open to question for in any case a text, alongside possible inter-textual elements, consists to a large extent of elements that are not borrowed from other texts, and of sentences that definitely do not occur in any other text. If it means that texts are constructed from sounds and words that also occur in other texts, the definition of intertextuality is not of much use and no more than a tautology. The

4. L. Jenny, 'La stratégie de la forme', *Poétique* 27 (1976), pp. 257-81; R. Barthes, *S/Z*. (Paris: Seuil, 1970); R. Barthes, *Le plaisir du texte* (Paris: Seuil, 1973); J. Derrida, *De la grammatologie* (Paris: Minuit, 1967); J. Derrida, *L'écriture et la différence* (Paris, Seuil, 1967); J. Derrida, *La dissémination* (Paris: Editions Seuil, 1972); S. Fish, *Self-Consuming Artifacts: The Experience of Seventeenth-Century Literature* (Berkeley, University of California Press, 1972); S. Fish, *Is There a Text in This Class? The Authority of Interpretative Communities* (Cambridge, MA: Harvard University Press, 1980); H. Bloom, *The Anxiety of Influence: A Theory of Poetry* (New York: Oxford University Press, 1973); H. Bloom, *Deconstruction and Criticism* (London, Routledge & Kegan Paul, 1979); P. De Man, *Allegories of Reading: Figural Language in Rousseau, Nietzsche, Rilke and Proust* (New Haven: Yale University Press, 1979); P. De Man, *Blindness and Insight: Essays in the Rhetoric of Contemporary Criticism* (London: Routledge, 1983).

5. Cf. W. Van Peer, 'Intertekstualiteit: traditie en kritiek', *Spiegel der Letteren* 29 (1987), pp. 16-24.

concept of intertextuality has developed into so broad an idea, in which everything has become an intertext, that it does not function as a distinct concept anymore, but as a general philosophical statement. This conceptual vagueness needs correction. The term 'intertextuality' can function only as an instrument of analysis and an explanatory model when it is defined more closely, and (the repetition of) the elements to which it refers are well articulated. The second point of criticism concerns the opposition between the unending universe of the text on the one hand and the individual intertextual process of reading on the other. It is not very important to observe a few arbitrary repetitions or intertexts in an unending universe, just as there is no point in distinguishing individual drops of water in a wide river. Furthermore, how can individual interpretations (again a few drops) be compared? There are surely no grounds at all for comparing interpretations of a text. From this I would like to draw the conclusion that the concept of intertextuality as introduced by Kristeva is useful in clarifying the fact that a text is not only a self-contained structure but a differential one as well, and it can be meaningful when its later conceptual vagueness and universalism is limited. For a fruitful use a more limited notion of intertextuality is necessary.

Intertextuality in a Stricter Sense

Intertextuality in a limited sense is confined to demonstrable relationships between texts.[6] These are usually based on a kind of repetition. It is not simply a question of the repetition of sounds and words, since they are necessary for any form of language use, but of sentences and texts or parts of texts. At the same time intertextuality is based on transformations: textual elements or patterns are both repeated and transformed in order to be assimilated into new text structures. Repetition and transformation are therefore intertextuality's characteristic features.

With these two main features, intertextuality is rather more closely defined. Nonetheless, there are still two contradictory visions possible: in the first, intertextuality is restricted to text production, and in the second, intertextuality is limited to text reception. This distinction

---

6.   See M. Riffaterre, *A Semiotics of Poetry* (Bloomington: Indiana University Press, 1978); P. Claes, *Het netwerk en de nevelvlek: semiotische studies* (Leuven: Acco, 1979); P. Claes, *De mot zit in de mythe: Antieke intertextualiteit in het werk van Hugo Claus* (Amsterdam: Meulenhof 1981); G. Genette, *Palimpsestes, la littérature au second degré* (Paris: Seuil, 1982).

is important for biblical exegesis and for any interpretation of texts. The following figure can serve as a summary.

Intertextuality: Text Production	Intertextuality: Text Reception
writer	reader
diachronic	synchronic
sources	functions
causality	analogy
indexicality	iconicity
compulsory relations	potential relations

Any text can be imported into other texts. When this indeed happens, and texts are taken up and assimilated into other texts, the intertextual relationship could be approached from two perspectives: from the first text (text 1 or T1), sometimes called the genotext, or from the second text (T2), sometimes called phenotext. Intertextuality is thus to be viewed as a phenomenon that is operative both in the production or the writing process of a text and in the reception or reading of a text.

Since the nineteenth century, biblical exegesis has always viewed a text as something that is characterized in the first place by the fact that it is produced by one or more writers or editors. This view of the text is thus related to the production of the text. Historical-critical exegesis directs all its attention to the genesis of the text and the intention of the writer. The author or editor will have used other texts in his or her writing process: he or she indicates these explicitly or implicitly, by means of quotations, allusions and so forth. A good reader is one who knows or discovers which texts the author used when writing. This form of intertextuality is essentially diachronic or historical in nature. In tradition criticism and redaction criticism, the aim is to search for the oral or written sources and traditions and to investigate how they have been used by the writer as genotexts. The same applies to many comparative studies, in which extra-biblical texts are often studied as genotexts of biblical texts. A text is generally deemed to be expounded when all the sources that precede it have been found. The concern of these studies is to recover the intention of the writer by identifying the sources the writer has used and the intentional and historical relationships are considered to be compelling for the reader.[7] The text components are in fact viewed as

7. See, W. Vorster, 'Intertextuality and Redaktionsgeschichte', in Draisma (ed.), *Intertextuality*, pp. 15-26.

indices, that is, as signs that are directly and causally determined by earlier texts. This causative influence is traceable: the genotext is historically earlier than the phenotext, the author would have known the genotext and used it in a certain way in it the writing process of his or her own text. Not to pay attention to these causal relationships is, according to this view, not to do justice to the text's own intertextual conditionedness.

In the second view of intertextuality the reader is in the central position, on the basis of the idea that the reader is the one who allows the texts to interfere with one another.[8] A reader who does not know any other texts cannot identify any intertextual relationships. The reader is the one who, through his or her own reading and life experience, lends significance to the great number of possibilities that a text offers. Consequently, the presumed historical process by which the text came into being is no longer important, but rather the final text product, which is compared with other texts in synchronic relationships. The principle of causality is then rejected too; its place is taken by the principle of analogy. Words are not viewed as indexical signs but as iconic signs. Iconicity denotes the principle that phenomena are analogous or isomorphic.[9] Similar and different texts are not explained as being directly influenced by each other, causally or diachronically, but as being indirectly related to each other and having a similar or iconic quality or image in common. Whereas indexicality works on the basis of a succession of cause and effect, iconicity works on the basis of simultaneousness and analogy. Reading intertextually in this way is a synchronic reading. By putting two texts side by side, the reader becomes aware of the analogies (repetitions and transformations) between texts.

From a diachronic point of view, intertextual relationships are necessary relationships: the writer has put them in there, and the reader must discover them, because they formed the very foundation of the genesis of the text. From a synchronic point of view, intertextual relationships are specific to the extent that they are more suited to text relationships than Kristeva's general understanding of

8. For some studies from this perspective, see, D.N. Fewell (ed.), *Reading Between Texts: Intertextuality and the Hebrew Bible* (Louisville, KY, Westminster/ John Knox, 1992).

9. For an extensive study of intertextuality as linked to iconicity see E.J. van Wolde, 'Trendy Intertextuality', in Draisma (ed.), *Intertextuality*, pp. 43-49; and E.J. van Wolde, 'From Text Via Text to Meaning: Intertextuality and its Implications', in E.J. van Wolde, *Words Become Worlds: Semantic Studies of Genesis 1–11* (Biblical Inerpretation Series, 6; Leiden: Brill, 1994), pp. 160-99.

intertextuality but, at the same time, less restricted than the necessary indexical relationships because they are potential relationships. The reader perceives similarities and lets these function as signs pointing to the intertextual relationships between the texts. Recent literary criticism tends to restrict itself to this second type of intertextual research. Accordingly, I propose here to study intertextuality in the Hebrew Bible in this restricted sense, based on iconicity, synchronicity and the interaction between texts and reader. As a scientific—that is, critical and verifiable—study it starts from an acknowledgment of the autonomous value of each of the compared texts on their own, and continues with the explication of the textual markers shared by the texts. These shared elements permit the individual autonomous text to dialogue with other texts without allowing itself to be absorbed by them or absorbing them itself.[10]

A Procedure for Intertextual Research

To study this kind of intertextual relationship, a step-by-step procedure might be useful. Its starting point is the reader's awareness of some similarities between two (or more) texts and the hypothesis that these iconic qualities point at an intertextual relationship. First, these texts are to be studied on their own, as intratextual structures or networks of meaning in which the textual elements receive their meaning and function in interaction with the reader.

Secondly, an inventory of the repetitions in the compared texts can be made. This concerns (1) the repetitions of words and semantic fields: both repeated words and repeated semantic fields might refer to identical or similar areas of meaning; for example, where in one text motherhood, family ties and childbirth occur, in another text the same characteristics might be presented and their intertextual relationship be visible without using exactly the same words; (2) repetitions of larger textual units or structures, for example similarities in stylistic structures, in temporal or spatial arrangements, in sentences, in discourses or ways of expression; (3) similarities in theme or genre which create analogies in textual backgrounds. These first three types of repetition are of stylistic and semantic nature. Intertextual repetitions can, however, also stretch out to narratological features, such as (4) analogies in character descriptions or in character types, (5) similarities in actions or series of actions, (6) similar narratological repre-

10. Cf. J. Delorme, 'Intertextualities about Mark', in Draisma (ed.), *Intertextuality*, pp. 35-42.

sentations; that is, the ways in which the narrator represents the actions of the characters. All these shared features might be read as signs, iconic pointers to intertextual relationships. In addition to semantic and narratological repetitions, rhetorical and pragmatic or communicative features can be taken into consideration. This gathering of all types of repetition as evidence or this inventory of possible intertextual signs is an important stage of research. If sufficient repetition does not exist, then there is no basis for arguing for intertextuality. In case of considerable repetitions and similarities, a basis for intertextual linking is given and a reflection on these iconic features possible. This proves that intertextuality is not just the idea a reader has made up in his or her mind, but that the markers in the text have made this linking possible.

Whereas it is useful to become aware of different possible intertextual relationships, productive intertextual reading must be concerned not only with the meaning of one text (T1) in its encounter with another text (T2), but also with the new text created by the interaction of both texts.[11] This is the third stage of the analysis, which concentrates on the new network of meaning originating from the meeting of both texts. The reader becomes aware of a new realm of meaning. Only in this way does intertextual research become a heuristic tool, a window to look through at texts, making visible the ongoing dialogue between the texts and their readers.

The Ruth and Tamar Narratives: Shared Semantic Features

When reading the book of Ruth the reader is confronted at the end of the book with an explicit allusion to Genesis 38, when the elders at the city gate of Bethlehem say to Boaz: 'May your house be as the house of Perez, whom Tamar bore to Judah, because of the seed that Yahweh will grant you by this woman'. This triple intertextual linking in the book of Ruth where the son to be born is compared with Perez, Ruth with Tamar, and Boaz with Judah, is an indexical sign imposed on the reader. Alerted to this relationship between the Tamar and Ruth stories, the reader can subsequently become aware of the similarites between the frameworks of these narratives. Both start, in 38.1-2 and 1.1-2 respectively, with an indication of time ('it happened in that time'; 'it happened in the days of the judging of the judges'), and continue with a short report of the leaving of the home

---

11. Cf. N. Bailey, '1 Chronicles 21: Ambiguity, Intertextuality and the (de)Sanitisation of David' (PhD dissertation, University of Sheffield, 1995, pp. 53-56).

country by Judah or by a Judahite man to sojourn in a foreign country. Subsequently, the narrator tells us the names of the characters involved, in Genesis 38 providing only the names of the males, in the book of Ruth of both the male and female characters. The foreign women, Ruth and Tamar, are absent at the beginnings of 'their' stories, as the stories are told from a Judahite perspective and not from a Moabite or Canaanite one. Later on the women gradually attract more of the reader's attention, especially when the narrator represents their discourses and 'mental spaces'. The transformations in the stories are the result of the women's actions.

Nevertheless, the foreign women become absent again in the concluding scenes of the stories. The last chapter of Ruth is told from the perspective of Boaz, and closes with his evaluation and with those of the elders and the women. The very last lines of the book of Ruth refer exclusively to the newborn son, Obed, and his part in the genealogy of David. No mention is made of Ruth; she is even not called the mother of the baby: Naomi, the Bethlehemite woman, is. Ruth has disappeared. The same holds true for Tamar. Her story ends in 38.27-30, after Judah's evaluation of her behaviour, with the account of childbirth. Although Tamar is the mother who gives birth, her name nowhere occurs: 'when the time of *her* bearing came, look: there were twins in *her* womb. While *she* was giving birth...' The sons receive names, but not the mother. Further, not Tamar, but some unnamed third person masculine singular (twice, in 38.29 and 30), gives a name to her children. The birth story is not presented from Tamar's point of view but from that of the midwife, who decides who is the first-born son and who the second. Ruth's son is likewise not named by the mother but by the women of Bethlehem (Ruth 4.17). The female protagonists, Ruth and Tamar, are absent in the final scenes of the stories; they disappear in favour of their sons.

Whereas the beginnings of the narratives present the fathers leaving, the endings represent the births and name-givings of the sons. The ongoing life of Judahites is therefore the main point in the frameworks of the Ruth and Tamar narratives. The stories functioning within these frames tell us about the role of certain foreign women who made this framework possible.

The stories within this framework share many semantic features as well.[12] They presuppose a similar social and legal background of

---

12. Cf. A. Brenner, 'Naomi and Ruth', in A. Brenner (ed.), *A Feminist Companion to Ruth* (Sheffield: Sheffield Academic Press 1993), pp. 70-84 (80), which summarizes the common themes of the stories of Ruth and of Tamar.

levirate marriage and redemption, and are the only texts in the Hebrew Bible that refer to this topic, which is formulated as a law in Deut. 25.5-6. This background creates an important semantic field in which both Ruth's and Tamar's actions acquire meaning: both women are non-Judahite, but act according to Judahite or Israelite law. Ruth and Tamar start to play their part in this procreative proces only after their Judahite husbands die.[13] The husbands described in Ruth 1.1-15 look like those in Gen. 38.1-11: Mahlon marries Ruth, but he is mentioned so elliptically that the reader discovers only at the end of the book (4.10) that Ruth is Mahlon's wife and not Chilion's. Mahlon dies at the same time as Chilion and no reason is given. In Genesis 38 Er is given by his father to Tamar, but dies soon after he marries Tamar (how soon is not clear). His death is described as: 'Er (ער), Judah's firstborn, erred (רע) in the eyes of Yahweh, so the Yahweh made him die' (38.7). The relationship between Er, his evil action and Yahweh's reaction is presented by the wordplay between ער and רע,[14] which strikes the reader's eye, as it caught Yahweh's eye; it is provided as an explanation of Er's death. Not much attention, then, is paid to the husbands of Tamar and Ruth. Their deaths are described as those of sons, not of husbands, with Gen. 38.7 presenting the son's death from the father's and Ruth 1.5 from the mother's point of view.

Then Judah gives his second son, Onan, to Tamar to fulfill his fraternal duty. Onan, however, decides to do it his way. And Yahweh reacts in his way: 'he made him die' (38.10). The two 'killings' are the only explicitly presented actions of Yahweh. This activity shows some resemblance to Naomi's evaluation of Yahweh's actions, when she refers to Yahweh 'who made her return empty' (Ruth 1.21). She considers Yahweh to be responsible for the deaths of her husband and sons. The difference is, however, that whereas in Genesis 38 the narrator refers to Yahweh's killing, in the book of Ruth the character Naomi does so.

The next semantic similarity occurs rapidly thereafter. After Onan's death Judah decides to negate the role of the Canaanite woman, addressing Tamar as follows: 'Return as a widow to the house of

13. Cf. the extensive, although more interpretative and associative, comparison between the Ruth and Tamar stories in, D.N. Fewell and D.M. Gunn, *Compromising Redemption: Relating Characters in the Book of Ruth* (Literary Currents in Biblical Interpretation; Louisville: Westminster/John Knox, 1990).

14. Etymologically the name ער probably comes from the stem עור, 'rouse oneself, awake'. In the text, however, it might *function* in relationship with רע. Cf. B. Jacob, *Das erste Buch der Tora: Genesis* (New York: Ktav, 1934), p. 712.

your father' (38.11). The behaviour of Naomi is similar, although the intermediary step represented by Onan is lacking here as she has no other son to give to Ruth. But she negates the role of the Moabite woman as well, saying, 'Go and return, a woman to the house of her mother' (1.8). Whereas Judah explicitly states Tamar's position as a widow, Naomi does not. And whereas Judah talks of the house of the father, Naomi refers to the house of the mother. Many explanations are given for this difference. Possibly the answer to this problem is quite simple. As both speaking characters try to distance themselves from the young women, Judah, the father-in-law, breaks with Tamar as a responsible father, sending her back to her own father, and Naomi, the mother-in-law, breaks with Ruth as a responsible mother, sending her back to her own mother. The difference in speech depends therefore on the person who is speaking.[15]

This is why the Canaanite and Moabite women have to act. They intend to take their procreative role seriously. After a certain period of waiting or spending time on their own—Ruth working in the fields and Tamar waiting in her father's house—they come into action. Inspired by Ruth's gleaning activities and her stories about Boaz, Naomi invents a courageous plan: Ruth has to go to Boaz on the threshing floor by night. However important Naomi's planning is, Ruth is the one who has to carry it out. Tamar initiates and implements a similar plan; her action is as courageous as Ruth's. She sits at the city gate, waits for her father-in-law who takes her to be a whore, and acts accordingly. The similarities of Ruth's and Tamar's actions are manifold. Their 'seduction' procedures concern elderly male relatives and involve aspects of clothing, washing and make-up. They go to a public place, the threshing floor and gate respectively, and are in attendance for the men to come. They make themselves attractive, but not immediately recognizable; Ruth does so according to the advice given by her mother-in-law ('do not make yourself known to the man'), Tamar by covering her face with a veil. And they share the same purpose: to give birth to a male heir in order to make the names of the dead husbands survive. Their aim is the continuation of the bloodline through sexual relations with aged male relatives.

15. In the Hebrew Bible, five times (Gen. 38.11; Num. 30.17; Deut. 22.21; Judg. 19.2, 3) women are related with their father's house; in all these occurrences a male character or narrator is the presenter.However, four other biblical texts—Gen. 24.28; Ruth 1.8; Song 3.4, 8.2—relate women to their mother's house. In all these four texts the women (Rebekah, Naomi, and twice the woman in the Song) are the speaking subjects.

In short, the intertextual links between the Ruth and Tamar narratives are strong from a semantic point of view. They include the similarity in spatial arrangement (a public place) and in timing which involves a certain period of waiting. The female characters use a similar procedure in which much attention is paid to clothes and attractiveness, and they both wait for the man to react. Their actions regard to similar persons, elderly male Judahite relatives, and share the same purpose to continue the family line, so that the Judahite (and David's) genealogy is secured. Ruth and Tamar succeed in their plans and give birth: Ruth to one son and Tamar to two sons. Both are neglected at the end of the story, but nevertheless become famous later on and praised as Israelite ancestors.

The Role of the Narrator in Genesis 38 and in the Book of Ruth

Many authors have pointed to an important characteristic of these stories: in both the narrator represents both female points of view and female voices. This makes these texts rather unusual in the Hebrew Bible. A closer attention to the narratological structure of these texts might show some other interesting features.

Genesis 38 and the book of Ruth start and close with a series of direct narrator's texts in which the narrator describes the time, place and characters, and summarizes in rapid succession some actions. In the central part of the stories a large number of discourses or direct speeches are presented in such a way that the reader is able to share the feelings, thoughts or mental spaces of the characters, especially Naomi, Ruth, Boaz, Judah and Tamar. These discourses make it possible for the reader to identify with these characters and to participate in their points of view. Besides these direct narrator's texts and embedded direct speeches, another kind of representation occurs: indirect narrator's texts. These are clauses in which the narrator speaks not directly from a narrator's perspective, but indirectly through the character's perspective: the character is represented as a thinking, observing or speaking subject, but the representing is done by the narrator. In particular, *verba sentiendi* (observe, see, hear, think, and the like) point to these indirect narrator's texts. By presenting the character's awareness in this form, the narrator increases the reader's involvement with the experience or thought of the character. At the same time, by doing the representation him (or her) self the narrator is able to evaluate, to add approval or disapproval with regard to the character's observations, feelings or awareness, thus steering the reader in a strong way.[16]

In Genesis 38 the first indirect narrator's text occurs in v. 9, where the narrator depicts the mental awareness of Onan: 'Onan knew that the seed would not be his'. And a direct narrator's text continues: 'so whenever he went in to his brother's wife, he spilled [it] on the ground, without giving the seed to his brother'. Because the representation is the narrator's in 38.9, only the reader knows of Onan's considerations, and Judah knows nothing of his considerations nor of his *coiti interrupti*. It is crucial that we as readers know more than Judah does. When the text continues with 'he [Onan] erred in the eyes of Yahweh with what he did, and he [Yahweh] made him die too' (38.10), it is because of our knowledge of Onan's reasons for his behaviour that we are able to understand Yahweh's reaction. We are therefore guided by the narrator to justify this divine action. Judah, however, knows nothing of the kind, neither of Onan's thoughts and behaviour nor of Yahweh's. He blames (and understandably from his point of view) the foreign woman for his sons' deaths. This is presented to the readers in 38.11. Judah's last words ('he said: so he will not die like his brothers') are, although represented as a direct discourse, not heard by Tamar. Only the reader knows of Judah's considerations and reflections, and of his lack of knowledge.

Up to this point readers have not been able to share considerations of feeling with Tamar, but from 38.13 onwards we are increasingly involved in her perspective. This starts with a direct narrator's text in which the narrator shares Tamar's point of view, because it says: 'Tamar was told'. The following direct discourse, 'your father-in-law is on his way up to Timnah to shear his sheep', is described from Tamar's vantage point too, as is visible in the possessive pronoun 'your'. The text continues with five direct narrator's clauses (38.14a-e) sharing Tamar's perspective: 'She took off her widow's clothes, covered herself with a veil, and wrapped herself up. Then she sat down on the way into Enaim, which is on the road to Timnah'. The next clauses (38.14f-h) are indirect narrator's texts, representing Tamar's observation:

כי ראתה	38.14f
כי גדל שלה	38.14g
והיא לא נתנה לו לאשה	38.14h

---

16. For an extensive description see, E. van Wolde, 'Who Guides Whom? Embeddedness and Perspective in Biblical Hebrew and 1 Kings 3:16-28', *JBL* 114.4 (1995), pp. 623-42.

Here Tamar's perception is reported in a way that enables readers to see what she sees, and to reflect upon what she reflects upon. Earlier we learned of Onan's and Judah's feelings, now for the first time we know of Tamar's. But there is one important difference: the particle כִּי precedes the verb of perception רָאָה, which points to the narrator's emphasis on Tamar's perception.[17] By presenting the character's awareness in this explicit form, the narrator reveals a greater involvement in her awareness than in the case of an indirect narrator's text without כִּי, as before in 38.9 and 38.11, representing Onan's and Judah's considerations. In this way the narrator increases the reader's involvement with the observed or mental object and encourages the reader to evaluate Tamar's consideration positively. Thus the reader is guided to agree with Tamar and to continue reading with a positive attitude towards her following actions.

One other indirect narrator's text in Gen. 38.18 tells us about a character's awareness. This time it refers to Judah's perception. He sees Tamar without recognizing her because of her veil: 'truly (כִּי) he did not know that she was his daughter-in-law'. For the second time the reader is guided to share Judah's perception and to become aware of his lack of knowledge. He sees but does not know. Before he did not know of Onan's behaviour and of Yahweh's actions. His interpretation was then, as it is now, based on seeing and not knowing. This turns out to be Judah's main characteristic, presented by the narrator in indirect narrator's texts.

This analysis of the narratological structure of Genesis 38 reveals that the direct narrator's texts occur at the beginning and end of the story (and in between only to continue the story line) and that a large amount of direct discourse or embedded speech is presented in the middle section. It also elucidates that at the moment transformations take place, they are represented in indirect narrator's texts. This narratological form is indeed the best way to show progress in the presentation of the story line and at the same time to give the reader a view into the mental domain of the characters. In this way the reader is guided to participate in the changes in the characters' perceptions or reflections and to understand the motivation of their actions. Thus, the reader knows of Onan's thoughts and Yahweh's decision to kill Onan, of Judah's lack of knowledge with regard to his sons' deaths and Yahweh's actions. The reader is guided even more to share the view of Tamar and her plan of action, and to become aware of Judah's behaviour resulting from his second lack of knowledge. This

---

17. E. van Wolde, 'Who Guides Whom?', pp. 635-36.

explains the readers' involvement with and evaluation of the characters and their behaviour.

The narratological structure of the book of Ruth is comparable, but not quite the same. It contains more embedded discourses than Genesis 38, although it opens and closes with direct narrator's texts that share the Judahite men's perspective, as Genesis 38 did. The direct discourses in Ruth are very often spoken by female characters, but in the second half of the book the amount of male direct discourses increases. The readers are thus frequently enabled by the narrator to share the characters' mental domains. This might explain why indirect narrator's texts are less needed in the book of Ruth. Only three of them occur here, all referring to Naomi's state of mind. The first, in Ruth 1.6b, reflects what Naomi has heard and thought in Moab

כי שמעה בשׂדה מואב	1.6c
כי פקד יהוה את עמו לתת להם לחם	1.6d

Here the representation is given by the narrator, but the hearing is restricted to Naomi's domain. The word כי preceding the *verbum sentiendi* שמע refers to the emphasis the narrator places on Naomi's mental awareness, leading the reader to share her perception that Yahweh has given bread to the people of Bethlehem. The transformation that takes place in her mind is the starting point of the change in the story line.

The second indirect narrator's text (1.18) shares the perception of Naomi, too:

ותרא	1.18a
כי מתאמצת היא ללכת אתה	1.18b

'Naomi saw that she was strengthened [determined] to go with her'. Naomi's evaluation of Ruth's decision to go with her to Judah is provided in an inside view by the narrator, which makes the reader share her feeling, but the narrator does not add an evaluation of his own (by means of כי, for instance). This indirect narrator's text makes the reader aware of another turning point in the story. The first one was Naomi's decision to return to Bethlehem; the second describes Naomi's reluctant acceptance of Ruth's accompanying her on the trip back home.

The third indirect narrator's text is presented in 2.18:

ותרא חמותה את אשר לקטה	2.18a

Naomi sees what Ruth has gleaned and asks where she has been working that day. Her interest is awakened, a first tiny spark of hope arises in her mind. This is represented by the narrator in a way that enables the reader to look through Naomi's eyes. In the following verses she stresses that Ruth should continue to glean in the same field of the same man, Boaz. Shortly thereafter Naomi designs a plan which Ruth has to fulfill. The fulfillment and results of this plan are reported in Ruth 3–4, in which no more indirect narrator's texts occur, only numerous direct discourses and direct narrator's texts.

In short, in the book of Ruth few indirect narrator's texts occur, because we as readers are able to look through the eyes of the characters by the directly represented discourses. It is almost a script for a theatre play: dialogues are lined up by short narrator's texts. The three indirect narrator's texts point to the crucial moments in the transformation of Naomi's mental state. She is the Judahite who in this story changes her attitude, influenced by the behaviour of Ruth: first, when she hears about the end of the famine, she decides to return to Bethlehem; secondly, after Ruth decides to accompany her to Bethlehem, Naomi gives up opposing her; and thirdly, her reaction to Ruth's gleaning success becomes the introduction of Naomi's change of mind with regard to Ruth and future life. In both texts, Genesis 38 and the book of Ruth, readers are guided to sympathize with the characters through direct discourses and, on some crucial points in the transformation of the awareness of the characters, led through indirect narrator's texts. The result is, in a way, comparable: the readers are involved in the mental tranformations of Onan and, still more intensively, in those of Judah and Tamar in Genesis 38, and of Naomi in the book of Ruth.

The Role of the Characters in the Ruth and Tamar Narratives
The explicit allusion in Ruth 4.12 to Genesis 38 refers the reader to the characters featuring in both stories. Invited by the text to look more carefully at the intertextual links between these characters, we are able to discover a subtle intertextual network.

Starting with the couple Boaz and Judah, it is discovered that their main characteristic is that they are both elder relatives of two young widows. The difference in age is clearly indicated in Genesis 38. It might be inferred from Ruth 3.10a, where Boaz calls Ruth 'my daughter', and this is confirmed in 3.10b, where he praises her for not walking behind the younger men but selecting him. Boaz's and Judah's similarity in age is only one shared feature. Another is their membership in the same clan: Boaz is presented as a man from the clan of Ephratites, of which Tamar is called the mother and Judah the father (4.11-12). The final genealogy in 4.18-22, however, starts with Perez, not with Judah, as if only Boaz is present in David's genealogy and Judah is not. Could this mean that Judah did not deserve his place in David's genealogy? In their actions with regard to their family, Boaz and Judah have nevertheless something in common. Although related to the young widows, Boaz and Judah do not have levirate obligations. Formulated in Deut. 25.5-10, these clan obligations refer to brothers, as the fourfold occurrence of the word אח ('brother') and the fourfold יבם ('brother-in-law') show: they refer to relatives of the same generation and not to clan members of previous generations. In Genesis 38 and in Ruth 3–4 the young widows, Tamar and Ruth, appeal to this older generation, when younger relatives are no more available. Boaz and Judah do not consider it to be their duty to fulfill the clan obligations; it is the women's creative interpretation of these laws that open the elder male relatives to these legal possibilities. This explains why Ruth and Tamar need a bold procedure to get the attention of Boaz and Judah.

It is not that the widowed relatives address these elder male relatives immediately. Only after they have failed to get the younger relatives to act, Boaz and Judah become involved themselves. It is striking, however, that not only the elder relatives, but also the younger ones have much in common. In Gen. 38.8-9 Onan, the second son of Judah, is commanded by his father to go in to the wife of his brother to produce offspring for his brother. His behaviour shows remarkable resemblances to Peloni Almoni in Ruth 4.1-7. The name אונן, which might etymologically refer to און, '(manly) vigour', might possibly be understood in this context as refering implicitly to אין, 'nothing' or 'nought'. The name פלני אלמני refers clearly to 'a certain one not mentioned'. Whether or not the names are analogous, the behaviour shows some striking similarities. Onan does not reject sexual intercourse with Tamar, but turns down his duty to give offspring to his brother; Peloni Almoni does not reject redeeming the possessions of Elimelek and Naomi, but rejects his duty 'to keep the name of the deceased person alive'. In this sense they act in the same way: they do not want to provide a name for the dead male relative, and therefore they do not deserve a proper name themselves. This intertextual relationship is confirmed by the use of the word שחת, 'to ruin', 'destroy' or 'spill': Onan spills (שחת) on the ground (Gen. 38.9), and Peloni Almoni does not want to ruin (שחת) his inheritance (Ruth 4.6).

Becoming aware of an intertextual relationship between these younger male relatives, the reader's eye might catch yet another similarity. Concerning the levirate marriage, Deut. 25.7-10 says: 'If a brother-in-law does not desire (יחפ׳ץ) to take his sister-in-law, then his sister-in-law will stand with him before the eyes of the elders, and draw off his sandal from his feet (חלצה מעל רגלו נעלו), and his name will be called over Israel '"house of the one whose sandal is drawn off" (בית חלוץ הנעל)'.[18] Ruth 4.7 actually refers to this sentence, but the formulation is slightly different. Peloni Almoni 'draws off a sandal' (שלף נעלו) to confirm his not giving seed or offspring to the deceased brother Elimelek. The word combination שלף נעלו (and not חלץ נעלו) is unique in the Hebrew Bible; elsewhere the word שלף occurs exclusively in combination with חרב, 'to draw the sword (from a sheath)'.[19] This is, in a metaphorical way, exactly what both Peloni Almoni and Onan do: Onan in a literal sense, because he draws his sword (penis) from the female sheath or vagina, as sign of his unwillingness to give his seed (offspring); and Peloni Almoni, in a symbolic sense. This intertextual analogy is perceivable by the reader, although it is impossible to decide if it is intentional; it explains, however, the unique combination שלף נעלו in a context in which one would have expected חלץ נעלו. All these similarities taken together show equally egotistical behaviour by the younger relatives toward their female relatives, and explain why Ruth and Tamar have to address the elder relatives.

In their activities to persuade Boaz and Judah, Ruth and Tamar reveal some similarities. They both go to a public domain and prepare themselves carefully. Ruth goes to the threshing floor:

ותבא בלט	3.7e
ותגל מרגלתיו	3.7f
ותשכב	3.7g

This verse is usually translated 'Ruth came [secretly], uncovered the place of his feet, and lay down'.[20] In this translation, מרגלתיו is understood as the direct object of גלה, in which case the *nota accusativi* את could have been expected. An even stronger argument against this translation is that מרגלתיו is an indication of place (*always* in the Hebrew Bible); it describes the location where an action takes place, and it is not the object of the action. Most exegetes start with

18. Cf. C.M. Carmichael, 'A Ceremonial Crux: Removing a Man's Sandal as a Female Gesture of Contempt', *JBL* 96 (1977), pp. 321-36.

19. Num. 22.23, 31; Josh. 5.13; Judg. 8.10; 9.54; 20.2, 15, 17, 25, 25, 46; 1 Sam. 17.51; 31.4; 2 Sam. 24.9; 2 Kgs 3.26; 1 Chron. 10.4; 21.5, 5, 16.

20. The following analysis of Ruth 3.7 is inspired by: K. Nielsen, 'Le choix contre le droit dans le livre de Ruth: De l'aire de battage au tribunal', *VT* 35 (1985), pp. 201-12, esp. pp. 205-207.

acknowledging מרגלתיו as an indication of place, but nevertheless deal with the word as if it were not a spatial marker, but an object; and refer to Ruth's uncovering the place of Boaz's feet which, gradually, becomes 'Ruth uncovers Boaz's feet'. This translation is unlikely therefore on the basis of the function of מרגלתיו as a spatial marker and confirmed by the absence of את as an accusative marker.

The question is, then, what is the direct object of גלה? What or whom is Ruth uncovering? The verb גלה occurs often in the Hebrew Bible, mostly referring to an uncovering of the nakedness (ערוה) either by a man uncovering his father's nakedness or his father's wife nakedness (often), or by a man uncovering himself (Gen. 9.21; Exod. 20.26; 2 Sam. 6.20) and by a woman uncovering herself (esp. Ezek. 16.36; 23.18). So Ruth might uncover Boaz, but that is not plausible because Boaz continues to sleep. One has to conclude therefore that Ruth uncovers herself at the place of the feet of Boaz.[21] Filled with feelings of shame or not able to think of it, most commentators have overlooked this possibility of 'striptease by night'. Nevertheless the context affirms this interpretation, because in the next verse Ruth asks Boaz to cover her with a (part of a) mantle. Her question presupposes her nakedness, and not the nakedness of Boaz's feet. By using the word כנף, she refers to verse 2.12, where Boaz addressed Ruth and told her to seeks rescue under the כנף of Yahweh. Now in 3.9 Ruth uses this word to express her hope that she will find rescue under Boaz's protection: he himself has to spread his garment over her. The connotation of this invitation is clear, as similar usages in Deut. 23.1; 27.20 and in Ezek. 16.8 show: by covering her with a mantle, he takes her as his wife. His reaction will show what he intends to do: to marry her or not. By uncovering herself and confronting Boaz with her nakedness, she puts before him the choice: either have sexual

---

21. A comparison with Ezek. 16.6-14 might be instructive. In the Ezekiel context the same words occur, and a young woman who reaches maturity is described: she lies naked and God sees her, then covers her with a כנף, washes and anoints her and gives her clothes and jewelry. As her nakedness is a sign of her readiness to marry, the covering with the garment refers to the marriage itself. In the next part of Ezek. 16 the negative side is shown: this woman has become unfaithful to God, uncovers her nakedness (*niphal* גלה) and plays the whore. This last case is confirmed in the parable of Ohola and Oholiba, where the women uncover their nakedness (twice in Ezek. 23.18: *piel* 3 fem. sing. of גלה, as in Ruth 3.7). In Ruth 3.7 the positive connotation and situation presuppose a link to Ezek. 16.6-14; Ruth's act of uncovering shows, however, an activity usually evaluated negatively in the Hebrew Bible, whether it is the case that a woman uncovers herself, or that she uncovers a man. This might possibly explain why Ruth's uncovering activity is so elliptically described.

intercourse or cover her, which is virtually the same.

The actions of Tamar are, in a way, comparable to Ruth's:

ותסר בגדי אלמנותה מעליה	38.14a
ותכס בצעיף	38.14b
ותתעלף	38.14c
ותשב בפתח עינים	38.14e

Tamar uncovers herself, taking off her widow clothes. But then she covers herself and veils her face and goes to a public meeting place, the gate of the city. Her clothing and sitting have the same functions as Ruth's unclothing and laying down. Both create the conditions for sexual intercourse, and wait for male reactions. Tamar waits in the gate, Ruth on the threshing floor; the one wrapped up, the other naked. The sexual intention is necessary to reach their goal, to secure offspring through a male relative. Because the older male relatives are not considering it as their legal task to fulfill levirate obligations— and they are justified by the Deuteronomic law—probably female sexual invitations will lead to the same result.

In their reactions Boaz and Judah show dissimilarities and similarities. The subtle and creative behaviour of Ruth is reflected by Boaz's sophisticated and creative procedure in the gate of Bethlehem, and Tamar's straightforward approach is reflected by Judah's straightforward reaction. In Ruth 3.4-14 the sexual tension is obvious, but explicit statements, such as ויבא אליה ('he went in to her') or וישכב עמה ('he lay with her'), both standard expressions for sexual intercourse in biblical Hebrew, are not provided.[22] The events in ch. 4 confirm this impossibility of intercourse on the threshing floor: if 'the marriage' was consummated there, the scene in the city gate would be a fake. Ruth 4.13 presupposes this also: 'Boaz took Ruth as wife and he went in to her and she became pregnant'. If there had been a first time, this explicit statement of the second time would be superfluous. On the other hand, many words used in the threshing floor scene have a strong sexual connotation: בוא ('enter', 3.3, 4, 7, 7, 14), ידע ('know', in 3.3, 3, 4, 14), שכב ('lie', 3.3, 4, 4, 4, 7, 7, 8, 13, 14), מרגלתיו ('place of the feet', 3.3, 7, 14), גלה ('uncover', 3.3, 4, 7), רגל ('feet' and 'genitals', 3.3, 7, 14), כנף ('wing', 'garment', 3.3, 9, elsewhere often used in the context of a marriage ceremony), ערמה ('grain pile', 3.7, showing a strong resemblence with ערום, 'naked').[23] The accumula-

22. Cf. M. Bernstein, 'Two Multivalent Readings in the Ruth Narrative', *JSOT* 50 (1991), pp. 15-26.

23. E.F. Campbell, *Ruth* (AB; Garden City, NY: Doubleday, 1975), pp. 131-32; J.M. Sasson, *Ruth: A New Translation with a Philological Commentary and a*

tion of such vocabulary has an effect on the reader. It creates an ambiguity: this quantity of *doubles entendres* makes the sexual or erotic atmosphere of the threshing floor tangible. Any clear answers about what happened are not given, but the text gives the impression it is intended this way. Affirmation of this intention is found in 3.16b, where Ruth gives (on the morning after) an account of the events to Naomi: 'She told her everything the man had done for/to her'. 'Everything' can mean everything indeed. This direct narrator's text deliberately keeps the ambiguity of the threshing floor alive.

This ambivalence on the threshing floor is reflected by the ambivalence in the gate. Boaz is the protagonist here and starts talking to Peloni Almoni about the land of 'our brother' (אחינו) Elimelek, which Naomi is selling (4.3). He then complicates his presentation: (Boaz said) 'I said to myself, and I will tell your ear saying...' (4.4). This doubly embedded discourse makes Boaz's intention less perceivable, as is, presumably, his strategy. The content of his proposal to the *go'ēl* is קנה, 'acquire (the land)'. So Boaz acts as a caretaker or minder of Naomi and presents her business in such a way that the *go'ēl* thinks he is able to make a decision. Thus he concludes: אנכי אגאל, 'I will redeem'. But then, in Ruth 4.5, Boaz presents the consequence: 'On the day you acquire the land from the hand of Naomi, you acquire Ruth the Moabite, the wife of the deceased'. Now Boaz acts as an agent for Ruth; he switches from one widow to the other, suggesting that the acquisition of Elimelek's land and possessions goes hand in hand with marriage to Ruth. As the widow of Elimelek and owner of the land, Naomi should be the widow Peloni Almoni has to marry. In other words, Boaz presents here an implication that is not an implication at all. He makes it still more difficult for the *go'ēl* by calling Ruth explicitly 'the Moabite', a forbidden woman in Judahite law. Finally, he stresses the point that the land or inheritance will not be in the possession of the *go'ēl*, but will belong to the deceased man. Boaz creates difficulties here, by using legal topics and transforming them slightly to make a positive response less preferable for the *go'ēl*.[24] The reader therefore gets the impression that the final result, Boaz's marriage with Ruth, is intentional. One might conclude that

Formalist-Folklorist Interpretation (Baltimore: The Johns Hopkins University Press, 1979), pp.69-79, 93; Bernstein, 'Two Multivalent', p. 18.

24. Since the Masoretes offer in verse 4.5 קניתי ('I acquire') as the *keth̲ib* reading and קנית ('you acquire') as the *qere* reading, this textual ambivalence increases the reader's perception of ambiguity in the text. For an extensive study of this problem, see, M.D. Gow, *The Book of Ruth: Its Structure, Theme and Purpose* (Leicester: Apollos, 1992), pp. 150-68.

Boaz's ambiguous tactics correspond in a way to the narrator's ambiguous description of the events on the threshing floor.

In the Tamar narrative the relatives are involved in a similar levirate procedure, but their actions are less strategic and the narrator's account less ambiguous. Tamar takes off her widow's clothes, veils herself and sits down in the city gate. There is no ambivalence at all; it is clear that she acts as a whore, because women are not supposed to sit in the city gate. When Judah passes, he immediately assumes she is a whore. And Tamar acts accordingly, starting to bargain with Judah, as is usually done in these cases. Once the payment is agreed upon, Judah acts directly. There is no ambiguity in the text in 38.18 at all: ויבא אליה ותהר לו ('he went in to her and she conceived by him').[25] Only after stating this, the narrator tells us that Tamar gets up and returns home. The pregnancy is achieved, and that was her aim. However different might be the subtlety in behaviour between Ruth and Tamar, and between Boaz and Judah, similarities are present as well. Both Boaz and Judah like to keep things secret. Boaz asks Ruth to leave from the threshing floor before anybody can recognize her, and the people in the gate of Bethlehem know nothing of the previous night. Judah likes to keep things secret as well: when his friend trys to pay and does not find the whore, Judah prefers to loose his seal, cords and staff—all signs of his (sexual) identity—rather than have what he has done become known. This secrecy is conditional for the successful continuation of the narrative in both stories. The negotiations of Boaz in the city gate will succeed only if the secret is maintained. The praise of the men in the gate of Bethlehem is ironic: not knowing the nightly events, they compare Boaz with Judah, and Ruth with Tamar. The reader knows more and appreciates this *double entendre*. The secrecy of Tamar, which is a different secrecy from Judah's, is necessary to expose the failure of Judah's behaviour with respect to his daughter-in-law. He not only fails in not giving his third son to her, but even decides to have her burned, when he hears of her pregnancy (38.24). Her secret behaviour turns out to be the only way to act: the presentation of the pledge and the revelation of her and Judah's secret activities show the truth. She has indeed played

---

25. P. Joüon and T. Muraoka, *A Grammar of Biblical Hebrew* (Rome: Pontificio Istituto Biblico, 1991), '132fN. They explain הרה with לו in Gen. 38.18 as an 'ל analogous to the ל auctoris'. This is confirmed by Gen. 38.25. G. Wenham, *Genesis 16–50* (WBC; Dallas: Word Books, 1994), p. 362, however, translates with, 'she became pregnant for him', which is an unlikely (and almost sexist) translation, and not confirmed by the text in 38.25.

the whore. But not in the way Judah has presumed, and with him as protagonist.

In short, Boaz and Judah figure in a context of levirate marriage with a young widow, although they are 'fathers' or 'elderly male relatives' and not brothers. Their role in the continuation of the Judahite genealogy is enforced by the younger, foreign women. The circumstances of the stories—secrecy, thresing floor and gate, active sexual women and their reactions—are very much alike. Just as Judah goes in to Tamar and she becomes pregnant immediately, Boaz goes in to Ruth and she becomes pregnant immediately. They are explicitly linked via the speech of the other men in the gate of Bethlehem, even though these men do not know about the similarities between the threshing floor and the gate of Enaim. The final evaluation of Tamar by Judah is positive: 'she is more righteous than I' (38.26), as is Boaz's evaluation of Ruth in 3.11: 'all people of the gate know that you are a woman of character'; and both strong women are praised by the men of Bethlehem. Another similarity is that in both narratives the theme is to bring forth a son to keep the name of the deceased husband alive. The young widow Ruth finally gives birth to a son, but he is not called 'the son of Mahlon', or 'the son of Elimelek', but 'the son of Boaz'. In the same way the son brought forth by Tamar is called 'the son of Judah and Tamar', and not 'the son of Er'; no mention whatsoever is made of the continuation of the name of the husband. The fathers replace the sons and do the work of the brothers.

The Role of the Reader

Knowing these similarities and analogies, one may ask if the shared features or cluster of intertextemes lead to a network of meaning that puts the compared texts in another light. The reader might become aware of new dimensions and enter into an ongoing dialogue between the Ruth and Tamar narratives.

One of the main characteristics of both stories is the ability of the two foreign women to transform the insiders, the Judahite men and women. Consequently the reader may discover that this transformation is semantically marked in both texts by one and the same word. By covering or uncovering, veiling or unveiling themselves, Tamar and Ruth actually disclose the others, the Judahites. In both narratives this is presented by נכר, 'observe', 'recognize', 'acknowledge' or 'understand'. The moment Tamar shows Judah his seal, cords and staff, the pledge he has given her, he recognizes (נכר) them and acknowledges (נכר) Tamar's righteousness. The word נכר summarizes the crucial transformation of the story: Judah sees what he has not seen before.[26] His double lack of knowledge—the first relating the behaviour of his two sons in the eyes of Yahweh, the second concerning the identity of the woman in the gate of Enaim whom he saw but did not know—is removed by the woman who makes him נכר, see and acknowledge. It is significant that as soon as Judah sees 'he did not go on knowing her', ולא יסף עוד לדעתה (Gen. 38.26). Once his eyes have been opened, no other knowledge is needed.

Tamar is the eye-opener. The reader could have been aware of this much earlier, as Tamar was sitting at the gate of Enaim, בפתח עינים, 'the gate of the eyes'.[27] She will open the eyes of the male protagonist, Judah. The only other eyes mentioned in this story are Yahweh's (בעיני יהוה) occuring twice in 38.7,10, just before the gate of Enaim (בפתח עינים) in 38.14. Later on Tamar is called הקדשה, 'the holy one' or 'the holy whore', 'sitting in Enaim (בעינים) by the road' (38.21). Here the relationship between holiness and eyes is observable for the reader, although unseen by Judah and his friend. Tamar shows Judah Yahweh's eyes, which Judah had not been able to see before. Judah's lack of knowledge concerning his sons and Tamar, and concerning Yahweh's actions and eyes, is demonstrated by this holy woman: when Judah passes her gate and becomes aware of his passing, he is able to see and acknowledge.

A similar ability to reveal characterizes Ruth. In her story this is expressed by the very same word, נכר. Ruth's activities do not concern one person (Judah) as in Tamar's tale, but two persons: Naomi and Boaz. Naomi gradually changes under the influence of Ruth's behaviour. She starts as a disappointed person who feels left alone by God and men, and who has no trust at all in her daughter-in-law. The first step in her transformation is her perception and decision to return to Bethlehem, when she hears (שמעה) that Yahweh has again given food to his people (1.6). It is an important first step, enabling her to return to her home country. Nevertheless her attitude towards Yahweh still remains a critical one, as becomes clear from her blaming him for her emptiness (1.21). The second step is imposed upon

26. Cf. U. Cassuto, 'The Story of Tamar and Judah', in U. Cassuto, *Biblical and Oriental Studies*. I. *Bible* (Jerusalem: Magnes, 1973), pp. 29-40 (written originally in 1929), esp. pp. 30-31. Presumably inspired by him, but without referring to him, is R. Alter, *The Art of Biblical Narrative* (New York: Basic Books, 1981), p. 10.

27. Cf. M. Bal, F. van Dijk-Hemmes, and G. van Ginneken, *En Sara in haar tent lachte* (Utrecht: Hes, 1984), esp. p. 54; J. Bos, 'Out of the Shadows: Genesis 38; Judges 4:17-22; Ruth 3', *Semeia* 42 (1988), pp. 37-67, esp. pp. 42-43.

her by Ruth, when Naomi sees (ותרא) that Ruth is strong in her decision to join her and accepts reluctantly. These two steps do not really change Naomi, but they create the conditions for her future transformation in belief and attitude. The third step is accomplished by Ruth. When she returns from the field and gives Naomi the grain she collected, Naomi says: יהי מכירך ברוך, 'blessed be he that did take knowledge of you' (2.19). From this moment on Naomi acts differently. She apparently changes as soon as she realizes that someone else has taken notice of Ruth. It is as if Naomi acknowledges for the first time Ruth's abilities. Before she has heard (שמע) and seen (ראה), but now she discovers Ruth by the intermediary noticing (נכר) of Boaz. She immediately begins to plan a future life. Naomi has attained a mental transformation. This new mental competence results in advice to Ruth about the threshing floor: now Naomi creates the conditions for the change of other persons.

The other character who is transformed by Ruth's behaviour is Boaz. In their first meeting Ruth said to him (2.10): 'Why do I find grace in your eyes that you take notice (נכר) of me, even though I am a foreigner (נכריה)?' The word נכריה refers to an important characteristic of a foreigner; because foreigners are different the indigenous population notices them, foreigners are always 'seen'. But Boaz makes Ruth into a 'really esteemed noticed foreigner', and praises her for seeking rescue under the wings of Yahweh. Unlike Judah's behaviour in the Tamar narrative, Boaz has no lack of knowledge and is more aware of Yahweh's eyes, but he still commends the foreign woman to Yahweh's wings. By her bold action on the threshing floor, Ruth makes Boaz notice her and makes him aware of his possibilities as redeemer and seed supplier. At the very moment of his surprised perception, the readers are enabled by the narrator to look through his eyes: והנה אשה ('look a woman [lying at the place of his feet]') (3.8). This way of presenting is quite unique for the book of Ruth. This transforming moment in which Ruth is no longer seen by Boaz as a foreigner but as a woman, is presented so that the reader will sympathize with this new situation. Boaz is aware of the consequences as well, and is therefore afraid other men might see her on the floor: 'she was lying at the place of his feet until the morning, and she rose up before one could know (נכר) another; and he said "let it not be known (אל יודע) that a woman came into the floor"' (3.14). The other people's lack of knowledge is essential for Boaz's strategy. They do not have to know what he knows, nor are the readers given a clue about all aspects of this knowledge on the threshing floor. From this point Boaz is the acting person; transformed by Ruth, he does not to refer her again to Yahweh's wings, but to takes her under his own wings.

As non-Judahite women, Tamar and Ruth are women who are seen but not noticed. In the end they turn out to be the instruments by which Judah, Naomi and Boaz perceive and attain knowledge. As foreigners they are able to confront the insiders and to hold a mirror up to their faces. This is why it is not enough to read these stories along the gender line only. The narratives are about Ruth and Tamar transforming the male relatives Boaz and Judah, but also about the changes of the 'inside-people' or Judahites, Naomi included. Insideness and outsideness is, together with gender, an important feature of both narratives. Without Tamar, the Judahites would not have survived; without Ruth, they would never have had David as king.

In both cases, Ruth and Tamar disappear at the end and become ellipses in their own stories. They are annexed by the inside people or, positively put, they have become an integral part of Israelite history. Tamar made Judah see, Ruth made Naomi change and Boaz become aware, but their revealing activities eventually lead to their own disappearance. Ruth and Tamar function as eye-openers, but are in the end invisible again. Rereading Genesis 38 from this standpoint, one can discover that the annexing begins much earlier. The foreign identity of Tamar is disguised, for nowhere is it explicitly stated whether she is a Canaanite or not. The reader has to infer it but cannot be sure. Could it be true that the foreignness of Tamar is already annexed from the beginning of the story? The same occurs in the first chapter of the book of Ruth. Although explicitly described as a Moabite woman, Ruth chooses for Naomi, for her people and her God. This choice gets much attention from the narrator, and still more from commentators through the ages. It is as if Ruth, from this moment on, has already stopped being a foreigner: she has given up her Moabite identity and becomes a Yahweh-believer and Judahite. She is a dignified ancestor of David indeed. One might wonder if exegetes are not too pleased about Ruth's assimilation. It is as if the loss of her identity as Moabite is a prerequisite for becoming part of Israel's history. Only after the foreignness of the foreigners is negated are they acceptable as parts in their own history. The mirror intended to unveil the audience, unfortunately, has led to the emptying of the foreigners who do not confront but confirm the Judahite identity.

RACHEL WEEPING FOR HER CHILDREN: INTERTEXTUALITY AND THE BIBLICAL TESTAMENTS—A FEMINIST APPROACH

Elaine Wainwright

> [E]arly believers-in-Jesus sought to understand Jesus of Nazareth, the
> prophetic teacher and wonderworker, in his relationship with God. To
> do so, they used all the resources provided in their traditions and
> cultures.[1]

The telling of the Jesus story in early communities of participants in
the reign of God movement gave birth to a number of complex narratives resulting from the use of a wide variety of resources. A fundamental recognition in this regard is that gospel stories are interlaced
with language, allusions and texts from the Scriptures of their communities of production, the most predominant of these resources
being the Hebrew Bible or Jewish Scriptures. This 'use' of texts, however, is not simply a literary interweaving; it participates in the interaction between the producers of the new text and their cultural
context, so that cultural codes and cultural traces likewise interlace
the gospel narrative.

This essay seeks to address the relationship between the testaments of the biblical narrative which I will call the Hebrew Bible[2]
and the Christian Testament; and, in particular, the way those early
communities of participants in the reign of God movement 'used'
their Scriptures to give meaning to the life, death and resurrection of
Jesus of Nazareth. Traditionally in biblical scholarship, this relationship has been considered under the rubric of what we might call
'use', with the focus being on the writer of the gospel narrative and
the way that writer used the biblical text as source—by way of either
direct quotation, allusion or type—in order to interpret the life of

---

1. Anthony J. Saldarini, *Matthew's Christian–Jewish Community* (Chicago: University of Chicago Press, 1994), p. 165.

2. In using this designation I do not wish to limit this to Hebrew texts only but
to include the scriptures of the Jewish people at the beginning of the common era,
whether in Hebrew or in Greek.

Jesus and the reign of God movement.[3] It entailed a linear or di-achronic literary and historical study. In this essay, however, I have chosen *intertextuality* as a way of studying relationships between the testaments. I make this choice not only because intertextuality offers rich possibilities for understanding how the Hebrew Bible was read by and, in its turn, read the early reign of God movement, but also because it 'opens to ideological criticism', as Timothy Beal suggests.[4] Hence, it provides an approach readily amenable to a feminist per-spective.

In the section below, I briefly situate the understanding of intertex-tuality in this essay within a broader context of literary and biblical studies, and explore the possibilities it offers for a feminist critical analysis of the relationship between the biblical testaments. This will be followed by a limited feminist intertextual study of the infancy narrative of the Matthean gospel as an example of such inter-testamental relationships.

What Was Spoken by the Prophets...Text, Inter-text, Con-text

> Intertextuality designates the multitude of ways a text has of not being self-contained, of being traversed by otherness.[5]

It is generally held that the term 'intertextuality' was introduced by Julia Kristeva to give expression to her claim that 'each word (text) is an intersection of word (texts) where at least one other word (text) can be read'.[6] Kristeva's claim, however, demonstrates the intertextuality in her own work, especially in relation to Bakhtin. For him, each

---

3.   Note in this regard the titles of two such studies in relation to Matthew's gospel: Robert Horton Gundry, *The Use of the Old Testament in St Matthew's Gospel: With Special Reference to the Messianic Hope* (NovTSup, 18; Leiden: Brill, 1975) and Krister Stendahl, *The School of St Matthew and its Use of the Old Testament* (Phila-delphia: Fortress Press, 1968); and in a more recent publication, Walter C. Kaiser, *The Uses of the Old Testament in the New* (Chicago: Moody Press, 1985).

4.   Timothy K. Beal, 'Ideology and Intertextuality: Surplus of Meaning and Controlling the Means of Production,' in Danna Nolan Fewell (ed.), *Reading Between Texts: Interetextuality and the Hebrew Bible* (Louisville: Westminster/John Knox, 1992), p. 32.

5.   Barbara Johnson, as quoted in Gary Phillips, '"What is Written?" How are you Reading Gospel, Intertextuality and Doing Lukewise: A Writerly Reading of Lk 10:25-37 (and 38-42)', in Eugene H. Lovering (ed.), *SBL 1992 Seminar Papers* (Atlanta: Scholars Press, 1992), pp. 266-301 (266).

6.   Julia Kristeva, *Desire in Language: A Semiotic Approach to Literature and Art* (Leon S. Roudiez [ed.]; and Thomas Gora, Alice Jardine and Leon S. Roudiez [trans.]; New York: Columbia University Press, 1980), p. 66.

utterance or word is related to other utterances or words in a relationship called dialogism.[7] In her development of intertextuality Kristeva insisted that it was not simply a 'study of sources' but rather was what she called a 'transposition', which demanded a new understanding of a text that could no longer be seen as 'single, complete' but always as 'plural, shattered'.[8] This is the result of what Kristeva calls 'positionalities' or subject and object positions that shift and change as the 'intersection of textual surfaces' takes place.[9] As a result, neither the text's world of reference nor the reader or writer are stable or univocal but are considered in their multiplicity and fluidity.[10] Mary McClintock Fulkerson suggests, therefore, that intertextuality invites interpreters of a text to 'recognize the existence of many texts as they appear from multiple subject positions'.[11]

Intertextuality's evocation of a multiplicity of meanings provides an entry point for a feminist critical reading. Just as difference is a 'productive force issuing into new readings and texts'[12] within intertextuality, so too is difference a significant factor in the recognition of multiple female and feminist subject positions.[13] As the reader–

7.   See Tsvetan Todorov, *Mikhail Bakhtin: The Dialogical Principle* (trans. Wlad Godzich; Theory and History of Literature, 13; Minneapolis: University of Minnesota Press, 1984), p. 60. The title of this text as well as that edited by Michael Holquist, *The Dialogic Imagination: Four Essays by M.M. Bakhtin* (trans. Caryl Emerson and Michael Holquist; Austin, TX: University of Texas Press, 1981), indicate the pervasiveness of the notion of dialogism in Bakhtin's work—which will not be further developed here because it is beyond the scope of this essay.

8.   Julia Kristeva, *Revolution in Poetic Language* (trans. Margaret Waller; New York: Columbia University Press, 1984), pp. 59-60: '[t]he term intertextuality denotes this transposition of one (or several) sign system(s) into another; but since this term has often been understood in the banal sense of "study of sources", we prefer the term transposition because it specifies that the passage from one signifying system to another demands a new articulation…of enunciative and denotative positionality'. For a more extensive analysis of Kristeva's notion of intertextuality, see Phillips, 'Intertextuality', pp. 275-80.

9.   Kristeva, *Revolution*, pp. 59-60 and *Desire*, p. 65. See also Phillips, 'Intertextuality', p. 277.

10. Mary McClintock Fulkerson, *Changing the Subject: Women's Discourses and Feminist Theology* (Minneapolis: Fortress Press, 1994), develops this much more fully in her chapter 3, 'From the One Text to the Many: Women Performing Scripture', pp. 117-82.

11. McClintock Fulkerson, *Changing the Subject*, p. 142.

12. Phillips, 'Intertextuality', p. 274.

13. The literature addressing this aspect of feminist critical theory is extensive. For an excellent account of difference within the current wave of feminism see Rosi Braidotti, *Nomadic Subjects: Embodiment and Sexual Difference in Contemporary*

writer positionalities shift, the feminist critical reader will be attentive to the different subject positions of women in both the production and reception of the text 'which is not one', as well as how female gender and hence the female reader in the text is constructed. For the feminist critical reader, therefore, one's feminist perspective significantly influences the choices that must be made among the myriad possible meanings, as it is impossible to choose all meanings at any one point in time. This same reader will likewise be attentive to the particular ideological perspectives influencing the choices of meanings made by other interpreters, especially in light of the prevailing tendency of malestream interpretation to render the female invisible either as subject or object:

> And so the practice of intertextual reading must find its place somewhere between the closed structure of a single text (however defined) and the uncontainably surplussive fabric of language (called intertextuality).[14]

The recognition of ideology as a significant factor in the production of meanings provides the space where feminist critical readings find entry.

Intertextuality, therefore, is not simply concerned with the influence of or the borrowing from sources, which has been the traditional way in which the interrelationship between the biblical testaments has been understood.[15] Rather, it seeks to address the intersection of texts from not only Jewish but also Graeco-Roman literary contexts as well as myriad oral contexts.[16] Consideration of the ideologies

Feminist Theory (New York: Columbia University Press, 1995), pp. 146-72. She points to three layers of difference: that between men and women, differences among women, and the different subject positions within each woman.

14. Beal, 'Ideology and Intertextuality', p. 28.

15. For a more nuanced overview of recent studies about the relationship between the testaments and within the biblical canon, see the introduction to Gail R. O'Day, 'Jeremiah 9:22-23 and 1 Corinthians 1:26-31: A Study in Intertextuality', *JBL* 109.2 (1990), pp. 259-67 (60).

16. The full richness of intertextuality in relation to the Matthean gospel will not be addressed in this paper whose focus is, more specifically, the intertextual relationshipship between the biblical testaments. This limitation to intra-biblical intertextuality has also generally been the choice made in the few isolated articles that have addressed intertextuality within biblical studies, together with Fewell (ed.), *Reading Between Texts*; Sipke Draisma, (ed.), *Intertextuality in Biblical Writings: Essays in honour of Bas van Iersel* (Kampen: Kok, 1989); and Daniel Boyarin, *Intertextuality and the Reading of Midrash* (Indiana Studies in Biblical Literature; Bloomington: Indiana University Press, 1990) which, as the title suggests, addresses biblical intertextuality in Jewish midrash.

within these texts, and their intersection in the new text, will raise questions regarding not only the meanings of texts but also the production of that meaning. The subsequent examination of some of these aspects of textuality and intertextuality in the opening chapters of Matthew's gospel will demonstrate the multiplicity of possible meanings that such intertextuality makes available. It will also raise questions regarding the implications of different meanings for women writers and readers in the first century CE and now.[17]

The above considerations of intertextuality have focused predominantly on texts in a way that could suggest intertextuality's virtual imprisonment within the confines of discourse and textuality. This has, however, not been constitutive of its history of development. Jay Clayton and Eric Rothstein, in their introduction to *Influence and Intertextuality in Literary History*, suggest that 'for Kristeva, Bakhtin represented the possibility of opening linguistics to society'.[18] Bakhtin emphasized, on the one hand, the dangers inherent in blurring the boundary lines between the world outside the text and the world represented in the text. On the other hand, he noted how indissolubly the two are tied up with one another:

> The work and the world represented in it enter the real world and enrich it, and the real world enters the work and its world as part of the process of its creation, as well as part of its subsequent life, in a continual renewing of the work through the creative perception of listeners and readers.[19]

Such an interaction gives rise not only to the literary text as considered above, but also to the text of culture and, as Bakhtin suggested, consideration of this text is almost inseparable from the reader. It is the 'creative perception' of the listener or reader that brings to light the intersection of both literary and cultural texts toward multiplicity of meanings. That reader may be the writer of a new text, like a gospel narrative, or may be the reader(s) of the new narrative thus produced.[20] Myriads of texts, both literary and socio-cultural, have

17. Phillips, 'Intertextuality', p. 274, says the following in relation to Luke, which could apply equally to Matthew: 'For Luke the writer, not even his writing can be one and final; in spite of his textual weave his text generates other texts in an intertextual productivity that knows only provisional boundaries'.

18. Jay Clayton and Eric Rothstein, 'Figures in the Corpus: Theories of Influence and Intertextuality', in Jay Clayton and Eric Rothstein (eds.), *Influence and Intertextuality in Literary History* (Madison: University of Wisconsin Press, 1991), p. 18.

19. Bakhtin, *Dialogic Imagination*, p. 253.

20. Phillips, 'Intertextuality,' p. 285, who notes that 'writing is always already a reading and that a reader in every instance rewrites the text as a different text'.

intersected in the shaping of such reader(s). McClintock Fulkerson points out, in relation to the biblical text, that the reader or producer of meaning is, in fact, the community. For her, therefore, 'the codes that constitute the community are necessary elements in its coding/ reading of that holy text'.[21]

Recent studies of the Matthean gospel have likewise recognized the significance of the 'community' in the production and reception of the gospel.[22] The Matthean community re-reads the Hebrew Bible and other literary texts in its Graeco-Roman environment, as well as its cultural texts, in dialogue with traditions—both oral and written—of the life of and resurrection belief in Jesus of Nazareth. It produces a new text as a result of the intertextuality at work, a text which Lucretia Yaghjian suggests is a 'sectarian reading', since it is within and yet against the 'official reading establishment'.[23] As such, it functions as a foundational community narrative in order to establish group solidarity and identity for a dissident group within or on the edge of a Jewish community—perhaps in Antioch or southern Syria, according to the claims of Saldarini.[24] The resultant Matthean text can, therefore, be conceived as a 'counterstory':

> ...a story that contributes to the moral self-definition of its teller by undermining a dominant story, undoing it and retelling it in such a way as to invite new interpretation and conclusions. Counterstories can be told anywhere, but particularly when told within chosen communities, they permit their tellers to reenter, as full citizens, the communities of place whose goods have been only imperfectly available to its marginalized members.[25]

21. McClintock Fulkerson, *Changing the Subject*, pp. 165-66.

22. In particular Saldarini, *Matthew's Community*. See also Graham N. Stanton, *A Gospel for a New People: Studies in Matthew* (Edinburgh: T. & T. Clark, 1992) and Andrew Overman, *Matthew's Gospel and Formative Judaism: The Social World of the Matthean Community* (Minneapolis: Fortress Press, 1990). Saldarini (*Matthew's Community*, pp. 85-87), discusses the problems associated with the term 'community' and prefers to use 'group'. In this essay, however, I will retain the more traditional terminology.

23. Lucretia B. Yaghjian, 'How Shall We Read? A Preface to Matthew's Protocols of Reading' (unpublished manuscript n.d.), p. 10.

24. Saldarini, *Matthew's Community*, reconstructs the Matthean community on the edge of, but not separated from, the dominant Jewish community within its context of origin. The question of the nature and location of that community is too complex for discussion here.

25. Hilde Lindemann Nelson, 'Resistance and Insubordination', *Hypatia* 10.2 (1995), pp. 23-40 (23).

The Matthean gospel story is rich in intertextuality. In the under-standing of Bakhtin it has chosen a language in which to speak Jesus, chosen a language from the heteroglossia of

> socio-ideological contradictions between the present and the past, between differing epochs of the past, between different socio-ideolog-ical groups in the present, between tendencies, schools, circles and so forth.[26]

From a feminist perspective, however, a significant point must be made. The above understanding of community-produced text will still only offer access to the dominant discourse(s) unless there is a recognition of resisting reading practices, especially among women.[27] The reading practices of at least some women of the Matthean com-munity, while largely constructed by the reading practices of the community, can nevertheless be considered subversive in relation to its dominant narrative.[28] They will be constituted by women's social location within first-century kyriarchal structures as well as their resistance to them.[29] It is to these intertextual readings that a feminist approach seeks to give voice. A feminist approach concerned for

26. Bakhtin, *Dialogic Imagination*, p. 291.

27. For the purpose of this paper, I will not try to explore the differences within the reading practices of the Matthean community beyond that associated with gender. However, my own further research would indicate that there is a need to look at the more complex differences within the reading communities within this group—influenced by ethnicity, class, education, religious and philosophical asso-ciation, among other factors.

28. See Elaine M. Wainwright, *Towards A Feminist Critical Reading of the Gospel according to Matthew* (BZNW, 160; Berlin: de Gruyter, 1991), for a more extensive development of women's resistant reading of this gospel narrative. The insights this study revealed have been supported by the theoretical considerations provid-ed by McClintock Fulkerson, *Changing the Subject*, pp. 147-50 and by Nelson, 'Resistance and Insubordination', p. 24, who points out that 'narratives of resis-tance and insubordination...allow communities of choice to challenge and revise the paradigm stories of the "found" communities in which they are embedded. The ability of counterstories to reconfigure dominant stories permit those who have been excluded or oppressed by the "found" community to gain fuller access to the goods offered there.' Wim Beuken and Ellen van Wolde, 'Introduction' (in Draisma [ed.], *Intertextuality in Biblical Writings*, p. 7) suggest that '[r]eading intertextually is an act of resistance against the reading of texts in a concluding and restricting way'.

29. Elisabeth Schüssler Fiorenza, *But She Said: Feminist Practices of Biblical Inter-pretation* (Boston: Beacon, 1992), pp. 103-32, develops a careful explanation of how patriarchy functioned in first-century Mediterranean society as a system of multiple oppressions, to which she gives the name 'kyriarchy'.

difference will, however, not focus solely on gender but also on the construction of differences within the community that can be camouflaged by what appears to be a unitary text. It will challenge the understanding of the community as predominantly Jewish or predominantly gentile—inside or outside Judaism, as the dominant scholarship presents it; and will seek to uncover the multiple literary and socio-cultural texts that have constructed this reading community, texts of the different reading groups within the community. And finally, it must be recognized that my analysis of some intertextual readings of the Matthean gospel's infancy narrative, which may have been possible for this community of participants in the reign of God movement at the end of the first century of the common era, will, of course, be filtered through the matrix of my own cultural and socio-ideological location.[30]

Rachel Weeping: Resistant Tears and Other Languages

The opening words of the Matthean gospel, '*biblos Geneseōs*/book of the origin(s)', suggest immediately a reading or a re-reading of the Hebrew Bible. The reader constructed in this text is Jewish. For many among the predominantly Jewish component of the Matthean community, this opening text intersects or resonates with two texts (2.4 and 5.1) from Genesis, the first *biblos*/book of the Hebrew Bible. Genesis 2.4—'This is the book of the origin/*genesis* of the heavens and the earth'—is a double-edged text. It functions to close off the first account (Gen. 1.1–2.4a) of the creation of the heavens, the earth and the human creature, male and female; and to open the second account of that creation (2.4a-2.25). Genesis 5.1—'This is the book of the origin/*genesis* of the human ones/*anthrōpōn*'—introduces a narrative: a genealogical account of the generations from Adam to Noah. Here, text types intersect to produce excesses of meaning that need not concern us at this point. Genesis 5.1, however, not only parallels Gen. 2.4 with the rupture of the parallel occurring at 'heaven and earth' and 'humanity'/'human ones', but 5.1b-2a also echoes Gen. 1.27—'in the image of God, God made him ('Adam' in 5.1 and '*anthrōpon*/human one' in 1.27), male and female God made them'.[31]

30. The infancy narrative of Matthew's gospel contains more potential for intertextual analysis than is possible within the scope of this paper but, hopefully, what is uncovered will point readers toward further possibilities.

31. 2.4   Αὕτη ἡ βίβλος γενέσεως <u>οὐρανοῦ καὶ γῆς</u> ὅτε ἐγένετο,

    5.1   Αὕτη ἡ βίβλος γενέσεως <u>ἀνθρώπων</u>

    2.4   ἡ ἡμέρᾳ ἐποίησεν κύριος ὁ θεὸς <u>τὸν οὐρανὸν καὶ τὴν γῆν</u>

The female in the narrative genealogy of Genesis 5, however, is virtually erased except for the passing references to daughters in each
generation (Gen. 5.4, 7, 10, 13, 16, 19, 22, 26, 30).

The intertextual possibilities in the opening of the Matthean gospel
shape readers to encounter a new book, a book of origins like the first
book of the Bible, a beginning of a new story. This new story holds
promise of a new creation like the first creation and a new humanity
reconstituted in the image of divinity, male and female.[32] The rupture
in the echoed texts holds these two aspects of re-creation in tension.[33]
The ideology of Genesis 5 undermines the vision but, as Miscall suggests, this new text (Mt. 1.1a) displaces or decentres the earlier texts.[34]
Such displacement is not new, as Miscall's analysis of Isaiah's re-
reading of Genesis 1 suggests; but the textual displacement functions
rhetorically to construct its reader(s) as a community seeking a new
self-definition by 'undoing' its dominant narrative, and by 'retelling

5.1   ἡ ἡμέρᾳ ἐποίησεν ὁ θεὸς <u>τὸν Ἀδὰμ</u>,
1.27   ἐποίησεν ὁ θεὸς <u>τὸν ἄνθρωπον</u>,
5.1   κατ᾽ εἰκόνα θεοῦ ἐποίησεν αὐτὸν ἄρσεν καὶ θῆλυ
        ἐποίησεν αὐτούς, καὶ εὐλόγησεν
1.27   κατ᾽ εἰκόνα θεοῦ ἐποίησεν αὐτον, ἄρσεν καὶ θῆλυ
        ἐποίησεν αὐτούς καὶ εὐλόγησεν
5.1   αὐτούς...
1.27   αὐτούς...

32. Phyllis Bird, '"Male and Female He Created Them": Gen 1:27b in the
Context of the Priestly Account of Creation', *HTR* 74 (1981), pp. 129-59 raises the
question, in relation to Genesis 1.27, as to the understanding of the reference 'male
and female' by the Priestly writer. One could raise a similar question in relation to
the first century Jewish–Christian community of the Matthean Gospel. For the
contemporary reader, however, it is evocative of difference, male and female
subjectivity in humanity, and male and female imaging of divinity. See Elaine
Wainwright, 'What's in a Name? The Word Which Binds/The Word Which Frees',
in Maryanne Confoy, Dorothy Lee and Joan Nowotny (eds.), *Freedom and Entrapment: Women Thinking Theology* (North Blackburn: Dove, 1995), pp. 100-20.

33. Michael Crosby, *House of Disciples: Church, Economics, and Justice in Matthew*
(Maryknoll: Orbis Books, 1988), p. 82, holds these two together when he says:
'Somehow in Jesus and, by extension, in the community of his disciples, God's
work of creation was to begin anew; through them creation was to be reordered to
reveal God's original plan for the world. Human households came to reflect God's
household order for the cosmos. Creation was pictured as the household of God
(Ps. 24:1).'

34. Peter Miscall, 'Isaiah: New Heavens, New Earth, New Book', in Fewell
(ed.), *Reading between Texts*, p. 45. It is interesting that, in his conclusion, Miscall
understands Isaiah as seeking to close off a series of 'creations' by positing this
new book as 'precluding further figuration'. One must ask whether the Matthean
implied author reads/writes in a similar way.

it in such a way as to invite new interpretation and conclusions'.[35]

A feminist reading, however, is alert to the possible transgressions of the opening vision which is so rich in imagery and yet possibility of erasure, as the brief analysis of Genesis 5 has demonstrated.[36] The first of these transgressions occurs immediately as the vision is particularized in Jesus, the anointed one, son of David, son of Abraham. Israel's story, which began with the book of origins and unfolded in its 'historical' texts, is read through the very limited lens of male genealogy, hinted at by the designations 'son of David' and 'son of Abraham'.[37] Such a reading is further underscored if the opening phrase is read as 'book of the genealogy [of Jesus Christ]'. Male genealogy informs the initial interpretation of Jesus *Christos* and, likewise, limits the intertextual possibilities of the new book of origins.[38] On the other hand, one might speculate whether, within women's meaning-making in relation to Jesus,[39] the influence might

35. Nelson, 'Resistance and Insubordination', p. 23. This notion is further amplified by the image used by McClintock Fulkerson (*Changing the Subject*, pp. 151-54), who speaks of each re-reading as a graft that directs or stimulates the flow of sap or meaning in a new direction

36. It is beyond the scope of this paper to explore the imagery of 'new creation' or even 'creation' within the Hebrew Bible, especially in Isaiah 40–66 and the Psalms. See Miscall, 'Isaiah'; but also note the way Miscall sees Isaiah as closing off further figurations rather than opening up to future or further new figurations.

37. Yaghjian, 'How Shall We Read,' p. 5, points out that '[w]hat a birth certificate or passport is to ours, a genealogical record was to Matthew's world: it certified the bearer as an official member of his culture in good standing, and conferred upon him the cultural credentials of role and status apposite to his ancestral heritage…to claim, then as Matthew does, that David (Israel's prototypical shepherd–king) and Abraham (through whom all the nations become heirs of Israel's blessing) are both primogenitors of Jesus is to invoke the book of the culture no less strategically than the book of the covenant.'

38. For a comprehensive study of the intertextual possibilities of the titles Jesus Christ, son of David and son of Abraham, see W.D. Davies and Dale C. Allison, *A Critical and Exegetical Commentary on the Gospel according to Saint Matthew* (ICC; 2 vols.; Edinburgh: T. & T. Clark, 1988), I, pp. 149-60.

39. Marianne Sawicki, *Seeing the Lord: Resurrection and Early Christian Practices* (Minneapolis: Fortress Press, 1994), pp. 149-81, posits a community of women's poiēsis in Jerusalem after the crucifixion which initially designates Jesus as 'Messiah'/*Christos*. My initial work on the women characters in the Matthean Gospel, *Towards a Feminist Critical Reading*, also suggested women's remembering of Jesus and women's remembering and retelling of the stories of their sisters in the reign of God movement associated with Jesus. Work still remains to be done in relation to the Matthean community to reconstruct possible contexts for women's meaning production by way of texts and traditions.

have flowed in the opposite direction. Hence, the possibilities of a new beginning involving male and female in the image of God—evoked by the opening phrase, 'book of the origin'—may have functioned to subvert the maleness of the metaphors initially predicated of Jesus—*Christos*, son of David and son of Abraham.[40] Such a reading, reconfiguring the original vision distorted by the limitations of male genealogy, could have constituted reading subjects—both female and male—who envisioned their community as a new kinship structure.

The actual genealogy or patrilineage that follows the opening verse (1.2-17) is a particular and highly constructed reading of Israel's story.[41] It is read as patrilineage [male was the father of male], encoding the text of the dominant kinship structure,[42] and draws its reader into an ordered, coherent and patterned structure bespeaking completion and fulfilment: a single unitary reading rather than the plural or shattered one suggested by the opening phrase (1.1a). Within such a reading, the female is constructed as an invisible vehicle of reproduction not by the text, but by its absence and its gaps, its erasure and exclusion. One wants to cry out, Is there neither mother nor daughter in Israel?[43]

The five patterned ruptures in the narrative (1.3, 5a, 5b, 6, 16) echo such a cry. A number of texts intersect here, giving rise to tensive readings. From within the patriarchal register these ruptures can be,

40. Readers would have also noted the text-type or genre transgression that links the 'book of the genealogy' not to the ancestor 'Abraham' but to the final progeny, Jesus Christ. Jesus *Christos* subverts expected patterns, at least textually, at this point in the opening of the narrative.

41. For an extensive discussion of the various texts that intersect in the genealogy see Raymond Brown, *Birth of the Messiah: A Commentary on the Infancy Narratives in the Gospels of Matthew and Luke* (new updated edn; Garden City, NY: Doubleday, 1993), pp. 74-84 and Davies and Allison, *Critical and Exegetical Commentary*, pp. 161-67.

42. Bruce Malina and Richard Rohrbaugh, *Social Science Commentary on the Synoptic Gospels* (Minneapolis: Fortress Press, 1992), pp. 24-25.

43. In relation to such erasure, note the repeated reference to daughters as well as sons in the genealogical narrative of Gen. 5.1-32 (already noted above); and to the stories of the matriarchs—Sarah, Rebecca, Rachel and Leah—in subsequent chapters of Genesis. See J. Cheryl Exum, 'The Mothers of Israel: The Patriarchal Narratives from a Feminist Perspective', *BRev* 2.1 (1986), pp. 60-67 and Ilona N. Rashkow, 'Daughters and Fathers in Genesis... Or, What is Wrong with This Picture?' in A. Brenner (ed.), *A Feminist Companion to Exodus to Deuteronomy* (The Feminist Companion to the Bible, Sheffield: Sheffield Academic Press, 1994), pp. 22-36, which deal respectively with inclusion and erasure.

and have been, read theologically. These anomalous women, whose insertion into the patriarchal familial system is 'irregular', are nevertheless the instruments through which the divine order, imaged as absolutely male-centred, reaches its completion or fulfilment.[44] From within the register of resistant readers these women (Tamar, Rahab, Ruth, Bathsheba and Mary), whose own stories threatened the structure of the patriarchal family, open a small fissure in the symbolic universe that the patrilineage constructs.[45] Into this fissure can be drawn the names of the mothers and daughters who were likewise the ancestors of Jesus.[46] Jesus, the anointed one, is therefore not only born of and into a family symbolically constructed as male-centred. He is also born of and into a family in which the stories of women, who symbolize an alternative to the dominant male ideology, intersect with that dominant ideology. Jesus is son or child of Mary, of Tamar, Rahab, Ruth and Bathsheba as well as of David and Abraham. A hint of alternative kinship structures and alternative memories, alternative readings of the biblical story, coincides with the dominant reading and at least momentarily decentres it. Verse 16 climaxes such a decentering as the pattern is broken definitively, with Joseph being identified as the husband of Mary and Mary designated as the one from whom Jesus is birthed. Such a gap is quickly covered over, however, with the recapitulation of the ordered reading of Israel's history in 1.17, and with the story of Joseph's agency in the birth of Jesus within the context of a divinely authorized Davidic family in 1.18-25.

Having given some brief consideration to intertextuality within the

44. Brown, *Birth*, pp. 73-74, offers this reading as the most widely held among scholars today but, in his work, it is offered in supposedly value-neutral theological terms. It is not analyzed in relation to the support such theology proffers for the patriarchal structure of the narrative, hence its rhetorical effect in terms of construction of readers.

45. For a more comprehensive analysis of these women's stories and their inclusion in the Matthean text, see Wainwright, *Towards a Feminist Critical Reading*, pp. 60-69, 160-70. Both this reading and that of Jane Schaberg, *The Illegitimacy of Jesus: A Feminist Theological Interpretation of the Infancy Narratives* (San Francisco: Harper & Row, 1987), p. 33, recognize that the stories of each of these women are brought back under patriarchal control in their respective narratives.

46. Luce Irigaray, *Sexes and Genealogies* (trans. Gillian C. Gill; New York: Columbia University Press, 1993), p. 19, makes the following plea in this regard: 'Let us not forget, moreover, that we already have a history, that certain women, despite all the cultural obstacles, have made their mark upon history and all too often have been forgotten by us'. Irigaray's emphasis on mother–daughter genealogies is likewise significant here.

opening verses of Matthew's gospel (1.1-17), I would turn attention now to the interweaving of stories that symbolically link the birth and infancy of Jesus with that of Moses—as recounted in the biblical text and developed in later popular Jewish traditions.[47] In the Hebrew Bible, the dream(s) of Joseph (Gen. 37.5-11) is (are) a narrative prelude to the saving of God's people through the birth of a liberator (Exod. 2.1-7). Echoes of the Genesis and the more extensive Exodus narrative resound through, and give shape to, Matthew's account of the birth and infancy of Jesus (1.18–2.23). Joseph is an ambiguous figure in the Matthean text. He is the recipient of dreams (1.20, 2.12 and 2.19) like the ancient ancestor, Joseph, and his forebears in the Genesis narrative (Abimelech, Gen. 20.3-8; Jacob, Gen. 28.12-16, 31.10-13 and 46.2-4). It is through him and his dreams that a distant and transcendent deity protects the child Jesus; and yet it is this same child who is to be called 'Emmanuel', the one in whom this distant deity comes among Israel to save its people (Mt. 1.23, 22). Intertextuality constructs the divine as both far and near through the mediation of Joseph and the child who is the object of the dreams. The resistant reader, however, would have noted that Joseph is introduced into the narrative not as the father of Jesus, as one would have expected of the patterned close to the genealogy (1.16), but as the 'husband of Mary from whom the anointed one/*Christos* was born'. The patriarchal figure constructed by significant intertextuality is deconstructed by the text. Mary's agency is, however, erased in its turn by the Joseph narrative in 1.18-25.

It is, however, the Exodus narrative that is most significantly re-read in the infancy narrative of Matthew's gospel. This Matthean re-reading takes it place with other such readings in the first century of the common era (Josephus, *Ant.*, 2.2.12, Targum Pseudo-Jonathan for Exodus and the *Biblical Antiquities* of Pseudo-Philo to name but a few).[48] Each of these has the prophecy about the coming liberator conveyed by way of a dream. In Pseudo-Philo's *Biblical Antiquities*, however, it is upon Miriam that the 'spirit of God' comes in a dream bringing this divine message for her parents:

47. John Dominic Crossan, *Jesus: A Revolutionary Biography* (San Francisco: HarperCollins, 1994), pp. 10-15, outlines the parallels in detail.

48. See Eileen Schuller, 'Women of the Exodus in Biblical Retellings of the Second Temple Period,' in Peggy L. Day (ed.), *Gender and Difference in Ancient Israel* (Minneapolis: Fortress Press, 1989), pp. 178-94 for an analysis of the erasure of women in these retellings, in a way similar to what can be seen in the Matthean infancy narrative.

...that which shall be born of you shall be cast into the water, for by him water shall be dried up, and by him will I do signs and I will save my people... (LAB 9.10).

We are alerted by the above to one of the significant erasures in the Matthean re-reading of the early Exodus narrative, namely that of the Hebrew and Egyptian women who in the narrative are the instigators of Israel's liberation—Shiprah and Puah, Miriam, Jocabed[49] and the daughter of Pharaoh (Exod. 1.8–2.10). Cheryl Exum draws the attention of contemporary readers to the ideology inherent in the Exodus texts, which portrays these active and subversive women as 'mothers' of the male liberator in a way that obscures their collaborative subversion of oppressive authority.[50] These women are also almost completely erased in the Matthean re-reading of Exodus with only a slight trace of their memory in the shadowy figure of Miriam/Mary, the mother of the child. Rather, the Matthean re-reading situates the birth of the liberator, Jesus, completely in the context of male power struggles, focused particularly in Herod who is designated king, as was Pharaoh (Mt. 2.1; Exod. 1.8). There is a significant reversal in this reading, however, with Joseph being commanded to take the child and his mother and flee into Egypt in order to escape Herod's plot against the life of the child (2.13).[51] Oppressive hegemony is shifted from Egypt to Israel, with Egypt becoming the place of sanctuary. This reading is itself quickly decentred by the introduction into the text of Hos. 11.1b as a fulfilment of what was spoken through the prophet (Mt. 2.15): 'out of Egypt I called my son'. Political and oppressive hegemony is plural and not limited to any one particular location.

The Matthean reading of Hosea would have evoked Israel's constant confession of faith that its God led Israel as a people out of Egypt, the place of slavery. Israel as a nation is clearly one possible tenor of the filial metaphor in Hos. 11.1. The metaphor is transferred to Jesus in Mt. 2.15. Here the new Exodus/new liberation, evoked intertextually, is focused in Jesus, as was the new creation evoked in the opening verse of the infancy narrative. There, imagery of

49. Miriam and Jochebed are not named here in the narrative, being identified simply as the sister and the mother of the child; but the reader discovers their names later in the narrative, in Exod. 6.20.

50. Cheryl Exum, 'Second Thoughts about Secondary Characters', in Brenner (ed.), *A Feminist Companion to Exodus to Deuteronomy*, pp. 74-87.

51. A further intertexual relationship that cannot be developed here is that with 1 Kgs 11.40: Solomon sought to kill Jeroboam but Jeroboam arose and fled into Egypt, to Shishak king of Egypt, and was in Egypt until the death of Solomon.

humanity—male and female—offered the possibilities of new constructions of human kinship. In the Hosean poem (Hos. 11.1-7), which Mt. 2.15 draws into the narrative, the imagery predicated of divinity is predominantly that of the mother.[52] A feminist critical reading of first century CE intertextuality is open to the potential readings of Mt. 2.15. The predominance of male imagery for divinity in the Hebrew Bible would suggest that the dominant reading would be in terms of father imagery. This has certainly been so in subsequent readings within Christianity, characterized as it has been by the 'progressive patriarchalization' of the Christian image of God.[53] The Hosean imagery may, however, have been read by resistant first-century readers as maternal, especially when it is remembered that Sophia/Wisdom, a female *gestalt* of God, characterized the wisdom literature of Israel's immediate intertestamental period. Through this lens, divinity imaged as male and female calls forth a new exodus, a new liberation so that God being with God's people constitutes a new humanity, not just a male saviour.

Traces of wisdom traditions, with their attendant female imagery, may have been heard by some first-century readers or listeners elsewhere in the infancy narrative. On the one hand, the elusive figures of the *magoi* are linked to the East, the symbolic origin of religious wisdom in languages and texts beyond the Hebrew Bible.[54] On the other hand, while the Emmanuel fulfilment text of Mt. 1.23 explicitly recalls Isa. 7.14, 8.8 and 8.10, it also evokes those Wisdom songs in which Sophia sang of her delight to be with the human community (Prov. 8.22-31), her setting up of her dwelling place in Jacob (Sir. 24.8-12) and her appearance on the earth, dwelling among humanity (Bar. 3.37). And even if such connections were not made by members of the first-century reading community, they provide rich intertextual readings for contemporary feminist critics as well as for the constitution of female–feminist subjectivity. They construe incarnation of divinity

52. Helen Schüngel-Straumann, 'God as Mother in Hosea 11', in A. Brenner (ed.), *A Feminist Companion to the Latter Prophets* (The Feminist Companion to the Bible, 8; Sheffield: Sheffield Academic Press, 1995), pp. 194-218 (203), where she acknowledges that the prophet Hosea never expressly calls God 'mother' but that 'all the activities listed in vv. 1-4 were, in Hosea's time, the exclusive province of mothers'.

53. Schüngel-Straumann, 'God as Mother', pp. 217-18. See Gundry, *Use of the Old Testament*, pp. 93-94 by way of an example, in which it is assumed without discussion that the imagery is that of father and son.

54. Ulrich Luz, *Matthew 1–7: A Commentary*, (trans. Wilhelm C. Linss; Minneapolis: Augsburg, 1989), pp. 134-35.

in female as well as male terms, the dominant male centre with its attendant ideology being displaced by the traces and even the erasures within the narrative. This intertextuality may allow contemporary reading communities to speak Jesus in new languages as a result of their reading of the polyglossal Matthean text as the Matthean community might have read it.

There are many other instances of intertextuality of various types which could be further explored in the Matthean infancy narrative. I will conclude, however, with a brief discussion of the citation of Jer. 31.15, which closes the narrative of Herod's slaying of the male children who are under two years from Bethlehem and its surrounding regions. The narrative context raises questions regarding the repeated use of the phrase 'this was to fulfil...' or its equivalent (Mt. 1.22, 2.5, 15, 17, 23). Such a phrase, like the opening genealogy, gives order, meaning and understanding to the life of Jesus, so that it can be read by different reading communities as a re-telling of their scriptural story. It is indeed an 'undoing' and 'retelling', but the claim to fulfilment obscures the undoing: it allows the retelling to shape the self-identity of a community whose locus is on the margins of Judaism, itself a deviant community or a resistant community needing a counterstory.

Difference and intertextuality combine, however, to shatter the order that fulfilment evokes. The voice of Rachel weeping uncovers another silence in the text—the mothers of Bethlehem weeping for their children, refusing to be consoled because they are no more (not just taken into exile as were Rachel's metaphorical children, but slaughtered at the hands of a tyrant king). Their voices cry out to and against the intervening God of the infancy narrative. Their story, or rather their absence from the story, is surrounded by four dream appearances (2.12, 13, 19, 22) serving the rescue of Jesus, the favoured child. Does this God only intervene on behalf of favoured male children like Isaac and Jesus, not on behalf of innocent women and children (cf. Judges 19, Mt. 2.16)? The silence in the text cries out for an answer.

It is the raised voice of Rachel that pierces the male world of power, of slaughter and of divine favour. She stands in the place of the erased women, but she also stands in the place of divine compassion likewise erased. Just as the Hosean citation three verses earlier drew into the Matthean narrative images from the poem that it heads, so too the citation in Mt. 2.18 of Jer. 31.15 reads the slaughter of the children of Bethlehem in light of the entire poem of Jer. 31.15-22. The divine voice that responds to Rachel is a voice that promises return from exile, a voice more difficult to hear in the Matthean narrative in the face of the finality of death. For participants in the reign of God movement, however, resurrection was becoming an interpretive lens that was beginning to shape their reading of tragic death. The divine voice of the Jeremian poem—they shall return from the enemy's land—may well have been read through this lens.

The weeping and loud lamentation of Rachel creates a further fissure in the well-ordered Matthean narrative. She stands in the place of divine compassion, imaged as female in continuity with the maternal imagery of 2.15. Phyllis Trible translates v. 20b of Jeremiah's poem in these words: 'Therefore, my womb trembles for him; I will truly show motherly-compassion upon him'.[55]

The extraordinary poem of Jeremiah does not end there. Its final verse, 22b, drawn into the Matthean narrative by way of the image of Rachel, forms an inclusion with this narrative's opening verse (1.1a). Jeremiah's poem ends with God creating a 'new thing' on the earth, female/woman surrounding/encompassing male/man.[56] The image of female (נקבה) in the final verse of the poem evokes Genesis 1.27. In contrast, however, the terminology used for male is not זכר, as in Gen. 1.27, but גבר, more generally associated with the virile male or male warrior than the generic.[57] The resistant tears of the female, Rachel, which virtually conclude the Matthean infancy narrative can also encompass or surround it—decentering male hegemony in whatever form it appears: sexual, military, political, religious.

55. Phyllis Trible, *God and the Rhetoric of Sexuality* (Overtures to Biblical Theology; Philadelphia: Fortress Press, 1978), p. 45.

56. This text is evocative of many meanings, as has been indicated by its various translations. The New American Bible gives at least three in a footnote to the verse. A number of scholars consider the text 'secondary' or a later addition. But, with Trible (*God and the Rhetoric of Sexuality*, p. 59 n. 39), I would affirm that it belongs to the final form of the poem in the MT. The LXX has paraphrased the text: Gleason L. Archer and G.C. Chirichigno, *Old Testament Quotations in the New Testament: A Complete Survey* (Chicago: Moody Press, 1983), p. 137, suggest that the Matthean text 'is closer (especially in word order) to the MT than the LXX'. William L. Holladay, *Jeremiah 2: A Commentary on the Book of the Prophet Jeremiah Chapters 26–52* (Hermeneia; Minneapolis: Fortress Press, 1989), p. 195, proposes both a sexual and a military sense to the use of the verb translated as 'surround' or 'encircle, enfold'.

57. For a more extended discussion see Trible, *God and the Rhetoric of Sexuality*, p. 49 and p. 59 n. 44; and Mieke Bal, *Death and Dissymmetry: The Politics of Coherence in the Book of Judges* (Chicago: University of Chicago Press, 1988), who demonstrates the centrality of the image of the גבר or warrior within the symbolic world of the book of Judges.

For the reader resistant to the male-centredness of the opening verses of the narrative, Rachel's resistant tears thus point back to the beginning of the narrative, to its hope and possibilities. They also break open the closures that the narrative seeks to impose upon its readers. This new advent of God with God's people, symbolized in Jesus, is to be read as plural and shattered, not single and unitary.

Conclusion

Biblical intertextuality has provided one lens through which to examine the relationships between the biblical testaments. On the one hand, it enables contemporary readers, especially feminist readers, to shatter the dominant narrative encoded not only within the text but also within themselves as a result of the malestream traditioning process over centuries. Such a reading, it has been demonstrated, is *a* reading: not necessarily *the* reading of the Matthean communities' retelling of their sacred story as the story of Jesus. On the other hand, it allows resistant and partially erased readings of the story of Jesus and the reign of God movement to be heard anew, as the voices of communities of difference retelling their sacred story. Plurality plays within the parameters of this interpretive process in a way that opens to the possibilities of the 'new creation' that the Matthean text, examined in this essay, has evoked.

VIII

FORAYS INTO RABBINICS

RABBINIC INTERPRETATION OF SCRIPTURE

Judith Hauptman

Although the Hebrew Bible is the collection of sacred writings for three of the world's major religions, Jews live their lives today more according to the Talmud—a set of laws, ethical principles and homilies dating from the first five or six centuries of the common era. This corpus presents the reader with an extensive commentary on the Bible, in part a direct explication of verses and in part a compendium of laws only loosely based on Scripture. The Talmud has two major parts: the older Hebrew strand called Mishnah (*m.*), and the later Hebrew and Aramaic strand called *gᵉmārā*. The *gᵉmārā* is preserved in two recensions, the Palestinian (*y.*) and Babylonian (*b.*). The spokesmen of the Talmud are called 'sages' or 'rabbis'.

The rabbis often begin their exegetical exercise with a verse or phrase from the Torah, apply to it a hermeneutical device and then derive a new rule, often hardly hinted at in the words of the verse themselves. Although some would argue that what drives the rabbis' thinking is the meaning implicit in the verse as placed there by the divine author, I subscribe to a different point of view: that the act of exegesis is an attempt on the part of the rabbis to maintain the authority and sacredness of Scripture but, at the same time, to read their own, often more progressive social thinking into the ancient text. In this manner the rabbis are able radically to transform biblical institutions, such as marriage and divorce, and even modify their patriarchal configuration. Unlike many secular legal systems, which can be changed by a majority of legislators, a religious system—anchored, according to its interpreters, in a divinely revealed text—needs to accommodate itself to evolving social truths by changing but still appearing to remain the same. It is fascinating to trace the process by which the rabbis accomplish this dual goal. This will be observed in a close reading of the passages dealing with sex crimes against women.

Biblical References to Sex Crimes against Women

Exodus 22.15-16: If a man seduces an unbetrothed virgin and has sexual relations with her, he shall pay the bride price and marry her. If her father refuses to give her to him, he must still weigh out money like the bride price of virgins.[1]

This is a rather puzzling set of verses. It says that in all cases the seducer has to pay the bride price of virgins to the father of the girl he has seduced, but he will not always get a bride for his money. It depends on how the woman's father feels about the match. Even if the father refuses to give his daughter in marriage he still deserves to be paid, because as a non-virgin she is worth less to him on the marriage market. This rule shows that the victim of seduction, according to these verses, is not the girl herself, but her father. She is seen as his property, almost as a part of him, so that it is he who suffers as a result of her exploitation and humiliation and not she. Or, more accurately, she does not suffer independently of him. The individual is not viewed so much as an individual but as a member of a family.[2] The seducer must therefore make amends to the collective body, in particular to the head of household, not to the girl herself.

We find a similar outlook and legal resolution in the related crime of rape, dealt with only in Deuteronomy.

Deuteronomy 22.28-29: If a man finds an unbetrothed (מֹאֹרָשָׂה) virgin and forces her to engage in sexual relations with him, and they are found out: the man who had sex with her has to give her father fifty silver coins and she will be his wife; because he forced her (תַּחַת אֲשֶׁר עִנָּה)[3] he may not dismiss her ever.

Here, too, the sexual crime committed against the daughter is analyzed in terms of its economic effect upon the father. He is paid fifty silver Shekels, apparently equal to the bride price of virgins. But in this instance the Torah also shows concern for the girl in that it assigns the man to her as a husband, for as long as he lives, with the stated rationale 'because he forced her'. This phrase, in my opinion, is expressing sympathy for the young victim: she now has a husband

---

1. All translations of texts, both biblical and rabbinic, are mine. Bracketed words are explanatory notes added by me to help the reader grasp the full import of the text.

2. This is still true today among many traditional families in the MIddle East and elsewhere.

3. The Hebrew root עִנָּה in the pi. apparently means 'to exert force'. It does not necessarily mean that he afflicted her in the course of the rape.

for good. He may not fabricate a reason to divorce her. It also seems true that his having to marry her is regarded as a punishment for him, in that she is an albatross around his neck. He must provide for her forever. We thus see that the Torah is punishing the rapist much more severely than it has punished the seducer. Since the rapist's crime was worse in that the woman's consent was not sought, his punishment, long-term economic obligation to his victim, is greater. It seems that, in the biblical period, a girl who was raped could not easily be married off, and so, if ancient expectations of marriage had more to do with financial and social security and the opportunity to raise children than a loving relationship, the girl who was raped might not look askance upon the prescribed union. Again, if the girl is viewed as a member of a family collective, then this solution is designed to satisfy the head of household as well as the girl herself. There seems to be no better way in an ancient patriarchal social order to make amends for what happened. She cannot regain her virginity.

In the preceding verses (24, 25) the Torah says that if a man rapes a betrothed virgin, he deserves the death penalty. But why such a vast difference in the punishment for these two crimes, the rape of an unbetrothed and a betrothed virgin? The woman's suffering is identical in both instances. This forces me to conclude that the rape of a woman who already belongs to another man is a far more serious breach of the social order than the rape of a woman not yet purchased in marriage. The victim of the rape in this instance is the husband of the betrothed virgin, who cannot be compensated for his loss—he will no longer be the first to have sex with her—and so the rapist has to die. These verses also tell us that rape is impossible, by definition, in the city because had the woman called out, for sure she would have been saved (vv. 23, 24). The aggressor may have intended rape, but her presumed silence in the face of force indicates that the act was consensual. In the field, the Torah gives the woman the benefit of the doubt and assumes she cried out but to no avail (vv. 25-27). This leads to the conclusion that, in the eyes of the biblical author, rape and seduction, in many instances, are the same crime, be it forced or consensual.

It is therefore not surprising that the author of the Temple Scroll (in the second century BCE) refers, in his quasi-biblical writings, to only one kind of sex crime against women: seduction. He cites the Torah's rape verses almost verbatim but with one very significant change: he substitutes the verb 'seduce' for 'rape'.[4] He then proceeds to prescribe for seduction the punishments of rape—forced marriage, no divorce, payment of fifty silver Shekels to the father. This means that he sees both sets of Torah verses as describing only one crime, seduction. There is no such thing as rape of an unbetrothed virgin, in his opinion. Larry Schiffman compares rape and seduction in the Torah, the Temple Scroll and tannaitic literature. He concludes that since the Scroll does not mention a bride price, only a fifty silver Shekel payment to the girl's father, the author considers the payment a penalty—like the *tannaim*, who will later call it q[e]*nās*, not a compensation to the father for the loss of his daughter's virginity. The author, he says further, 'seeks to restore the moral balance and order'.[5] I am not convinced by his argument. Moshe Weinfeld[6] suggests that the Torah too deals with only one case, seduction. The laws as they appear in Deuteronomy, he claims, pay more attention to the victim of the crime because the Deuteronomic author is more humanistic. He has rewritten the seduction laws of Exodus according to his own outlook. But, ultimately, it seems to me that there is only one sex crime against a virgin presented in the Bible, and it is neither rape nor seduction as we know them today, but something in between—part forced and part consensual. It is interesting that in the two rape cases in the Bible, that of Dinah by Shechem (Gen. 34) and Tamar by Amnon (2 Sam. 13), the resolution of the story is different from the recommendations made in the Exodus and Deuteronomy verses cited. In both narrative instances, the brother(s) of the rape victim develop(s) an elaborate, devious scheme and kill(s) the rapist (and his family, in the first instance). The reason for the intense anger, as stated in reference to both episodes, is that 'such a thing is an "abomination" (נבלה), something not done in Israel' (Gen. 34.7; 2 Sam. 13.12). No marriage took place, in either case, between victim and rapist. This means that rape in reality was far more complicated than the verses in Exodus and Deuteronomy suggest. The maelstrom that it creates in the family, and the sense of outrage and shame, almost guarantee that its resolution will not conform to the suggestion of marriage and little else. Note that the victim's brothers are not avenging the girl's

4.   Yigael Yadin, *Megilat Hamikdash* (Heb.; Tel Aviv: Sifriyat Ma'ariv, 1990), column 66.

5.   Larry Schiffman, 'Laws Pertaining to Women in the Temple Scroll', in Devorah Dimant and U. Rappoport (eds.), *The Dead Sea Scrolls: Forty Years of Research* (Leiden: Brill, 1992), pp. 210-28 (224).

6.   Moshe Weinfeld, *Deuteronomy and the Deuteronomic School* (Oxford: Oxford University Press, 1972), pp. 283-87.

shame and pain in particular, but that of the family in general.

In the rabbinic corpus we see that the rabbis recognize the existence of two distinctly different crimes against women, rape and seduction. Since they view all the books of the Torah as the work of a single author, God, the differences in wording between the two sets of verses mean for the rabbis that each of the two sections addresses a different set of circumstances. They even find it necessary to create a word for rape, *'ōnes*, since the Bible only describes it by a series of verbs: 'he grabbed her', 'he afflicted her', 'he forced himself on her', and so on.

But that is just the beginning of what the rabbis do. To understand their altered outlook on these matters, a close reading is needed of some of their dicta on the subject. The rules of rape and seduction appear in the Talmudic tractate dealing with marriage contracts called *Ketubbot*, because the statutory amount of the *kᵉtubbāh* ([marriage] document) varies with the presence or absence of virginity.

Rabbinic Treatment of Sex Crimes against Women

Compensation

> The seducer pays for shame and injury[פגם] and a fine; in addition to these, the rapist pays for pain; the rapist must pay [all] immediately; as for the seducer: when he divorces her, he pays her for the shame, injury, etc.; the rapist must drink from his flowerpot [that he 'watered' with his seed, i.e., marry her]; the seducer may choose to divorce (*m. Ket.* 3.4).

In this mishnah (an individual paragraph in the larger work called the Mishnah), the rabbis institute a new set of payments—shame, injury and pain—based on what the victim of the crime, *the woman*, has experienced. Unlike the fine of fifty pieces of silver which is fixed, these payments vary from case to case. It is here that we see the rabbis' major accomplishment: execution of a paradigm shift. They abandon the biblical model of a crime against the woman's father, the man who stood to benefit from the 'sale' of her virginity, and turn rape into a case of assault and battery against the woman herself—compensation for which is documented elsewhere, in *m. B. Qam.* 8.1. The reason that there we find *five* payments—for damages, pain, medical costs, unemployment and shame—and here only *three*—damages, pain and shame—is that the remaining two, medical costs and unemployment, only apply if the woman suffered incidental injuries in the course of the forced sex act. In addition, a later mishnah

(*Ket.* 4.1) pictures a trial at which judges determine the level of compensation to be paid by the aggressor. Rape and seduction are thus no longer a form of forced marriage, a way of a man getting the woman he wants against her father's will, but a crime committed against a woman.

> How is he forced to 'drink from his flowerpot'? [He must marry her]
> even if she were lame, or blind, or covered with boils... (*m.* 3.5).

This mishnah seems to be providing a rationale for the Torah's forcing a raped woman to live with the man who raped her. The rabbis are saying that if a man of ordinary means took advantage of a physically handicapped woman, who is more vulnerable to rape and less marriageable than others, then his punishment, which is to her benefit, is for her to be 'foisted' on him for the rest of his life, as repulsive as he finds her.[7]

Note that marital suitability in this passage is viewed strictly from a male perspective: the more physically blemished the woman is, the less appealing she is to him and other men; the more important, therefore, for him to have to marry her. It is even possible to suggest that this passage is homiletical: it tells men that rape may give short-term pleasure but, they should realize, the price they pay may be long-term suffering; no matter how unsuitable the woman is for him, the man will have to live with her for the rest of his life. How attractive he is in her eyes and her opinion of him as a mate is of no relevance. The rabbis assume that women, especially those whose marital prospects are limited, prefer any man to no man at all (*b. Qid.* 41a).

Elimination of the Fine

> If he raped the following young women, he pays the [50 shekel] fine...
> but if he raped these other young women, he does *not* pay a fine...
> (*m.* 3.1, 2).

> ...A minor may be sold as a maidservant and *no* fine is paid by the
> man who rapes her. A girl between twelve and twelve and a half may
> not be sold as a maidservant and a fine *is* paid by the man who rapes

---

7.   The only women the aggressor is not forced to marry, according to the Mishnah, are those of inappropriate lineage (e.g. a *mamzēr* a child born of an adulterous or incestuous union). The rabbis will not force a violation of their own marital rules, even in a case of rape. *The Temple Scroll*, written about 130 BCE, already states that he can only marry her if she is fitting for him according to the law. It then lists a variety of forbidden consanguineous relationships. See more on this subject below.

her. An independent young woman [older than twelve and a half] may
not be sold and a fine is *not* paid by the man who rapes her (*m.* 3.8).

At first reading these mishnahs surprise us: they exempt many men
from having to pay a penalty for rape or seduction. Moreover, as
shown by a parallel statement in the Tosefta (a companion volume to
the Mishnah),[8] the redactor of the Mishnah has codified the more
restrictive view of R. Me'ir, instead of the dissenting view of the sages
who impose a fine in many more instances of the rape of a young
girl. One might claim that this is evidence that the rabbis down-
played the gravity of sex crimes against women. I do not think so. If
these mishnahs are read in the context of the entire chapter, it can be
seen that their aim is to limit sharply the circumstances in which it
will be necessary for the rapist or seducer to pay the fine. Why would
the rabbis wish to do that? That they impose restrictions in other
cases, such as implementation of the death penalty and remission of
debts in the sabbatical year, is understandable, given the obvious
broad social benefits of interpreting those institutions out of existence. But why would they limit the scope of cases in which the rapist
must pay a fine, in addition to damages, for the crime he has committed? It is the fine, a punishment above and beyond damages, that
makes this case different from others of personal injury. Releasing a
man from paying it almost implies that he was not guilty of the crime
of rape or seduction, only of damages that were incidental to the
sexual act.

If we backtrack for a moment and remind ourselves that the 'fine',
a rabbinic term for the fifty silver Shekels of the Torah, was paid to
compensate the father for the loss of anticipated income from his
daughter's virginity, we realize that it had nothing to do with the
criminality of the act. Therefore, the fact that the rabbis decide to
eliminate it should not be understood as overlooking the woman as
victim. It is possible that the rabbis moved toward sharply curtailing
the fine because, in their eyes, it seemed somewhat of a travesty to
pay such a large amount to the father for a crime committed against
the daughter—especially since the bride price had already been
replaced by a statutory *keᵗubbāh* amount. It seems that the value of a
human being as a person independent of his or her family had
gained currency by the rabbinic period. By eliminating the fine from

8.   *Tos.* 3.8: 'A girl, from the age of one day and until puberty, she may be sold
as a maidservant but no fine is paid by one who rapes her. The opinion of
R.Me'ir… But the Sages say: a girl from the age of one day and until puberty, a
fine is paid by one who rapes her.'

most cases of rape and seduction, the rabbis seem to be saying that this payment no longer makes legal sense; but the new payments for shame, pain and injury, not referred to in the Torah in this context, are the ones that they are interested in establishing firmly. And although, at first, these payments were also made to the father, in the very next chapter of the Mishnah the rabbis begin to transfer them to the girl herself.

Transfer of Payment

> If a young woman was seduced, the payment for shame and injury, and the fine, go to her father. And also the pain for a woman who was raped.
> If she stood trial [to sue the rapist] before the father died, they [the moneys] are his. If the father then died, they go to her brothers.
> If she did not stand trial before her father died, *they go to her.*
> If she stood trial before becoming a *bôgeret* [independent young woman], they go to the father. And if the father then dies, they go to the brothers. But if she did not stand trial before becoming a *bôgeret*, *they go to her.*
> R. Simon says: if she did not collect payment before her father died, *they go to her.*
> The work of her hands, what she finds, even if she has not yet collected [payment], if the father died, they go to the brothers [because these moneys were due her or accrued to her when the father was still alive and thus they now go to the brothers] (*m.* 4.1). [The *gᵉmārā* adds (*b. Ket.* 43a) that anything she finds after her father dies is hers, and similarly anything she makes and sells after her father died belongs to her and not her brothers.]

According to this mishnah, if the woman goes for trial as an independent young woman the moneys go to her. Or if she had not yet stood trial before her father died, the payments go to her. Thus, the point of this mishnah is to establish when the payments go to the woman instead of her father or her brothers, who are his heirs. That is, we learn from this mishnah that all moneys earned or due her after she reaches *bagrût*, 'maturity', either physically or by virtue of her father's death, accrue to her and not anyone else.

Pᵉgām, a Variable Fine

> What is the amount of payment for shame? It all varies with the [status and circumstances] of the one who inflicts shame and the one who suffers it.
> Pᵉgām [damages]? We look upon her as a slave woman on sale in the marketplace; how much was she worth [as a virgin] and how much is she worth now.

> The fine (*q*ᵉ*nās*) is the same in every case. Any payment stipulated by
> the Torah is the same in all cases (*m. Ket.* 3.7).

Further support for the rabbinic move to eliminate the fine is the
introduction of *p*ᵉ*gām*, payment for personal injury, always coupled
with shame and appearing in rabbinic literature almost exclusively
in connection with seduction and rape. The rabbis of the Talmud
interpret it as payment for the loss of virginity.[9] If this is what it
means, it is a different name for the fine, which also compensated the
father for the loss of virginity. So why are there two payments for the
same virginity? *P*ᵉ*gām*, as noted by the mishnah, is variable, dependent on the circumstances, not fixed like the Torah's fine. As the
rabbis imply in *m. 'Arak.* 3.4, a fixed payment can lead in some cases
to paying too much and in others to paying too little. So, in what
appears to be an ingenious move, the rabbis replaced the Torah's
fixed payment with their own variable one, a statement on their part
of the sense of social justice of their times (although foreign to many
of us today).

It seems to me that the rabbis, without saying so explicitly, have
made a significant statement about crimes against women: that
payments that go to the father, which imply that he is the victim and
not his daughter, are in the process of being eliminated; and payments for what she suffered are in the process of being developed and
transferred to her. Also, and less obvious, is that the rabbis understand that rape is something a man does to a woman, something she
does not invite and that causes her pain. This is a point worth
emphasizing. When these passages are read in context, they show
that the rabbis have gone a long way to rectify the no longer appropriate indifference of the Bible to the young woman as victim. The
rabbis were able to make significant changes by fleshing out the
Torah's rules about sex crimes against women.

The Pain Associated with Rape

The rabbis of the Babylonian Talmud, when commenting on the pain
referred to in *m. Ket.* 3.4, attempt to understand what a woman
experiences during rape.

> What pain [does the mishnah refer to when it says that the rapist pays
> for pain]?

---

9. Cf. *b. Ket.* 40b: Said the father of Samuel: we estimate the difference
between what a man would pay to have sex with a virgin slave and with a non-
virgin slave.

—Said the father of Samuel: that he threw her down on the ground
(שחבטה על גבי קרקע).
—R. Zera attacked the logic [of this answer]: does this mean that if he
threw her down on silk [cushions] he would be free from paying for
pain [i.e., that he would not be liable for the pain of the forced sexual
act itself]?
—And should you say, that is so, have we not learned in a *baraita* [an
extra-mishnaic teaching, from the same period]: R. Simon b. Judah said
in the name of R. Simon: a rapist does not pay for pain because this is
what awaits her in the future from her husband [i.e., upon marriage, she
will have her hymen torn, causing her pain (שסופה להצטער תחת בעלה).
But they said to him: there is no comparison between engaging in sex
willingly and unwillingly! [and the rapist *does* have to pay for the pain
of the forced sexual act] (*b. Ket.* 39a-b).

The *Palestinian Talmud* cites the same teaching to make the point that
the mishnah is not in accordance with R. Simon, who discounts
women's pain in rape. But the formulation of R. Simon's view in the
Palestinian Talmud is somewhat different.

The mishnah is not like R. Simon, for R. Simon exempts the rapist from
paying for pain. What is this like? One who cuts a wart off his friend's
foot that his friend was anyway planning to remove. Or one who cuts
down his friend's young trees that he was anyway planning to cut
down.
They said [to him]: there is no comparison between engaging in sex by
force and doing so willingly. There is no comparison between engaging in
sex on a dunghill and engaging in sex in the context of marriage (*y. Ket.*
27c, 3.5).[10]

The rabbis in this version of the *baraita* are clearly saying, as are the
rabbis in the *Babylonian Talmud*, that there are two parts to the
payment for pain: the first is the pain of the forced sexual act itself,
which includes the rupture of the hymen; the second is the pain of
being physically assaulted. In other words, the rabbis are strongly
chiding R. Simon for missing the point that there is not just one but
even two kinds of suffering on the woman's part.

Note that the two examples of pain given by R. Simon in the
Palestinian Talmud, removal of a wart from the foot and cutting down
young shoots (an example of precious property), cause very little
physical pain to the one who suffers it. If we now compare R. Simon's
comment in the two Talmuds, the *Palestinian* version says that there
is virtually no pain at all for the woman while the *Babylonian* version

10. See *m. Ket.* 7.5, where 'pouring out onto a dunghill' is a euphemism for
coitus interruptus or an immediate attempt on the woman's part to thwart a possible pregnancy.

says that there is pain but, since she was going to experience it sooner
or later, the man need not pay for it. It is hard to know why these two
versions of R. Simon's statement exist, except to say that they reflect
different attitudes towards rape by the different transmitters of his
statement: one more sensitive and one less so. Men's perception of
women's pain in rape—the topic of the earlier rabbis' dispute—is of
interest to women in particular, since men, in most cultures, are
skeptical about rape, not believing that women suffer during rape
and not even believing that women do not invite rape upon themselves. If the dispute is looked at in this light, it seems that the
majority of rabbis understand that women suffer pain in rape. This
point is summed up nicely in the following, rather extreme, statement:

> Rava said: if it began as a forced sexual act but ended as a consensual
> one, and even if she says, 'let him be, for if he had not accosted me I
> would have hired him to do so'—[she only said so] because she was
> sexually aroused [יצר אלבשה]—such a woman is permitted [to resume
> life with her husband because this act is classified as rape, not as con-
> sensual. In rabbinic law, a woman may not return to her husband after
> consensual sex with another man] (*b. Ket.* 51b).

According to this rabbi rape is rape, even if it appears to be seduction.
It should be noted, however, that he subscribes to the widespread
belief that even in conditions of fear and brutality women can enjoy
sex.

Pain of First Sexual Encounter
The *Babylonian Talmud* (*b. Ket.* 39b) continues:

> —Rather, R. Nahman said that Rabbah bar Abuha said: the pain
> [referred to in the mishnah is not the pain of being thrown down but the
> pain] of having her legs forced open...
> —If so, the seducer also [should have to pay for pain and yet the mish-
> nah says that he does not]!
> —Said R. Nahman said Rabbah bar Abuha: I will give you a parable: it
> [seduction] is like a person who says to someone else, rip my silk and I
> will not hold you responsible.
> —'My' [silk]? But it belongs to her father!
> —Rather, said R. Nahman said Rabbah bar Abuha: the wise women
> (פקחות) would say, a woman who is seduced does not suffer any pain.[11]

11. The question was, why not pay the seduced woman for pain since she too
must have experienced it, if we accept the last definition of pain? The answer is
that wise women say that a woman who consents to an illicit sexual act does not
suffer pain.

—But do we not see that she suffered pain?
—Said Abaye: Mother told me that it [the discomfort a virgin feels when engaging in sex for the first time] is like hot water on a bald head.
—Rava said: the daughter of R. Hisda told me [i.e. his wife] that it is like the prick of a bloodletter.
—R. Pappa said: The daughter of Abba Sura'a [i.e. my wife] told me, like a dry crust on the gums.

In this section men try to understand what women experience in their first sexual encounter. They debate the nature of the discomfort a woman feels when her hymen is torn *with* her consent. Each of the three rabbis quotes a woman, two their wives and one a nursemaid (whom he refers to as Mother). The pain described by all three women is minor. By quoting women only, these men recognize that the pain is real but that they themselves cannot adequately describe it because they are men. Note that the *Babylonian Talmud* reports, in the name of women, that a seduced virgin does not suffer any pain. This is a preachy statement: since she 'asked' for it, we cannot show any sympathy for anything she may have suffered. And the women who transmit it are called 'wise'.

What all of this adds up to is that not only do the rabbis begin to transfer the rape payments from a raped woman's father to her, they also indicate that they have some sense of the trauma that she suffers, both aspects of it: exertion of force in general and forced sex in particular.

Consent to Marry
Yet another major change introduced by the rabbis is the elimination of the forced marriage between the aggressor and the victim.

Thus was also taught in a *baraita* [=*Tos.* 3.7) …the same goes for the rapist and the seducer, either she or her father may refuse [to go through with the marriage].
—It is possible to find a [biblical] basis for a seduced woman refusing marriage, for the verse [Exod. 22.16] says: 'refuse, he refuses' [to give her in marriage, מאן ימאן אביה לתתה לו]; this teaches that her father may refuse to give her. But what about the girl herself? The redundancy implies that she, too, may do so.
—That she may refuse marriage to a rapist we learn from 'she will be his wife' [Deut. 22.29]—this implies that she must consent to the match; as for her father, where does Scripture say that he may refuse?
—Said Abaye: so that the sinner not be rewarded [יהא חוטא נשכר שלא].
—Said Rava: we learn this *a minori, a fortiori*: if in a case of seduction, when only the father's will has been overridden, she or her father may

refuse, then, in rape, in which both her father's will and hers have been overridden, certainly she or her father may refuse! (*b. Ket.* 39b).

It is easy to see that the biblical basis for the additional rules of refusal is rather flimsy. The Bible only makes reference to the father refusing in a case of seduction. The girl is not consulted at all. But, according to the rabbis, either the girl or her father may refuse marriage in either a case of rape or of seduction. This is a paradigmatic instance, to my mind, of rabbis reading their own more enlightened social thinking into the verses instead of deriving the new rules from the verses themselves. From a formal point of view, they are merely expounding the meaning of Scripture. From an essential point of view, they are radically altering the meaning of Scripture. It seems that in their day the need to gain a woman's consent to marriage, in particular to a man who had committed a crime against her, was a concept that had taken hold. Stated negatively, they apparently saw forced marriage to a rapist as abhorrent. Most importantly, it seems that not just her father's wishes counted, but hers as well.

In short, the rabbis recognized that rape and seduction are crimes against women as individual women and not just women as part of a collective family unit. They also seem to view marriage differently from the Torah: the man who has raped or seduced a woman is not necessarily the right husband for her. She can choose to reject him. This probably means that in their day she would be able to find another. Although they nowhere mention rape of a divorcee, widow or single woman, it would follow that these cases too would be judged in the same way: as instances of assault and battery. The payments would go to the woman herself, since there is no man in her life to whom she is subordinate. As for the rape of a married woman, this is a capital offense.

So, even though the rabbis do not prescribe a criminal punishment for someone who rapes an unmarried woman, a glaring deficiency from a contemporary point of view, one cannot avoid noticing that they have, with little fanfare, introduced major changes in the biblical legislation, all of which move in the direction of placing a young woman rather than her father at the center of their inquiry.

How did the rabbis accomplish this radical reorientation? First, upon looking at the verses, they decided that two different sex crimes are spoken of. Secondly, by playing these verses off against each other, they were able to apply details of one case to the other. Thirdly, by creating the category of *bôgeret*, an independent young woman, nowhere to be found in the Bible. And by introducing the five payments for assault and battery, only some of which are found in the Bible, they were able to develop the rules of rape and seduction according to an alternative model. Were we to examine the rules of marriage, divorce, inheritance or most other topics affecting women, we would see similar rabbinic transformations of biblical institutions. Within their patriarchal social configuration, which they had no intention of eliminating, there is much evidence of the fact that they extended new rights to women and often raised their legal status.

Conclusions

I think that I have shown in the analysis of this topic that, if Talmudic passages are read in their own larger literary context and in conjunction with the biblical verses upon which they are based, it will be discovered that they do not mean what they appear to mean on first reading. Far more importantly, this rich contextual reading uncovers the aims and techniques of the legislator. One might say, with a certain irony, that the over-arching goal of all rabbinic hermeneutical techniques is to make it possible for the interpreter to read the text *not* according to its plain sense meaning. The reason for the suppression of the literal meaning is that the rabbis are looking to find meaning for their day. Attitudes about the worth of the individual, the family, women and their social status and the nature of crimes committed against them, changed substantially from the biblical to the rabbinic period—either because of evolution of social thinking or infiltration of ideas from cultures outside. The rabbis therefore needed to find a way to modify the texts of the past to accommodate them to the social and philosophical truths of the present. They did so by inventing rules of interpretation of Scripture that allowed them freedom of interpretation, enabling them to deconstruct and reconstruct verses in ways that they saw fit.

I think it critically important for us today to elicit meaning from these ancient texts, rather than read meaning into them. Examining second- to fifth-century CE texts from the perspective of the twentieth century is not likely to uncover what the ancient authors were interested in conveying. It is all too easy to find more and more evidence of patriarchy and oppression of women. The challenge is to look beyond such a finding and determine where the system as a whole was heading. As shown above, in the area of sex crimes against women rabbinic interpretation of Scripture was moving away from the view that the father was the victim of sex crimes committed against his daughter; and toward the view that *she* was the one who suffered and was deserving of compensation. If earlier texts and later ones are compared and, as noted above, if texts are read in as rich an ancient context as possible, we will come closer to understanding what the authors of these texts wished to say about the subject at hand than if we simply look back at them from where we stand today. We can, in this way, discover that the rabbinic interpretation of Scripture is socially motivated and tendentious. And therein lies its importance.

RABBIS, FEMINISTS AND PATRIARCHY'S ORDINARINESS

Miriam Peskowitz*

Rightfully and passionately, we feminist scholars of religions argue back and forth about where to look for women, men and gender. Do we seek new sources from 'outside' the classical traditions transmitted by male hands and elite interests? Can we find archaeological artifacts and other material culture and, when we do, what is it that we are finding? Do we look to the few and fragmentary samples of writing by women? To papyrus documents that detail some legal and economic transactions of specific women? To rituals performed by women alone, or by women along with men? Do we survey traditions that are sacred and canonical and which, for the most part, privilege men? And when we scrutinize these traditions, what do we look for, and how do we look? Do we proffer examples of misogyny, sexism and other gender-based oppressions of women? Probe for systemic gender hierarchies? Highlight moments of sympathy? Do we sketch the familiarities of the quotidian? Locate ironies? Note male projections of women? Find moments when women resisted oppression, with the knowledge that these moments come to us mostly through the writings of the men the women were resisting in the first place? Do we examine polemics of gender, list roles for men and women, show transgressions, trace moments of gender fluidity? Do we demonstrate gender's constructedness—and its contingency? Do we show the intellectual habits that have structured how we interpret and explain evidence? Do we want to find heroines and role models for the present, metaphors for the future? Or undermine common beliefs that gender is inevitable? And choosing any combination of these strategies, do we tell happy stories? Horror stories? Both? All?[1]

*   Reprinted by permission from Miriam Peskowitz, *Spinning Fantasies: Gendering the Ordinary in Roman-Period Judaism* (Berkeley: University of California Press, 1997).

    1.   On some of these issues see Amy Richlin, 'Hijacking the Palladium: Feminists in Classics', and 'The Ethnographer's Dilemma and the Dream of a Lost

A passage from the mishnaic tractate, *Ketubot*, offers a starting point for working through these questions. Tractate *Ketubot* refers most specifically to the deeds, or contracts (*k^{e}tubbôt*) that accounted for a woman's transfer from her father's house to the legal and social authority of her husband. This tractate enumerates the legal and fiscal relations of marriage-by-contract, a relatively new innovation among Jews. Tractate *Ketubot* sets the terms for rabbinic Jewish marriage, and offers a vision of what should be normal for the fiscal lives of women who live as part of families. After its initial interests in virginity and the amount of money to be promised as a marriage settlement (*k^{e}tubbāh*) if the marriage were to end, the tractate contains law (*halakhah*) about the relation of Jewish women to inheritance and the control of their labor and profits as married women. The rabbinic texts comprise one of numerous traditions for which the Hebrew Bible was situated as an authoritative and ancestral source. In many of the Mishnah's tractates, the early rabbis were both dependent on the Bible and intent on reformulating biblical law. In the case of tractate *Ketubot*, however, the rabbis have inherited the Hebrew Bible's lack of interest in formal marriage law.

The earliest rabbinic legal texts were produced by rabbis in Palestine around the turn of the third century CE. These writings—the Mishnah and, slightly later, the Tosefta—were put together several decades after the end of difficult relations between the Roman Empire and its Jews. In the Jewish revolt of 66–70 CE the Jewish Temple in Jerusalem was destroyed, and its aristocratic and priestly ruling class sundered. A second revolt, centered in Judaea in the years 132–135, also resulted in a Roman victory. Rabbinic Judaism is a Jewish tradition that was developed in Palestine in the aftermath of these revolts against Rome. By the late second century relations between Rome and Palestinian Jews had calmed, but the Empire itself was embroiled in ongoing tensions. Imperial succession was hotly contested, military prowess faltered, and the earlier desire to expand Rome's borders gave way to attempts to defend what territory the

Golden Age', in Nancy Sorkin Rabinowitz and Amy Richlin (eds.), *Feminist Theory and the Classics* (New York: Routledge, 1993) pp. 272-303; Caroline Walker Bynum, 'Introduction: The Complexity of Symbols', in Caroline Bynum, Stevan Harrell, and Paula Richman (eds.), *Gender and Religion: On the Complexity of Symbols* (Boston: Beacon Press, 1986), pp. 1-20; Lynn Davidman and Shelly Tenenbaum (eds.), *Feminist Perspectives on Jewish Studies* (New Haven: Yale University Press, 1994); the discussion in Ross Kraemer, *Her Share of the Blessings: Women's Religions Among Pagans, Jews, and Christians in the Greco-Roman World* (New York: Oxford University Press, 1992).

Empire already held.[2] Outliving its reputation as a hotspot of Roman military attention, by the turn of the third century Palestine and its inhabitants faded as a problem for Rome. Both Jews and the region of Palestine also fade from the attention of historical writers. One result of this is that much remains unknown, barely known, or unknowable. Little is known with much certainty about the lives of Palestine's women and men, about the circles of rabbis who produced the Mishnah and Tosefta, about its Christian communities, about people who were not part of Jewish, Christian and Jewish-Christian communities, about the individual rabbis and others who appear in early rabbinic texts.

According to rabbinic tales of their origins, the Mishnah was edited by Judah ha-Nasi in Sepphoris, a small Roman city on the southern edge of Galilee whose population included Romans, Christians and Jews. Still under excavation, year after year more of Sepphoris is dug from the dirt. Sepphoris was part of the culture that passed through the Roman Empire. Although Sepphoris was a small city, it was well connected with other parts of the eastern Mediterranean and with the Empire. The excavated city reveals a Romanized culture, with a theater of major proportions and well-planned city sections and roads. Its everyday art included hand statues of Roman gods. Mosaic floor pavements displayed mythological heroes, folktales, motifs of other Mediterranean cities such as Alexandria, beautiful women and naked men. Palestine and the region of Galilee were relatively unimportant to Rome's history. But the local version of Roman culture was certainly of important common knowledge to the people who lived in Sepphoris.

The Mishnah is composed of select discussions, arguments and opinions, recollections and brief narratives. It contains infrequent references to Torah, but is built on a thorough knowledge of biblical books. The Mishnah has an authorial voice mixed with anonymous statements and with positions attributed to specific rabbis. Although it was edited in the early third century CE, the men who appear in the Mishnah lived in the years between the first century BCE and the early third century CE.

The Mishnah contains a radically new vision for Judaism, one that

2. On this period see Peter Brown, *The World of Late Antiquity, AD 150–170* (London: Harcourt Brace Jovanivich, 1971); Michael Grant, *The Antonines: The Roman Empire in Transition* (London: Routledge, 1994); and Fergus Millar, *The Roman Near East, 31 BC–AD 337* (Cambridge, MA: Harvard University Press, 1993), pp. 99-140.

developed in Palestine a century after the destruction of the Second Temple. This vision replaced the more extraordinary, visceral and perhaps burdensome rites of the destroyed Temple with *halakhah*, or religious law. The Mishnah promotes law—*halakhah*—for the every-day and for the impossible. *In its halakhah the everyday and the extra-ordinary are merged.* The Mishnah uses similar tones for the imagined world of the extinct Temple, and for the equally imagined realm of the ordinary and the interpersonal. Promulgated in the early third century, the Mishnah became the basis of the Talmudic commentary tradition. The Mishnah's first commentary was the Tosefta, a Pales-tinian text that features mostly the same group of rabbis (called *Tan-naim*, or repeaters), and which dates (most likely) to the middle of the third century. This first commentary was followed by the two Tal-muds: the Babylonian Talmud (*c.* 500); and the Palestinian Talmud (*c.* 400) which, although it was the first finished, never gained the prominence and authority of the Babylonian Talmud. Eventually, rabbinic *halakhah* became influential and authoritative for Jews. The study and explication of Talmudic traditions became a ritual and social practice for literate men in some Jewish communities. Forms of rabbinic Judaism became widespread among Jews, although the details of this spread and its meaning for ordinary Jewish men and women are largely unknown. The texts that the early rabbinic circles produced in a small Roman province on the edge of the Roman Empire are usually read *now* as part of a classic traditions. But in its own time, the early rabbinic movement that produced these texts was relatively small, its influence restricted to small communities of Jews in northern Palestine.[3]

As a classic tradition for our world, both images of ancient rabbis and ways to read Talmud are largely overdetermined. For centuries and generations since talmudic texts were composed, these were read almost entirely by men. Due to this tradition, for women and for many men several things combine to make talmudic texts difficult or intimidating to approach: the religious authority invested in them, their mystique in a modern world, and the difficulty of talmudic modes of expression. These texts come with fairly strict traditions for reading and making sense out of them. For us, these texts come with

3. In this assessment I find most compelling the less romanticized work of scholars such as Lee Levine, *The Rabbinic Class of Late Antiquity* (New York: Jewish Theological Seminary, 1989; Jerusalem: Yad Izhak ben-Zvi, 1985), and Shaye J.D. Cohen, 'The Place of the Rabbi in Jewish Society of the Second Century', in Lee Levine (ed.), *The Galilee in Late Antiquity* (New York: Jewish Theological Seminary, 1992), pp. 157-73.

inherited paths of religious study and critical academic study, each of which carries its own possibilities, its own variety and its own restraints. Furthermore, the Talmud is usually classified as a legal text. As such, its 'legalness' can be conflated with modern Western notions of law. This association brings with it notions about the authority, inaccessibility and 'dryness' of the text. We tend to read legal texts for their directions and counsel, seeking straightforward answers to specific questions. Reading the Talmud as 'law' privileges 'legal' answers, as much as it usually assumes that there is only one kind of legal reading. But why indeed should we limit legal texts to a 'legal' reading? Why examine these texts 'as lawyers'? All sorts of assumptions about the Talmud tend to shield it from certain questions: how its tractates work ideologically; how they work as stories; how they become part of a naturalized ethos for everyday life—to name only a few. These inheritances preclude a whole range of critical and creative concerns about how legal texts make their meaning. Locating the contours and limitations of the available traditions for interpreting the Talmud and other ancient texts can clear some space for other ways of reading these texts to emerge.[4]

The written texts of early rabbinic Judaism can be read as an example of what happened when an all-male Jewish elite turned its

---

4. Talmudic texts are alternately normative, binding, hegemonic, meaningful or ignored by Jews. Still, even this statement does not express the varied meanings of 'Talmud' for those who may or may not accept its halakhic authority. Reform, Secular, and Jews with various relations with Judaism and Jewishness see the Talmud in ways that range from ignorance to disdain to respectful distance to nostalgia to romanticization. These relations and others preserve the text's cultural authority, even if its *halakhah* goes unobserved and unknown. Furthermore, these texts carry symbolic status for Jews and for non-Jews. Apart from devotion expressed by an individual or community, talmudic writing serves to signify a canonical, classical religion, even for those who would associate these texts as part of 'the past' or as 'what other Jews do'. This obtains particularly within the realm of the history of religions, where religious traditions are often associated with the specific 'texts' upon which and from which authority is claimed (hence the equation of 'Talmud' with 'Judaism'). In thinking through the complicated privilege of talmudic texts, Adi Ophir's discussion has been helpful. In his 'From Pharaoh to Saddam Hussein: The Reproduction of the Other in the Passover Haggadah', in Laurence Silberstein and Robert Cohn (eds.), *The Other in Jewish History and Thought* (New York: New York University Press, 1994), pp. 205-35, he writes: 'A privileged text is part of the very process of acculturation that serves to unify a culture over and above its different, particular spheres or fields'. Ophir writes insightfully into what is also a paradox for me: writing about Talmud as a privileged text, when in fact it is defamiliarized and less-than-privileged in most communities in which I live, work and write.

attention to the economy and relations of the everyday. Reading
these, we can see how this movement made certain possibilities of
gender imaginable and real.[5] One feature of everyday life—and one
site for the construction of gender—was marriage between men and
women. Tractate *Ketubot* attends to the intersection of women, men,
property and marriage. Reading the following passage slowly and
closely is one way to experiment with different kinds of feminist
ways to read early rabbinic texts. The text of *m. Ket.* 8.1 translates as
follows. In general, all translations are my own, unless otherwise
noted. Square brackets—[ ]—add words and phrases that are not in
the Hebrew text, but which are helpful and even necessary to make
the grammatical terseness of the Hebrew comprehensible in English.
Parentheses—( )—offer explanations of pronouns, contexts and concepts that help readers new to these texts make 'basic' sense of the
passage; parentheses also hold occasional transliterations (in italics)
of Hebrew terms that might be of interest to more advanced readers.[6]

> Regarding the woman to whom property fell before she was betrothed:
> Shammai's House and Hillel's House agree that she may sell and/or
> give it away, and it (her act) is valid.
>
> [If property] befell her after she was betrothed: Shammai's House says
> she may sell, and Hillel's House says she may not sell.
>
> They (the Houses) agree that if she sold or gave it away (after she was
> betrothed and before she was married), it is valid.
>
> Recounted Rabbi Yehudah: They said before Rabban Gamliel: Since he
> (the husband) has authority over the woman, will he not have authority
> over the [woman's] property?

5.   In articulating a preliminary account of this mode of reading I am influenced by Christina Crosby, 'Dealing With Differences', in Judith Butler and Joan
Scott (eds.), *Feminists Theorize the Political* (New York: Routledge, 1992), pp. 130-
43. She writes of 'foregoing the satisfying search for error in favor of reading for
how truths are produced, including the ones one holds most dear, and sustaining a
critique of something that is both dangerous and indispensable'.
6.   The terseness and implicit cross-referencing within these texts makes necessary a somewhat bulky apparatus. The differentiation between brackets and parentheses is simultaneously necessary and murky; there will be much overlap. As
with any language translation, the translation of passages from Mishnah and
Tosefta is always already an interpretation. Within a project that interrupts the
desire to see the past as familiar, it is as problematic to offer up ancient Hebrew
(or, Greek, Latin, and Aramaic texts) in English as it is necessary to do so. Most
Euro-American readers are not fluent readers of these ancient languages (especially since access to these languages is a privilege of class and other statuses, and
the educations they afford). For readers unfamiliar with these languages, I will
refer in notes to English translations when these are available and reliable.

He [Gamliel] said to them: Concerning the [ownership and control of] new [property] (*hahadasim*) we are embarrassed [by the lack of legal justification], and you would burden us with [*halakhah* for the ownership and control of] the old [property] (*hayesanim*).

[If property] befell her after she wed. Both Houses agree that if she sold it or gave it away, that the husband may take it from the hands of the buyers (since he owns and controls it, and the wife had no right to sell or give it away.)

[If property] befell her [after betrothal but] before she wed, and she wed. Rabban Gamliel says, if she sold or gave it away (after she wed), (her act) is valid.

Recounted Rabbi Hanina ben Aqabya: They said before Rabban Gamliel: Since he has authority over the woman, will he not have authority over the [woman's] property?
He [Gamliel] said to them: Concerning the [ownership and control of] new [property] we are embarrassed [by the lack of legal justification], and you would burden us with [*halakhah* for the ownership and control of] the old [property].

Mishnah *Ket.* 8.1 is a legal story about a woman's relation to property, both during betrothal (the period that precedes marriage) and during her marriage. My notion of 'legal story' stems not from the talmudist's notion of 'legal fictions', but from Vicki Schultz's writings on 'judicial story'.[7] As a critical practice, reading for legal stories means reading legal texts in ways that always note them as representations and as cultural effects. Legal statements are read for how they encode explanations, interpretive frameworks and characterizations of human beings. These things and more are part of a matrix of assumptions about how the world works and, as such, they govern the 'sense' and 'logic' that these legal texts articulate. Locating this matrix of assumptions is the focus of this type of analytic reading. Reading for 'legal stories' emphasizes the importance of narration and textuality in these legal writings; it keeps in view the fact of the Mishnah's literary crafting.

Typically, interpretation of early rabbinic legal texts has been remarkably circumscribed. Passages are cited straightforwardly, as if their truth were unmediated by the fact of their being written. One trend in reading rabbinic texts uses long lists of passages as if they

7. See V. Schultz, 'Telling Stories about Women and Work: Judicial Interpretations of Sex Segregation in the Workplace in Title VII Cases Raising the Lack of Interest Argument', *Harvard Law Review* 103 (1990), pp. 1750-1844; and 'Women "Before" the Law: Judicial Stories about Women, Work, and Sex Segregation on the Job', in Butler and Scott (eds.), *Feminists Theorize the Political*, pp. 297-338.

were documentary evidence for history and/or society. Often this practice removes these passages from their argumentative context; they are decontextualized and treated as if they were univalent and uncomplicated. Another tendency reads these passages as *halakhah*, but sees *halakhah* as a natural outcome of 'the human condition' and not as a process that constructs human subjects, one that imagines realities and fashions rabbinic selves. As a result of these circumscribed reading practices, much work needs to be done to shift the way we conventionally read passages from the Mishnah and Tosefta, to unshake these inherited modes, even for those of us who do not consider ourselves subjects of such inheritances. In response, however, I do not propose one single theory or strategy for reading these texts. Rather, I experiment with the differences made by the angle of seeing legal texts as stories. In experimenting with reading early rabbinic legal texts in ways different from the inherited practices of talmudic law, I owe a debt particularly to feminist theorists such as Vicki Schultz, Patricia Williams and Judith Butler.[8]

A survey of published scholarship on the Mishnah and Tosefta finds very little precedent for reading legal texts this way. A fairly powerful distinction between *halakhic* and *aggadic* material has operated in which certain modes of reading and interpretation are deemed appropriate for midrash and *aggada*, but these reading modes are not used as either an ethos or a strategy for reading halakhic and religio-legal texts. Stephen Fraade, near the end of his work with the non-legal materials in *Sifre Deuteronomy*, notes that his

> next step will be to sharpen my focus even more on the texts of that legal core, asking whether they, too, should be engaged in the dialogical complexity and performative *work* of their discursive rhetoric and not simply for the legal norms, hermeneutics, or justifications they are conventionally thought monologically to contain.[9]

The problem to which Fraade alludes, and within which I work, is this: underwriting the current reading of tannaitic legal texts is a positivist-inspired notion that law is straightforward in the meanings it makes, and that legal writing is not part of the same process of mediation and representation that characterizes other types of writing. This assumption has significant ramifications in terms of ques-

8.   See Schultz, 'Telling Stories'; Patricia Williams, *The Alchemy of Race and Rights* (Cambridge, MA: Harvard University Press, 1991); and Judith Butler, *Gender Trouble: Feminism and the Subversion of Identity* (New York: Routledge, 1990).

9.   Stephen Fraade, *From Tradition to Commentary: Torah and its Interpretation in the Midrash Sifre to Deuteronomy* (Albany: SUNY Press, 1991), pp. 163-64.

tions that are *not* asked of legal texts. A primary question posed to midrashic materials has been, 'How do these texts make meaning?' Scholarly assumptions about legal writing have foreclosed all but the most rudimentary of questions about how various meanings were made through these types of expression.

Although I have introduced *m. Ket.* 8.1 as a passage about women and their property, this is not the most accurate description. The passage is not so much 'about women' as it is a compact story about male rabbis who debate the legal conditions for a woman's relation to property. Hence, the passage is really about men and property. To describe it as 'about women' effaces the presence and power of the men who produced this text. It renders invisible the ideological frame that organizes the tractate's contents. In *m. Ket.* 8.1, male rabbis argue about property. They offer various arguments to extend—or resist the extension of—a husband's privilege to own and control his wife's property. A husband's privilege could be extended in either of two ways. The first is chronological. The man's authority as a husband would begin during the betrothal period that precedes marriage. Secondly, his husbandly authority to own and control would be strengthened to cover additional types of his wife's property—specifically, any property she has gained before their marriage. From these extensions, rabbis and other Jewish men profit. Male rabbis discuss the general extension of men's legal privileges over the women who will be their wives. Since, in their Jewish societies, rabbis were also men, these extensions of male privilege would have augmented the privilege of individual rabbis. Along with other men, rabbis also would gain ownership and control over more parts of their own wives' estates.

In focusing critical attention on the men in rabbinic passages that are also about women, I do not want to let women disappear. But, in fact, women are part of what this passage produces. The women of *m. Ket.* 8.1 are constructs, rabbinic fictions, one-dimensional personae named by their legal status and their relations to men. The women of *m. Ket.* 8.1 have names like 'betrothed woman' or 'married woman'. These female identities are first and foremost fantasies of *halakhah*, not 'real women'. So, rather than search ancient rabbinic texts for fictions of 'real law' or 'real women', I read this passage to show the difficulty that rabbis encountered as they made gender. I catch rabbis in the act, so to speak, of producing characters for women and men and forming them into an economy for marriage. I find them crafting male and female humans who will fit appropriately into a rabbinic vision for Jewish marriage. This part of tractate *Ketubot* reveals traces of rabbinic uncertainty, and I focus on it for this reason. As a matter of course, religio-legal texts from early rabbinic Judaism contain debates and different opinions. But, as I will argue, the admission of uncertainty found in *m. Ket.* 8.1 is rare even when it functions as part of a polemic to reassure rabbis and their readers that fundamental security is possible.

On Property

Property is part of a complex set of social relations. A woman's relation to property—land, animals, metals, money, clothing and other possessions—shifts with her legal relation to different men. Her legal potential to own and control property changes with marriage. As a wife, a woman may still *own* some kinds of property, but her *control* is curtailed. Her husband gains control over the property, and he owns the profit from most of the types of property that belong to her. In other words, for married women ownership is not always synonymous with control. Depending on the gender of the owner, ownership does not necessarily include control over the property that is owned.

In early rabbinic law, once a woman is married, the degree of control her husband maintains over her property depends on how her property is designated. One distinction classifies categorized property as either new property or old property. New property is what a woman gains during the marriage, primarily through her own labor. This differs from property she gains from inheritance or other gifts. New property results from anything she finds, from wages she earns as a worker, or from profits on property she owns and controls. Old property refers primarily to gifts, private holdings and family inheritances she had received before she married. Old property includes gifts her family gives to her on the occasion of marriage, as well any inheritance or gift she has received during her marriage. In early rabbinic law, old property contains a further set of distinctions. When a woman marries, her property is designated as either *ṣô'n-barzel* or as *mulug*. Over *ṣô'n-barzel* property the husband has almost absolute ownership, and he takes responsibility for its diminution or loss. With *mulug* property, the wife maintains the title. She owns the property, but the husband controls it and has 'usufruct' (the 'rights of fruit'). In more vivid terms, a married woman might own a field of olive trees but she does not always own the harvest of olives these trees produce. Further, since the husband has usufruct (the rights to the profits from the property), he can prevent his wife from selling the property or giving it away. If his wife sells the property he can retrieve it, since her sale interferes with his rights to profit from usufruct. A third distinction includes gifts that are given to a married woman on the condition that both the property and income are hers to own and control.[10]

Both the husband's ownership of his wife's new property, and his control of her old property designated as *mulug*, were innovations of early rabbinic law. Neither are found in the Bible. This mishnah—*Ket.* 8.1—shows an initial moment at which rabbis formulate innovations that strengthen a husband's control over his wife's property, and write these innovations into early rabbinic *halakhah*. Mishnah *Ketubot* 8.1 starts with the question of whether the husband's legal control over a woman's property begins with betrothal (*kiddûšîn/ 'ērûsîn*) or with marriage (*nissû 'în*). Its question is this: does a man control his wife's old property during their betrothal, or must he wait until their marriage? Underlying this first question is another: which legal conditions of marriage take effect at betrothal, and which must wait until the formal ceremonies of marriage itself to take effect? These quandaries are the predicament within which the first half of *m. Ket.* 8.1 is set: a man betroths a woman; the woman owns old property that the man will control upon marriage; does he control it during their betrothal?[11]

10. See Louis Epstein, *The Jewish Marriage Contract: A Study in the Status of the Woman in Jewish Law* (New York: Jewish Theological Seminary of America, 1927), chs. 6–7; and B. Levine, 'Mulugu/Melug: The Origins of a Talmudic Legal Institution', *JAOS* 88 (1968), pp. 271-84. There is a complicated history to these legal terms, and I both mean and not mean to simplify it here. *mulug* develops from its status as a wife's private property into something over which the husband has tenancy. Tannaitic sources do not articulate reasons for these changes which favor the husband. Amoraic sources (*b. Sanh.* 71a and *b. Naz.* 24b) develop the rationale: 'How can a woman own anything, whatever she owns belongs to her husband'. As well, the Talmud will reinterpret these extensions of a husband's privilege as mutual obligations between husband and wife; a discourse of 'mutuality' effaces the presence of a real imbalance of power relations between husband and wife. Scholarly interpreters are often complicit in this: see Zeev Falk, 'Mutual Obligation in the Ketubah', *JJS* 7 (1957), pp. 215-17; and A.S. Kofsky, 'A Comparative Analysis of Women's Property Rights in Jewish Law and Anglo-American Law', *Journal of Law and Religion* 6 (1988), pp. 317-53.

11. The problem might be specifically rabbinic. At this point in the development of Jewish law and practice, *kiddûšîn* ('betrothal') and *niśśû 'în* ('marriage') have been unjoined. In earlier periods the legalities of betrothal and marriage had taken place at the same time, and later in Jewish religious history, they would again be rejoined. One result of the unjoining was the creation of a new legal

To answer these questions *m. Ket.* 8.1 offers several cases. Each case elicits historical rabbinic positions. The legal history begins with debates attributed to two pharisaic opponents from the mid-first century CE, the Houses of Hillel and Shammai. The first case establishes that, potentially, a woman may own and control property. If, before her betrothal, a woman gained property, then her ownership of that property includes control over it. The first-century Houses of Hillel and Shammai agree that if a woman gained property *before* she was betrothed, then as a betrothed woman she retains control. She can sell it, give it away or profit from it in other ways, and her acts are legally valid. In the next case, the betrothed woman has gained property *after* her betrothal but before the ceremony of marriage, and she wishes to sell it or give it away. Here, the Houses take different positions. Shammai's House maintains that the betrothed woman controls her property. But Hillel's House disagrees: the betrothed woman owns but does not control this property. The position of Hillel's House treats the betrothed woman as if she were already married and, thus, separates ownership of property from its control.

In the third case, uncertainty about the rabbinic innovation of extending a husband's authority prevails. If the betrothed woman sold property or gave it away, neither House will allow the future husband to reclaim the sold property from its new owner. Neither House will extend the man's privilege this way. Only once he is formally married can the husband retrieve such property. But the position is slippery, even murky. The betrothed woman is not supposed to sell or give away property she has gained during the period of betrothal (according to the House of Hillel's position in the second case). But if she did so, her act is legally valid.

The gist of these three cases is that womanhood was conceptualized to entail any number of changing relations between women and property. These relations were contingent and situational. They depended upon a woman's legal relation to her husband or her father. Questions about a woman's relation to property could be answered by pointing to her relation to a particular man. In this way, early rabbinic notions of gender imagined that womanhood included various relations to property. But twisting around a bit and looking differently, something else becomes clear. Property ownership was one node in the construction of sexual difference. Both gender distinctions, as well as distinctions between women—unmarried, betrothed,

period between betrothal and marriage whose contours were to be imagined and defined by the rabbis.

married, widowed and divorced—were constituted (in part) through assessing their relation to property. In tannaitic law the definition of men's relationship to the ownership and control of property is stable. A nearly essential part of masculinity was the legal right and social potential to own property. For women, the legal capacity to own and control property was variable. Early rabbinic ideas about woman-hood did not include the idea that property ownership and control was an essential element of female being.

Reading Historically

It is always tempting to read a passage such as *m. Ket.* 8.1 as docu-mentary, and to assume that it unfolds in a historic progression from early to late. This temptation should be turned around. Passages from the Mishnah begin in the early third century and work back-ward, and they should be read this way. Mishnaic passages move forward and backward among the positions attributed to various rabbinic and pharisaic ancestors—such as the Houses of Hillel and Shammai—over a period of roughly one hundred and seventy years. The Mishnah is a formal selection of rabbinic argument. It is a fic-tionalization, a product crafted by a third-century storyteller and nar-rator of *halakhah*. The Mishnah is never a transparent record of 'real discussions' among rabbis, but a text that fashioned rabbis and instaurated a rabbinic movement. The Mishnah is heavily edited and known only through manuscripts from periods much later than the third century, manuscripts that contain some later interpolations along with slight variations in words and phrases. Temptations to read the Mishnah as a simple and straightforward text—and to read its contents as moving progressively from start to finish—must always be thwarted.

The first three cases of *m. Ket.* 8.1 feature the first-century Houses of Hillel and Shammai. To follow these, *m. Ket.* 8.1 introduces Rabbi Yehudah. According to rabbinic chronology Yehudah was active among the third generation of Tannaim, in the mid-second century. Yehudah adds a more specific argument to the debate about men, woman and property. His contribution addresses the legal murki-ness that was revealed in the third situation: a betrothed woman should not sell property she gained during betrothal but, if she did, then her act is valid after the fact and the future husband can not reclaim what she has sold. The section that begins with Yehudah attends less to the details of the third case and more to the sense of murkiness and uncertainty. In this middle section, *m. Ket.* 8.1

presents the second and third tiers in its legal history of the issue at hand. Having begun with debates from the mid-first century, the early third-century narrator produces a response by introducing a second-century rabbi who will introduce a late first-century rabbi, the authoritative Rabban Gamliel. Including these rabbis asserts a lineage for thinking about a husband's authority and a betrothed woman's property. Paradoxically, by presenting this lineage as an authority for resolving the debate, the passage portrays the debate as powerful enough to have continued, unresolved, for over a century and a half.

In this story about a legal argument, Rabbi Yehudah tells a tale in which his rabbinic ancestor Rabban Gamliel questions the halakhic justification for a husband's authority over his wife's property. To discuss this, I will repeat a section from the middle section of *m. Ket.* 8.1:

> Recounted Rabbi Yehudah: They said before Rabban Gamliel: Since he (the husband) has authority over the woman (his wife), will he not have authority over the [woman's] property?
>
> He [Gamliel] said to them: Concerning the [ownership and control of] new [property] we are embarrassed [by the lack of legal justification], and you would burden us with [halakhah for the ownership and control of] the old [property].

The context of the debate is betrothal. In this middle section, 'they'— an unnamed group of sages—present a two-part argument before Rabban Gamliel. The first part claims that the husband has authority over his wife. The second part builds on the first. Because the husband has authority over his wife, he also has authority over her property. In his response Gamliel does not question their first principle. A husband's authority over his wife is not the point that is up for debate. Their basic premise holds. Gamliel responds only to the second part of their argument, the expansion of the basic principle. The sages have argued that since the husband has authority over the wife, he also has authority over her property. In this context, he would control her old property during the period of their betrothal. In the Mishnah's version of Yehudah's tale, Rabban Gamliel raises some concerns.[12]

---

12. Consider the material benefits by imagining a woman whose family has given her an orchard of olive trees. If her husband has usufruct, then he owns the olives that are harvested from the trees and sold. If the woman and man are betrothed and not married until eight or ten months later, it becomes clear that the material stakes are the profits from a year's worth of olive growing, and whether

To the sages' desire to expand the husband's authority over his wife during the period of betrothal, Gamliel demurs. Not offering a simple agreement or disagreement, instead he raises a broader concern and calls attention to the lack of legal foundations. He reminds his interrogators, as well as readers like us, of a larger contour of early rabbinic debate about husbands, wives and property. Gamliel understands that early rabbinic *halakhah* places a woman's old and new property into the economy of marriage, but he wants his fellow rabbis to ascertain reliable legal foundations for their innovation. Rabban Gamliel argues that the legal justification for a husband's ownership of his wife's new property must precede any attempt to expand the husband's authority over the woman's old property. To his mind, the sages have not yet presented an adequate justification for the husband's control of the wife's old property: 'Concerning the [ownership and control of] new [property] we are embarrassed [by the lack of legal justification], and you would burden us with [halakhah for the ownership and control of] the old [property]'. Gamliel's dissent is built on the demand for legal justification—whether through Scripture, or rules of exegesis, or from the rulings of pharisaic ancestors or elsewhere. It is on this account that Gamliel refuses to give a husband-to-be rights to his wife's property during the period of their betrothal.

Gamliel will reappear in the next and last part of *m. Ket.* 8.1. This last section turns from the betrothed woman to consider the married woman. The section's first case begins with a consensus position that is attributed to the first-century Houses of Hillel and Shammai. A married woman gains old property (that is, by inheritance or gift). She sells it or gives it away. Both Houses declare that her act is legally invalid. As a result, her husband can nullify the sale and retrieve the property from the buyer or recipient. The husband controls the wife's old property, and the wife cannot undercut his control and his rights to its profits by releasing the property to others.

The section's second case is more complicated. A woman gains old property during betrothal. She marries and then sells the property or gives it away. On this point the Houses' consensus turns to disagreement, and Rabban Gamliel is introduced again. He permits the wife the right to sell or give away the property she gained during betrothal. According to Gamliel, the husband does not control the old property she gained during betrothal. Gamliel does not allow the husband to act as if the property were under his control, and does not

these profits belong to the 'husband' or to the betrothed woman.

permit him to reclaim it. Property that the wife gains during betrothal remains hers alone; upon her marriage it will be neither *ṣô'n barzel* nor *mulug*. Gamliel's position maintains that a woman's legal ability to own and control property during betrothal is markedly different from the restrictions that apply once the marriage is fully consummated. Furthermore, the factor of the time at which the woman acquired the property outweighs the factor of the time at which she sells it.

With Gamliel's second appearance the mishnah begins to build an argument that reaches its conclusion at the end of *m. Ket.* 8.2. In his first appearance Gamliel has been placed clearly in a position of authority. The argument between Gamliel and the sages ended the discussion of property during betrothal. His point about the lack of legal foundation explains the ambiguity of the case in which a betrothed woman did release her property, she should not have done so, but the husband had no legal recourse. Gamliel's second appearance is followed quickly by his third, a word-for-word repetition of the earlier exchange with the sages. In this recounting, the exchange between Gamliel and the sages is cited by Rabbi Hanina ben Aqabya, a contemporary of Yehudah's in the rabbinic circles of the mid-second century. In this new context both Gamliel and the sages 'say' the same words. Only now, the topic has changed from betrothal to marriage. Although the words are repeated verbatim, the exchange means something different. In the earlier exchange about betrothal Gamliel ended the argument and refused to extend the principle of a husband's authority over his wife to controlling her property during betrothal. In the repetition, Gamliel is the one who is refuted and refused. The relations between Gamliel, the sages and the mishnaic narrator shift. Gamliel's authority is more ambiguous at this point. He is no longer the authoritative speaker who satisfactorily answers the sages. Instead, Gamliel's argument becomes a minority stance. The mishnah refuses Gamliel's position. The sages speak against him, and their argument is victorious.

I reproduce the exchange once again, this time to make a different set of points. As the passage yields its legal story about how to extend the privileges of husbands, it reveals a rabbinic anxiety about the foundations for their law. When these lines from *m. Ket.* 8.1 are read in this way, the repetition of Gamliel's argument with the sages becomes an ambivalent, questioning refrain.

> Recounted Rabbi Hanina ben Aqabya: They said before Rabban Gamliel: Since he (the husband) has authority over the woman (his wife), will he not have authority over the [woman's] property?

He [Gamliel] said to them: Concerning the [ownership and control of] new [property] we are embarrassed [by the lack of legal foundation] and you would burden us with [halakhah about the ownership and control of] the old [property].

The refrain is repeated, and this repetition displays a rabbinic activism on behalf of a husband's authority. But as the repetition displays the rabbis' active interest, it simultaneously betrays a rabbinic anxiety about gender and male authority. If they needed to argue for it, masculine authority was not an entirely automatic and naturalized part of life. If it were it would be an unspoken assumption, not a topic of discussion. The fact that their argument is necessary admits that male authority is desired—but its details are still under question, a privilege to be actively maintained by those who covet it. In articulating an argument to extend a husband's privileges, the mishnah implicitly acknowledges the plasticity of masculine privilege.

The technological invention of plastic appears many centuries after these rabbis, but provides a vivid way to talk about how they took human life and shaped specific forms of gender. As a substance, plastic can be shaped into an almost unlimited array of forms. As a critical term, it can describe what people do with ideas, acts and culture. Plastic can be shifted, reshaped, manipulated into different forms. As opposed to something that is thought to be defined by an essence, plasticity refers to the sense in which ideas and practices are shaped and changed. Thus, when *m. Ket.* 8.1 alters the legal conditions of women's and men's lives, it tacitly admits the constructedness of gender. In the act of changing the legal and economic relations of a man with the woman to whom he is betrothed or married, the assenting rabbis reshape (one part) of what it means to be a man. In reshaping they attest to the changeability of masculinity, to its plasticity. Shaping masculinity and providing law for certain visions of women and men, those who wrote rabbinic passages were not mere vessels for their *halakhah*, but responsible for these visions of human life. To describe this in language that rabbis in Roman Palestine certainly did not use, the passage's polemic witnesses their engagement with (if not their awareness of) the constructedness of human subjects and the constructedness of gender. And it shows their active commitment to influencing these constructions, to remaking men, women and the social relations of gender in new forms.

In *m. Ket.* 8.1 and elsewhere, gender and the relations of women and men were something that mattered very much to the early rabbis. Rabbinic writers of this text were conscious, more or less, of their experiments with changing the relations of Jewish men and Jewish women. But the rabbis who produced the Mishnah and other texts did not transmit exactly what they inherited, but consciously created something new. They did not seamlessly pass along a 'heritage' (not that transmissions of heritages are ever seamless). These were not inheritances that less than consciously became part of the new rabbinic Judaism. Rather, the parameters of marriage were up for discussion. Within certain limits, the details of marriage were debated and the foundations for legal innovations were parsed.

If gender mattered, and it did, the question at hand is how the rabbis conversed about gender. For instance, *m. Ket.* 8.1 is overtly concerned with the economic relations of women and men. The interchange offers two sides to a debate about male privilege. The sages are overt in their desire to extend a husband's privilege, and their argument addresses this directly. Rabban Gamliel's position can be read as a defense of women against this incursion of male privilege. But in this passage Gamliel's response is not based on a direct argument about the relations of women and men. The issue at hand is gender—about the various ways that women and men will be constituted as separate and distinct through different powers over property. Yet gender as such is not directly addressed. Gamliel objects on the grounds that he and his fellow rabbis must find a foundation for their legal innovation in order to make the new law legitimate. As his words are recounted by Yehudah and Hanina ben Aqabya, Gamliel wants the plasticity of men and masculine privilege to be grounded in legitimate rabbinic forms of legality. (This is the Mishnah's perspective as well, and provides a partial reason for its inclusion of the position attributed to Gamliel.) Gamliel's dispute is based on a desire that *halakhah* have recognizable and authoritative foundations.

Gamliel's argument can be part of a polemic about men, women and marriage. His refusal to extend a husband's power can be read as a defense of women. But Gamliel's position is not articulated as a demand for greater justice for betrothed women and wives. It does not suggest that this goal will be achieved if elements of their husbands' control over property are contained. Rather, Gamliel's position is articulated as a quest for juridical certainty and better law. The debate is about how *halakhah* for marriage will craft men and women into different types of property-owning subjects. The sages' words address this rather directly. Gamliel's response to them does not. In Gamliel's critique of the sages, gender is present as a topic but not deployed as the basis for an argument. His defense of women may be just an inadvertent, even ironic, effect.

Gender can be as powerful in its apparent absence as in its presence. This recognition is what prompts me to look in two places at the same time: at the overt results of rabbinic deliberation; and at the multivalent process by which they arrived at conclusions, even when this process seems barely visible.

In a culture built on distinctions between women and men, in a religious law grounded in the pervasiveness of sexual difference, clues about gender are never too far away. A closer reading of *m. Ket.* 8.1 finds traces that makes gender visible in Gamliel's position. I look again at the refrain—'He said to them: Concerning the new we are embarrassed, and you would burden us with the old'. But now my attention turns to the phrase I have translated as 'we are embarrassed', or *'ānû bôšin* The phrase contains a personal pronoun and a verbal participle in the first person plural (we are embarrassed, *'ānû bôšin*). The phrase does not speak only for Gamliel as an individual. It was not written in the singular, 'I am embarrassed'. The plural places Gamliel with a group larger than himself. The tantalizing question of who is included in the 'we' with whom Gamliel speaks must be set aside, since the plural may be used to convey a greater sense of Gamliel's authority to speak not only for himself but for rabbis more generally.

There are additional meanings in these sparse words attributed to Gamliel. Philologically, the root for embarrass—*bôš*—refers to human bodies that are exposed and injured. Built from this root, the term *bôšin* that is used to describe Gamliel's sensibility slips in and around a range of meanings that include shame, abashment, insult, exposure and disgrace.[13] Abstractly, this injury and these feelings of disgrace can apply to both women and men. However, gendered meanings are situational. In tractate *Ketubot*, the term makes vivid an emotional state that is very precisely gendered. The root appears in several tractate *Ketubot* passages preceding *m. Ket.* 8.1. In these places, the root refers to the shame, disgrace and loss of dignity the rabbis attribute to a woman as a result of her rape by a man.[14] These nearby meanings would be available and familiar to those who wrote, edited, read, discussed or listened to *m. Ket.* 8.1. These meanings give a certain cast to Gamliel's embarrassment by linking it with the emotions and power relations surrounding male rape of women. Choosing the

13. See *m. B. Qam.* 8.1, *t. B. Qam.* 5.12, *m. Ab.* 5.20 and *Num. R.* 15.
14. *M. Ket.* 3.7, 3.9, 4.1. Elsewhere, see *m. 'Arak.* 3.4.

word 'embarrassed'—*bôšin*—the Mishnah presents Rabban Gamliel's position through its gendered meanings. Gamliel's dissent is expressed as the undesirable position of a woman who has been raped. Voiced through language that is associated with a raped woman, Gamliel's character is one whose position is acknowledged, foresworn and indirectly recompensed, but who nonetheless loses.

How it Knows what it Knows

Gamliel's 'embarrassment' has long fascinated me. Becoming more vivid through my own repeated readings of this text, Gamliel's words in *m. Ket.* 8.1 seemed heroic. I applauded his refusal to extend a husband's authority over his wife's property. I savored the way he stood in the way of other rabbis who wished to do so. His admission of insecurity about the foundations of *halakhah* merged with my own interests in finding the traces of how gender and law were produced. It was *simpatico* with my desire to locate the seams of production that, once closed, make gender and its details seem natural, normal and even inevitable. I was in sympathy as his character reached for an argument about foundations, this strong legal and literary weapon that always asks *how* something is known. Although differences of opinion are the insignia of the Mishnah and other rabbinic writing, the kind of metacritique in Rabban Gamliel's statement is relatively rare. His bewilderment about the foundation for this specific *halakhah* indicates a rabbinic desire for the security of legal ancestry. And, at the same time, his bewilderment shows the very manufacture of ancestry and genealogy. If, in this early stage, the rabbinic movement needed to make its foundations seem authoritatively self-evident, these traces are the text's own evidence that its law is neither inevitable nor self-evident. In short, I saw the argument between Gamliel and the sages as a conceptual tool offered by the Mishnah for its own deconstruction.

Highlighting the passage's uncertainties about how it knows what it knows is my entry point into a discussion of different feminist relations with these ancient rabbis and rabbinic texts. This passage is a vivid moment in the production of early rabbinic law. It can be analyzed in many possible ways. How one analyzes this and other rabbinic passages depends on a whole series of prior assumptions. For example, if one assumes that the Mishnah (and the rabbis who produced and used it) desires indeterminacy, then the uncertainty articulated through Rabban Gamliel (in *m. Ket.* 8.1) becomes part of what rabbis want to say about the foundations of law for marriage and property. To find and highlight this uncertainty is to read with the rabbinic grain. It means that we have found something the Mishnah's editors would have wanted their readers to know: that they wished to highlight the insecurity of legal foundations.

Another kind of reader could assume that the Mishnah wants to privilege stable meanings and secure foundations. This assumption would reject the idea that the legal text surreptitiously helps its readers effect its own unraveling. According to this second possible way of reading the passage, the expression of uncertainty in *m. Ket.* 8.1 is a less-than-conscious bulge in the text's seams. Thus, finding this trace of indeterminacy amounts to reading *against* the rabbinic grain. Reading this way makes visible something embedded in the text's logic, and shows something the text might have wished to keep under wraps. The expression of uncertainty about legal foundations pressures the Mishnah to reveal its own arbitrariness. Against its own desires, the text is made to show the unnatural, constructed status—of the law, of gender, of masculine privilege and women's relation to property. Pretty major differences, these, that all depend on what we readers assume about the world, about the rabbis and about how writing works.[15]

Of course these are not the only two options for making sense of the passage. In reading for women, men and gender, both options focus on how the Mishnah comments on its own status as law. Delving into these metacritical questions about law and text are not the only queries someone might bring to this and other Mishnaic texts. Sometimes more readily accessible answers about women are desired. But this desire too is complicated, and built on different assumptions about interpretation. A panoply of feminist readings of rabbis, of early rabbinic Judaism, of 'women in the Mishnah' and of the Mishnah's women are possible. One reading, for instance, might focus on the specific resolution offered by the Mishnah on the issue of women's property rights and the extension of husbands' authority. Such a reading would seek and find answers to questions about the status of women in early rabbinic law.[16]

---

15. It is also possible that the text engages *both* claims of determinacy and of indeterminacy in different ways and at different times.

16. I have in mind here the work of several scholars. Judith Romney Wegner's *Chattel or Person: The Status of Women in the Mishnah* (New York: Oxford University Press, 1988) is of foremost importance. I am both indebted to her research, and respectfully take issue with a good many of her conclusions and with many of the assumptions that undergird her reading of Mishnah. Explicating *m. Ket.* 8.1, for example, Wegner writes: 'But if a wife retains legal ownership of her property,

Another kind of reading could emphasize individual rabbis. The textual frame around these ancient rabbis is set aside. We could forget that it matters that 'Gamliel' is narrated by Hanina ben Aqabya and Yehudah, or that 'Hanina ben Aqabya' and 'Yehudah' are narrated by the Mishnah's editing writers, and so forth. The crafting of ancestral voices and arguments could be forgotten in favor of plucking out individual rabbinic voices, deemed usable for feminism. In letting our attention drift from the written-and-transmitted quality of the Mishnah, the named rabbis seem to come alive, magically released from the constraints of the text. Individual rabbis become a pantheon of 'real people', with lives independent of the characters that early rabbinic writing has created. This way of reading can result in a collection of redeemable Rabbis and rabbinic heroes, a group to which Rabban Gamliel can belong.[17] Depending on the reader's desires, Gamliel would be a double hero. Not only does he deconstruct the law's authority, but in his sympathies he also defends betrothed women and wives against the extension of a husband's authority. For Jewish women and feminists in communities that are committed to *halakhah*, Rabban Gamliel can be used as an ancient

why limit her power to control it at all? The restriction is all the more surprising as sages themselves note their "embarrassment" at the lack of authority for this rule. The answer must be that the wife has voluntarily surrendered her right to control the property' (p. 90). Although I would like to feign astonishment that the supposition that 'women volunteer for their subjugated status' passes as an 'answer' to a more complicated question, there is an intellectual genealogy to this argument. Wegner's work seems to be committed to classically liberal notions of agency wherein human subjects exist prior to the law, hence consent to the law and its demands. This assumption of liberal legal theory is combined with a protection of the ancient rabbis and a desire to find somewhere to stand as a feminist who adheres to rabbinic law. Wegner's writing emphasizes those positive and potential moments in rabbinic law in which women of different legal statuses have more fully developed and expanded rights. Writing from within these particular positions, she offers this conclusion of rabbinic property laws for women. Rather than constructing the conditions for women's lives in a restrictive way, she argues that 'the net effect of the mishnaic rules that govern a wife's property is this: Any woman of full age has the capacity to own property. Marriage does not extinguish a wife's ownership, but merely holds its full exercise in abeyance; though the wife's rights are subordinated to her husband, they remain potentially intact' (p. 91). Arguments such as this protect the oppressiveness of certain rabbinic traditions by making claims about women's agency; in other words, rabbinic patriarchy could not have been so bad, since women participated knowingly.

17. Of course, such a possibility can be imagined only by restricting Gamliel to the characterization of him in *m. Ket.* 8.1. In texts such as *m. B. Bat.* 9.1, Gamliel comes down decidedly in favor of privileges for men.

and authoritative ally in arguments for increases in women's rights. Gamliel's position and his critique of his colleagues can be read as marking a road not historically taken by rabbinic Judaism, but a more positive road still located within the parameters of the Talmud.[18]

I see the attractions of this Gamliel. But I am not searching for heroes among the rabbis, and this kind of detextualized and decontextualized reading perturbs me. Seeking ancient rabbis as friends for feminists, it can become too easy to forgive them their patriarchy. Thus, another kind of feminist reading might emphasize the structural inequities and the intransigence of masculinism expressed in early rabbinic texts. Here, Gamliel's heroism falters. Within an economy of marriage that is already restrictive, Gamliel's position grants women in some circumstances greater control over certain types of their property. He argues against extending the husband's rights—to the period of betrothal, to the control of a wife's old property gained during betrothal—but only until the proper *halakhic* foundations can be asserted. But these are details at the margins: a husband still has legal rights that directly curtail the rights granted to his wife. This position protects a wife only from the extension of a husband's rights over her and her property. Gamliel's mishnaic words do not contest the basic hierarchical premise of a husband's authority over his wife. Reading this way, Gamliel is not so heroic. He is a patron who remains patronizing. Whether once live in the flesh or given birth only from a scribe's ink pen, he is not someone that I would want as

18. I have chosen to present composite positions and possibilities for feminist readings rather than engage in one-sided arguments with colleagues who will not in these same pages be able to argue back. I refer readers to work by scholars such as: Judith Hauptman, 'Feminist Perspectives on Rabbinic Texts', in Davidman and Tenenbaum (eds.), *Feminist Perspectives on Jewish Studies*, pp. 40-61; Judith Baskin, 'The Separation of Women in Rabbinic Judaism', in Yvonne Yazbeck Haddad and Ellison Banks Findly (eds.), *Women, Religion, and Social Change* (Albany: SUNY Press, 1985); Daniel Boyarin, *Carnal Israel: Reading Sex in Talmudic Culture* (Berkeley: University of California Press, 1993); Leonie Archer, *Her Price is Beyond Rubies: The Jewish Woman in Graeco-Roman Palestine* (JSOTSup, 60; Sheffield: Sheffield Academic Press, 1990); the various works of Louis Epstein; Paul V.M. Flesher, 'Are Women Property in the System of the Mishnah', in Jacob Neusner, Ernest Freirichs and Nahum Sarna (eds.), *From Ancient Israel to Modern Judaism* (Atlanta: Scholars Press, 1988), I; G. Meyer, *Die Jüdische Frau in der Hellenistisch-Romischen Antike* (Stuttgart: Kohlhammer, 1987); Judith Wegner, *Chattel or Person?*; Tal Ilan, *Jewish Women in Greco-Roman Palestine: An Inquiry Into Image and Status* (Tübingen: Mohr, 1995); and Gail Labovitz, 'Arguing for Women in Talmud', *Shofar* 14.1 (1995), pp. 72-79.

an ally for long. But when I read this passage now, this is the Gamliel that I see.

Demanding Answers

All of these readings are organized as referenda. In the end specific rabbis, or all rabbis, or the entirety of rabbinic *halakhah* are announced as either positive or negative. They are either good or bad, redeemable or not. The rabbis and their law are worthwhile, useless or dangerous. But there is a problem with needing the rabbis and their texts to be either good or bad, with seeing pro-feminism, proto-feminism, absolute villainy, or good news for Jewish masculinity in these texts. The problem is that any of these answers can allow too quick a move away from the process of figuring out how these ancient rabbis painstakingly, and in the first place, made certain notions of gender, men and women imaginable as 'common' sense. My quandary in reading rabbinic texts for answers and for temporary allies is that this allows the broader power of masculinist culture to slip too easily from view. Looking at individuals and their positions can allow the general assumptions of these writings to go unchallenged. The specific masculinist relations they imagine in their views of the world become both invisible and universal. Reading for details, the underlying claims about women, men and the rabbis themselves can be too easily accepted as truths. Reading rabbinic texts this way, as readers and thinkers we gain no practice in looking closely at evidence, in taking apart its assumptions and logics, in finding environmental and historic contexts, in figuring out the mechanisms of how masculinism worked. The demand for truths and answers from early rabbinic texts can ignore the ambiguity within rabbinic texts. It can presuppose that these texts always had specific answers. Reading these texts is always in part a reflection of ourselves. Demanding these kinds of answers situates us as people who will countenance no ambivalence and little complexity. It constructs us as people who can only navigate the starkly opposite possibilities of the *either* and the *or*.

The practice of plucking out individual characters—whether heroes, fallen heroes or villains—removes from view the broader rabbinic culture out of which these texts were produced (and which in turn was produced by these writings). Plucking out heroes removes from view the rabbinic writers whose work produced these texts, 'voices' and arguments; and whose efforts transmitted characters and legal stories in these forms and configurations, not in others. It removes from view the ordinary and unnamed rabbis who repeated, read, heard and commented upon this text. Although he may have lived and participated in rabbinic gatherings, the 'Rabban Gamliel' of *m. Ket.* 8.1 is not an individual. Gamliel's 'voice' does not exist historically outside of these textual renditions. The figure of Gamliel is proliferated through this, other and later rabbinic texts. Tannaitic figures are figments of their creators and their readers. As a necessity of life in the twentieth century, it is possible to claim 'Gamliel' as heroic or, at least, as helpful. But the Mishnah is not a transparent record, nor does it transmit even a fraction of early rabbinic conversation. It crafts both Rabbis and words into fantasy, into stories about law and life. As significant as Gamliel may have been within the early Rabbinic movement, or as important as he became in later Jewish traditions, Rabban Gamliel is at the same time part of tannaitic fictions for real life. Remembering that texts are mediated, feminist desires for rabbinic allies cannot claim a historical 'truth' about any 'real' Gamliel.

Ordinariness

This is what happens when we bring back into view those who produced the Mishnah, crafted *m. Ket.* 8.1, and constructed this version of Rabban Gamliel. A mishnaic passage never records opposite positions on an equal footing. Its 'arguments' are never really arguments as we know them—between colleagues, friends, strangers and opponents who maintain their own stances, think on their feet, react and respond and change course. Mishnaic arguments are highly staged. Although at times the relations of tannaitic opponents are unclear, majority and minority voices and voices of dissent are often noted as such in various ways.[19] These debates are not about the rabbis involved so much as they are about a mishnaic argument writ large. In other words, the position attributed to Rabban Gamliel marks a point along the way to the resolution of the predicament of *m. Ket.* 8.1: the shaky foundations for some of the *halakhah* for marriage and property. Gamliel's position is emphasized through repetition, but it means something different each time it appears. *m. Ket.* 8.1 concludes with the second repetition of Gamliel's embarrassment. In one way of reading, this would indicate support for Gamliel, as if through sheer numbers of repetition and through the fact that he alone is named. But perhaps we are caught in the habit of emphasizing individuals, of attending to those characters whose writers

19. See for example, *t. 'Ed.* 1.4.

gave them names. The reiteration of this refrain does not emphasize Gamliel's position alone. Far from it: the repetition allows both sides a second hearing. With Gamliel, the unnamed sages also get their moment. Gamliel's critique is repeated, but so too is the basic premise of patriarchal marriage—that a husband has authority over his wife—repeated and authorized through the unnamed sages, whose very anonymity may be interpreted as tannaitic consensus.

When we broaden the context for analyzing this passage, it becomes clear that the resolution of the debate in *m. Ket.* 8.1 actually appears in the mishnah that follows. There the tractate finds one legally viable foundation for the husband's control over property that his wife received before their marriage. As will become clear, *m. Ket.* 8.2 partially attends to Rabban Gamliel's concern about legal justification, but on new and different terms. To demonstrate this I repeat the end of *m. Ket.* 8.1, followed by *m. Ket.* 8.2:

> Recounted Rabbi Hanina ben Aqabya: They said before Rabban Gamliel: Since he has authority over the woman, will he not have authority over the [woman's] property?

> He [Gamliel] said to them: Concerning the [ownership of] new [property] we are embarrassed [by the lack of legal foundation] and you would burden us with [halakhah for the ownership and control of] the old [property]

> *m. Ket.* 8.2:
> Rabbi Simeon distinguishes between kinds of properties. Properties that are known to the husband, she may not sell. And if she sold or gave it away (as a married woman), the act is void. [Properties] that are unknown to the husband, she may not sell, and if she sold or gave it away (again, as a married woman), her act is valid.

Rabbi Simeon distinguishes between property about which the husband knows, and property about which he is ignorant. A married woman can own and control property she gained during betrothal if her husband is unaware. If her husband knows about her property, then he has rights to it and she may not sell it, give it away or otherwise deprive the husband of its usufruct. Now, according to Gamliel's priorities, his rabbinic colleagues must attend first to the problem of justifying a husband's claim to his wife's *new property*, that which she gains during their marriage. But in *m. Ket.* 8.2 Rabban Gamliel's priorities are ignored. His view becomes the minority view. Gamliel has demanded that they justify first the husband's authority over new property gained during marriage. In contrast, in *m. Ket.* 8.2 Rabbi Simeon prioritizes finding a foundation for the husband's control of the woman's *old property*. Simeon supplies a principle to justify extending the husband's authority: his knowledge of the woman's property. If he *knew* about the woman's property, then he has the right to control that property and to profit from it. Simeon resolves the problem of extending a husband's privileges over his wife and her property by locating the basis for this extension in a man's knowledge.[20]

In telling this story about rabbinic men who make laws that privilege men and constrict women, the repetitions highlight an underlying principle in their notion of marriage: 'They said before Rabban Gamliel: Since he has authority over the woman...' As a character in this tale, Gamliel serves the rabbinic extension of husbandly authority well. Gamliel does not argue against this aspect of male authority. He merely wants its legal authority to be established appropriately. The refrain of the husband's authority over the wife provides a prior context for Simeon's reliance on the authority of a man's senses. The repetition stresses the principle of male authority and makes it familiar. This makes reliance on male eyes seem like ordinary and common sense.

In this way, *m. Ket.* 8.2 and Rabbi Simeon offer a circular argument. The principle that a husband has authority over his wife envisions a man as authoritative, a woman as less so. Based on this already established authority, his knowledge (of her property) is deemed authoritative. This authority is transformed into a viable legal foundation for further rabbinic extension of a husband's authority. The exchange between Rabban Gamliel and the sages presumes a man's authority over a woman in marriage. This is precisely the portion of the refrain that remains consensual, familiar and uncontested. That it is even possible for a feminist or any other reader not to notice this immediately points to the relative invisibility and ordinariness of what is, from another frame of reference, an absolutely extraordinary claim.[21]

20. The argument invokes a man's desire for the property and profit he will gain through marriage as his primary rationale for that marriage. Within this reasoning, the desire against changes [to this fiscal attraction] becomes the reason to restrict the woman's control over her property. This overt deployment of a notion of justice for men and husbands stands in contrast to the absence in Gamliel's defense of a notion of justice for women. Here, as elsewhere in early rabbinic writing, gender is made to matter explicitly in some places and not in others.

21. Calling into question male dominance over women has been the basic insight of feminist acts, Women's Studies and feminist theory. With the professionalization of these critical practices, male dominance has also become that which is

supposed to go unsaid. I am indebted to conversations with Naomi Seidman about the necessity for reclaiming a critique of patriarchy for academic feminism; see her 'Theorizing Jewish Patriarchy *in extremis*', in Miriam Peskowitz and Laura Levitt (eds.), *Judaism Since Gender* (New York: Routledge, 1996), pp. 40-48 as well as 'Carnal Knowledge: Sex and the Body in Jewish Studies', *Jewish Social Studies* 1 (1994), pp. 115-46. I am also grateful to Judith Baskin, Gail Labovitz, Laura Levitt and Daniel Boyarin who, in different ways, pushed me to locate myself more clearly within feminist possibilities for reading rabbinic texts.

TORAH STUDY AND THE MAKING OF JEWISH GENDER*

Daniel Boyarin

לחוה, שתח'

'One has to learn to move like a gendered human body' (Maud W. Gleason).[1]

In direct contrast to the firm handshake approved (for men and businesswomen) in our culture, a *Yeshiva-Bokhur* (Talmud student, in Yiddish), until this day, extends the right hand with a limp wrist for a mere touch of the other's hand. If the handshake is, as frequently said, originally a knightly custom, the counter-handshake of the ideal Jewish male elegantly suggests that the *Yeshiva-Bokhur* is the Jewish antithesis to the knight of romance as male ideal. Indeed, one of the things that most repelled the Victorian journalist Frank Harris upon meeting Oscar Wilde was that 'he shook hands in a limp way that I disliked',[2] presumably owing to its 'effeminacy'. The very handshake of the ideal male Jew encoded him as femminized[3] in the

---

* This paper is a condensed chapter from my book, *Unheroic Conduct: The Rise of Heterosexuality and the Invention of the Jewish Man* (Contraversions: Studies in Jewish Literature, Culture and Society; Berkeley: University of California Press, 1997).

1. Maud W. Gleason, *Making men: Sophists and Self-Presentation in Ancient Rome* (Princeton, NJ: Princeton University Press, 1995), p. xxvi.

2. Alan Sinfield, *The Wilde Century: Effeminacy, Oscar Wilde and the Queer Moment* (New York: Columbia University Press, 1994), p. 2.

3. I write this way to indicate clearly that I am not ascribing some form of actual or essential femininity to certain behaviors or practices, as to a Jungian *anima*. For the toxic effects of that ideology, see Robert W. Connell, *Masculinities* (Berkeley: University of California Press, 1995), pp. 12-15 and cf. now especially Marjorie Garber, *Vice-Versa: Bisexuality and the Eroticism of Everyday Life* (New York: Simon & Schuster, 1995), pp. 211-14. I am rather marking these performances as 'femme' within the context of a particular culture's performatives, and particularly as it intersects with other cultural formations. The point is, then, not to reify and celebrate the 'feminine' but to dislodge the term. 'Phallus', the 'feminine' (and, in only a slightly different register, 'Jew') are fatally equivocal terms in Western discourse, insisting on their disconnection from real human beings of particular groups—men, women, and Jews—at the same time that they inescapably

eyes of European heterosexual culture, but that very handshake constituted as well a mode of resistance to the models of manliness of the
dominant fiction.

Torah study itself was associated with a whole range of deport-
ment, of manners of standing, sitting, walking and speaking, an
entire habitus in Bordieu's terminology, a set of techniques of the
body. As most recently powerfully documented by the work of
Naomi Seidman, the study of Torah was what marked the early
modern Ashkenazi (Northern European) Jewish male as male, over
against the female, for whom this enterprise was a forbidden asset.[4]
This is not to say that all male Ashkenazi Jews actually studied
Torah any more than all medieval German men were knights, but
this social marker was what defined the ideal male, indeed defined
maleness itself. Torah study was for these Jews a tertiary sexual
characteristic, defined by Maud Gleason as 'the tilt of the pelvis, the
gestures of the hand, even certain movements of the eyes—all these
function as a conventional language through which gender identity

---

declare their connection with these groups. The contortions of Weininger in insisting that everyone is 'Jewish' but Jews only more so, but there can be Jews
(Weininger) who escape being Jewish are only one dramatic example of this aporia.
For the coinage itself, compare Ed Cohen's 'fem'-menists' (Ed Cohen, 'Are we
(not) what we Are Becoming? "Gay" "Identity", "Gay Studies", and the Disciplining of Knowledge', in Joseph A. Boone and Michael Cadden [eds.], *Engendering Men: The Question of Male Feminist Criticism* [New York: Routledge, 1990],
p. 174.) I had, in fact, for a long time considered 'femmenize' but worried that it
would be read as a pun on 'men' and not on 'femme'. This usage further distinguishes the cultural processes that I am describing from those referred to when one
speaks of the 'feminization of the synagogue', by which is meant the fact that in
certain 'assimilating' communities only women typically attended the synagogues
(at the same time that Protestant churches were being feminized in the same
sense). This phenomenon, discussed most recently and cogently by Paula Hyman,
is not what I am talking about here (Paula E. Hyman, *Gender and Assimilation in
Modern Jewish History: The Roles and Representation of Women* [Samuel and Althea
Stroum Lectures in Jewish Studies; Seattle: University of Washington Press, 1995],
pp. 24-25).

   4.   Naomi S. Seidman, '"A Marriage Made in Heaven"? The Sexual Politics of
Hebrew–Yiddish Diglossia' (dissertation, University of California at Berkeley,
1995 [1993]), pp. 85-86 and *passim*. Again, I emphasize that my qualification of
my discourse as being about Ashkenazi Jews is not in order to make an exception
of Sefaradic and Eastern Jews but the opposite: to indicate that Ashkenazim are
not the only Jews that there are, just the only ones that I have studied (for the
modern period). It would be fascinating to find out whether or not these characteristics and gender practices are common to the whole Jewish people at given
periods of time.

may be claimed and decoded'.[5] If Torah study and its associated
bodily techniques are what defined the rabbinic Jewish male as male,
then the exclusion of women from the study of Torah finds a functional explanation; it was the structure that engendered the Jews, the
practice that constructed the system of gender differentiation and
gender hierarchy within traditional Jewish society.

The stereotypical reasons given within most feminist critique to
date for the cultural practice of segregation of women from Torah
study are unconvincing for one reason or another. Thus, one typical
explanation is that women were considered essentially and always
contaminated and contaminating, and that contact with the Holy
Torah had to be prohibited on those grounds. This assumption simply does not hold water from several points of view. First, there is
very little evidence in rabbinic Jewish literature that women were so
regarded. Indeed, one of the characteristics of the rabbinic movement
is ways that it set itself up in opposition to older, more Hellenized
Judaisms, in which such ideas—including extreme misogyny and
antisexuality—were rampant. Simply conflating these different Judaisms misses the point entirely, as does the collapsing of all systems of
male domination into an undifferentiated unhistoricized 'patriarchy,'
often referred to as 'the patriarchy'.[6] Secondly, there is no evidence,
and indeed, there is counter-evidence, that the Torah had to be protected from impurity. The standard phrase in halakhic literature is
'The words of Torah are not susceptible to impurity', and it was not
until the early medieval period that women were considered contaminating entities in the context of Torah.[7] The formal halakhic level
of the texts suggests strongly that there were no bars to women studying Torah; but, nevertheless, even in talmudic times this seems to
have been practically unknown, and later there is a positive horror of
it.[8] Thirdly, since even at its medieval worst the exclusion from study

5.   Gleason, *Making Men*, p. xxvi. For a quite different usage of the term 'tertiary sexual character' see Otto Weininger, *Sex and Character* (ET; New York: AMS,
6th edn, 1975 [1906]), p. 195.

6.   Carole Pateman, *The Sexual Contract* (Stanford: Stanford University Press,
1988), pp. 29-30; see also Judith Butler, *Gender Trouble: Feminism and the Subversion of Identity* (Thinking Gender; London: Routledge, 1990), p. 3.

7.   Shaye J.D. Cohen, 'Menstruants and the Sacred in Judaism and Christianity', in Sarah Pomeroy (ed.), *Ancient History, Women's History* (Chapel Hill: University of North Carolina Press, 1991), pp. 273-99.

8.   Daniel Boyarin, *Carnal Israel: Reading Sex in Talmudic Culture* (The New
Historicism: Studies in Cultured Poetics; Berkeley: University of California Press,
1993), pp. 167-96.

of Torah did not, paradoxically, include the most holy Book, the Bible itself, but only the culturally more valued practice of the study of Talmud, the explanation that women contaminate the holy text is incoherent. In rejecting this explanation as genetically unconvincing, however, I am not denying the degree to which it has functioned synchronically, since the end of late antiquity, as the means for the production of an ideology of women as contaminated and contaminating—an ideology that men disseminated and women internalized. I am simply reversing the relations of cause and effect. Exclusion from study of Torah was not caused by a theory of women as contaminating; the theory of women as polluting is an effect of the exclusion of women from the study of Torah. Whether or not this is a 'correct' interpretation of the Talmud, it is thus nonetheless certain that women have been made in historical Judaism to experience themselves as impure, dangerous and devalued through these exclusions. It is virtually impossible to overemphasize the intensity of affliction and humiliation that this systematic ritual expression of inferiority has caused for many Jewish women.

A second explanation has it that the presence of women within the sites of the study of Torah would be too disturbing a factor, at least distracting and probably worse. This seems to me much closer to the mark: Torah study was understood to have a powerful erotic charge which would indeed have been very 'dangerous' if men and women were to do it together.[9] But this does not explain the apparent impossibility of separate spaces within which women could study Torah, just as there were separate spaces within which they could participate in prayer. There has to be a fuller, sharper, structural cultural necessity for such an extreme pattern of exclusion.

I propose that, for rabbinic patriarchy, the exclusion of women from the study of Torah is the central dynamic in the construction of gender and thus of the subjection of women; and that this exclusion fulfils the functions that in other patriarchies are fulfilled in the realm of economic activity (work) and sanctioned physical domination of women by men (*patria potestas* in its most extreme version). Talmudic discourse provides a frame of social and cultural theory that is an important material fact in the production of rabbinic Jewish cultures, although the social realizations of the structural possibilities afforded by the 'theory' vary in accord with different economic, social and political conditions. Actual cultural forms are mediated through a

---

9.   In my work-in-progress, tentatively entitled 'Why is this Knight Different: Jewish Re-visions of Christian Love', I wish further to interrogate this construction.

complex set of social, economic, historical and cultural conditions, frequently including the nature of the cultural practice of the societies within which Jews found themselves in different times and climes. Thus, I am not claiming either that Jewish culture as it was actually lived 'on the ground' conformed to the norms of the talmudic discourse, nor that Christian culture as it was lived was structured according to the theories of gender that Carole Pateman, among others, has described. I cannot, however, escape the sense that these differing theories both respond to and structure at least to some extent different sets of social practices as well.

I theorize that the exclusion of women from the study of Torah subtended the rabbinic Jewish gender hierarchy in two closely related ways: via the construction of a 'fraternity', and via the production of a social system within which a group of men (the rabbis) held power over the actual practices and pleasures of female bodies. It is here that the point of sharpest feminist critique must be aimed, at this generally compassionate and humane (but absolute) control of female subjects through maintaining them in virtual ignorance of the practices which enable ritual (and thus virtually all socio-cultural) decision-making within the traditional society. As to the first category, I suggest that the rabbinic phratry was substantially similar in its gendered structure and engendering function to such analogues as the guild or shop in Western economic and social practice. As Carole Pateman has put it (depending in this instance on Cynthia Cockburn), 'The workplace and the trades unions are organized as fraternal territory, where "it was unthinkable" that a girl could be part of an apprenticeship system so clearly "designed to produce a free man", where "skilled" work is the work done by men, and where manhood is tested and confirmed every day'.[10] The same function is performed for rabbinic Jews (once again, at least ideally) in *Bes-Hamidrash* (the House of Study), while Jewish women are to be found in the workplace. It is similarly unthinkable for a girl to be part of the homotopic space of the Study House as well. Manhood is tested and confirmed (and, I would add, constructed) every day precisely in the House of Study, and the workplace becomes the relatively devalued site that the 'private sphere' is in bourgeois society.

The second way that rabbinic Jewish culture produced a hierarchy of genders through the study of Torah was in its actual construction of the meaning of femaleness through this exclusion. In this respect it is similar in substance to the modes of production of gendered

10. Pateman, *Sexual Contract*, p. 141.

difference and gendered subjection, endemic within Western society
in general. Another of Pateman's formulations seems to capture more
closely the meanings of men's exclusive access to Torah: 'women's
relations to the social world must always be mediated through men's
reason; women's bodies must always be subject to men's reason and
judgments if order is not to be threatened'.[11] Analogously, for rabbinic Judaism, women's relations to the sacred world are mediated
through men's reason in the practice of the study of Torah.

What is common to both of these modalities is that they both steer
toward a judgment that it is not appropriate to ask with respect to
classical rabbinic culture whether or not a pre-given entity, the class
of women, is or is not permitted to study the Torah; but, rather, to see
that it is study of Torah as a gendered activity that produces the
hierarchially ordered categories of men and women.[12] As Delphy has
observed:

> The concept of class starts from the idea of social construction and
> specifies the implications of it. Groups are no longer *sui generis*, consti-
> tuted before coming into relation with one another. On the contrary, it is
> their relationship which constitutes them as such. It is therefore a ques-
> tion of discovering the social practices, the social relations, which, in
> constituting the division of gender, create the groups of gender (called
> 'of sex').[13]

Men are those human beings of whom it is expected that they 'study
Torah'. Men, as the dominant class of traditional Judaism, are precisely those who are obligated to study Torah as well as to perform
the entire panoply of positive commandments.

As a discourse, rabbinic Judaism was, to borrow Laura Levitt's
terms from another context, primarily detrimental to women's agency
but not to their physical welfare.[14] I do not minimize, by saying this,
the effect of psychic pain, of the constant insult and denial of value
and autonomy that the system produced and enforced. To put it in
James Scott's terms, it is in the exclusion from study of Torah that
we find the clearest structural, ritual expression of an inferiority of
women 'in rituals or etiquette regulating public contact between

11. Pateman, *Sexual Contract*, p. 101.
12. For the clarity of this formulation I am indebted to M. Peskowitz,
'Engendering Jewish Religious History', *Shofar* 14.1 (1995), pp. 8-34.
13. Christine Delphy, *Close to Home: A Materialist Analysis of Women's
Oppression* (trans. and ed. Diane Leonard; Amherst: University of Massachusetts
Press, 1984), p. 26.
14. Laura Sharon Levitt, 'Reconfiguring Home: Jewish Feminist Identity/ies'
(dissertation, Emory University, 1993), pp. 55, 72.

strata'.[15] In short, in rabbinic culture gender, and thus gender domination, is forged via the construction of the ideal male as Torah scholar. Torah study is the functional modality by which male dominance over women is secured in rabbinic discourse, thus fulfilling the functions that physical domination secures in various other cultural formations. Male power remains secure, at least insofar as the rabbis, an all male group, held power over Jewish women, but the distinctions between the patriarchal theories make a meaningful difference.

I propose that the tertiary sexual characteristics of Jewish men render them readable as pseudo-women within the *habitus* of the larger cultural context, and that Jews from the Babylonian talmudic period and in its cultural descendants were frequently aware of this 'linguistic' slippage, responding to it differently in different times and places. At the same time, however, that these techniques of the body, and especially the praxis of Torah learning that they supported and were supported by, produced (ideally) gentle, passive, emotional men, they also formed the technology through which the domination of women was carried out in this culture. The study of Torah is the quintessential performance of rabbinic Jewish maleness. In other words, precisely the stylized repetitions that produced gender differentiation (and thus cultural as well as sexual reproduction) within classical Jewish praxis were the repetitive performances of the House of Study, including the homosocial bonding. At the structural(ist) level, the specific performances themselves are irrelevant; what is culturally significant is the very inscription of sex through any gender differentiating practice. The House of Study was thus the rabbinic Jewish equivalent of the locker-room, barracks or warship, and we may compare the historically similar taboos on the presence of women in those environments. However, on the level of cross-cultural contact, gaps between the gendered performances of one culture and another become exceedingly consequential. In our case, the performance of maleness through study became particularly fraught, I suggest, precisely because this performance was read as female in the cultural environment within which European Jews lived from the Roman period onward. The ambivalence is also fully internal to Jewish culture itself. The 'tent' is the prototypical space of the female; of Yael it is said: 'She is blessed more than all of the women in the tent' (Judg. 5.24)—glossed by the Midrash as more blessed than the Mothers, Sarah, Rebecca, Leah and Rachel, of whom it is said that

15. In James C. Scott, *Domination and the Arts of Resistance* (New Haven: Yale University Press, 1990), p. xi.

they occupied the tent.[16] But on the other hand Jacob, the ideal male of rabbinic culture, is also 'an innocent, a dweller in tents' (Gen. 25.27)—glossed by the midrash as the tents in which Torah study is carried out.[17] Since the 'tent' is the epitome of private and 'female' space, and 'the common thread [of late antique political philosophy] was the insistence on the subordination of the private to the public sphere and of the female to the male',[18] once the House of Study is figured as a 'tent', the gender of its inhabitants becomes extremely equivocal even in their own estimation as well in as that of others. The political subordination of the Jew to the Roman worked perfectly with this patterning as well. If study of Torah is the singular performative that determines the Jewish man as a gendered male, then we can understand—which is not the same thing, of course, as accepting—the basis for a cultural taboo on women entering that space and engaging in that performance. The easy contrast between the female inside and the male outside having been breached, and males (ideally) now occupying an inside space as well, set up, I hypothesize, the tension that produced the extreme exclusion of women from the practice of the study of Torah.

Male Self-fashioning Has Consequences for Women

Some early Christian culture was, interestingly enough, developing at the same time very similar patterns of gendering and of domination. Resistance to Roman models and ideals of male power was common to these Christians and to the rabbis. While in some aspects this rejection was similar to that of the rabbis, its ultimate meanings were quite different. Virginia Burrus writes of an early fifth-century contemporary of the talmudic rabbis:

> Sulpicius' asceticism is, I propose, explicitly 'antipublic' and as such represents a conscious expression of political and cultural alienation which separates him from more traditional aristocratic Christian contemporaries like Ausonius. This preliminary thesis leads me to another: we may, I think, anticipate a certain destabilization of gender identity in the writings of an aristocrat who voluntarily retires from the uniquely male sphere of public life and withdraws to a sphere commonly associated with women and female influence.[19]

16. See *Gen. R.* 48. Yael is, of course, a singularly 'phallic' female herself who, within her very tent, drove a peg into the head of a tyrant and saved Israel.
17. *Gen. R.* 63 and *passim*.
18. Virginia Burrus, *The Making of a Heretic: Gender, Authority, and the Priscillianist Controversy* (Berkeley: University of California Press, 1995), p. 8.
19. Virginia Burrus, 'The Male Ascetic in Female Space: Alienated Strategies of

On the one hand Sulpicius's conversion is, as Burrus remarks, 'a radical rejection of power' and in this respect one could find abundant parallels in rabbinic texts as well; moreover, as she argues, at least in this case we do not have a simple transfer of enjoyment of power from the secular to the episcopal realm. Indeed, Sulpicius's total retirement is an affront to the public life of Bishops in the Gallic Church of his time and place. Most suggestive for my purposes is, however, the fact that Sulpicius explicitly marks women and especially virginal women as his models for the ascetic life of retirement and withdrawal from public exposure and activity. Burrus concludes, quite strikingly, that 'Sulpicius puts forth the radical suggestion that the male must indeed "become female" through his ascetic renunciation of public life'. The most striking parallel, however, to my interpretation of rabbinic culture is that Sulpicius proposes 'feminine' characteristics as ideals for the life of the Christian and yet, or rather because of, this reintroduces, first, the classical *topos* of the separation and subordination of women and, secondly, the traditional rhetoric of negative womanly influence:

> Let not a woman enter the camp of men, but let the line of soldiers remain separate, and let the females, dwelling in their own tent, be remote from that of men. For this renders an army ridiculous, if a female crowd is mixed with the regiments of men. Let the soldier occupy the line, let the soldier fight in the plain, but let the woman keep herself within the protection of the walls.[20]

Now, the 'camp of men' is here the individual solitude of a single, near-hermetic male ascetic, and the point of this admonition is that he must separate from his also converted, celibate wife. The historical meanings of the gendered roles have thus been thoroughly undermined by these men also, just as they had been for the rabbis and the successors. As Burrus shrewdly interprets, the point is that the intentional, valorized self-feminization of the Christian male ascetic produced also gender anxiety for those same men at the same time, and they reasserted their maleness through reinforcements of traditional gender roles transposed to a new metaphorical key. Christians were ultimately to create new literal female spaces in the form of female monastic communities, separate and (nearly) equal to those of men. Owing to the absolute commitment to marriage and communal

Self-Definition in the Writings of Sulpicius Severus', paper presented at the SBL/ AAR Annual Meeting in 1992; and see her *Making of a Heretic*, p. 146.

20. Sulpicius, *Martinian Dialogues*, 2.11, quoted by Burrus, *Making of a Heretic*, p. 146.

life of the rabbis, the structures of their practice were entirely different. Nevertheless, I think this counterpart situation in contemporary Christianity serves to help us diagnose the kinds of gender anxiety produced by the males 'dwelling in their own tents', and their available 'solutions' via forms of segregation and exclusion of women.

The Rabbinic Sexual Contract

The gender system of rabbinic culture has frequently been portrayed as a simple structure of domination and exploitation, identical to the structure of domination that is also found in modern marriage, with husbands having the right to both sexual and economic exploitation of their wives' bodies. This does not provide an accurate enough nor specific enough description of rabbinic patriarchy since, at least in theory, husbands do not have automatic sexual access to their wives; and even their economic rights in their wives' labor are limited by law. In contrast to Western legal systems, rabbinic wives continued to own their own property.[21] The significance of this point is that the doctrine of coverture—the legal disappearance of a wife into her husband's person, which was active in European legal systems until the nineteenth century[22]—did not obtain in classical Jewish law. As Levitt writes, 'In the late eighteenth century, when Jewish women entered into this legal system, they ironically became even less able to act on their own behalf'.[23]

Yet there may be no doubt that rabbinic wives are just *as* subordinated, however differently, as other women. Moreover, it is very important to emphasize that while economic and sexual coverture do not obtain for rabbinic culture, something that might best be styled spiritual coverture does. Because of the system of commandments within which significance and value are placed upon the fulfilment of a commandment that one is obligated to perform, and since women were 'exempted' from the fufilment of many commandments, they were understood as only being able to achieve spiritual merit through the enabling of their husbands to perform these commandments. Women could gain, on this system, a religious identity only through being married and through their support of their husbands' religious lives. The import of this structure of subordination of women's spiritual value to that of their husbands should not

21. Pateman, *Sexual Contract, passim,* esp. pp. 90-100.
22. Pateman, *Sexual Contract,* pp. 119-20.
23. Levitt, 'Reconfiguring Home', pp. 130-31.

be underestimated nor underemphasized, particularly at the moment that the greater autonomy and significance of women in the economic realm is being articulated. Since, for this culture, the greatest value was placed precisely on the economically 'useless' practice of Torah study, which many women enabled through their labor and business acumen, the notion of women as an exploited class of economic actors is not inapposite. At the same time, neither should we ignore the potentially greater satisfactions of a life of economic autonomy, activity and usefulness vis-à-vis life in the 'doll's house' of the bourgeoisie. Moreover, this economic autonomy at certain times has led, for example in medieval Ashkenaz, to potentially greater scope for women's religious roles as well. With regard to medieval Jewish women of France and Germany, David Biale writes,

> In fact, women in the French and German Jewish communities of the High Middle Ages appear to have enjoyed rather astonishing freedom, probably a result of their active role in business and other public professions. Women may have also demanded a greater liturgical role, for lively debates were carried on in legal circles about the place of women in the synagogue and in talmudic study.[24]

It is only, for instance, in this chronotope of Jewish history that in some communities women were counted for the *minyan*, the public quorum for prayer. Louis Finkelstein proposes that this increased religious participation—which he calls a 'movement toward "women's rights"'—including authorities who permit women to act as judges in religious courts, be counted for a quorum for grace, be called to the Torah as well as shifts toward equality in marriage and divorce laws, 'had its origin and compelling force largely in the fact that women began to occupy a prominent position in the economic world'.[25]

Pateman has described traditional European marriage in the following terms:

> Until late into the nineteenth century the legal and civil position of a wife resembled that of a slave. Under the common law doctrine of coverture, a wife, like a slave, was civilly dead. A slave had no independent legal existence apart from his master, and husband and wife

24. David Biale, *Eros and the Jews: From Biblical Israel to Contemporary America* (New York: Basic Books, 1992), p. 74; Ivan Marcus, 'Mothers, Martyrs, and Moneymakers: Some Jewish Women in Medieval Europe', *Conservative Judaism* 10 (Spring, 1986).

25. Louis Finkelstein, *Jewish Self-Government in the Middle Ages* (Philadelphia: Jewish Publication Society, 1924), pp. 378-9.

became 'one person', the person of the husband. Middle- and upper-
class women of property were able to avoid the full stringency of the
legal fiction of marital unity through the law of equity, using devices
such as trusts and pre-nuptial contracts. But such exceptions (compare:
not all slave-masters use their power to the full) do nothing to detract
from the strength of the institution of coverture as a reminder of the
terms of the conjugal relation established by (the story of) the original
contract.[26]

Throughout the nineteenth century one of the most pervasive of feminist *topoi* was that of the wife as slave. A wife was required to live
where her husband desired, her earnings and property belonged to
her husband exclusively and without exception, and she could even
be sold, sometimes at public auction.

The rabbinic Jewish system of gender relations certainly seems to
be exploitative of women's labor, and has frequently been represented as a system of virtual slavery. However, the ethos of this
system seems to be quite different from that of slavery or serfdom,
because a wife is considered an economic actor. This relation is
formally built into the legal system of the formation as a series of *quid
pro quos* and, moreover, as voluntaristic in structure. Indeed, the
talmudic text (*Ket.* 58b) explicitly distinguishes between the economic
situation of wives and slaves:

> Rav Huna said in the name of Rav: A wife is empowered to say: 'I will
> not be supported, and I will not work for him'. He holds that for the
> rabbis who enacted [the law about marital economic relations], the
> main point was to obligate husbands to support their wives, and the
> [award] of her labor [to the husband] was to prevent enmity [i.e., to
> prevent resentment on the part of the husband if he were obligated to
> support his wife and she free to earn money in addition]. And
> therefore, when she says that she does not want to be supported and
> wants to keep the product of her labor, the power is in her hands.

The argument is, in other words, that since the principal point of the
enactment of the law of marital economic relations was to benefit the
wife, if she desires to renounce both the benefits and obligations of
that law, she may. The Talmud goes on to prove this claim by
comparing the situation of wives to that of slaves and determining
that, since even in the case of a Hebrew slave one may not expro-
priate his or her labor without recompense, this is true even more so
for a wife whose status is much higher than that of a slave; and,

---

26. Carole Pateman, *The Disorder of Women: Democracy, Feminism and Political
Theory* (Stanford: Stanford University Press, 1989), p. 77; *idem, Sexual Contract*,
pp. 120-21.

therefore, she may renounce support and keep her earnings if she wishes.[27] While we may legitimately doubt how often this 'right' could in practice be exercised,[28] it remains enshrined as the established Jewish law—as, for instance, in the following quotation from the code of Maimonides:

> If the wife says: 'I will not be supported, and I will not work for him', we listen to her, and do not force her, but if the husband says: 'I will not feed you, and will take nothing from you', we do not listen to him, for perhaps her labor will not be sufficient to provide for her maintenance (Laws of Marriage [אישות], 12.4).

Although much more research and analysis would be necessary to demonstrate the point fully (and such scholars as Judith Hauptman and Miriam Peskowitz are engaged in fine-grained investigations of gender and economics in rabbinic texts and times; see, for example, their essays in this volume), it would seem to be suggested by this synecdochical point that the rabbinic system—in its symbolic structure—is *not* one in which women were interpreted as slaves to their husbands. In theory, there were institutions built into rabbinic society that enabled women to support themselves and, in later periods of rabbinic Jewish society, actual women were economically active and independent. The fact of women's economic activity in traditional Jewish culture has been used as an alibi for the entire system of oppression of women; I have, of course, no wish to return to such a mode of discourse. Nonetheless, the critique that marriage is coerced because (as in modern European society) it was the only way for a woman to support herself, while clearly not totally invalid for Jewish cultures formed by rabbinic law, loses much of its force there. Other modes of socio-cultural control have led Jewish women to seek marriage and indeed structured the discourses of male desirability within the culture.

It is also not the case in rabbinic theory that husbands have full and arbitrary control over the work-lives of their wives. They simply cannot, by rabbinic law, order their wives to perform any and every service that they desire or require.[29] The Mishnah strictly constrains

---

27. As Christine Delphy points out, even when in modern France a wife's earnings are legally established as her own, 'the custom in most marriages has been to annul this concession' (Delphy, *Close to Home*, p. 68).

28. Pateman, *Sexual Contract*, p. 158; Delphy, *Close to Home*, p. 20.

29. Cf. Delphy, who writes: 'The services which a married woman provides are not fixed. They depend on the will of the employer, her husband' (Delphy, *Close to Home*, p. 70).

the nature of the services that constitute household tasks incumbent on a wife by listing the modes of labor as grinding, baking, cooking, laundering, breastfeeding her children, making the bed, pouring water over her husband's hands and feet, and serving his food and drink. These labors clearly mark the subservient status of the wife— there is no contesting that—but they do not produce a situation within which the husband's power is unlimited and arbitrary, enabling him to demand anything of her that his whims indicate; and it is such arbitrary power without recourse that would most completely mark her status as that of slave. In addition, women who had independent means—either inherited or earned—could hire servants to perform all of these activities, thus transforming the unpaid labor of the housewife into paid labor (*m. Ket.* 5.5).[30] Once again this loophole, while not negligible symbolically, undoubtedly existed for exceedingly few women.[31] Women did have recourse to the rabbinic courts if their husbands were cruel to them or exceeded the boundaries of the considerable (but not unlimited or arbitrary!) authority that was given them to constrain the lives of their wives—and, among the sanctions that rabbinic courts would provide (when they had temporal power) were financial seizures to support a woman without her husband's consent; forced sale of his property and transfer of the proceeds to his wife; whipping; imprisoning; and various degrees of ostracism from Torah study and from the community, including full excommunication.

In the rabbinic text marriage is understood literally as a contract between the actual parties, that is, the husband and the wife, rather than as deriving from an unwritten social contract such as that described by Gerda Lerner:

> The dominated exchange submission for protection, unpaid labor for maintenance… The basis of paternalism is an unwritten contract for exchange: economic support and protection given by the male for subordination in all matters, sexual service, and unpaid domestic service given by the female.[32]

30. This is clearly not at all the same thing as a woman being given servants by her wealthy husband, 'to free her for the work of social display' (Delphy, *Close to Home*, p. 70). Note also that Rabbi Shim'on ben Gamaliel in that mishnah professes that a husband may not forbid his wife from working, because 'idleness leads to boredom'.

31. Pateman, *Sexual Contract*, pp. 111-12.

32. Gerda Lerner, *The Creation of Patriarchy* (Oxford: Oxford University Press, 1986), pp. 217-18.

Because the rabbinic marriage contract is a written contract that provides (in theory) for the possibility that the wife may refuse the exchange of economic support for unpaid domestic service and still be a wife, and that, moreover, (in principle) affords her a fair measure of agency in sexuality as well, it is significantly different from the European sexual contract described by Pateman.[33] Insofar, however, as most women had no possibility of actualizing their freedom to reject the 'sexual contract', this rabbinic law comes to appear as just another example of 'a theoretical strategy that justifies subjection by presenting it as freedom'.[34] It could be argued that in medieval and early modern Ashkenaz the society actualized this structural possibility, and women achieved a great deal of economic independence and social power.

Not atypical for early modern Jewish women, in terms of her economic status, is the famous Glikl of Hameln. Glikl had been a full partner in her husband's successful business while he was alive, and sole proprietor after his death.[35] When contracts needed to be drawn for the business, it was she who drafted the document and pursued the negotiation (p. 61). She relates that she and her sisters were 'taught in religious and worldly things' (p. 13). Perhaps more surprising, this study was, moreover, not at home but in the regular religious Jewish school, the *Cheder* (p. 14). Finally, she was highly educated in German culture of the day as well. She traveled to fairs

33. I am not disagreeing here with Laura Levitt's interpretation of the formal ritual, by which the $k^e tubb\bar{a}h$ was enacted as a contract between the groom and the community rather than between the groom and the bride ('Reconfiguring Home', p. 87). I think her analysis is essentially (with some minor reservations) correct on this point. My argument is rather that substantively, since rabbinic law understood the wife as able to decline certain obligations and privileges, the $k^e tubb\bar{a}h$ constitutes, *de facto*, an agreement (or the record of an agreement) between him and her. She has agreed to be supported in return for renouncing her own earnings but, according to the law, she could have refused this bargain were it advantageous for her to do so. It is clear that there were very few actually occurring incidences within which a bride could exercise the right to refuse to be maintained and refuse to give up her earnings, so in practice this meant little, but the symbolic potential and its meanings for the theory of marriage (i.e. the absence of coverture) are not without historical importance—nor without significance in contemporary attempts to restructure marriage within traditionalist Jewish communities, now that economic conditions have changed and many wives earn as much as or more than their husbands.

34. Pateman, *Sexual Contract*, p. 39.

35. Beth-Zion Abrahams (trans. and ed.), *Memoirs [Glückel of Hameln: Life, 1646–1724]* (New York: Thomas Yoseloff, 1963), p. 42.

all over Germany, bought and sold on the Exchange and ran a factory. In a quite matter of fact way she, moreover, describes another such woman as 'a woman of virtues [*Esches Chajil*]' because 'she carried on the business and saw to her husband and children in a handsome way' (p. 92), clearly seeing nothing aberrant in a wife as breadwinner.

It is crucial to realize that Glikl's exceptionality consists primarily in the fact of her writing; there is no reason to assume that the other aspects of her life were *sui generis*, neither her education and the partnership of her marriage, nor her business and public service life. As Natalie Zemon Davis points out, Glikl herself had good role models in her mother and grandmother.[36] Glikl writes of one Jewish woman who 'understood business well and supported the household. She went regularly to the fairs' (p. 17). Of another pious Jewish girl she writes that she 'knew French perfectly',[37] and this same girl knew Hebrew fluently as well (pp. 19-20). Early in the seventeenth century the Jews negotiated with the city of Breslau to allow women to attend that city's commercial fair, because otherwise the Jewish business would have been seriously impaired. Glikl of Hameln had in many ways the kind of marriage that Mary Wollstonecraft describes as a nearly utopian vision. Her life was the antithesis of the *höhere Tochter* [bourgeois daughter] and 'the angel in the house'. Her society, and traditional European Jewish society in general well into the nineteenth century, hardly instantiated Hegel's typical and banal view that 'The husband has the "prerogative to go out and work for the [family's] living, to attend to its needs, and to control and administer its capital"'.[38]

This economic power may have resulted in greater autonomy and satisfaction for Jewish women of this period, certainly vis-à-vis their bourgeois grand-daughters.[39] But nevertheless, since other aspects of

36. Natalie Zemon Davis, *Women on the Margins: Three Seventeenth-Century Lives* (Cambridge, MA: Harvard University Press [Belknap], 1995), p. 14. For that matter, as Davis makes clear, even her writing of an autobiography in the form of an 'ethical will' may not have been as unusual as previously thought (p. 20).

37. This, to be sure, is more like the accomplishments of the later bourgeois *höhere Tochter*.

38. Biale, *Eros*, p. 68.

39. Marion A. Kaplan, *The Making of the Jewish Middle Class: Women, Family, and Identity in Imperial Germany* (Oxford: Oxford University Press, 1991), p. 52. See also Naomi Shepherd, *A Price Below Rubies: Jewish Women as Rebels and Radicals* (Cambridge, MA: Harvard University Press, 1993), pp. 6-7, who shows the effect of this greater autonomy on mustering the participation of Jewish women in radical

male privilege were clearly in place, it has to be assumed that the essential structures of domination were the same even if subtly (perhaps significantly) shifted around or displaced. Thus

> The civil sphere gains its universal meaning in opposition to the private sphere of natural subjection and womanly capacities. The 'civil individual' is constituted within the sexual division of social life created through the original contract. The civil individual and the public realm appear universal only in relation to and in opposition to the private sphere, the natural foundation of civil life.[40]

At first glance this would seem not to apply to rabbinic society, precisely because women are not removed from the eminently public realm of commerce. But, in fact, all we have to do is to substitute the House of Study (or even the space of study of Torah in the home) for the 'public realm' in order to see that, for this rabbinic cultural system, commerce simply shifts into the structural equivalent of the 'private sphere'. In other words, technologies of domination have to be interpreted within their own systemic structure and, within the structure of rabbinic Judaism, it is precisely the 'indoor', somewhat private realm of the House of Study that defines the social prestige and power of men over women—and not the estate of getting and spending of economic power that produces such distinction in bourgeois society. Indeed, the commitment of 'men' to indoor, seemingly private pursuits of study in Ashkenazi culture was certainly one of

movements; and disputes the unsupported view of Richard Stites that the reason for the greater participation of Jewish women in such movements was owing to the 'greater despotism' of the Jewish family. In direct contrast, Shepherd argues that it was the encouragement of these women's fathers to seek education and their partial (if fraught) identification with their fathers that prodded their radicalism. Shepherd is clearly correct and supports her conclusions with hard data. Knee-jerk prejudices about Jewish society being systematically worse for women than any others die hard. Of course, at the same time, as Shepherd makes clear, the pull to radical movements was in large part a form of rebellion against the disabilities that women did suffer under traditional Jewish culture. It is important to emphasize, however, that there were many Protestant women in Western Europe—and especially England—who were leading lives quite similar in outlines, mutatis mutandis, to that of Glikl as well (Anthony Fletcher, *Gender, Sex and Subordination in England 1500–1800* [New Haven: Yale University Press, 1995], pp. 173-91). My point is hardly, then, to argue for some particular superiority of Jewish–European culture over others. My claim is rather that in its significantly different ideas about gender, Jewish culture may have provided some tools for resistance to the more severely constricted lives for women that embourgeoisement and heterosexuality provided.

40. Pateman, *Sexual Contract*, p. 177.

the factors that inscribed them as femminized in the eyes of the Others. The hierarchy in Judaism, precisely by valorizing the 'private' over the 'public', exploits gender as yet another modality by which the Jewish People in Diaspora valorizes itself over those very Others. As Burrus has remarked,

> If in some sense it is Judaism's 'colonization' that forces it into a purely (even exaggeratedly) private sphere after the fall of the Temple and thus inscribes its men as 'femminized', then the response of the resistant subculture of audaciously marking the private as 'high' (in value) and the public as 'low' and then sending its women out to deal with the public is eye-opening indeed.[41]

This seems to me a valid insight, but it must not be allowed to become another version of a Nietzschean *ressentiment* argument that then loses the critical force of the reversal of values that nevertheless has taken place, while still attending to the ways that within the culture itself gender hierarchy has revealed once more its resilience and persistence even in these altered situations. In other words, the relevant distinction is not between public and private at all, but between the most valued and less valued practices of the culture so, within the culture itself, the ascriptions of maleness and femaleness are almost reversed.[42] For this reason men, ignorant of Torah, who 'support their women' through working and selling and, thus, are more like 'real men' and Iron Johns, may be described by this society as men who are 'like women'.

A semi-documentary text taken from the autobiography of a Polish Jew, Yehiel Yeshayahu Trunk (1887–1961), and relating the story of the marriage of his great-great grandmother at the beginning of the

41. Burrus, *Making of a Heretic*, p. 7.

42. Pateman, *Sexual Contract*, pp. 113-14. See Pateman, *Disorder*, pp. 118-40 for an extensive critique of the notion of public–private as a transhistorical dichotomy. Especially relevant is her discussion of the separation of production from the household, and the development of the theory of a public–private separation (p. 123). On the other hand, see the insightful remarks of Virginia Burrus: 'Indeed, as terms of "ordinary discourse" evoking "unreflectively held notions and concepts" that shape day-to-day lives, "public" and "private" may not appear in need of interpretation at all, but it is doubtful whether the dichotomous categories with which so many operate are in fact either as universal or as transparently "commensensical" as is sometimes claimed. Indeed, I would suggest that the public–private distinction is most fruitfully applied to the study of the Priscillianist controversy precisely because it is an artifact of the very Mediterranean cultures that shaped the terms of the late-ancient controversy' (Burrus, *Making of a Heretic*, p. 7).

nineteenth century, is highly suggestive of this point:

> His mother, Devora, was a poor and simple orphan, who came from Plotsk. She had a stall in the market, and from this labor supported herself. When she had gathered an amount of money from her standing in the market for long days in sweltering heat and freezing cold and she had for some time been sexually mature she came to the local Rabbi, Rabbi Leibush the Brilliant, showed him the fund of gold coins that she had gathered through her toil, and requested that he, Rabbi Leibush the Brilliant, would provide for her a husband who was a Talmudic scholar. Rabbi Leibush answered her that he knew in Plotsk a Jew, somewhat advanced in age, who was a great Talmudic scholar, and who was supporting himself through teaching children. The man was poor and destitute, but an outstanding sage...
>
> The damsel, Devora asked Rabbi Leibush the Brilliant: 'Is this poor schoolmaster truly a great Talmudic scholar?'
>
> 'Yes, my daughter', answered her Rabbi Leibush, 'he is an outstanding Talmudic sage'.
>
> 'If so,' said the orphan Devora, 'I agree'.
>
> From this union was born only one son, he was Rabbi Yehoshuale Kutner.[43]

This is truly a remarkable story in many ways, and paradigmatic, I suggest, of rabbinic culture. We have here several reversals of the gendered expectations of bourgeois European culture. First of all, the dominant, desiring subject is clearly the female one. It is she who seeks to find a husband. It is important to emphasize, moreover, that she is totally independent of father and brother and any other male who could directly control her desire. To be sure, her desire is constructed by her cultural formation but, then, so is all desire. Precisely the point of my research is to inquire as to what sort of desire this culture constructed or sought to construct. Secondly, in order to find the sort of husband that she desires, she must be economically well established. She accomplishes this task, presumably starting from nothing, through great effort. The prospective bridegroom, on the other hand, is working as the Jewish equivalent of a governess. I do not mean, of course, to imply that he is doing women's work from the point of view of Jewish culture; he is not. However, in terms of a Western European marriage plot, it would be a young woman who would be supporting herself through the honorable but somewhat humble work of taking care of others' children until an economically established man would come along to

43. Yehiel Yeshayahu Trunk, *Polin: Memories and Portraits* (trans. from Hebrew by Ezra Fleischer; Jerusalem, 1962), pp. 6-7.

rescue her into a marriage. Here, once more, the plot is reversed. Although the text does not make this explicit, we should understand that from now on the husband will devote himself entirely to study, no longer forced to waste his time on the teaching of children and no longer oppressed by grinding poverty. He now has a proper wife to support him. At least for the narrative's purposes, it is simply assumed that he would agree. Finally, the story has a happy ending because, although only one child was born of the union, he was a very famous talmudic sage and rabbi in his own right, the eminent Rabbi Yehoshuale Kutner. In a sense that is the whole point of the story, to narrate the birth of the hero. To be sure, however, this is also a story that has been filtered through a male textuality; yet it is not, I suggest, entirely imaginary that within this cultural formation such a man, a slightly ageing, economically ineffective, but brilliant talmudic scholar, would be desired as an object for marriage on the part of a nubile and economically independent young woman. I think that this nineteenth-century case history provides a perfect exemplum for the point that I am making. Women are not subordinated within rabbinic culture through economic uselessness but, rather, through economic utility. Men do not dominate within rabbinic culture through the exercise of economic power but rather through their exiting from the world of economic action. The structures are reversed from those of general European society; the essential hierarchy and system of male domination remains firmly in place.

Orthodox Feminists: Reina Batya and Bertha Pappenheim

In the nineteenth century we begin also to hear the voices of Jewish women reacting to and reflecting upon their situation within the cultural–religious system. In fact, one could begin to trace such a genealogy back to the eighteenth century in the person of Sarah Rebecca Rachel Leah, daughter of Yukl Horowitz, who was learned in Hebrew and Aramaic and wrote women's prayers in which she protested against the marginalization of women in Ashkenazic religious life.[44] Later in the nineteenth century (and in the twentieth cen-

44. Chava Weissler, 'Women's Studies and Women's Prayers: Reconstructing the Religious History of Ashkenazic Women', *Jewish Social Studies* NS 1.2 (Winter, 1995), pp. 28-47 (40-42). I only part from Weissler's remarkable essay in disagreeing with her statement to the effect that, 'Whatever Leah had to say on this topic, and on the others she takes up in the introduction, her voice was effectively silenced, or perhaps it would be more precise to say that there was no audience who could hear her' (p. 41). I would suggest that she is at the beginning of a

tury even more so) these voices are increasingly those of women, such as Devora Baron[45] or Puah Rakowski and Ita Kalish,[46] who have 'left the fold' of traditional Judaism. I will discuss here women who can be said to have remained within (in their own perceptions and desires) the traditional community and system of values, while registering pain and strong protest against the ways that system marginalizes, excludes, disempowers and oppresses them. The longing for study of Torah and the recognition of the pain of exclusion are reflected in the Yiddish books of religion for women from the early modern period, which indicate that the reward for female piety in this world is learning Torah 'just like men' in the next.[47] These explicit nineteenth-century female voices go beyond this longing, and begin to articulate the clear understanding that it is the exclusion from Torah study that subtends the whole system of domination of women. From the early modern period on we are not confined (as we are for much of earlier Jewish history) to projections of female voices as imagined by men.

Reina Batya, The Wife of the Natziv, and her Protest

A remarkable memoir, written in the early twentieth century, provides evidence of women's protests against the system of exclusion at the very parnassus of the Yeshiva world.[48] The woman, Reina Batya of Volozhin, was the daughter of a rabbinic leader of Lithuanian Jewry in the generation before her and the wife of Lithuanian Jewry's greatest talmudic and religious authority of her generation—The Natziv, Rabbi Naftali Tzvi Berlin. Although the text, unfortunately, once again preserves the woman's voice only as filtered through a male amanuensis, a nephew, I believe that in this case its evidence is no less precious for reasons that should become clear below. The conversation reported would have taken place in the last quarter of the nineteenth century. Since the text has never been published in full in English, and is difficult to find even in Hebrew, I shall provide here a fairly long extract:

groundswell that finds its full force a century later, and that was empowered precisely by learned women like her.

45. Seidman, *Marriage*, p. 252.

46. Hyman, *Gender*, pp. 57-58, 62-64.

47. Chava Weissler, 'The Religion of Traditional Ashkenazic Women: Some Methodological Issues', *Association for Jewish Studies Review* 12.1 (Spring, 1987), p. 93; 'Women in Paradise', *Tikkun* 2.2 (1987), pp. 43-46, 117-20.

48. I wish to thank my friend, Yaakov Elman, for pointing me to this text.

I frequently heard her complaining and protesting, in pain and distress, with angry heart and bitter spirit, about the bitter fate and meager portion of women in the life of the world, because they deprived them of the fulfillment of time-bound commandments such as phylacteries and fringes, sitting in the *sukkah* and waving the *lulav*, and much much more.

And in the midst of this protest, there used to shine through a tacit complaint and envy of men who had received everything, 'who had (as she expressed it) 248 positive commandments, while to the abject and humiliated women, only three were given'.

Although within the Ashkenazi tradition women had been 'allowed' to perform the commandments that Reina Batya mentions, their participation had been considered as voluntary, as superogatory and therefore as less significant than that of men. In contrast to a Protestant religious sensibility in which it would be precisely the free, unobligated performance of works that would be considered 'higher', within Judaism it is the fulfilment of that which is 'forced' upon one that is read as the most consequential and therefore socially prestigious. Reina Batya's interpretation of the exemption of women from positive commandments as abjection and humiliation is thus entirely on point, and apologists who refer to 'permission' for women to perform commandments have missed the point.

The text continues:

Even more than this, she was worried and vexed about the defiled honour of the women and their lowly status due to the fact that the rabbis forbid teaching them Torah. One time she told me that if Eve (meaning the female sex) was cursed with ten curses, this curse [the prohibition] of learning Torah, is equivalent to all the curses, and is even more than all of them. There was no end to the grief.

One time, while she was speaking with great feeling on this subject, I said to her, 'But my aunt, you women are blaming the men for this prohibition when they are not at fault. You yourselves caused this and you are guilty in the matter', and I explained my words. Our sages said (at the end of the second chapter of *Avot de Rabbi Natan* [an early midrash]) that Torah should only be taught to a humble person. About women, our Sages decided in *Yerushalmi Shabbat* [i.e. the Palestinian Talmud], Chapter 6, that 'they [women] are jaunty' [*šaḥṣāniyôt*, a rare Aramaic term], meaning that they are proud. If so, isn't it forbidden to teach them Torah because of their character traits, and who is to blame if not they themselves, and why do they complain?

She said to me: 'I am not clearly convinced of the meaning of the word "jaunty", whether it in fact refers to pride, and from where do you know this?'

I said to her: 'I also did not understand this word, but that is the way

that the scholars understand it, and the only other source that I know
for it is Rashi's commentary on Tractate *Shabbat* (62b), for with respect
to what it says there that "the people of Jerusalem are people of *šahaṣ*",
Rashi interpreted that they speak in a prideful manner, and similarly
with this interpretation one can explain the words of the *Tosafot* on
Pesaḥim'...

She said to me: 'When I have free time I will do research on the word
and find out the exact meaning. In the meantime bring me *Avot de Rabbi
Natan* and I will investigate the text that you cited'. I went and brought
and fell right into the trap!

For in *Avot de Rabbi Natan* the wording is as follows: 'Bet Shammai
says: "A person shall only teach to one who is clever, humble and rich";
and Bet Hillel says: "We teach to everyone, because there were many
sinners in Israel and they started learning the Torah and became righteous, observant men"'.

As she finished reading these words, she raised her voice in anger and
said, 'How did you do this evil thing, or was it because you wanted to
trick me that you took the opinion of Bet Shammai as the basis for your
word? Every boy who has studied even a little Talmud, and even one
who is only learning in elementary school, knows that when there is a
disagreement between Bet Shammai and Bet Hillel, the law is in accordance with Bet Hillel, and here Bet Hillel permits teaching Torah to
everyone!'

And I told her the truth that I am not guilty in the matter, for the words
that I had cited I did not know from their original source, from the text
of *Avot de Rabbi Natan*, but from one of the books in which it was
quoted, and there *they only cited the words of Bet Shammai* [emphasis in
the original]!

As she was in good spirits at her victory, she was no longer angry with
me, and when she saw that I was somewhat upset, she was sorry, and
she comforted me and said to me: 'You are released, you are forgiven,
for this sort of deception is not a new thing in the hands of the scholars
and the authors, and such it was always, but in the future be more careful about it!'[49]

This document provides us with a subtle but clear articulation of the
problems of authority and voice in the matter of control of women
regarding the study of Torah. At an earlier point in the conversation,
not reproduced here, Reina Batya had already rebuked the nephew
for citing a text that he had not read in the original, and here demonstrates to him the inadequacy, indeed the falsehood of his argument
against her, owing to the same 'deception'. He has produced an
argument for the prohibition of women from the study of Torah
based on an interpretation of a text from the Palestinian Talmud,

---

49. Boruch Epstein, *Mekor Boruch: My Memoirs from the Previous Generation* (4
vols.; Lithuania: Rom, 1928), pp. 1950-52.

which he had not seen in the original either, and a text from the midrash (*Avot de Rabbi Natan*) which, as it turns out, he misquotes in a crucial way. Reina Batya contests his interpretation on two grounds. First of all, that it is dependent on a virtually unsupported interpretation of a word that is nearly a *hapax legomenon*; and secondly, that once the full text of the *Avot de Rabbi Natan* is read, its conclusion turns out to be the exact opposite from what was claimed. The interpretation of the rare word that the nephew had relied upon is cited in the name of 'the scholars', that is, the contemporary community of talmudists, and the truncated text that he had cited came also from a contemporary secondary source. The net effect of these two interventions on Reina Batya's part is to demonstrate fully that the 'prohibition' of women from studying Torah is an artifact of the exercise of hermeneutic authority on the part of the later tradition which, by selectively interpreting and quoting the rabbinic sources just as the nephew has done, produces this very prohibition. Reina Batya's voice represents a plea for scholarly standards, for a virtually 'modern' critical attention to 'original sources' and contexts—indeed, for historical criticism over against the naive ahistorical method of the nephew, representing the style of scholarship of the Yeshiva that depends on blind authority (at least on this issue) rather than on critical text analysis. It is not only, then, that she 'wins' the argument, but that she does so through demonstrating the superiority of her learning to that of the very man (men) contesting her right and obligation to study.

Reina Batya then goes on to cite positive examples of learned women in support of her claim that the 'prohibition' is an arbitrary imposition by a male power structure of a system of insults to women and not something that is mandated by the Torah:

> And in a continuation of the discussion and with intent to lend force to her protest, she accounted and mentioned the names of many learned women: Beruria, the wife of Rabbi Me'ir, Yalta, the wife of Rav Nahman, and the daughter of Rabbi Hanina the son of Teradion, the mother of the author of the S^ema' [a central early modern halakhic work], and the sister of Rabbi Yeshaya Berlin Pik, and then she finished by asking, 'And what wrong did they [the rabbis] find in them that they had learned Torah?' And in no wise was she willing to acquiesce in the terrible shame to women and this violation of their dignity in this exclusion of them from the study of Torah.
>
> I remember that when she mentioned the name of Beruria, the wife of Rabbi Me'ir, I told her that a wrongdoing was found against her that she mocked the words of our sages, for 'women are light-headed'. In the end

she herself was guilty of light-headedness, as is brought out in the story
of Rashi on *Aboda Zara* 18b.
She answered me, 'In truth, I know of this legend, but did our Sages find
all men guilty because of the sin of *Aḥer*, who left the right way (*Hagiga*
15a)? Furthermore, Beruria did not mock with contempt and derision.
She only thought that our Sages did not fully understand the rationality
of women. According to her view, women are also strong-minded. This
was the entire incident and nothing more'.[50]

This is an extraordinary text that can be taken as a representation of
an actual woman's protest. I am fully cognizant of the ways that
male self-presentation as defeated can provide complex rhetorical
advantages in contestations with other men.[51] Indeed, it is conceiv-
able in this case that the issue is precisely conflict over canons of
scholarly criticism, and that our author is covertly attacking (almost
caricaturing) the standards of the mediocre practices of scholarship
that were all too common in the Yeshiva. (Given his position as a
scion of a particularly acute scholarly and critical family, this would
make a great deal of sense.) Nevertheless, this does not preclude the
possibility—even the plausibility—of the conversation having happened, and the loss of our ability to recover a feminist grandmother
(for me, almost literally a grandmother) here seems a price too high to
pay for hyper-suspiciousness. My great grandmother, Miriam, of
approximately the same generation as Reina Batya and the same
status and class, is famous to this day for her Bible scholarship and
for knowing the entire Bible by heart with traditional commentaries.
(My other great grandmother, more the Glikl type, ran a lumber yard
and supported her family in style while her husband studied Torah.)
The discursive force of this powerful text, mediated from male interlocutor (nephew) to this male feminist writer (the 'grandson'), is
clearly both a *cri de coeur* and a highly sophisticated protest. Both
aspects are significant—both the depth of the anger and pain, and the
perspicacity of the feminist and critical analysis.

    First of all, let me emphasize that which is crucial to my argument.
This is a protest from within the very nerve center of rabbinic Judaism in the nineteenth century. This woman was married to the dominant spiritual, practical and intellectual leader of the Lithuanian
Jews of that time and thus of the Ashkenazic (non-Hasidic) world.
There is no sign, moreover, in this text that she wished to be anything
else, although here the fact that we have a secondhand report might
indeed raise some questions. There are no indications from outside

50. Epstein, *Mekor Boruch*, p. 1953.
51. Epstein, *Mekor Boruch*, p. 1949.

this text that Reina Batya was disaffected about Judaism in general. She did, however, protest strenuously against the domination of and insult to women that was produced, as she correctly perceived, by the exclusion of women from the study of Torah. In a move prescient of much later stratagems to reclaim Lilith or Dora, moreover, she turns Beruria, a figure of the medieval tale designed to protect the boundaries of male privilege, into a protofeminist. Although indirectly, she is in effect contesting the very assertion that the rabbis have the right to determine the nature and status of women, 'to establish that women are "jaunty"'. Beruria wished only to explain to the sages the rationality of women, *which they did not understand* and, by implication, continue not to understand.

Notably material, moreover, is the fact that this woman is clearly highly learned by any standards. The nephew describes her as spending all of her time, winter and summer, sitting at a table in the dining hall of the house with the Bible, the Mishnah, various midrashic texts, other religious literatures and traditional historiographies before her, studying day and night. He describes her as 'righteous, wise, modest, and outstandingly learned, equal [in learning] to exemplary men'.[52] She is not only familiar with the contents of the arguments that her scholarly nephew provides, but she can counter them with examples and arguments that disprove their validity. She

52. It should be remarked that even this exclusion was not as total as is sometimes imagined. In an apparent memoir, couched as a short story, Rebecca Goldstein writes:

> So both my father and my mother taught the Jewish subjects to Gideon and me. There was no gender discrimination in what they taught us. My father studied Talmud with me just as hard and as long as with Gideon. I know that Orthodox Jews are rumored to be sexist. Hell, it's no rumor.One sage wrote that it was better for the sacred books to be burned before they were taught to Jewish daughters. And the Vilna Gaon warned, in a letter to his daughters, that women should stay away from the synagogue, since they're likely to engage there in nothing more uplifting than malicious gossip, which is a fairly serious sin in Judaism.
> My family wasn't at all tainted by this kind of bigotry...
> I've read some of the angry literature that's been put out recently by Jewish feminists. And truly there seems to be a lot there to be angry about. All I can say is that the kind of mindless dismissal of girls that seems to typify certain parts of the Orthodox Jewish world simply wasn't my experience at all (Rebecca Goldstein, *Strange Attractors: Stories* [New York: Viking, 1993], pp. 205-206).

Quite obviously the perceptions of Judaism among women in those 'certain parts of the Orthodox Jewish world' and in Telz (Lithuania), where this author's family (and mine) came from, will be quite different.

is competent, likewise, to seek out the text, a classical Hebrew–Aramaic rabbinic text, that he cites and confute his interpretation, indeed to argue for certain bad faith on his part since he violated, albeit through carelessness, the usual canons of authority in preferring Bet Shammai's view over that of Bet Hillel. Finally, she indicates that she intends to do further lexicographical work on the meaning of a technical term in rabbinic Hebrew that is critical for determining the rabbis' true position on women learning Torah. In spite of her obvious erudition in Torah, this exceedingly learned woman bitterly (and seemingly paradoxically) protests her exclusion from the learning of Torah and the cruel sense of indignity that it produces for her and her sisters. What must be concluded from this argument is that the exclusion of women from Torah was not intended to keep them in ignorance, nor was it the product of a sense that women were contaminated and contaminating, as some scholars have erroneously interpreted it, but was purely and simply a means for the maintenance of a male power-structure via the symbolic exclusion of women from the single practice most valued in the culture, the study of Talmud. It is the study of Talmud alone, the 'Oral Torah', to which is ascribed the dignity of the title 'Torah study' over and against, then, study of the actual 'Written Torah', the Five Books of Moses, itself or its commentaries. Women of the learned classes were encouraged to become competent scholars of everything *except the Talmud itself*. My great grandmother's prodigious Bible-learning, for all the respect that it earned her, would have been considered eccentric at best in a man, who ought to have been spending his time studying Torah, which certainly means for this community the Talmud and its commentaries. This text thus strongly supports the stance that I and others have maintained, to the effect that the exclusion of women from the study of Torah, that is, Talmud, is not a religiously necessary principle but a sociological development that subtended the entire system of male domination of women within the society, what Reina Batya calls the 'defiled honour of the women and their lowly status'; and it is here, as well understood by Reina Batya, that pressure must be put on the system (and indeed can be put on the system) if that domination is to end. Insofar, then, as Beruria represents a structural possibility nascently actualized in contemporary Orthodox Jewish life that female subjects will engage fully in the study of Torah, there is also the prospect of a revolution in gender within current Jewish life as well. The important question in my mind is whether or not such a revolution will require a loss of the useful and positively marked categories of traditional Jewish gendering as well, namely the construction of maleness as gentle, receptive and nurturing, femaleness as powerful and competent. The critical project is to see that it does not.

Bertha Pappenheim and 'The Jewish Woman'

> 'If there will be justice in the world to come, women will be lawgivers, and men have to have babies (Bertha Pappenheim).[53]

Another nineteenth- (and early twentieth-) century Jewish woman who strenuously protested the exclusion of women from Torah, while retaining her allegiance to Jewish traditional culture and religion itself, was Bertha Pappenheim. In her essay 'The Jewish Woman', Pappenheim documents 'a cultural dichotomy in the life of the Jewish woman, as was demonstrated in the widely held view that women were to "be Jewish", but were not allowed to learn'.[54] 'Learn' is indeed the proper translation here, not 'study', because Pappenheim is referring accurately to the religious practice known as 'learning Torah', that is, study of the Talmud. Pappenheim continues with her strong voice of protest:

> The People of the Book closed the entry way to Jewish spiritual life, to its fountainheads, to women; only piecemeal and cropped were they to have faith and act, without knowing why. No *Bes-Jakob* School, no continuing education can repair how the souls of Jewish women and thus Judaism in its entirety has been sinned against, by withholding the Jewish meaning of life from the unknown Jewish woman, harnessing just her physical strength to the man. The wife of the Jew was allowed to carry the building blocks of family life as a beast of burden; in numbness is she to keep in step. But how she was praised and lauded, the *eshes hayil* (*Minnesang* with *gefilte* [stuffed] fish), how much the male-human interpretations of the law turned against her, whose spirit was certainly receptive and ready!

In this brilliantly bitter moment Pappenheim presents a sophisticated feminist analysis of the gender system of rabbinic Judaism, and its version of controlling women through a combination of exaltation and exclusion. There is both a caustic protest against the 'sin against the souls of Jewish women', reminiscent in tone to that of Reina

53. Bertha Pappenheim (Dora Edinger, *Bertha Pappenheim: Freud's Anna O.* [Highland Park, Illinois: Congregation Solel, 1968]), p. 95.

54. Bertha Pappenheim, 'The Jewish Woman', in Dora Edinger (ed.), *Bertha Pappenheim: Leben und Schriften* (Frankfurt am Main: Ner-Tamid Publishers, 1963). I am using here a translation made for me by Renata Stein.

Batya; and the sarcastic reference to the song (from Proverbs 31) that is sung in praise of the Jewish wife every Friday night at the dinner table, just before she serves the *gefilte* fish.

But it must nevertheless be noted that the tone and purpose of Pappenheim's critique, however bitter, is to ensure that traditional Jewish life be reformed so that it could continue with vitality and justice. As evidence of her ongoing allegiance to Orthodoxy, I offer the following quotation:

> Naturally the women went to the Temple on the High Holidays, the older ones also on Saturday, but they could not follow the services properly. Here the fracture, leading to the Liberal and Reform liturgy in later decades, already begins. Wouldn't it have been more reasonable to educate the women and of course not the women alone of the congregation to understand the service, rather than building a service that unhistorically and without tradition conforms to the failing understanding of the congregation?[55]

It is clear from this citation that, in the very heart of her feminist protest, Pappenheim remained convinced that the historical and traditional form of the culture and its practices held vitality and a future, and that that future was crucial for her.

Something of the complexity and nuance of Pappenheim's perceptions of traditional Judaism may be garnered from the following letter that she wrote on one of her trips to Galicia, as part of a series of letters she wrote to the members of her women's group and eventually published under the title *The Work of Sisyphus* (1912):

> I was yesterday with Frau B. at the Wonder Rabbi's, a visit most interesting in thousands of details. Frau B. is German, from Silesia, highly respected all over; specially since she still lives strictly orthodox. It was quite doubtful whether the Rabbi would receive us, but a Frau D. who lives in B.'s house is the rabbi's sister, and she introduced us.
>
> This woman is a true living Glückel von Hameln. It's just wonderful of what and how she talks, her faith, her common sense, her naivete. I hope I remember the story she told me as a parallel to the exposure of Moses. But since it took at least half an hour to tell, I cannot possibly write it down. She asked about my business, of course. She grasped, with incredible speed, when I explained what I wanted to achieve. She looked at me with doubtfully raised eyebrows, and said, 'A swallow

55. I would also note that her account of the origins of Reform Judaism, as due to the forced ignorance of the women, is a compelling early example of the insight that accrues when a feminist perspective is brought to bear on Jewish history. This is at least as convincing a thesis, in my opinion, as the more famous one of Scholem who attributes Reform Judaism to the aftermath of the Sabbatai Zevi false messiah convulsion of the seventeenth century.

wants to drain the *Yam* [sea]? *Rebbaun schel aulom* [the Lord] may help, but since it is done in purity to the Lord's praise, my brother, the rabbi, may he live, will also help.' Isn't that the true Glückel? She introduced us to her dear sister-in-law, the Rabbi's wife. Then I told her about the women's movement, and she told me right away how she talks to young wives, and to husbands, too. We spoke about the illegitimate children, the *Mamser* [the child of an illicit union who can never marry except for another *mamser*] and much more—she just could not finish spitting [to ward off the evil eye]. Finally, audience at the Rabbi's. We had waited for two hours. Piously, he turned his back to me. I gave a vivid lecture. He called my endeavor a great *Mitzvah* [religious commandment]; he will warn people in his own circle [of the dangers of the procurers of girls]. I am to write down all I told him. And he helped; I think it was good and important and right to have been at the Alexandrover's. Respect for the Rabbi is such that there is complete silence in his house—only if one knows how Hasidic Jews behave, can one understand what this does mean.[56]

We learn much from this rich document that has been nearly ignored until now in the readings of Bertha Pappenheim. In the very heat of her struggle against fearful effective collusion of Jewish society in the forced prostitution of young Jewish girls, she finds time and energy to sing the praises of a vital, learned Jewish woman she meets, calling her a true Glikl. All of her writings suggest that she wanted to cure a 'sick patient', not to kill it. As Marion Kaplan has written,

> Her convictions as a religious Jew were as intense as her feminist beliefs. While her feminism was often incompatible with Jewish tradition, bringing her into conflict with the Jewish establishment, she insisted that only greater participation by women in their community would prevent Judaism's decline.[57]

More interesting than the behavior of the 'Wonder Rabbi' [Miracle-working Hasidic leader] is the practice of his sister, who is both clearly learned in rabbinic lore and a religious leader in her own right. The Polish Wonder Rabbi's wife counsels not only the young women but also their young husbands, and this in one of the most traditional possible of all European Jewish communities. In the context, since this statement that she speaks to the young husbands follows immediately after 'I told her about the women's movement',

---

56. Bertha Pappenheim, *Sisyphus-Arbeit: Reisebriefe aus den Jahren 1911 und 1912* (Leipzig: Verlag Paul E. Linder, 1924), pp. 149-50; ET in Edinger, *Bertha Pappenheim*, p. 46.

57. Marion A. Kaplan, 'Anna O. and Bertha Pappenheim: An Historical Perspective', in Max Rosenbaum and Melvin Muroff (eds.), *Anna O.: Fourteen Contemporary Reinterpretations* (New York: Free Press, 1984), pp. 101-17 (102).

the suggestion is that the content of the rabbi's wife's address to the couples was 'feminist' as well. Pappenheim compares these powerful Jewish women with Glikl, Pappenheim's ancestor, whose work she translated and with whom she identified.[58] Glikl of Hameln was the first great female literary voice in Jewish history (since Miriam and Deborah in the Bible; see above). Her text is thoroughly informed by the Old Yiddish literary tradition, including prayers for women, a translation and classic commentary on the Bible and books of legends and moral instruction. As rich a literary life as these works provided, however, by the nineteenth century we can meet pious ('Orthodox') Jewish women in both eastern and central Europe for whom the women's literary tradition is not sufficient, because they recognize the spiritual and cultural power that full access to the most fully canonical rabbinic tradition offers.

Interestingly enough, at the same time that these women are strenuously protesting the exclusion of women from the study of Torah, it is their access to the Yiddish literary canon that provides them with the terms and the power, as well in certain measure with the animus, with which to protest. It is in this letter that Pappenheim most clearly articulates her identification of Glikl as a role model for Jewish women and suggests that this powerful, capable type of woman is not unknown among the *Ostjuden* (East-European Jews) of her day. This text bears out, then, my claim that Bertha Pappenheim is at one and the same time a militant critic *and* passionate defender of traditional Jewish life: critic of the subordination of women in the religious sphere, and advocate of their traditional economic and social power. She, moreover, desires reform of the religious sphere precisely so that its traditional form ('Orthodoxy') may continue and not be replaced by what she herself perceives are debased imitations of Protestant culture. This dual critique and redemption provides the most important model for me in my own work on rabbinic Judaism.

These first-wave Orthodox feminist analyses support the thesis to which the analysis of this essay has been pointing. Traditionally, European Jewish women maintained a great deal of economic autonomy and power together with the respect and prestige that these conferred and, moreover, were *normatively* protected by the culture from both exploitation and violence—as opposed to a legal system surrounding them that enfranchised men to exploit and brutalize 'their' women at will. But this does not, in any way, forestall or

58. For the clue that got me going in this direction, as for much else, I am grateful to Juliet Mitchell.

weaken a feminist critique of the rabbinic Jewish social system. Indeed, it may be that rabbinic patriarchy is a partial anticipation of the 'kinder, gentler patriarchy'—what Aviva Cantor calls a 'reformed patriarchy'—that in some quarters is seen as being in the birthing today, an even more powerful and astute domination of women by men to secure their (male) desires than the gross physical dominations, namely permission to beat, rape and sell, encoded by European custom and common law. Nevertheless, as Bertha Pappenheim clearly saw, the way forward into a feminist modernity for rabbinic culture does not necessitate an abandonment of the culture *tout court* but, rather, the recovery and retention of the (relative) power for women it did maintain as well as the virtues of alternative and oppositional male socialization that it produced, while investing full participation of women in the power and prestige-producing central practice of Torah study.

IX

THE PERSONAL/AUTOBIOGRAPHICAL

REFLECTIONS ON DAVID

David M. Gunn

Invited to reflect on my writing on David over the past two decades, I find myself reading what I have not read in years. *The Story of King David*[1] grew out of several pieces I had written on oral tradition and the books of Samuel, together with a literary critical essay which Robert Culley invited me to write for one of the first issues of *Semeia*[2] and which was spurred on by some essays on David coming from Walter Brueggemann.[3] A critique of consensus views, especially since Leonhard Rost's influential work,[4] of the genre, purpose and boundaries of the so-called 'Succession Narrative' or 'Court History' (2 Samuel 9–20 and 1 Kings 1–2) and a detailed source-critical argument for including in its extent at least 2 Samuel 2–4 (with 5.1-3 and parts of ch. 6) rounded out the book. This was a literary-critical enterprise built squarely on an historical-critical base. I have never attempted (or wanted) to undertake such a project again. Let me expand that comment a little.

First, I find that the literary–critical 'interpretation' stays with me. Most of it I would say again today, if a little differently, though I am struck by what I did not say, and know that I did not even think about. Where, for example, are David's concubines (2 Sam. 15.16, 20.3) in my reading? But let me come back to them and the 'interpretation' a little later.

Secondly, the work on oral tradition (I had comparative experience in Homeric studies and Serbo-Croatian heroic songs) left me con-

---

1. D.M. Gunn, *The Story of King David: Genre and Interpretation* (JSOTSup, 6; Sheffield: JSOT Press, 1978).

2. D.M. Gunn, 'David and the Gift of the Kingdom', in R.C. Culley (ed.), *Classical Hebrew Narrative* (Semeia 3; Missoula, MT: Scholars Press, 1975), pp. 14-45.

3. E.g. W. Brueggemann, 'Life and Death in Tenth Century Israel', *JAAR* 40 (1971), pp. 96-109; 'On Coping with Curse: A Study of 2 Sam. 16:5-14', *CBQ* 36 (1974), pp. 175-92.

4. L. Rost, *The Succession to the Throne of David* (trans. M.D. Rutter and D.M. Gunn; Historic Texts and Interpreters in Biblical Scholarship, 1; Sheffield: Almond Press, 1982 [1926]).

vinced that, while my argument for characterizing the narrative style of the 'King David' story as 'traditional' was (and still is) sustainable, the possibility of determining with any precision the relationship between these texts and a living oral tradition was remote; and nothing published since has necessitated my revising that conclusion. As a result I have come to treat these texts in practice as 'literary' texts, though I must recognize that this may be something of an anachronism and that a poetics of orality may yet prove to open them to a different understanding.

Thirdly, while I believe that my argument concerning the boundaries of the hypothetical 'source' text in 2 Samuel (including chs. 2–4 [etc.] with 9–20 and 1 Kings 1–2) also holds up remarkably well, the practical result was a demonstration that, even so, the beginning of the postulated source could still not be determined with any precision; and that the relationship between the so-called 'Succession Narrative' and the 'sources' in 1 Samuel is beyond determination. In source-critical terms, the so-called 'Story of David's Rise' is a bogus document, lacking any convincing clarification in relation to the sources in 2 Samuel. More than that, I learned in due course that close argument had little bearing on the formation of historical-critical consensus. Like 'J' and 'E' and 'P', the 'Succession Narrative' and the 'Story of David's Rise' had become reified by the time I was writing. Arguments like mine or those of Hannelis Schulte[5] or even Rost himself (who did not define his narrative as beginning at 2 Samuel 9) were simply a bothersome complication in the way of an elegant simplicity. No need to counter the arguments—just go on repeating the 'consensus'. (Frank Cross's simplistic double redaction hypothesis of the so-called 'Deuteronomistic History'[6] has survived by the same process, despite wholesale undermining by his own pupils attempting to shore up the hypothesis!) The experience deepened my scepticism regarding the 'assured results' of historical-critical study of the Bible, and convinced me that to build my literary-critical work on such foundations was to build on quicksand. There was quicksand enough in literary criticism! Accordingly my next book, *The Fate of King Saul*,[7] ignored historical-critical boundaries

5. H. Schulte, *Die Entstehung der Geschichtschreibung im alten Israel* (BZAW, 128; Berlin: de Gruyter, 1972).

6. F.M. Cross, Jr, 'The Themes of the Book of Kings and the Structure of the Deuteronomistic History', in *Canaanite Myth and Hebrew Epic* (Cambridge, MA: Harvard University Press, 1973), pp. 274-89.

7. D.M. Gunn, *The Fate of King Saul: An Interpretation of a Biblical Story* (JSOTSup, 14; Sheffield: JSOT Press, 1980).

altogether and ventured a 'final form' reading as a literary critic.

This point leads me to say something further about the 'interpretation' of both the David and Saul narratives. At this distance it is easy to see how dislocated biblical studies had become from the study of literature in other fields. At the time—in the mid-seventies— I was so caught up with 'mastering' the conventions of historical-critical biblical scholarship and, at the same time, breaking with those conventions that I barely noticed how cognate literary studies had been going through a revolution since I learned the craft of a literary critic in high school and university in Melbourne (Australia) in the early sixties. I practised my biblical literary criticism much in the mode of the 'close reading' that F.R. Leavis typified;[8] and my lifelong fascination with literary ambiguity had been honed by William Empson's *Seven Types of Ambiguity*.[9] (Indeed, Empson was still a professor at the University of Sheffield in England when I took up my first appointment there in 1970.) By 1980 I knew a little more of the impact critical theory was having outside our field, and struggled without much success to digest the diet of structuralism that *Semeia* fed us (David Jobling and Edmund Leach kept my interest alive[10]). When a reviewer mentioned approvingly my deployment of the insights of structuralism I was touched but more than a trifle bewildered.

The fact was, I was still at heart a Leavisite—akin to a 'New Critic' in American parlance. That meant placing a high value on the text as the repository of its own meaning, largely independent of author and location (and hence anathema to historical criticism), though these factors, in practice, were not wholly ignored. The practice of criticism meant not only expertise in analyzing the text's salient compositional elements, but the exercise of a judgment of the text's value that

8.   For example F.R. Leavis, *Revaluation: Tradition and Development in English Poetry* (London: Chatto & Windus, 1936); *idem*, *New Bearings in English Poetry* (London: Chatto & Windus, 1938); *idem*, *The Great Tradition: George Eliot, Henry James, Joseph Conrad* (London: Chatto & Windus, 1948).

9.   W. Empson, *Seven Types of Ambiguity* (London: Chatto & Windus, 1930; Harmondsworth: Penguin Books, 1965 [1961]).

10.   D. Jobling, *The Sense of Biblical Narrative: Three Structural Analyses in the Old Testament* (JSOTSup, 7; Sheffield: JSOT Press, 1978; repr. 1986 as *The Sense of Biblical Narrative: Structural Analyses in the Hebrew Bible*, I); D. Jobling, *The Sense of Biblical Narrative: Structural Analyses in the Hebrew Bible*, II (JSOTSup, 39; Sheffield: JSOT Press, 1986); E. Leach, *Genesis as Myth and Other Essays* (London: Jonathan Cape, 1969); and E. Leach and D.A. Aycock, *Structuralist Interpretations of Biblical Myth* (Cambridge: Cambridge University Press, 1983).

was, at the same time, both 'aesthetic' and 'moral'. It was this under-standing of 'literature' as work of serious entertainment (borrowing from Matthew Arnold's typifying of great poetry as work of 'high seriousness') that offered me a frame for reading David and Saul in the books of Samuel.

What was missing in all this, of course, was a critical inquiry into the bases on which the critic's judgments were made. Which is to say, I read without serious self-reflection. Today, the necessity of such a process is taken (by many) to be self-evident! I am even invited to self-reflect in print.

Looking back at my readings with this question of 'judgment' in mind, I rather think that one thing salvaging them from the-dust heap of history (at least for me) is the role ambiguity plays in the criticism at many levels, and its operation in the resultant 'interpre-tation'. In particular I contested readings of David as either 'good' or 'bad' and similarly challenged the moral probity of God—whom I suggested was David's alter ego—in these narratives. (Of course, I am not alone in such a reading, especially today, but twenty years ago ambiguity was not a favoured category of biblical criticism.) Attention to the machinations of ambiguity (Empson's phrase) has a salutary effect on a critic's drive to shut down the meaning of a text in explaining it. Rather, such attention, I believe, inclines a reading towards indeterminacy and openness.

Another factor that works to keep the readings alive is perhaps less obvious. David Clines (then my colleague at Sheffield and a source of great support and stimulation) and I discussed at infinite length over several years the issue of whether a text has a single 'theme' (the term we used—see his *The Theme of the Pentateuch*[11]) or several themes and, if the latter, whether they must be compatibly related. The discussion was about univocality and multivocality, about monologic and dialogic, about determinate and indeterminate, though we used none of those terms. My own inclination, which fitted with the role ambi-guity played in my understanding of language, was to argue for mul-tiple themes, though for a time I undercut that position by seeking still some relation of compatibility between these, hence in fact moving back from multivocality to univocality. Nonetheless, this (theoretical) receptiveness to multiple voices 'in' the text underlies my early readings. By the time I wrote the *Saul* book I had taken the position that a story could mean many things, and that some of these

11. D.J.A. Clines, *The Theme of the Pentateuch* (JSOTSup, 10; Sheffield: JSOT Press, 1978).

meanings could co-exist while vying with one another. By 1980, too, I had become deeply interested again in the history of interpretation and impressed by the contributions of 'pre-critical' interpreters—including poets, playwrights and visual artists—to my understanding of the stories of Saul and David. In practice and in theory, then, I was being driven to take more seriously the role of the reader in the production of meaning—a shift that also led me towards the possibility of multiple and even conflicting meanings being the legitimate production of criticism.

Finally, a theological issue has permeated my critical thought and practice. It did then and has continued to do so. I finished my theology degree at the University of Otago (New Zealand) deeply unsettled, effectively an agnostic. The issue was theodicy. I only came to terms with God again when I learned to leave the issue unsettled, unsolved because insoluble. But I have not ceased to challenge God on the question of justice; and my work, I long ago recognized, was marked by my animus towards an unjust God who presides over, indeed (in biblical terms) directs, an unjust world. My reading of God in the story of King David was restrained, though I pressed the question of God's arbitrariness and, as I have already remarked, wondered whether, in the end, God was not rather like David—in the circumstances a not wholly flattering conclusion. My reading of Saul was a more direct exploration of the demonic in God. Saul is a victim—and David the beneficiary—of a game of power politics that God is playing out with Israel where what is at stake is God's reputation and authority, divine identity no less. I went on to write on Samson as God's victim—it was simply a matter of reading with sympathy and not dismissing or ignoring the function of the divine spirit in the plot.[12] I later created a complicated and complicating intertextual dimension to the interpretation by glossing it with texts from Isaiah, especially 40–55 and the 'suffering servant'. I offered a counter-reading to the conventional liberation reading of Exodus, arguing that again God's reputation rather than Israel's freedom is the highest value, at the cost, in this case, of the firstborn children (among others).[13] I am reminded today of the children of Iraq who

12. D.M. Gunn, 'Samson of Sorrows: An Isaianic Gloss on Judges 13–16', in D. Nolan Fewell (ed.), *Reading Between Texts: Intertextuality in the Hebrew Bible* (Literary Currents in Biblical Interpretation; Louisville: Westminster/John Knox Press, 1992), pp. 225-53.

13. D.M. Gunn, 'The "Hardening" of Pharaoh's Heart: Plot, Character and Theology in Exodus 1–14', in D.J.A. Clines, D.M. Gunn and A.J. Hauser (eds.), *Art*

continue to pay the price of their own ruler's folly and a foreign ruler's reputation.

I did not, and do not, see these readings as definitive—for the issue they deal with is profoundly complex and, I believe, insoluble—but rather, by pressing the case against God, as demanding the acknowledgment that the Bible's accounts of God and justice are fraught with injustice. Christian readings are particularly prone to a glib side-stepping of this issue in the interests of a cleaned-up, morally tidy, divinity. I was, and am, interested in maintaining a dialectic on this question. Again, therefore, this theological concern has led me towards an appreciation of the indeterminacy of the biblical text—even though my particular readings may appear to be pressing in quite the opposite direction, towards determinacy.

During the seventies I gradually became aware, mainly through my wife, Margaret, and her women's support group, of the women's movement and the injustice of the inequities between men and women in our society. We were then living in Britain. At the same time that growing consciousness found no particular expression in my biblical criticism. I continued to read as a man, without being aware of it. When Phyllis Trible's[14] *God and the Rhetoric of Sexuality* appeared in the United States in 1978, I did not immediately read it. I was heavily involved in editing and in the management of a struggling (but growing) JSOT Press; my reading beyond the immediate demands of teaching and editing was limited and focused on literary criticism; and the term 'rhetoric' in the title conjured a classic compositional discipline that held no special interest. James Muilenburg and 'rhetorical criticism' meant little to me. As for 'sexuality' ('gender', I suspect, would have been an apter term), I realize now that I simply did not appreciate how radical the challenge of feminists to the business of criticism was. By 1980 that had begun to change. I had read Trible's book (discovering in the process that she was a very fine literary critic), and helped arrange the publication in *JSOT* of the women's caucus papers from the centennial meeting of the SBL that year.[15] That book and those papers had great influence. It began to dawn on me that I had to learn to read and write differently.

The learning took some time (and continues). When I came to the

and Meaning: Rhetoric in Biblical Literature (JSOTSup, 17; Sheffield: JSOT Press, 1982), pp. 72-96.

14. P. Trible, *God and the Rhetoric of Sexuality* (Overtures to Biblical Theology; Philadelphia: Fortress Press, 1978).

15. P. Trible (ed.), 'The Effects of Women's Studies on Biblical Studies', *JSOT* 22 (1982), pp. 3-71.

United States in 1984, to Columbia Theological Seminary, my primary concern was still the struggle to legitimate literary criticism
within the discipline of biblical studies and to explore in a seminary
context my conviction that literary-critical modes of biblical interpretation were cogent tools in the hands of pastors and church lay
people. When, soon after my arrival in Atlanta, Danna Nolan Fewell
engaged me in discussion the issue was literary criticism, not feminism—and literary criticism was to be a defining bond between
us for a decade of creative partnership that profoundly shaped my
thought and practice as a scholar. Soon, however, especially after we
began to teach together at Columbia Seminary and to tease out alternatives in reading the book of Ruth, our dialogue turned increasingly
to feminism. She proved a wonderful mentor.[16] To her goes much
credit for the way feminist criticism and literary criticism have since
blended in my work (though I bear full responsibility for any sins of
sexism that persist!)

Another influence was Randy Bailey from Interdenominational
Theological Center. He came first to talk about David.[17] Over the
years our friendship deepened. He, too, was a gracious (and persistent) mentor and I learned from him to discern better the unspoken
racism that marks so much of Western thought and social institutions. I remember well his gentle scolding of me for my uncritical
assumptions (in *King David*) about the Cushite who brings David the
message of Absalom's death, or my thoughtless borrowing of the
motif label 'the woman who brings death' to describe Rizpah,
Bathsheba, Tamar, Abishag, along with Potiphar's wife and Eve—
both examples of the reinscription of ideology that I found helpful to
rehearse in subsequent teaching.

One of the first courses I offered at Columbia Seminary, in the
Spring of 1985, was on 'Wisdom and the Feminine', borrowing the
title and tenor from Claudia Camp's pioneering book (which I had
just published in the Almond Press 'Bible and Literature Series')[18]
and combining that with interests I had in wisdom literature and
especially Proverbs, going back to my teaching in Sheffield. It was the
first time I set up a course where feminism (inasmuch as I knew
what that was!) provided the major focus. It was a small group of

16. See D. Nolan Fewell, 'Feminist Criticism of the Hebrew Bible: Affirmation,
Resistance, and Transformation', *JSOT* 39 (1987), pp. 65-75.

17. See C.R. Bailey, *David in Love and War: The Pursuit of Power in 2 Samuel 10–
12* (JSOTSup, 75; Sheffield: JSOT Press, 1990).

18. C.V. Camp, *Wisdom and the Feminine in the Book of Proverbs* (Bible and
Literature, 11; Sheffield: Almond Press, 1985).

mostly women, quite diverse in background, temperament and theology. Several women held our feet to the fire. All in the group were patient with each other and listened. I encountered the pain engendered by patriarchal texts, church and theology at first hand. It was a powerful experience, unforgettable.

That same Spring I found myself contributing to a course at the seminary on hermeneutics/critical method and 'biblical theology'. My colleague in homiletics, Lucy Rose, spoke with clarity, conviction and courage about feminist criticism and its impact on biblical studies and theology. Again, some of the women students were pointedly vocal. As a result I found myself compelled to work out more clearly how to bring these feminist perspectives into conjunction with my interests in literary criticism, especially the move to reader-oriented criticism and deconstruction. Deconstruction, which I was unsure I really understood (perhaps not much has changed in a decade!), seemed to me to offer a powerful alliance with feminist criticism simply because it focused on meaning in texts as always potentially destabilizing, on how texts have a way of undermining themselves. Against the (sometimes justified) criticisms that deconstruction is (was?) solipsistic, amoral, inimical to political change, I have always been inclined to argue that one can start and stop a deconstructive reading at will, and that it is precisely the stopping that obliges one to stake, and take responsibility for, the moral values and political or ideological stands that motivate the stopping. By the same token I am obliged to recognize that my stopping is always subject to shift, that the exercise of power in reading is always a process.

In 1985, too, I was asked by Robert Alter and Frank Kermode to write the chapter on 'Judges' for what was then styled *The Harvard Literary Guide to the Bible*.[19] I was excited and enthusiastic about the prospect, both for the opportunity to contribute and for the recognition that I believed this project would help bring to literary criticism in the field of biblical studies. A session on the book was planned by the 'Bible and Literary Criticism' section at the AAR/SBL annual meeting later that year. Alter was to speak and I was invited to respond. By the time of the meeting I had become acutely aware that this was a men's project. I was torn over what to say about that in the session. In the event I spoke of the emergence of literary criticism in

19. D.M. Gunn, 'Joshua and Judges', in R. Alter and F. Kermode (eds.), *The Literary Guide to the Bible* (Cambridge, MA: Harvard University Press, 1987), pp. 102-21.

biblical studies as an issue of power, a struggle against a monopoly of knowledge that was bound up with the control of academic institutions such as theological schools, graduate schools, the professional guild and the means of publication. There was deep irony in the notion that this was to be a 'Harvard' literary guide. Then I addressed the Bible as a text of various constituencies of readers: a literary model, especially in a post 'new-critical' or reader-oriented idiom, exposes our ideologies as readers, our manipulation of reading as a power game. Just so does a feminist hermeneutic allied with a literary critical approach—as Trible exemplified—raise acutely the issue of power. Why was there no woman (and Trible most outstandingly) on the list of contributors to the volume? Raising the question, I avoided exploring it. Deference to Alter and the literary critical project won out. Rather, I went on to speak more generally of ideology and the control of reading, concluding, on an intentionally ironic note, that we needed this new guide to give formal expression...'to the new orthodoxy in biblical studies!'

The depth of the irony eluded me. In fact what I had done was allow my celebration of this signal step in the legitimization of literary criticism to overwhelm my own argument about power. The volume, which later lost its 'Harvard' moniker and became, pretentiously, *The Literary Guide to the Bible*, did indeed give expression to orthodoxy, but hardly a new one. In its exclusions, both methodological/hermeneutical and (thereby) personal, the *Guide* reinscribed the still-dominant patriarchy of our society. But if I missed this, others did not. That large packed meeting room introduced me for the first time to Mieke Bal. She rose and uttered withering words on the exclusion. I left the meeting in confusion, both elated and deeply unsettled, but dimly aware that what had happened was another major turning point for me (and, I suspect, for others who were there). Feminist principles of justice and equity could not come second to questions of methodology. Questions of methodology were themselves implicated in issues of power. Power was not just something other people had; I enjoyed it too and had not deployed it well. (In my chapter for the *Guide*, I attempted to subvert my instructions by playing with deconstructive possibilities and a reading of Judges that borrows from Trible to delineate at its end a society already divided and one part oppressed without a foreign oppressor. Even so, I still acquiesced in the editors' brief to maintain a largely formalist—and ostensibly ideologically 'neutral'—approach to our texts and muted my own voice.) All in all, it was a salutary episode that left a deep mark on my professional work and writing.

The experience was compounded by another. Letty Russell and Mary Daly spoke at Emory University—Russell, of a new mutuality between women and men; Daly, of a visionary world where men were absent. At question time Daly—as was apparently her custom—took no questions from men. I was shocked that in the midst of a university, the place above all where freedom of speech was prized, she should eliminate men, me, from the conversation, for no other reason than that I was biologically male. By the time I left the building it was dawning on me that I had experienced—not just thought about—in this exclusion a glimpse of something constitutive of women's experience in our society. It was a moment of consciousness-raising that stuck with me.

My first couple of years in the United States were thus highly programmatic. When I wrote on David in 1985, it was in the midst of this transition in my career and critical thought. The essay, on the David of biblical narrative (Chronicles as well as Samuel), was commissioned for a special issue on David in the journal *Interpretation*. It was deemed impenetrable. I tried some rewriting. After two tries the editor finally rejected it and looked elsewhere to fill the gap. I was not altogether surprised. It was my first attempt to try a deconstructive turn in my writing. Taking as my starting point chapters 22 and 23 from the so-called 'appendix' to 2 Samuel and the popular label 'the sweet psalmist of Israel', I set about answering the question 'Who is David?' by invoking, and then disturbing, the apparent security of the voice of David's psalm and 'last words'. The essay follows direct trails in the plot and associative trails of thought. The disturbances appear to arise within the text itself, the product of ambiguous language and unsettling juxtapositions, although the sense of irony driving the reading is, of course, my own. The upshot is a series of questions and answers about David—and increasingly Yhwh—that weave in and out of the text of Samuel and eventually jump to Chronicles, Ezra and Nehemiah. If, by assimilating him into the institution of the temple, Chronicles seems to do finally what the books of Samuel have seemed unable to do—namely, to tame, secure and neatly order the story of David—nevertheless, as we trace David's shadow across Ezra and Nehemiah we end with Nehemiah, a surrogate David, urging God to remember the forces of evil and to remember him, Nehemiah, for good. So we find ourselves back with David's last (self) righteous words, where we began, where vision and actuality compete and righteousness risks mocking itself.

Were I to write this piece again, today, I suspect that I would be more self-conscious about writing my own stance into the reading. I

also am struck by the way I veer towards and away from an underlying assumption that the 'insecurity' of my reading is foremost a
product of the text itself, or an 'author' (as opposed to 'narrator')
even, rather than primarily a function of my ideologically driven
determination to undermine any 'secure' reading by setting the text
against itself. In short, I am unsure to what extent this is truly a
deconstructive reading. Still, it remains a reading that I believe challenges any easy interpretation of these texts, including Chronicles
and Ezra–Nehemiah. It is thus methodologically receptive to a feminist re-reading, though it makes no overtly feminist moves itself and
lays itself open to critique from feminist perspectives. In this regard,
it perhaps needs to be read alongside the essay that formed a chapter
in *Gender, Power and Promise* which I wrote with Danna Nolan Fewell
some six or seven years later.[20] (The paper finally found a print
outlet, with a characteristically astute response from Peter Miscall, in
Cheryl Exum's *Signs and Wonders*).[21]

When I look back and delve around in my memory and (pack-rat)
files I am struck by the confluence of events in the opening months of
1986. At a conference on the Bible and Literary Theory (organized by
Regina Schwartz) my friend Burke Long and I watched with some
fascination a critical divide open up between Mieke Bal, on the one
hand, and Robert Alter and Meir Sternberg (among others) on the
other. Some of what Mieke Bal had to say then lent itself to an inaugural address I gave later in the spring at Columbia Seminary on
'Moses as Mother' (Numbers 11). And framing all this was the intense engagement with the book of Ruth that emerged from the
exegesis class on Ruth that Danna and I conducted and endlessly
discussed.

We shared a penchant for close reading, for word-play, for irony,
and for 'counter'-reading. We both placed a high value on imagination as an ingredient of interpretation. We decided that we had something worth saying on Ruth in print. And, not least important, we
discovered that we could write together with facility. We crafted our
first paper together, on Ruth, for the South-Eastern regional meeting
of the SBL that same spring. We followed it a year later with another
paper, also on Ruth. These ventures turned out to be only the

20. D. Nolan Fewell and D.M. Gunn, *Gender, Power, and Promise: The Subject of
the Bible's First Story* (Nashville: Abingdon Press, 1993).

21. D.M. Gunn, 'In Security: The David of Biblical Narrative', in J.C. Exum
(ed.), *Signs and Wonders: Biblical Texts in Literary Focus* (Semeia Studies; Atlanta:
Scholars Press, 1989), pp. 133-51 (with response by P.D. Miscall, pp. 153-63).

beginning of an extensive collaboration which in one way or another touched all my further work, including that on David.

As far as the 'David' texts were concerned, about the time we were finishing the second Ruth paper, I was writing the chapter on 2 Samuel in the *Harper's Bible Commentary*.[22] It was an opportunity for some convergence of the various strands developing in my criticism. To write for a lay audience meant that I had to abandon the elusive style of the 'In Security' essay. The publishing context—as well as my situation in the seminary and in the many lay workshops on the Bible that I found myself conducting—also seemed to me at the time to demand real concessions regarding the stringency with which I addressed the issues of textual and theological or ideological instability in this book of the Bible. It is hard for me to judge the result. At any rate the commentary afforded me the opportunity to attempt to re-read 2 Samuel with much more attention to the margins. Accordingly, Rizpah, Michal, David's nameless daughters, Bathsheba, Tamar, the woman of Tekoa, Tamar who was Absalom's daughter, David's concubines, the woman of Abel beth-Maacah, and again Rizpah—all find a focus in my story where they had not in my earlier accounts. The pathos of Michal's liaison with Paltiel (ch. 3) and her facing down of the prancing David (ch. 6) touched me as they had not done before, and the story of David's concubines (chs. 15 and 20) particularly stuck in my gullet. In time their story was to become for me the point from which one could unravel this whole story of the great king and his liege lord, Yhwh.

At the end of that year (1987), at the SBL annual meeting, I was to speak ('To Know or Not to Know') on Robert Polzin's draft for his book on *Samuel and the Deuteronomist*,[23] except that my paper turned in the main to a critique of Meir Sternberg's poetics.[24] This is an issue

22. D.M. Gunn, '2 Samuel', in J. Mays (gen. ed.), *Harper's Bible Commentary* (San Francisco: Harper & Row, 1988), pp. 287-304.

23. R. Polzin, *Samuel and the Deuteronomist: A Literary Study of the Deuteronomistic History. II. 1 Samuel* (Indiana Studies in Biblical Literature; Bloomington: Indiana University Press, 1989); *David and the Deuteronomist: A Literary Study of the Deuteronomistic History. III. 2 Samuel* (Indiana Studies in Biblical Literature; Bloomington: Indiana University Press, 1993).

24. M. Sternberg, *The Poetics of Biblical Narrative: Ideological Literature and the Drama of Reading* (Indiana Studies in Biblical Literature; Bloomington: Indiana University Press, 1985); D.M. Gunn, 'Reading Right: Reliable and Omniscient Narrator, Omniscient God, and Foolproof Composition in the Hebrew Bible', in D.J.A. Clines, S.E. Fowl and S.E. Porter (eds.), *The Bible in Three Dimensions* (JSOTSup, 87; Sheffield: JSOT Press, 1990), pp. 53-64.

that has continued to exercise me: despite Sternberg's play with ambiguity and irony and an ostensible focus on the reader, it seems to me that his premise is the determinability of the biblical text, given correct reading procedures, so that ambiguities, ironies and the shifting constitution of the Bible's reader, are of no final consequence. To me they are constitutive of textual meaning and its constant susceptibility to displacement. The notions of omniscient reader and 'foolproof composition' are as insubstantial as the notion of omniscient God. I have argued this case in several contexts and will probably come back to it in print, since Sternberg's argument appears to commend itself to a large following. The ideological stakes of the argument, as I see it, are high: a theory that lends itself to authoritarian readings over one that is receptive to disjunctive readings. Sternberg's poetics are a serious challenge to feminist criticism, as Danna and I tried to show (if not wholly successfully), in a critique of his reading of Dinah.[25]

Over the next five years Danna and I finished the book on Ruth[26]—in which we explored re-telling as an expression of interpretation, rather in the manner of midrash—and a much more difficult one to write, on narrative in the Hebrew Bible.[27] The latter pressed us to consider carefully method and theory and to work through a wide range of narrative texts. The result was a deepened skepticism about the possibility of a systematic biblical narratology; or, to put it another way, a heightened awareness of the 'constructed' nature, and slipperiness, of the critics' analytic categories.

It was a time of memorable and invaluable collaboration. It was a time also marked for me by new courses centered on feminist criticism—including one with pastoral theology colleague Jeanne Stevenson Moessner which became something of a counterpoint to the required theology course—and increasing numbers of occasions when I had the opportunity to speak about feminist criticism and the Bible. I struggled to confront some of the deep-seated problems of trying to be 'a man in feminism'. My students, Danna, Jeanne and others encouraged me to keep trying. But as Barbara Johnson put it some years ago: 'Jacques Derrida may sometimes see himself *philosophically* positioned as a woman, but he is not *politically* positioned

25. D.M. Gunn and D.N. Fewell, 'Tipping the Balance: Sternberg's Reader and the Rape of Dinah', *JBL* 110 (1991), pp. 193-211.

26. Fewell and Gunn, *Compromising Redemption*.

27. D.M. Gunn and D.N. Fewell, *Narrative in the Hebrew Bible* (Oxford Bible Series; Oxford: Oxford University Press, 1993).

as a woman. Being positioned as a woman is not something that is entirely voluntary.'[28] I am no Jacques Derrida, but I believe I take the point.

By 1992 Danna and I were putting together a set of close readings (*Gender, Power, and Promise*) that took the subjectivity of women and children as their starting point and spanned the length of Genesis–Kings, the Bible's 'primary' story. The project challenged us to read 'legal' as well as narrative texts, and texts that we had not read before. We sought threads and coherences reaching through large extents of texts. We also sought points of disjunction, entries to deconstruction. Inevitably I found myself once more seeking a reading of the 'David' texts in Samuel. It was an emotionally wrenching experience. I do not think I could do this again, to tell a story from this Bible to which my life is so bound, and to feel my anger, to hate the story, to resent my boundness and yet somehow respect it, to have to go on, story after story after story. No matter how hard we tried to read the red dot in a sea of blue, we could not escape the dominance of David: the text, we decided, lies 'in the shadow of the king'. We started with David's concubines. The story went downhill from there.

When I look back at *The Story of King David*, it is not that I think that first reading misbegotten. But, fifteen years later, I was in a very different place. The nice attempts at reading 'balance' in the depiction of the king had given way to a dislocating shift in the reading subject. Irony and complexity, yes; balance, no. In the early book I described as a fundamental structure of the story the way men's dealings with women mirrored what I saw as their 'public' or 'political' dealings. I did not then understand how politics are written on women's bodies.

Not long after I came to Columbia Seminary I found myself in a meeting where a long and tortuous discussion about changing rules for graduation appeared to me to rest somehow on a problem with one student. I knew her from my exegesis class. She was a good student. 'What's the problem?', I finally asked a colleague next to me. 'She's a lesbian', he confided. Today the issue of the ordination of gays and lesbians threatens to split my church. The issue divides the faculty of many Presbyterian theological schools.

With hindsight, 1989–91 is another time of confluence: a friendship that my wife formed at Smith College School of Social Work; an experience of my own heterosexism as a visitor to a class on gay and

28. B. Johnson, *A World of Difference* (Baltimore: The Johns Hopkins University Press, 1987), p. 2.

lesbian issues in social work at Smith; a chapel meditation that opened my office door to students who were living in the closet; a church meeting of ministers and elders in Atlanta that voted to suppress a report on human sexuality (by John Carey and others)[29] that insisted on naming patriarchy and heterosexism as sins confounding a just and loving understanding of humans as sexual beings; discussion with Danna, theoretical and exegetical, about sexuality as well as gender as social construction; David Greenberg's huge(ly) fascinating book, *The Construction of Homosexuality*.[30]

At the SBL in 1991 I presented an analysis of Lev. 18.22 ('You shall not lie with a male as with a woman') as an item in a list of proscriptions explicable as a classic production of a patriarchal society.[31] This reading of Leviticus 18 then framed a brief attempt at gay/lesbian readings of David and Jonathan, and (in sympathy with a poem by Maureen Duffy[32] that David Clines had sent) Ruth and Naomi. Wanting to embody these readings better I played on a screen, in tandem with my text and mostly without comment, works of art on these biblical subjects (including Donatello, Michelangelo and Caravaggio) that lent themselves to this purpose. A picture of Ruth (by Calderon) that Danna had come across had already occasioned our analysis of its gender, (homo)sexual and racial overtones. Of all the contributions I have made at professional meetings, I believe this one has drawn the most response. To what extent the visual dimension of the presentation was responsible for that response I cannot say, but the experience spurred my interest in the power of the visual image as well as in the issue of the construction of sexuality.

My 'projections' of David go back many years to a research project and an upper level course on David in Western culture at the University of Sheffield. The scope of the study has included manuscript and printed Bible illustration, free standing painting, sculpture, poetry, plays and novels, devotional writing, sermons, children's books, movies, politics and theology. For long I was at a loss as to how to focus my study. But with the social construction of gender

29. J.J. Carey *et al.*, *Keeping Body and Soul Together: Sexuality, Spirituality, and Social Justice* (Louisville: Presbyterian Church [USA], 1991).

30. D.F. Greenberg, *The Construction of Homosexuality* (Chicago: University of Chicago Press, 1988).

31. 'A Fearful Dominion: Biblical Constructions of Homosexuality'; this found its way, after a fashion, into *Gender, Power, and Promise*.

32. M. Duffy, 'Mother and the Girl', in *Collected Poems 1949–84* (London: Hamish Hamilton, 1985).

and sexuality, and the politics of biblical authority, I found my frame. A book began to emerge. For a start, I took the image of David with Goliath's head that had provided a point of visual focus in my earlier presentation and in turn took Donatello's bronze David as my particular reference; and by exploring the gender conventions of decapitation in visual art I developed an interpretation of the statue as a celebration of a homosexual (for want of a better term) triumph of 'love' after the manner of the renaissance figure—whether in visual art or poetry, as in Petrarch—where the love in question is conventionally heterosexual.

Moving into another discipline is somewhat daunting, but the overlap of hermeneutical issues between literature and visual art is considerable—and, in any case, I have the example of Mieke Bal as an encouragement. I have also had the support of an outstanding group of graduate students over the past several years, at Columbia Seminary, Emory University and more recently at Southern Methodist University: students who have grown up on critical theory and have constantly informed me, pushed me to account for my critical positions and incited me to experiment.

One offshoot of this cultural study of David that has taken me along an increasingly different path from the one on which I have mostly travelled as a literary critic, is my increasing concern to elaborate the social context of my materials. Perhaps this project and my longtime friend and 'social-world' interlocutor, Jim Flanagan,[33] have worn me down—and my erstwhile colleague, Philip Davies, had, not for the first time provoked me.[34] I find myself becoming a historian. (Actually, come to think of it, the first class I ever taught at university, in 1965, was on Thucydides' poignant account of imperial Athens' disastrous Sicilian expedition: I read it as a political allegory of the United States' burgeoning colonial adventure in Vietnam, a prescient reading as it turned out.) From trying to find out whether Donatello would likely have been familiar with a Latin Bible or whether same-sex sexual relations were tolerated in mid-fifteenth century Florence, I moved in another project to an exploration of the social history of bathing. Visual depictions of Bathsheba bathing are ubiquitous in Bible illustration in Europe from the Middle Ages until about the middle of the sixteenth century. She is depicted both naked

33. See J.W. Flanagan, *David's Social Drama: A Hologram of Israel's Early Iron Age* (The Social World of Biblical Antiquity, 7; Sheffield: Almond Press, 1988).

34. See P.R. Davies, *In Search of 'Ancient Israel'* (JSOTSup, 148; Sheffield: JSOT Press, 1992).

and largely clothed. I was struck by the power that the social construction of the meaning of a mundane action—such as bathing—can have on the interpreter of an ancient text. That the bathing Bathsheba is naked is commonly assumed. That David's gaze is an invasion of her privacy is also often assumed. Alternatively, her action may be construed as deliberately breaking the normal rules of privacy in order to allure the king: her bathing, in other words, is taken to be a key element in assessing her and the king's motivations. Yet the text does not say she is naked; and the association of bathing, nakedness and privacy is certainly a modern North European construction and cannot be assumed for the social world of this ancient text. In short, like Mieke Bal, I have become particularly interested in word–image associations and the ways in which biblical texts become visualized in particular social locations.[35] This interest extends to movies (encouraged by Alice Bach), and the 1951 'David and Bathsheba' with Gregory Peck and Susan Hayward provides a nice case in point—where the bathing scene, I would argue, emblematic of the ambiguous role of the woman in the Woman's Film of the period, is caught as she is between the liberating wartime experience of Rosie the Riveter and the backlash of the domesticating fifties.

I wrote 'Goliath's Head: Text, Image, and the Subversion of Gender' in 1993 and 'Bathsheba Goes to Hollywood and Other Adventures' in 1994, presenting both at the SBL annual meetings among other places.[36] In 1993 I left Columbia Theological Seminary to take up a post in the Department of Religion at Texas Christian University. My move into cultural criticism—if that is what it is—is not unconnected with my move from the theological school to the university. It seems to me that biblical criticism with a postmodern turn, and especially feminist criticism, is increasingly constrained in the context of a theological school. The question of biblical authority has become acute again, as it became with the onset of historical criticism more than two centuries ago. I find it very hard to see where feminist criticism of the Bible can go 'constructively' without it destroying traditional notions of the Bible's authority as a sacred text. Increasingly I see feminist biblical criticism, Christian and Jewish, as religious

35. M. Bal, *Murder and Difference: Gender, Genre, and Scholarship on Sisera's Death* (Indiana Studies in Biblical Literature; Bloomington: Indiana University Press, 1988); and *Reading Rembrandt* (Cambridge: Cambridge University Press, 1991).

36. D.M. Gunn, 'Bathsheba Goes Bathing in Hollywood: Words, Images and Social Locations', in A. Bach (ed.), *Biblical Glamour and Hollywood Glitz* (Semeia, 74; Atlanta: Scholars Press, 1996), pp. 75-101.

apology, engaged in papering over the cracks that it has opened to scrutiny.

Discard claims to divine authority and inspiration, and 'biblical' literature stands in its mottled complexity like any other literature that plumbs human experience, profoundly, for good or ill. No need, then, for endless rationalizings to convert its perceived perversities into manifestations of divine truth. A couple of years ago Claudia Camp and I taught a class called 'Foreign and Female: Biblical Images of Women'.[37] Years ago she (wisely) had declined my editorial suggestion that, for her book on *Wisdom and the Feminine*, she drop her arguments for locating her material in the post-exilic period. Now I found myself enthusiastically exploring images of the 'strange woman' not merely in Proverbs but from a range of biblical texts (including the New Testament) that we had each worked with over the years, with social location—not least post-exilic, the subject of important reassessment recently—very much part of the search for meaning. But more than the compromise of my literary-critical purity in this process, what struck me about our conversations was the way Claudia managed to read the manifold aspects of identity and otherness as interwoven and interdependent. The foreign woman or 'strange' woman may represent all that 'we' are not, yet without her we are not, for she is part of 'us'. I am drawn to the boundaries, to the places where 'we' become other, not 'us'. Only on the boundary can we be subjectively both us and other. Yet the boundary is a fiction. To stand there is impossible. But I am drawn. Most of my life has been lived as a sojourner (a 'resident alien', as the US government so charmingly puts it), a person between four countries. Sojourners live on boundaries, or perhaps at boundaries, or is it near boundaries...

Does it seem strange, then, that I am working on a study of land and dispossession? If I write next about David it will likely be about David's taking of the stronghold of Zion—taken as he took his women—in the context of a study of colonial appropriations of the Bible in the European settlement of New Zealand (I am the great-grandson of colonial settlers), North America and modern Palestine/Israel.

Recently I have been involved with Gary Phillips and Danna Nolan Fewell in starting a new series of books for Routledge in London. At the prompting of Tim Beal, valued conversation partner,

37. See C.V. Camp, 'Wise and Strange: An Interpretation of the Female Imagery in Proverbs in Light of Trickster Mythology', in J.C. Exum and J.W.H. Bos (eds.), *Reasoning with the Foxes: Female Wit in a World of Male Power* (Semeia, 42; Atlanta: Scholars Press, 1988), pp. 4-36.

we have called the series 'Biblical Limits', borrowing from Drucilla Cornell's characterization of deconstruction as 'the philosophy of the limit'.[38] The edges, boundaries, limits of the discipline(s) of biblical studies are being pressed and transgressed. Consensus understandings of the provenance and purpose of many biblical texts are coming apart. Debate over the role of readers in the production of meaning continues unabated. Confidence that scholars can delineate 'the meaning' of biblical texts is waning—while the Bible of popular religion becomes ever more a thing of bounded certainty. Tim and I edited a volume for the series, *Reading Bibles, Writing Bodies*,[39] a collection of papers that suggest some of these critical movements that probe and transgress biblical limits. My contribution is again on David.[40] Looking for the destabilizing point of entry into the text, I ask, How did David kill Goliath? My search for an answer leads into questions of text and canon. It leads to no certain text, to no certain Bible, to no certain answer.

38. D. Cornell, *The Philosophy of the Limit* (New York and London: Routledge, 1992).

39. T.K. Beal and D.M. Gunn (eds.), *Reading Bibles, Writing Bodies: Identity and the Book* (London and New York: Routledge, 1997).

40. D.M. Gunn, 'What Does The Bible Say? A Question of Text and Canon', in Beal and Gunn (eds.), *Reading Bibles, Writing Bodies*, pp. 242-61.

'MY' SONG OF SONGS

Athalya Brenner

Introduction

One of the battle cries of feminists from the 1970s onwards has been the demand to distinguish 'women's experience' as an experiental and critical category that conditions and contributes to the definition, enactment and perpetuation of gender. The concept 'women's experience' referred both to the essential life cycle that biological women might experience—menstruation, birthing, ageing and other sensations and emotions emanating from the body—as well to the social and societal conditions that program women into F (female/feminine) roles and expected F performance. The work of French feminists especially reinforced the recognition of F experience as a basic category for woman's voice, reading and writing.[1]

The growing attention to difference and pluralism in the late 1980s and 1990s has made 'women's experience' a less useful critical category than it might have been. Differences in ethnicity, nationality, location, colour, religion, class, age, social circumstances, economic conditions, education and many other factors besides have curtailed—inevitably and fortunately—the usefulness of the 'universal sisterhood' concept. Against a background of the multiple sophisticated feminisms developed meanwhile, a single abstracted concept of F experience is unwarranted. On the other hand, a growing emphasis on the reader's location, coupled with the recognition of difference, allow the [F and M] critic relative theoretical liberty in that personal location—including gender—need not be as masked and devalued, as previously, as a factor motivating academic criticism. The pretense to critical objectivity is losing ground, not least because of feminist insistence. If the category 'women's experience' has lost most of its validity as a generally applicable concept for feminists, the

1. For a selection in English translation see E. Marks and Isabelle de Courtivron, *New French Feminisms: An Anthology* (New York: Shocken Books, 1981).

category 'personal/autobiographical criticism' has and is gaining relevance.

This article, then, is an exploitation of the new [relative] permissiveness in regard to 'personal experience' and the appreciation of the relevance of readerly difference for critical work. For, surely, the license to be legitimately different encompasses *specific* F experience, a single woman's experience, as well as other personal factors.

I Am...

Jewish, a native Israeli, a woman, a mother, divorced, fifty-three years old. I was born in the then 'Palestine' under the British UN mandate, in 1943. My mother and father were immigrants, from Poland and Lithuania respectively. Both came to the then 'Land of Palestine' as teenage 'pioneers' for ideological as well as practical reasons in the late 1930s, when the writing of the holocaust was already on the wall for European Jewry, including the so-called *Ostjuden*. Both came from traditional Jewish but 'enlightened' (well-integrated into the gentile environment) lower middle-class backgrounds. Both had attended non-Jewish as well as supplementary Jewish schools. They were multilingual: at home in the languages and cultures of Poland, Russia and Germany in addition to Jewish culture in Yiddish and, to a lesser extent, Hebrew. After they had become immigrants, when they were married, they decided that their children would be born into the Hebrew language and into Hebrew, 'non-exilic' and non-religious culture. That meant—among other things—that in our household Hebrew was privileged, consciously and ideologically, over any other language; and the HB was privileged over post-biblical Jewish literature, not to mention world literature, as a source for spiritual life and human existence. It also meant that the land of Israel, especially but not only as reflected in Scripture, acquired a halo—particularly when it became clear that European Jewry was no more. This meant that Jewish sources, especially the HB, had to be tapped for what Zionism and Zionists of Labour movement convictions, especially the immigrants, imagined would be a fresh Jewish start.

All this is quite ordinary: many of my Israeli friends and contemporaries come from similar backgrounds. For me, though, it is not so. For me this means that my native tongue was from the day I spoke my first word, and still is, Hebrew. My Yiddish is sketchy. Other languages came later (including the English studied at school and later worked on in order to communicate with the man I married—to the extent that English has come to rival Hebrew in my professional and personal life; but this came later). The HB for me is intimate. We learnt it at school, great portions of it, from second grade onwards, until we were fed up with it. It was treated as a secular sacred text. I know the language of the HB first hand: it is similar to mine, albeit different too. The different morphologies, phonologies, syntax and semantics matter; but, also and always, they do not matter. The Bible is home in the same way that a mild version of Marxist theory and praxis is.

And so is the land. The quality of the light. The views, the land-scapes. The ridiculous shape and size. The vegetation. The smells. The varieties of climates. The abrupt change of seasons. I grew up on an ethos of loving the land to distraction, of swallowing it, of making it one's own by walking and hiking. Israel for me was the whole world; I knew no other place; I never went overseas until I was twenty-two years old.

In the emerging Israeli culture of my growing-up years there was a lot of singing: preferably as a communal bonding exercise and in Hebrew, of course: Israel was very insular then, apprehensive and defensive of its Hebrew culture in the process of formation (at the end of the 1950s voices demanding the banning of rock 'n' roll, and, slightly later, the Beatles as decadent were still heard in Israel). It was understood, vaguely, that the words of many songs were derived from the HB, albeit with modifications at times (the fashions for songs from other Jewish sources, and Hasidic songs, came later). Dances were attached to some of those songs and were repeatedly performed on various social and national occasions. When first, early teenage romance occurred, biblical love songs—or loving phrases taken straight out of the HB—featured largely. Where those love poems came from in the HB was unclear: they were not on the school syllabus of Bible studies. And yet, they had a biblical flavour. There was no mistake about that.

In my culture, Passover as well as the High Holidays (the New Year, *yom kippur, sukkot*) were the highlights of the year. On Passover, after the reading of the *hagadah*, some poems were recited in an 'exilic' melody (Ashkenazic, really, in my home). This happened every year, after the heavy Passover meal, when all I wanted was to be gone from the table. But one Passover, I think I was thirteen or fourteen years old at the time, it occurred to me that I had prior knowledge of many of these poems: as individual poems, with other tunes of eastern flavour. That series of poems was the SoS, of course. I had known these poems, they had featured largely in my life, before I

in fact realized that they were from the Song. They became my heritage before I could place them, consciously, inside my beloved Bible.

And so, for me, the SoS has been an important part of my formative
years and still is a significant component of my daily existence. It
belongs to my life experience, the emotive baggage that goes everywhere with me but becomes joyfully pronounced particularly when I
am in Israel. In order to try and convey this experience, I shall now
link specific SoS passages to specific and recurrent personal experiences and social activities of my past and present life; then come back
to the question, How does this intimate and emotive connection with
the SoS affect my academic study of it?

Situations and Activities

Singing

Some SoS-derived songs were so popular that they were, and perhaps still are, considered Israeli folk songs (although, in most cases,
the name of the music composer may be known).[2] The poems are set
to music and sung often, especially in two kinds of recurrent life situations: as songs heralding the arrival of spring just before and during
the time of Passover (from kindergarten on); and in love and courting
situations. License with the biblical words was often taken: the order
of verses was inverted; additions in modern Hebrew were inserted,
parts of verses were deleted, verses from various passages were
matched together in a new continuum, and so on.

> Do not gaze at me because I am dark, because the sun has gazed on me
> (1.6a-b);
> I am black and beautiful, daughters of Jerusalem (1.5a).

In this song, the verses are inverted. In

> I am a rose of Sharon, a lily of the valleys. As a lily among brambles, so
> is my love among maidens (2.1-2),

the quotation ends abruptly. In the song based on

> The voice of my beloved! Look, he comes, leaping upon the mountains,
> bounding over the hills. My beloved is like a gazelle or a young stag
> (2.8-9a),

some modifications were introduced to the biblical text. The next
song is a free-floating pastiche of SoS verses:

---

2.   Translations, unless otherwise stated, are from the NRSV, but follow the
chapter and verse divisions of the Hebrew text.

The flowers appear on the earth; the time of singing (2.22a)… in the dance of the two camps (7.1)… I have a bag of myrrh (113),

bound together with repetitions and insertions. On the other hand,

my dove, in the clefts of the rock, in the covert of the cliff, let me see your face, let me hear your voice; for your voice is sweet, and your face is lovely (2.14),

is a straight quote; the only additions are some hearty bellows added by the singers at the end of the repeated lines. In the next example, 2.16 is sung as a first stanza and repeated as a refrain, while various other passages are introduced in between:

My beloved is mine and I am his; he pastures his flock among the lilies (2.16).
Who (NRSV: 'What') is that coming up from the wilderness, like a column of smoke, perfumed with myrrh and frankincense (3.6).
My beloved is mine…
You have ravished my heart, my sister, my bride, you have ravished my heart, [bride] (4.9).
My beloved is mine…
Awake, O north wind, and come, O south wind! (4.16a).
My beloved is mine…

Other popular songs were based on 5.9-10, followed by a modified version of the male-descriptive *wasf* of 5.10-16; 6.1-2a; 6.11 together with 7.12, 13a, b, d; a song based on 7.14 together with variants on 1.16a, 2.9a and other verses indicating the beauty of a male lover and the coming of spring; 8.6-7; and 8.13-14. In short, when and where I grew up, the SoS was difficult to avoid; it was part of the popular culture of song and singing. Even now, when the SoS is taught in an Israeli University or college setting, more often than not a humming noise would be heard: one of the students, often quite unself-consciously, has started to sing one or the other of the poems studied.[3]

Dancing

'I went down to the nut orchard, to look at the blossoms of the valley, to see whether the vines had budded, whether the pomegranates were in bloom' (6.11). This poem was known to most not only as a poem but also as a dance, an Israeli 'folk' dance—that is, a dance for

---

3. It should also be mentioned that many poets who write in Hebrew customarily incorporate biblical quotations into their poetry. When such poems are set to music they enrich the SoS-derived stock of Hebrew songs, particularly love songs. An example which comes to mind is Leah Goldberg's poem entitled 'Come, Bride', recently set to a music and made popular by the singer Ahinoam Nini.

Saturday night gatherings, for dancing in the street on State
Independence Day, for any joyous occasion. So was the poem based
on the refrain 'My beloved is mine and I am his' (2.16a), and others.
Some dance troupes, with their distinctive 'folk' style garments,
would perform those dances with virtuousity: the rest of us would
just do our best. It is years now since I have danced these dances
with the enthusiasm I remember. But I remember the steps, the
atmosphere, the accordion playing the music, the worry whether I'd
be invited to dance by a boy or dare to ask a boy to dance with me.
The provenance of these dances in the SoS was discovered relatively
late. To begin with they were just our dances, originally Israeli and
natural to us. Until today, when I read one of the 'dance' passages it
conjures up a world full of childhood and maturation images. The
impulse to perform the steps once more, while singing the words
aloud, is always there when I read or teach the relevant passages.

Landscapes and Hikes
The ethos of hiking as a means for establishing a relationship with
the land, indeed, for appropriating it, was exemplified by a biblical
quote: we should do what Abraham was commanded to do—'Rise
up, walk through the length and breadth of the land, for I will give it
to you' (Gen. 13.17). Trips combining geography, history and archaeology were an important part of the school curriculum and of leisure
activities. And they always, always included walking to a place
where some HB quotes could be made relevant by being recited *in
situ*. When you went to Massada (part of the school syllabus), it was
linked with other writings (Josephus Flavius, *The Jewish Wars*, 7:8.2-
7:9.2) and the transformative, ideological myth of Jewish survival
and Zionist courage; but the close-by oasis of En Gedi, gone to on the
same trip, is for me the place where a woman's voice says, 'My
beloved is to me a cluster of henna blossoms in the vineyards of En-
Gedi' (SoS 1.14)—simply because there I *heard* this verse for the first
time (I *read* it much later). Every time I read this verse it invokes a
mental picture of how En-Gedi looked like then—and snatches of
memory relating to that trip, that time. This is my primary memory of
the place, superimposed on by later trips. My point is that a memory,
of the childhood memory kind which are seldom lost, is automatically associated for me with a text in this case, too. Jerusalem, among
other things, is the territory of the 'daughters of Jerusalem'. The
'Tower of David', now a museum, has a woman's image hanging
over it, and her neck is encircled by metallic jewelry (4.4). The
'Sharon' and the 'valleys' were appropriated by hiking in the past

and now are frequently traveled by car from where I live, to and from the centre of the country; 'the lily of the Sharon', the 'rose of the valleys' (2.1) float into my mind automatically, especially in the flowering season (I start humming the songs). Places like the Hermon, Lebanon, Glead, Carmel have more biblical connotations than the SoS alone; but, because the SoS was sung so much and so often, the special primary flavour remains.

Nature, Gardens, Food

The word 'pomegranate', Heb. רמון, occurs 47 times in the HB. The contexts are varied: from cultic ornaments[4] to place names[5] to a human name[6] to, perhaps, a god's name.[7] All these appear to be secondary usages. The chief denotation of the word is the tree, a native to the region like olives and other vegetable foods (Num. 13.23, 20.5; Deut. 8.8; Joel 1.12; Hag. 2.19). But when I look at the pomegranate trees in my garden (I have two), when I look on the ripe fruit which is partly deep-red and partly whitish-pink, I do not think about silver pomegranates on priestly garments (although I've seen an excavated sample, when it was exhibited at the Israel Museum in Jerusalem together with the priestly blessing eight years ago). Neither do I think about other cultic applications, nor about place names. It is the SoS pomegranate, six times used in the SoS[8] in metaphors for skin-colour and wine-drinking, that comes immediately to mind together with the verses of which they are part. Hair is described in terms of a herd of goats floating down a hill (4.1, 6.5)? I have seen it so many times, where I live; I still see it sometimes; the colour, the movement, even the texture come to me in a compact image; there is no difficulty and no need to verbalize. And when I do see a herd of goats sliding down the hill, sometimes into the road so that I have to stop my car, I recite the relevant verses to myself, automatically. The colour, the movement, the point of the metaphor (the entity referred to) is so clear because I have experienced its referent so many times. The change of seasons, the spring, is so much like SoS 2.11-13 (indeed, by the time of Passover the fig tree in my garden starts to 'put forth its figs' [2.13]).

I could cite more examples for illustrating how the SoS is, for me,

---

4. Exod. 28 and 39 (in the tabernacle); 1 Kgs 7, 2 Kgs 25, Jer. 52, 2 Chron. 3 and 4 (in the Jerusalem temple).
5. In Josh., Judg., Zech. 14, 2 Chron.
6. In 2 Sam. 4.
7. 2 Kgs 5.
8. SoS 4.3, 13; 6.7, 11; 7.13; 8.2.

an intimate and personal part of my life. But, perhaps, this is hardly necessary. It is impossible not to recall, sing, dance, recite SoS passages in daily life and recurrent situations in Israel, for me at any rate: because I am a native, because I had a certain kind of childhood and upbringing and growing up and adulthood here at a specific time in history, because the SoS (more, perhaps, than any other biblical book) was part of my (pop) culture before it became Bible for me.

The Personal and the Academic

In the last ten years I have studied the SoS, taught it or parts of it, and written about it extensively.[9] I come back to it again and again. The question is, therefore, how does my personal acquaintance with the SoS relate not only to my nostalgic, emotive and aesthetic enjoyment of it, but also to my academic appreciation of it? In other words, in what ways is my personal intimacy with this collection of love lyrics relevant to my critical work with and on it? Or: how does autobiography influence criticism, in my case at least? I will try to answer these questions by discussing a few issues briefly.

One Poem or a Structured Collection?

Scholars are divided on this issue. The two basic stands are: first, the SoS is a unified composition, with two lovers—a female lover and a male lover—engaged in a never-ending series of courting, dialogues, monologues, meetings and departures; and secondly, the book is an anthology of love lyrics, from various times and locations, with many figurations of female and male lovers. The whole is unified structurally, through the ingenious efforts of capable editors (or an editor). There are several variations on these two basic outlooks but, fundamentally, one of these two positions would be adopted by any given scholar.

Now, I join those who view the SoS as a collection of love lyrics, editorially strung together (the second option). There are many

---

9.   At the risk of self-advertising, here is a partial list of my work on the SoS: *The Song of Songs* (OTG; Sheffield: JSOT Press, 1989); '"Come Back, Come Back the Shulammite"(Song of Songs 7.1-10): A Parody of the *wasf* Genre', in J.T. Radday and A. Brenner (eds.), *On Humour and the Comic in the Hebrew Bible* (JSOTSup, 92; Sheffield: Almond Press, 1990), pp. 251-76; (ed.), *A Feminist Companion to the Song of Songs* (The Feminist Companion to the Bible, 1; Sheffield: Sheffield Academic Press, 1993); 'To See Is to Assume: Whose Love Is Celebrated in the Song of Songs?', *Biblical Interpretation* 1.3 (1993), pp. 1-20; and more—in Hebrew, Dutch and German (forthcoming).

reasons I can cite for this critical choice: formalistic, linguistic, stylistic, contextual and others. All these critical reasons are no doubt worth considering. But I suspect that, unconsciously at best, something more is at play here for me. I came to know the SoS as individual poems, indeed, as fragments (with no knowledge of the whole, at least at the beginning and for years): I incorporated components of it into my early life long before I knew of the biblical book itself (it was not on the school syllabus as such; it took years for me before I recognized it as a unity at Passover; it was various songs and dances, individually performed). This must have, somehow, determined my critical decision, at least in part—although I am hardly aware of it most of the time.

The Song of Songs is exactly what its Title Indicates: Songs, not 'Poetry' for Recitation

I am deeply aware of the singability, so to speak, of the SoS's constituents. After all, this is how I met such constituents or components to begin with, as songs. That is, poems set to music, with roles sometimes allocated to female lovers, male lovers, daughters of Jerusalem or 'woman's brothers' (1.5-6; 8.8-9) and so forth, and repeatedly performed accordingly. Some of them I knew first and foremost as dances. My experience makes it absolutely clear to me that the SoS is *not there* primarily for recital as 'poetry': it is there for *singing*. Fortunately, Rabbi Aqiba agrees with me, although indirectly: 'Rabbi Aqiba says, He who trills his voice with the Song of Songs in drinking houses and makes it a kind of song has no portion in the world to come' (*b. Sanh.* 12.10). It seems, then, that these songs were *sung*, primarily; and that the legitimation by allegorization programs of Judaism—and Christianity—concerning this collection of love songs required that they become recited poems instead of songs; that is, that the songs be divorced from their original mode of performance,[10] the kind of performance I grew up with.

Erotic Love Lyrics, not an Allegory: Erotic Nature of the Song of Songs

The 'Israel' I grew up in—urban, educated, middle class, insular, secular, socialist, relatively advanced from the viewpoint of gender relations—facilitated an understanding, from a very early age, that the SoS is about erotic, physical love. In my primary experience, the

---

10. See also tractate *Kalla* 1.4, 6: 'He who reads a verse in the Song of Songs and turns it into a kind of song...brings a flood to the world'; and similarly *b. Sanh.* 101a.

SoS poems have to do precisely with that. Imagining that an allegorical meaning—of divine–human love, historical or mystical; of any kind of Jewish or Christian or scholarly approach—is the *primary* or even a coexistent 'original' meaning of the SoS leaves me with genuine puzzlement, even embarrassment. Nothing will convince me that, to begin with, the SoS was conceived of as an elaborate allegory of religious passion, be it the passion for a goddess or for a male monotheistic god of whatever definition. I consider SoS allegories extremely interesting and a worthy subject of study. However, I find it improbable that the original significance of the biblical text is a 'hidden' significance, anything else but what it declares itself to be by its contents: songs of love and love-making between heterosexual humans.

Sitz im Leben

At the beginning of this century it was fashionable to imagine the SoS as a set of wedding poems, or songs to be performed during the prolonged (perhaps seven days, as in the case of Samson, Judg. 14) wedding feast. Indeed, a wedding of King Solomon is mentioned in the SoS (ch. 3). In my life experience, such songs are sung in non-wedding situations. This undoubtedly influences my view, based on additional critical criteria, that the songs are love songs rather than wedding songs. The many lovers of the SoS end (8.8) exactly were they started (1.2): running after each other, running away from each other. Indeed, secondary wedding usages of this non-wedding related material is possible. For instance: the Jewish orthodox wedding ceremony is notorious for the bride's oral and audial passivity—she does not speak. But my female cousin arranged with the rabbi that, at a certain point in the ceremony, she direct at her partner the words 'My beloved is mine and I am his'. Beautiful, no doubt: but a secondary utilization.

Female and Male Voices

Somehow, most of the SoS's songs that I have heard throughout my growing years have been sung by female singers. Most of the lines chosen for musical settings have been female first-person lines. I wonder, without reaching a conclusive result, how much that has conditioned my current feminist interests. It seems to me—and not only to me—that female voices in the SoS are stronger, more self assured, more confident, more articulate than male voices. Why this is so is less than clear at the present stage of SoS study. Various possibilities are considered: that the SoS is primarily a female composition; that in other cultures as well, such as Egyptian and Tamil cultures, in pre-nuptial situations women's voices are allowed freedom unequaled in other life situations of patriarchal frameworks; and so forth. And I wonder about myself, once more, about how my critical position—looking for the likelihood or feasibility of women's voices in the SoS[11]—is conditioned by my upbringing and admittedly banal (in ethnic, temporal, locational and class terms) life history.[12]

By Way of Conclusion

Do I assess my perspective on the SoS as a privileged perspective, academically or otherwise? Not at all. As a Jewish Israeli woman of a certain age, background and so on, I am mindful of certain privileges that are mine: the privilege of having been born in a 'Palestine' that very soon became an 'Israel'; the privilege of speaking Hebrew as a native tongue; the privilege of growing up on a biblical diet that was unproblematic (it was not religious in the usual sense, but secular-religious). This privilege of growing up with the HB was conceived of as problematic (as well as unproblematic) the minute it was used ideologically and politically, especially by what I consider 'the opposition': I am left-of-centre in my personal politics. Therefore, certain HB books, like Deuteronomy or Joshua, have always displeased me personally—I am neither keen on reading them nor on teaching them. Other biblical books, like the SoS, are more difficult to interpret politically: they pertain to the primary needs of human existence. They are less problematic for me.

So far I have discussed the influence of my life on my interest in the SoS; perhaps it is in order to give just one example how my interest in the HB enables me to understand aspects of the popular culture I

---

11. Cf., for instance, A. Brenner and F. van Dijk-Hemmes, *On Gendering Texts: Female and Male Voices in the Hebrew Bible* (Leiden: Brill, 1993).

12. I am well aware of the fact what is 'banal' for me is not equally banal for others. For instance, one of my best friends roughly shares many growing-up factors with me: age, place of birth and residence, gender, school, youth movement, army service; economic circumstances. However, her parents came from Germany and were not motivated by Zionist ideology. Hence, her native tongue was German, the early literature she came into contact with was primarily the Brothers Grimm's stories in the original language rather than HB and Jewish stories in Hebrew. Thus, these two variables made a great difference—at least until those differences were leveled by shared cultural factors in our early twenties. Upon reading this article, my friend remarked: 'But, for me, this is not banal at all; and while I share some of your sentiments and critical insights about the SoS, still others do not belong to my personal experience'.

grew up in (although it was possible, of course, to grow up in the Israel of my childhood without often connecting popular culture with the SoS).

In the early and mid-fifties there was propaganda and even a political call towards settling the Northern Negev. This, like other current events, was reflected in the popular songs of the time. A hugely popular song was called 'Simona of Dimona', and its refrain was something like the following:

> Love is a blaze within me,
> [love] for the black but comely,
> And my heart will sing, sing for Simona of Dimona...

Dimona is a small desert town south of Be'er Sheba, on the road to Eilat; even today the town has the status of a 'development town', a status reserved precisely for underdeveloped, peripheral locales. The northern Negev was settled mostly by newly arrived Jewish immigrants from middle-eastern countries, especially from Northern Africa. It was possible then, it is possible now, when listening to nostalgic records of 1950s popular songs, to identify both the name 'Simona' (with its Frenchified form) and the love object's dark beauty solely in terms of an allusion to the girl's ethnic origins and related looks. Most people undoubtedly understood both elements as such. But, having located both the burning love and the dark good looks in the linguistic provenance of the SoS, the recognition of the allusions to and quotations from SoS 8.6 and—even more so—1.5-6 acquires a completely different significance. At the time, first-generation [Jewish] immigrants from Mediterranean Muslim countries, especially from Northern Africa, were regarded as an inferior, less civilized, hardly differentiable group by native Israelis and by the culturally and economically dominant elite of European descent: indeed, the gap established in the 1950s between ethnic communities in the nascent country is one of our most lamentable failures, still in force today. At that time, marriage between members of Ashkenazi and oriental communities was as unacceptable to many as exogamy or intermarriage. Against this background, knowledge of how 'I am black but comely' functions in its source (SoS 1.6) as a protest against a conventionalized beauty ideal (blond and fair? urban?) lends the popular modern song another dimension. Thus, the song links up with the concerns of the hour not only by functioning as propaganda, an idealistic call (to young men, of course; they are the ones who carry the burden of pioneering activities) to go south. It also hints, broadly, that dark (read, dark girls of oriental descent) is beautiful and always has been—see the SoS. Modern Israeli culture has used the HB for its needs in a variety of ways, one among which was to enlist passages in order to effect changes in social attitudes to ethnic isolationism. This holds not only for low-brow popular culture but also, perhaps even more so, for politics and high-brow culture.

It so happens, then, that the SoS is much more than an academic topic in my world. I live with it: I always have. This personal circumstance affects my academic work. I remind myself of this again and again. The fact that my personal circumstances also enhance my *enjoyment* of this biblical book is a giant bonus. If my awareness of the intervention of personal circumstances is an efficient sentinel; if awareness of emotional and critical processes helps; if my willingness to declare the bias created by my life history is of any value, if confessing experience is a safeguard against allowing that same experience too much weight—then this self-exposure can be of a limited value to other readers who, undoubtedly, would bring their primary and secondary experiences and life histories to their own reading and work too.[13]

13. I regard this essay as part of a larger project dealing with my slippery, every-shifting identity as a person and HB scholar. Its next version will incorporate criticisms made at the Sheffield seminar (1997) as well as on other occasions. Matters not discussed here—like the orientalization of the SoS (and the HB in general) in Israeli and Western Culture, and the lack of military and security notions from the picture drawn in this essay—will be incorporated then.

X

BACK TO THE TRADITIONAL

EDITOR'S PREFACE TO CLAUS WESTERMANN'S 'BEAUTY IN THE HEBREW BIBLE'

Carole R. Fontaine

In the domain of theological discourse, what constitutes *value*? That is, what subjects are considered worthy of attention, based on their importance or centrality to theological discussion? For mainstream Christian biblical and theological scholarship (as in patriarchal pastoral contexts), the primary focus of scholarly investigation of the Bible has been in the realm of *soteriology*, the salvation of the individual. While biblical scholars and dogmatic theologians usually have different methods, questions and points of departure, it is fair to say that their domains of value, those things that they make into the subject of their studies, are in relative agreement. Given the preoccupations growing out of the Enlightenment, ultimately occasioning the development of the 'history of religions' phenomenological approach to studies of religion, this common value has inevitably led to a concern with historicity—can we *prove* that the Bible's portrait of the history of Israel and the early church and its promises of personal salvation are *true*?

Such questions, while not wholly irrelevant to the feminist method for the study of biblical religion, seldom constitute central concerns. This is not to say that soteriology is of no importance to feminist scholars, but we are more inclined to ask questions that would never occur to our more orthodox brothers: do women actually need 'saving' in the same way that men do? *Is* the world actually 'fallen' as the New Testament claims, or does the Hebrew Bible preserve a rather different view of the nature of worldly existence? *Is* Eve the mother of sin, as some patristic writers claimed, or are we forced to make this claim so that we may value Mary as the 'mother of Redemption', even as 'Christ' replaces Adam in this typology of the Old and New? *Can* a male savior be valid, useful, or effective in women's spiritual quest for maturity and wholeness? Does the gendered nature of salvation (according to some) offered in the New Testament constitute a serious problem for women along with the men who see women as ontologically whole (rather than as contingent) beings? Given the central place of women's religious experience, now and through the ages, as the value object of feminist religious discourse, it is no wonder that what we *do* so often fails to qualify as 'theological' by those who *wrote* and continue to *write* malestream/mainstream theological treatises.

To this end, we introduce here a startling deviation from the mainstream paradigm of what constitutes the theological value to be found in the Bible. In the essay presented below, Professor Claus Westermann of Heidelberg University turns from the history of mighty acts in the history of Israel and the early church to the daily world of divine blessing, as known in the form of *beauty*. While it was common to find ancient philosophers speculating on the nature of beauty and its place in the world and the life of humanity, this theme has been much less important for the soteriologically-driven inquiries of Christian biblical scholars. For Westermann, blessing constitutes a primary modality through which the God of Bible is made known and apprehended by the creatures of this world. While history remains hard to prove, easy to misunderstand, slippery in the value it may be said to hold in a post-modern world, blessing is easily seen, touched, held. A drop of rain, the cry of a newborn, the beauty of a beloved partner—for Westermann, these are as a much a testimonyof divine presentation as a pillar of fire or a sea split in two. Since feminist theology seeks to locate itself in the neglected realms of experience—the everyday lives of women and children where blessing is experienced as present or absent, regardless of whether we agree on its origins or meaning—we are delighted to include this work in the current volume. To those who wish to continue their reading in this area, we refer you to Westermann's *Blessing in the Bible and the Life of the Church* (Philadelphia: Fortress Press, 1978).

BEAUTY IN THE HEBREW BIBLE

Claus Westermann*

Does beauty belong essentially to what passes between God and humanity in the Hebrew Bible? Does beauty represent such an important aspect of the Bible's statements about God, that without all that is said about beauty, the Bible would not even *be* the Bible? In order to be able to answer these questions, we must be aware of the fact that two basic distinctions have to be made: a distinction referring to statements about beauty, and a distinction referring to the Bible's statements about God.[1]

We may discuss beauty as something that exists (as 'being'), but we also talk about beauty as 'event'. Beauty understood as something that exists, 'being', requires an objective attitude towards beauty. One can perceive beauty in a picture, one can hear it in music; one can contemplate a beautiful landscape or listen to the song of a nightingale. The Western concept of art fundamentally defines beauty as something that exists, as 'being'. The characteristic feature of this comprehension of art consists in the contrast between performance on one side and watching and listening on the other, a fact that can be observed in our prevailing institutions and forms of art such as cinema, concert, exhibition or museum. Moreover, this objective attitude towards art has social aspects. It is the essential motive of the creating and performing artist to achieve greatness and excellence:

---

*   Translated by Ute Östringer and Carole R. Fontaine.
1.   I should like to salute my current colleague and friend, Walther Zimmerli, with this work on the occasion of his seventieth birthday. I graduated in Zürich 1949 with the work, 'The Praise of God in the Psalms', where the question of beauty in the Bible arose for me more out of the experience of horror and brutality. The essay 'Biblische Ästhetik' of 1950 (in *Zeichen der Zeit* 88 [1950], pp. 277-89), took up some points made by G. von Rad, *Theologies des AT* (1957), I, pp. 361-66; here I take up this question again. W. Zimmerli gave me a first hint to the topic in the sentence in his commentary on Genesis on Gen. 1.31: 'The "good", which is remarked upon here, lies halfway between the "good" and the "beautiful"'.

the performance of beauty aims at reaching the heights, utmost 'quality'. It is connected with the idea of virtuosity, classic ideals and artistic perfection. On the other side, that is, the side of the 'audience', this objective attitude towards art has a selective effect. Applying a high standard, beauty exists for 'intellectuals' or even just for an elite among intellectuals. The distinction which is made between art and kitsch expresses this selection.

However, it is also possible to speak about beauty as 'event'. It is wonderful to participate in a celebration, to be given a radiant smile or to walk through the woods on a sunny day in springtime. The exclamation, 'Ah! How beautiful!' contrasts sharply with the criticism of a theater play. One difference immediately becomes evident: beauty as 'event' has a more elementary character than beauty as 'being'. It is common to all people and intrinsically belongs to human nature. If the experience of beauty is no longer possible in a human life, then it can no longer be called life. Life, in its real sense, only exists where something beautiful happens. Thus, it is the nature of beauty understood as event which unites humankind. Here, the selective tastes of the elite play no part.

We can conclude from this first distinction that 'beauty as being' most probably plays only a minor role concerning the question of its significance in the Hebrew Bible; 'beauty as event' presumably is in more accord with the Bible.

A second distinction has to be made with regard to the significance of beauty in narrations about God in the Hebrew Bible. It is a striking fact that major sections of the Hebrew Bible do not have anything or hardly have anything to do with beauty. Beauty is a topic that occurs only in certain contexts.

Where the Bible describes God's deeds of salvation and announces God's judgment, it does not mention beauty. This fact does not require explanation. It would certainly be inappropriate to speak of beauty in the narrations of the Exodus from Egypt, the journey through the desert, the acquisition of land, the combats during the time of the Judges or the announcements of judgment through the prophets, the description of the end and the lamentations of a suffering people. The same applies to the portions of the text in which the Bible talks about judgment and salvation in each individual life. The theology of the Hebrew Bible, which is marked by a strictly soteriological orientation, cannot attribute much significance to beauty, for its emphasis is on salvation and judgment as the only essential elements of the relationship between God and humans, God and God's people, God and the world.

The mention of beauty in the Hebrew Bible is thus restricted to the description of the beauty of creation, including humans as well as all the other creatures, to the description of, for example, a beautiful country or town; beauty that arose out of blessing; the beauty of the king, queen and royal court; the solemn beauty of the cult, including everything that it involves; and, finally, the beauty of the future state of salvation. All these topics refer—directly or indirectly—to the beneficial works of God. Blessing means abundance, wealth, thriving, success, exuberance; and all this includes beauty in a variety of ways.

That the description of beauty does not refer to God's works of salvation but to God's blessing is vividly illustrated in the last song about God's Servant, where the following is said of the servant who is suffering in the place of humanity: '...he has neither form nor comeliness...' (Isa. 53.2bα). For beauty was irrelevant for God's deeds of salvation throughout the course of the divine history with Israel. This fact is symbolized by the description of the Servant at the end of this narrative, when he is put into contrast with the royal figure of outstanding beauty (alluded to in Ps. 45.2): '...there is no beauty such that we should desire him...' (Isa. 53.2bβ). The songs of God's servant are based on the history of the monarchy as well as prophecy; they announce in accordance with the suffering prophets of judgment that the final Redeemer will not be a king of glorious beauty but, rather, an inconspicuous servant. Thus, it is made even clearer: in a theology that regards itself as soteriology, beauty can be of no significance. But Isaiah 53 does not end with the suffering of the servant. The suffering and death of the servant is supposed to bear its fruits, its reward: 'he shall see his seed; he shall prolong his days...' and '...he shall divide spoil with the rich...'; this is the old wording of the promise of God's blessing. Salvation occurs when the blessing is returned; just as in the beginning the promise of salvation is connected with the beauty of the land. Salvation becomes necessary when life, as the gift of the Creator, is threatened with death; salvation is bound up with the gift of life. In the Hebrew Bible, beauty does *not* belong to the 'history of salvation' (*Heilsgeschichte*), but rather to the gift of blessing.

The Beauty of Creation

In the creation story of the Priestly writer in Genesis 1, at the end of each work of creation the following sentence is repeated: '...and God saw that it was good'. The Hebrew word, טוב, in this context contains both the meaning of 'good' and of 'beautiful'.[2] Beauty is an intrinsic quality of the creation. However, this beauty is not objective nor can it be treated objectively; this beauty of creation is a real event, in view of all the atrocity and terror that are part of the creation. It is only legitimate to say this because the creation is beautiful in the eyes of God: 'that the light is good, remains established in the authority of the Creator'.[3] This corresponds to the functional character of the word טוב in Genesis 1, in the sense of 'being good for...' and 'being beautiful for...' The word characterizes creation as such and does not represent a quality that is attributed to it later on. Herein, basically, lies the difference, compared to our concept of beauty.

1. If the statement '...and [God] saw that it was good [beautiful]...' refers to the world, we regard it as identical with our typical concept of the beauty of nature; and yet what Gen. 1.31 means essentially diverges from this concept. The fact that the works of creation are beautiful coincides with their function in creation as a whole, even where humankind cannot perceive it. This is expressed exactly by the statement that they are beautiful in the eyes of God. While our apprehension of the beauty of nature is exclusively based on the perception (aesthetics), sensibility and personal tastes of people, the beauty of all creation in Genesis 1 is founded on the broader horizon of God's perspective.

2. The functional understanding of beauty is also reflected by the fact that specific expressions for 'beautiful' or 'beauty' are used rather infrequently in the Hebrew Bible, whereas the concept 'beautiful' is conveyed by other words like טוב 'good' or, in certain contexts, כבוד ('glory'). The Hebrew Bible speaks of the כבוד of the forests of Leban-on,[4] whereas *we* would speak of the beauty of the forests of Lebanon. What is meant here as well is the 'blessing-full-ness'—the glory of the trees—and its meaning for the land and for humankind, and not just perceptible, objective beauty.

Something else is directly connected with this fact. All creation is the work of God; however, every good work requires appreciation—God's works of creation as well. In Genesis 1, this is expressed from God's perspective: after the completion of the creation, the praising of

2. W. Zimmerli, *Zürcher Bibelkommentare. 1. Moses 1–11* (1967 [1943]), p. 88; C. Westermann, Genesis 1–11: Ein Kommentar (Neukirchen–Vluyn: Neukirchener Verlag, 1974), I, pp. 228-29.

3. Zimmerli, *Moses 1–11*, p. 156.

4. Isa. 10.18; 35.2; 60.13; Ezek. 31.18; Ernst Jenni and C. Westermann (eds.), *Theologisches Handwörterbuch zum Alten Testament* (2 vols.; Munich: Chr. Kaiser Verlag, Zurich: Theologischer Verlag, 1971–76), I, pp. 798-99.

the Creator from the side of creatures begins. The beauty of the creation is put into words by the Creator praising his works. The psalms of creation that praise the beauty of all creation correspond to the phrase '...and he saw that it was good...' However, where this praise of the Creator is expressed, the beauty of the creation can never become an objectivized beauty of nature. The beauty of the creation is an *event*; it exists where it is expressed by the Creator. It cannot be abstracted from the interaction between the works of creation and their praise in order to represent a beauty that is merely perceptible.

If the sentence '...and he saw that it was good...' refers to human beings as creatures, it has as a prerequisite a special idea of the beauty of humanity. Here beauty is also based on the creation and it is an intrinsic feature of humans as creatures.[5] However, this does not really refer to that kind of beauty that distinguishes a beautiful person from an ugly one (the Hebrew Bible also deals with this problem in the narrations of Jacob's wives). Here, the kind of beauty is meant which all children seem to have in common and which is expressed in a song by the poet M. Claudius: '...that I am, am and do have this beautiful human countenance...' Since the blessing of the Creator is granted to all living things, and since in the eyes of the Creator all things are good ('beautiful'), real beauty is an inherent feature of humans in that they are creatures.

The beauty of humanity can be discovered and experienced when entering into contact with others. In the history of the creation by the Yahwist in Gen. 2.23, it is described very poetically how man and woman meet each other, how the man 'welcomes the woman with jubilation' (Herder). But even here no specific word meaning 'beautiful' is used. If two loving partners meet each other, they are affected by the beauty which is part of their joy about the meeting.

However, the joy about the beauty of the beloved man or woman sometimes is expressed with exaltation, as is the case in the Song of Solomon. Here, the concept and comprehension of beauty are especially close to ours; but, even here, the peculiarity of the attitude of the Hebrew Bible becomes evident through the fact that beauty is experienced in the process of meeting. Song 2.8-14 shows this especially clearly. Beauty that comprises the handsomeness of humanity is an event.

3. In the history of the creation of J, which is traditionally con-

5.   For personal human beauty in the Hebrew Bible see H.W. Wolff, *Anthropologie des Alten Testaments* (Munich: Chr. Kaiser Verlag, 1973), pp. 111-15.

nected with the creation of humanity,[6] one finds allusions to the beauty of non-human creation that correspond to what is said about human beauty. However, this is presented in its relation to humanity. In the narration of 'the temptation', the beauty of the fruits of the forbidden tree is alluring '...it was pleasant to the eyes and good for food...' (Gen. 3.6).

Here we meet with another aspect of beauty: it can turn into a temptation! Beauty is ethically ambivalent, just as in general all gifts of blessing are ethically ambivalent ('...he [God] causes it to rain on the good and the bad...'). That beauty can endanger people, that the desire for beauty can lead to catastrophe, is no contradiction to the fact that beauty has its roots in creation and that it is contained in the Creator's blessing. Rather, this shows even more clearly that beauty can never become an absolute value of its own, for it can never be objectivized. The beauty of creation, just like the beauty of humanity, can be beneficial *or* fateful.

That the narrators and writers of the Hebrew Bible were intensely occupied with the problem of the ambivalence of the beauty of humanity and its dangerous effects is shown by the fact that this motif emerges in three independent narratives. These are: the history of the creation (Gen. 6.1-4); the history of the ancestors (Gen. 12.10-20), and the history of the kings (2 Sam. 11). In each of these three narratives, the beauty of women represents a motif that causes conflicts. The powerful men can take possession of beautiful women by virtue of their superiority of power. In Genesis 6, these are 'the sons of Elohim'; in Genesis 12, Pharaoh; in 2 Samuel 11, King David. Each of these three episodes is based on the experience that where a human society is dominated by a considerable imbalance of power, men and women no longer meet on the same level as described in Genesis 2 or in the Song of Solomon. The meeting is replaced by something else—a perverted form of encounter in which the mighty one can use his power to take possession of beauty. One of the major problems of humanity, which can originate from the beauty of persons, is treated in this motif and its various elaborations with deep insight.

Beauty in the Description of Blessing

The beauty of a man or a woman may be called a direct gift of blessing, such as, for example, the beauty of the king in Ps. 45.3 (p.d.), or the beauty of the daughters of Job in 42.13-15.

6. Westermann, *Genesis 1–11*, pp. 31-34.

1.   This relation between blessing and beauty, expressed in bles-
sing-sayings and descriptions of salvation derived from them, must
be regarded as deeply rooted in the broader context of Israel's traditions. Blessing is accompanied by exuberant fullness, as in the blessing of Joseph in Deut. 33.13-17.

> Blessed by the Lord be his land, for the choicest gift of heaven, for the
> dew and for the deep that coucheth beneath,
> And for the precious fruits brought forth by the sun, and for the pre-
> cious fruits brought forth by the moon,
> And for the chief things of the ancient mountains, and for the precious
> things of the lasting hills, and for the precious things of the earth and
> the fulness thereof...

The Hebrew word מגד—here translated as 'precious things',
perhaps rather meaning 'donation'—appears only in Deut. 33.13-17
and Song 4.13-16, 7.14 ('pleasant fruits'). These passages most certainly show that מגד means something exceptionally good and, at the
same time, beautiful.

The blessings of Balaam, which are spoken by him in favor of
Israel in spite of the curse demanded, have the same sense and
sound (Num. 24.4-7):

> How fair are thy tents, O Jacob, and thy tabernacles, O Israel.
> As the valleys are they spread forth, as the gardens by the river's side,
> as the trees of lignum aloes which the Lord hath planted and as cedar
> trees beside the water.
> He shall pour the water out of his buckets, and his seed shall be in
> many waters.

Both examples sufficiently show how, in the sayings of blessing,
the exuberant abundance of the gifts of blessing and beauty belong
together. However, it can also be seen here very clearly that beauty is
not meant as objectively perceptible, but as 'being good for...', that is,
for those who receive the blessing. Further, these sayings show us
something else. Obviously, here speech about beauty goes along with
beautiful language; the extraordinarily lovely, poetic language of
these words of blessing must not be separated from the fact that such
speech talks about beauty, as in Psalm 45. The poem about the beauty
of the king and queen is called דבר, 'beautiful word'.

2. A traditional historical relation exists between the sayings of
blessing, the prophetic sayings, and the description of salvation.[7] The
description of salvation (or blessing) is fundamentally different from
the promise of God's saving grace and the announcement of salva-

---

7.   *ThB* 55 (1974), pp. 236-37.

tion (or deliverance). The fact that we can distinguish these two forms confirms that statements about beauty in the Hebrew Bible play a significant role in the context of God's blessing but not necessarily with regard to God's saving deeds. The prophecy of salvation (deliverance) points to a certain moment in the future, at one moment in the course of time, that is, the moment of God's intervention to save and aid humanity. For example, this is shown in the words of salvation spoken by the prophet Hananiah (Jer. 28.11): 'Thus saith the Lord, Even so will I break the yoke of Nebuchadnezzar, king of Babylon...' The narration of blessing, on the other hand, differentiates a state of salvation extending over a long period of time in contrast to the present state of affairs. In the description of this future state, beauty is attributed much significance. Just as in the verses about Judah in Gen. 49.11, the description of blessing merges into a description of beauty:

> Binding his foal unto the vine, and his ass's colt unto the choice vine; he
> washed his garments in wine, and his clothes in the blood of grapes:
> His eyes shall be red with wine, and his teeth white with milk...

In the portrayal of the coming time of blessing, the elements outlining the beauty of this time establish a significant component.

> ...then shall thy light rise in obscurity and thy darkness be as the
> noonday;

And the Lord shall guide thee continually and satisfy thy soul in drought; and make fate the bones; and thou shalt be like a watered garden and like the spring of water, whose waters fail not (Isa. 58.10-11).

Or Isa. 62.2-3, 5:

> And the Gentiles shall see thy righteousness, and all kings thy glory...
> ...Thou shalt also be a crown of glory in the hand of the Lord, and a
> royal diadem in the hand of thy God...
> ...and as the bridegroom rejoiceth over the bride, so shall thy God
> rejoice over thee.

These are only a few examples out of a large variety of words describing the future (state of) salvation, all about the beauty of this blessed state which is to come. It is certainly the largest group of texts in the Hebrew Bible that speak about beauty, and it would probably be a rewarding task to analyze them all under this aspect. All these descriptions of the future state of salvation have in common that, in them, the unspoilt effect of God's blessing is accompanied by beauty and by life that is considered and experienced as beautiful. It is not at all surprising, but rather consistent, that the same view is expressed in the New Testament[8] and the Christian narrative of salvation as we find it in the songs about eternity, when one speaks of the 'beautiful Paradise':

> Kein Zunge kann erreichen
> die ewige Schönheit groß;
> man kann's mit nichts vergleichen,
> die Wort sind viel zu bloß…
>
> No tongue can reach
> the boundless eternal Beauty,
> one can compare it with nothing,
> even a few words are too many….

Two more areas which hold an important place in the Hebrew Bible's discourse also belong in the realm of the relationship of beauty to blessing: kingship and cult.

Beauty in Kingship

In the Hebrew Bible the beauty of humans is mentioned for the first time in the story about the origin of the monarchy. In the time of the judges, the appearance and figure of the redeemer is of no significance; the king's appearance, however, is important. This is connected with the fact that the king is the mediator of blessing: the king, anointed and consecrated by God, is obliged to represent royal dignity in his appearance as well.

Psalm 45, usually interpreted as the wedding song of a king (it could, however, also be a psalm to celebrate a dynasty), describes in solemn language the beauty of the king and queen:

> Thou are fairer than the children of men;
> grace poured into thy lips:
> therefore God hath blessed thee forever (v. 3).

The beauty of the king is evidence for the fact that he has been anointed by God. This sentence confirms that beauty can be understood as an effect of blessing. Here the beauty of the figure (יֹפִי) and grace (חֵן) of the lips are described in parallelism. What is meant here is pleasing speech—speech which is pleasing to its hearers. It is speech in which beauty is given form in words. This means that the king's beauty may not be compared with that of a statue; he is not a kind of Adonis. The king's beauty is described as vivid reality. Here

8.   Rev. 19.6-8; 21.2, 9, 11, 23.

again the functional conception of beauty becomes evident. But the king is also characterized by magnificence and glory (vv. 8-9):

> Therefore God has anointed thee with the oil of gladness above thy fellows.
> All thy garments smell of myrrh and aloes, and cassia, out of the ivory palaces, whereby they have made thee glad.

The royal ritual, the royal court, serve to intensify the king's beauty and attribute to it the glorious environment which is part of it. This expresses a new function of beauty: beauty as magnificence, as representation of greatness and sovereignty. Here differences may be perceived. This aspect of beauty as representation of importance and royal position plays a much more important role in the description of Solomon's kingdom than of David's and in Saul's story it is not yet mentioned. Further, it is exactly this aspect of beauty as well which provokes the criticism and accusation of the prophets, especially in Isa. 2.6-22.

Beauty representing magnificence and splendor is not reduced to the description of the royal court. It is even mentioned in the context of battles and war:

> Gird thy sword upon thy thigh, O most mighty, with thy glory and thy majesty. (Ps. 45.3; Heb., 'with your הוד and your הדר').

The words הוד and הדר, usually used in praise to express God's majesty, refer here to the king fighting in his royal armor. This is significant for the history of war. Starting with the monarchy, the kings' wars are accompanied by splendor and magnificence. It was only with modern materialistic battle that this kind of 'beautiful' war ceased to exist.

That beauty is necessarily included in the praise of the queen (Ps. 45.10-16) derives from the dynastic structure of the kingdom. As the one chosen by the king, the bride enters into the special sphere of royal beauty which surpasses individual beauty. The description of the queen's entry (vv. 14-16) reflects this specific majestic beauty, which is something new compared to the familiar concept. The beauty of appearance, jewelry, garments and royal posture (cf. Prov. 30.29-31) do indeed serve to delineate royal beauty.

The Beauty of the Cult

First of all, we have to remember the two distinctions made at the beginning. There is no room for beauty in the cult if the worship of God refers only to God's deeds of salvation, if the amphictyonic cult (as, for example, described by von Rad and Noth)[9] mainly consists of recalling God's deeds, the credo, the proclamation of commandments and the reading of the law and the celebration of the covenant. However, it remains clear and obvious that beauty starts to play a role in the cultic service when blessing is integrated into it. Since in the cult blessing is given and received, beauty, exuberance, satiety and richness can become part of cultic celebration. This, perhaps, becomes most evident in narrative praise and descriptive praise. The individual (narrative) psalm of praise, which relates one of God's deeds of salvation, merely narrates in simple words 'what happened'; the psalm of descriptive praise, which honors God's complete work including the works of creation, rings out in the orchestra of instruments of the temple's music. This too shows us that the beauty of the cult is functional beauty, not a kind of decoration that can be omitted if desired.

The second distinction between beauty as something which has static being and beauty as 'event' must also be taken into account in this context. If the instruments do accompany the praise of God—

> Praise him with the sound of the trumpet; praise him with psaltery and harp (Ps. 150.3a)—

then this means that the instruments themselves participate in the process of worship. The worship of God, with its tendency to extend outward, starts with the singing of human voices which are then joined by the voices of other creatures, of wood and of metal, each given a voice that has been formed into instruments. The rejoicing of those praising the Lord with their singing is accompanied and passed on by the jubilant rejoicing of the instruments. It remains clear that the beauty of instrumental music is an event, since it accompanies and intensifies the worship of God by those attending the service. Here we should not speak of a performance of sacred music and its audience. What actually happens is that the community assembled to celebrate the service turns into one choir, of which the instruments form a part.

However, music is only one form of beauty in the cultic service.[10] The buildings, cult objects and priestly garments represent beauty as well. Here we must be aware that in the Hebrew Bible two different stages in the history of the cult can be identified: the cult of a large

9. Martin Noth, *A History of Pentateuchal Traditions* (trans. Bernhard W. Anderson; Chico, CA: Scholars Press, 1981), from p. 60.

10. C. Westermann, 'Religion und Kult', *Zeitwende* 2 (1975), pp. 77-86.

settled community and, before that, the cult of early communities, as described in the narratives of the ancestors. The beauty of the settled cult's requisites—the splendor of the building, the cult objects, the decoration and the priestly vestments—belongs exclusively to the phase of settled culture. It is not an inherent characteristic of the cult. This is significant for two reasons. The beauty of the decor, with its splendor and magnificence, did not necessarily emerge from Israel's encounter with its God; it could have been copied from other cultures, as the example of Solomon's construction of the Jerusalem temple proves. The borrowed beauty, the splendid decorative elements of the service, can jeopardize the event if the decoration contains pagan elements used to worship Israel's God. Since the external decorations are not an inherent characteristic of the service, they may be separated from it. After the destruction of the temple and the loss of all cult objects, the service could be resumed in a new form, completely devoid of all decorative trappings; thereupon service of the synagogue, characterized by the lack of any decoration, grew out of this separation. Much more remains to be concluded *from* the beauty of the cultic service in the Hebrew Bible and *about* the beauty of cultic service; this requires further investigation for its own sake.

Beautiful Work and Beautiful Word

Now we must add a distinction which was already a prerequisite of the preceding discussion without it having been explicitly mentioned. Beauty exists as something that can be found or something that has been made, as something created or as something produced. We may say, then, that we find it in nature and in art.

In the modern usage of language a certain difficulty arises in this respect. The distinction just mentioned could be regarded as a differentiation between 'creative' art and mere 'artistic craftsmanship'. Through the secularization of the term 'creation' humans, especially artists, are said to be creative and thus the concept of God as the creator falls more and more into oblivion. The other consequence of this process is that creation has come to mean 'nature', and nature has become producible. It is quite unfortunate that in the Christian use of language works of art are unscrupulously called 'creations' and artists are called 'creative'. Here it is necessary to return to a precise and unambiguous language. Since in German 'to create' (*schaffen*) means 'to work', and since in standard German 'creative capacity' (*Schaffenskraft*) is equivalent to 'capacity for work', this verb and its derivatives may be used of humans. But only God is a *Creator*.

Persons cannot be 'the creators' of significant works, nor can they be 'creative'. We should do without all our modern talk about 'creativity'. Everything persons produce—be they farmer, technician, painter or composer—can only be made within the boundaries of all creation, including their own existence.

When the Hebrew Bible speaks about beauty that is produced by humans, this differs considerably from our modern discourse about art and artistic creativity. The Hebrew Bible does not know the principle of *l'art pour l'art*. For the Hebrew Bible this would be a perversion of beauty since, for humans in the Hebrew Bible, beauty only exists in its function to 'be beautiful for'. The principle of *l'art pour l'art* requires a radically objectivized beauty. Beauty represented in art is isolated for its real context, and becomes an object that is destined to be regarded or listened to for its own sake. Such a concept of art would not correspond to the Hebrew Bible concept of human nature. Among the most beautiful works of art in the Hebrew Bible are the psalms of praise, such as Psalm 148. As works of poetry and also music, the psalms' meaning lies in their function: to worship God, to appeal through such praise to God, to reflect upon this praise of God: 'It is a good thing to give thanks to the Lord' (Ps. 92.2). If the psalms were taken out of their context and converted into concert music, this would be a perversion.

1. We have already mentioned the beauty produced by humans, especially in the context of beauty in the cult and the monarchy. Beauty was made, that is, the beauty of the buildings, cult objects, garments and decoration that belong to the cult. And the beauty— produced by humans—of the buildings, the culture of the royal court, objects, decoration, weapons that go with the monarchy—that all this is functional beauty is unmistakable.

If we investigate the occurrences of crafted beauty, of 'art' in the Hebrew Bible as a whole, the first and most striking impression is that the arts of writing and sound are absolutely predominant. The beautifully formulated word, the דבר טוב (Ps. 45.2), has a specific meaning for the Hebrew Bible; related to this are the arts of songwriting and music, the art of 'voice' used for singing in profane contexts as well as in the cult, and the playing of instruments. Fine arts, however, play only a minor role in Israel. Painting and sculpture are not even mentioned throughout the entire Hebrew Bible, and this situation has been borne out by the current state of archaeological investigation. More important for Israel is architecture, but individual architecture specific to Israel was never developed; the major buildings of Jerusalem, palace and temple, were constructed by master builders from Phoenicia. With regard to other forms of artistic craftsmanship, as far as they existed at all, Israel depended on its neighbors.

2. The almost complete lack of fine arts is not the whole story, however. If one goes further into detail one perceives that, in Israel, the art of poetry in certain fields comprises fine arts. This is because in these fields, fine arts were replaced to a large extent by the art of poetry: so in the language of *parables* or *similitudes*, the language of images or metaphors (this Greek term is not really adequate for the phenomenon, since it does not represent a 'transfer'). In Israel, the power of images, which in other cultures was expressed by means of plastic and representational arts, found expression in the metaphorical power of language.

Especially in the collections of Proverbs—yet not only there—the description of beauty is expressed by such a rich and abundant language that the question of the existence of beauty in the Hebrew Bible leads to a surprising discovery: the description of beauty is one of the most important elements of Proverbs. Beauty as such, however, is not a topic *of* them. Isolated, abstract beauty was unknown in the communities in which the proverbs were written. The Proverbs speak about beautiful persons and beautiful objects, but not about beauty per se. Even beautiful objects and persons are not described for their own sake, or in order to talk about their beauty. The significance and sense of this description of beauty is rather based upon the comparison (similitude), the parable:

> As an earring of gold, and an ornament of fine gold, so is a wise reproof upon the obedient ear (Prov. 25.12).

It is a prerequisite of this comparison that the aesthetic esteem, the value of the ring and ornament should meet with common, unanimous approval. However, such a proverb not only demonstrates the common esteem of beauty; through the similitude the giving and accepting of a wise warning are granted their share in the beauty of the ornaments. It is something beautiful and valuable—so it is said—if a good word is spoken at the right moment (Prov. 25.11),

> A word fitly spoken is like apples of gold in a bowl of silver.

This comparison with beautiful objects—especially with beautiful, valuable jewelry (ring, ornament, crown, silver, gold, coral, necklace, bowls of silver) but also with pleasant fragrances (balm, myrrh) or pleasant taste (wine, honey)—can be found in abundance throughout the whole collection of Proverbs, and it unintentionally and discreetly shows that beauty is a natural element of human existence.

Moreover, this group of similitudes which compare wisdom (i.e. wise advice, warning or encouragement) with beauty vividly illustrates the functional concept of beauty. All kinds of beauty on its own are insignificant. It is only in the community of people, where beauty decorates, gives pleasure and enriches life, that it becomes meaningful.

Up to now we have only talked about similitudes in which a comparison with something beautiful was drawn. But the variety of proverbs is much wider. We can also find parable and comparison in other genres of texts: in the love song (SoS), the Psalms, the sayings of the prophets. Every explicated similitude is poetry: an event is compared to one that has occurred in another realm, and thus the one is illuminated by the other or helps to explain the other. The parables of the vineyard and the vine-grower in Isaiah 5 or Psalm 80, for example, describe the same event, namely, the work of the vine-grower in the vineyard. Both intend to tell those who are addressed something about God's works among the people; but, in each one, this is done in a completely different way. However, iidentically in both examples, the event to be compared—the acts of God among the community—and the event to which it is compared merge in a unified whole. The works of God with the people, experienced in reality as single independent acts, become a completed unity, a 'story'.

The similitude represents only one possible form of the poetic language which is developed in the Hebrew Bible.[11] In one passage, poetic language is explicitly called 'beautiful word' (דבר טוב): in the introduction of Psalm 45. This song, praising the king and queen, is 'beautiful speech'.

It is impossible to present the poetry of the Hebrew Bible in detail here: a few remarks must be sufficient. Poetry or poetic language belong to all parts of the Hebrew Bible. One may find them in the historical books and the prophets, the psalms and the books of wisdom literature.

3. In the historical books our distinction between 'poetry' and 'prose' must be replaced by the distinction between enumerative and narrative texts. The *narrative* is a form of poetry (Gunkel: 'poetic

11. W. Zimmerli, 'Die Weisung des AT zum Geschäft der Sprache', *ThB* 19 (1963), pp. 277-99; 'Verkündigung und Sprache der Botschaft Jesajas', *ThB* 51 (1964), pp. 73-87.

narration'[12]) in which the poetic character can be more or less developed. Potentially, however, every narrative is poetry. For in a narrative, in the course of the amorphous flow of a variety of events, a common message emerges which gradually takes shape as narrative suspense evolves. The exposition starts with a certain state (e.g. the childlessness of Sarai) and leads to a new state in the conclusion (the child is born and given a name). Yet, the narrative only becomes poetry through the confrontation between narrator and listeners. The narrator designs the concept of the story for the listeners. Here, poetry is a process in which both sides have their part. In addition to narratives, we can find poems, songs and proverbs in the historical books. The numerous 'profane' songs in the Hebrew Bible all have a 'setting in life', such as the song about the digging of a fountain (Num. 21.17-18.).

4. That the words of the prophets are written in poetic language, that the speech of the prophets is poetry is a surprising fact, one which is of considerable significance for the phenomenon of prophecy. Usually we know 'religious speech' in the form of sermon, letter, doctrine, that is, as prose. The reason why the words of the prophets have a poetic form is grounded in the fact that prophetic speech is an *appeal* and appeals as such have a rhythmic form. If would be a misunderstanding to think that the poetic form of the words of the prophets results from an intention to solicit more approval by using a formulation with a more pleasant style. The poetic form of the prophets' words should be understood as due strictly to its function.[13]

One of the roots of the prophetic sayings are the sayings of the seers.[14] If the sayings of the seers describe something beautiful, as is the case in the sayings of Balaam, they are written in verse. Since the sayings of the seers are succeeded by prophetic sayings, it is only natural that such later sayings should also be formulated in poetic language when they describe the judgment or salvation that is to come. On the other hand, the prophetic accusation can be traced back to judicial accusation, and the announcement of judgment goes back to threat of punishment or sentence in court, namely, to prose forms. This explains why, in announcements of judgment through the

12. Editor's note: see Hermann Gunkel, *The Legends of Genesis: The Biblical Saga and History* (New York: Schocken Books, 1964), pp. 10-12.

13. See Zimmerli's essay on poetic language in Isaiah, 'Verkündigung', on this particular point.

14. Editor's note: 'Seers' refers here to the early, 'non-writing' prophets preceding the classical prophets of the eighth century BCE; the work of the latter group is associated with books of collected oracles bearing their names.

prophets before Amos, the prose form prevails. Here the words of the prophets are part of narrations or notices, and are written in corresponding style. When the words of the prophets started to separate themselves from narrative and became an independent type of written account, they more and more came to form a unified whole which contained both accusation and announcement. Thus, the word of God spoken out by a human being turned into one unity, standing out among the words of humans, as an appeal that comes from far away. Therefore, the word of the prophets as poetic form was able to incorporate various completely different elements at the same time: especially the descriptive style which it borrowed from the sayings of the seers, but also other forms of poetry (such as the dirge). Thus, the words of the prophets came to be a literary genre of its own.

5. The psalms have often been said to be poetry, especially since in them one finds the דבר טוב, the 'beautiful word'.[15] Here, the question arises why a literary style which is, of course, suitable for the hymns of praise can at the same time be appropriate for the psalms of lament. The designation 'song of lament' or 'poem of lament' seems to be a contradiction in itself.

Narrative praise and descriptive praise, in different ways and for different reasons, are poetry.[16] Narrative praise results from the experience of deliverance and is a reply to it. The heart of it is the sigh of relief expressed in one short exclamation, ברוך Yhwh! We find it in narrative texts as well, such as Exod. 18.9; it is an echo of the experience of rescue, lifting itself out from the narrative by the exalted language of the exclamation in rhythmic form (a double accent). The joy of the one who was rescued, a joy directed towards God, finds its poetic expression in this exclamation. The exclamation is based on an account of salvation which, from a situation of need, leads to rescue. The account as such has a prose form and so do other elements of the psalms of narrative praise, such as the announcement, the vow of praise, the appeal to join in with the praise. Yet, the fact that through their structure the psalms of narrative praise form a new unity, turns them into song and poetry which, as a whole, are the

15. 'Here...in the glorifying of Yahweh...Israel also encounters the reality of Beauty in its highest form' and furthers the beautiful representation. Gerhard von Rad, *Theologie des Alten Testaments*, I (1957), pp. 361-66.

16. Editor's note: In Westermann's form-critical analysis, psalms of 'narrative praise' refer to those hymns that recount God's saving acts in the past and God's character as *Redeemer*; psalms of 'descriptive praise' refer to hymns which praise God's everyday blessing in and of creation. In the latter, God's character is that of *Creator*.

expression of the praise of God. When, in the course of the religious service, a person who has been rescued tells the community about this event and asks others to respond, this develops the poetic form which is taken up by the congregation at the service.

In the case of hymns of descriptive praise of God, things are different. Here, it is in the process of the praising of God as such that the words take shape as poetry. However, the incentive is not only the expressive power of a rescued person narrating the experience, but the praising of God by the whole congregation in answer to God's works and existence as a whole. It is this interaction between God and the congregation that responds to the divine: that is the essential element of the service. The hymn fulfilling this function exists in all the different religions throughout the world and always has a lyric form. It may adopt a variety of forms. One thing is especially characteristic of the psalms of descriptive praise in Israel which—like the psalms, hymns and songs of other religions and cults—intend to sing the praise of God and everything God represents and does: the predominance of the imperative form, the appeal to praise. This is the most evident connection with the psalms of narrative praise. The dominant place of the appeal demonstrates to what large an extent the praising of God in Israel is based on the experience acquired by this people during its history of its God.

But how can the lament become a poem, a song, a דבר טוב? Part of the answer derives from what was said about psalms of narrative praise. Like this type, the lament contains elements of prose which, being formed into a unified sacral song, are transformed into poetry. But this is not the whole answer. We must investigate the character of this integrated whole in the lament psalm. Each psalm of lament in the Hebrew Bible is characterized by a change of attitude that leads away from the lamenting or goes beyond it. There is no psalm of lament that does not contain at least one element of trust.[17] In many of them, for example Psalm 13, this additional aspect merges with a vow of praise. In others, such as Psalm 22, the lamentation turns into the praise of God in the conclusion. This is the reason why psalms of lament can adopt the form of songs and poetry. The polarity between lament and praise allows the 'complaint' to influence the structure of the psalm, and the change in the attitude in the speaker of the lament allows the complaint to merge into praise. However, this should not lessen the gravity of the lament psalm. It remains a cry from the

17. Editor's note: Some scholars would disagree here, as motifs of confidence or trust seem to be lacking in Psalm 88.

depths, a cry that may also contain a profound sensation of the absence of God, which is an absolute contrast to a hymn of praise. This cry from the depths can be integrated into religious service, can become another form of worship-ful Word. It is here, in the worship of God, that the lament can become a song, a poem with a structure which maintains the connection to praise.

It is with this form of the lament psalm, where grief is transformed into song, that the 'beautiful word' in the Hebrew Bible finds its deepest human expression.

BIBLIOGRAPHY

Abrahams, B.-Z. (trans. and ed.), *Memoirs [Glückel of Hameln: Life 1646–1724]* (New York: Thomas Yoseloff, 1963).

Ackerman, S., '"And the Women Knead Dough": the Worship of the Queen of Heaven in Sixth-century Judah', in P.L. Day (ed.), *Gender and Difference in Ancient Israel* (Minneapolis: Augsburg–Fortress, 1989), pp. 109-24.

—'The Queen Mother and the Cult in Ancient Israel', *JBL* 112 (1993), pp. 385-401.

—*Under Every Green Tree: Popular Religion in Sixth-Century Judah,* (HSM, 46; Atlanta: Scholars Press, 1992).

Adorno, T., *Negative Dialectics* (trans. E.B. Ashton; New York: Continuum, 1973).

Ahituv, S., *Handbook of Ancient Hebrew Inscriptions from the Period of the First Commonwealth and the Beginning of the Second Commonwealth* (Jerusalem: Keter, 1992 [Hebrew]).

Ahlström, G.W., *The History of Ancient Palestine from the Paleolithic Period to Alexander's Conquest* (JSOTSup, 146; Sheffield: Sheffield Academic Press, 1993).

Albright, W.F., 'Astarte Plaques and Figurines from Tell Beit Mirsim', in *Mélanges syriens offerts à Monsieur René Dussaud* (Paris: Geuthner, 1939), I, pp. 107-20.

—*Yahweh and the Gods of Canaan* (London: Athlone Press, 1968).

Alcoff, L., and E. Potter (eds.), *Feminist Epistemologies* (London: Routledge, 1993).

Allen, J.P., *Genesis in Egypt: The Philosophy of Ancient Egyptian Creation Accounts* (Yale Egyptological Studies, 2; New Haven: Yale Egyptological Seminar, 1988).

Altenmüller, H., 'Bes', in W. Helck and E. Otto (eds.), *Lexikon der Ägyptologie* (Wiesbaden: Otto Harrassowitz, 1975), I, cols 720-24.

—'Beset', in W. Helck and E. Otto (eds.), *Lexikon der Ägyptologie* (Wiesbaden: Otto Harrassowitz, 1975), I, col. 731.

Alter, R., *The Art of Biblical Narrative* (New York: Basic Books, 1981).

Alter, R., and F. Kermode (eds.), *The Literary Guide to the Bible* (Cambridge, MA: Harvard University Press, 1987).

Andersen, F.I., *Job* (London: Inter-Varsity Press, 1976).

Angerstorfer, A., 'Ašerah als "consort of Jahwe" oder Aširtah?', *Biblische Notizen* 17 (1982), pp. 7-16.

Antony, L.M., and C. Witt (eds.), *A Mind of One's Own: Feminist Essays on Reason and Objectivity* (Boulder: Westview Press, 1993).

Archer, Gleason L., and G.C. Chirichigno, *Old Testament Quotations in the New Testament: A Complete Survey* (Chicago: Moody Press, 1983).

Archer, L.J., S. Fischler and M. Wyle (eds.), *Women in Ancient Societies: An Illusion of the Night* (London: Macmillan, 1994).

Archer, L. *Her Price is Beyond Rubies: The Jewish Woman in Graeco-Roman Palestine* (JSOTSup, 60; Sheffield: Sheffield Academic Press, 1990).

Asher-Greve, J.M., 'Bibliography on Women in the Ancient Near East', in *NIN: Journal of Ancient Near Eastern Gender Studies* 2 (in preparation).

—'The Essential Body', in E. Hall and M. Wyke (eds.), *Gender and the Body in Antiquity* (special issue of *Gender and History*; Oxford: Oxford University Press, 1997).

—*Frauen in Altsumerischer Zeit* (Bibliotheca Mesopotamica, 18; Malibu, CA: Undena Publications, 1985).

—'Where Are The Missing Men? A Gendered Analysis of Simple Pattern Seals'. (in preparation).

—'Women, Gender, and Scholarship', in *NIN: Journal of Ancient Near Eastern Gender Studies* 1 (forthcoming, 1997).

Asher-Greve, J.M., and A.L. Asher, 'From Thales to Foucault... and Back to Sumer', in *Intellectual Life of the Ancient Near East: Proceedings of the 43. Rencontre Assyriologique Internationale, Prague, 1-5 July 1996* (forthcoming).

Asher-Greve, J.M., and W.B. Stern, 'A New Analytical Method and its Application to Cylinder Seals', *Iraq* 45 (1986), pp. 157-62.

Ashmore, W., and R. Shaver, *Discovering Our Past: A Brief Introduction to Archaeology* (Mountain View, CA: Mayfield, 1988).

Asín Palacios, M., *Abenházam de Córdoba y su historia crítica de las ideas religiosas*, II (5 vols.; Madrid: Real Academia de la Historia, 1928).

Astour, M., 'Tamar the Hierodule: An Essay in the Method of Vestigial Motifs', *JBL* 85 (1966), pp. 185-96.

Atkinson, C.W., *The Oldest Vocation: Christian Motherhood in the Middle Ages* (Ithaca, NY: Cornell University Press, 1991).

Bach, A., 'Good to the Last Drop: Viewing the Sotah (Numbers 5:11-31) as the Glass Half Empty and Wondering How to View it Half Full', in J.C. Exum and D.J.A. Clines (eds.), *The New Literary Criticism and the Hebrew Bible* (JSOTSup, 143; Sheffield: Sheffield Academic Press, 1993), pp. 26-54.

Bach, A. (ed.), *The Pleasure of Her Text: Feminist Readings of Biblical and Historical Texts* (Philadelphia: Trinity Press International, 1990).

Bacon, M.H., *Mothers of Feminism: The Story of Quaker Women in America* (San Francisco: Harper & Row, 1986).

Bailey, N., *1 Chronicles 21: Ambiguity, Intertextuality and the (de)Sanitisation of David* (PhD dissertation, Sheffield: Department of Biblical Studies, 1995).

Bailey, R.C., *David in Love and War: The Pursuit of Power in 2 Samuel 10–12* (JSOTSup, 75; Sheffield: JSOT Press, 1990).

Bakan, D., *And they Took for themselves Wives: The Emergence of Patriarchy in Western Civilization* (New York: Harper & Row, 1979).

Bakhtin, M., *The Bakhtin Reader: Selected Writings of Bakhtin, Medvedev and Voloshinov* (ed. P. Morris; London: Edward Arnold, 1994).

—*The Dialogic Imagination: Four Essays by M.M. Bakhtin* (ed. Michael Holquist; trans. C. Emerson and M. Holquist; Austin, TX: University of Texas Press, 1981).

—*The Formal Method in Literary Scholarship* (trans. A. Wehrle; Baltimore, 1978).

—*Problems of Dostoevsky's Poetics* (ed. and trans. C. Emerson; Minneapolis: University of Minnesota Press, 1984).

Bal, M., 'A Body of Writing: Judges 19', in A. Brenner (ed.), *A Feminist Companion to Judges* (The Feminist Companion to the Bible, 4; Sheffield: Sheffield Academic Press, 1993), pp. 208-30.

—*Death and Disymmetry: the Politics of Coherence in the Book of Judges* (Chicago: University of Chicago Press, 1988).

—'Introduction', in Bal (ed.), *Anti-Covenant: Counter-Reading Women's Lives in the Hebrew Bible* (Sheffield: Sheffield Academic Press, 1989), pp. 11-24.

—*Lethal Love: Feminist Literary Readings of Biblical Love Stories* (Bloomington: Indiana University Press, 1987).

—'Metaphors He Lives By', *Semeia* 61 (1993), pp. 185-208.

—*Murder and Difference: Gender, Genre, and Scholarship on Sisera's Death* (Indiana Studies in Biblical Literature; Bloomington: Indiana University Press, 1988).

—'One Woman, Many Men, and the Dialectic of Chronology', in *idem*, *Lethal Love: Feminist Literary Readings of Biblical Love Stories* (Bloomington: Indiana University Press, 1986), pp. 89-103.

—*Reading Rembrandt* (Cambridge: Cambridge University Press, 1991).

Bal, M., F. van Dijk-Hemmes and G. Ginneken, *En Sara in haar tent lachte* (Utrecht: Hes, 1984).

Balch, D.L., *Let Wives be Submissive: The Domestic Code in 1 Peter* (Atlanta: Scholars Press, 1981).

Barker, M., *The Great Angel: A Study of Israel's Second God* (London: SPCK, 1992).

Barr, J., *The Semantics of Biblical Language* (Oxford: Oxford University Press, 1961; London: SCM Press, 1991 [1983]; Philadelphia: Trinity Press International, 1991).

Barrelet, M.-T., *Figurines et reliefs en terre cuite de la Mésopotamie antique*, I (Bibliothèque Archéologique et Historique, 85; Paris: Geuthner, 1968).

Barrett Browning, E., *Aurora Leigh and Other Poems* (London: The Women's Press, 1978).

Barstow, A., 'The Use of Archaeology for Women's History: James Mellaart's Work on the Neolithic Goddess at Çatal Hüyük', *Feminist Studies* 4 (1978), pp. 7-18.

Barta, W., *Untersuchungen zum Götterkreis der Neunheit* (Münchner Ägyptologische Studien, 28; München: Deutschen Kunstverlag, 1973).

Barth, F., 'Role Dilemmas and Father–Son Dominance in Middle Eastern Kinship Systems', in L.K. Francis (ed.), *Kinship and Structure* (Chicago: Aldine, 1971), pp. 87-95.

Barthes, J., *Image, Music, Text: Essays Selected and Translated by Stephen Heath* (New York: Hill and Wang, 1977).

Barthes, R., *S/Z* (Paris: Seuil, 1970).

—*Le plaisir du texte* (Paris: Seuil, 1973).

Baskin, J., 'The Separation of Women in Rabbinic Judaism', in Y.Y. Haddad and E. Banks Findly (eds.), *Women, Religion and Social Change* (Albany: SUNY Press, 1985), pp. 3-18.

Baumann, G., *Wer mich findet, hat Leben gefunden* (Forschungen zum Alten Testament, 16; Tübingen: Mohr, 1996).

Bayer, B., 'The Finds That Could Not Be', *BARev* 8.1 (1982), pp. 20-33.

Beach, E.F., *Image and Word: Iconology in the Interpretation of Hebrew Scriptures* (Ann Arbor, MI: University Microfilms, 1991).

—'The Samaria Ivories, *Marzeaḥ*, and Biblical Text', *BA* 56 (1993), pp. 94-104.

—'Transforming Goddess Iconography in Hebrew Narrative', in Karen L. King (ed.), *Women and Goddess Traditions: Studies from Asia, the Ancient Mediterranean, and Contemporary Goddess Thealogy* (intr. K.J. Torjesen; Studies in Antiquity and Christianity; Minneapolis: Fortress Press, 1997).

Beal, T.K., 'Ideology and Intertextuality: Surplus of Meaning and Controlling the Means of Production', in D. Nolan Fewell (ed.), *Reading between Texts: Intertextuality and the Hebrew Bible* (Louisville: Westminster/John Knox, 1992), pp. 27-39.

Beal, T.K. and D.M. Gunn (eds.), *Reading Bibles, Writing Bodies: Identity and the Book* (London: Routledge, 1997).

Beal, T.K., and T. Linafelt, 'Sifting for Cinders: Strange Fires in Leviticus 10:1-5', *Semeia* 1995 (forthcoming).

Beck, P., 'The Cult-Stands from Taanach: Aspects of the Iconographic Tradition of Early Iron Age Cult Objects in Palestine', in I. Finkelstein and N. Naʿaman (eds.), *From Nomadism to Monarchy: Archaeological and Historical Aspects of Early Israel* (Jerusalem: Yad Izhak Ben-Zvi and Israel Exploration Society, 1994; Hebrew Original), pp. 352-81 [1990], pp. 417-46.

—'The Drawings from Horvat Teiman (Kuntillet ʾAjrud)', *Tel Aviv* 9 (1982), pp. 3-68.

Becking, B., and M. Dijkstra (eds.), *On Reading Prophetic Texts: Gender-Specific and Related Studies in Memory of Fokkelien van Dijk-Hemmes* (Leiden: Brill, 1996).

Begelsbacher-Fischer, B.L., *Untersuchungen zur Götterwelt des Alten Reiches im Spiegel der Privatgräber der IV. und V. Dynastie* (OBO, 37; Fribourg Suisee: Editions Universitaires; Göttingen: Vandenhoeck & Ruprecht, 1981).

Bekkenkamp, J. and F. van Dijk, 'The Canon of the Old Testament and Women's Cultural Traditions', in A. Brenner (ed.), *A Feminist Companion to the Song of Songs* (The Feminist Companion to the Bible, 1; Sheffield: Sheffield Academic Press, 1993), pp. 67-85.

Bellah, R., 'Religious Evolution', in W.A. Lessa and E.Z. Vogt (eds.), *Reader in Comparative Religion: An Anthropological Approach* (New York: Harper & Row, 3rd edn, 1965), pp. 36-50.

Bellis, A.O., 'Feminist Biblical Interpretation', in C. Meyers, T. Craven and R. Kraemer (eds.), *Women in Scripture: A Dictionary of Named and Unnamed Women in the Hebrew Bible, Apocrypha, and New Testament* (Boston: Houghton Mifflin, forthcoming).

Belsey, C. and J. Moore, 'Introduction: The Story So Far', in C. Belsey and J. Moore (eds.), *The Feminist Reader: Essays in Gender and the Politics of Literary Criticism* (Houndmills, Basingstoke: MacMillan Education, 1989), pp. 1-20.

Benjamin, W., 'The Task of the Translator', in *Illuminations* (trans. H. Zohn; London: Fontana, 1973), pp. 70-82.

Berger, S., 'A Note on Some Scenes of Land-Measurement', *JEA* 20 (1934), pp. 54-56 and pl. X.

Bernard of Clairvaux, *Magnificat: Homilies in Praise of the Blessed Virgin Mary* (trans. Marie-Bernard Saïd and Grace Perigo (Cistercian Fathers Series, 18; Kalamazoo, MI: Cirstercian Publications, 1979).

Bernhardt, K.-H., 'Aschera in Ugarit und im Alten Testament', *Mitteilungen des Instituts für Orientforschung* 13 (1967), pp. 163-74.

Bernstein, M., 'Translation Technique in the Targum to Psalms. Two Test Cases: Psalms 2 and 137', in E.H. Lovering (ed.), *SBL 1994 Seminar Papers* (Atlanta: Scholars Press, 1994), pp. 326-45.

—'Two Multivalent Readings in the Ruth Narrative', *JSOT* 50 (1991), pp. 15-26.

Berquist, Jon L., *Judaism in Persia's Shadow: A Social and Historical Approach* (Minneapolis: Fortress Press, 1996).

Beuken, W., and E. van Wolde, 'Introduction', in S. Draisma (ed.), *Intertextuality in Biblical Writings: Essays in Honour of Bas van Iersel* (Kampen: Kok, 1989), pp. 7-8.

Biale, D., *Eros and the Jews: From Biblical Israel to Contemporary America* (New York: Basic Books, 1992).

—'The God with Breasts: El Shaddai in the Bible', *HR* 21 (1981–82), pp. 240-56.

Bible and Culture Collective, *The Postmodern Bible* (New Haven: Yale University Press, 1995).

Bickel, S., *La cosmogonie égyptienne: Avant le Nouvel Empire* (OBO, 134; Fribourg Suisee: Editions Universitaires; Göttingen: Vandenhoeck & Ruprecht, 1994).

Bikai, P.M., 'The Rod and the Ring', in *Society of Biblical Literature Abstracts* (Atlanta: Scholars Press, 1990), p. 329, S136.

Binford, L., 'A Consideration of Archaeological Research Design', *American Antiquity* 29 (1964), pp. 425-41

Binford, L., and S.R. Binford, *New Perspectives in Archaeology* (Chicago: Aldine, 1968).

Bird, P., 'The Harlot as Heroine: Narrative Art and Social Presupposition in Three Old Testament Texts', *Semeia* 46 (1989), pp. 119-39.

—'Images of Women in the Old Testament', in R. Ruether (ed.), *Religion and Sexism: Images of Women in Jewish and Christian Traditions* (New York: Simon & Schuster, 1974), pp. 41-88.

—'"Male and Female He Created Them": Gen 1:27b in the Context of the Priestly Account of Creation', *HTR* 74 (1981), pp. 129-59.

—'Poor Man of Poor Woman: Gendering the Poor in Prophetic Texts', in B. Becking and M. Dijkstra (eds.), *On Reading Prophetic Texts: Gender-Specific and related Studies in Memory of Fokkelien van Dijk-Hemmes* (Leiden: Brill, 1996), pp. 37-51.

—'Sexual Differentiation and Divine Image in the Genesis Creation Texts', in K.E. Børresen (ed.), *The Image of God: Gender Models in Judaeo-Christian Tradition* (Minneapolis: Fortress Press, 1995), pp. 5-28.

Bledstein, A.J., 'Binder, Trickster, Heel and Hairy-Man: Rereading Genesis 27 as a Trickster Tale Told by a Woman', in A. Brenner (ed.), *A Feminist Companion to Genesis* (The Feminist Companion to the Bible, 2; Sheffield: Sheffield Academic Press, 1993), pp. 282-95.

Bleier, R., *Science and Gender: A Critique of Biology and its Theories on Women* (New York: Pergamon Press, 1984).

Bleier R. (ed.), *Feminist Approaches to Science* (New York: Pergamon Press, 1986).

Blenkinsopp, J., 'Theme and Motif in the Succession History (2 Sam XI2ff) and the Yahwistic Corpus', *Supplement to Vetus Testamentum* 15 (Leiden: Brill, 1966), pp. 44-57.

Bloch-Smith, E., *Judahite Burial Practices and Beliefs about the Dead* (JSOTSup, 123; Sheffield: Sheffield Academic Press, 1992).

Blok, J., 'Sexual Asymmetry: A Historiographical Essay', in J. Blok and P. Mason (eds.), *Sexual Asymmetry: Studies in Ancient Society* (Amsterdam: Gieben, 1987), pp. 1-58.

Bloom, H., *The Anxiety of Influence: A Theory of Poetry* (New York: Oxford University Press, 1973).

—*The Book of J* (trans. D. Rosenberg; London: Faber, 1991 [1990]).

—*Deconstruction and Criticism* (London: Routledge & Kegan Paul, 1979).

—*The Western Canon: The Books and School of the Ages* (New York: Harcourt Brace & Company, 1994).

Blount, B.K., *Cultural Interpretation: Reorienting New Testament Criticism* (Minneapolis: Fortress Press, 1995).

Blumenthal, D.R., *Facing the Abusing God: A Theology of Protest* (Louisville, KY: Westminster/John Knox, 1993).

Boff, L. and C. Boff, *Introducing Liberation Theology* (trans. P. Burns; Liberation and Theology, 1; Tunbridge Wells: Burns & Oates, 1992).

Borg, M.J., *Jesus in Contemporary Scholarship* (Valley Forge, PA: Trinity Press International, 1994).

—*Meeting Jesus Again for the First Time: The Historical Jesus and the Heart of Contemporary Faith* (San Francisco: HarperSanFrancisco, 1994).

Børresen, K.E., *Subordination and Equivalence: The Nature and Role of Woman in Augustine and Thomas Aquinas* (Lanham, MD: University Press of America, 1981; Kampen: Kok, 1995).

Bos, J., 'Out of the Shadows: Genesis 38; Judges 4:17-22; Ruth 3', *Semeia* 42 (1988), pp. 37-67.

Boström, G., *Proverbia Studien: Die Weisheit und das fremde Weib in Spr. 1-9* (Lund: Gleerup, 1935).

Boström, L., *The God of the Sages* (Stockholm: Almqvist & Wiksell, 1990).

Botteneck, G.J., and H. Ringren (eds.), *Theologische Wörterbuch zum Alten Testament* (Stuttgart: Kohlhammer, 1989), VI.

Boyarin, D., *Carnal Israel: Reading Sex in Talmudic Culture* (The New Historicism: Studies in Cultural Poetics; Berkeley: University of California Press, 1993).

—*Intertextuality and the Reading of Midrash* (Indiana Studies in Biblical Literature; Bloomington: Indiana University Press, 1990).

—*Unheroic Conduct: The Rise of Heterosexuality and the Invention of the Jewish Man* (Contraversions: Studies in Jewish Literature, Culture, and Society; Berkeley: University of California Press, 1997).

Braidotti, R., *Nomadic Subjects: Embodiment and Sexual Difference in Contemporary Feminist Theory* (New York: Columbia University Press, 1995).

Brenner, A., '"Come Back, Come Back the Shulammite" (Song of Songs 7.1-10): A Parody of the *wasf* Genre', in J.T. Raddady and A. Brenner (eds.), *On Humour and the Comic in the Hebrew Bible* (JSOTSup, 92; Sheffield: Almond Press, 1990), pp. 251-76.

—'Naomi and Ruth', in A. Brenner (ed.), *A Feminist Companion to Ruth* (The Feminist Companion to the Bible, 9; Sheffield: Sheffield Academic Press, 1993), pp. 70-84.

—'On Incest' in A. Brenner (ed.), *A Feminist Companion to Exodus to Deuteronomy* (The Feminist Companion to the Bible, 6; Sheffield: Sheffield Academic Press, 1994), pp. 113-38.

—'On Reading the Hebrew Bible as a Feminist Woman: Introduction to the Series', in A. Brenner (ed.), *A Feminist Companion to the Song of Songs* (The Feminist Companion to the Bible, 1; Sheffield: Sheffield Academic Press, 1993), pp. 11-27.

—'Pornoprophetics Revisited: Some Additional Reflections', *JSOT* 70 (1996), pp. 63-86.

—'Some Observations on the Figurations of Woman in Wisdom Literature', in A. Brenner (ed.), *A Feminist Companion to Wisdom Literature* (The Feminist Companion to the Bible, 9; Sheffield: Sheffield Academic Press, 1995), pp. 50-66.

—*The Song of Songs* (Old Testament Guides; Sheffield: JSOT Press, 1989);

—'To See Is to Assume: Whose Love Is Celebrated in the Song of Songs?', *Biblical Interpretation* 1.3 (1993), pp. 1-20.

—'Women's Traditions Problematized: Some Reflections', in Becking and Dijkstra (eds.), *On Reading Prophetic Texts*, pp. 53-66.

Brenner, A. (ed.), *A Feminist Companion to Exodus to Deuteronomy* (The Feminist Companion to the Bible, 6; Sheffield: Sheffield Academic Press, 1994).

—*A Feminist Companion to the Hebrew Bible in the New Testament* (The Feminist Companion to the Bible, 10; Sheffield: Sheffield Academic Press, 1996).

—*A Feminist Companion to the Latter Prophets* (The Feminist Companion to the Bible, 8; Sheffield: Sheffield Academic Press, 1995).

—*A Feminist Companion to the Song of Songs* (The Feminist Companion to the Bible, 1; Sheffield: Sheffield Academic Press, 1993).

—*A Feminist Companion to Wisdom Literature* (The Feminist Companion to the Bible, 9; Sheffield: Sheffield Academic Press, 1995).

Brenner, A., and F. van Dijk-Hemmes (eds.), *On Gendering Texts: Female and Male Voices in the Hebrew Bible* (Biblical Interpretation Series, 1; Leiden: Brill, 1993).

Bridenthal, R., and C. Koonz (eds.), *Becoming Visible: Women in European History* (Boston: Houghton Mifflin, 1977).

Brock, R.N., 'Dusting the Bible on the Floor: A Hermeneutics of Wisdom', in E. Schüssler Fiorenza (ed.), *Searching the Scriptures: A Feminist Introduction*. I. pp. 64-75.

—*Journeys by Heart: A Christology of Erotic Power* (New York: Crossroad, 1991).

Brock, S., 'To Revise or Not to Revise: Attitudes to Jewish Biblical Translation' in G.-J. Brooke and B. Lindars (eds.), *Septuagint, Scrolls and Cognate Writings* (Septuagint and Cognate Studies, 33; Atlanta: Scholars Press, 1992), pp. 301-38.

Brooke, G.J., 'The Temple Scroll and LXX Exodus 35–40', in Brooke and Lindars (eds.), *Septuagint, Scrolls and Cognate Writings*, pp. 81-106.

Brooke, G.J., and B. Lindars (eds.), *Septuagint, Scrolls and Cognate Writings* (Septuagint and Cognate Studies, 33; Atlanta: Scholars Press, 1992).

Brooten, B., 'Jüdinnen zur Zeit Jesu', in B. Brooten and N. Greinacher (eds.), *Frauen in der Männerkirche* (Munich: Chr. Kaiser Verlag, 1982), pp. 141-49.

—'Early Christian Women and their Cultural Context: Issues of Method in Historical Reconstruction', in Yarbro Collins (ed.), *Feminist Perspectives*, pp. 63-93.

Brown, A., *Apology to Women: Christian Images of the Female Sex* (Leicester: Inter-Varsity Press, 1991).

Brown, D., *Vir Trilinguis: A Study in the Biblical Exegesis of Saint Jerome* (Kampen: Kok, 1992).

Brown, F., S.R. Driver and C.A. Briggs, *A Hebrew and English Lexicon of the Old Testament* (*BDB*; Oxford: Clarendon Press, 1907).

Brown, J.C., and R. Parker, 'For God So Loved the World?', in J.C. Brown and C.R. Bohn (eds.), *Christianity, Patriarchy, and Abuse: A Feminist Critique* (Cleveland: Pilgrim Press, 1989), pp. 1-30.

Brown, P., *The Cult of the Saints: Its Rise and Function in Latin Christianity* (London: SCM Press, 1981).

—*The World of Late Antiquity, AD 150–170* (London: Harcourt Brace Jovanovich, 1971).

Brown, R., *Birth of the Messiah: A Commentary on the Infancy Narratives in the Gospels of Matthew and Luke* (Garden City, NY: Doubleday, rev. edn, 1993).

Brown, S., 'Feminist Research in Archaeology: What Does it Mean? Why Is it Taking so Long?', in N.S. Rabinowitz and A. Richlin (eds.), *Feminist Theory and the Classics* (London: Routledge, 1993), pp. 238-271.

Brueggemann, W., 'Life and Death in Tenth Century Israel', *JAAR* 40 (1971), pp. 96-109.

—'On Coping with Curse: A Study of 2 Sam. 16:5-14', *CBQ* 36 (1974), pp. 175-92.

Brumfiel, E.M., 'Weaving and Cooking: Women's Cooking in Aztec Mexico', in J.M. Gero and M.W. Conkey (eds.), *Engendering Archaeology: Women and Prehistory* (Oxford: Basil Blackwell, 1991), pp. 224-54.

Bruns, G.L., 'Midrash and Allegory: The Beginning of Scriptural Interpretation', in R. Alter and F. Kermode (eds.), *The Literary Guide to the Bible* (Cambridge, MA: Harvard University Press, 1987), pp. 627-33.

Buccellati, G., 'Methodological Concerns and the Progress of Ancient Near Eastern Studies', in *Or* NS 42 (1973), pp. 9-20.

Buchman, C., and C. Spiegel (eds.), *Out of the Garden: Women Writers on the Bible* (New York: Ballantine, 1993).

Bulkien, E., 'Hard Ground: Jewish Identity, Racism and Anti-Semitism', in E. Bulkien, M.B. Pratt and B. Smith (eds.), *Yours in Struggle* (New York: Long Haul Press, 1984), pp. 89-194.

Bulkien, E., M.B. Pratt and B. Smith (eds.), *Yours In Struggle* (New York: Long Haul Press, 1984).

Burney, C.F., *The Book of Judges* (London: Rivingtons, 1920).

Burrus, V., *The Making of a Heretic: Gender, Authority, and the Priscillianist Controvery* (The Transformation of the Classical Heritage; Berkeley: University of California Press, 1995).

—'The Male Ascetic in Female Space: Alienated Strategies of Self-definition in the Writings of Sulpicius Severus', paper presented at SBL/AAR Anuual Meeting, 1992.

Bussert, J.M.K., *Battered Women: From a Theology of Suffering to an Ethic of Empowerment* (New York: Lutheran Church in America, 1986).

Butler, J., *Gender Trouble: Feminism and the Subversion of Identity* (New York: Routledge, 1990).

—*Gender Trouble: Feminism and the Subversion of Identity* (Thinking Gender; London: Routledge, 1990).

Butler, J., and J. Scott (eds.), *Feminists Theorize the Political* (New York: Routledge, 1992).

Bynum, C., *Holy Feast and Holy Fast* (Berkeley: University of California Press, 1986).

—'Introduction: The Complexity of Symbols', in C. Bynum, S. Harrell, and P. Richman (eds.), *Gender and Religion: On the Complexity of Symbols* (Boston: Beacon Press, 1986), pp. 1-20.

Cady Stanton, E., *The Woman's Bible* (New York: European Publishing Co., 1895; repr.; Seattle: Coalition Task Force on Women and Religion, 1974).

—*The Woman's Bible: The Original Feminist Attack on the Bible* (New York: European Publishing Company, 1898 [1895]; abridged edition, with Introduction by Dale Spender; Edinburgh: Polygon Books, 1985).

Cady Stanton, E., *et al.*, *The Woman's Bible* (2 vols.; repr.; New York: Arno Press, 1974 [1895, 1898]).

Cady, S., M. Ronan, and H. Taussig, *Wisdom's Feast: Sophia in Study and Celebration* (San Francisco: Harper & Row, 1989).

Callaway, M., *Sing, O Barren One: a Study in Comparative Midrash* (Atlanta, GA: Scholars Press, 1986).

Cameron A., and A. Kuhrt (eds.), *Images of Women in Antiquity* (London: Routledge, 2nd rev. edn, 1993).

Cameron, D., *Feminism and Linguistic Theory* (London: Macmillan, 2nd rev. edn, 1992).

Camp, C.V, 'Metaphor in Feminist Biblical Interpretation', *Semeia* 61 (1993), pp. 3-38.

—'The Female Sage in Ancient Israel and in the Biblical Wisdom Literature', in J.G. Gammie and L.G. Perdue (eds.), *The Sage in Israel and the Ancient Near East* (Winona Lake, IN: Eisenbrauns, 1990), pp. 185-203.

—*Wisdom and the Feminine in the Book of Proverbs* (Bible and Literature Series, 11; Sheffield: Almond Press, 1985).

—'Wise and Strange: An Interpretation of the Female Imagery in Proverbs in Light of Trickster Mythology', in J.C. Exum and J.W.H. Bos (eds.), *Reasoning with the Foxes: Female Wit in a World of Male Power* (*Semeia,* 42; Atlanta: Scholars Press, 1988), pp. 4-36.

—'Woman Wisdom as Root Metaphor: A Theological Consideration', in K.G. Hoglund, *et al.* (eds.), *The Listening Heart: Essays in Wisdom and the Psalms in Honor of Roland E. Murphy* (JSOTSup, 58; Sheffield: JSOT Press, 1987), pp. 45-76.

Campbell, E.F., *Ruth* (AB; Garden City, NY: Doubleday, 1975).

Campbell, K. (ed.), *Critical Feminism: Argument in the Disciplines* (Buckingham: Open University Press, 1992).

Cannon, K., 'Womanist Interpretation and Preaching in the Black Church', in Schüssler Fiorenza (ed.), *Searching the Scriptures*, I, pp. 326-38.

Caplice, R., *Introduction to Akkadian* (Studia Pohl SM; Rome: Biblical Institute Press, 1983).

Caquot, A., 'Israelite Perceptions of Wisdom and Strength in the Light of the Ras Shamra Texts', in Gammie *et al.* (eds.), *Israelite Wisdom*, pp. 25-33.

Carey, J.J., *et al.*, *Keeping Body and Soul Together: Sexuality, Spirituality, and Social Justice* (Louisville: Presbyterian Church [USA], 1991).

Carmichael, C.M., 'A Ceremonial Crux: Removing a Man's Sandal as a Female Gesture of Contempt', *JBL* 96 (1977), pp. 321-36.

Carrithers, M., *Why Humans Have Cultures: Explaining Anthropology and Social Diversity* (Oxford: Oxford University Press, 1992).

Carroll, B.A. (ed.), *Liberating Women's History: Theoretical and Critical Essays* (Chicago: University of Illinois Press, 1976).

—'The Study of Women in Antiquity: Past, Present, and Future', in *AJP* 112 (1991), pp. 263-68.

Carroll, R.P., 'Desire under the Terebinths: On Pornographic Representation in the Prophets—A Response', in A. Brenner (ed.), *A Feminist Companion to the Latter Prophets* (The Feminist Companion to the Bible, 8; Sheffield: Sheffield Academic Press, 1995), pp. 275-307.

—*Jeremiah* (OTL; Philadelphia: Westminster Press, 1986).

Carter, C.E., 'A Discipline in Transition: The Contributions of the Social Sciences to the Study of the Hebrew Bible', in C.E. Carter and C. Meyers (eds.), *Community, Identity, and Ideology: Social-Science Approaches to the Hebrew Bible* (Sources for Biblical and Theological Study; Winona Lake, IN: Eisenbrauns, 1996), pp. 3-36.

—'Ethnoarchaeology', *The Oxford Encyclopedia of Archaeology in the Near East*, II, pp. 280-84.

Carter, C.E., and C. Meyers (eds.), *Community, Identity, and Ideology: Social-Science Approaches to the Hebrew Bible* (Sources for Biblical and Theological Study; Winona Lake, IN: Eisenbrauns, 1996).

Cassuto, U., 'The Story of Tamar and Judah', in *idem*, *Biblical and Oriental Studies. I. Bible* (Jerusalem: Magnes, 1973), pp. 29-40.

Catastini, A., 'Le inscrizioni di Kuntillet 'Ajrud e il profetismo', *AION* NS 42 (1982), pp. 127-34.

—'Note di epigrafia ebraica I–II', *Henoch* 6 (1984), pp. 129-38.

—'Profeti tra epigrafia ed epistolografia', *Egitto e Vicino Oriente* 13 (1990), pp. 143-47.

Cazelles, H., 'La Sagesse de Proverbes 8, 22: Peut-elle être considérée comme une hypostase?', in A.M. Triacca and A. Pistoia (eds.), *Trinité et Liturgie* (Rome: C L V Edizioni liturgiche, 1984), pp. 51-57.

Charlesworth, J.H. (ed.), *The Old Testament Pseudepigrapha* (2 vols.; London: Darton, Longman & Todd, 1983–85).

Charon, J., *Le Tout, l'Esprit et la Matière* (Paris: Albin Michel, 1987).

Chase, D.A., 'A Note on an Inscription from Kuntillet 'Ajrud', *BASOR* 246 (1982), pp. 63-67.

Christ, C., *Laughter of Aphrodite* (San Francisco: Harper & Row, 1987).

Christ, C., and J. Plaskow (eds.), *Womanspirit Rising: A Feminist Reader in Religion* (New York: Harper & Row, 1979).

Cixous, H., 'Sorties: Out and Out: Attacks/Ways Out/Forays', taken from H. Cixous and C. Clément, *The Newly Born Woman* (trans. Betsy Wing; Minneapolis: University of Minnesota Press, 1986; repr. in Belsey and Moore, *The Feminist Reader*, pp. 101-16 and notes, pp. 229-30.

Claassen, C. (ed.), *Exploring Gender through Archaeology: Selected Papers from the 1991 Boone Conference* (Monographs in World Archaeology, 11; Madison, WI: Prehistoric Press, 1992).

—*Women in Archaeology* (Philadelphia: University of Pennsylvania Press, 1994).

Claes, P., *De mot zit in de mythe: Antieke intertextualiteit in het werk van Hugo Claus* (Amsterdam: Meulenhof 1981).

—*Het netwerk en de nevelvlek: semiotische studies* (Leuven: Acco, 1979).

Clark E., and H. Richardson (eds.), *Women and Religion: A Feminist Sourcebook of Christian Thought* (New York: Harper & Row, 1977).

Clayton, J., and E. Rothstein, 'Figures in the Corpus: Theories of Influence and Intertextuality', in *idem*, (eds.), *Influence*.

Clayton, J., and E. Rothstein (eds.), *Influence and Intertextuality in Literary History* (Madison: University of Wisconsin Press, 1991).

Clifton, L., *Good Woman: Poems and a Memoir* (Brockport, NY: BOA Editions, 1987).

—*Next: New Poems* (Brockport, NY: BOA Editions, 1987).

Clines, D.J.A., *What Does Eve Do to Help? And Other Readerly Questions to the Old Testament* (JSOTSup, 94; Sheffield: JSOT Press, 1990).

—'Why is there a Song of Songs? And What Does it Do to You if You Read It?', *Jian Dao* 1 (1994), pp. 14-26.

Clines, D.J.A., and J.C. Exum, 'The New Literary Criticism', in J.C. Exum and D.J.A. Clines (eds.), *The New Literary Criticism and the Hebrew Bible*.

Coats, G.W., 'Widow's Rights: A Crux in the Structure of Genesis 38', *CBQ* 34 (1972), pp. 461-66.

Cohen, A. (trans.), *Midrash Rabbah, Lamentations* (Hindhead, Surrey: Soncino, 1939).

Cohen, E., 'Are we (not) what we Are Becoming? "Gay" "Identity", "Gay Studies", and the Disciplining of Knowledge', in J.A. Boone and M. Cadden (eds.), *Engendering Men* (New York: Routledge, 1990), pp. 161-75.

Cohen, G.M., and M.S. Joukowsky (eds.), *Women in Archaeology: The Classical World and the Near East* (in preparation).

Cohen, S.J.D., 'Menstruants and the Sacred in Judaism and Christianity', in S. Pomeroy (ed.), *Ancient History, Women's History* (Chapel Hill: University of North Carolina Press, 1991), pp. 273-99.

—'The Place of the Rabbi in Jewish Society of the Second Century', in L. Levine (ed.), *The Galilee in Late Antiquity* (New York: Jewish Theological Seminary, 1992), pp. 157-73.

Collins, S., *A Different Heaven and Earth* (Valley Forge, PA: Judson Press, 1974).

Conkey, M.W., and J.M. Gero (eds.), *Engendering Archaeology: Women and Pre-history* (Oxford: Basil Blackwell, 1991).

—'Tensions, Pluralities, and Engendering Archaeology: An Introduction to Women and Prehistory', in *idem* (eds.), *Engendering Archaeology*, pp. 3-54.

Conkey, M.W., and J. Spector, 'Archaeology and the Study of Gender', in M. Schiffer (ed.), *Advances in Archaeological Method and Theory* (New York: Academic Press, 1984), VII, pp. 1-38.

Connell, R.W., *Masculinities* (Berkeley: University of California Press, 1995).

Contenau, G., *La déesse nue babylonienne: Etude d'iconographie comparée* (Paris: Paul Geuthner, 1914).

Conzelmann, H., 'The Mother of Wisdom', in J.M. Robinson (ed.), *The Future of Our Religious Past: Essays in Honor of Rudolf Bultmann* (New York: Harper & Row, 1971), pp. 230-43.

Coogan, M.D., 'Canaanite Origins and Lineage: Reflections on the Religion of Ancient Israel', in P.D. Miller, Jr, P.D. Hanson, and S.D. McBride (eds.), *Ancient Israelite Religion* (Philadelphia: Fortress Press, 1987), pp. 115-24.

—'The Goddess Wisdom—"Where can she be found?": Literary Reflexes of Popular Religion', communication given at the Society of Biblical Literature Meetings in Washington D.C., 1993.

Coogan, M.D., 'The Goddess Wisdom—Where can she be found?' (forthcoming in the Baruch A. Levine Festschrift, ed. L. Schiffman *et al.*).

Cooper, J.S., 'Gendered Sexuality in Sumerian Love Poetry', in I.L. Finkel, and M.J. Geller (eds.), *Sumerian Gods and their Representation* (Cuneiform Monographs 7; Groningen, NL: Styx, 1996), pp. 85-97.

Cooper, J.S., and G.M. Schwartz (eds.), *The Study of the Ancient Near East in the 21st Century: The William Foxwell Albright Centennial Conference* (Winona Lake, IN: Eisenbrauns, 1996).

Corley, K.E., '1 Peter', in Schüssler Fiorenza (ed.), *Searching the Scriptures. II. A Feminist Commentary* (New York: Crossroad, 1994), pp. 349-60.

Cornell, D., *The Philosophy of the Limit* (London: Routledge, 1992).

Couroyer, B., 'Le "Dieu des sages" en Égypte: II', *RB* 95 (1988), pp. 70-91.

Craig, K.M., and M.A. Kristjansson, 'Women Reading as Men/Women Reading as Women: A Structural Analysis for the Historical Project', *Semeia* 51 (1990), pp. 119-36.

Crenshaw, J.L. (ed.), *Studies in Ancient Israelite Wisdom* (New York: Ktav, 1976).

Crenshaw, J.L., *A Whirlpool of Torment: Israelite Traditions of God as an Oppressive Presence* (Overtures in Biblical Theology; Philadelphia: Fortress Press, 1984).

Crosby, C., 'Dealing with Differences', in J. Butler and J. Scott (eds.), *Feminists Theorize the Political* (New York: Routledge, 1992), pp. 130-43.

Crosby, M., *House of Disciples: Church, Economics, and Justice in Matthew* (Maryknoll: Orbis Books, 1988).

Cross, F.M., Jr, *Canaanite Myth and Hebrew Epic: Essays in the History of the Religion of Israel* (Cambridge, MA: Harvard University Press, 1973).

—'The Themes of the Book of Kings and the Structure of the Deuteronomistic History', in *Canaanite Myth and Hebrew Epic*, pp. 274-89.

Crossan, J.D., *The Historical Jesus: The Life of a Mediterranean Jewish Peasant* (San Francisco: HarperSanFrancisco, 1991).

—*Jesus: A Revolutionary Biography* (San Francisco: HarperCollins, 1994).

Crowfoot, J.W., G.M. Crowfoot and K.M. Kenyon, *The Objects from Samaria* (London: Palestine Exploration Fund, 1957).

Culican, W., 'A Votive Model from the Sea', *PEQ* 108 (1976), pp. 119-23.

'Cultic Inscriptions Found in Ekron', in 'Arti-facts: News, Notes, and Reports from the Institutes', *BA* 53 (1990), p. 232.

D'Angelo, M.R., 'Colossians', in Schüssler Fiorenza (ed.), *Searching the Scriptures*, II, pp. 313-22.

Dalley, S., *Myths From Mesopotamia* (Oxford and New York: Oxford University Press, 1989).

Daly, M., *Beyond God the Father: Towards a Philosophy of Women's Liberation* (Boston: Beacon, 1973).

—*Gyn/Ecology: The Metaethics of Radical Feminism* (Boston: Beacon, 1979).

Dame, E., *Lilith and Her Demons* (Merrick, NY: Cross-Cultural Communications, 1986).

Daniels, P.T., 'The Decipherment of Ancient Near Eastern Scripts', in J.M. Sasson (ed.), *Civilizations of the Ancient Near East* (New York: Charles Scribner's Sons, 1995), I, pp. 81-93.

Darr, K.P., *Far More Precious than Jewels* (Louisville, KY: Westminster/John Knox, 1991).

Dasen, P.R., J.W. Berry, and N. Sartorius (eds.), *Health and Cross-Cultural Psychology: Toward Applications* (Cross-Cultural Research and Methodology Series; Newbury Park, CA: Sage, 1988).

Daum, A., 'Blaming the Jews for the Death of the Goddess', *Lilith* 7 (1979); reprinted in E.T. Beck (ed.), *Nice Jewish Girls* (Trumansburg: The Crossing Press, 1982), pp. 255-65.

—'A Jewish Feminist View', *TTod* 41 (1984), pp. 294-300.

Daum, A., and D. McCauley, 'Jewish-Christian Feminist Dialogue: A Wholistic Vision', *USQR* 38.2 (1983), pp. 147-89.

Davidman, L., and S. Tenenbaum (eds.), *Feminist Perspectives on Jewish Studies* (New Haven: Yale University Press, 1994).

Davies, G.I., *Ancient Hebrew Inscriptions: Corpus and Concordance* (Cambridge: Cambridge University Press, 1991).

Davies, P.R., *In Search of 'Ancient Israel'* (JSOTSup, 148; Sheffield: Sheffield Academic Press, 1992).

—*Whose Bible is it Anyway?* (Sheffield: Sheffield Academic Press, 1995).

Davies, S., 'The Canaanite-Hebrew Goddess', in C. Olson (ed.), *The Book of the Goddess: Past and Present* (New York: Crossroad, 1985), pp. 68-79.

—*The Revolt of the Widows: the Social World of the Apocryphal Acts* (Carbondale, IL: Southern Illinois Press; London: Feffer and Simons, 1980).

Davies, W.D., and D.C. Allison, *A Critical and Exegetical Commentary on the Gospel according to Matthew*, I (ICC; 2 vols.; Edinburgh: T. and T. Clark, 1988).

Davis, N.Z., *Women on the Margins: Three Seventeenth-Century Lives* (Cambridge, MA: Harvard University Press [Belknap], 1995).

Day, J., 'Asherah in the Hebrew Bible and Northwest Semitic Literature', *JBL* 105 (1986), pp. 385-408.

—'Ashtoreth', in D.N. Freedman (ed.), *The Anchor Bible Dictionary* (Garden City, NY: Doubleday, 1992), I, pp. 491-94.

Day, L., *Three Faces of a Queen: Characterization in the Books of Esther* (JSOTSup, 186: Sheffield: Sheffield Academic Press, 1995).

Day, P.L. (ed.), *Gender and Difference in Ancient Israel* (Minneapolis: Fortress Press, 1989).

Dayagi-Mendels, M., 'Canaanite Cult Stand', in J.P. O'Neill (ed.), *Treasures of the Holy Land: Ancient Art from the Israel Museum* (New York: Metropolitan Museum of Art, 1986), pp. 161-63.

De Laurentis, T. (ed.), *Feminist Studies Critical Studies* (Bloomington: Indiana University Press, 1986).

De Man, P., *Allegories of Reading: Figural Language in Rousseau, Nietzsche, Rilke and Proust* (New Haven: Yale University Press, 1979).

—*Blindness and Insight: Essays in the Rhetoric of Contemporary Criticism* (London: Routledge, 1983).

De Swarte Gifford, C., 'American Women and the Bible: The Nature of Woman as Hermeneutical Issue', in A. Yarbro Collins (ed.), *Feminist Perspectives on Biblical Scholarship* (Chico, CA: Scholars Press, 1985), pp. 28-30.

De Troyer, K., 'An Oriental Beauty Parlour: An Analysis of Esther 2.8-18 in the Hebrew, the Septuagint and the Second Greek Text', in A. Brenner (ed.), *A Feminist Companion to Esther, Judith and Susanna* (The Feminist Companion to the Bible, 7; Sheffield: Sheffield Academic Press, 1995), pp. 47-70.

—'On Crowns and Diadems of Kings, Queens, Horses and Men', in B.A. Taylor (ed.), *Proceedings of the IOSCS Conference in Cambridge 1995* (Septuagint and Cognate Studies; Atlanta: Scholars Press, forthcoming).

—'The End of the Alpha-text of Esther: Translation Techniques and Narrative Techniques in MT 8.1-17, LXX 8.1-17 and AT 7.14-41' (Leuven: Peeters, forthcoming, 1997).

deBuck, A., *The Egyptian Coffin Texts. IV. Texts of Spells 268-354* (The University of Chicago Oriental Institute Publications, 67; Chicago: University of Chicago Press, 1951).

Delcor, M., 'Astarté et la fécondité des troupeaux en Deut. 7,13 et paralleles', *UF* 6 (1974), pp. 7-14.

—'Le culte de la "Reine du Ciel" selon Jer 7,18; 44,17-19, 25 et ses survivances', in W.C. Delsman, *et al.* (eds.), *Von Kanaan bis Kerala* (Kevelaer: Butzon & Bercker; Neukirchen-Vluyn: Neukirchener Verlag, 1982), pp. 101-22.

—'Le personnel du temple d'Astarté à Kition d'après une tablette phénicienne (cis 86 A et B)', *UF* 11 (1979), pp. 147-64.

Delorme, J., 'Intertextualities about Mark', in Draisma (ed.), *Intertextuality*, pp. 35-42.

Delphy, C., *Close to Home: A Materialist Analysis of Women's Oppression* (trans. and ed. Diane Leonard; Amherst: University of Massachusetts Press, 1984).

Derrida, J., 'Des Tours de Babel', *Semeia* 54 (1991), pp. 3-34.

—*De la grammatologie* (Paris: Minuit, 1967).

—*L'écriture et la différence* (Paris: Seuil, 1967).

—*La dissémination* (Paris: Seuil, 1972).

Detweiler, R., 'Overliving', *Semeia* 54 (1991), pp. 239-55.

Dever, W.G., 'Archaeology, Syro-Palestinian and Biblical', in *Anchor Bible Dictionary* (New York: Doubleday, 1992), I, pp. 354-67.

—'Asherah, Consort of Yahweh? New Evidence from Kuntillet 'Ajrud', *BASOR* 255 (1984), pp. 21-37.

—'Biblical Archaeology', in Meyers *et al.* (eds.), *Oxford Encyclopedia of Archaeology in the Near East* (New York: Oxford University Press, 1997).

—'el-Qôm, Khirbet', in M. Avi-Yonah and E. Stern (eds.), *Encyclopedia of Archaeological Excavations in the Holy Land* (4 vols.; Jerusalem: Israel Exploration Society and Massada Press, 1978), IV, pp. 976-77.

—'The Impact of the "New Archaeology" on Syro-Palestinian Archaeology', *BASOR* 242 (1981), pp. 14-29.

—'Inscriptions from Khirbet el-Kom', *Qadmoniot* 4 (1971), pp. 90-92 (Hebrew).

—'Iron Age Epigraphic Material from the Area of Khirbet el-Kôm', *HUCA* 40-41 (1970), pp. 139-204.

—'Is the Bible Right After All?', *BARev* 22 (1996), pp. 30-37, 74-77.

—'Material Remains and the Cult in Ancient Israel', in C.L. Meyers and M. O'Connor (eds.), *The Word of the Lord Shall Go Forth: Essays in Honor of David Noel Freedman in Celebration of his Sixtieth Birthday* (Winona Lake, IN: Eisenbrauns, 1983), pp. 571-87.

—'Qôm, Khirbet el-', in E. Stern (ed.), *The New Encyclopedia of Archaeological Excavations in the Holy Land* (Jerusalem: Israel Exploration Society, 1993), IV, pp. 1233-35.

—'Recent Archaeological Confirmation of the Cult of Asherah in Ancient Israel', *Hebrew Studies* 23 (1982), pp. 37-44.

—'"Will the Real Israel Please Stand Up?". Part I: Archaeology and Israelite Historiography', *BASOR* 297 (1995), pp. 61-80.

—'"Will the Real Israel Please Stand Up?". Part II: Archaeology and the Religion of Ancient Israel', *BASOR* 298 (1995), pp. 37-58.

DeVries, L.F., 'Cult Stands: A Bewildering Variety of Shapes and Sizes', *BARev* 13.4 (1987), pp. 26-37.

Di Vito, R.A., *Studies in Third Millennium Sumerian and Akkadian Personal Names* (Rome: Pontifical Biblical Institute, 1993).

Dickinson, E., *Complete Poems* (ed. T.H. Johnson; Boston: Little Brown, 1955).

Dietrich, M., and O. Loretz, *'Jahwe und seine Aschera': Anthropomorphes Kultbild in Mesopotamien, Ugarit und Israel: das biblische Bilderverbot* (Münster: Ugarit-Verlag, 1992).

—'Die Weisheit des ugaritischen Gottes El im Kontext der altorientalischen Weisheit', *UF* 24 (1992), pp. 31-38.

Dietrich, M., O. Loretz, and J. Sanmartín, *Die Keilalphabetischen Texte aus Ugarit.* I. *Transkription* (KTU) (AOAT, 24.1; Kevelaer: Butzon & Bercker; Neukirchen–Vluyn: Neukirchener Verlag, 1976).

Diezinger, A., *et al.* (eds.), *Erfahrung mit Methode: Wege sozialwissenschaftlicher Frauenforschung* (Freiburg: Kore, 1994).

Dijk-Hemmes, F. van, 'Tamar and the Limits of Patriarchy: Between Rape and Seduction (2 Samuel 13 and Genesis 38)', in M. Bal (ed.), *Anti-Covenant: Counter-Reading Women's Lives in the Hebrew Bible* (JSOTSup, 81; Bible and Literature Series, 22; Sheffield: Almond Press, 1989), pp. 135-56.

Diringer, D., 'Duweir Ewer', in O. Tufnell (ed.), *Lachish IV: Text* (London: Oxford University Press, 1958), p. 130.

Dohmen, C., 'Heisst Semel "Bild, Statue"?', *ZAW* 96 (1984), pp. 263-66.

Donaldson, L.E., *Decolonizing Feminisms: Race, Gender, and Empire-Building* (Chapel Hill: University of North Carolina Press, 1992).

Doob Sakenfeld, K., 'Feminist Uses of Biblical Materials', in L. Russell (ed.), *Feminist Interpretation of the Bible* (Oxford: Basil Blackwell, 1985), pp. 55-64.

Draisma, S. (ed.), *Intertextuality in Biblical Writings: Essays in Honour of Bas van Iersel* (Kampen: Kok, 1990).

Dreyer, G., 'Die Datierung der Min-Statuen aus Koptos', *Kunst des Alten Reiches* 28 (1995), pp. 49-56.

Driver, G.R., *Canaanite Myths and Legends* (Old Testament Series, 3; Edinburgh: T. and T. Clark, 1956).

—'Reflections on Recent Articles', *JBL* 73 (1954), pp. 125-36.

—'Supposed Arabisms in the Old Testament', *JBL* 55 (1936), pp. 101-20.

Driver, S.R., *Notes on the Hebrew Text and the Topography of the Books of Samuel* (Oxford: Clarendon Press, 2nd rev. edn, 1913).

Duby, G., *History Continues* (Chicago: University of Chicago Press, 1994).

Duffy, M., 'Mother and the Girl', in *Collected Poems 1949–84* (London: Hamish Hamilton, 1985).

Dumont du Voitel, W., *Macht und Entmachtung der Frau: Eine ethnologisch-historische Analyse* (Frankfurt and New York: Campus, 1994).

Dunbar, P.L., 'An Ante-Bellum Sermon', in D. Randall. (ed.), *The Black Poets* (New York: Bantam, 1971), pp. 44-6.

Dupont-Sommer, A., 'Le syncretisme religieux des Juifs d'Éléphantine d'après un ostracon Araméen inédit', *RHR* 130 (1945), pp. 17-28.

DuQuesne, T., ' "Semen of the Bull": Reflexions on the symbolism of Ma'et with reference to Recent Studies', *Discussions in Egyptology* 32 (1995), pp. 107-16.

Durand, J.-M., *La Femme dans le Proche-Orient Antique: XXXIIIe Rencontre Assyriologique Internationale* (Paris: erc, 1987).

Durber, S., 'The Female Reader of the Parables of the Lost', in G.J. Brooke (ed.), *Women in the Biblical Tradition* (Lampeter: Edwin Mellen, 1992), pp. 187-207

Dutcher-Walls, P., *Narrative Art and Political Rhetoric: The Case of Athaliah and Joash* (JSOTSup, 209; Sheffield: Sheffield Academic Press, 1996).

Eagleton, T., *Literary Theory: An Introduction* (Minneapolis: University of Minnesota Press, 1983).

Edinger, D., 'Bertha Pappenheim (1859–1936): A German-Jewish Feminist', *Jewish Social Studies* 20.3 (1958), pp. 180-86.

—*Bertha Pappenheim: Freud's Anna O.* (Highland Park, IL: Congregation Solel, 1968).

Edwards, I.E.S., 'A Relief of Qudshu–Astarte–Anath in the Winchester College Collection', *JNES* 14 (1955), pp. 49-51.

Efroymson, D.P., 'The Patristic Connection', in A. Davies (ed.), *Anti-Semitism and the Foundations of Christianity* (New York: Paulist Press, 1979), pp. 98-118.

Eilberg-Schwartz, H., *God's Phallus and Other Problems for Men and Monotheism* (Boston: Beacon, 1994).

Elliott, J.H., *What is Social Scientific Criticism?* (Minneapolis: Fortress Press, 1993).

Emerton, J.A., 'New Light on Israelite Religion: The Implications of the Inscriptions from Kuntillet 'Ajrud', *ZAW* 94 (1982), pp. 2-20.

—'Some Problems in Genesis XXXVIII', *VT* 25 (1975), pp. 338-61.

—'Wisdom', in G.W. Anderson (ed.), *Tradition and Interpretation: Essays by Members of the Society for Old Testament Study* (Oxford: Clarendon Press; New York: Oxford University Press, 1979), pp. 214-37.

Emerton, J.A. (ed.), *Congress Volume; Vienna 1980* (VTSup, 32; Leiden: Brill, 1981).

Empson, W., *Seven Types of Ambiguity* (London: Chatto & Windus, 1930; Harmondsworth: Penguin Books 1965 [1961]).

Engelstad, E., 'Images of Power and Contradiction: Feminist Theory and Postprocessual Archaeology', *Antiquity* 65 (1991), pp. 502-14.

Engle, J.R., 'Pillar Figurines of Iron Age Israel and Asherah/Asherim' (PhD dissertation, University of Pittsburgh, 1979).

Englund, G., *Akh—une notion religieuse dans l'égypte pharaonique* (BOREAS, 11; Uppsala: Acta Universitatis Upsaliensis, 1978).

Epstein, B., *Mekor Boruch: My Memoirs from the Previous Generation* (4 vols.; Vilna, Lithuania: Rom, 1928).

Epstein, I. (ed.), *The Babylonian Talmud* (London: Soncino, 1935).

Epstein, L., *The Jewish Marriage Contract: A Study in the Status of the Woman in Jewish Law* (New York: Jewish Theological Seminary of America, 1927).

Erlich, V.S., *Families in Transition: A Study of 300 Yugoslav Villages* (Princeton, NJ: Princeton University Press, 1966).

Exum, J.C., *Fragmented Women: Feminist (Sub)versions of Biblical Narratives* (JSOTSup, 163; Sheffield: JSOT Press, 1993).

—'"Mother in Israel": A Familiar Story Reconsidered', in Russell (ed.), *Feminist Interpretation of the Bible*, pp. 73-85.

—'The Mothers of Israel: The Patriarchal Narratives from a Feminist Perspective', *BRev* 2.1 (1986), pp. 60-67.

—'Murder They Wrote: Ideology and the Manipulation of Female Presence in Biblical Narrative', in A. Bach (ed.), *The Pleasure of Her Text: Feminist Readings of Biblical and Historical Texts* (Philadelphia: Trinity Press International, 1990), pp. 45-67.

—'Second Thoughts about Secondary Characters: Women in Exodus 1.8–2.10', in A. Brenner (ed.), *A Feminist Companion to Exodus to Deuteronomy* (The Feminist Companion to the Bible, 6; Sheffield: Sheffield Academic Press, 1994), pp. 75-87.

—'"You Shall Let Every Daughter Live": A Study of Exodus 1:8–2:10', *Semeia* 28 (1983), pp. 63-82.

Exum, J.C., and D.J.A. Clines, *The New Literary Criticism and the Hebrew Bible* (JSOTSup, 143; Sheffield: JSOT Press, 1993).

Falk, Z., 'Mutual Obligation in the Ketubah', *JJS* 7 (1957), pp. 215-17.

Fander, M., 'Historical Critical Methods', in Schüssler Fiorenza (ed.), *Searching the Scriptures*, I, pp. 205-24.

Fantham, E., H.P. Foley, N.B. Kampen, S.B., Pomeroy, and H.A. Shapiro, *Women in the Classical World: Image and Text* (Oxford: Oxford University Press, 1994).

Faulkner, R.O., *The Ancient Egyptian Coffin Texts* (3 vols.; Warminster: Aris & Philips, 1973–1978).

—*The Ancient Egyptian Pyramid Texts Translated into English* (Oxford: Clarendon Press, 1969).

—*The Papyrus Bremner-Rhind (British Museum No. 10188)* (Bibliotheca Aegyptiaca, 3; Brussels: Fondation Egyptologique Reine Elisabeth, 1933).

Felder, C.H. (ed.), *Stony the Road We Trod: African American Biblical Interpretation* (Minneapolis: Fortress Press, 1991).

Felt, U., H. Nowotny, and K. Taschwer, *Wissenschaftsforschung: Eine Einführung* (Frankfurt and New York: Campus, 1995).

Fensham, F.C., 'Widow, Orphan and the Poor in Ancient Near Eastern Legal and Wisdom Literature', *JNES* 21 (1962), pp. 129-39.

Fewell, D. Nolan, 'Feminist Criticism of the Hebrew Bible: Affirmation, Resistance, and Transformation', *JSOT* 39 (1987), pp. 65-75.

Fewell, D. Nolan (ed.), *Reading Between Texts: Intertextuality and the Hebrew Bible* (Louisville: Westminster /John Knox, 1992).

Fewell, D. Nolan, and D.M. Gunn, *Compromising Redemption: Relating Characters in the Book of Ruth* (Literary Currents in Biblical Interpretation; Louisville: Westminster/John Knox Press, 1990).

—'Controlling Perspectives: Women, Men and the Authority of Violence in Judges 4 & 5', *JAAR* 58 (1990), pp. 389-411.

—*Gender, Power and Promise: The Subject of the Bible's First Story* (Nashville, TN: Abingdon Press, 1993).

—'Tipping the Balance: Sternberg's Reader and the Rape of Dinah', *JBL* 110 (1991), pp. 193-211.

Finkelstein, L., *Jewish Self-Government in the Middle Ages* (Philadelphia: Jewish Publication Society, 1924).

Fish, S., *Is There a Text in This Class? The Authority of Interpretative Communities* (Cambridge, MA: Harvard University Press, 1980).

—*Self-Consuming Artifacts: The Experience of Seventeenth-Century Literature* (Berkeley: University of California Press, 1972).

Fisher, L., *Ras Shamra Parallels* (2 vols; Rome: Pontificum Institutum Biblicum, 1975).

Flanagan, J.W., *David's Social Drama: A Hologram of Israel's Early Iron Age* (The Social World of Biblical Antiquity, 7; Sheffield; Almond Press, 1988).

Fleming, D.E., *The Installation of Baal's High Priestess at Emar: A Window on Ancient Syrian Religion* (Atlanta, GA: Scholars Press, 1992).

—'More Help from Syria: Introducing Emar to Biblical Study', *BA* 58 (1995), pp. 139-47.

Flesher, P.V.M., 'Are Women Property in the System of the Mishnah?', in J. Neusner, E. Freirichs, and N. Sarna (eds.), *From Ancient Israel to Modern Judaism* (Atlanta: Scholars Press, 1988), vol. 1, pp. 219-31.

Fletcher, A., *Gender, Sex and Subordination in England 1500–1800* (New Haven: Yale University Press, 1995).

Fontaine, C.R. —'The Deceptive Goddess in Ancient Near Eastern Myth: Inanna and Inaras', *Semeia* 42 (1988), pp. 84-102.

—'Disabilities and Illness in the Bible: A Feminist Perspective', in A. Brenner (ed.), *A Feminist Companion to the Hebrew Bible in the New Testament* (The Feminist Companion to the Bible, 10; Sheffield: Sheffield Academic Press, 1996), pp. 286-301.

— '"A Heifer From Thy Stable": On Goddesses and the Status of Women in the Ancient Near East', in Bach (ed.), *The Pleasure of Her Text: Feminist Readings of Biblical and Historical Texts*, pp. 69-95.

—'A Response to "Hosea"', in Brenner (ed.), *A Feminist Companion to the Latter Prophets*, pp. 60-69.

—'Proverbs', in J.L. Mays (ed.), *Harper's Bible Commentary* (San Francisco: Harper & Row, 1988), pp. 495-517.

—'Proverbs', in C.A. Newsom and S.H. Ringe (eds.), *The Women's Bible Commentary* (Louisville: Westminster/John Knox, 1992), pp. 145-52.

—'The Social Roles of Women in the World of Wisdom', in A. Brenner (ed.), *A Feminist Companion to Wisdom Literature* (The Feminist Companion to the Bible, 9; Sheffield: Sheffield Academic Press, 1995), pp. 24-49.

Fortune, M., *Sexual Violence: The Unmentionable Sin* (New York: Pilgrim Press, 1983).

Foster, B.R. (trans.), *From Distant Days: Myths, Tales and Poetry of Ancient Mesopotamia* (Bethesda, MD: CDL Press, 1995).

Fowler, M.D., 'Excavated Figurines: A Case for Identifying a Site as Sacred?', *ZAW* 97 (1985), pp. 333-44.

—'Excavated Incense Burners: A Case for Identifying a Site as Sacred?', *PEQ* 117 (1985), pp. 25-29.

Fox, M., 'Egyptian Onomastica and Biblical Wisdom', *VT* 36 (1986), pp. 302-10.

—'World Order and Ma'at: A Crooked Parallel', *JANESCU* 23 (1995), pp. 37-48.

Fraade, S., *From Tradition to Commentary: Torah and its Interpretation in the Midrash Sifre to Deuteronomy* (Albany: SUNY Press, 1991).

Frankfort, H., *Cylinder Seals: A Documentary Essay on the Art and Religion of the Ancient Near East* (London: Gregg Press, 1965 [1939]).

—*The Birth of Civilization in the Near East* (Garden City, NY: Doubleday, 1956).

Frankl, V., *Man's Search for Meaning* (New York: Pocket Books, rev. and updated, 1984).

Freedman, D.N., 'Yahweh of Samaria and His Asherah', *BA* 50 (1987), pp. 241-49.

French, V., 'What is Central for the Study of Women in Antiquity?', *Helios* 17 (1990), pp. 213-19.

Frevel, C., *Aschera und der Ausschließlichkeitsanspruch YHWHs* (2 vols; Bonner Biblische Beiträge, 94; Weinheim: Beltz Athenäum Verlag, 1995).

Friedl, E., 'The Position of Women: Appearance and Reality', *Anthropological Quarterly* 40 (1967), pp. 47-108.

Friedman, S.S., *Penelope's Web: Gender, Modernity, H.D.'s Fiction* (Cambridge: Cambridge University Press, 1990).

—*Psyche Reborn: The Emergence of H.D.* (Bloomington: Indiana University Press, 1975).

Frymer-Kensky, T.S., *In the Wake of the Goddesses: Women, Culture, and the Biblical Transformation of Pagan Myth* (New York: Free Press, 1992).

Fuchs, E., 'The Literary Characterization of Mothers and Sexual Politics in the Hebrew Bible', in Yarbro Collins (ed.), *Feminist Perspectives*, pp. 117-36.

—'Who is Hiding the Truth? Deceptive Women and Biblical Androcentrism', in Yarbro Collins (ed.), *Feminist Perspectives*, pp. 137-44.

Fulkerson, M. McClintock, *Changing the Subject: Women's Discourses and Feminist Theology* (Minneapolis: Fortress Press, 1994).

Furman, N., 'His Story versus Her Story: Male Genealogy and Female Strategy in the Jacob Cycle', in Yarbro Collins (ed.), *Feminist Perspectives*, pp. 107-16.

Gage, M., *Women, Church and State: The Exposé of Male Collaboration against the Female Sex* (repr.; Watertown, MA: Persephone Press, 1980 [1893]).

Gager, J., *The Origins of Anti-Semitism: Attitudes Towards Judaism in Pagan and Christian Antiquity* (New York: Oxford University Press, 1985).

Gammie, J.G., *et al.* (eds.), *Israelite Wisdom: Theological and Literary Essays in Honour of Samuel Terrien* (Missoula, MT: Scholars Press for Union Theological Seminary, 1978).

Garber, M., *Vice-Versa: Bisexuality and the Eroticism of Everyday Life* (New York: Simon & Schuster, 1995).

Garbini, G., 'Su un'iscrizione ebraica da Khirbet el-Kom', *AION* NS 38 (1978), pp. 191-93.

Garner, G.G., 'Kuntillet 'Ajrud: An Intriguing Site in Sinai', *Buried History* 14.2 (1978), pp. 1-16.

Garry, A. and M. Pearsall (eds.), *Women, Knowledge, and Reality: Explorations in Feminist Philosophy* (New York and London: Routledge, 1992).

Gaster, T.H., 'The Archaic Inscriptions', in O. Tufnell, C.H. Inge, and L. Harding (eds.), *Lachish II: The Fosse Temple* (London: Oxford University Press, 1940), pp. 49-54.

Gates, H.L., Jr (ed.), *'Race', Writing, and Difference* (Chicago: University of Chicago Press, 1986).

—*The Signifying Monkey: A Theory of African-American Literary Criticism* (New York: Oxford University Press, 1988).

Geertz, C., *The Interpretation of Cultures* (New York: Basic Books, 1973).

Gelb, I.J., 'Approaches to the Study of Ancient Society', *JAOS* 87 (1967), pp. 1-8.

Gelb, I.J., B. Landsberger, and A.L. Oppenheim (eds.), *The Assyrian Dictionary* (*CAD*; 21 vols; Chicago: Oriental Institute, 1956–89).

Gelles, R.J., 'Family Violence', in R.L. Hampton *et al.* (eds.), *Family Violence*, pp. 1-24.

Gelles, R.J., and M.A. Straus, 'Determinants of Violence in the Family: Toward a Theoretical Integration', in W.R. Burr, R. Hill, F.I. Nye and I.L. Reiss (eds.), *Contemporary Theories About the Family*. I. *Research Based Theories* (New York: Free Press, 1979), pp. 549-81.

Gemser, B., *Sprüche Salomos* (HAT; Tübingen: Mohr, 1963).

Genette, G., *Palimpsestes, la littérature au second degré* (Paris: Seuil, 1982).

George, D.H., *The Evolution of Love* (Grenada, MS: Salt-Works Press, 1977).

Georgi, D., 'Frau Weisheit oder das Recht auf Freiheit als schöpferische Kraft', in L. Siegele-Wenschkewitz (ed.), *Verdrängte Vergangenheit, die uns bedrängt: Feministische Theologie in der Verantwortung für die Geschichte* (Munich: Chr. Kaiser Verlag, 1988), pp. 243-76.

Gero, J.M., and M.W. Conkey (eds.), *Engendering Archaeology: Women and Prehistory* (Oxford: Basil Blackwell, 1991).

Geus, C.H.J. de, 'The Profile of an Israelite City', *BA* 49 (1986), pp. 224-27.

Gibson, J.C.L., *Canaanite Myths and Legends* (Edinburgh: T. & T. Clark, 2nd edn, 1978 [1977]).

—*Job* (Philadelphia: Westminster Press, 1985).

Gilbert, C., *Bonfire* (Boston:Alice James Press, 1983).

Gilbert, S., and S. Gubar (eds.), *The Madwoman in the Attic: The Woman Writer and the Nineteenth Century Literary Imagination* (New Haven: Yale University Press, 1979).

Gilchrist, R., 'Women's Archaeology? Political Feminism, Gender Theory and Historical Revision', *Antiquity* 65 (1991), pp. 495-501.

Gilligan, C., *In a Different Voice: Psychological Theory and Women's Development* (Cambridge, MA: Harvard University Press, 1982).

Gilmore, D.D. (ed.), *Honor and Shame and the Unity of the Mediterranean* (Washington, DC: American Anthropological Association, 1987).

Gilmore, D.D., *Manhood in the Making: Cultural Concepts of Masculinity* (New Haven: Yale University Press, 1990).

—*Aggression and Community: Paradoxes of Andalusian Culture* (New Haven: Yale University Press, 1987).

Gilula, M., 'To Yahweh Shomron and his Asherah', *Shnaton* 3 (1978–79), pp. 129-37 (Hebrew).

Gitin, S., 'Seventh Century B.C.E. Cultic Elements at Ekron', in A. Biran and J. Aviram (eds.), *Biblical Archaeology Today 1990: Proceedings of the Second International Congress on Biblical Archaeology: Jerusalem, June–July 1990* (Jerusalem: Israel Exploration Society, 1993), pp. 248-58.

Giveon, R., 'Ptah and Astarte on a Seal from Accho', in G. Buccellati (ed.), *Studi sull 'Oriente e la Bibbia offerti a P Giovani Rinaldi* (Gênes: Editrice Studio e Vita, 1967), pp. 147-53.

Gleason, M.W., *Making Men: Sophists and Self-presentation in Ancient Rome* (Princeton, NJ: Princeton University Press, 1995).

Glock, A.E., 'Taanach', in M. Avi-Yonah and E. Stern (eds.), *Encyclopedia of Archaeological Excavations in the Holy Land* (Jerusalem: Israel Exploration Society and Massada Press, 1978), IV, pp. 1138-47.

—'Taanach', in E. Stern (ed.), *The New Encyclopedia of Archaeological Excavations in the Holy Land* (Jerusalem: Israel Exploration Society, 1993), IV, pp. 1428-33.

Goethe, J.W. von, *Goethe Werkes*, I (ed. E. Trunz; Munich: Beck, 1981).

Goldberg, D.T. (ed.), *Multiculturalism: A Critical Reader* (Cambridge, MA: Basil Blackwell, 1994).

Goldstein, J., 'Antisemitism, Sexism and the Death of the Goddess', in M. Curtis (ed.), *Antisemitism in the Contemporary World* (Boulder: Westview Press, 1986), pp. 251-57.

Goldstein, R., *Strange Attractors: Stories* (New York: Viking, 1993).

Good, E.M., 'Deception and Women: A Response', *Semeia* 42 (1988), pp. 117-32.

Goodenough, E.R., *Jewish Symbols of the Greco-Roman Period* (Bollingen Series, 37; 12 vols.; New York: Pantheon, 1953–1968).

Gordis, R., *The Book of God and Man: A Study of Job* (Chicago: University of Chicago Press, 1965).

—*The Book of Job: Commentary, New Translation and Special Studies* (New York: Jewish Theological Seminary, 1978).

Gordon, C.H., *Ugaritic Textbook (UT)* (AnOr, 38; Rome: Pontifical Biblical Institute, 1965).

Görg, M., *Aegyptiaca Biblica: Notizen und Beiträge zu den Beziehungen zwischen Ägypten und Israel* (Wiesbaden: Otto Harrassowitz, 1991).

Gottwald, N., *Studies in the Book of Lamentations* (Chicago: Alec R. Allenson, 1954).

Gottwald, N.K., and R.A. Horsley (eds.), *The Bible and Liberation: Political and Social Hermeneutics* (Maryknoll: Orbis Books, rev. edn, 1993).

Gow, M.D., *The Book of Ruth: Its Structure, Theme and Purpose* (Leicester: Apollos 1992).

Goyon, J.-C., 'Le céremonial de glorification d'Osiris du papyrus du Louvre I. 3079 (colonnes 110 à 112),' *Bulletin de l'Institut français d'archéologie orientale du Caire* 64 (1966), pp. 89-156.

Grant, M., *The Antonines: The Roman Empire in Transition* (London: Routledge, 1994).

Graves, R., *The White Goddess* (New York: Octagon Books, 1978).

Gray, J., *I & II Kings: A Commentary* (OTL; Philadelphia: Westminster Press; London: SCM Press, 2nd rev. edn, 1970).

Grayson, A.K., 'History of Mesopotamia: History and Culture of Assyria; History and Culture of Babylonia', in Freedman (ed.), *Anchor Bible Dictionary*, IV, pp. 732-777.

Greenberg, D.F., *The Construction of Homosexuality* (Chicago: University of Chicago Press, 1988).

Greenberg, I., 'Cloud of Smoke, Pillar of Fire: Judaism, Christianity, and Modernity after the Holocaust', in E. Fleischner (ed.), *Auschwitz: Beginning of a New Era?* (New York: Ktav, 1977), pp. 7-55.

Grenfell, A., 'The Iconography of Bes, and of Phoenician Bes-hand Scarabs', *Proceedings of the Society of Biblical Archaeology* 24 (1902), pp. 21-40.

Gressmann, H., *Altorientalische Bilder zum Alten Testament* (Berlin: de Gruyter, 1927).

—*Altorientalische Texte und Bilder zum Alten Testament* (Tübingen: Mohr [Paul Siebeck], 1909).

—'Josia und das Deuteronomium', *ZAW* 42 (1924), pp. 313-37.

Griffiths, J.G., *The Origins of Osiris and his Cult* (Studies in the History of Religions, 40 (Leiden: Brill, 1980).

Groneberg, B., 'Eine Einführungsszene in der altbabylonischen Literatur', in K. Hecker *et al.* (eds.), *Keilschriftiche Literaturen* (Berlin: Georg Reimer, 1986), pp. 93-108.

Gross, R. (ed.), *Beyond Androcentrism: New Essays on Women and Religion* (Missoula, MT: Scholars Press, 1977).

Grössmann, E., 'History of Biblical Interpretation by European Women', in Schüssler Fiorenza (ed.), *Searching the Scriptures*, I, pp. 27-40.

Gruber, M.I., 'The Motherhood of God in Second Isaiah', in *The Motherhood of God and Other Studies* (Atlanta: Scholars Press, 1992), pp. 3-15.

Guijarro Oporto, S., 'La familia en la Galilea del siglo primero', *Estudios Biblicos* 53 (1995), pp. 461-88.

Gundry, R.H., *The Use of the Old Testament in St Matthew's Gospel: With Special Reference to the Messianic Hope* (SuppNovT, XVIII; Leiden: Brill, 1975).

Gunkel, H., *The Legends of Genesis* (trans. W.H. Carruth; Chicago: Open Court, 1907).

—*The Legends of Genesis: The Biblical Saga and History* (New York: Schocken Books, 1964).

—*Zum religionsgeschichtlichen Verständnis des Neuen Testaments* (Göttingen: Vandenhoeck & Ruprecht, 1903).

Gunn, D.M., 'David and the Gift of the Kingdom', in R.C. Culley (ed.), *Classical Hebrew Narrative* (Semeia, 3; Missoula, MT: Scholars Press, 1975), pp. 14-45.

—*The Fate of King Saul: An Interpretation of a Biblical Story* (JSOTSup, 14: Sheffield: JSOT Press, 1980).

—'The "Hardening" of Pharaoh's Heart: Plot, Character and Theology in Exodus 1–14', in D.J.A. Clines, D.M. Gunn and A.J. Hauser (eds.), *Art and Meaning: Rhetoric in Biblical Literature* (JSOTSup, 17; Sheffield: JSOT Press, 1982),pp. 72-96.

—'Joshua and Judges', in Alter and Kermode (eds.), *The Literary Guide to the Bible*, pp. 102-21.

—'In Security: The David of Biblical Narrative', in J.C. Exum (ed.), *Signs and Wonders: Biblical Texts in Literary Focus* (Semeia Studies; Atlanta: Scholars

Press, 1989), pp. 133-51 (with response by Peter D. Miscall, pp. 153-63).

—'Reading Right: Reliable and Omniscient Narrator, Omniscient God, and Fool-proof Composition in the Hebrew Bible', in D.J.A. Clines, S.E. Fowl and S.E. Porter (eds.), *The Bible in Three Dimensions* (JSOTSup, 87; Sheffield: JSOT Press, 1990), pp. 53-64.

—'Samson of Sorrows: An Isaianic Gloss on Judges 13–16', in Fewell (ed.), *Reading Between Texts: Intertextuality in the Hebrew Bible*, pp. 225-53.

—'2 Samuel', in J. Mays (gen. ed.), *Harper's Bible Commentary* (San Francisco: Harper & Row, 1988), pp. 287-304.

—*The Story of King David: Genre and Interpretation* (JSOTSup, 6: Sheffield: JSOT Press, 1978).

—'Traditional Composition in the "Succession Narrative"', *VT* 26 (1976), pp. 214-29.

—'What Does The Bible Say? A Question of Text and Canon', in Beal and Gunn (eds.), *Reading Bibles, Writing Bodies*, pp. 242-61.

Gunn, D.M., and D. Nolan Fewell, *Narrative in the Hebrew Bible* (Oxford Bible Series; Oxford: Oxford University Press, 1993).

Gunneweg, J., I. Perlman, and Z. Meshel, 'The Origin of the Pottery of Kuntillet 'Ajrud', *IEJ* 35 (1985), pp. 270-83.

Gurko, M., *The Ladies of Seneca Falls: The Birth of the Women's Rights Movement* (New York: Schocken Books, 1974).

Güterbock, H.G., 'An Outline of the Hittite AN.TA.ÒUM Festival', *JNES* 19 (1960), pp. 80-89.

H.D., *Trilogy* (NY: New Directions, 1973).

Habel, N.C., *The Book of Job* (OTL; London: SCM Press, 1985).

Hackett, J.A., 'Phoenician and Punic Goddesses', paper presented to the Gender and Cultural Criticism Consultation, Society of Biblical Literature annual meeting, 1993.

Hadley, J.M., 'Chasing Shadows? The Quest for the Historical Goddess', in J.A. Emerton (ed.), *Congress Volume, IOSOT 1995* (Leiden: Brill, in press).

—*Evidence for a Hebrew Goddess: The Cult of Asherah in Ancient Israel and Judah* (Oriental Publications Series; Cambridge: Cambridge University Press, forthcoming).

—'The Fertility of the Flock?: The De-personalization of Astarte in the Old Testament', in B. Becking and M. Dijkstra (eds.), *On Reading Prophetic Texts* pp. 115-33.

—'The Khirbet el-Qom Inscription', *VT* 37 (1987), pp. 50-62.

—'Kuntillet 'Ajrud: Religious Centre or Desert Way Station?,' *PEQ* 125 (1993), pp. 115-24.

—'Some Drawings and Inscriptions on Two Pithoi from Kuntillet 'Ajrud', *VT* 37 (1987), pp. 180-213.

—'William Robertson Smith and the asherah', in W. Johnstone (ed.), *William Robertson Smith: Essays in Reassessment* (JSOTSup, 189; Sheffield: Sheffield Academic Press, 1995), pp. 164-79.

—'Wisdom and the goddess', in J. Day, R.P. Gordon and H.G.M. Williamson (eds.), *Wisdom in ancient Israel: Essays in honour of J.A. Emerton* (Cambridge: Cambridge University Press, 1995), pp. 234-43.

—'Yahweh and "His Asherah": Archaeological and Textual Evidence for the Cult of the Goddess', in W. Dietrich and M.A. Klopfenstein (eds.), *Ein Gott allein?: JHWH-Verehrung und biblischer Monotheismus im Kontext der israelitischen und altorientalischen Religionsgeschichte* (OBO, 139; Fribourg: Editions universitaires; Göttingen: Vandenhoeck & Ruprecht, 1994), pp. 235-68.

Haley, S.P., 'Black Feminist Thought and Classics: Re-membering, Re-claiming, Re-empowering', in Rabinowitz and Richlin (eds.), *Feminist Theory*, pp. 23-43.

Hall, K., and M. Bucholtz (eds.), *Gender Articulated: Language and the Socially Constructed Self* (London: Routledge, 1995).

Halpern, B., '"Brisker Pipes than Poetry": The Development of Israelite Monotheism', in J. Neusner, B.A. Levine, and E.S. Frerichs (eds.), *Judaic Perspectives on Ancient Israel* (Philadelphia: Fortress Press, 1987), pp. 77-115.

Hamayon, R., *La Chasse à l'âme* (Nanterre: Société d'Ethnologie, 1990).

Hampson, D., *Theology and Feminism* (Signposts in Theology; Oxford: Basil Blackwell, 1990).

Hampton, R.L., Thomas P. Gullotta, Gerard R. Adams, Earl H. Potter, III, and Roger P. Weissberg (eds.), *Family Violence: Prevention and Treatment. I. Issues in Children's and Families' Lives* (Newbury Park, CA: Sage, 1993).

Handy, L.K., *Among the Host of Heaven: The Syro-Palestinian Pantheon as Bureaucracy* (Winona Lake, IN: Eisenbrauns, 1994).

—'Hezekiah's Unlikely Reform', *ZAW* 100 (1988), pp. 111-15.

Hanhart, R., 'The Translation of the Septuagint in Light of Earlier Tradition and Subsequent Influences', in Brooke and Lindars (eds.), *Septuagint, Scrolls and Cognate Writings*, pp. 339-79.

Hanson, K.C., 'The Herodians and Mediterranean Kinship. I. Genealogy and Descent', *BTB* 19 (1989), pp. 75-84.

—'The Herodians and Mediterranean Kinship. II. Marriage and Divorce', *BTB* 19 (1989), pp. 142-51.

—'The Herodians and Mediterranean Kinship. III. Economics', *BTB* 20 (1990), pp. 10-21.

Hanson, P.D., *The People Called: The Growth of Community in the Bible* (San Francisco: Harper & Row, 1986).

Haran, M., 'zebah hayyamim', *VT* 19 (1969), pp. 11-22.

Haraway, D., 'Animal Sociology and a Natural Economy of the Body Politic. Part II. The Past is the Contested Zone: Human Nature and Theories of Production and Reproduction in Primate Behavior Studies', *Signs* 4 (1978), pp. 37-60.

Harding, S., *The Science Question in Feminism* (Ithaca, NY: Cornell University Press, 1986).

Harding, S. (ed.), *The 'Racial' Economy of Science: Toward a Democratic Future* (Bloomington: Indiana University Press, 1993).

Harris, M., *Cultural Materialism: The Struggle for a Science of Culture* (New York: Vintage, 1980).

Hartman, G., 'The Struggle for the Text', in Hartman and Budick (eds.), *Midrash and Literature*.

Hartman, G., and S. Budick (eds.), *Midrash and Literature* (New Haven: Yale University Press, 1986).

Hartmann, B., 'Monotheismus in Mesopotamien?', in O. Keel (ed.), *Monotheismus im Alten Israel und seiner Umwelt* (BibB, 14; Fribourg: Verlag Schweizerisches Katholisches Bibelwerk, 1980), pp. 49-81.

Hartmann, R., 'Zu Genesis 38', *ZAW* 33 (1913), pp. 76-77.

Hassan, F.A., 'Primeval Goddess to Divine King: The Mythogenesis of Power in the Early Egyptian State', in R. Friedman and B. Adams (eds.), *The Followers of Horus: Studies Dedicated to Michael Allen Hoffman 1944–1990* (Egyptian Studies Association Publication, 2; Oxbow Monographs, 20; Oxford: Oxbow Publications, 1992), pp. 307-21.

Hautpman, J., 'Feminist Perspectives on Rabbinic Texts', in L. Davidman and S. Tenenbaum (eds.), *Feminist Perspectives on Jewish Studies* (New Haven: Yale University Press, 1994), pp. 40-61.

Hekman, S.J., *Gender and Knowledge: Elements of a Postmodern Feminism* (Boston: Northeastern University Press, 1990).

Helck, W., 'Zur Herkunft der Erzählung des sog. "Astartepapyrus"', in M. Görg (ed.), *Fontes atque pontes* (Wiesbaden: Otto Harrassowitz, 1983), pp. 215-23.

Helck, W., and E. Otto (eds.), *Lexikon der Ägyptologie* (Wiesbaden: Otto Harrassowitz, 1975).

Hengel, M., and A.M. Schwemer (eds.), *Die Septuaginta zwischen Judentum und Christentum* (WUNT, 72; Tübingen: Mohr [Paul Siebeck], 1994).

Hengel, M., 'Die Septuaginta als "christliche Sammlung": ihre Vorgeschichte und das Problem ihres Kanons', in Hengel and Schwemer (eds.), *Die Septuaginta zwischen Judentum und Christentum*, pp. 182-284.

Herdner, A., *Corpus des tablettes en cunéiformes alphabétiques découvertes à Ras Shamra–Ugarit de 1929 à 1939 (CTA)* (Publications de la Mission de Ras Shamra, 10; Paris: Geuthner, 1963).

Herman, J.L., *Trauma and Recovery* (New York: Basic Books, 1992).

Herr, M.D., 'Midrash', *EncJud*, XI, pp. 1507-14.

—'Midreshei Halakha', *EncJud*, XI, pp. 1521-23.

Herrmann, W., 'Wann wurde Jahwe zum Schöpfer der Welt?', *UF* 23 (1991), pp. 165-80.

Heschel, S., 'Altes Gift in neuen Schläuchen: Antijudaismus und Antipharisäismus in der christlichen-feministischen Theologie', in Frauenforschungsprojekt zur Geschichte der Theologinnen Göttingen (ed.), *Querdenken: Beiträge zur feministisch-befreiungs theologischen Diskussion* (Pfaffenweiler: Centaurus verlagsgesellschaft, 1992), pp. 65-77.

—'Anti-Semites against Antisemitism', *Tikkun* 8 (Nov.–Dec. 1993), pp. 47-53.

—'Konfigurationen des Patriarchats, des Judentums und des Nazismus in deutschen feministischen denken', in C. Kohn-Ley and I. Korotin (eds.), *Der feministische 'Sündenfall': Antisemitische Vorurteile in der Frauenbewegung* (Wien: Picus Verlag, 1994), pp. 160-85.

Hess, R.S., 'Yahweh and His Asherah? Epigraphic Evidence for Religious Pluralism in Old Testament Times', in A. Clarke and B.W. Winter (eds.), *One God, One Lord in a World of Religious Pluralism* (Cambridge: Tyndale House, 1991), pp. 5-33.

Hestrin, R., 'First Temple and Persian Periods', in E. Carmon (ed.), *Inscriptions Reveal* (Israel Museum Catalogue, 100; Jerusalem: The Israel Museum, 1972 [Hebrew]).

—'The Cult Stand from Ta'anach and its Religious Background', in E. Lipiński (ed.), *Studia Phoenicia* 5 (Leuven: Peeters, 1987), pp. 61-77.

—'The Lachish Ewer and the 'Asherah', *IEJ* 37 (1987), pp. 212-23.

Hillers, D., *Lamentations* (AB; Garden City, NY: Doubleday, 1992).

Hobbs, T.R., '*BTB* Readers Guide: Aspects of Warfare in the First Testament World', *BTB* 25 (1995), pp. 79-90.

Hodder, I., 'Gender Representation and Social Reality', in D. Walde and D. Willows , *The Archaeology of Gender* (Calgary: Calgary University Press, 1991), pp. 11-16.

—*Reading the Past: Current Approaches to Interpretation in Archaeology* (Cambridge: Cambridge University Press, 2nd edn, 1991).

—*Reading the Past: Current Approaches to Interpretation in Archaeology* (Cambridge: Cambridge University Press, 1986).

Holladay, William L., *Jeremiah 2: A Commentary on the Book of the Prophet Jeremiah Chapters 26–52* (Hermeneia; Minneapolis: Fortress Press, 1989)

Holland, T.A., 'A Typological and Archaeological Study of Human and Animal Representations in the Plastic Art of Palestine During the Iron Age' (2 vols; PhD dissertation, Oxford University, 1975).

—'A Study of Palestinian Iron Age Baked Clay Figurines, with Special Reference to Jerusalem: Cave 1', *Levant* 9 (1977), pp. 121-55.

Hölscher, G., *Das Buch Hiob* (Tübingen: Mohr [Paul Siebeck], 1937).

Hornung, E., *Der Eine und die Vielen* (Darmstadt: Wissenschaftliche Buchgesell-schaft, 1971); ET: *Conceptions of God in Ancient Egypt: The One and the Many* (London: Routledge & Kegan Paul, 1982).

—*Der ägyptische Mythos von der Himmelskuh: Eine Ätiologie des Unvollkommenen* (OBO, 46; Freiburg, Schweiz: Universitätsverlag; Göttingen: Vandenhoeck & Ruprecht, 1982).

Horsley, R.A., *Jesus and the Spiral of Violence: Popular Jewish Resistance in Roman Palestine* (Minneapolis: Fortress Press, 1993).

Hrouda, B. (ed.), *Methoden der Archäologie: Eine Einführung in die naturwissen-schaftlichen Techniken* (Munich: Beck, 1978).

Hyman, P.E., *Gender and Assimilation in Modern Jewish History: The Roles and Representation of Women* (Samuel and Althea Stroum Lectures in Jewish Studies; Seattle: University of Washington Press, 1995).

Ilan, T., *Jewish Women in Greco-Roman Palestine: An Inquiry Into Image and Status* (Tübingen: Mohr, 1995).

Irigaray, L., *Sexes and Genealogies* (trans. Gillian C. Gill; New York: Columbia University Press, 1993).

Isaac, J., *The Teaching of Contempt* (trans. Helen Heaver; New York: Holt, Rinehart & Winston, 1964).

Ishida, T. (ed.), *Studies in the Period of David and Solomon and Other Essays* (Winona Lake, IN: Eisenbrauns; Tokyo: Yamakawa-Shuppansha, 1982).

Jacob, B., *Das erste Buch der Tora: Genesis* (New York: Ktav 1934).

Jacobsen, T., *The Harp That Once… Sumerian Poetry in Translation* (New Haven and London: Yale University Press, 1987).

—*The Treasures of Darkness: A History of Mesopotamian Religion* (New Haven: Yale University Press, 1976).

Jacobsohn, H., *Die dogmatische Stellung des Königs in der Theologie der alten Ägypter* (Ägyptologische Forschungen, 8; Glückstadt: J.J. Augustin, 1939).

—'Kamutef', in *Lexikon der Ägyptologie* (Wiesbaden: Otto Harrassowitz, 1981), III, pp. 308-309.

Jahn, G., *Das Buch Esther nach der Septuaginta hergestellt, übersetzt und kritisch erklart* (Leiden: Brill, 1901).

Janzen, J.G., *Job* (Atlanta: John Knox, 1985).

Japhet, S., *I & II Chronicles* (London: SCM Press; Louisville: Westminster/John Knox, 1993).

Jaroš, K., *Hundert Inschriften aus Kanaan und Israel: Für den Hebräischunterricht bearbeitet* (Fribourg: Verlag Schweizerisches Katholisches Bibelwerk, 1982).

—'Zur Inschrift Nr. 3 von Hirbet el-Qōm', *Biblische Notizen* 19 (1982), pp. 31-40.

Jeansonne, S.P., *The Women of Genesis: From Sarah to Potiphar's Wife* (Minneapolis: Fortress Press, 1990).

Jenni, E., and C. Westermann (eds.), *Theologisches Handwörterbuch zum Alten Testament* (2 vols.; Munich: Chr. Kaiser Verlag; Zurich: Theologischer Verlag, 1971–76).

Jenny, L., 'La stratégie de la forme', *Poétique* 27 (1976), pp. 257-81.

Jobes, K.H., *The Alpha-Text of Esther: Its Character and Relationship to the Masoretic Text* (SBLDS, 153; Atlanta: Scholars Press, 1996).

Jobling, D., *The Sense of Biblical Narrative: Three Structural Analyses in the Old Testament* (JSOTSup, 7; Sheffield: JSOT Press, 1978; repr. 1986 as *The Sense of Biblical Narrative: Structural Analyses in the Hebrew Bible*, I).

—*The Sense of Biblical Narrative: Structural Analyses in the Hebrew Bible*, II (JSOTSup, 39; Sheffield: JSOT Press, 1986).

Johnson, B., *A World of Difference* (Baltimore: The Johns Hopkins University Press, 1987).

Joukowsky, M., *A Complete Manual of Field Archaeology: Tools and Techniques of Field Work for Archaeologists* (Englewood Cliffs, NJ: Prentice–Hall, 1980).

Joüon P., and T. Muraoka, *A Grammar of Biblical Hebrew* (Rome: Pontificio Istituto Biblico, 1991), Vols. 1–2.

Joyce, P., 'Feminist Exegesis of the Old Testament: Some Critical Reflections', in J.M. Soskice (ed.), *After Eve: Women, Theology and the Christian Tradition* (London: Marshall Pickering, 1990), pp. 1-9.

Jung, C.G., *Analytical Psychology: Notes of the Seminar Given in 1925* (Princeton, NJ: Princeton University Press, 1989).

—*The Archetypes and the Collective Unconscious* (Collected Works, 9.1; New York: Pantheon, 1959).

—*Memories, Dreams, Reflections* (London: Fontana, 1983).

—*Symbols of Transformation* (Collected Works, 5; New York: Pantheon, 1956).

—*Two Essays on Analytical Psychology* (Collected Works, 7; New York: Pantheon, 1953).

Kaiser, O. (ed.), *Texte aus der Umwelt des Alten Testaments* (Gütersloh: Gütersloher Verlagshaus, 1982–1990).

Kaiser, W.C., *The Uses of the Old Testament in the New* (Chicago: Moody Press, 1985).

Kamesar, A., *Jerome, Greek Scholarship and the Hebrew Bible: A Study of the Quaestiones Hebraicae in Genesis* (Oxford: Clarendon Press, 1993).

Kaplan, A.E., 'Is the Gaze Male?', in A. Snitow, C. Stansell and S. Thompson (eds.), *Powers of Desire: The Politics of Sexuality* (New York: Monthly Review Press, 1983), pp. 309-27.

Kaplan, M.A., 'Anna O. and Bertha Pappenheim: An Historical Perspective', in M. Rosenbaum and M. Muroff (eds.), *Anna O.: Fourteen Contemporary Reinterpretations* (New York: Free Press, 1984), pp. 101-17.

—*The Making of the Jewish Middle Class: Women, Family, and Identity in Imperial Germany* (Oxford: Oxford University Press, 1991).

Kates, J.A. and G.T. Reimer (eds.), *Reading Ruth: Contemporary Women Reclaim a Sacred Story* (New York: Ballantine, 1994).

Keder-Kopfstein, B., *The Vulgate as a Translation: Some Semantic and Syntactical Aspects of Jerome's Version of the Hebrew Bible* (Jerusalem, 1968).

Keel, O., *Jahwes Entgegnung an Ijob* (Göttingen: Vandenhoeck & Ruprecht, 1978).

—*The Symbolism of the Biblical World: Ancient Near Eastern Iconography and the Book of Psalms* (trans. T.J. Hallett; New York: Seabury, 1978).

—*Die Welt der altorientalischen Bildsymbolik und das Alte Testament: Am Beispiel der Psalmen* (Zürich: Benziger Verlag; Neukirchen–Vluyn: Neukirchener Verlag); ET: *The Symbolism of the Biblical World* (trans. T.J. Hallett; New York: Seabury, 1978).

Keel, O. (ed.), *Monotheismus im Alten Israel und seiner Umwelt* (BibB 14; Fribourg: Verlag Schweizerisches Katholisches Bibelwerk, 1980).

Keel, O., and C. Uehlinger, *Göttinnen, Götter und Gottessymbole: Neue Erkenntnisse zur Religionsgeschichte Kanaans und Israels aufgrund bis unerschlossener ikonographischer Quellen* (Quaestiones disputatae, 134, Freiburg: Herder, 1992).

Kellenbach, K. von, *Anti-Judaism in Feminist Religious Writings* (Atlanta: Scholars Press, 1994).

Keller, E.F., and H.E. Longino (eds.), *Feminism and Science* (Oxford: Oxford University Press, 1996).

Keller, E.F., *Reflections on Gender and Science* (New Haven: Yale University Press, 1985).

Keller, W., *Und die Bibel hat doch Recht in Bildern*; ET: *The Bible as History: Archaeology Confirms the Book of Books* (Hodder & Stoughton, 1980 [1956]).

Kelly-Gadol, J., 'Did Women Have a Renaissance?', in R. Bridenthal, C. Koonz and S. Stuard (eds.), *Becoming Visible: Women in European History* (Boston: Houghton Mifflin, 1987 [1976]).

Kempinski, A., 'Beth-Shean: Late Bronze and Iron Age Temples', in M. Avi-Yonah (ed.), *Encyclopedia of Archaeological Excavations in the Holy Land* (London and Jerusalem: Israel Exploration Society and Massada Press, 1975), I, pp. 213-15.

Kenyon, K., *Royal Cities of the Old Testament* (London: Barrie and Jenkins, 1971).

Kessler, M., *Someone to Pour the Wine* (Shippensburg, PA: Ragged Edge Press, 1996).

King, K.L. (ed.), *Women and Goddess Traditions: Studies from Asia, the Ancient Mediterranean, and Contemporary Goddess Thealogy* (intr. K.J. Torjesen; Studies in Antiquity and Christianity; Minneapolis, Fortress Press, 1997).

King, P.J., *American Archaeology in the Mideast: A History of the American Schools of Oriental Research* (Philadelphia: American Schools of Oriental Research, 1983).

Kinukawa, H., *Women and Jesus in Mark: A Japanese Feminist Interpretation* (Maryknoll, NY: Orbis Books, 1994).

Kloppenborg, S., 'Isis and Sophia in the Book of Wisdom', *HTR* 75 (1982), pp. 57-84.

Knapp, A.B., *Archaeology, Annales and Ethnohistory* (Cambridge: Cambridge University Press, 1992).

—'History of Mesopotamia: Mesopotamian Chronology', in Freedman (ed.), *Anchor Bible Dictionary*, IV, pp. 714-20.

—*Society and Polity at Bronze Age Pella: An Annales Perspective* (Sheffield: Sheffield Academic Press, 1993).

Koch, K., 'Aschera als Himmelskoenigin in Jerusalem', *UF* 20 (1988), pp. 97-120.

Kofsky, A.S., 'A Comparative Analysis of Women's Property Rights in Jewish Law and Anglo-American Law', *Journal of Law and Religion* 6 (1988), pp. 317-53.

Kohn-Ley C., and I. Korotin (eds.), *Der Feministische 'Sündenfall': Antisemitische Vorurteile in der Frauenbewegung* (Wien: Picus Verlag, 1994).

Korbin. J.E., 'Anthropological Contributions to the Study of Child Abuse', *Child Abuse and Neglect* 1 (1977), pp. 7-24.

—*Child Abuse and Neglect: Cross-cultural Perspectives* (Berkeley: University of California Press, 1981).

Korotin, I., 'Die mythische Wirklichkeit eines Volkes: J.J.Bachofen, das Mutterrecht und der Nationalsozialismus', in Kohn-Ley and Korotin (eds.), *Der feministische 'Sündenfall'*, pp. 84-131.

Korpel, M.C.A., 'The Female Servant of the Lord in Isaiah 54', in Becking and Dijkstra, *On Reading Prophetic Texts*, pp. 153-67.

Korsak, M.P., *At the Start: Genesis Made New* (Leuven: Poetry Centre; Garden City, NY: Doubleday, 1994).

—'Genesis: A New Look', in A. Brenner (ed.), *A Feminist Companion to Genesis* (The Feminist Companion to the Bible, 2; Sheffield: Sheffield Academic Press, 1993), pp. 39-52.

Kottsieper, I., 'Die alttestamentliche Weisheit im Licht aramäischer Weisheitstraditionen', in B. Janowski (ed.), *Weisheit außerhalb der kanonischen Weisheitsschriften* (Gütersloh: Kaiser, 1996), pp. 128-62.

Kraemer, R.S., *Her Share of the Blessings: Women's Religions Among Pagans, Jews, and Christians in the Greco-Roman World* (New York: Oxford University Press, 1992).

Kramer, S.N., *The Sumerians: Their History, Culture, and Character* (Chicago: University of Chicago Press, 1963).

Kristeva, J., *Desire in Language: A Semiotic Approach to Literature and Art* (ed. L.S. Roudiez; trans. T. Gora, A. Jardine and L.S. Roudiez; New York: Columbia University Press, 1980).

—*The Kristeva Reader* (ed. Toril Moi; Oxford: Basil Blackwell, 1986).

—*Revolution in Poetic Language* (trans. M. Waller; New York: Columbia University Press, 1984).

—*Semeiotikè: Recherches pour une semanalyse* (Paris: Seuil, 1969).

—'Women's Time', in "Women's Time", *Signs* 7 (1981) (trans. A. Jardine and H. Blake), pp. 13-35, reprinted in Belsey and Moore, *The Feminist Reader*, pp. 197-217, and notes, pp. 240-42.

Kuenen, A., *The Religion of Israel to the Fall of the Jewish State*, I (trans. A.H. May; London: Williams & Norgate, 1874).

Kuhrt, A., 'Non-Royal Women in the Late Babylonian Period: A Survey', in B.S. Lesco (ed.), *Women's Earliest Records: From Ancient Egypt and Western Asia* (Brown Judaic Studies, 166; Atlanta: Scholars Press, 1989), pp. 215-49.

Kuklick, B., *Puritans in Babylon: The Ancient Near East and American Intellectual Life, 1880–1930* (Princeton, NJ: Princeton University Press, 1996).

Kunin, S.D., *The Logic of Incest: A Structuralist Analysis of Hebrew Mythology* (JSOTSup, 185: Sheffield: Sheffield Academic Press, 1995).

Kwok, P.-l., 'Discovering the Bible in the Non-Biblical World', *Semeia* 47 (1989).

—*Discovering the Bible in the Non-Biblical World* (Maryknoll, NY: Orbis Books, 1995).

—'Racism and Ethnocentrism in Feminist Biblical Interpretation', in Schüssler Fiorenza (ed.), *Searching the Scriptures*. I, pp. 101-16.

Labovitz, G., 'Arguing for Women in Talmud', *Shofar* 14.1 (1995), pp. 72-79.

Lagrange, F.-M., 'Etudes sur les religions sémitiques: les déesses: Achéra et Astarté', *RB* 10 (1901), pp. 546-66.

Lambert, W.G., Review of *Studies in Third Millennium Sumerian and Akkadian Personal Names*, by R.A. De Vito, *Or* 64 (1995), pp. 131-36.

Lang, B., 'Ein babylonisches Motiv in Israels Schöpfungsmythologie (Jer 27.5-6)', *BZ* 27 (1983), pp. 236-37.

—*Die Bibel neu entdecken* (Munich: Kösel, 1995).

—*Drewermann, interprète de la Bible* (Paris: Cerf, 1994).

—'Figure ancienne, figure nouvelle de la Sagesse en Pr 1 à 9,' in J. Trublet (ed.), *La sagesse biblique de l'Ancien au Nouveau Testament* (Paris: Cerf, 1995), pp. 61-97.

—*Frau Weisheit* (Düsseldorf: Patmos, 1975).

—'Monotheismus', in M. Görg *et al.* (eds.), *Neues Bibel-Lexikon* (Düsseldorf: Patmos, 1995), II, cols. 834-44.

—'Schule und Unterricht im alten Israel', in Lang, *Wie wird man Prophet in Israel?* (Düsseldorf: Patmos, 1980), pp. 104-19; also in M. Gilbert (ed.), *La sagesse de l'Ancien Testament* (Leuven: Peeters, 2nd edn, 1990), pp. 186-201, 412-14.

—'Die sieben Säulen der Weisheit (Sprüche IX 1) im Licht israelitischer Architektur', *VT* 33 (1983), pp. 488-91.

—*Wisdom and the Book of Proverbs: A Hebrew Goddess Redefined* (New York: Pilgrim Press, 1986).

—'Wisdom', in K. van der Toorn *et al.* (eds.), *Dictionary of Deities and Demons in the Bible* (Leiden: Brill, 1995), cols. 1692-702.

Lapp, P.W., 'The 1963 Excavation at Ta'annek', *BASOR* 173 (1964), pp. 4-44.

—'The 1968 Excavations at Tell Ta'annek', *BASOR* 195 (1969), pp. 2-49.

—'A Ritual Incense Stand from Taanak', *Qadmoniot* 5 (1969), pp. 16-17 (Hebrew).

—'Taanach by the Waters of Megiddo', *BA* 30 (1967), pp. 2-27.

Laqueur, T., *Making Sex: Body and Gender from the Greeks to Freud* (Cambridge, MA: Harvard University Press, 1990).

Larsen, M.T., 'The "Babel/Bible" Controversy and Its Aftermath', in Sasson *Civilizations*, I, pp. 95-106.

Leach, E., *Genesis as Myth and Other Essays* (London: Jonathan Cape, 1969).

—'The Legitimacy of Solomon', in *Genesis as Myth and Other Essays* (London: Jonathan Cape, 1969), pp. 25-83.

Leach E. and D.A. Aycock, *Structuralist Interpretations of Biblical Myth* (Cambridge: Cambridge University Press, 1983).

Leavis, F.R., *The Great Tradition: George Eliot, Henry James, Joseph Conrad* (London: Chatto & Windus, 1948).

—*New Bearings in English Poetry* (London: Chatto & Windus, 1938).

—*Revaluation: Tradition and Development in English Poetry* (London: Chatto & Windus, 1936).

Lee, G.R., 'The Utility of Cross-Cultural Data', *Journal of Family Issues* 5 (1984), pp. 519-41.

LeGuin, U., *Buffalo Gals and Other Animal Presences* (Santa Barbara: Capra Press, 1987).

Leith, M.J.W., 'Verse and Reverse: The Transformation of the Woman, Israel, in Hosea 1–3', in Day (ed.), *Gender and Difference in Ancient Israel*, pp. 95-108.

Lemaire, A., 'Abécédaires et exercices d'écolier en épigraphie nord-ouest sémitique', *JA* 266 (1978), pp. 221-35.

—'Date et origine des inscriptions hébraïques et phéniciennes de Kuntillet 'Ajrud', *Studi epigrafici e linguistici* 1 (1984), pp. 131-43.

—*Les écoles et la formation de la Bible dans l'ancien Israël* (OBO, 39; Fribourg: Editions universitaires; Göttingen: Vandenhoeck & Ruprecht, 1981).

—'Les inscriptions de Khirbet el-Qôm et l'Ashérah de YHWH', *RB* 84 (1977), pp. 595-608.

—'Who or What Was Yahweh's Asherah?', *BARev* 10.6 (1984), pp. 42-51.

Lenski, G.E., *Power and Privilege: A Theory of Social Stratification* (New York: McGraw–Hill, 1966).

Lerner, G., *The Creation of Patriarchy* (Oxford: Oxford University Press, 1986).

Lerner, M., *The Socialism of Fools: Anti-Semitism on the Left* (Escondido, CA: Publisher's Group West, 1992).

Lesko, B.S. (ed.), *Women's Earliest Records: From Ancient Egypt and Western Asia* (BJS, 166; Atlanta: Scholars Press, 1989).

Levine, A.-J. (ed.), *'Women Like This': New Perspectives on Jewish Women in the Greco-Roman World* (Early Judaism and its Literature, 1; Atlanta: Scholars Press, 1991).

Levine, B., 'Mulugu/Melug: The Origins of a Talmudic Legal Institution', *JAOS* 88 (1968), pp. 271-84.

Levine, E., *The Aramaic Version of Lamentations* (New York: Hermon, 1976).

Levine, L., *The Rabbinic Class of Late Antiquity* (New York: Jewish Theological Seminary, 1989; Jerusalem: Yad Izhak ben-Zvi, 1985).

Levinson, D., *Family Violence in Cross-Cultural Perspective* (Frontiers of Anthropology, 1; Newbury Park, CA: London; New Delhi: Sage, 1989).

—'Family Violence in Cross-Cultural Perspective', in Hasselt *et al.* (eds.) *Handbook of Family Violence*, pp. 435-55.

Levitt, L.S., 'Reconfiguring Home: Jewish Feminist Identity/ies' (dissertation; Emory University, 1993).

Lichtheim, M., *Ancient Egyptian Literature: A Book of Readings*. I. *The Old and Middle Kingdoms* (Berkeley: University of California Press, 1973).

—*Ancient Egyptian Literature: A Book of Readings*. II. *The New Kingdom* (Berkeley: University of California Press, 1976).

Linafelt, T., 'Margins of Lamentation, or, The Unbearable Whiteness of Reading', in T.K. Beal and D.M. Gunn (eds.), *Reading Bibles, Writing Bodies: Identity and the Book* (London: Routledge, 1996).

—'Reading the Hebrew Bible after the Holocaust: Toward an Ethics of Interpretation', in *The Holocaust: Progress and Prognosis, 1934–1994* (Lawrenceville, NJ: The Holocaust Resource Center of Rider College, 1994), pp. 627-41.

Lipiński, E., 'The Goddess Aṯirat in Ancient Arabia, in Babylon, and in Ugarit', *OLP* 3 (1972), pp. 101-19.

—'The Syro-Palestinian Iconography of Woman and Goddess' (Review of *Frau und Göttin* by U. Winter), *IEJ* 36 (1986), pp. 87-96.

Lipstadt, D., *Denying the Holocaust: The Growing Assault on Truth and Memory* (New York: Free Press, 1993).

Lohfink, N., 'The Cult Reform of Josiah of Judah: 2 Kings 22–23 as a Source for the History of Israelite Religion', in Miller, Jr, Hanson and McBride (eds.), *Ancient Israelite Religion*, pp. 459-75.

Lohr, M., 'Der Sprachgebrauch des Buches der Klagelieder', *ZAW* 14 (1894), pp. 31-50.

Longino, H., 'Science, Objectivity, and Feminist Values (A Review Essay)', in *Feminist Studies* 14 (1988), pp. 561-74.

Lorber, J., *Paradoxes of Gender* (New Haven: Yale University Press, 1994).

Loretz, O., *Ugarit und die Bibel: Kanaanäische Götter und Religion im Alten Testament* (Darmstadt: Wissenschaftliche Buchgesellschaft, 1990).

Lozios, P.,'Violence and the Family: Some Mediterranean Examples', in J.P. Martin (ed.), *Violence and the Family* (Chichester: Wiley, 1978), pp. 183-96.

Lundquist, J.M., 'Babylon in European Thought', in Sasson (ed.), *Civilizations*, I, pp. 67-80.

Luther, B., 'Die Nouvelle von Juda und Tamar und andere israelitische Novellen', in E. Meyer (ed.), *Die Israeliten und ihre Nachbarstämme* (Halle: Max Niemeyer, 1906), pp. 175-206.

Luther, M., *Luther's Works* (gen ed. Jaroslav Pelican; 30 vols.; St Louis: Concordia, 1955–).

Luz, U., *Matthew 1–7: A Commentary* (trans. W.C. Linss; Minneapolis: Augsburg, 1989).

Macintosh, A.A., *Hosea* (ICC; Edinburgh: T. & T. Clark, 1997).

Maertens, T., *The Advancing Dignity of Woman in the Bible* (trans. S. Dibbs; De Père, WN: St Norbert Abbey Press, 1969).

Maier, J., 'The Ancient Near East in Modern Thought', in Sasson (ed.), *Civilizations*, I, pp. 107-20.

Maier, W.A., III, *'Ašerah: Extrabiblical Evidence* (HSM 37; Atlanta: Scholars Press, 1986).

Maisels, C.K., *The Emergence of Civilization* (London: Routledge, 1990).

Malina, B.J., and J.H. Neyrey, 'First-Century Personality: Dyadic, Not Individualistic', in J.H. Neyrey (ed.), *The Social World of Luke–Acts: Models for Interpretation* (Peabody, MA: Hendrickson, 1991), pp. 67-96.

Malina, B.J., 'A Conflict Approach to Mark 7', *Forum* 4.3 (1988), pp. 3-30.

—'The Bible: Witness or Warrant? Reflections on Daniel Patte's *Ethics of Biblical Interpretation*', *BTB* 26 (1996), pp. 82-87.

—'Dealing with Biblical (Mediterranean) Characters: A Guide for U.S. Consumers', *BTB* 19 (1989), pp. 127-41.

—'Establishment Violence in the New Testament World', *Scriptura* 5 (1994), pp. 51-78.

—*The New Testament World: Insights from Cultural Anthropology* (Louisville: Westminster/ John Knox, rev. edn, 1993).

—'Religion in the Imagined New Testament World: More Social Science Lenses', *Scriptura* 5 (1994), pp. 1-26

Malina, B., and R. Rohrbaugh, *Social Science Commentary on the Synoptic Gospels* (Minneapolis: Fortress Press, 1992).

Mann, M., *The Sources of Social Power. I. A History of Power From the Beginning to A.D. 1760* (Cambridge: Cambridge University Press, 1986).

Marcus, I., 'Mothers, Martyrs, and Moneymakers: Some Jewish Women in Medieval Europe', *Conservative Judaism* 10 (1986), pp. 31-45.

Marcus, M.I., 'Dressed to Kill: Women and Pins in Early Iran', *The Oxford Art Journal* 17 (1994), pp. 3-15.

—'Geography and Visual Ideology: Landscape, Knowledge and Power in Neo-Assyrian Art', in M. Liverani (ed.), *Neo-Assyrian Geography* (Roma: Università di Roma 'La Sapienza', 1995), pp. 193-202.

—'Incorporating the Body: Adornment, Gender and Social Identity in Ancient Iran', *Cambridge Archaeological Journal* 3 (1993), pp. 157-78.

—'Sex and the Politics of Female Adornment in Pre-Achaemenid Iran (1000–800 B.C.E.)', in N.B. Kampen (ed.), *Sexuality in Ancient Art: Near East, Egypt, Greece and Italy* (Cambridge: Cambridge University Press, 1996), pp. 41-54.

Marcus, R., 'On Biblical Hypostases of Wisdom', *HUCA* 23 (1950–51), pp. 57-171.

Margalit, B., 'Some Observations on the Inscription and Drawing from Khirbet el-Qôm', *VT* 39 (1989), pp. 371-78.

—'The Meaning and Significance of Asherah', *VT* 40 (1990), pp. 264-97.

Marks, E., and I. de Courtivron, *New French Feminisms: An Anthology* (New York: Shocken Books, 1981).

Martin, C.J., 'The Haustafeln (Household Code) in African American Biblical Interpretations: "Free Slaves" and "Subordinate Women"', in C.H. Felder (ed.), *Stony the Road We Trod: African American Biblical Interpretation* (Minneapolis: Fortress Press, 1991), pp. 206-31.

Martinelli, T., 'Geb et Nout dans les Textes des Pyramides: Essai de compréhension du caractère masculine de Geb et de la Terre ainsi que du caractère féminin de Nout et du Ciel', *Bulletin de Société d'Egyptologie, Genève* 18 (1994), pp. 61-77.

Maslow, A.H., *Toward a Psychology of Being* (New York: Van Nostrand, 2nd edn, 1968).

Matthews, V.H., and D.C. Benjamin, 'Social Sciences and Biblical Studies', in V.H. Matthews, D.C. Benjamin and C. Camp (eds.), *Honor and Shame in the World of the Bible* (Semeia 68; Atlanta: Scholars Press, 1994), pp. 7-21.

Mayes, A.D.H., *The Story of Israel between Settlement and Exile* (London: SCM Press, 1983).

Mazar, A., 'Beth-Shean', in Stern (ed.), *The New Encyclopedia of Archaeological Excavations in the Holy Land*, I, pp. 214-23.

Mazar, B. (ed.), *Views of the Biblical World* (Ramat Gan, Israel: International Publishing, 1958–1961).

McCarter, P.K., Jr, 'Aspects of the Religion of the Israelite Monarchy: Biblical and Epigraphic Data', in Miller, Jr, Hanson and McBride (eds.), *Ancient Israelite Religion*, pp. 137-55.

McComiskey, T.E., 'The Status of the Secondary Wife: Its Development in Ancient Near Eastern Law. A Study and Comprehensive Index' (PhD thesis, Brandeis University, 1965).

McGaw, A., 'Recovering Technology: Why Female Technologies Matter', in R. Wright (ed.), *Gender and Archaeology* (Philadelphia: University of Pennsylvania Press, 1996), pp. 52-57.

McIntyre, S., 'Backlash Against Equality: The "Tyranny" of the "Politically Correct"', *McGill Law Journal* 38.1 (1993), pp. 1-63.

McKay, H.A., ' "Only a Remnant of Them Shall Be Saved": Women from the Hebrew Bible in New Testament Narratives', in Brenner (ed.), *A Feminist Companion to the Hebrew Bible in the New Testament*, pp. 33-61.

McKay, J.W., *Religion in Judah Under the Assyrians: 732–609 B.C.* (London: SCM Press, 1973).

McKinlay, J.E., *Gendering Wisdom the Host: Biblical Invitations to Eat and Drink* (JSOTSup, 216; GCT, 4; Sheffield: Sheffield Academic Press, 1996).

Meek, T., *The Book of Lamentations* (Nashville: Abingdon Press, 1956).

Mehlinger, O., and C. Mehlinger, *Göttingen, Götte und Gottessymbole: Neue Erkenntnisse zur Religionsgeschichte Kanaans und Israels aufgrund bislang unerschlossener iconographischer Quellen* (Freiburg; Herder, 1995).

Meissner, B., *Babylonien und Assyrien* (Heidelberg: Carl Winter, 1925).

Melko, M., and L.R. Scott (eds.), *The Boundaries of Civilizations in Space and Time* (Lanham, MD: University Press of America, 1987).

Meshel, Z., 'Did Yahweh Have a Consort?', *BARev* 5.2 (1979), pp. 24-35.

—'The Inscriptions of Kuntillet 'Ajrud', communication given at the 12th Congress of the International Organization for the Study of the Old Testament in Jerusalem, 1986.

—'The Israelite Religious Centre of 'Ajrud, Sinai', in A. Bonanno (ed.), *Archaeology and Fertility Cult in the Ancient Mediterranean* (Amsterdam: Grüner, 1986), pp. 237-40.

—'The Israelite Religious Centre of Kuntillet 'Ajrud', *Bulletin of the Anglo-Israel Archaeological Society* (1982–83), pp. 52-55.

—'Kuntilat 'Ajrud, 1975–1976', *IEJ* 27 (1977), pp. 52-53.

—'Kuntillat 'Ajrud: An Israelite Site on the Sinai Border', *Qadmoniot* 9 (1976), pp. 119-24 (Hebrew).

—'Kuntilet-'Ajrud', *RB* 84 (1977), pp. 270-73.

—*Kuntillet 'Ajrud: A Religious Centre from the Time of the Judaean Monarchy on the Border of Sinai* (Israel Museum Catalogue, 175; Jerusalem: The Israel Museum, 1978).

—'Kuntillet 'Ajrud: An Israelite Religious Center in Northern Sinai', *Expedition* 20 (1978), pp. 50-54.

—'Kuntillat-'Ajrud', *Le Monde de la Bible* 10 (1979), pp. 32-36.

—'A Lyre Player Drawing from 'Ajrud in Sinai', *Tatzlil* 17 (1977), pp. 109-10 (Hebrew).

—'A Religious Center at Kuntillet 'Ajrud, Sinai', in A. Biran (ed.), *Temples and High Places in Biblical Times* (Jerusalem: Nelson Glueck School of Biblical Archaeology of Hebrew Union College, 1981), p. 161.

—'Teman, Horvat', in Stern (ed.), *The New Encyclopedia of Archaeological Excavations in the Holy Land*, IV, pp. 1458-64.

Meshel, Z., and C. Meyers, 'The Name of God in the Wilderness of Zin', *BA* 39 (1976), pp. 6-10.

Mettinger, T.N.D., 'The Veto on Images and the Aniconic God in Ancient Israel', in H. Biezais (ed.), *Religious Symbols and their Functions* (Scripta Instituti Donneriani Aboensis, 10; Stockholm: Almqvist & Wiksell, 1979), pp. 15-29.

—'YHWH SABAOTH: The Heavenly King on the Cherubim Throne', in T. Ishida (ed.), *Studies in the Period of David and Solomon and Other Essays* (Winona Lake, IN: Eisenbrauns; Tokyo: Yamakawa-Shuppansha, 1982), pp. 109-38.

Meyer, G., *Die Jüdische Frau in der Hellenistisch-Romischen Antike* (Stuttgart: Kohlhammer, 1987).

Meyers, C., *Discovering Eve: Ancient Israelite Women in Context* (Oxford: Oxford University Press, 1988).

—'Procreation, Production, and Protection: Male–Female Balance in Early Israel', *JAAR* 51 (1983), pp. 569-93.

Meyers, E.B., *et al.* (eds.), *The Oxford Encyclopedia of Archaeology in the Near East* (5 vols.; New York: Oxford University Press, 1997).

Michalowski, P., 'Third Millennium Contacts: Observations on the Relationship Between Mari and Ebla', *JAOS* 105 (1985), pp. 293-302.

Millar, F., *The Roman Near East, 31 BC–AD 337* (Cambridge, MA: Harvard University Press, 1993).

Miller, P.D., Jr, 'Psalms and Inscriptions', in Emerton (ed.), *Congress Volume*, pp. 311-32.

—'The Absence of the Goddess in Israelite Religion', *HAR* 10 (1986), pp. 239-48.

—*They Cried to the Lord: The Form and Theology of Biblical Prayer* (Minneapolis: Fortress Press, 1994).

Miller, P.D., P.D. Hanson, and S.O. McBride (eds.), *Ancient Israelite Religion* (Philadelphia: Fortress Press, 1987).

Milne, P.J., 'Eve and Adam: A Feminist Reading', in H. Minkoff (ed.), *Approaches to the Bible: The Best of Bible Review* (Washington: Biblical Archaeological Society, 1995), II, pp. 259-69.

—'No Promised Land: Rejecting the Authority of the Bible', in Shanks (ed.), *Feminist Approaches* , pp. 47-73.

Minogue, S. (ed.), *Problems for Feminist Criticism* (London: Routledge, 1990).

Mintz, A., *Hurban: Responses to Catastrophe in Hebrew Literature* (New York: Columbia University Press, 1984).

Miscall, Peter, 'Isaiah: New Heavens, New Earth, New Book', in Fewell (ed.), *Reading Between Texts: Intertextuality and the Hebrew Bible*, pp. 41-56.

Mitchell, W.J.T., *Iconology: Image, Text, Ideology* (Chicago: University of Chicago Press, 1986).

Mittmann, S., 'Die Grabinschrift des Sängers Uriahu', *ZDPV* 97 (1981), pp. 139-52.

Moberly, R.W.L., 'To Hear the Master's Voice: Revelation and Spiritual Discernment in the Call of Samuel', *SJT* 48 (1995), pp. 443-68.

Moghaizel, L., 'The Arab and Mediterranean World: Legislation Towards Crimes of Honor', in Schuler (ed.), *Empowerment and the Law*, pp. 174-80.

Mollenkott, V., *The Divine Feminine* (New York: Crossroad, 1983).

Moltmann-Wendel, E., *Land, wo Milch und Honig fließt* (Gütersloh: Gütersloher Verlagshaus, 1985); ET: *A Land Flowing with Milk and Honey* (trans. J. Bowden; New York: Crossroad, 1986).

Monteiro, R., J. Sequeira and F. Yasas, 'Living Bread from Crumbs', in *In God's Image* (September 1988), pp. 50-51.

Morgan, R., *Lady of the Beasts* (New York: Random House, 1976).

Mosala, I.J., *Biblical Hermeneutics and Black Theology in South Africa* (Grand Rapids: Eerdmans, 1989).

—'The Use of the Bible in Black Theology', in I.J. Mosala and B. Tlhagale (eds.), *The Unquestionable Right to be Free: Black Theology from South Africa* (Maryknoll, NY: Orbis, 1986), pp. 175-99.

Mulack, C., *Die Weiblichkeit Gottes* (Stuttgart: Kreuz Verlag, 1983).

Müller, D., 'Die Zeugung durch das Herz', *Or* NS 35 (1966), pp. 247-74.

Müller, H.P., 'עשתרת, 'štrt ('aštoret)', in G.J. Botterweck and H. Ringgren (eds.), *Theologisches Wörterbuch zum Alten Testament* (Stuttgart: Kohlhammer, 1989), VI, pp. 453-63.

—'Kolloquialsprache und Volksreligion in den Inschriften von *Kuntillet 'Aǧrūd* und *Ḥirbet el-Qōm*', *ZAH* 5 (1992), pp. 15-51.

Murdock, G.P., *Social Structure* (New York: Macmillan, 1949).

Murphy, R.E., 'Hebrew Wisdom', *JAOS* 101 (1981), pp. 21-34.

—'Proverbs and Theological Exegesis', in D.G. Miller (ed.), *The Hermeneutical Quest* (Allison Park, PA: Pickwick Publications, 1986), pp. 87-95.

—*The Tree of Life: An Exploration of Biblical Wisdom Literature* (Garden City, NY: Doubleday, 1990).

—'Wisdom: Theses and Hypotheses', in Gammie, *et al.* (eds.), *Israelite Wisdom*, pp. 35-42.

Naguib, S.-A., *Le clergé féminin d'Amon thébain à la 21e dynastie* (Orientalia Lovaniensia Analecta, 38; Leuven: Peeters and Departement Oriëntalistiek, 1990).

Nathanson, B.G., 'Toward a Multicultural Ecumenical History of Women in the First Century/ies C.E.', in Schüssler Fiorenza (ed.), *Searching the Scriptures*, I, pp. 272-89.

Natmessnig, A., 'Antisemitismus und feministische Theologie', in Kohn-Ley and Korotin (eds.), *Der feministische 'Sündenfall'*, pp. 185-209.

Naveh, J., 'Graffiti and Dedications', *BASOR* 235 (1979), pp. 27-30.

Nelson, H.L., 'Resistance and Insubordination', *Hypatia* 10.2 (1995), pp. 23-40.

Nelson, R.D., *The Double Redaction of the Deuteronomistic History* (JSOTSup, 18; Sheffield: JSOT Press, 1981).

Neufeld, E., *Ancient Hebrew Marriage Laws* (London: Longmans, Green, 1944).

Newsom, C., and S. Ringe (eds.), *The Women's Bible Commentary* (Louisville, KY: Westminster/John Knox Press, 1992).

Newsom, C., 'Response to Norman K. Gottwald, "Social Class and Ideology in Isaiah 40–55"', *Semeia* 58 (1993), pp. 73-78.

Newsom, C.A., and S.H. Ringe (eds.), *The Women's Bible Commentary* (Louisville: Westminster/John Knox, 1992).

Nicholson, L.J. (ed.), *Feminism/Postmodernism* (London: Routledge, 1990).

Nicholson, L.J., *Gender and History: The Limits of Social Theory in the Age of the Family* (New York: Columbia University Press, 1986).

Nicolas, A.T. de, *Powers of Imagining: Ignatius de Loyola* (Albany: State University of New York Press, 1986).

Nielsen, J. McC. (ed.), *Feminist Research Methods: Exemplary Readings in the Social Sciences* (Boulder: Westview Press, 1990).

Nielsen, K., 'Le choix contre le droit dans le livre de Ruth: De l'aire de battage au tribunal', *VT* 35 (1985), pp. 201-12.

Nissen, H.J., *The Early History of the Ancient Near East: 9000–2000 B.C.* (Chicago: University of Chicago Press, 1988).

Norris, K., 'A Prayer to Eve', *Paris Review* 115 (Summer 1990).

North, R., 'Yahweh's Asherah', in M.P. Horgan and P.J. Kobelski (eds.), *To Touch the Text: Biblical and Related Studies in Honor of Joseph A. Fitzmyer* (New York: Crossroad, 1989), pp. 118-37.

Noth, M., *A History of Pentateuchal Traditions* (trans. Bernhard W. Anderson; Chico, CA: Scholars Press, 1981), p. 60.

—*Überlieferungsgeschichtliche Studien* (Halle: M. Niemeyer, 1943; ET: *The Deuteronomistic History*; JSOTSup, 15; Sheffield: JSOT Press, 1981; and *The Chronicler's History* (JSOTSup, 50; Sheffield: JSOT Press, 1987).

Nougayrol, T., E. Laroche, C. Virolleaud, and C.F.A. Schaeffer, *Ugaritica V* (Mission de Ras Shamra, 16; Paris: Geuthner, 1968).

O'Brien, J., 'Nammu, Mami, Eve and Pandora: What's in a Name?', *The Classical Journal* 79 (1983), pp. 35-45.

—'On Saying No to a Prophet', delivered, in the Israelite Prophetic Literature section, at the AAR/SBL Annual Meeting in Philadelphia, November 1995; forthcoming in *JBL*.

O'Connor, M., 'The Poetic Inscription from Khirbet el-Qôm', *VT* 37 (1987), pp. 224-30.

O'Day, G.R., 'Jeremiah 9:22-23 and 1 Corinthians 1:26-31: A Study in Intertextuality', *JBL* 109.2 (1990), pp. 259-67.

Oates, J., and D. Oates, *The Rise of Civilization* (Oxford: Phaidon, 1976).

Oates, J., *Babylon* (London: Thames & Hudson, 1979).

Obermann, J.J., *The Archaic Inscriptions from Lachish* (JOASSup, 2; Baltimore: The American Oriental Society, 1938).

Ochs, C., *Behind the Sex of God* (Boston: Beacon Press, 1977).

Ochshorn, J., 'Ishtar and Her Cult', in Olson (ed.), *The Book of the Goddess*, pp. 16-29.

Oduyoye, M.A., *Daughters of Anowa: African Women and Patriarchy* (Maryknoll, NY: Orbis Books, 1995).

Olson, C. (ed.), *The Book of the Goddess* (New York: Crossroad, 1985).

Olyan, S.M., *Asherah and the Cult of Yahweh in Israel* (SBLMS, 34; Atlanta: Scholars Press, 1988).

—'Some Observations Concerning the Identity of the Queen of Heaven', *UF* 19 (1987), pp. 161-74.

Ophir, A., 'From Pharaoh to Saddam Hussein: The Reproduction of the Other in the Passover Haggadah', in L. Silberstein and R. Cohn (eds.), *The Other in Jewish History and Thought* (New York: New York University Press, 1994), pp. 205-35.

Oppenheim, A.L., *Ancient Mesopotamia: Portrait of a Dead Civilization* (Chicago: University of Chicago Press, 2nd rev. edn, 1977).

—'Assyriology: Why and How?', *Current Anthropology* 1 (1960), pp. 409-23.

Osiek, C., 'The Feminist and the Bible: Hermenuetical Alternatives', in A. Yarbro Collins (ed.), *Feminist Perspectives*, pp. 93-105.

Osing, J., 'Isis und Osiris', *Mitteilungen des Deutschen Instituts für ägyptische Altertumskunde in Kairo* 30 (1974), pp. 91-113.

Ostriker, A., *Feminist Revision and the Bible* (Oxford: Basil Blackwell, 1993).

—*Stealing the Language* (Boston: Beacon Press, 1986).

Otzen, B., '*hatam, hotam*', in *TDOT*, IV, pp. 263-69.

—'Indskrifterne fra Kuntillet 'Ajrud: Tekst—Form—Funktion', *SEÅ* 54 (1989), pp. 151-64.

Overholt, T.W., *Cultural Anthropology and the Old Testament* (Guides to Biblical Scholarship; Minneapolis: Fortress Press, 1996).

Overman, A., *Matthew's Gospel and Formative Judaism: The Social World of the Matthean Community* (Minneapolis: Fortress Press, 1990).

Pagels, E., *Adam, Eve and the Serpent* (New York: Random House, 1988).

Pantel, P. Schmitt (ed.), *A History of Women*. I. *From Ancient Goddesses to Christian Saints* (gen. eds. G. Duby and M. Perrot; Cambridge, MA and London: Belknap and Harvard University Press, 1992).

— 'Women and Ancient History Today', in Pantel (ed.), *A History of Women*, I, pp. 464-69.

Pappenheim, B., 'The Jewish Woman', in D. Edinger (ed.), *Bertha Pappenheim: Leben und Schriften* (Frankfurt am Main: Ner-Tamid Publishers, 1963).

—*Sisyphus-Arbeit: Reisebriefe aus den Jahren 1911 und 1912* (Leipzig: Verlag Paul E. Linder, 1924).

Parker, R., and L. Lesko, 'The Khonsu Cosmology', in *Pyramid Studies and Other Essays Presented to I.E.S Edwards* (Occasional Papers, 7; London: Egyptian Exploration Society, 1988), pp. 168-75.

Parrot, A. (ed.), *Studia Mariana* (Leiden: Brill, 1950).

—*The Arts of Assyria* (trans. S. Gilbert and J. Emmons; New York: Golden Press, 1961).

Passman, T., 'Out of the Closet and into the Field: Matriculture, the Lesbian Perspective and Feminist Classics', in Rabinowitz and Richlin , *Feminist Theory*, pp. 181-208.

Pastan, L., *Aspects of Eve* (New York: Norton, 1975).

Patai, R., 'The Goddess Asherah', *JNES* 24 (1965), pp. 37-52.

—'The Goddess Cult in the Hebrew–Jewish Religion', in A. Bharati (ed.), *Realm of the Extra-Human: Agents and Audiences* (The Hague: Mouton, 1976), pp. 197-210.

—*The Hebrew Goddess* (New York: Ktav, 1967).

—*The Hebrew Goddess* (New York: Avon Books, 2nd edn, 1978 [1967]).

Pateman, C., *The Disorder of Women: Democracy, Feminism and Political Theory* (Stanford: Stanford University Press, 1989).

—*The Sexual Contract* (Stanford: Stanford University Press, 1988).

Perlman, A.L., 'Asherah and Astarte in the Old Testament and Ugaritic Literatures' (PhD dissertation, Graduate Theological Union and University of California, Berkeley, 1978).

Peskowitz, M., 'Engendering Jewish Religious History', *Shofar* 14.1 (1995), pp. 8-34

—*Spinning Fantasies: Gendering the Ordinary in Roman-Period Judaism* (Berkeley: University of California Press, 1997).

Pettey, R.J., *Asherah: Goddess of Israel* (American University Studies, Series VII [Theology and Religion], 74; New York: Peter Lang, 1990).

Phillips, G.A., '"What is Written?" How Are You Reading? Gospel Intertextuality and Doing Lukewise: A Writerly Reading of Lk 10:25-37 (and 38-42)', in Eugene H. Lovering (ed.), *SBL 1992 Seminar Papers* (Atlanta: Scholars Press, 1992), pp. 266-301.

Phillips, J.A., *Eve: The History of an Idea* (San Francisco: Harper & Row, 1984).

Piercy, M., *Circles on the Water: Selected Poems* (New York: Knopf, 1982).

—*Mars and Her Children* (New York: Knopf, 1992).

Pilch, J.J., 'Beat His Ribs While He is Young (Sirach 30.12): A Window on the Mediterranean World', *BTB* 23 (1993), pp. 101-13.

—'Death with Honor: The Mediterranean Style Death of Jesus in Mark', *BTB* 25 (1995), pp. 65-70.

—*Introducing the Cultural Context of the Old Testament* (New York: Paulist Press, 1991).

—'People (ethnos)', and 'Citizen', in S.M. Tomasi (ed.), *The Pastoral Dictionary on Migration and Human Mobility* (New York: Center for Migration Studies of New York and the G.B. Scalabrini Federation of Centers for Migration Studies, forthcoming).

—'The Transfiguration of Jesus: An experience of Alternate Reality', in P.F. Esler (ed.), *Modeling Early Christianity: Social Scientific Studies of the New Testament in its Context* (London: Routledge, 1995), pp. 47-64.

Pinsky, V., and A. Wylie (eds.), *Critical Traditions in Contemporary Archaeology: Essays in the Philosophy, History and Socio-Politics of Archaeology* (Cambridge: Cambridge University Press, 1990).

Plaskow, J., 'Anti-Judaism in Feminist Christian Interpretation', in Schüssler Fiorenza (ed.), *Searching the Scriptures*, I, pp. 117-29.

—'Anti-Semitism: The Unacknowledged Racism', in J. Kalven and M. Buckley (eds.), *Womanspirit Bonding* (New York: Pilgrim Press, 1984), pp. 89-95.

—'Blaming Jews for Inventing Patriarchy', *Lilith* 7 (1979); reprinted in E. Torton Beck (ed.), *Nice Jewish Girls* (Trumansburg: Crossing Press, 1982), pp. 250-55.

—'Feminist Anti-Judaism and the Christian God', *Journal of Feminist Studies* 7.2 (1991), pp. 99-109.

Plath, S., *Selected Poems* (ed. Ted Hughes; New York: Harper & Row, 1981).

Pobee, J.S., and B. von Wartenberg-Potter (eds.), *New Eyes for Reading: Biblical and Theological Reflections by Women from the Third World* (Bloomington: Meyer-Stone, 1986).

Polanyi, M., *The Tacit Dimension* (London: Routledge & Kegan Paul, 1967).

Pollock, S., 'Women in a Men's World: Images of Sumerian Women', in Gero and Conkey (eds.), *Engendering Archaeology*, pp. 366-87.

Polzin, R., *David and the Deuteronomist: A Literary Study of the Deuteronomistic History*. III. *2 Samuel* (Indiana Studies in Biblical Literature; Bloomington: Indiana University Press, 1993).

—*Samuel and the Deuteronomist: A Literary Study of the Deuteronomistic History*. II. *1 Samuel* (Indiana Studies in Biblical Literature; Bloomington: Indiana University Press, 1989).

Pomeroy, S.B., 'A Classical Scholar's Perspective on Matriarchy', in B.A. Carroll (ed.), *Liberating Women's History: Theoretical and Critical Essays* (Chicago: University of Illinois Press, 1976), pp. 217-23.

—*Women's History and Ancient History* (Chapel Hill: University of North Carolina Press, 1991).

Pope, M.H., ''Aṭtart, 'Aštart, Astarte', in H.W. Haussig (ed.), *Wörterbuch der Mythologie* (Stuttgart: Ernst Klett, 1965), pp. 250-52.

—*El in the Ugaritic Texts* (VTSup, 2; Leiden: Brill, 1955).

—*Job* (AB; Garden City, NY: Doubleday, 1965).

Porter, B.N., *Images, Power, Politics: Figurative Aspects of Esarhaddon's Babylonian Policy* (Philadelphia: American Philosophical Society, 1993).

Porter, J.R., 'The Daughters of Lot', *Folklore* 89 (1978), pp. 127-41.

—'Genesis XIX:30-38 and the Ugaritic Text of SHR and SLM', in *Proceedings of the Seventh World Congress of Jewish Studies: Studies in the Bible and the Ancient Near East* (Jerusalem: Perry Foundation, 1981).

Postgate, N.J., *Early Mesopotamia: Society and Economy at the Dawn of History* (London Routledge, 1992).

Pressler, C., *The View of Women Found in the Deuteronomic Family Laws* (BZAW, 216; Berlin: de Gruyter, 1993).

Pritchard, J.B., *Palestinian Figurines in Relation to Certain Goddesses Known through Literature* (American Oriental Series, 24; New York: Kraus, 1943).

Provan, I., *Lamentations* (NCBC; Grand Rapids: Eerdmans, 1991).

Provan, I.W., *Hezekiah and the Books of Kings* (BZAW, 172; Berlin: de Gruyter, 1988).

Prusak, B.P., 'Woman: Seductive Siren and Source of Sin?', in R. Ruether (ed.), *Religion and Sexism: Images of Women in Jewish and Christian Traditions* (New York: Simon & Schuster, 1974), pp. 89-116.

Puech, E., 'The Canaanite Inscriptions of Lachish and Their Religious Background', *Tel Aviv* 13 (1986), pp. 13-25.

Rabinowitz, N.S., and A. Richlin (eds.), *Feminist Theory and the Classics* (London: Routledge, 1993).

Rad, G. von, *Genesis: A Commentary* (OTL; trans. J.H. Marks; London: SCM Press, revd edn, 1972).

—*Theologies des Alten Testaments*, I (Munich: Chr. Kaiser Verlag, 1957).

—*Wisdom in Israel* (trans. J.D. Martin; London: SCM Press, 1972).

Ramazanoğlu, C., *Up against Foucault: Explorations of Some Tensions Between Foucault and Feminism* (London: Routledge, 1993).

Rankin, O.S., *Israel's Wisdom Literature* (Edinburgh: T. & T. Clark, 1936).

Rashkow, I., 'Daughters and Fathers in Genesis... Or, What is Wrong with This Picture?', in Brenner (ed.), *A Feminist Companion to Exodus to Deuteronomy*, pp. 22-36.

Rast, W.E., 'Cakes for the Queen of Heaven', in A.L. Merrill and T.W. Overholt (eds.), *Scripture in History and Theology: Essays in Honor of J. Coert Rylaarsdam* (Pittsburgh: Pickwick Press, 1977), pp. 167-80.

Reed, W.L., *The Asherah in the Old Testament* (Fort Worth, TX: Texas Christian University Press, 1949).

Reiner, E., *Surpu: A Collection of Sumeran and Akkadian Incantations* (Graz: E. Weidner, 1958).

Renger, J., 'Who Are All Those People?', in *Or* NS 42 (1973), pp. 259-73.

Rexroth, K., and L. Chung (trans. and eds.), *The Orchid Boat: Women Poets of China* (New York: Seabury, 1972).

Richlin, A., 'The Ethnographer's Dilemma and the Dream of a Lost Golden Age', in Rabinowitz and Richlin (eds.), *Feminist Theory*.

—'Hijacking the Palladium: Feminists in Classics', pp. 272-303.

—'Zeus and Metis: Foucault, Feminism, Classics', *Helios* 18 (1991), pp. 160-80.

Riffaterre, M., *A Semiotics of Poetry* (Bloomington: Indiana University Press, 1978).

Rilke, R.M., *Gedichten uit de jaren 1913–1926* (trans., ed. and annotated W. Blok and C.O. Jellema; Baarn: Ambo, 1993).

Ringe, S.H., 'A Gentile Woman's Story', in Russell (ed.), *Feminist Interpretation of the Bible*, pp. 65-72

Ringgren, H., *Word and Wisdom: Studies in the Hypostatization of Divine Qualities and Functions in the Ancient Near East* (Lund: Hakan Ohlssons Boktryckeri, 1947).

Robins, G., *Women of Ancient Egypt* (London: British Museum Press, 1993).

Robinson, E., *Biblical Research in Palestine, Mount Sinai and Arabia Petraea* (3 vols.; New York: Ayer, 1977 [1841]).

—*Later Biblical Researches in Palestine and in Adjacent Regions* (New York: Ayer, 1977 [1856]).

Röder, B., J. Hummel, and B. Kunz, *Göttinnen Dämmerung: Das Matriarchat aus archäologischer Sicht* (Munich: Droemer Knaur, 1996).

Rohrlich, R., 'State Formation and the Subjugation of Women', *Feminist Studies* 6 (1980), pp. 76-102.

Rohrlich-Leavitt, R., 'Women in Transition: Crete and Sumer', in Bridenthal and Koonz (eds.), *Becoming Visible: Women in European History*, pp. 16-59.

Römer, W.H.P., *Einführung in die Sumeriologie* (Nijmegen: Katholike Universiteit, 9th rev. edn, 1986).

Rösel, M., 'Die Jungfraugeburt des endzeitlichen Immanuel: Jesaja 7 in der übersetzung der Septuaginta', *JBTh* 6 (1991), pp. 135-51.

Rosenberg, D., and H. Bloom,. *The Book of J* (New York: Grove Weidenfeld, 1990).

Rosenberg, R., 'The God Sedeq', *HUCA* 36 (1965), pp. 61-177.

Roskies, D.G., *A Bridge of Longing: The Lost Art of Yiddish Storytelling* (Cambridge, MA: Harvard University Press, 1995).

Rossetti, C., *The Poetical Works of Christina Rossetti* (ed. W.M. Rossetti; London: Macmillan, 1911 [1904]).

Rossi, A. (ed.), *The Feminist Papers: From Adams to de Beauvoir* (New York: Columbia University Press, 1973).

Rost, L., *The Succession to the Throne of David* (trans. M.D. Rutter and D.M. Gunn; Historic Texts and Interpreters in Biblical Scholarship, 1; Sheffield: Almond Press, 1982 [1926]).

Rowe, A., *The Four Canaanite Temples of Beth-Shan*. I. *The Temples and Cult Objects* (Publications of the Palestine Section of the University Museum, University of Pennsylvania, 2; Philadelphia: University of Pennsylvania Press, 1940).

—*The Topography and History of Beth-Shan* (Publications of the Palestine Section of the Museum of the University of Pennsylvania, 1; Philadelphia: University Press, 1930).

Rowley, H.H., *From Moses to Qumran* (London: Lutterworth, 1963).

Ruether, R.R., *Faith and Fratricide* (New York: Seabury Press, 1974).

—'Feminist Interpretation: A Method of Correlation', in Russell (ed.), *Feminist Interpretation of the Bible*, pp. 111-24.

—'Motherearth and the Megamachine', in C. Christ and J. Plaskow (eds.), *Womanspirit Rising* (San Francisco: Harper & Row, 1979), pp. 43-53.

—*Religion and Sexism: Images of Women in Jewish and Christian Traditions* (New York: Simon & Schuster, 1974).

—*Sexism and God-Talk: Toward a Feminist Theology* (Boston: Beacon Press, 1983).

—*Womanguides* (Boston: Beacon Press, 1985).

Ruether, R.R., and E. McLaughlin (eds.), *Women of Spirit: Female Leadership in the Jewish and Christian Traditions* (New York: Simon & Schuster, 1989).

Russell, L.M., 'Authority and the Challenge of Feminist Interpretation', in *idem* (ed.), *Feminist Interpretation of the Bible*, pp. 137-46.

—'Introduction', in Russell (ed.), *Feminist Interpretation of the Bible*, pp. 11-18.

—*Feminist Interpretation of the Bible* (Oxford: Basil Blackwell, 1985).

—*Feminist Interpretation of the Bible* (Philadelphia: Westminster Press, 1985).

Russell, L.M., and J.S. Clarkson (eds.), *Dictionary of Feminist Theologies* (Louisville: Westminster/John Knox, 1996).

Saiving, V., 'The Human Situation: A Feminine View', in Christ and Plaskow (eds.), *Womanspirit Rising*, pp. 25-42.

Saldarini, A.J., *Matthew's Christian–Jewish Community* (Chicago: University of Chicago Press, 1994).

Sanday, P.R., 'Female Status in the Public Domain', in M.Z. Rosaldo and L. Lamphere (eds.), *Women, Culture, and Society* (Stanford: Stanford University Press, 1974), pp. 189-206.

Sasson, J., 'Queens and Goddesses at Mari', paper presented to the Gender and Cultural Criticism Consultation, Society of Biblical Literature annual meeting, 1993.

Sasson, J.M. (ed.), *Civilizations of the Ancient Near East* (New York: Charles Scribner's Sons, 1995).

Sasson, J.M., *Ruth: A New Translation with a Philological Commentary and a Formalist-Folklorist Interpretation* (Baltimore: The Johns Hopkins University Press, 1979).

Sauneron, S., *Les fêtes religieuses d'Esna aux derniers siècles du paganisme* (Esna, 5; Cairo: Institut français d'archéologie orientale, 1962).

—*Le Temple d'Esna* (Esna, 3; Cairo: Institut français d'archéologie orientale, 1968).

Sawicki, Marianne, *Seeing the Lord: Resurrection and Early Christian Practices* (Minneapolis: Fortress Press, 1994).

Sawyer, D.F., *Women and Religion in the First Christian Centuries* (London: Routledge, 1996).

Sawyer, J.F.A., 'Daughter of Zion and the Servant of the Lord in Isaiah: A Comparison', *JSOT* 44 (1989), pp. 89-107.

Scagliavini, F., 'Osservazioni sulle Iscrizioni di Kuntillet 'Aǧrud', *RSO* 63 (1989), pp. 199-212.

Schaberg, J., *The Illegitimacy of Jesus: A Feminist Theological Interpretation of the Infancy Narratives* (San Francisco: Harper & Row, 1987).

Scharff, A. and A. Moortgat, *Ägypten und Vorderasien im Altertum* (Munich: Bruckmann, 1950).

Schaumberger, C. (ed.), *Weil wir nicht vergessen wollen...zu einer Theologie im deutschen Kontext* (Münster: Morgana Verlag, 1988).

Schiffman, L., 'Laws Pertaining to Women in the Temple Scroll', in D. Dimant and U. Rappoport (eds.), *The Dead Sea Scrolls: Forty Years of Research* (Leiden: Brill, 1992), pp. 210-28

Schmitt, J.J., 'Like Eve, Like Adam: *mšl* in Gen 3, 16', *Bib* 72 (1991), pp. 1-22.

Schottroff, L., *Lydia's Impatient Sisters: A Feminist Social History of Early Christianity* (Louisville: Westminster John Knox, 1995).

Schottroff, L., S. Schroer, and M.-T. Wacker, *Feministische Exegese: Forschungserträge zur Bibel aus der Perspective von Frauen* (Darmstadt: Wissenschaftliche Buchgesellschaft, 1995).

Schretter, M. K., *Emesal-Studien: Sprach- und literatur-geschichtliche Untersuchungen zur sogenannten Frauensprache des Sumerischen* (Innsbrucker Beiträge zur Kulturwissenschaft, 69; Innsbruck, 1990).

Schroer, S., *In Israel gab es Bilder: Nachrichten von darstellender Kunst im Alten Testament* (OBO, 74; Fribourg: Editions universitaires; Göttingen: Vandenhoeck & Ruprecht, 1987).

—'Weise Frauen und Ratgeberinnen in Israel', *Biblische Notizen* 51 (1990), pp. 41-60; rev. and trans. as 'Wise and Counselling Women in Ancient Israel: Literary and Historical Ideals of the Personified *Ḥokmâ*, in Brenner (ed.), *A Feminist Companion to Wisdom Literature*, pp. 67-84 .

—'Zur Deutung der Hand unter der Grabinschrift von Chirbet el Qôm', *UF* 15 (1983), pp. 191-99.

—'Die Zweiggöttin in Palästina/Israel', in M. Küchler and C. Uehlinger (eds.), *Jerusalem* (Novum Testamentum et Orbis Antiquus, 6; Freiburg: Universitäts Verlag; Göttingen: Vandenhoeck & Ruprecht, 1987), pp. 201-25.

Schuler, M. (ed.), *Empowerment and the Law: Strategies of Third World Women* (Washington, DC: OEF International, 1986).

—*Freedom from Violence: Women's Strategies from Around the World* (Washington, DC: OEF International, 1992).

Schuller, E., 'Feminism and Biblical Hermeneutics: Genesis 1–3 as a Test Case', in M. Joy and E.K. Neumaier-Dargyay (eds.), *Gender, Genre and Religion: Feminist Reflections* (Waterloo: Wilfrid Laurier Press, 1995), pp. 31-46.

Schuller, E., 'Women of the Exodus in Biblical Retellings of the Second Temple Period', in Day (ed.), *Gender and Difference in Ancient Israel*, pp. 178-94.

Schulte, H., *Die Entstehung der Geschichtschreibung im alten Israel* (BZAW, 128; Berlin: de Gruyter, 1972).

Schultz, V., 'Telling Stories about Women and Work: Judicial Interpretations of Sex Segregation in the Workplace in Title VII Cases Raising the Lack of Interest Argument', *HLR* 103 (1990), pp. 1750-1844.

—'Women "Before" the Law: Judicial Stories about Women, Work, and Sex Segregation on the Job', in Butler and Scott (eds.), *Feminists Theorize the Political*, pp. 297-338.
Schüngel-Straumann, H., 'God as Mother in Hosea 11', in Brenner (ed.), *A Feminist Companion to the Latter Prophets*, pp. 194-218.
—'On the Creation of Man and Woman in Genesis 1–3: The History and Reception of the Texts Reconsidered', in Brenner (ed.), *The Feminist Companion to Genesis*, pp. 53-76.
Schüssler Fiorenza, E., *Bread Not Stone* (Boston: Beacon Press, 1984).
—*But She Said: Feminist Practices of Biblical Interpretation* (Boston: Beacon, 1992).
—*In Memory of Her: A Feminist Theological Reconstruction of Christian Origins* (New York: Crossroad, 1983).
—*In Memory of Her: A Feminist Theological Reconstruction of Christian Origins* (London: SCM Press, 1983).
—'Transforming the Legacy of *The Woman's Bible*', in *idem* (ed.), *Searching the Scriptures*. I. *A Feminist Introduction*, pp. 1-24.
—'The Will to Choose or to Reject: Continuing Our Critical Work', in L. Russell (ed.), *Feminist Interpretation of the Bible*, pp. 125-35.
Schüssler Fiorenza, E. (ed.), *Searching the Scriptures*. I. *A Feminist Introduction* (New York: Crossroad, 1993).
—*Searching the Scriptures*. II. *A Feminist Commentary* (New York: Crossroad, 1994).
Scott, J.C., *Domination and the Arts of Resistance: Hidden Transcripts* (New Haven: Yale University Press, 1990).
Scott, J.W., 'Gender: A Useful Category of Historical Analysis', *American Historical Review* 91 (1986), pp. 1053-75.
—*Gender and the Politics of History* (New York: Columbia University Press, 1988).
Scott, J.W. (ed.), *Feminism and History* (Oxford: Oxford University Press, 1996).
Scroggs, R., 'Christ the Cosmocrator and the Experience of Believers', in A.J. Malherbe *et al.* (eds.), *The Future of Christology* (Minneapolis: Fortress Press, 1993), pp. 160-75.
Segall, M.H., *Cross-Cultural Psychology: Human Behavior in Global Perspective* (Monterey, CA: Brooks/Cole, 1979).
—'Psychological Antecedents of Male Aggression: Some Implications Involving Gender, Parenting, and Adolescence', in Dasen *et al.* (eds.), *Health and Cross-Cultural Psychology: Towards Applications* (Cross-Cultural Research and Methodology Series; Newbury Park, CA: Sage, 1988), pp. 71-92.
Segall, M.H., P.R. Dasen, J.W. Berry, and Y.H. Poortinga (eds.), *Human Behavior in Global Perspective: An Introduction to Cross-Cultural Psychology* (Boston: Allyn & Bacon, 1990).
Segovia, F.F., and M.A. Tolbert (eds.), *Reading from This Place*. I. *Social Location and Biblical Interpretation in the United States* (Minneapolis: Fortress, Press 1995).
—*Reading from This Place*. II. *Social Location and Biblical Interpretation in Global Perspective* (Minneapolis: Fortress Press, 1995).
Seidman, N., 'Carnal Knowledge: Sex and the Body in Jewish Studies', *Jewish Social Studies* 1 (1994), pp. 115-46.
—'Theorizing Jewish Patriarch *in extremis*', in M. Peskowitz and L. Levitt (eds.), *Judaism Since Gender* (New York: Routledge, 1996), pp. 40-48.

Seidman, N.S., '*A Marriage Made in Heaven'? The Sexual Politics of Hebrew–Yiddish Diglossia* (Dissertation; University of California at Berkeley, 1995 [1993]).

Sellin, E., *Tell Ta'annek* (Vienna: C. Gerold's Sohn, 1904).

Setel, T.D., 'Prophets and Pornography: Female Sexual Imagery in Hosea', in Russell (ed.), *Feminist Interpretation of the Bible*, pp. 86-95.

Sethe, K., *Amun und die acht Urgötter von Hermopolis* (Leipzig: Verlag der Akademie der Wissenschaften, 1929).

—*Die altägyptischen Pyramidtexten* (Leipzig: Hinrichs, 1908–1910).

Seux, M.-J., *Epithètes royales Akkadiennes et Sumériennes* (Paris: Letouzey et Ané, 1967).

Sewall, M. (ed.), *Cries of the Spirit: A Celebration of Women's Spirituality* (Boston: Beacon Press, 1991).

Sexton, A., *Complete Poems* (Boston: Houghton Mifflin, 1981).

—*The Awful Rowing Toward God* (London: Chatto & Windus, 1992).

Shakespeare, W. *Macbeth.*

Shanks, H. (ed.), *Feminist Approaches to the Bible: Symposium at the Smithsonian Institution* (Washington, DC: Biblical Archaeological Society, 1995).

Shea, W.H., 'The Khirbet el-Qom Tomb Inscription Again', *VT* 40 (1990), pp. 110-16.

Shepherd, N., *A Price Below Rubies: Jewish Women as Rebels and Radicals* (Cambridge, MA: Harvard University Press, 1993).

Siebert-Hommes, J., '"But If She Be a Daughter... She May Live!": "Daughters" and "Sons" in Exodus 1–2', in Brenner (ed.), *A Feminist Companion to Exodus to Deuteronomy*, pp. 62-74.

Siegele-Wenschkewitz, L. (ed.), *Verdrängte Vergangenheit, die uns bedrängt: Feministische Theologie in der Verantwortung für die Geschichte* (Munich: Chr. Kaiser Verlag, 1988).

Sievernich, G., and H. Budde (eds.), *Europa und der Orient, 800–1900* (Gütersloh: Bertelsmann, 1989).

Simon, S., *Gender in Translation: Cultural Identity and the Politics of Transmission* (London: Routledge, 1996).

Sinfield, A., *The Wilde Century: Effeminacy, Oscar Wilde and the Queer Moment* (New York: Columbia University Press, 1994).

Singer, S., 'Cache of Hebrew and Phoenician Inscriptions Found in the Desert', *BARev* 2.1 (1976), pp. 33-34.

Sjöberg, Å. (ed.) *The Sumerian Dictionary* (Philadelphia: The University Museum, University of Pennsylvania, 1984).

Skinner, J., *A Critical and Exegetical Commentary on Genesis* (ICC; Edinburgh: T. & T. Clark, 2nd edn, 1930).

Skinner, M. (ed.), *Rescuing Creusa: New Methodological Approaches to Women in Antiquity* (Special Issue of *Helios*, NS 13.2; Lubbock, TX: Texas Tech University Press, 1987).

Smelik, K.A.D., *Behouden Schrift: historische documenten uit het oude Israël* (Baarn: Ten Have, 1984); ET: *Writings from Ancient Israel: A Handbook of Historical and Religious Documents* (trans. G.I. Davies; Louisville: Westminster/John Knox Press, 1991).

Smith, H., 'Feminism and the Methodology of Women's History', in Carroll (ed.), *Liberating Women's History*, pp. 369-84.

Smith, M., 'Adam Eve', *Grove Magazine* 1.6 (Spring 1982), p. 44.

Smith, M.N., *Rowing in Eden: Rereading Emily Dickinson* (Austin: University of Texas Press, 1992).

Smith, M.S., *The Early History of God: Yahweh and the Other Deities in Ancient Israel* (San Francisco: Harper & Row, 1990).

Smith, S., *Collected Poems* (New York: Oxford University Press, 1976).

Smith, W.R., *Religion of the Semites* (London: A. & C. Black, 2nd edn, 1907).

Soden, W. von, *Einführung in die Altorientalistik* (Darmstadt: Wissenschaftliche Buchgesellschaft, 1985).

—*The Ancient Orient* (trans. D.G. Schley; Grand Rapids: Eerdmans, 1994).

Sorge, E., *Religion und Frau* (Stuttgart: Kohlhammer, 1985).

Spivak, G.C., *In Other Worlds: Essays in Cultural Politics* (New York: Methuen, 1987).

—*The Post-Colonial Critic: Interviews, Strategies, Dialogues* (New York: Routledge, 1990).

Spretnak, C., *Lost Goddesses of Early Greece* (Berkeley: Moon Books, 1978).

Stadelmann, R., *Syrisch-Palästinensische Gottheiten in Ägypten* (Leiden: Brill, 1967).

Stamm, J.J., *Die akkadische Namengebung* (Leipzig: Hinrichs, 1939).

Standhartinger, A., *Das Frauenbild in jüdisch-hellenistischer Zeit: Ein Beitrag anhand von 'Joseph und Aseneth'* (Leiden: Brill, 1995).

Stanton, G.N., *A Gospel for a New People: Studies in Matthew* (Edinburgh: T. & T. Clark, 1992).

Steinkeller, P., 'History of Mesopotamia: Mesopotamia in the Third Millennium B.C.', in Freedman (ed.), *Anchor Bible Dictionary*, IV, pp. 724-32.

Stemberger, G., *Introduction to the Talmud and Midrash* (trans. and ed. M. Bockmühl; Edinburgh: T. & T. Clark, 1996 [1991]).

Stendahl, K., *The School of St Matthew and its Use of the Old Testament* (Philadelphia: Fortress Press, 1968).

Sternberg, M., *The Poetics of Biblical Narrative: Ideological Literature and the Drama of Reading* (Indiana Studies in Biblical Literature: Bloomington: Indiana University Press, 1985).

Stevens, A., *Archetype: A Natural History of the Self* (London: Routledge & Kegan Paul, 1982).

Stevenson, M.J. (ed.), *Through the Eyes of Women: Insights for Pastoral Care* (Minneapolis: Fortress Press, 1996).

Stolz, F., 'Monotheismus in Israel', in Keel (ed.), *Monotheismus*, pp. 143-89.

Stone, E.C., *Nippur Neighborhoods* (SOAC, 14; Chicago: The Oriental Institute, 1987).

—'Texts, Architecture and Ethnographic Analogy', *Iraq* 43 (1981), pp. 24-33.

Stone, M., *When God was a Woman* (New York: Harcourt Brace Jovanovich, 1978)

Straus, M.A., 'Wife-beating: How Common and Why', in M.A. Straus and G.T. Hotaling (eds.), *The Social Causes of Husband–Wife Violence* (Minneapolis: University of Minnesota Press, 1980), pp. 23-36.

Strika, I., 'Prehistoric Roots: Continuity in the Images and Rituals of the Great Goddess Cult in the Near East', *RSO* 57 (1983), pp. 1-41.

Sugirtharajah, R.S., 'The Bible and its Asian Readers', *Biblical Interpretation* 1:1 (1993), pp. 54-66.

—'Jesus and Mission: Some Redefinitions', in W.S. Robins and G. Hawney (eds.), *The Scandal of the Cross: Evangelism and Mission Today* (London: United Society for the Propagation of the Gospel, 1992), pp. 1-8.

—'The Syrophoenician Woman', *ExpTim* 98 (October 1986), p. 14.

Sugirtharajah, R.S. (ed.), *Voices From the Margin: Interpreting the Bible in the Third World* (Maryknoll, NY: Orbis Books, rev. edn, 1995).

Suso, H., The Exemplar, with Two German Sermons (trans. F. Tobin; New York: Paulist Press, 1989).

Swidler, L., *Biblical Affirmations of Woman* (Philadelphia: Fortress Press, 1979).

Tadmor, M., 'Female Cult Figurines in Late Canaan and Early Israel: Archaeological Evidence', in Ishida (ed.), *Studies in the Period of David and Solomon*, pp. 139-73.

—'Female Figurines in Canaan in the Late Bronze Age', *Qadmoniot* 57 (1982), pp. 2-10 (Hebrew).

—'Female Relief Figurines of Late Bronze Age Canaan', *Eretz-Israel* 15 (1981), pp. 79-83 (Hebrew).

Talalay, L.E., 'A Feminist Boomerang: The Great Goddess of Greek Prehistory', in *Gender and History* 6 (1994), pp. 165-83.

Tamez, E., *The Amnesty of Grace: Justification by Faith from a Latin American Perspective* (trans. S.H. Ringe; Nashville: Abingdon Press, 1993).

—*Bible of the Oppressed* (Maryknoll, NY: Orbis Books, 1982).

Tannen, D. (ed.), *Gender and Conversational Interaction* (Oxford: Oxford University Press, 1993).

Tanzer, S.J., 'Ephesians', in Schüssler Fiorenza (ed.), *Searching the Scriptures*, II, pp. 325-348;

Taylor, J.G., 'Another Cult of Yahweh and Asherah?', communication given at the Annual Meeting of the Society of Biblical Literature in Boston, MA, 1987.

—'The Two Earliest Known Representations of Yahweh', in L. Eslinger and G. Taylor (eds.), *Ascribe to the Lord: Biblical and Other Studies in Memory of Peter C. Craigie* (JSOTSup, 67; Sheffield: JSOT Press, 1988), pp. 557-66.

—'Yahweh and Asherah at Tenth Century Taanach', *Newsletter for Ugaritic Studies* 37 (1987), pp. 16-18.

—*Yahweh and the Sun: Biblical and Archaeological Evidence for Sun Worship in Ancient Israel* (JSOTSup, 111; Sheffield: JSOT Press, 1993).

Tennyson, A. Lord, *Poetry* (Everyman's Library, 626; London and New York: Dent, 1949), Vol. 2.

The Assyrian Dictionary of the Oriental Institute of the University of Chicago (Chicago, 1956).

Theissen, G., *The Gospels in Context: Social and Political History in the Synoptic Tradition* (Minneapolis: Fortress Press, 1991).

—*The Miracle Stories of the Early Christian Tradition* (trans. Francis McDonagh; Philadelphia: Fortress Press, 1983).

—*The Open Door: Variations on Biblical Themes* (Minneapolis: Fortress Press, 1991).

Thiel, W., *Die deuteronomistische Redaktion von Jeremia 1–25* (WMANT, 41; Neukirchen–Vluyn: Neukirchener Verlag, 1973).

Thistlethwaite, S.B., 'Every Two Minutes: Battered Women and Feminist Interpretation', in Russell (ed.), *Feminist Interpretation of the Bible*, pp. 96-110.

Thom, D., 'A Lop-Sided View: Feminist History or the History of Women?, in Campbell (ed.), *Critical Feminism*, pp. 25-52.

Thompson, H., 'History of Archaeology', in *Biblical Archaeology: The World, the Mediterranean, the Bible* (New York: Paragon House, 1987), pp. 43-158.

Thompson, T., and D. Thompson, 'Some Legal Problems in the Book of Ruth', *VT* 18 (1968), pp. 79-99.

Thompson, T.L., *Early History of the Israelite People from the Written and Archaeological Sources* (Leiden: Brill, 1992).

Tiffany, F.C., and S.H. Ringe, *Biblical Interpretation: A Road Map* (Nashville: Abingdon Press, 1996).

Tigay, J.H., *You Shall Have No Other Gods: Israelite Religion in the Light of Hebrew Inscriptions* (Harvard Semitic Studies, 31; Atlanta: Scholars Press, 1986).

Tiger, M., *Mary of Migdal* (Galloway, NJ: Still Waters Press, 1991).

Todorov, T., *Mikhail Bakhtin: The Dialogical Principle* (trans. Wlad Godzich; Theory and History of Literature, 13; Minneapolis: University of Minnesota Press, 1984).

Tong, R., *Feminist Thought: A Comprehensive Introduction* (Boulder: Westview Press, 1989).

Toombs, L.E., 'A Perspective on the New Archaeology', in L.G. Perdue, L.E. Toombs and G.L. Johnson (eds.), *Archaeology and Biblical Interpretation* (Atlanta: Scholars Press, 1987), pp. 41-52.

Torge, P., *Aschera und Astarte: Ein Beitrag zur semitischen Religionsgeschichte* (Leipzig: Hinrichs, 1902).

Tov, E., *The Text-Critical Use of the Septuagint* (Jerusalem: Simor, 1981).

Trible, P., 'Depatriarchalizing in Biblical Interpretation', *JAAR* 12 (1973), pp. 39-42.

—'The Effects of Women's Studies on Biblical Studies', *JSOT* 22 (1982), pp. 3-5.

—'Eve and Adam: Genesis 2–3 Reread', *Andover Newton Quarterly* 13 (March 1973), pp. 251-58.

—'Eve and Miriam: From the Margins to the Center', in H.L. Shanks (ed.), *Feminist Approaches to the Bible: Symposium at the Smithsonian Institute* (Washington, DC: Biblical Archaeological Society, 1995), pp. 5-24.

—*God and the Rhetoric of Sexuality* (London: SCM Press, 1978).

—*God and the Rhetoric of Sexuality* (Overtures to Biblical Theology; Philadelphia: Fortress Press, 1978).

—'If the Bible's So Patriarchal, How Come I Love It?', *Bible Review* 8.5 (1992), pp. 44-47, 55.

—*Texts of Terror: Literary-Feminist Readings of Biblical Narratives* (Philadelphia: Fortress Press, 1984).

Trible, P., (ed.), 'The Effects of Women's Studies on Biblical Studies', *JSOT* 22 (1982), pp. 3-71.

Trigger, B.G., *A History of Archaeological Thought* (Cambridge: Cambridge University Press, 1989).

Troy, L., 'Good and Bad Women: Maxim 18/284-288 of the Instructions of Ptahhotep', *Göttinger Miszellen* 80 (1984), pp. 77-82.

—*Patterns of Queenship in Ancient Egyptian Myth and History* (BOREAS, 14; Uppsala: Acta Universitatis Upsaliensis, 1986).

—'The Ennead: The Collective as Goddess. A Commentary on Textual Personification' in G. Englund (ed.), *The Religion of the Ancient Egyptians: Cognitive Structure and Popular Expressions* (BOREAS, 20; Uppsala: Acta Universitatis Upsaliensis, 1989), pp. 59-69.

—'The First Time: Homology and Complementarity as Structural Forces in Ancient Egyptian Cosmology', *Cosmos: Journal of the Traditional Cosmology Society* 10.1 (June 1994), pp. 3-51.

Trunk, Y.Y., *Polin: Memories and Portraits* (trans. Ezra Fleischer; Jerusalem, 1962).

Tufnell, O., *Lachish III: The Iron Age* (London: Oxford University Press, 1953).

Umansky, E.M., 'Creating a Jewish Feminist Theology: Possibilities and Problems', in J. Plaskow and C.P. Christ (eds.), *Weaving the Visions: New Patterns in Feminist Spirituality* (San Francisco: Harper & Row, 1989), pp. 187-98.

Van Biema, D., 'Genesis Reconsidered', *Time* 145.20 (October 28, 1996), pp. 66-75.

Van der Kooij, A., *Die alten Textzeugen des Jesajabuches: Ein Beitrag zur Textgeschichte des Alten Testaments* (OBO, 35; Göttingen: Vandenhoeck & Ruprecht, 1981).

Van Hasselt, V.B., R.L. Morrison, A.S. Bellack, and M. Herson (eds.), *Handbook of Family Violence* (New York: Plenum Press, 1988).

Van Peer, W., 'Intertekstualiteit: traditie en kritiek', *Spiegel der Letteren* 29 (1987), pp. 16-24.

Vandier, J., 'Iousaas et (Hathor)-Nebet-Hetepet', *REg* 16-18, 20 (1964–1966), pp. 55-146; 89-176; 67-142; 135-148.

Vaux, R. de, 'On Right and Wrong Uses of Archaeology', in J.A. Sanders (ed.), *Near Eastern Archaeology in the Twentieth Century: Essays in Honor of Nelson Glueck* (Garden City, NY: Doubleday, 1970), pp. 64-80.

Velde, H. te, *Seth, God of Confusion: A Study of his Role in Egyptian Mythology and Religion* (Probleme der Ägyptologie; Leiden: Brill, 1967).

—'The Theme of the Separation of Heaven and Earth in Egyptian Mythology and Religion', *Studia Aegyptiaca* 3 (1977), pp. 161-70.

Veltri, G., 'Der griechischen Targum Aquilas: Ein Beitrag zum rabbinischen übersetzungsverständnis', in M. Hengel and A.M. Schwemer (eds.), *Die Septuaginta zwischen Judentum und Christentum* (WUNT, 72; Tübingen: Mohr [Paul Siebeck], 1994), pp. 92-115.

Virolleaud, C., *Le Palais Royal d'Ugarit* 2 (PRU) (Publications de la Mission de Ras Shamra, 7; Paris: Geuthner, 1957).

Vorländer, H., *Mein Gott: Die Vorstellung vom persönlichen Gott im Alten Orient und im Alten Testament* (Kevelaer: Butzon & Bercker,1975).

Vorster, W., 'Intertextuality and Redaktionsgeschichte', in Draisma (ed.), *Intertextuality*, pp. 15-26.

Wacker M.T., and B. Wacker, 'Matriarchale Bibelkritik: ein antijudaistisches Konzept?', in Siegele-Wenschkewitz (ed.), *Verdrängte Vergangenheit die uns bedrängt*, pp. 181-243.

Wacker, M.T., 'Die Göttin kehrt zurück: Kritische Sichtung neuerer Entwürfe', in M.T. Wacker (ed.), *Der Gott der Männer und die Frauen* (Düsseldorf: Patmos, 1987), pp. 11-38.

Wainwright, E.M., *Toward a Feminist Critical Reading of the Gospel according to Matthew* (BZNW, 60; Berlin: de Gruyter, 1991).

—'What's in a Name? The Word Which Binds/The Word Which Frees', in M. Confoy, D. Lee, and J. Nowotny (eds.), *Freedom and Entrapment: Women Thinking Theology* (North Blackburn: Dove, 1995), pp. 100-20.

Wakeman, M. 'Ancient Sumer and the Women's Movement: The Process of Reaching Behind, Encompassing and Going Beyond', *JFSR* 1.2 (1985), pp. 27-38.

—'Biblical Prophecy and Modern Feminism', in R. Gross (ed.), *Beyond Androcentrism: New Essays on Women and Religion* (Missoula, MT: Scholars Press, 1977) pp. 67-68.

Walde, D., and N.D. Willows (eds.), *The Archaeology of Gender: Proceedings of the 22nd Annual Chacmool Conference* (Calgary: University of Calgary Archaeological Association, 1991).

Walzer, M., *Exodus and Revolution* (New York: Basic Books, 1985).

Warner, M., *Alone of All Her Sex: The Myth and the Cult of the Virgin Mary* (New York: Knopf, 1983).

Weems, R.J., *Battered Love: Marriage, Sex and Violence in the Hebrew Prophets* (Overtures in Biblical Theology; Minneapolis: Fortress Press, 1995).

Wegner, J.R., *Chattel or Person? The Status of Women in the Mishnah* (Oxford: Oxford University Press: 1988).

Weiler, G., *Ich verwerfe im Lände die Kriege* (München: Frauenoffensive, 1984).

Weinfeld, M., 'Additions to the Inscriptions of 'Ajrud', *Shnaton* 5–6 (1982), pp. 237-39 (Hebrew).

—*Deuteronomy and the Deuteronomic School* (Oxford: Clarendon Press, 1972).

—'Kuntillet 'Ajrud Inscriptions and their Significance', *Studi epigrafici e linguistici* 1 (1984), pp. 121-30.

—'A Sacred Site of the Monarchic Period', *Shnaton* 4 (1980), pp. 280-84 (Hebrew).

Weininger, O., *Sex and Character* (ET; 6th edn, New York: AMS, 1975 [1906]).

Weippert, H., 'Die "deuteronomistischen" Beurteilungen der Könige von Israel und Juda und das Problem der Redaktion der Königsbücher', *Bib* 53 (1972), pp. 301-39.

Weissler, C., 'The Religion of Traditional Ashkenazic Women: Some Methodological Issues', *Association for Jewish Studies Review* 12.1 (1987), pp. 73-94.

—'Women in Paradise', *Tikkun* 2.2 (1987), pp. 43-46; 117-20.

—'Women's Studies and Women's Prayers: Reconstructing the Religious History of Ashkenazic Women', *Jewish Social Studies* NS 1.2 (Winter, 1995), pp. 28-47.

Wellhausen, J., *Die kleinen Propheten* (Berlin: Georg Reimer, 3rd edn, 1898).

Wenham, G., *Genesis 16–50* (WBC; Dallas: Word Books, 1994).

West, Ramona F., *Ruth: A Retelling of Genesis 38?* (PhD dissertation, Southern Baptist Theological Seminary; Ann Arbor, MI: University Microfilms, 1987).

Westenholz, J.G., 'Towards a New Conceptualization of the Female Role in Mesopotamian Society', *JAOS* 110 (1990), pp. 110, 510-21.

Westermann, C., *Genesis 1–11: A Commentary* (trans. J.J. Scullion; Minneapolis: Augsburg, 1984 [1974]).

—*Genesis 12–36: A Commentary* (trans. J.J. Scullion; Minneapolis: Augsburg, 1985 [1981]).

—*Isaiah 40–66: A Commentary* (Philadelphia: Westminster Press, 1969 [1966]).

—*The Structure of the Book of Job* (Philadelphia: Fortress Press, 1981).

Westermann, D.C., 'Biblische Ästhetik', *Zeichen der Zeit* 88 (1950), pp. 277-89.

—*Genesis 1–11: Ein Kommentar* (Biblische Kommentar, 1; Neukirchen–Vluyn: Neukirchener Verlag, 1974).

—'Religion und Kult', *Zeitwende* 2 (1975), pp. 77-86.

Westkott, M., 'Feminist Criticism of the Social Sciences', *Harvard Educational Review* 49 (1979), pp. 422-30.

Whybray, R.N., *The Book of Proverbs* (Cambridge: Cambridge University Press, 1972).

—*The Second Isaiah* (OTG; Sheffield: JSOT Press, 1983), pp. 68-78.

—*Wealth and Poverty in the Book of Proverbs* (JSOTS, 99; Sheffield: JSOT Press, 1990).

Wiggins, S.A., 'The Myth of Asherah: Lion Lady and Serpent Goddess', *UF* 23 (1991), pp. 383-94.

—*A Reassessment of 'Asherah': A Study According to the Textual Sources of the First Two Millennia B.C.E.* (AOAT, 235; Kevelaer: Butzon & Bercker; Neukirchen–Vluyn: Neukirchener Verlag, 1993).

Wilhelm, G., 'Kuntilet 'Ağrud', *AfO* 26 (1978–79), p. 213.

Wilkinson, D., 'The Connectedness Criterion and Central Civilization', in M. Melko and L.R. Scott (eds.), *The Boundaries of Civilizations in Space and Time* (Lanham, MD: University Press of America, 1987), pp. 25-28.

Willey, P., '"Remember the former Things": The Recollection of Previous Texts in Isaiah 40–55' (PhD dissertation, Emory University, 1996).

Williams, B., 'Narmer and the Coptos Colossi', *Journal of the American Research Center in Egypt* 25 (1988), pp. 35-59.

Williams, J.G., *Women Recounted: Narrative Thinking and the God of Israel* (Bible and Literature Series, 6; Sheffield: Almond Press, 1982).

Williams, P.J., *The Alchemy of Race and Rights* (Cambridge, MA: Harvard University Press, 1991).

Williamson, C., *A Guest in the House of Israel: Post-Holocaust Church Theology* (Louisville, KY: Westminster/ John Knox Press, 1993).

Williamson, H.G.M., *1 and 2 Chronicles* (New Century Bible Commentary; Grand Rapids: Eerdmans; London: Marshall, Morgan & Scott, 1982).

Wilner, E., *Sarah's Choice* (Chicago: University of Chicago Press, 1989).

Wilson, V., 'The Iconography of Bes with Particular Reference to the Cypriot Evidence', *Levant* 7 (1975), pp. 77-103.

Wilson-Kastner, *Faith, Feminism and the Christ* (Philadelphia: Fortress Press, 1983).

Winter, M.T., *Woman Prayer, Woman Song: Resources for Ritual* (Oak Park, IL: Meyer-Stone Books, 1987).

Winter, U., *Frau und Göttin: Exegetische und ikonographische Studien zum weiblichen Gottesbild im Alten Israel und in dessen Umwelt* (OBO, 53; Fribourg: Editions universitaires; Göttingen: Vandenhoeck & Ruprecht, 1983).

Wire, A., 'The Structure of the Gospel Miracle Stories and Their Tellers', *Semeia* 11 (1978), pp. 83-113.

Witherington, B., *Women and the Genesis of Christianity* (Cambridge: Cambridge University Press, 1990).

Wolde, E.J. van, 'From Text Via Text to Meaning: Intertextuality and its Implications', in *idem, Words Become Worlds: Semantic Studies of Genesis 1–11* (Biblical Interpretation Series, 6; Leiden: Brill, 1994), pp. 160-99.

—'Trendy Intertextuality', in Draisma (ed.), *Intertextuality*, pp. 43-49.

—'Who Guides Whom? Embeddedness and Perspective in Biblical Hebrew and 1 Kings 3:16-28', *JBL* 114.4 (1995), pp. 623-42.

Wolff, H.W., *Anthropologie des Alten Testaments* (Munich: Chr. Kaiser Verlag, 1973).

Wood, J.T., *Gendered Lives: Communication, Gender and Culture* (Belmont, CA: Wadsworth, 1994).

Woolf, V., 'Professions for Women', in R. Bowlby (ed.), *The Crowded Dance of Modern Life* (Harmondsworth: Penguin Books, 1993).

Wright, G.E., 'The New Archaeology', *BA* 38 (1974), pp. 104-15.

Wright, G.R.H., 'The Positioning of Genesis 38', *ZAW* 94 (1982), pp. 523-29.

Wright, H.T., 'History of Mesopotamia: Prehistory of Mesopotamia', in Freedman (ed.), *Anchor Bible Dictionary*, IV, pp. 720-24.

Wylie, A., 'Archaeological Cables and Tacking: The Implications of Practice for Bernstein's Options Beyond Objectivism and Relativism', *Philosophy of the Social Sciences* 19 (1989), pp. 1-18.

—'Feminist Theories of Social Power: Some Implication for a Processual Archaeology', *Norwegian Archaeological Review* 25 (1992), pp. 51-68.

—'Gender Theory and the Archaeological Record: Why is There No Archaeology of Gender?', Prehistory', in Gero and Conkey (eds.), *Engendering Archaeology*, pp. 31-56.

—'The Interplay of Evidential Constraints and Political Interests: Recent Archaeological Research on Gender', *American Antiquity* 57 (1992), pp. 15-35.

—'A Proliferation of New Archaeologies: "Beyond Objectivism and Relativism"', in N. Yoffee and A. Sherratt (eds.), *Archaeological Theory: Who Sets the Agenda?* (Cambridge: Cambridge University Press, 1993), pp. 2-26.

Yadin, Y., *Megilat Hamikdash* (Heb.; Tel Aviv: Sifriyat Ma'ariv, 1990).

Yadin, Y., et al., *Hazor I: An Account of the First Season of Excavations, 1955* (Jerusalem: Magnes, 1958).

Yaghjian, L.B., 'How Shall We Read? A Preface to Matthew's Protocols of Reading' (unpublished manuscript, n.d.).

Yamashita, T., 'The Goddess Asherah' (PhD dissertation, Yale University, 1963).

Yarbro Collins, A. (ed.), *Feminist Perspectives on Biblical Scholarship* (Chico, CA: Scholars Press, 1985).

Yllö, K., 'Political and Methodological Debates in Wife Abuse Research', in Yllö and Bograd (eds.), *Feminist Perspectives on Wife Abuse*, pp. 28-50.

—'Sexual Equality and Violence against Wives in American States', *Journal of Comparative Family Studies* 14 (1983), pp. 67-86.

Yllö, K., and M. Bograd (eds.), *Feminist Perspectives on Wife Abuse* (Newbury Park, CA: Sage, 1988).

Zakovitch, Y., 'Bible, Bible on the Wall', *Jerusalem Report*, 26 January, 1995, p. 48.

Zborowski, Mark, *People in Pain* (San Francisco: Jossey-Bass, 1969).

Zevit, Z., 'The Khirbet el-Qôm Inscription Mentioning a Goddess', *BASOR* 255 (1984), pp. 39-47.

Zimmerli, W., 'Verkündigung und Sprache des Botschaft Jesajas', *ThB* 51 (1964), pp. 73-87.

—'Die Weisung des AT sum Geschäft der Sprache, *ThB* 50 (1963), pp. 277-99.

—*Zürcher Bibelkommentare. 1. Moses 1–11* (1943), pp. 319-67.

THEOLOGY LIBRARY